THE EDUCATION OF
AMERICAN BUSINESSMEN

A STUDY OF UNIVERSITY-COLLEGE PROGRAMS
IN BUSINESS ADMINISTRATION

THE CARNEGIE SERIES IN AMERICAN EDUCATION

The books in this series have resulted from studies supported by grants of the Carnegie Corporation of New York, and are published by McGraw-Hill in recognition of their importance to the future of American education.

The Corporation, a philanthropic foundation established in 1911 by Andrew Carnegie for the advancement and diffusion of knowledge and understanding, has a continuing interest in the improvement of American education. It financed the studies in this series to provide facts and recommendations which would be useful to all those who make or influence the decisions which shape American educational policies and institutions.

The statements made and views expressed in these books are solely the responsibility of the authors.

Books Published

Conant · The American High School Today
Glenny · Autonomy of Public Colleges
Pierson · The Education of American Businessmen

In Preparation

Clark · Education as a Mass Enterprise
Medsker · The Junior College: Progress and Prospect

THE EDUCATION OF AMERICAN BUSINESSMEN

A STUDY OF
UNIVERSITY-COLLEGE PROGRAMS
IN BUSINESS ADMINISTRATION

by Frank C. Pierson and Others

1959

McGRAW-HILL BOOK COMPANY, INC.

New York   Toronto   London

THE EDUCATION OF AMERICAN BUSINESSMEN

COMMITTEE OF REVIEW

Elliott V. Bell
Chairman of the Executive Committee
McGraw-Hill Publishing Company, Inc.

William R. Biggs
Chairman, The Brookings Institution

Buell G. Gallagher
President, The City College of New York

J. Ward Keener
President, B. F. Goodrich Company

Richard L. Kozelka
Dean, School of Business Administration
University of Minnesota

Stanley F. Teele
Dean, Graduate School of Business Administration
Harvard University

Payson S. Wild
Vice President and Dean of Faculties
Northwestern University

Langbourne M. Williams, Chairman of the Committee
Chairman of the Board
Freeport Sulphur Company

LIST OF CONTRIBUTORS

Kenneth R. Andrews, Professor of Business Administration, Graduate School of Business Administration, Harvard University

George Leland Bach, Dean, Graduate School of Industrial Administration, Carnegie Institute of Technology

Donald S. Bridgman, Consultant and Director of College Relations, American Telephone and Telegraph Company (retired)

Joseph D. Coppock, Professor of Economics, Earlham College

Robert G. Cox, Associate Professor of Accounting, Wharton School of Finance and Commerce, University of Pennsylvania

John P. Dyer, Dean, University College, Tulane University

John A. Griswold, Professor of Finance, Amos Tuck School of Business Administration, Dartmouth College

W. Grant Ireson, Professor of Industrial Engineering, School of Engineering, Stanford University

Leland L. Medsker, Vice Chairman, Center for the Study of Higher Education, University of California, Berkeley

Schuyler F. Otteson, Professor of Marketing, Indiana University

George P. Shultz, Professor of Industrial Relations, Graduate School of Business, University of Chicago

Howard L. Timms, Professor of Management, Indiana University

Lewis B. Ward, Director, The Executive Study, Educational Testing Service

PREFACE

The study of The Education of American Businessmen presented in this volume is both important and opportune. It is important because higher education for business administration has become so large a part of our total educational effort, because the rapid proliferation of institutions and programs has been accompanied by serious questioning as to the direction and quality of the effort, and because much of the rest of the world is increasingly looking to the United States for guidance on higher education in business administration.

The study is opportune because it comes in a brief pause before the anticipated surge of college enrollments in the 1960's. If proposals for qualitative changes are to have serious and mature consideration, such consideration can best be given before faculty members and educational administrators alike are struggling with the consequences of a probable teacher shortage of very great magnitude. As Professor Pierson emphasizes, education for business at the university and college level is likely to be a major element in our educational structure during the decade ahead. The time to begin to determine the nature of that educational activity is now.

The basic issues to be resolved are relatively few; the detailed manifestations of these issues are numerous. To a marked degree this study focuses on the questions of the importance of a liberal education for businessmen, on the ways by which this liberal education can best be achieved, on the appropriate degrees of specialization within the university, and on the qualitative aspects of work at all levels and of all types.

It is also highly appropriate that this study should have been sponsored financially by Carnegie Corporation of New York. The Carnegie name has long been associated with scholarly studies in professional education and in educational policy generally. One of the notable landmarks in medical education, in many minds the most important, was the report published in 1910, "Medical Education in the United States and Canada," authorized by Abraham Flexner and sponsored by the Carnegie Foundation for the Advancement of Teaching.

The members of the Review Committee wish to suggest an attitude on the part of the readers toward this study which they believe will be helpful. A major characteristic of the American system of higher education must be borne constantly in mind as background against which this study should be examined.

The American system of higher education has already gone far beyond any other in the world in the proportion of the population which it seeks to educate, and the prospect in the generation ahead is that this proportion will increase. The effort to provide advanced education for so large a proportion of the population obviously creates problems different not only in degree but also in kind from those of the rest of the world. It seems to us to mean that the basic variety which now exists among our more than 1,800 institutions for advanced study must continue. With so large an educational problem, the value of diversity—of many different approaches—is greatly enhanced. [There surely is no one best way to prepare men for careers as business managers, but there may well be some poorer ways, and there may well be some common threads among the better ways.]

It is with this attitude in mind that the Review Committee most heartily recommends to the business and academic communities for their thoughtful consideration the facts, figures, and conclusions of this study of higher education in business administration.

COMMITTEE OF REVIEW

Elliott V. Bell
William R. Biggs
Buell G. Gallagher
J. Ward Keener
Richard L. Kozelka
Stanley F. Teele
Payson S. Wild
Langbourne M. Williams, CHAIRMAN

PREVIEW OF FINDINGS

The purpose of this study is to assess different approaches to academic preparation for business careers. Part 1 discusses the principles underlying this relatively new branch of higher education, and in Part 2 these principles are applied to existing programs of undergraduate and graduate schools of business administration. Part 3 examines selected areas of the business school curriculum in some detail; the programs of other institutions in this field, such as engineering schools, junior colleges, and liberal arts colleges, are reviewed in Part 4. All but one chapter in Parts 1 and 2 were written by the survey director; the last two parts of the study are the product of different contributors. Since the range and variety of topics is rather wide, the principal findings are set forth here to provide a general guide to the study as a whole.

The central problem confronting this branch of higher education is that academic standards need to be materially increased. Serious difficulties, however, stand in the way of meeting this need: careers in business are extremely varied; as an area of academic training, the field is new; the subject lacks a well-defined base or well-knit internal structure; and many important aspects of business life have only a remote connection with academic work. Overshadowing all these difficulties is the heavy enrollment pressure to which business schools have been subject since World War I. Enrollments are due to rise much higher in the coming decade, so unless bold steps are taken, academic standards are bound to fall still further.

The most acute problem exists in the four-year undergraduate schools, since only the barest handful of these institutions screen applicants or impose exacting standards for graduation. With some notable exceptions, however, this condition is found at the graduate level as well. Thus, the most important step to take in this area is to increase the number of institutions which limit their programs to students interested in, and capable of, serious academic work.

Against this consideration is the no less compelling need to provide adequate educational facilities for great numbers of students of diverse ability who will pursue a variety of business careers. The programs of study should be diversified enough so each student can carry his development just as far as his capacities will permit. Many kinds of diversity are possible and perhaps desirable, but the most important is to make sure that promising students are given work fully commensurate with their abilities. Broadly speaking, this is not true of undergraduate business schools today. All too many of these schools concentrate their efforts almost exclusively on average or even mediocre students; all too few call forth the best work from the best students. On this score, graduate programs show up more strongly than undergraduate, although again the contrast does not seem to be as marked as is generally believed.

If more business schools were to concentrate their energies on students who are capable of serious academic study, many less gifted students would have to go elsewhere. It would be unthinkable in a society like ours to deny educational opportunity to such students. How, then, could their needs best be met? An important part of the answer, developed more fully in Part 4 of this study, is to broaden the role of institutions other than business schools. A greater measure of responsibility for training in the simpler business skills should be assumed by two-year junior colleges, community colleges, and special institutes. These same institutions might also provide more of the preparation in the elementary aspects of general background subjects. Older persons who have already started their work careers should be able to get this type of training on a part-time basis in evening and extension programs, industry trade schools, and the like. Such programs have become increasingly important in recent years but they need to be given still more emphasis in the future.

Under existing conditions business schools do many things which these other institutions are quite capable of doing themselves. Typically, work is offered in secretarial science, elementary bookkeeping, or other routine office procedures which have no legitimate place in a four-year college program. Specialized courses in fields like marketing or production are often concerned with relatively simple techniques which have little analytical content or educational value. Perhaps no hard and fast line can be drawn; perhaps, too, some measure of overlapping is desirable; but it seems abundantly clear from the evidence assembled in Part 2 of this study that some part of the work now being done at business schools ought to be transferred to other institutions. This finding, though with a good deal less force, applies to graduate as well as to undergraduate business programs.

If such a transfer took place, it would mean that more business schools would be in a position to concentrate on the things they are uniquely qualified to do. What, then, is the distinctive role of these institutions? Here is the central question which confronts every school, and each must answer it for itself. The materials and viewpoints brought together in this study are offered as no more than a possible framework for thinking and discussion within the schools.

Stated briefly, the special area of undergraduate and graduate business schools appears to lie in the application of general knowledge and scientific methods to significant issues of business policy. At the undergraduate level it is particularly important that students get the foundation preparation they will need in their later careers. At the graduate level, attention can quite properly center on application of background knowledge to important business problems and to widening the boundaries of this field through research. At the same time, both undergraduate and graduate work needs to be kept in a broad context and limited to problems of solid analytical content. If business schools, or at least a substantial number of them, are not prepared to move in this direction, they can never hope to achieve the leadership role that is their due.

The most promising development in this field is the increased emphasis being placed on management's responsibilities for formulating and carrying through decisions. Schools with this orientation tend to stress the importance of broad background preparation and the contributions of basic disciplines to understanding key business questions. Correspondingly less emphasis is placed at these institutions on the details of business practice, on practical techniques, and on specific skills. A managerial approach is not without serious dangers, especially at the undergraduate level, since capacity for administrative responsibility is chiefly developed through experience, not through academic study. A school can minimize these dangers by stressing the kinds of knowledge and abilities which are needed in a wide range of management positions, at lower as well as at upper levels of authority. Similarly, emphasis needs to be put on widely applicable methods, not principles, of managerial performance since the body of tested knowledge in this area is still painfully small. The chief value of this approach is that it helps unify the study of the various business specialties or functions by relating them to each other, to the underlying disciplines, and to the conduct of the firm as a whole.

The besetting weakness in this branch of education, as perhaps in many others, is the tendency to build up areas and subareas far beyond their true academic worth. What may have once been a pioneering effort to increase the scope and depth of a field, too often turns into an elaborate departmental structure with a variety of prerequisites, course requirements, and specialized electives. A school that is genuinely interested in a managerial point of view and makes a conscientious effort to bring each of its courses within this conception of business education will necessarily limit its offerings in the various specialized areas. The press of student numbers and the mounting scarcity of qualified faculty members will doubtless force the schools to streamline their programs in any event, but a point that can scarcely be overemphasized is that, even without these pressures, the schools should cut back many of their offerings.

The reason this recommendation deserves most serious consideration is that at present many schools are graduating students who have had but the slightest exposure to general background or basic tool subjects. The vast majority of students receiving undergraduate degrees from these institutions today have had little or no work in any of the humanities outside English, in college mathematics, in any of the sciences beyond a single one-year course, or in any of the social sciences outside economics and possibly history. If these students go on to graduate study in business, few graduate institutions make any provision to fill such gaps in the students' preparation. Even in the areas outside business and economics in which some work is required, only a minute fraction of undergraduate business students go beyond a one-year introductory survey course. The result is that almost all the students studying for careers in business are not getting anything approaching a solid foundation for their later work.

This appalling condition is due at least as much to the liberal arts schools and top university leaders as to the business schools themselves. The malaise of the liberal arts in American higher education has extremely complex causes but there can be no doubt that it exists and on a wide scale. Therefore, any steps that are taken to shift the work of business students from the business specialties to greater emphasis on general background subjects need to be coupled with a revitalization of the liberal arts studies as well. Merely to require these students to take a variety of courses in nonbusiness areas taught in a perfunctory manner by instructors whose main interests lie elsewhere will not meet the situation and in fact may cause much harm.

The objection will be raised that, if all the schools were to move in this direction, there would not be enough variety in the programs to take account of differences between students, employers, and faculty groups. The danger of too many business schools moving too quickly to limit departmental specialism, to emphasize foundation preparation, and to unify course offerings seems, to say the least, remote. Precisely the opposite danger appears far more likely. It should be noted that the approach developed in this study is an extremely broad one, leaving wide latitude for variation and experimentation among the schools. Some might choose to stress upper management, others lower management, still others the whole range of management positions. Some might elect to avoid any measure of intensive specialization, others to give enough specialization for students to gain initial job footholds. Some might stress internal firm relationships, others external influences on the firm. The broad objective —to help students develop the kind of work habits and mental tools which would be of continuing value throughout their business careers—would presumably be the same for all institutions, but the roads the schools would follow in pursuit of this goal could be, and should be, many and diverse.

This conception of academic preparation for business seems to fit well with the requirements of many types of business careers. The individual student cannot hope to know the specific kinds of knowledge or particular skills he will need for the different positions he will hold over his working lifetime. Even in a static environment this would be unlikely enough; in a diversified, fast-changing society like ours it is simply unimaginable. Therefore, business schools need to concentrate on helping students develop transferable capacities which can be used in many situations and many jobs. Chief attention needs to be placed on fostering qualities of clear analysis, imaginative reasoning, and balanced judgment and on strengthening those qualities through repeated application to business-type situations. Knowledge of subject matter is essential, but not enough. In addition to being grounded in certain important areas of business operations, the student needs to be able to use his knowledge in dealing with concrete problems. Accordingly, no more subject specialization should be encouraged, particularly at the undergraduate level, than is necessary to secure a start in industry. Primary emphasis could then rest where it belongs—on analysis and application of underlying disciplines and widely usable tool subjects.

The evidence reviewed in Part 1 indicates that, generally, employers do not require a high degree of specialization in job areas open to business school graduates—that in most instances a few courses in fields like finance, marketing, and personnel are quite sufficient if they are well taught and are made analytically demanding. Rather, employers tend to look for qualities of integrity, vigor, resourcefulness, and general intelligence in new recruits. In view of this evidence, business schools have ample latitude to chart their own course and to set their standards as high as they deem appropriate. Surely schools which elect to raise standards will not lack for support from the business community.

If business schools in increasing numbers move in the latter direction, the charge will doubtless be made that their work would soon become too academic, and thus lose much of its value in terms of specific career training. Again, viewed against the record to date, the likelihood that this will occur is remote indeed. What sometimes seems to be overlooked is that these schools are affiliated with institutions of higher education, many of the latter being major centers of learning. The purpose of a college or university is to free the mind and help the individual lay a foundation for a life of self-education. A business school is part of this same great tradition and accordingly should be dedicated to opening up new areas of understanding in one of the most important phases of modern life. It is quite true that the relationship between academic work and career preparation presents a number of difficult questions, especially at the undergraduate level. Experience in a variety of professional fields, however, indicates that career preparation can be reconciled with the highest quality of academic performance, and in fact can contribute vitally to it. If preparation for business cannot meet this test, it is hard to see why it should be accorded full academic status at the college or university level.

Another possible objection to the proposals developed in this study is that they do not differentiate undergraduate and graduate work in business sharply enough. This is an issue which is probably not going to be settled for a long time, and much experimentation will be needed to resolve it. As conceived in this study, academic preparation for business should develop along three broad lines: (1) study in certain basic disciplines and tool subjects (notably literature and language skills, mathematics and statistics, psychology and sociology, legal institutions, economics and accounting), (2) study of the application of these disciplines and tools to a few broad functional aspects of the firm (finance, marketing, personnel, and production), and (3) study of the initiating-coordinating-implementing process within the firm at different levels of management. Undergraduate schools, according to this view, should stress the foundation subjects with considerably less attention to the functional specialties and the details of managerial performance. Graduate schools, on the other hand, should deal more intensively with applications of background knowledge and scientific methods to the functional specialties and to the responsibilities of management. This perhaps is not as sharp a line of demarcation as will ultimately prove desirable; it may be that this field should eventually follow the pattern set by law and medicine and limit direct preparation for business to students who already hold undergraduate degrees. For the foreseeable future, however, the distinction recommended here seems thoroughly defensible.

Still another objection to the approach developed in this study is that, if students were limited to four or five semester courses in their major subject, they would not be able to specialize as much as might seem desirable. The general views of employers on this issue, referred to above, are becoming well known. What is less widely known is that many faculty members working directly in business subject areas likewise feel that this amount of specialization is all that should be permitted. The programs of study recommended for the principal business specialties, as set forth in Part 3, fall within these same limits. Each was prepared by a business school faculty member actively engaged in the field discussed. Needless to say, the proposals developed in Part 3 are not in any sense an expression of predominant opinion. However, intensive investigations conducted at seventy-five business schools in all parts of the country uncovered wide-spread faculty support for a general reduction in the amount of work in the specialized areas, especially at the undergraduate level.

In this connection it needs to be emphasized that the strength of any educational institution largely lies in its faculty. If a school's staff feels that it is part of a significant intellectual venture, a forward-moving quality is likely to permeate the entire program. Bold planning may in fact be the most practical way to fire up a faculty and generate sustained enthusiasm. At the same time, careful preparation is needed to gain genuine accept-ance for any realignment of an existing program. Change for the sake of change is hardly the answer. A new program must be soundly conceived and thoroughly discussed by a school's entire faculty if it is to win wide-spread support.

The direction a particular school takes is thus largely a matter of faculty development. Much more attention needs to be paid than in the past to keeping each school's faculty growing. Sabbatical leaves, summer in-stitutes, special seminars, research aids, and other devices need to be more fully utilized. A great deal of attention should be paid to assessing the strengths and weaknesses of a faculty and to recruiting new staff. An over-all plan of faculty development may prove helpful, but this is an area in which individual staff members must play a leading role.

In quantitative terms alone, the personnel requirements of business schools over the next decade will be formidable indeed. The more signifi-cant issue, however, is what kind of faculties these schools should en-deavor to develop. Institutions which move in the general direction out-lined in this study will want teachers who maintain close ties with basic disciplines and are actively concerned with the broader aspects of busi-ness behavior as well as with the more specialized business functions. This will entail a considerable change from the backgrounds and interests of present faculties; it will also mean establishing much closer relations than now exist with the liberal arts and other faculty groups. In order to augment the supply of new faculty members and develop stronger busi-ness school staffs, far greater emphasis will have to be placed on doctoral programs. While it would be unwise for more than a few of the largest and strongest institutions to attempt to offer the doctorate, the entire field's future depends on the quality of these programs.

Implicit in the conception of business education set forth in this study is the prime role which should be accorded research. The need is not for just any kind of research, as that rather elastic term is often defined, but for research which meets high scientific standards and is aimed at prob-lems of general significance. It would not be practical to support exten-sive programs of research at a large number of institutions; for maximum results most of the work should be confined to a small group of schools.

At the same time, all schools should strive to make some contributions to the enrichment of the field, and faculty members should keep as much abreast of current research work as they possibly can. Only by this means is it possible for teachers in this as in any other field to remain intellectually alive.

One of the principal themes running through this study is that business careers are so diversified that many kinds of educational programs are called for. Mention has already been made of the broader role which should be accorded junior colleges, extension divisions, and evening schools. Other institutions and facilities also have much to contribute, such as company training programs, university programs in management development, engineering schools, and liberal arts schools. Part 4 reviews the part these other institutions now play in business education and considers how each might be related more effectively to the field as a whole. Of these institutions the small liberal arts colleges pose the most serious questions. According to the final chapter in Part 4, colleges in this category which have business programs frequently offer work in a rather wide variety of business subjects even though their business faculty may consist of only two or three people. At these institutions there is a tendency for the business programs to attract heavy enrollments, to the detriment of the work in economics and other fields. The result is that many of the liberal arts colleges with business departments do not offer solid grounding either in the business subjects or in the basic disciplines which underlie them.

On a number of counts, the general quality of the work done at business schools and other institutions in the business area appears sorely deficient. It should be stressed, however, that a few schools have been able to put their work on a sound academic footing, while some of the graduate business programs compare favorably with the best to be found in either professional or nonprofessional graduate areas. Moreover, the campus interviews uncovered widespread interest in the possibility of change at many institutions. The willingness to question and experiment is itself evidence of real strength and augurs well for the future.

This study is paralleled by a similar survey being prepared by Robert A. Gordon and James E. Howell, *Higher Education for Business*, sponsored by the Ford Foundation. Appreciation is expressed to them for their generous cooperation in assembling materials in the beginning stages of this investigation. Their data on employer attitudes and requirements, a topic to which they gave particular attention, proved especially helpful in preparing Chap. 5. In comparing the results of the two investigations, it should be kept in mind that the principal findings and recommendations were reached in a completely independent manner.

Of the many individuals whose cooperation was enlisted in the preparation of this study, particular thanks are due the deans and faculty members of the nation's business schools. Dean Ewald T. Grether was good enough to read and criticize a number of the chapters in early draft form. Special thanks are also due the members of the study's interviewing staff who took time from other duties to visit many campuses and prepare detailed reports on individual schools. The members of the interviewing staff were as follows: Allan M. Cartter, Department of Economics and Business Administration, Duke University; Robert G. Cox, Wharton School of Finance and Commerce, University of Pennsylvania; Marten S. Estey, Wharton School of Finance and Commerce, University of Pennsylvania; Robert F. Lanzillotti, School of Economics and Business, State College of Washington; Richard H. Leftwich, College of Business, Oklahoma State University; Samuel M. Loescher, Department of Economics, Indiana University; James E. McNulty, Wharton School of Finance and Commerce, University of Pennsylvania; Lawrence L. Parrish, School of Business Administration, University of Connecticut; Louis B. Perry, President, Whitman College; Howard G. Schaller, College of Commerce and Business Administration, Tulane University; Gerald G. Somers, Department of Economics, University of Wisconsin; Louis R. Tripp, Department of Economics, University of Wisconsin.

Acknowledgment is made to the following persons who assisted at various stages of the investigation: Margaret M. Estey, Theda O. Henle, John G. Lipsett, Myrtle R. Keeny, Elaine G. Riesenberg, Mariana W. Robinson, and Howard H. Williams. An especially heavy debt is owed to Gloria W. Grover and Margaret W. Moore for their work in organizing and analyzing the school questionnaire, the results of which have already been made available to the cooperating schools.

Appreciation is expressed to the Carnegie Corporation of New York for initiating and underwriting the study and to Swarthmore College for granting me a leave of absence to undertake this investigation. Most of all, I am indebted to my wife for her unflagging patience and wholehearted support at every stage of the undertaking.

Frank C. Pierson

Swarthmore College
June, 1959

CONTENTS

PREFACE vii

PREVIEW OF FINDINGS ix

PART ONE. A FRAMEWORK OF APPRAISAL

CHAPTER 1. The Field and the Issues 3
2. Higher Education and the Professions 16
3. History of Business Schools 34
4. Student Characteristics and Interests 55
5. Employer Requirements 84
6. Education for Careers in Management *Lewis B. Ward* . 124
7. Foundations of Education for Business 149

PART TWO. THE AMERICAN BUSINESS SCHOOL

8. Undergraduate General Studies 163
9. Undergraduate Business Studies 196
10. Master's Programs in Business 229
11. Faculty and Teaching Methods 268
12. Doctoral Programs and Research 296

PART THREE. DEVELOPING THE CURRICULUM

13. Managerial Decision Making as an Organizing Concept
    George Leland Bach 319
14. Accounting *Robert G. Cox* 355
15. Finance *John A. Griswold* 392
16. Marketing *Schuyler F. Otteson* 423
17. Personnel Management and Industrial Relations *George
    P. Shultz* 452
18. Production *Howard L. Timms* 475

PART FOUR. OTHER PROGRAMS IN BUSINESS ADMINISTRATION

19. Preparation for Business in Engineering Schools *W. Grant
    Ireson* 507

20. Company Management Development Programs *Donald S. Bridgman* 536
21. University Programs for Practicing Executives *Kenneth R. Andrews* 577
22. Evening-Extension Programs in Business *John P. Dyer* . 609
23. Preparation for Business in Junior Colleges *Leland L. Medsker* 638
24. Preparation for Business in Liberal Arts Colleges *Joseph D. Coppock* 662

APPENDIXES 709

INDEX 733

PART ONE

A FRAMEWORK OF APPRAISAL

THE FIELD AND THE ISSUES

The issues confronting universities and schools of business administration are essentially similar. Both must strive to achieve unity in diversity and to reconcile quantity and quality in education. There are many academic routes to preparing for business careers. Business schools should concentrate their energies on activities for which they are uniquely qualified.

It has long been part of the American dream that education should be open to all. The establishment of free and universal public education through the grade school years marked a milestone in the nation's development in the nineteenth century. The extension of this same opportunity to all groups through the secondary school years was largely accomplished in the first half of the twentieth century. Now an essentially similar development is occurring at the college level, and if present trends continue, college for all students who might qualify will be a reality within the next century.

Between 1900 and 1956, higher education enrollments increased fifteen times (from about 200,000 to 3,000,000) or from 4 per cent to 35 per cent of the college-age population; even if the latter proportion is not exceeded, college students are expected to number about 4,800,000 by 1970, and if the proportion rises to 50 per cent, a total of 6,800,000 is projected.[1]

As indicative of a general trend, the latter figure seems well justified. In a complex society such as ours there is increasing need for college-trained personnel, a circumstance which has been greatly heightened by the country's critical position in world affairs. Pressure on colleges and universities to admit a larger proportion of the nation's youth is also associated with the fact that a disturbingly high proportion of superior

[1] U.S. Office of Education data and projections. See also Harold Goldstein, "Recent Trends in and Outlook for College Enrollments," *Monthly Labor Review*, March, 1956, Table 1, p. 287.

high school graduates does not now attend college. Nearly one-half of high school seniors in the top 20 per cent of their graduating class fail to enter college, a wastage of a precious resource which can hardly be expected to continue indefinitely.[2] The most important influence, however, that is raising the proportion of young people in college is simply the continued rise in living standards and the change in family budgets that has accompanied it. Today, a college degree is widely accepted as a badge of social status, as a first rung on the ladder of economic betterment, and as an introduction to the good life—American style.

The enthusiasm of our countrymen for more education has not been matched, as yet at least, by our willingness to cover the full costs involved. By far the most serious problems in this regard exist at the primary and secondary school levels, but the gap between needs and resources is already wide at the college level and bids fair to increase still further. In recent years vigorous efforts have been made to make up for prior deficiencies in the nation's outlays for higher education; in 1940, only $759 million was spent for such purposes as against about $4 billion in 1956. On the other hand, estimates based on projected enrollments, faculty requirements, plant expansion, and other costs indicate that total needs will come to about $7 billion in 1970 at existing prices. This would entail increasing expenditures on higher education from approximately $15 per capita in 1954 to perhaps $34 per capita in 1970 and raising the share of higher education in an enlarged gross national product from 0.68 per cent to slightly more than 1.0 per cent.[3]

The widening gap between needs and resources has shown up most sharply in the failure of faculty salaries to keep pace with the incomes of comparable professional groups. Thus, the $6,600 mean annual income received by undergraduate college teachers in 1958–1959 was well below the earnings of other professional groups with similar periods of training.[4] In fact, while real annual earnings per capita rose substantially for most income categories during the first half of the twentieth century, they remained virtually unchanged over this period for college faculty members. The same pattern has held in more recent years; between 1939 and 1956 real disposable income per capita rose about 62 per cent for all

[2] The Report of the Commission on Human Resources and Advanced Training (Dael Wolfle, Director), America's Resources of Specialized Talent, Harper & Brothers, New York, 1954, pp. 145–146, 149–150.

[3] The President's Committee on Education Beyond the High School, Second Report to the President, U.S. Government Printing Office, Washington, D.C., 1957, p. 86. The committee notes wryly that the American people spend about as much per capita on parimutuel betting as on higher education.

[4] This estimate, which was supplied by W. Robert Bokelman, U.S. Office of Education, is the average salary for all faculty ranks in liberal arts and other undergraduate colleges for the academic year 1958–1959.

income groups, while faculty pay in real terms declined somewhat.[5] In other words, as demand for college education has risen, incomes of college teachers have fallen sharply in relation to other groups and have even tended to decline somewhat in absolute real terms. The glaring inconsistency reflected in these facts will complicate still further the task of meeting the prospective rise in enrollments; while vigorous corrective efforts are being made, their success remains in doubt.[6]

More important than considerations of cost, the spread of higher education to an expanding cross section of the population raises serious questions about the purposes and functions of the nation's colleges and universities. Today's undergraduate and graduate students come from all manner of backgrounds and are extremely diverse in terms of both abilities and interests; the jobs and careers they will enter are hardly less heterogeneous. Inevitably, the colleges and universities find themselves pulled in a great many different directions. Polyglot educational structures are an inevitable result.

In graduate programs, the diversity of offerings presents less serious issues, although increasing doubts are being voiced even here.[7] At the undergraduate level, on the other hand, while the ideal of a broadly unifying program of undergraduate studies as exemplified by the liberal arts tradition remains very much alive, for large numbers of students and their parents this tradition has little meaning. The students entering our colleges and universities today plan to be journalists, nurses, engineers, dentists, secretaries, salesmen, social workers, architects, teachers, chemists, accountants, zoologists, and the like; among a few of the more highly developed professions, a broad precareer preparation has come to be accepted as desirable and even necessary, but for most it has not.

Colleges and universities admitting many students from the lower half of their high school classes are under especially heavy pressure to diversify their offerings and develop programs of widely varying content and quality. Most of the large publicly supported institutions are in this position, and many of the smaller private schools are also. The same

---

[5] Seymour E. Harris, "Faculty Salaries," *Bulletin of the American Association of University Professors,* December, 1957, p. 582. Harris concludes that faculty members lost about $2 billion as a result of the decline in the purchasing power of their salaries between 1940 and 1957. He states: "Had their income kept up with that of the population, their gain would have been about $5 to 6 billion in 17 years."

[6] The President's Committee on Education Beyond the High School urged that top priority be given to raising faculty salaries, recommending that they be doubled on the average within five to ten years. *Op. cit.,* p. 6.

[7] Committee of Fifteen, *The Graduate School Today and Tomorrow,* Fund for the Advancement of Education, New York, 1955, and The Report of the President's Committee, *The Educational Future of Columbia University,* Columbia University Press, New York, 1957.

pressures to diversify, though somewhat different in nature, impinge on large, urban, nonresidential universities and other institutions which attract many students from lower-income families. The press of numbers thus tends to push the colleges and universities apart, both internally and in relation to one another, with some branches of institutions stressing a broad common core of subject matter and others emphasizing highly technical, specialized training for particular careers.

TREND TOWARD PROFESSIONS

As these institutions have admitted students with more diversified backgrounds and abilities, the proportion enrolled in professional as opposed to liberal arts programs has risen correspondingly. As long ago

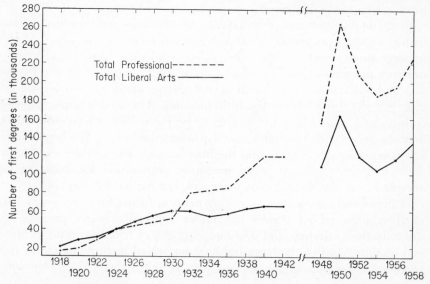

FIG. 1-1. First professional and liberal arts degrees conferred by universities, colleges, and technological schools in the United States, 1918–1958. Source: Appendix 1.

as 1917–1918, professional programs accounted for 45 per cent of all bachelor's and first-level degrees; in 1939–1940, the proportion was 65 per cent, and in 1956–1957, following a moderate decline immediately after the war, it came to 63 per cent.[8] As noted in a recent study, these figures greatly understate career preparation at undergraduate institutions, since work of this sort has long been emphasized by many liberal

[8] See Appendix 1.

arts schools.[9] The figures set forth in Fig. 1-1 are, however, indicative of the general trend.

The rapid spread of professional or career education has not occurred in the older, more firmly established fields, such as medicine, law, and engineering, but in newer fields like nursing, social work, and home economics. The big gainers in recent decades have been teaching and business. By 1955–1956 these two branches of higher education accounted for just under 30 per cent of all bachelor's and first professional degrees (see Fig. 1-2). At the master's and second professional degree level they

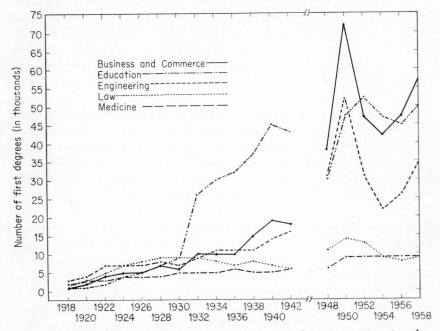

FIG. 1–2. First degrees in business and commerce, education, engineering, law, and medicine conferred by universities, colleges, and technological schools in the United States, 1918–1958. Source: Appendix 2.

made up nearly 50 per cent of the total, but of this latter figure, teaching formed much the greater part. It should be noted that the great majority of degrees granted by professional schools fall in the first-level category.

The rise in business enrollments has been spectacular. In 1919–1920, undergraduate degrees awarded in schools and departments of business accounted for only 3 per cent of the total. In 1939–1940, they totaled about 19,000, or 10 per cent of all degrees, and in 1949–1950, with the

[9] Earl J. McGrath and Charles H. Russell, *Are Liberal Arts Colleges Becoming Professional Schools?* Bureau of Publications, Teachers College, Columbia University, New York, 1958.

returning veterans, they rose to a peak of 72,000, or 17 per cent of the total. Since then, the absolute number of undergraduate business degrees has declined sharply but since 1953–1954 it has been increasing while its relative share has leveled off; thus, in 1957–1958, a total of 57,669 degrees were granted, or 16 per cent of all first-level degrees.[10] Graduate work in business, on the other hand, is largely a post-World War II phenomenon. In 1939–1940 graduate business education accounted for only 2 per cent of all master's and second professional degrees, but in 1949–1950 and 1957–1958 its share came to 8 and 7 per cent, respectively.

The increasing emphasis on preparation for a wide variety of careers in business is a wholly logical outcome of underlying trends in American society. Since college going is now so much taken for granted and going into business is such a dominant career pattern in this country, the wonder is that this area has but recently gained academic recognition and that even today its status is subject to vigorous, sometimes bitter, controversy.

Prior to 1910 there were only 13 schools of business at universities and colleges, and some of these were limited to a few courses in accounting and finance. While the number of schools with such programs jumped to about 48 by 1919, of which nearly half offered both undergraduate and graduate work, they accounted for only 3 per cent of total undergraduate degrees granted in the academic year ending in 1920 and a still smaller proportion of all graduate degrees. During the decade of the twenties, there was a big expansion in this branch of higher education with approximately 54 additional institutions establishing business school programs. The annual rate of increase in newly formed programs slowed perceptibly in the next three decades, since most campuses already had established such schools, though there were at least 23 new schools established between 1945 and 1949 alone. In 1955–1956, there were 163 schools of business at accredited institutions of higher education, and they awarded approximately 27,000 undergraduate and 4,000 graduate degrees that year.[11]

---

[10] See Appendix 2. It should be emphasized that the term "business schools" as used in this study refers to collegiate schools of business, not to proprietary business schools, programs at teachers colleges for secondary school teachers in commercial subjects, or special institutes and schools which limit most of their offerings to secretarial, accounting, and particular industry or trade courses.

[11] Data on number of newly established schools taken from a questionnaire sent in March, 1957, as part of the present study to every school or college of business located at universities and colleges recognized by a duly authorized regional accrediting body. (The questionnaire is hereafter referred to as the Survey Questionnaire.) Included in the 163 schools are 157 undergraduate schools and 6 exclusively graduate schools. For further information about the questionnaire, see Appendix 3. The 163 schools are listed by name in Appendix 5.

PROSPECTS FOR BUSINESS SCHOOLS

The foregoing facts speak for the significant part business schools are playing in higher education today. By the same token, these schools are experiencing their full share of the difficulties besetting colleges and universities at large. They too have had to cope with a rise in enrollments beyond the resources at their disposal. They also are hard-pressed for adequate teaching personnel. Their students also come from a wide range of backgrounds and are pursuing a great diversity of career interests. Indeed, under any realistic definition of the term "business," there is hardly any limit to the variety of jobs and duties for which these schools can be expected to prepare students. Some delimitation of the field becomes possible if it is confined to the managerial or administrative sphere alone, but a number of the most important jobs in business are held by staff specialists, and many management positions are not to be had until a person has spent a good many years in various specialized operations. Moreover, the term "management" itself covers a bewildering variety of duties ranging from the daily transmittal of orders by a foreman to long-term policy decisions by a top executive.

A few schools, particularly at the graduate level, are in a position to center most of their attention on upper-level management and staff responsibilities, and where this is done, a much sharper focus for the student's work becomes possible. Doubtless more schools could adopt this same approach than now do, but as a general pattern, this view of collegiate business education is not without serious difficulties of its own. Relatively few students, whether graduate or undergraduate, can hope to assume upper-management responsibilities, and at best such positions are likely to come late in a person's career. Since managing a modern business is such a complex, many-sided process, even schools with a top-management orientation are obliged to include a wide spectrum of activities in their programs. This poses a formidable dilemma: if the study of decision making is put in a narrow and precise framework, it gains clarity but may well lose all contact with reality; if, on the other hand, it is studied in the full complexity of on-going situations, it may well remain as confusing as the experience it is supposed to clarify. The truth is that the more responsible managerial and staff jobs in business cannot be learned in any straightforward, academic manner. Thus, quite aside from the sheer number and varied abilities of their students, business schools are dealing with a subject which to a considerable extent is diffuse and formless.

Viewed in the large, it seems clear that the critical issues confronting business schools and higher education as a whole are basically the same.

As educational entities, both are plagued by considerable uncertainty over the purposes they should serve and over the means for achieving them. Both are dealing with large, heterogeneous student groups whose interests and abilities are widely diverse. Both, nonetheless, feel the need for developing common, unifying programs which will provide background preparation for many areas of life. Similarly, both hope that the varied interests of their students can be met without any serious deterioration of academic standards and that all students—the more gifted as well as the average—will be stimulated to do the best work of which they are capable. All this is somehow to be achieved at a time when enrollments are again due to start rising rapidly and teaching staffs are going to be spread more thinly than ever before.

Studies of higher education typically stress that the need for both unity and diversity, as well as for quality and quantity, can be reconciled, but that mass education at any level represents a serious threat to the pursuit of academic excellence. As the recent Rockefeller report on education states:[12]

> By insisting that *equality* means an exactly similar exposure to education, regardless of the variations in interest and capacity of the student, we are in fact inflicting a subtle but serious form of inequality upon our young people. We are limiting the development of individual excellence in exchange for a uniformity of external treatment. [Italics in the original]

This is the overriding issue confronting business schools at the undergraduate level and to a considerable extent at the graduate level as well. The nature of the subject, the rapid rise in enrollments, and the diversity of students have all conspired to weight the educational scales in this area on the side of quantity rather than of quality instruction. The unfinished task in this as in many other branches of higher education is to redress this balance. It is to this end that the present study is chiefly addressed.

STRUCTURE OF BUSINESS EDUCATION

╵ A young person graduating from high school today who seeks direct academic preparation for a career in business has many educational paths he can follow. An increasingly important route is to enter one of 157 institutions which offer undergraduate B.A. or B.S. degrees in separate schools of business or commerce. Students in these programs are required to take a number of courses in liberal arts subjects in order to satisfy certain university-wide requirements, but their principal work centers in fields like accounting, finance, and marketing. Another important route is

[12] *The Pursuit of Excellence*, Doubleday and Company, Inc., Garden City, N.Y., 1958, p. 22.

to enter one of 424 colleges and universities which have undergraduate departments or divisions as opposed to schools of business; a student majoring in one of these programs has a narrower range of courses to choose from, but the areas covered are much the same as in the business schools themselves. In 1955–1956, colleges and universities with departments and divisions of business awarded approximately 12,000 undergraduate degrees and 500 graduate degrees. When added to the degrees awarded by business schools that year, the total came to about 39,000 undergraduate and 4,500 graduate degrees in business. Thus, despite the large number of institutions involved, the departmental and division programs accounted for less than half of the undergraduate degrees awarded by schools of business and for only a small fraction of the graduate degrees.[13] Finally, many institutions without either schools or departments of business typically offer an isolated course or two in business, usually as part of the work in economics.

A third route is to take a liberal arts or engineering program in one of the nation's many colleges or universities, majoring in any of a number of subjects and then either going directly into business or pursuing advanced studies in business, law, or some related field. A fourth route is to attend a two-year junior or community college. In 1958, well over half of the 652 institutions in this latter category offered a business curriculum, and of the regular students in schools with such programs, perhaps a fourth (roughly 50,000) were enrolled in some type of business curriculum.[14]

Persons who have taken no earlier academic preparation in business, or want to supplement such preparation at a later point in their careers, can follow a fifth route by taking work in evening or extension courses, in university programs for executive development, or in company-sponsored management training courses. Since adult students have frequently had considerable job experience and are almost always currently employed, these last-named programs can be closely geared to specific business problems and practices.

[13] As already noted, in addition to the 157 undergraduate schools there were 6 exclusively graduate schools of business at this time; adding the 424 institutions with departments and divisions of business, there was a grand total of 587 colleges and universities offering general degree-granting programs in business in 1955–1956 (see Appendix 4).

The U.S. Office of Education reported a total of 40,370 undergraduate and first-level business degrees, exclusive of teacher training, in commercial business subjects in 1955–1956. The difference between this total and the estimate given in the text of 39,000 degrees granted by departments, divisions, and schools of business is due to the fact that there are a few institutions, chiefly technical institutes with limited types of business programs, which were included in the U.S. Office of Education data but were not included in the estimate shown here.

[14] See Chap. 23 by Leland L. Medsker.

These five branches of business education have all developed rapidly since World War II but will need to be expanded still further if enrollment demands are to be effectively met. It will also be important for each branch to concentrate on the kind of education it is best prepared to offer; otherwise the available resources which are already severely taxed will not be put to their highest use. Since the undergraduate and graduate business schools stand at the center of this whole field of higher education, special care will have to be exercised to define their obligations clearly and to make sure they are carried out. These considerations have guided the general plan and execution of this study.

CHARACTERISTICS OF BUSINESS SCHOOLS

By way of added background, a few additional facts about these schools may be noted here. A little over 75 per cent of the undergraduate business schools offer four-year programs in which students enter as freshmen. About 20 per cent of the schools operate 2 2-year programs in which students come in as juniors and in a few cases they admit students as sophomores.[15] As shown later, these differences appear to have only a limited effect on the distribution of the students' courses between business and nonbusiness subjects.

The work of undergraduate business schools tends to concentrate at large public institutions. In 1955–1956 the country's 157 undergraduate business schools were divided roughly in half between private and public institutions, but the latter accounted for well over 50 per cent of all undergraduate degrees. Of the private schools, about 30 per cent were affiliated with the Catholic Church. Of public and private schools combined, about one-third of the total were located at large universities, i.e., institutions awarding more than 1,000 undergraduate degrees of all kinds; the latter schools accounted for slightly more than half of all undergraduate business degrees in 1956.

Of the 157 undergraduate schools of business, nearly 70 per cent also offered some type of graduate degree program in 1955–1956. In addition, there were 6 institutions which limited their offerings to graduate work only: Chicago, Columbia, Cornell, Dartmouth, Harvard, and Stanford.[16]

The total number of graduate business degrees awarded in 1955–1956

[15] Derived from replies to the Survey Questionnaire. The other data in this section were also taken from this source.

[16] At six other institutions which offered both undergraduate and graduate work in business, the latter was given in separate schools; these institutions were Carnegie Tech, M.I.T., New York University, University of California (Berkeley), University of California (Los Angeles), and University of Virginia. Since 1955–1956, a number of other separate graduate business schools have been established, including those at Purdue and Washington University (St. Louis).

came to approximately 4,500, or 9 per cent of all business degrees granted. Almost all the graduate degrees were M.B.A.s; 86 per cent of the total were in this category as against 11 per cent M.A. or M.S. degrees and 3 per cent doctoral degrees. While a surprisingly large number of schools offer some type of graduate program, a small number of schools account for most of the degrees, with ten institutions accounting for over 60 per cent of the total in 1955–1956.

The typical business school, especially in large urban centers, is actively involved in some type of management development or adult education work. Of the 163 undergraduate and graduate schools, approximately 66 offered management training programs, 68 offered institutes and special conferences for executives, and 43 offered some other type of adult education program in 1955–1956; there is some overlapping in the figures but only 50 of the 163 schools apparently offered no work of this nature. In addition, about half the undergraduate schools conducted evening classes. In terms of numbers of students, scope of programs, and diversity of activities, business schools apparently provide as wide a range of services as any other one branch of higher education. Each function considered by itself seems quite justified, but taken together they mean that a school's faculty is likely to be spread rather thinly over a wide terrain.

ISSUES CONFRONTING BUSINESS SCHOOLS

In assuming responsibility for offering direct or special preparation for careers in business, the universities and colleges are taking the position that this is a legitimate and important part of the undergraduate-graduate curriculum. Full agreement on this fundamental issue is unlikely, since it raises questions about the ultimate objectives of higher education as well as about the purposes of particular institutions or programs. Thus a distinction is customarily drawn between graduate and undergraduate work on the ground that the former is frankly designed for immediate career preparation and that courses in business can therefore form an appropriate part of graduate instruction. Conversely, such courses tend to be viewed with greater skepticism at the undergraduate level on the ground that students should concentrate on the broader aspects of their education during their undergraduate years.

The position developed in the next chapter, and at greater length in the rest of the study, is that business education rests on a stronger base at the graduate than at the undergraduate level but that at least for the immediate future, undergraduate business programs can play a highly constructive role if certain conditions of academic performance are met. In developing this view, it is necessary to consider what ends undergraduate and graduate education should serve, what means exist for attaining these ends, and what implications follow for existing programs. These issues are presented to business schools in a number of different forms, and in the interest of gaining perspective on the field as a whole, these issues are set forth briefly here in much the same order as they are discussed in Part 1 of the study.

A close-up view of the historical development of business schools, presented in Chap. 3, throws light on some of the more specific questions which remain unsettled in this area. The schools have faced difficult decisions in determining what subjects should be considered the heart of the business studies, what areas of specialization should be provided, where the balance should be struck between the business and nonbusiness or liberal arts studies, how graduate work should be approached, and similar questions. The historical record is not detailed enough to throw much light on all these issues or to explain the precise grounds on which critically important decisions were made. On the other hand, it is possible to contrast certain broad patterns of development and to show the general results that have followed from each.

Another cluster of questions is brought to the fore in Chap. 4, which considers the work of business schools from the viewpoint of the students enrolled in their programs. A critical issue to be faced in this area is the kind of admissions policies which these schools should follow. As already noted, in their efforts to provide educational opportunities for large masses of students, these schools run the serious risk of neglecting the needs of the more gifted. Yet if most of the schools were to limit admissions to the top quarter or third of high school graduates, thousands of students would either have to take the program of their second choice or be denied the opportunity of going to college altogether. Nor does the alternative of admitting large numbers of borderline students with the understanding that they will be rigorously screened at the end of their freshman or sophomore year seem either fair or efficient. Thus the problem becomes one of deciding how far business schools should go in carrying students who have little or no capacity for serious academic work.

A rather different issue is posed by the assertion that most undergraduate and graduate business students are chiefly interested in preparing for some specific line of work (e.g., accounting, marketing, or personnel management) and that a broad program of academic studies would have little meaning for them. The paucity of data makes the question of student motivation an extremely difficult one to analyze. Under any circumstances the number and variety of students involved defy systematic investigation, especially if it is assumed that the quality of the students will change in the future. Whether the academic interests of business students are limited to vocational objectives largely depends on how the latter term is defined and what the alternative academic programs are. It is one thing to argue that business students attend college in the hope that their careers in some aspect of business will be benefited and quite another to contend that a carefully developed academic program which is effectively taught would hold no challenge for most business students. Despite the difficulties involved, these matters deserve attention and are therefore discussed at some length in Chap. 4.

Behind questions having to do with student abilities and interests lies the broader and even more complex issue of career requirements in business. For what range of skills and abilities should business schools endeavor to prepare students? Can requirements for specific jobs be taught, and if so, should business schools teach them? Can the qualities of mind needed for successful and responsible careers in business be identified? Can they also be taught? Are business schools the appropriate institutions to teach them? Should certain schools prepare exclusively for top management and others for lower management alone?

Chapters 5 and 6 seek to throw light on these and related questions by examining the available evidence on career needs at different levels of responsibility in business. An underlying difficulty confronting business schools which seek to develop serious programs of academic study is that in so much of its actual conduct business is an art, not a science. Especially is this true of the more responsible positions in industry, the very ones which seem most deserving of formal academic preparation. It is not too much to say that job duties which are most worthy of academic attention frequently cannot be taught, while those that are teachable frequently do not deserve a place in a college or university curriculum. While greatly oversimplifying the problems facing undergraduate and graduate business schools, this statement contains enough truth to pose a genuine dilemma for these institutions.

Thus the discussion comes back again to a consideration of the purposes which colleges and universities should serve and of the means they should employ in linking academic study to the career needs of undergraduate and graduate students. Preparation for a life in business is but one aspect of the relation which should obtain between higher education and the preparation of practitioners generally. Significant differences of course exist, but some important implications for collegiate business education are to be found in the experience of certain other career areas. as the next chapter seeks to show.

CHAPTER 2

HIGHER EDUCATION AND THE PROFESSIONS

⌐ Career preparation is a worthy objective of higher education as
long as it does not block the individual's maximum intellectual
growth. Specialization and vocationalism can corrupt both liberal arts and professional study. Schools in the highly developed
professions have set themselves against this twofold danger.

As an increasingly important part of the country's system of higher education, business schools mirror the many changes and influences affecting
the nation's colleges and universities. The previous chapter developed the
theme that higher education is being extended to all sections of the
population and that career preparation in a wide variety of fields is a
wholly logical outcome of this trend. Other developments at this level of
education have also had a bearing on the emergence of business schools
and accordingly deserve attention at an early point in this study.

THE TWO TRADITIONS

Colleges and universities are the product of two distinct and sometimes
conflicting traditions. According to the first and more honored of these,
knowledge is pursued for its own sake, and the capacity to think is developed as an end in itself. The preservation of man's intellectual heritage
and the passing on of society's store of knowledge to succeeding generations is considered the special province of the liberal arts colleges while
responsibility for pushing back the boundaries of the known world
through research is said to lie particularly with the graduate schools.
Both, however, should be dedicated to the enrichment of the individual's
life, not for utilitarian purposes but as its own reward.

The distinctive feature of this conception of higher education lies in
part in the mastery of certain subject matter but perhaps in greater part
in the development of those qualities of mind and spirit which are said to
be needed for critical or creative endeavor in all phases of life and which
make it possible for the individual to distinguish the first-rate from the

16

inferior ". . . in every province—physical, aesthetic, intellectual, moral; in his profession or occupation; in personal, national and international life." [1]

In this view of the meaning and purpose of higher education, students and faculty have joined together in the pursuit of truth wherever that quest may lead them. All aspects of experience and all fields of learning fall within their province. This universality of viewpoint rests on knowledge coupled with a mastery of the methods of work employed in various disciplines; it does not entail the mere accumulation of facts in any encyclopedic or compartmentalized sense. Just how such a program of study will relate to the individual's later career is impossible to say. In some lines of endeavor it may prove immensely useful; in others, quite irrelevant; in still others, conceivably even harmful. But this kind of education does not stand or fall on its usefulness; it centers first and foremost on developing the individual as a person and on exploring the world of knowledge for its own sake.

Most proponents of this view of higher education would regard direct preparation for particular careers as basically alien to the purpose of academic work, if not at the graduate, then certainly at the undergraduate, level of instruction. An uncompromising advocate like Robert Hutchins equates vocational and professional education, arguing that career preparation of any kind ". . . deprives the university of its only excuse for existence, which is to provide a haven where the search for truth may go on unhampered by utility or pressure for 'results.'" [2] While perhaps not embracing such an extreme view, many academicians would tend to regard career preparation of whatever type (possibly excepting careers in scholarship!) with a mixture of skepticism and scorn.

The other great tradition in higher education would leave ample room for those students desiring to prepare for particular careers. According to this tradition, the search for truth is not impugned because it proves useful nor is education necessarily unworthy because it is pursued for its career value. On the contrary, career preparation is felt to be an essential purpose of all education; to the extent the latter is divorced from practical use, it is said to become sterile and lose much of its meaning.

While less honored in the academic realm, this second view of higher education goes back to the period in Greek history when the study of mathematics, science, and philosophy was considered the best preparation for careers in politics and in the service of the state as well as for

---

[1] Sir Richard Livingston, *Plato and Modern Education*, The Macmillan Company, New York, 1944, p. 25, quoted in *Report of the Committee on Educational Survey to the Faculty of the Massachusetts Institute of Technology*, Technology Press, Cambridge, Mass., 1949, p. 89.

[2] Robert M. Hutchins, *The Higher Learning in America*, Yale University Press. New Haven, Conn., 1936, p. 43.

enjoyment of "the genteel pursuits of life." [3] In the Middle Ages, higher education was chiefly designed to prepare theologians in the teachings of the Christian gospel and in the ideas of Plato and Aristotle, but this same curriculum, known as the *studium generale*, was also made a prerequisite for the study of law and medicine.[4] From the founding of the University of Paris in the thirteenth century through the successive stages of their development to the present time, the universities of the Western world have considered preparation for the "learned professions" one of their prime concerns, with the four faculties of law, medicine, letters and arts, and philosophy and science providing the main instruction. In Europe today, the proportion of the population continuing education beyond high school is relatively small but university students can start their professional specialization immediately upon admission. In this respect European universities have followed the German rather than the Cambridge and Oxford model in which work of a more advanced, specialized nature comes after three or four years of undergraduate liberal arts study.

The viewpoint underlying the present study is that American higher education should continue to strive for balance between these two traditions. Clearly, they can be made to complement one another, depending on the spirit in which they are approached. Just as clearly, they can be carried to a point where each negates the other. The outcome largely depends on what careers are involved, when career preparation is introduced into the student's education, and how broadly such preparation is conceived. Programs designed to produce engineers versed in all the techniques of their profession, for example, are essentially different from those which prepare students in engineering fundamentals only. Career preparation is a vital ingredient in the individual's total education as long as it is not allowed to crowd out what is broadening and ennobling in his academic experience.

In many institutions, the problem is essentially one of putting career preparation on a more meaningful footing in relation to other branches of college and university work. This applies to the undergraduate liberal arts and graduate nonprofessional studies as well as to the professional schools themselves. At many liberal arts institutions, as noted earlier, heavy emphasis has long been placed on direct career preparation, often in courses of a clearly non-liberal arts character. Whether study is aimed at jobs in accounting, chemical laboratories, or nursing, the viewpoint is essentially vocational. The same holds for courses in nonprofessional graduate fields

[3] Robert Ulich, *Professional Education as a Humane Study*, The Macmillan Company, New York, 1956, p. 4.

[4] George P. Schmidt, *The Liberal Arts College*, Rutgers University Press, New Brunswick, N.J., 1957, p. 44.

as well. Advanced work in, say, English literature or political science can be as vocationally oriented as the study of engineering or medicine. The issue posed by this kind of orientation is certainly not disposed of by calling the work "liberal arts" or "nonprofessional." An analysis of the malaise of these programs—its nature, extent, and cure—hardly falls within the scope of this study but the fact that it exists, and apparently on a wide scale, cannot be brushed aside.[5]

The other tradition in which career preparation is openly put at the center of the student's academic interests also tends to be perverted in practice. Once the door is opened to this type of education it becomes extremely difficult to maintain any clear standards of academic performance or any sense of unified purpose. Universities and even colleges tend to become little more than clusters of schools or departments united only by the accident of physical location. If doctors are to be trained, then why not dentists and veterinarians? If lawyers, why not teachers, social workers, journalists, accountants, bankers, and merchants? These are the relatively prestigious groups in the nation's labor force. Beyond them stand the secretaries and file clerks, nurses and laboratory technicians, dietitians and hygienists, and countless others, all demanding special training. Some of the currents which have carried American colleges and universities in this direction call for further examination.

BACKGROUND INFLUENCES

As is well known, the move to bring higher education to the people received its first big impetus under the Morrill Acts of 1862 and 1890 which provided land-grant colleges and universities with Federal aid. Training students to follow careers in farming and the mechanical arts, however, was only one facet of the general movement to make college education immediately and practically useful to students of all types and interests. Today, this movement is epitomized in the modern, multipurpose state and municipal university. An important element in the development of these institutions can be summed up in the words of a former president of the University of Minnesota who said in 1932:[6]

---

[5] The difficulties besetting these programs have been discussed by many educators from many points of view; see, for example, Robert D. Calkins, "Professional and Graduate Education and the Liberal Arts," *The Georgia Review*, Summer, 1952, and Committee of Fifteen, *The Graduate School Today and Tomorrow*, Fund for the Advancement of Education, New York, 1955.

[6] Lotus D. Coffman, *The State University: Its Work and Problems*, University of Minnesota Press, Minneapolis, 1934, pp. 205–206, quoted in John S. Brubacher and Willis Rudy, *Higher Education in Transition*, Harper & Brothers, New York, 1958, p. 169.

The State universities hold that there is no intellectual service too undignified for them to perform. They maintain that every time they lift the intellectual level of any class or group, they enhance the intellectual opportunities of every other class or group.

Still another aspect of this trend in higher education shows up in a passage from the recent self-study report of New York University. In characterizing the thinking of the deans of the University's professional schools during the period of the twenties, the report observes that they were given practically complete autonomy in the development and administration of their units; it continues:[7]

They were vigorous and imaginative men who did much to promote the growth of the University. The desire for self-sufficiency on the part of the larger schools was strengthened by budgetary practices that geared school appropriations to school revenues, and self-sufficiency resulted in a fragmentation of the work in the liberal arts and science.

The splintering process which grew out of this view of higher education has its qualitative as well as its quantitative aspects. Course offerings at major universities today are numbered by the hundreds, departments by the score. Some of the fields and courses have solid analytical content, others do not. Some are taught in a spirit of scientific inquiry, others are approached in terms of their first-job value only. Some are closely geared to basic, background subjects, others stand completely alone. Some require mind-stretching, independent work on the part of the students, others present little difficulty even to the less academically gifted.

The patchwork quality of this kind of education is most keenly felt at the undergraduate level; here is where the largest mass of students is found; here is where the students of the lowest academic aptitude are likeliest to crowd in; here is where the pressure to provide the simplest, most undemanding trade skills is greatest; yet here is where the individual student needs most to view experience in the round and to develop capacities which will serve him throughout life.

The scattered quality of higher education in the United States cannot be attributed to the relentless pursuit of careerism alone. It is part and parcel of college and university work as conceived in many fields today. For every undergraduate course in Press Photography there is one in the History of Furniture; for every course in Techniques of Camping there is one in Dating, Courtship, and Marriage; for every course in Cement and Highway Materials Testing there is one in Volcanology.[8] It was in

[7] *The New York University Self-Study, Final Report*, New York University Press. New York, 1956, p. 32.

[8] Examples taken from current undergraduate college catalogs.

reaction to this dense jungle of curriculum offerings that Ortega y Gasset inveighed when he said:[9]

The university of today, outside Spain even more than within, is a tropical underbrush of subject matters. If to this we add what we have deemed imperative—the teaching of culture—the verdure threatens to hide the horizon altogether; the horizon of youth which needs to be clear and open, in order that it may expose to view the beckoning glow afar off. There is no remedy but to rise up against this turgid overgrowth and use the principle of economy like a hatchet. First of all, a thorough pruning.

The way to this kind of college and university education, ironically enough, was opened by Harvard University under the leadership of Charles Eliot. At his inaugural in 1869, he said:[10]

The young man of nineteen or twenty ought to know what he likes best and is most fit for. . . . When the revelation of his own peculiar taste and capacity comes to a young man, let him reverently give it welcome, thank God, and take courage. Thereafter he knows his way to happy, enthusiastic work, and, God willing, to usefulness and success. The civilization of a people may be inferred from the variety of its tools.

In keeping with this philosophy, Eliot subsequently introduced the elective system which in turn was copied by most of the country's colleges and universities. At many institutions this created just the kind of atmosphere needed to touch off further expansion of an already luxuriating curriculum, an outcome which Eliot would probably have been the first to decry.

The elective principle had its greatest impact at the undergraduate level, but if higher authority was needed to seal the success of this approach to higher education, it was supplied by developments at the graduate level. In keeping with the example set by the German universities, referred to earlier, a number of institutions established ambitious graduate programs in the latter part of the nineteenth century, and heavy weight came to be placed on research. A similar pattern developed in professional education when Harvard and Johns Hopkins established medical schools on the German model which in turn served as the basis for Abraham Flexner's famous report in 1910.[11]

The spectacular success of these programs, chiefly in the sciences, led to widespread emulation of their form if not of their substance in many

[9] José Ortega y Gasset, *Mission of the University*, Princeton University Press, Princeton, N.J., 1944, p. 70.
[10] Henry James, *Charles W. Eliot*, vol. 1, Boston, 1930, pp. 230–231, quoted in Richard Hofstadter and C. DeWitt Hardy, *The Development and Scope of Higher Education in the United States*, Columbia University Press, New York, 1952, p. 49.
[11] Abraham Flexner, *Medical Education in the United States and Canada*, The Carnegie Foundation for the Advancement of Teaching, New York, 1910.

branches of higher education, with increasing emphasis on intensive specialization. It was in this atmosphere that graduate students acquired the interests and methods they were to develop later as undergraduate teachers. In fact, it is not too much to say that most undergraduate instruction became simply a condensed version of the basic ideas and information which faculty members had previously acquired in their graduate school days. Thus, the highly specialized pattern of graduate education, in widely varying form and extent, permeated and in considerable measure transformed the country's whole structure of higher education.

The educational thinker who more than any other one person crystallized these various ideas into a unified system was John Dewey. Unlike the Germanic conception of education, Deweyism came into the colleges and universities from the elementary and secondary school level. At the same time, there was more than a superficial affinity between these two philosophies of education; both denied that knowledge was in any sense a self-contained body of principles, fixed and immutable for all time; both regarded scientific research, and more specifically empirical scientific research, as the highest form of intellectual attainment; while Dewey's philosophy of education placed greater emphasis on practical or useful knowledge, both gave maximum latitude to the individual instructor and student to follow out his own specialized interests in an atmosphere of free inquiry.

Dewey did not support specialized study for its own sake nor did he favor the fragmentation of the curriculum at any level of education. But he did stress the importance of intensive empirical investigation, the practical uses of knowledge, and the test of pragmatism as the ultimate arbiter of truth. In a revealing passage dealing with the plea to return to one version of the Greek model of education, he wrote:[12]

The problem of going ahead instead of going back is then a problem of liberalizing our technical and vocational education. . . . A truly liberal, and liberating, education would refuse today to isolate vocational training on any of its levels from a continuous education in the social, moral, and scientific contexts within which wisely administered callings and professions must function.

These were some of the ideas and viewpoints which finally eventuated in the diffuse, specialized, utilitarian kind of educational programs found at many colleges and universities today. It need hardly be added that this concept of education, of which career preparation is only one part, would never have become dominant if it had not been in accord with broad economic and social changes of the time. The previous chapter showed

[12] John Dewey, *Problems of Men*, Philosophical Library, Inc., New York, 1946, p. 146.

how the rise in college enrollments since 1900 helped to further this trend in higher education. Related developments which had similar results were the shift toward an urbanized society, the growing importance of professional services, the emergence of the white-collar class, the increasing complexity of the country's economic affairs and career patterns, the achievements of the new technology, the egalitarian movement with its emphasis on equal opportunity and on social mobility, the declining importance of organized religion and the increasing secularization of education, the pragmatic, materialistic, restless quality of twentieth-century America—all these environmental influences, among others, were at work altering the nature and purposes of the country's colleges and universities. Academic preparation for a great variety of callings was thus merely one of many ways in which this new approach to higher education worked itself out, and preparation for business was merely one aspect of the general reorientation of the country's system of post-high school education.

The discussion to this point has been mostly of a negative turn. It is easy enough to heap scorn on the illiberalism of the liberal arts, the professionalism of the nonprofessional graduate studies, and the vocationalism of the professional schools. Yet the contributions of these same programs to the advancement of knowledge are incalculable. Their value in opening the way to successful and useful careers for thousands of students is unquestioned. Their part in humanizing American life, fostering personal growth, and giving reality to the country's democratic ideals is widely recognized. True, the counterattack on academic specialization, course proliferation, departmental prerogatives, and narrow careerism was too long delayed. But the contributions and possibilities of this kind of education also have to be recognized. The scope and complexity of the forces which brought it about have to be allowed for. The very aims of the society in which it arose have to be taken into account. This is not an area in which doctrinaire proposals are likely to be effective or educational gadgets very helpful. The issues go too deep into the fabric of contemporary American civilization to be dealt with in any sweeping or simple manner. The prime need, in short, is not to decry the drift toward mediocrity in higher education but to consider ways and means for coping with it. The present study undertakes this task in one area—academic preparation for business—but it should be pushed in all the other branches of higher education as well, the liberal arts and nonprofessional graduate studies included.

TYPES OF PROFESSIONAL EDUCATION

A closer view of different types of professional education indicates the complexity of the issues facing universities and colleges in this area and

the variety of approaches which can be taken to deal with them.[13] Every
field appears to be subject to a continuous barrage of criticism, and the
issues in controversy seem much the same. The well-nigh universal concern is that too much emphasis is placed on practical techniques, too
little on analytical methods useful in all kinds of situations. This concern
assumes many forms. Sometimes it is argued that education in practical
skills has no place in a college or university. At other times it is argued
this kind of preparation belongs at the graduate level only. At still other
times the importance of study in supporting background subjects is emphasized. In all cases, satisfying the conflicting demands for immediately
useful knowledge and for longer-term, more general knowledge is not
easily achieved.

These issues would become more manageable if the different career
areas could be put into well-defined categories, each with its own educational requirements. No such neat grouping, however, suggests itself. The
point at which a field becomes a profession instead of a vocation or requires a different level of academic preparation is likely to be rather
vague. In most fields, important changes have come slowly, not as any
planned pattern, but rather as a series of responses on the part of particular institutions to specific needs. Needless to say, decisions have often
occurred in particular fields which on hindsight have proven decisive, but
the specific reasons why they were made and how they actually affected
prevailing practice are less easy to isolate. Thus there can be no doubt
that when Charles Eliot in the last quarter of the nineteenth century
finally persuaded the different professional schools at Harvard to require
bachelor's degrees of all their incoming students, his action was of historic importance, but many other developments had to occur before the
full significance of this event was to be made clear. Similarly, the fact that
Daniel Gilman was able to limit the entire program of Johns Hopkins to
graduate instruction with a heavy emphasis on research was eventually to
have a profound influence on the development of medical education as
well as on all other phases of higher education, but his ideas had widely
differing effects on specific institutions and fields.

Often developments at the educational level came as an outgrowth of
changes in professional practice which took many years to crystallize. In
legal education, a number of important subjects, such as administrative
law, taxation, and labor law, have only developed within the past twenty-
five years; today they figure prominently in the curricula of most law

[13] Only those aspects of professional education which have relevance to the future
development of academic programs in business are touched on in the discussion.
Readers desiring a comprehensive view of professional education are referred to the
study being prepared on this subject by Earl J. McGrath under a grant from the
Carnegie Corporation of New York.

schools. In engineering, there are now over twenty areas of specialization for which undergraduate degrees are granted at many accredited institutions, including a number like aeronautical and petroleum engineering which have finally emerged as separate specialties. Educational programs in fields other than engineering, law, and medicine tend to yield no less mixed patterns of development.

The decision to grant academic recognition to a particular field is of critical importance to any university or college, but even this basic step is likely to come as the result of gradual developments or even of some capricious circumstance. A frequent pattern is for new departments or schools to emerge from a slow but largely unplanned regrouping of courses in established fields, with other institutions copying the new pattern after it has become established on a few of the more influential campuses. Another is for a school, as in law, engineering, or social work, to develop independently of any university connection and then to affiliate after it has become well established. Still another is for a school to be formed more or less *de novo* as a result of some benefactor's largesse. The result is a rather haphazard structure in which certain fields are closely related to different branches of university instruction while others are largely autonomous educational bodies.

Presumably, if a university or college decides to offer a curriculum in an area like agriculture or journalism, it plans to put the work above what would be offered at the high school level, but just how this is to be done is by no means always clear. Presumably, too, the work will require a fair degree of extended, systematic study and will relate in some meaningful way to the rest of the student's college-going experience, but again, these are matters which are generally left in an unsettled state largely for the future to decide. Some fields like nursing, pharmacy, and even engineering may continue "half-in and half-out" of the traditional academic fold for many years, but once recognition at a few of the more important universities is won, the clear trend is toward putting all the instruction on a similar footing. Whether this means that all the work can be put on an appropriately demanding level or whether some of it should be left to high schools, evening schools, special institutes, and the like is an open question.

As a field rises in academic prestige, the principles and skills distinguishing it from other fields become more sharply defined. Often this involves concentrating on the technical or specific applications of a subject, since they constitute the distinctive elements in a newly developed area. Moreover, this emphasis fits in well with the interest in the practical uses of knowledge which is generally characteristic of career preparation. From the viewpoint of both students and faculty members, the quickest way for a subject to prove itself is to show it can work in practical application—hence attention tends to center rather completely on techniques and concrete uses. This is likely to lead to a rather elaborate superstructure of specialized courses before any general principles are developed, and it may well leave a wide gulf between the new field and other more traditional areas of academic study.

In large measure the academic stature of a professional field depends on the extent to which it continues to be concerned with specific practice and on the nature and scope of the principles which underlie it. If preparation for a career merely involves mastering a bundle of techniques, or if the principles involved can be intuitively grasped with little systematic analysis, a limited educational curriculum will suffice. Moreover, the work will tend to be of a narrow, highly specialized nature, possessing few meaningful ties with the rest of an institution's program. The dangers facing universities or colleges which enter many such areas would appear to be obvious.

The mere fact that over the years a particular professional curriculum has been lengthened is, of course, no proof that it has become more educationally demanding; unfortunately, duration of study and intellectual content are not always equated. Nonetheless, the contrast in the educational requirements of different fields in this regard is suggestive. In the "learned professions"—medicine, law, and theology—the predominant educational pattern is now three or four years of undergraduate education plus three or four years of professional study. In the next academic tier are professions like dentistry and social work in which the prevailing pattern is two or more years of undergraduate plus two or more years of professional work. Finally, there are fields such as osteopathy, nursing, and library science which are mostly limited either to general college preparation or to a strictly professional type of curriculum. Fields like architecture and engineering are difficult to classify even in the roughest terms. On the one hand, students typically begin their professional studies as freshmen in both of these fields, but on the other, a considerable proportion of the work is required in other subjects. In the case of architecture, the usual program takes five years to complete, and in engineering, graduate work is becoming increasingly important.[14]

Callings which require relatively brief and elementary academic preparation pose a serious threat to an institution's standards, subverting its very reason for being if allowed to multiply unduly. In some instances, there may be certain aspects of a career area which call for intensive academic study, and a college or university can concentrate its attention on them without lowering the quality of its offerings. The difficulty is that most jobs in such areas do not fall in this category, and so an institution

[14] Lloyd E. Blauch (ed.), *Education for the Professions*, U.S. Office of Education, 1955, pp. 14, 74, and 157.

must choose between emphasizing mass education or developing a really demanding type of program. The field of agriculture provides a striking example of the choice which must be made. Certain aspects of this career area entail academic preparation of a very high order, and there is no doubt but that colleges and universities could limit themselves to solid programs in this field if they were determined to do so. On the other hand, the great majority of jobs in agriculture do not require extended, rigorous academic preparation, and an institution which prepares for any substantial portion of them must necessarily offer a lower-level type of program. As indicated earlier, this is the fundamental educational issue posed by every broad career area, and the way in which it is resolved is crucial to the country's entire system of higher education.

THE ADVANCED PROFESSIONS

The paths which the more fully developed professions, such as engineering, law, and medicine, have followed deserve attention in this connection. Despite certain differences, the educational issues which all these fields have faced are fundamentally the same, as are the approaches which have been developed for dealing with them. One of the salient characteristics of a highly developed profession is the breadth and analytical complexity of its central subject matter. In characterizing the general trend in its field, the Commission on Medical Education observed, perhaps somewhat hopefully:[15]

Medical education is shifting from a vocational training, which in the recent past has been largely didactic and descriptive, to a scientific discipline, the aim of which is to provide the student with an understanding and insight into the mechanisms and functional changes in disease processes and with a direct personal experience in the laboratories and at the bedside. It is not an isolated field but an integral part of university education and must be closely correlated with the other major divisions of learning.

A field like engineering has changed almost completely in the past twenty-five years, in some part because of the increase in the number of its specialized areas but in even greater part because of the development of a scientific set of principles which now constitutes the center of the entire field. Whether mastery of these principles requires a level of work comparable to the other sciences is perhaps debatable, but it seems clear that engineering education is becoming increasingly concerned with matters of theory, not details of specific practice. An authoritative report on engineering education concludes:[16]

[15] *Final Report of the Commission on Medical Education,* Office of the Director of Study, New York, 1932, p. 246.
[16] American Society for Engineering Education, *Report on Evaluation of Engineering Education,* 1955, p. 19.

A review of the evolution of engineering curricula over many years shows a trend toward increasing emphasis on the science underlying engineering at the expense of the study of engineering art for its own usefulness.

The same report observes that engineering increasingly involves translation of new scientific developments into practice, a process which is being facilitated ". . . by emphasizing unity in scientific subject matter."[17]

There is a similar trend evident in legal education, although here the outcome is rather different. Law lacks a single body of principles comparable to that found in engineering or medicine, in this respect coming closer to business as a subject of academic study.[18] Yet the schools at the better-known universities concentrate their attention almost wholly on the analytical aspects of the subject, not on description or on practical techniques. This is achieved by a searching examination of the reasoning which lies behind appellate court decisions. The student bears a heavy responsibility for analyzing these decisions on his own, and the classroom experience becomes one of testing his grasp of the significant facts, the questions of law, and the specific principles involved in individual cases.

As is well known, the major law schools have long since given up trying to teach the "trade skills" of the profession; these matters, including preparation in the details of state laws for the bar examinations, are left to special institutes, night schools, and the more practically oriented institutions. The emphasis on rigorous analysis rather than on practical training in legal education is not without its vigorous critics, but the predominant view was succinctly expressed by Judge Charles E. Clark, former dean of the Yale Law School, when he said:[19]

I shall argue that . . . there is no real basis for the criticism implicit in this pressure for practical training; that the latter is limited, partial and fragmentary at best; and that the present-day legal education in problem analysis and exposition and in thorough documentation of sources is much more important and valuable, as well as more within the practical competence of the schools.

Legal educators have long been impressed with the need to introduce nonlegal materials into their programs. Led by Columbia and Yale, a number of schools have endeavored to give considerable emphasis to the institutional or social background of the law. These efforts have not proven altogether successful, but the schools are continuing them none-

---

[17] *Ibid.,* p. 12.

[18] One of the most persistent criticisms of law school programs is that "they fail to provide a synthesis of the law and a synthesis of law and related principles." Albert J. Harno, *Legal Education in the United States,* Bancroft-Whitney Company, San Francisco, 1953, p. 137. On the other hand, another widespread criticism is that law schools "neglect training in the practical skills a lawyer must have." *Ibid.,* p. 137.

[19] Quoted in Albert J. Harno, *op. cit.,* pp. 148–149.

theless.[20] The prevailing view was recently summed up by the dean of the Pennsylvania Law School in these words:[21]

The lawyer, the law teacher, and even the law student know generally that the problems they deal with involve economics, politics, business, sociology, psychology, and other fields. . . . Yet at a time when all these fields are flourishing with new methods, materials, insights, the law schools and the legal scholars have not effectively solved the problem of how to bring the materials of these other disciplines into legal research and teaching, how to incorporate insights from related disciplines, how to handle or at least to understand their methods and techniques.

The need to establish closer ties with other disciplines is also widely felt in engineering, medicine, and the other more highly developed professions.

A related development is the increased attention paid to the student's background education and general intellectual equipment. In some areas, like engineering and medicine, certain preprofessional subjects are accorded central importance, but in others, such as law and social work, there appears to be little to choose between different background subjects. In all cases, prime attention centers on developing the student's powers of analysis, not on digesting certain quantities of information. This accords with the view that the duties of an engineer or a lawyer in today's world cannot be defined too precisely in advance and that their education should therefore center around capacities which can be put to a variety of specialized uses. A profession which stresses its responsibilities to the general public is also likely to emphasize the need for broad background preparation, often in areas far removed from its traditional sphere of interest.

In characterizing this aspect of the engineer's work, the M.I.T. survey report states:[22]

Like the physician, the engineer cannot always defer action until all the facts in a given situation are fully known but must work within the limitations

[20] "The most significant development in American legal education since 1870," observes one scholar, "is the movement toward reorganization of courses along functional lines and toward the broadening of law school studies to include nonlegal materials, chiefly from the social sciences, which are relevant to legal problems." Brainerd Currie, "The Materials of Law Study," *Journal of Legal Education*, vol. 8, no. 1, 1955–56, p. 1.

[21] Jefferson B. Fordham, *Report of the Dean*, 1956–1957, Law School, University of Pennsylvania, p. 5.

[22] *Report of the Committee on Educational Survey, op. cit.*, p. 40. A number of other studies of engineering education have reached similar conclusions. See, for example, Report of the Humanistic-Social Research Project, *General Education in Engineering*, American Society for Engineering Education, University of Illinois Press, Urbana, Ill., 1956.

of the state of the art at any given time. . . . It is through this ability to make critical judgments that the engineer's professional competence often finds its highest expression.

The report goes on to observe that an engineer's success depends as much on his understanding of human relations and his skill in handling men as upon his technical competence and that full achievement in his profession requires ". . . that he be a man of broad culture with a deep sense of social responsibility." [23]

Another distinguishing feature of the advanced professions is the care with which incoming students are screened. Since gaining an initial foothold in a profession like medicine or law depends on being admitted to a degree-granting school, the admission policies of these schools become of the utmost importance. If professional schools were not able to limit admissions to the best-qualified students, it seems obvious that any effort to raise standards would be effectively blocked. Since intellectual qualities normally associated with rigorous academic work are increasingly important in the advanced professions, admission policies can be reasonably clear-cut. These schools also have the advantage of getting students after three or four years of undergraduate work, thereby providing that much more evidence of academic capacity.

Another important development in the advanced professions is the increased emphasis on research and on scientific inquiries of all kinds. In engineering, law, or medicine today, it is not simply that the position of the research scholar is secure but rather that he is likely to be the most honored member of the faculty. Similarly, in these fields the professional schools are not simply keeping up to date with the best in current practice; they are very much to the fore of practice, concentrating a substantial portion of their faculty and other resources on exploring the frontiers of knowledge. The nature and quality of such work vary enormously from school to school, and perhaps from field to field, but it constitutes an increasingly important focus for the educational programs of all the advanced professions. The result is that institutions like Columbia's College of Physicians and Surgeons, Harvard Law School, and M.I.T. are looked to as the source of path-breaking ideas and as leaders in the professions they serve.

The emphasis on scholarship and research in professional schools in the more advanced fields bears importantly on the question of specialized study. There is no doubt but what such study is an essential element in scientific work of any kind and that it is a necessary part of the student's intellectual development in any field. What cannot be condoned is specialized work which repeats relatively straightforward material with

[23] *Ibid.*, p. 40.

which the student is already quite familiar, which crowds out other important areas of knowledge, and which requires little in the way of independent analysis or creative thought. To act on this distinction may mean nothing more than postponing specialized study until later in a student's career. More than this, it may mean putting rather severe limits on the quantity of detailed descriptive matter students are expected to master, permitting specialized work only to the extent it supplies an essential element in the student's intellectual growth. In the more highly developed professions, each of the four stages in a student's preparation—his work in background subjects, in the general principles of his profession, in the area of his special competence, and in the particular techniques of his specialty—tends to require an increasing proportion of the student's time, and unless his formal academic studies are to go on indefinitely, some compression becomes inescapable. Without exception, all the advanced professions stress the danger of slighting the first two of these stages in the student's preparation and concentrating undue time and effort on the more specialized aspects of his education.

There is no gainsaying that much work of a factual, technical nature must be required. Students preparing for professions or related careers will have to deal with a wide variety of concrete situations in the course of their work. Whether their prior academic preparation proves valuable in career terms will largely depend on whether it has continuing relevance for these action situations. This can best be assured if the student is obliged to relate his academic work to particular problems himself. Otherwise it is hard to believe he will ever be able to translate his general knowledge into specific use. But any life of action is bound to be concerned with matters of detailed practice—a surgeon has certain bodies of factual information as well as certain technical skills he must master, as does an engineer, lawyer, architect, or any other professionally trained person. These matters cannot be ruled out of professional education altogether, because the relation between formal knowledge and specific practice is close to the very center of such academic programs.

The issue is essentially one of deciding what kind of specialized study is essential to a student's preparation for a broad range of career interests. Highly technical preparation can be an extremely demanding intellectual experience, adding immeasurably to a student's analytical powers. Other technical work can be repetitive, obvious, and stultifying. Difficult as the distinction is to apply in practice, each field is obliged to determine whether a given type of technical preparation falls in one category or the other.

The various professions have approached this issue rather differently, and it would be quite misleading to suggest that a completely satisfactory balance has been achieved in any one of them.[24] Medicine has a distinct advantage over such fields as law or engineering in this regard, because the clinical subjects can be taught in close cooperation with hospitals. Even in medicine, however, considerable doubt exists over how far the student can profitably go in applying his academic preparation to specific case situations. In medical education as in engineering and law, every effort is made to keep this part of the program from degenerating into a series of mechanical exercises, but just where the line should be drawn is by no means clear.

IMPLICATIONS FOR BUSINESS EDUCATION

The foregoing discussion contains important implications for academic preparation for business careers, which are developed more fully in later chapters but can be briefly noted here. Business activities range from the simplest duties to the most complex. Similarly, academic preparation for business careers exhibits the whole range of characteristics found in the least developed and the most developed branches of professional education. For this reason there are no grounds for believing that the principal elements of professional education in a single field like medicine or law can be applied directly or mechanically to education for business.

On the other hand, the broad trend in professional education may well contain important lessons for this branch of higher education. At least it seems clear that if policy in this field follows the pattern marked by other fields as they have moved from lower to higher stages of development, the general direction which business education will take in the future is reasonably well defined. First, it will mean concentrating on giving students the equipment they will need to deal with complex and demanding problems, at levels of instruction of increasing difficulty. Second, it will mean focusing the student's work on a central core of subject matter which to the greatest possible extent unifies his studies in various fields. Third, it will mean helping him build up a broad background of knowledge and giving him every opportunity to utilize such knowledge in his area of special interest. Fourth, it will mean putting him as much as possible on his own in developing the uses of his formal education. Fifth, and finally, it will mean devoting a substantial portion of the schools' resources to research and to providing a leadership of new ideas for this entire field. Whether business schools can meet these responsibil-

[24] The difficulties which the various professions face in dealing with this and related issues are discussed in Proceedings of the Inter-Professions Conference on Education for Professional Responsibility, *Education for Professional Responsibility*, Carnegie Press, Pittsburgh, 1948.

ities and still provide diversified education for large masses of students is considered at length in later chapters. Here it is enough to point out that in this area, as in any other field, the first obligation of a college or university is to put its work on a challenging intellectual basis. This is the purpose of such institutions, and where it is not fulfilled, their reason for being disappears.

CHAPTER 3

HISTORY OF BUSINESS SCHOOLS

The development of business schools falls into three periods: origins and early growth (1880–1914), expansion and diversification (1914–1940), and reassessment and reorganization (1940 to present). Many schools had close ties with economics and other departments in the early period, later developed highly specialized curricula of their own, but more recently have adopted a broader conception of their work. Nonetheless, controversy persists over what the distinctive role of business schools should be.

The principal features of present-day business school programs were largely set thirty or forty years ago, and many of the current problems of these schools are the heritage of decisions reached even before then. Institutions launching new programs since World War II have had the opportunity to develop wholly new approaches, and a few others have drastically reorganized their work in recent years. Most, however, still adhere to the prewar pattern, so that a profile of today's business schools bears considerable resemblance to the typical school of the mid-twenties. It is to the past, then, attention must turn to explain the present.

Since this study is chiefly concerned with prospects for the future, only the more important aspects of past trends are of interest here. The discussion centers around the approaches of various types of schools—the distinguishing characteristics of their programs, the circumstances surrounding their development, and the general educational results. The material for this chapter deals with seventy-five schools chosen for special study in different parts of the country, but attention centers primarily on the history of twelve institutions.[1]

[1] These twelve institutions, representing a rather broad cross section of programs, are: California (Berkeley), Chicago, Columbia, Dartmouth (Tuck School), Harvard, Illinois, Indiana, Louisiana State, Minnesota, Pennsylvania (Wharton School), Temple, and Tulane. The list of schools selected for special study and the procedures followed in conducting the campus interviews are described in Appendix 6.

Seen in broad perspective, the development of business schools falls into three periods. In the first, dating from the founding of the Wharton School of Finance and Commerce in 1881 to World War I, business schools were engaged in finding a foothold in the academic world. Their programs reflected a wide variety of purposes which in turn could be traced to their mixed origins, their different campus environments, and the particular ideas of their early leaders. By the end of this initial period, however, the main lines of development of business schools had become visible. In the second period, covering the interwar years, the dominant pattern of business school programs became more firmly set. Following the lead of a few pioneering institutions, the basis for some new approaches to business education was also laid in this period, but these experiments did not alter the main direction of the schools' development. In the third period, dating from World War II, the number of schools which stood apart from the pattern prevailing in the interwar period increased, and their influence was beginning to make itself felt in a widening number of institutions. Most of the catalytic ideas of this third period came first at the graduate level, but their impact was widely felt at the undergraduate level as well. The salient features of each of these three periods and their implications for the future of business schools will become clear in the discussion which follows.

ORIGINS AND EARLY GROWTH: 1880–1914

The principal issues confronting business schools today were also present during the formative phase of their development. Naturally, there was much more improvisation in the early period, and the variety of approaches was, if anything, greater then than now. Certain of the ideas and experiments of the initial years anticipated some important current developments which today are considered quite revolutionary. Similarly, the decisions which a few of the more influential schools made forty or fifty years ago largely determined the pattern of business school education which has obtained until the present.

Academic leadership in the founding of business schools can often be traced to members of economics departments who were primarily interested in business practices and problems. In the case of many schools established later in the interwar period, the work in economics was already well under way, and the business programs simply emerged out of a gradual regrouping of business-oriented courses. Prior to World War I, however, the economics offerings tended to be rather limited, and they were quite as likely to include work in fields like business finance or transportation as in economic theory or economic history. In these cases the programs in business and economics often emerged together; in some cases business preceded economics.

One of the early schools to emerge from an already established program in economics was the business school at Chicago.[2] Even before the school's formation in 1898, the department of political economy offered a number of courses with a business orientation in such subjects as Railway Transportation, Finance, Banking and Money, and Practical Economics. The last-named course was taught by J. Laurence Laughlin who was chairman of the department of political economy and who was chiefly responsible for bringing the business school into existence. Laughlin had been trained at Harvard, had taught economics there, and had later left teaching for three years to serve as president of a fire insurance company. While a recognized scholar, his interests ran to the practical applications of economics. He well epitomized the close ties which existed between the business and economics programs at Chicago from the start.

On the other hand, the College of Commerce and Business Administration at Tulane, which was founded in 1914, developed before the university had developed a program in economics. The launching of this school can largely be attributed to the single-minded persistence of Morton Aldrich.[3] He had been trained at Harvard and the University of Halle and came to Tulane in 1901 to teach economics and sociology. His interests soon centered also on the business aspects of the field, and as early as 1905 he began to push the idea of a business school among his academic and business friends, his efforts bearing fruit nearly ten years later. Even in 1914, however, the work in economics at Tulane was still largely on paper and, in fact, languished rather seriously until it was put under the administrative control of the business school many years later. Similarly, while the School of Business Administration at State College of Washington was not formally established until 1928, there were no less than thirty-one business courses offered as early as 1920. Prior to the latter year, the work in business and economics had grown out of the same department, but by 1910 the business offerings began to outstrip those in economics, and by the mid-twenties, the former had far outnumbered the latter.

At a number of other institutions the progenitor of business programs was accounting. Thus, the founding of N.Y.U.'s School of Commerce, Accounts, and Finance in 1900 can be directly traced to the decision reached by the New York State Society of Certified Public Accountants in 1899 that a school was needed to supply students of accounting with the knowledge necessary to pass the C.P.A. examinations. The school's

[2] Information on the development of the Chicago program was supplied by R. H. Turner, Graduate School of Business, University of Chicago.

[3] Information on the origins of Tulane's program was supplied by Dean John P. Dyer, University College, Tulane University.

first dean was Charles W. Haskins, a member of the accounting firm of Haskins and Sells. Another and often closely related group of courses which preceded the introduction of a general business curriculum at many schools was in secretarial training, office skills, and teacher preparation in such subjects. The dual lineage of accounting and secretarial training was characteristic of a number of business schools in the South and Middle West, including Florida State, Ohio University, and many others.

Even schools like Virginia which initially had close ties with economics soon put heavy emphasis on accounting. Also, schools located in metropolitan areas often gave courses in the evening for "downtown" students, the work usually being in accounting and practical office skills. The initial program at Tulane, for example, was at night, and it continued to be the main part of the school's activities for many years. The business school at Northwestern, established in 1908, also originated in night school courses offered students in the Chicago business district.

Still a third group of schools trace their parentage to more diversified academic groups who nevertheless agreed that some type of special business curriculum was needed. While the ideas of these mixed groups were clearly not limited to economics, accounting, or office skills, it is hard to characterize their educational philosophy in very specific terms. At the outset they tended toward an interdisciplinary approach to the business curriculum with special emphasis on the social sciences. However, the ties between the study of business and other academic subjects at these institutions often remained vague and their programs varied considerably in consequence.

Thus the terms of Joseph Wharton's $100,000 bequest which led to the founding of the Wharton School in 1881, the nation's first business school, left a great deal of latitude to the University of Pennsylvania to chart a pioneer course in this area. Edmund J. James was brought to the campus to develop the new program and he was chiefly responsible for the direction it took until the time of his departure in 1896. James, like Laughlin, was a scholar with a keen interest in practical affairs. His special fields of interest were finance and public administration, and he stressed the importance of government service in developing Wharton's program. In the years James was in charge of the program, business preparation at Wharton consisted almost wholly of courses in history, government, and economics, with a small nucleus of offerings in accounting, business law, and business organization.[4] During this period the

---

[4] This was the way James summarized the program in a speech he gave before the American Banker's Association at Saratoga Springs in 1891. See also Emory R. Johnson, *The Wharton School—Its First Fifty Years*, 1881–1931, Wharton School, University of Pennsylvania, 1931.

Wharton School remained under the jurisdiction of the arts and science college and, in fact, it was not until 1912 that it secured its own dean and faculty.

In the case of the Tuck School, the emphasis on liberal arts preparation for business was built into the program from the time of its founding in 1900 by requiring three years of undergraduate work at Dartmouth, or four years elsewhere, before admission. Moreover, President Tucker, whose ideas greatly influenced the school during its formative years, felt that the first year of the graduate business curriculum should consist of certain courses in modern history, economic theory, political theory, anthropological geography, and modern language. Some of these subjects were continued in the second (and last) year when the student also took work in such fields as finance, transportation, and law. The faculty in the early years was drawn from different departments at Dartmouth, including economics, English, history, modern languages, political science, and sociology. The first director of the school was Professor Frank H. Dixon of the Dartmouth economics department.

The steps leading to the establishment of the Harvard Business School in 1908 have been traced to a suggestion made by President Eliot in 1898 to establish a school for diplomacy and government service. The faculty groups set up to report on this proposal felt that there would not be enough demand for this kind of a program but that there was considerable need for academic preparation for careers in business. While there was general agreement that the work should consist of two years of study at the graduate level, the initial sponsors were not clear how the new school should fit into the university structure as a whole. Initially, it was a subsidiary of the Faculty of Arts and Sciences, and it was not until 1913 that it achieved independent status.

Nor was it clear at the outset how closely the work in business should be related to programs elsewhere in the university, notably in the social sciences and applied sciences. A. Lawrence Lowell, who at the time was a lecturer in government at Harvard and an active participant in the events leading up to the founding of the school, argued vigorously for treating business as separate and distinct from political economy, drawing an analogy between the study of law and jurisprudence. The school's first dean, Edwin F. Gay, felt that in the formative years the program should be under the jurisdiction of the arts and science faculty, noting that a particularly close relation should exist between the Business School and the Graduate School of Applied Science. While Dean Gay was primarily a research scholar in the field of economic history with no business experience, he was no rigid formalist and espoused a number of unorthodox ideas, including considerable interest in the case method of teaching which was to provide the foundation for Harvard's program after World War I.[5]

Initial Programs

The schools founded in this early period had a difficult time winning academic status and developing a clear-cut role. As to what to teach, the problems were simplest for schools which stressed accounting and office procedures, more complex for those with an economics orientation, and still more so for those with a mixed academic background. The quickest and easiest way for a school to attract students and develop its own corps of teachers was to offer courses in specific trade practices and practical business skills. Work in particular industries offered a rather similar opportunity. Schools which from the start had a trade-industry orientation moved quickly to add numerous courses in various areas of business practice and related subjects. By 1914, the business school at N.Y.U., for example, offered 39 courses in commerce, 18 courses in journalism, 17 courses in finance, 16 courses in government and public affairs, and 14 courses in accounting.

Other schools, regardless of origin and announced purpose, tended to move in the same direction. Thus, a *Circular of Information* published in 1902 about the business school at Chicago characterized the work as fitting men "for careers in the practical profession of Banking, Transportation, Trade and Industry, and Journalism." While the requirements in the different areas were in good part the same, students could major in one of these four areas. By World War I, journalism had been dropped, but majors in public service, philanthropic service, and secretarial training had been added, and students could also take work in accounting and insurance. According to the 1914–1915 catalog, the trade and industry division alone listed 52 courses.

Toward the end of the 1890s, the Wharton School began to add courses in particular industries and specific business practices, for example, transportation and mercantile law. By 1906, according to Emory Johnson:

Courses were being offered in most of the larger fields of business—accounting, commerce and marketing, transportation, insurance, industry (production), corporation finance and investments, banking and real estate, and each of these subjects was being taught by men who were specializing in their respective fields.[6]

The 1906 catalog summed up the work at the Wharton School at that time in these words: "The work of the first two years is mainly pre-

[5] Melvin T. Copeland, *And Mark an Era*, Little, Brown & Company, Boston, 1958, Chaps. 1 and 2.

[6] Emory R. Johnson, *op. cit.*, p. 18.

scribed; that of the last two is elective, and is specialized along the lines selected by each student for his chosen career."

In the years before World War I, students at the Tuck School could major in such fields as accounting and auditing, business organization and procedure, transportation, and corporation finance and securities. The 1914–1915 Harvard Business School catalog listed courses in accounting, law, foreign trade, insurance, transportation, printing and publishing, lumbering, and three courses under the intriguing title of "Chambers of Commerce." The program at the University of California at Berkeley was limited to relatively few courses during this period, but the areas covered were nonetheless highly diversified. By World War I, students were required to take courses in economics and economic history, jurisprudence, trade journals, statistics, and accounting. Four areas of specialization were permitted—accounting, actuarial service, consular service, and railroading.[7]

It is clear from the record that in their formative years, most business schools soon developed a strong practical orientation. Once they did so, they expanded rapidly. Between 1900 and 1914, the number of degrees granted by the Wharton School increased from 10 to 79 at a time when the number of first degrees in arts and science rose only from 43 to 61.[8] The enrollment in business courses at the University of Illinois rose from 85 in 1904–1905 to 420 in 1914–1915 and the number of faculty members from 5 to 16.[9] The enrollment pattern at a number of other schools was similar.

Academic Status

While the emphasis on specific business practice helped business schools achieve a certain identity, it tended to isolate them from the rest of the academic community. As the number of courses in business skills increased, the proportion of the work devoted to more traditional disciplines fell. As more students with poor scholastic records were granted admission, the programs in business declined in esteem. As the faculties in these programs specialized in more areas of business practice, the

[7] A four-year undergraduate program was established at Berkeley in 1898, but it was not until World War II that steps were taken to give it a faculty separate from the department of economics and other departments.

[8] James H. S. Bossard and J. Frederic Dewhurst, *University Education for Business,* University of Pennsylvania Press, Philadelphia, 1931, p. 257.

[9] H. T. Scovill, *50 Years of Education for Business at the University of Illinois,* University of Illinois Press, Urbana, Ill., 1952, p. 9. A School of Commerce was established at Illinois in 1870, offering mostly secretarial courses, but it was discontinued in 1879. The program of business courses instituted in 1902 was expanded into a College of Commerce and Business Administration in 1915.

status of business schools in the academic world tended to deteriorate. The emphasis on details of business practice naturally attracted faculty members of a strong practical bent. Many of the schools, especially in metropolitan areas, leaned heavily on businessmen or professional practitioners who were willing to give a course or two in some specialized area but whose main interests lay elsewhere. Even full-time faculty members were often closely identified with outside business activities. Taken together, these circumstances did not instill confidence on the part of other college and university faculty members in the new programs. About the period when most of the early business schools had achieved complete administrative autonomy, they rightly or wrongly had fallen to a low academic estate.

Whether employer spokesmen exerted any significant pressure on business schools to emphasize practical skill training at this time is uncertain. The schools doubtless had the business community's attitudes in mind in developing such work; and in a number of instances, as noted, local employer groups played an active part in initiating the programs, their financial support often being crucial.[10] However, there is no evidence of overt attempts on the part of the business community to influence the educational policies of the schools; rather it was more a matter of the schools having to overcome employer indifference and skepticism.

As business schools withdrew from the academic community, they endeavored to form increasingly close ties with business organizations. This two-way trend was mutually reinforcing, the one furthering the other. It was carried to its furthest extreme in the relationship between certain schools and societies of professional accountants. Indeed, it later became difficult to tell whether the accounting instructors in these schools were primarily teachers who had an accounting practice on the side, or primarily practicing accountants who wanted to keep their hand in the teaching profession.

In explaining why the early business schools took this direction, it should be noted that the subject was largely undeveloped at this time and anything approaching a clear analytical framework for studying business practices was lacking. Economics came closer than any other field to providing such a theoretical framework, but it was in very much

[10] In the case of Tulane, for example, local accounting and business groups guaranteed the new school $5,450 annually for six years beginning in 1914. The Tuck School was launched after Edward Tuck gave Dartmouth $300,000 in 1899. Chicago's program was put on quite a different basis after the Hobart Williams gift of $2 million in 1916. The financial support which businessmen have accorded the Harvard Business School has been a crucial factor in its development; George F. Baker's gift of $5 million in 1924 was the largest of many other contributions before and since.

of a formative state itself. Moreover, a number of the early figures in the business school movement felt that economics did not provide a broad enough or realistic enough frame of reference for the study of business problems. In these early years the concept of management or administration as an organizing device for the business curriculum was just beginning to receive attention. Lacking any analytical focus, the courses spread in a variety of directions, and the programs became increasingly heterogeneous.

Most schools, even in this early period, took some steps to check the trend toward disparate, practical education. Even those which concentrated initially on accounting and secretarial training soon began to introduce courses in broader subjects, such as finance and business organization. On the other hand, schools which retained close ties with economics sometimes required an advanced theory course, and those with more mixed academic origins occasionally required advanced work in history and government as well as in economics. According to their 1914–1915 catalogs, for example, both Chicago and the University of California at Berkeley required all advanced students to take a course in the economic history of the United States. While providing a variety of courses at the practical level, Harvard stressed the need for a broad approach in its program, and even before World War I students were required to take a course in business policy.

The chief architect of the Wharton School program in this early period was Simon N. Patten, one of the country's leading economists and a person of an original turn of mind. During the period of his leadership, considerable emphasis on courses of a general, theoretical nature in fields other than business was retained. The Tuck School probably went further than any other institution in the prewar period in putting its work on a demanding intellectual level. Harlow S. Person, an active figure in the scientific management movement, was head of the school, and the Tuck program, as it became better defined, reflected many of his ideas. Heavy emphasis was placed on accounting and statistics, and the students' last year included work in the principles of scientific management, scientific management in distribution, and scientific management in manufacturing. Other examples could be cited to indicate that the schools were alive to the danger of scattering their offerings too widely and of concentrating their attention unduly on the techniques of business practice, but the broad trend was clearly in the latter direction.

EXPANSION AND DIVERSIFICATION: 1914–1940

Between the onset of World War I and the beginning of World War II, almost every important public university in the United States established a school of business. Most of the state universities, including Ohio State (1916), Alabama, Minnesota, and North Carolina (1919), Virginia (1920), Indiana (1921), and Kansas and Michigan (1924) set up schools in the early part of this period. Two of the top-ranking private universities, Columbia in 1916 and Stanford in 1925, also began business schools at this time, Stanford's being exclusively graduate from the outset. Large numbers of public and private institutions in metropolitan areas initiated similar programs, though they tended to come somewhat later than the state schools.

The sharp increase in the number of new schools and the rapid expansion in enrollments occurred before a solid basis for academic work could be developed. Courses were added before adequate textbook materials were available. New subdivisions were opened up within fields like accounting and marketing, not so much because of any well-developed educational plan, but because more students were crowding in and something had to be done with them. Faculty members brought in to teach basic courses in fields like finance and factory management were permitted to offer advanced courses of an even more specialized sort. New branches of the curriculum began to emerge, like real estate, public utility operations, brokerage, retailing, advertising, and credit practices. some of which were to be accorded status as separate major departments. The instructors in most of these subjects had to rely heavily on personal experience and scattered sources of information for teaching materials. Those who had gone to graduate school, of course, had taken their advanced degree in fields other than business. A considerable measure of improvisation and trial and error was therefore inescapable.

The program at Illinois may be taken as illustrative of the period. According to its 1925–1926 catalog, the first two years of required work for a student in the general business curriculum consisted of the courses listed in Table 3-1. The second two years required the courses listed in Table 3-2.

TABLE 3-1

REQUIRED COURSES, FIRST TWO YEARS

Course	Semester hours
Principles of Accounting	6
Intermediate Accounting	6
Modern Industry	3
Economic History of the United States	3
Principles of Economics	5
Money, Credit, and Banking	3
Business Organization and Operation	3
Business Letter Writing	2
Rhetoric and Themes	6

TABLE 3-2

REQUIRED COURSES, LAST TWO YEARS

Course	Semester hours
Marketing Organization and Operations	3
Principles of Business Law	6
Transportation System of the United States	3
Corporation Management and Finance	3
Rates and Regulations	3
Salesmanship and Sales Administration	6
Advertising	6
Advanced Economics	6

Two quite comprehensive studies of business schools were made at about the mid-point of this period, both rather critical of the prevailing pattern of business education. The one, edited by Leon C. Marshall, dean of the Chicago business school, observed:[11] "Within the field of technical business education there has often been such a proliferation of 'courses' that it is scarcely humanly possible that the content can be of university or professional-school grade." The other, written by James H. S. Bossard and J. Frederic Dewhurst of the Wharton School staff, concluded:[12] "Specialization in the business curricula runs riot—at least so far as differentiated curricula and faculty preferences are concerned." Both surveys indicated that the relation between the student's work in business and liberal arts subjects was not too meaningful and that the business studies themselves lacked coherence. Both called for a searching re-examination of the purposes and direction of the work of business schools.

While the dominant trend in business education during the interwar years was the source of much misgiving, certain elements of strength appeared which proved to have enduring importance. These developments grew out of pioneering efforts along four lines at a small group of institutions: (1) closer ties with certain subjects outside business, (2) more precise definition of the central core of business studies, (3) greater emphasis on company-wide management policies, and (4) intensive analysis of the decision-making process in a variety of business situations. Since these are the building blocks which are being used today to

[11] Leon C. Marshall (ed.), *The Collegiate School of Business*, University of Chicago Press, Chicago, 1928, p. 95.

[12] James H. S. Bossard and J. Frederic Dewhurst, *op. cit.*, p. 323. Between 1910–1911 and 1930–1931, the number of subjects offered at Wharton increased from 52 to 118; if only offerings in business and economics are counted, the total in 1930–1931 came to 91. *Ibid.*, p. 283.

strengthen the programs of a number of schools, they warrant further discussion.

Relation to Nonbusiness Subjects

Most of the business schools of the interwar period made a genuine effort to give students considerable exposure to the traditional liberal arts studies. If economics and business courses are grouped together, students generally took somewhat less than half their undergraduate work in nonbusiness areas.[13] Schools which had previously concentrated on trade skills and office procedures broadened their requirements to give more balanced preparation. Schools which had emerged from economics departments or from a mixed liberal arts background left considerable room for work outside the strictly business area. Marshall found that 12 of the 38 schools he studied limited most of the business courses to the junior and senior years, the first two years being taken in common with students in liberal arts. The pattern of instruction at the other schools in the study, all of them members of the American Association of Collegiate Schools of Business, was not substantially different.[14] By concentrating their efforts at the graduate level, Harvard, Michigan, Stanford, and Tuck left considerable room, of course, for students to pursue liberal arts studies.

The issue was not so much one of providing sufficient time for these studies but of putting the time available to productive use. The two surveys just referred to stressed the fact that the nonbusiness requirements tended to be a hodgepodge of courses which students took more because they had to than because they were a vital part of the work. This outcome was due as much to trends in liberal arts instruction, referred to in the preceding chapter, as to developments in the business curriculum.

The underlying difficulty was that preparation for business continued to be a diffuse, scattered subject lacking solid analytical content. The spreading out of business courses did not grow out of an evolving discipline comparable, say, to the development of chemistry or engineering. Rather, courses multiplied before a central subject matter could be developed. Under these circumstances, it is hardly surprising that the ties with other fields were of a tenuous and accidental nature.

The most ambitious effort to relate preparation for business to certain underlying disciplines occurred at Chicago. As early as 1917 Dean Marshall became imbued with the idea that anyone looking forward to

[13] James H. S. Bossard and J. Frederic Dewhurst, *op. cit.*, Chap. 11.
[14] Leon C. Marshall (ed.), *op. cit.*, pp. 12 and 83.

a responsible career in business would benefit from careful study of a number of nonbusiness subjects. Thus the school's *Announcements* in 1917 characterized the curriculum in these terms:

> *The business manager administers his business under conditions imposed by his environment, both physical and social.* The student should accordingly have an understanding of the physical environment. This justifies attention to such sciences as biology, physics, chemistry and the earth sciences. He should also have an understanding of the social environment and must accordingly give attention to civics, law, economics, social psychology, and other branches of the social sciences. A knowledge of environment is not sufficient, however. It must be supplemented with a range of courses dealing with business administration wherein the student may become acquainted with such matters as the computing aids of administration. . . . [Italics in the original]

Accordingly, in their first year, students were recommended to take such courses as Industrial Society, Geography and Resources of North America, and Civil Government in the United States. Second-year suggestions included Business Psychology, Value and Price, Labor Conditions and Problems, and Economic History of the United States. The third year included Introduction to Statistics, Social Control of Business, and Municipal Government. Finally, the fourth-year recommendations ranged from Trade Unionism to Public Finance. The business courses, on the other hand, were kept to a bare minimum in the first two years, and those studied in the last two years were built on top of broader courses taken earlier in related nonbusiness fields.

It was noted above that in the early days the closest kind of ties existed between the business school and the economics department at Chicago. These ties were strengthened, if anything, during the Marshall regime. For many years he served both as dean of the business school and as chairman of the economics department, and economists like J. M. Clark, Paul Douglas, Frank Knight, and Jacob Viner played active parts in the affairs of the school.

Following Marshall's resignation as dean in 1923, the program at Chicago took on more of a mixed character and in this sense became more conventional. Marshall's conception of business education was apparently difficult to adhere to, and there is some basis for arguing that his program never really got off the ground. As is well known, the business school experienced particular difficulties during the period of Robert Hutchins' presidency and by the end of World War II was in straitened circumstances. As a forerunner of current developments in business education, however, Marshall's work was of great importance. His attempt to relate preparation for business to fundamental fields of knowledge was the first major move away from the scattered, descriptive kind of work typical of business schools of the early twenties.

Functional Areas

Another significant development occurred early in the interwar period when many business schools began to concentrate their attention on certain broad functions of the business enterprise. By the mid-twenties, half or more of the thirty-four schools belonging to the American Association of Collegiate Schools of Business required all students to take work in accounting, business law, finance, statistics, and marketing.[15] Writing a few years later about this same group of schools, Bossard and Dewhurst found that upper-class core requirements centered on six subjects: business law, statistics, marketing, accounting, money and banking, and business or corporate finance.[16] The typical pattern was to require students to take survey-type courses in some or all of these areas during their junior year and to permit further specialized study in their senior year. The movement to focus the programs on certain functional areas cannot be traced to any one school. The lead was taken by Harvard, Michigan, and Tuck at the graduate level and by Chicago, Columbia, and Wharton at the undergraduate level. Other institutions, however, were quick to move in this same direction, and many of the new programs were set up on this pattern from the time they were first established.

Viewed in retrospect, the development of a core of required subjects constituted a major step in giving coherence and content to the business studies. Until this time, systematic analysis of business problems was limited to economics. By singling out certain functions of the business enterprise as required areas of study, business schools marked out the boundaries of a distinctive field of academic inquiry. The core subjects were to change somewhat in later years, and some proved to have a good deal more content than others; but the principal functional subjects developed in the early twenties were to provide the main focus for business schools until the present time. It seems clear that any constructive plans for the future must be built around these same subjects.

At the same time the significance of the consolidation efforts of the interwar period can be exaggerated. Many schools continued to offer a scattering of courses at the trade-skill level. Most of the schools which required a limited core of studies still permitted students to specialize in a variety of narrow areas. The core areas themselves continued to be sufficiently ill-defined and ill-developed to permit a wide diversity of instruction. During the twenties some of the pioneer thinkers in such fields as finance and marketing did important work, later crystallized their ideas in textbook form, and still later proceeded to defend them as

---

[15] Leon C. Marshall (ed.), *op. cit.*, p. 84.
[16] James H. S. Bossard and J. Frederic Dewhurst, *op. cit.*, p. 323.

the new orthodoxy. In other fields like business law and production it would be difficult to argue that any seminal ideas were developed in the interwar years, much less that the subjects continued to gain in intellectual stature during this period. A review of the more widely used textbooks in a number of business subjects suggests that the work tended to solidify prematurely, blocking further experimentation and growth.[17]

It would also be an exaggeration to say that the functional subjects gave much more than surface coherence to the student's work. The different core areas—accounting, finance, marketing, and the like—became self-contained subjects with major sequences, further subdivisions, special requirements, and the other regalia of departmental life. Some efforts were made, as noted below, to check departmental separatism, but the pressure of enrollments, the backgrounds and interests of the students, and the ambitions of both the faculty members and the deans all pointed the other way. Except for a few schools—notably those that retained a heavy economics emphasis—any genuine coherence in the work was almost totally lacking.

Managerial and Case Orientation

The most ambitious effort to develop greater content and coherence during the interwar period came when the schools began to introduce a company-wide, managerial viewpoint into their programs. A related development was the introduction of the case method of instruction. Many schools played a part in these two developments, but Harvard was the principal architect of both, and its work in this regard marked a milestone.[18]

Very early in the formation of business schools, attention was paid to the manager or administrator role in business. Usually the management viewpoint came in a single course, such as business organization or business policy. At Tuck and somewhat later at Chicago, it was developed rather systematically in a series of courses. But the idea of looking at all phases of business operations from a broad managerial point of view was to remain quite formal and empty until Dean Donham and his colleagues at Harvard gave it life.

Wallace B. Donham became dean at Harvard in 1919. As a graduate of Harvard Law School and a one-time banker, he combined interest in academic work with a practical feel for business affairs. It was his view that the task of businessmen was largely one of reaching decisions in a

---

[17] See the chapters in Part 3 dealing with various aspects of the curriculum.

[18] Much has been written on both these aspects of the Harvard program, so only the highlights are touched on here. For a careful review of this period, see Melvin T. Copeland, *op. cit.*, Chap. 6.

multitude of situations. With this as a starting point, the program at Harvard was developed on the basis of the following principles: (1) the student's entire two years should be centered on the kind of decisions which upper management is called on to make; (2) business decision making is much more of an art than a science, there being no principles of decision making which can be taught in a classroom in the same way, say, as the principles of physics or mathematics; therefore traditional methods of teaching by assigned reading and lecture are quite inappropriate, if not positively harmful; (3) the unique contribution of the business administrator, especially at the level of upper management, is to know enough about all the major facets of a firm's operations (production, sales, finance, personnel, etc.) to keep its various activities in proper balance and to have the requisite judgment to make decisions in a complex, fast-changing environment; (4) to the extent this capacity is an intellectual one which can be developed or strengthened by academic study, it rests on a capacity to reason out complex problems or situations, not on mastery of a particular subject or body of material; accordingly, the most effective educational scheme for developing this ability is for students to gain experience in making business decisions themselves; and (5) the method of study which comes closest to simulating business situations is to confront students with a wide variety of carefully developed cases in which they are obliged to take a position on particular issues after a thorough, independent analysis of the reported facts.

Dean Donham made a very bold move in the early twenties when he decided to put Harvard's entire program on the case method. As events turned out, the step was a spectacular success—it attracted the warm support of influential businessmen; it fairly soon won acceptance by and later the dedicated devotion of a teaching-oriented faculty; it stirred student interest; and it opened the door to a wealth of valuable field data. As Copeland's history makes plain, the job of developing case materials was prodigiously costly. Between 1920 and 1942, the period of his tenure as dean, Donham collected over $2 million for this purpose alone.[19] The case method also entailed a tremendous channeling of the faculty's energies, pretty largely excluding any type of research not having a case-analysis emphasis. On the other hand, given the general status of academic work in this field in the interwar period, these debit considerations were not too serious, while the benefits derived were substantial.

The Harvard example, though its program was exclusively graduate, exerted an important influence on almost every business school during these years. Stanford at the graduate level and Northwestern at the undergraduate level, for example, followed its pattern closely. Most

[19] At present, the Harvard Business School is allocating over $100,000 of its annual budget for the case program.

schools made at least some effort to introduce a managerial case-analysis point of view. Courses in business policy were frequently made a part of the core program, and students could even elect to major in management as a separate area of concentration. Needless to say, the results of these innovations were mixed, depending on the quality of a school's students, the strength of its faculty, and the adequacy of its resources. Serious question was raised about this new emphasis at the undergraduate level, and even at the graduate level there was some doubt just what managerial decision making entailed as a subject of academic study. As with the other forward-looking changes of the interwar period, the shift to a management focus was more an initial step toward improvement than a proven success.

REASSESSMENT AND REORGANIZATION: 1940 TO PRESENT

By the late forties, business schools had won strong positions on the campuses of most public universities and many of the larger private institutions. Enrollments had risen spectacularly immediately after the war, and while they leveled off in line with other fields in the early fifties, the clear prospect was for still further increases in the sixties. Of 107 undergraduate schools answering the Survey Questionnaire, three-fourths expected their enrollments to rise by 40 per cent or more between 1956 and 1970 while nearly a third expected them to more than double.[20] Plans for the future were drawn up in an expansionist atmosphere, the recurring doubt being whether qualified teachers could be found in sufficient numbers.

The business schools began to widen their activities rapidly after World War II.[21] New courses and majors in such fields as human relations, managerial economics, market research, forecasting, and the like were established. New degree programs at the one-year or two-year master's level and at the doctoral level began to appear. Some additional graduate schools of business came into existence. In many instances, spacious buildings arose to house the new programs, some heavily endowed and a number furnished with expensive equipment. Salary rates were perhaps no higher than in other branches of university life, but prospects for rapid promotion were often better and opportunities for lucrative consulting fees, generally greater. Many new appointments were made to business faculties, including some persons of the highest

[20] Survey Questionnaire sent to all accredited business schools in March, 1957. The percentage increases projected for graduate enrollments were considerably greater. See Appendix 3, Table 6.

[21] The details of these developments are set forth in Part 2 and to avoid repetition are not given here.

scholarly reputation. The word began to circulate in academic circles that business schools were on the move and that teaching at these schools had some real advantages over appointments in more static branches of university work.

The area of management development suddenly opened up in this period, and the business schools responded in vigorous fashion. Many of their faculty members had long been active in evening or extension programs, institutes, short conferences, and other phases of adult education, but formal education for persons who had achieved managerial status and who were looking forward to still more responsible jobs in administration was something new. The fact that some of the programs were designed for top management in larger enterprises bore added testimony to the prestigious position which business schools had finally won.

The basic features of the schools' academic programs also seemed more firmly set. By the postwar period, six subjects constituted most of the core work and most of the areas of major concentration as well: accounting, economics, finance, management, marketing, and production. Two other subjects—business law and statistics—made up the rest of the core program at most schools, though they were relatively unimportant as majors. Some of the other frequently chosen majors were secretarial science, personnel, insurance, and retailing.[22]

Role of the AACSB

The firmer status of business schools in this period was reflected in the activities of the American Association of Collegiate Schools of Business. This organization was founded in 1916 to promote exchange of information among the schools and to improve educational standards. Accordingly, it developed certain minimum conditions for admission which a well-rounded program would have to meet.[23] The association exerted an important influence during the interwar period as a forum for ideas and as a model for the least-favored schools, but it failed to provide any general leadership. Throughout this period its membership was relatively small; even by 1940 only fifty-three schools belonged, twenty-eight of which were located at state universities. The association's activities were limited to the deans and at best had but an indirect effect on business school faculty members. Its standards were at no time more than minimal; the specific core requirements established in the early twenties, for example, had been dropped by World War II. There was reason to

---

[22] Data taken from the Survey Questionnaire.

[23] In 1925–1926, for example, Standard 9 provided: "All collegiate schools shall offer a reasonable amount of work in at least five groups of study, such as business finance, accounting, business law, marketing and statistics."

believe that a number of schools which had long been members were
not in full compliance with the organization's standards and that they
had less right to belong than many which were excluded. In general, the
association lacked vigor, imagination, and any real sense of purpose
during most of these years.

After 1940, this organization exerted a somewhat wider and more positive influence. By 1958, eighty-five schools belonged and there were eight
associate members, institutions which did not quite meet all the standards for full membership. The association was recognized by other private and public bodies, including the U.S. Office of Education, as the
accrediting agency in this field. It had a full-time executive secretary and
active committees to handle admission applications and the enforcement
of standards among member schools. Its conditions for membership had
become somewhat more demanding than in the prewar period. A key
provision, established in 1949, stipulated that "instruction shall be offered
in the fields of economics, accounting, statistics, business law, finance,
marketing, and management" (excerpt from Standard 4). In 1958 it
established a few basic standards for graduate instruction. While still primarily a forum for the exchange of ideas among deans, the association
was beginning to exert a considerably wider influence than in the prewar period.

Continuing Issues

All these developments suggest that the business schools had at last
found themselves and that their programs were becoming more securely
set. Precisely the opposite was more nearly the truth. A great deal of the
work in such fields as accounting, business law, marketing, and production came in for attack. Increasingly, the question was being asked
whether business schools were essentially different from trade schools.
Some of the more pretentious developments in areas like management
and human relations became the butt of widespread criticism and sometimes of ridicule. The rapid expansion of master's, doctoral, and management development programs caused many doubts—including many self-
doubts—about the general direction of the work. Two major surveys
were published during this period, both sponsored by the AACSB—the
Kozelka report of 1954 and the Arden House conference on faculty requirements in 1956.[24] Neither was explicitly designed to appraise existing

[24] Richard L. Kozelka, *Professional Education for Business,* Minneapolis, American
Association of Collegiate Schools of Business, 1954, and American Association of
Collegiate Schools of Business, *Faculty Requirements and Standards in Collegiate
Schools of Business,* AACSB, New York, 1956. The reader seeking a good general
review of business school programs should consult the Kozelka report.

practice, but the effect of both was to raise searching questions about next steps in this area.

Prominent business school spokesmen began to raise questions about the core requirements established by the association only a few years earlier. Thomas L. Norton, dean of N.Y.U.'s School of Commerce, Accounts, and Finance, stated:[25]

In my opinion, it is time for the American Association of Collegiate Schools of Business to revise its membership standard relating to the Business Base, sometimes referred to as the "core" of business subjects. I believe that the present standard may well now be a hindrance rather than an aid to the improvement of college education for business.

A number of developments sharpened the criticisms being directed at business schools at this time. First, the question was raised with increasing insistence whether business programs were attracting students of inferior academic ability and, if so, whether these programs were at a genuine college level. Especially disturbing was the charge that academically superior students found little to challenge them and that the work did not represent any progression in difficulty in its more advanced phases. These same questions, if less widespread, were being asked about graduate business programs as well.

Second, many employers expressed the view that preparation in liberal art subjects was preferable to straight business training and that even graduate business work ran serious danger of being unduly narrow. To this it was rejoined that company recruiters often looked for the very training top management decried, but the mere expression of this viewpoint by influential business leaders carried serious overtones. Interestingly enough, the criticisms of executives came at a time when many schools were giving special stress to the managerial point of view.

Third, the rapid increase in graduate programs in the postwar period put business education in a wholly new light. Prior to World War II, almost all the schools concentrated their resources and efforts on undergraduate work and what little advanced study was provided usually consisted of a year's additional specialization beyond the undergraduate studies. In the postwar period some additional schools became exclusively graduate, and many others made this level of instruction their major concern. Several of these programs placed heavy emphasis on research. A number developed sophisticated mathematical-statistical methods for analyzing certain business problems. Increasing attention was also paid to the applications of psychology and sociology to management decisions. Some of the more notable of the new or completely revised programs were established at Carnegie Tech., Chicago, and

[25] Speech delivered at the annual meeting of the Middle Atlantic Association of Collegiate Schools of Business, Oct. 11, 1957.

M.I.T. The best undergraduate preparation for these and similar schools was a broad preparation in certain nonbusiness fields—engineering, mathematics, history, economics, and literature. But these new programs raised no less disturbing questions about the more traditional, specialized graduate programs as well. Thus both undergraduate and graduate business education were put very much on the defensive.

Fourth, the prospect of steadily rising enrollments coupled with (1) limited faculty and other resources and (2) the emergence of other programs, such as night schools, special institutes, company training facilities, junior colleges, and the like, forced the schools to review their positions and to face some difficult decisions. For a few schools it meant a rather clear choice between graduate and undergraduate instruction or between a rigorous academic and a highly vocational emphasis. For most, the choice was one of emphasis only in deciding where their main energies should center, what type of students they should generally seek to attract, and what qualities they should look for in new faculty members.

All these circumstances conspired in the postwar period to raise serious doubts about the prevailing pattern of business education and to compel a reappraisal of the entire field. A large number of institutions embarked on ambitious self-study plans, and various approaches were still more widely discussed. In some cases, concrete steps were taken immediately to implement the findings of these appraisals, but most were of a long-range nature. It is indicative of both the weaknesses and strengths of this field that after World War II many business schools were themselves evincing genuine doubts about the direction and quality of their work.

CHAPTER 4

STUDENT CHARACTERISTICS AND INTERESTS

Hardly any undergraduate business schools, especially those with four-year programs, follow selective admissions policies. Judged on intelligence-test scores, undergraduate business students do not compare favorably with other important student groups. These findings are modified, but only in part, at the graduate level. Both undergraduate and graduate business students regard education primarily in career-value terms, but whether business schools should alter their programs accordingly seems doubtful.

Some of the principal issues confronting business schools are brought into focus when the activities of these institutions are studied from the viewpoint of the students who attend them. The two preceding chapters contrasted the pattern of education for business as distinguished from such highly developed professions as engineering, law, and medicine. One of the distinctive features of business schools is that they have been in the forefront of the movement to carry higher education to a wide cross section of the population. Put in concrete terms this has meant that most business schools have had to adapt their programs to the abilities and interests of extremely large and diversified student groups. A natural inference to draw from this fact is that the majority of these schools cannot expect to establish high academic standards comparable to those found in the advanced professions. This is the issue with which this and subsequent chapters are concerned.

The general thesis developed here is that business schools could raise the content and quality of their programs materially and still meet the needs of the bulk of their students. Two quite different questions of educational policy are involved—first, whether academic standards in the lowest-ranking schools should be raised and second, whether the same should occur among schools which are already above the minimum. It is argued in this chapter that most students now attending business schools would derive great benefit from broad, demanding programs of study, that such programs would tend to attract a type of student who would profit even more from such work, and that from the viewpoint of student abilities and interests there is nothing to prevent business schools from raising standards considerably. This finding holds for the lowest-level schools as well as for those of higher ranking, and it applies to many institutions offering graduate as well as undergraduate work.

It should be emphasized that there is no attempt in this chapter to consider in any detail what the work at these two levels should entail or how demanding it should be; these issues are left to succeeding chapters. Few presumably would quarrel with the proposition that students should be pushed as closely as possible to the limits of their intellectual abilities. This would be in keeping with the main purpose of college and university work described in Chap. 2, and it would seem wholly desirable in terms of the personal development of the students themselves. This highly laudable objective, however, immediately raises a host of difficult questions about the kind of students business schools should admit, what standards of academic performance should be established, what are the backgrounds and interests of their students, and how should such considerations affect the work of these schools. These are baffling problems, and the discussion which follows does no more than suggest some tentative answers.

It can be assumed further that as this branch of academic work develops, it will acquire more analytical content and become more difficult. This is the pattern which other fields have followed, as sketched out in Chap. 2, and there is no reason to believe preparation for business will follow another course. But again, the outcome in terms of individual schools will depend on the specific meaning which comes to be attached to these words. If, for example, this area were to move ahead very rapidly, there is no question that many students would have to drop out or switch to less demanding programs. On the other hand, if the subject were to develop slowly—and this seems more likely—the repercussions among students would be far less. In the first case, it would be as though all the lower-ranking schools suddenly raised their standards (in terms of admission policies, grade average for graduation, course requirements, etc.) to the highest found anywhere in the country; in the second, it would be as though schools only raised their standards piecemeal and gradually. In both instances, some students would have to go elsewhere, but the difference in impact would of course be enormous.

As a practical matter, probably the most that can be expected is that the schools would tend to move up all along the line; the top-level schools would go still higher; those in the middle tier of academic quality would edge up more closely to the top schools; those in the lower tier would move into what is now the middle category; while at the bottom, a sharper line would be drawn between the work of the lowest-level four-year institutions and the work of high schools, evening schools, and the like. The great majority of students would still find programs of study suitable to their abilities, though admittedly some of the least academically gifted would be excluded from regular collegiate business programs. The issue, then, is whether the interests of these latter students should be allowed to outweigh the needs of those who are not now being pushed to the limits of their abilities. The view developed in this chapter is that they should not.

As noted in Chap. 1, the press of enrollments and the diversity of student interests with which business schools must cope pose issues more akin to those faced by higher education as a whole than by particular branches of professional education, and in neither case is any simple solution likely. The most apparent danger is that in striving to meet the needs of the many, the needs of the better students will tend to be neglected. But there is the further question whether programs pitched to the abilities and interests of the less qualified students will even bring out *their* best efforts or serve *their* special interests. There is some tendency in the academic world to write off large groups of students, whether in engineering, liberal arts, or business, as forever childish, incapable, and unimaginative. "Average" and "below average" students need to be treated like adults quite as much as their more favored peers.

The problem of motivating such students is admittedly complex but, speaking of college and university work only, should the actual subject matter they study be materially different from what is given superior students? The pace perhaps should be slower and the level of difficulty of the work reduced for such students, but it is doubtful whether the essential content of the programs should be made very different. This raises questions about the motivations and interests of business students and about the content of the business curriculum which are discussed at some length later. However these issues are resolved, it must be agreed that while business schools bear a heavy responsibility for providing more equal economic opportunity, they also carry an obligation to challenge all students at different levels of ability to their fullest capacities; to do otherwise would be a move away from, rather than toward, the kind of diversity which recognizes variations in student abilities and would in fact tend to establish a uniformity of mediocrity.

As enrollment pressures mount, the difficulties in giving full scope to students of varying academic promise will rise commensurately, making the need for safeguarding measures all the more necessary. The number of college students studying business is expected to increase at a rate of about 20,000 per annum over the next twenty years. In the face of this tidal wave, each school will be obliged to set its course very firmly or be swamped altogether. Later chapters sketch out a broad pattern for meeting these developments in which the simpler specialties which require relatively little prior education (secretarial work, bookkeeping, and similar office and selling skills) would be made the responsibility of high schools, junior colleges, night schools, and special institutes while more demanding types of specialized instruction and advanced preparation in business policy making would be handled largely at the graduate level. The undergraduate business schools would accordingly concentrate on underlying principles and basic tools needed by students in their later work, with only limited attention either to first-job skills or to the more advanced aspects of business preparation. This pattern would not only accord with developments which have already occurred in such other fields as engineering, law, and medicine, but it would be a logical outcome of long term trends in business education as well. In fact, as noted in the preceding chapter, some important beginnings among business schools have already occurred along these lines, and further developments may well be in the making which will put the whole matter of student needs and preferences in a substantially different light.

It will doubtless be argued that any effort to distinguish sharply between subcollege, college, and graduate work along these lines will not permit sufficient diversity among institutions at each of these three levels. It is widely accepted that undergraduate business schools, for example, should not follow a single pattern but should seek new approaches. Will the foregoing framework prevent this kind of healthy differentiation among these schools?

The answer is clearly, no. In fact, the whole intent of such an approach is to encourage *more* innovation. If the schools move away from an emphasis on first job skills, the effect will be to increase, not lessen, diversity. True, it would tend to decrease differences based on individual job or industry characteristics; however, in terms of the analytical content of the programs, this type of work is really highly uniform. Hence the development of programs with more of an analytical emphasis would almost surely spell more diversity.

Proposals for raising the academic standards of business schools, when considered from the students' viewpoint, can best be approached in terms of three main issues: (1) the schools' admissions policies, (2) the students' academic quality, and (3) the students' backgrounds, academic interests, and career goals. The more pressing problems in connection with all three of these issues are found at the undergraduate level, and to keep the discussion within manageable bounds, attention is largely confined to these schools. While adequate data are lacking for a complete analysis of these three questions, they are too important to disregard altogether.

ADMISSIONS STANDARDS

The direction which undergraduate and graduate business schools take with respect to their admissions policies is closely related to the issues just noted. If business administration becomes an increasingly distinct area of study with certain required subjects or skills to be mastered and certain standards of performance to be fulfilled, admissions policies would have to be modified accordingly. If, above a minimum level of quality, provision is made among schools for variation in an upward direction, it is obvious that the admission policies and/or graduation requirements of some schools would necessarily be a good deal more restrictive than others. As any field of learning develops, these two issues of minimum admission or performance standards, and variations above the minimum, become crucial.

For undergraduate business schools which admit students as freshmen, admissions standards are now largely decided on a university-wide basis. Looking ahead, there seems no reason why this should be universally true. Schools of architecture or engineering which admit freshmen are generally not bound by the admissions standards applicable to other students. If business schools continue to accept students in their first year, they should be permitted to establish standards equivalent to the stronger branches of instruction, though perhaps little progress can be made in this direction until this field of study becomes more clearly defined. As matters now stand, the admission policies of four-year undergraduate business schools are largely a result of the fact that these schools are concentrated at institutions which admit all graduates of accredited high schools.[1] Admissions requirements at ninety-eight of the four-year undergraduate business schools in 1955–1956 are summarized in Table 4-1. These ninety-eight schools, which in that year accounted for over 90 per cent of all undergraduate business degrees granted under accredited four-year programs, are divided about equally between public and private institutions and between those who are members and nonmembers of the American Association of Collegiate Schools of Business. In all but a few cases the admissions standards of these schools are the same as for the parent institution with which they are affiliated.

Broadly speaking, the table ranks the schools on the relative restrictiveness of their stated admissions standards, although a particular school's position might in actual practice be higher or lower than indicated. There

---

[1] Considerable care has to be exercised in making generalizations about these matters, because it is difficult to pin universities down as to exactly what their admission standards are; for one thing, specific practice changes considerably depending on the "state of the market," etc.

TABLE 4-1

ADMISSION STANDARDS OF 98 BUSINESS SCHOOLS
WITH FOUR-YEAR PROGRAMS, 1955–1956

Type of admission standards	No. of schools	Under-graduate enrollment	Under-graduate business enrollment	% of (3) in each group
	(1)	(2)	(3)	
I. Graduation from accredited high school only requirement........	27	155,598	26,945	27
II. Graduation from accredited high school plus grade average or class ranking (but no units specified)..	15	95,581	16,868	17
III. Graduation from accredited high school plus specified units in given subjects (but no grade or ranking requirement).................	23	154,021	24,561	24
IV. Graduation from accredited high school plus *both* requirements, as in Groups II and III above.....	13	111,551	12,688	13
V. Graduation from accredited high school plus examination (CEEB, ACE Psychological, or other examination), plus either grade, ranking, or subjects requirement	20	191,780	19,253	19
Total......................	98	708,531	100,315	

SOURCE: School catalogs and survey interview reports.

is little difference between the schools in Groups I and II since many in the latter are quite flexible (especially in regard to home-state students) about the high school grade average or class-ranking requirement. The schools in Group III make virtually no exceptions with respect to high school subjects required, but the high school course units which are specified are often minimal. Here, for example, are the high school requirements for one of the institutions in this group: English, 3 units; elementary algebra, 1 unit; 7 additional units from 5 groups of studies (English, foreign language, mathematics, social studies, laboratory science, and nonacademic studies), a minimum of four of the groups to be represented in the units offered; electives, 5 units. Occasionally, a Group III school will recommend but not require a few other high school courses such as ½ unit of advanced algebra or a science. By and large, the admission standards of schools in Groups I to III are almost uniformly low.

The schools in Group IV require both a certain ranking in high school and certain subjects of study, but even in their case, admission standards are hardly exacting. Detailed investigation of the thirteen schools in this group reveals that only one (City College of New York) puts the minimum high school ranking as high as the upper one-third; most of the others set the minimum at the upper two-thirds or three-fourths of the graduating class. Moreover, even if the student cannot meet this requirement, other procedures are usually open to him. The following is taken from the statement of admissions of one of the schools in Group IV:

> Evidence of satisfactory intellectual promise for admission to Freshman standing will be furnished by one or more of the following methods: (1) A satisfactory score on the Scholastic Aptitude Test of the College Entrance Examination Board. (2) Ten units of recommended grade (A or B or equivalent) in approved subjects earned in the last three high school years. (3) Certification by the high school principal that the applicant is scholastically in the upper half of his graduating class.

Finally, the schools in Group V (twenty of the ninety-eight four-year schools) specify that all students take some kind of a recognized examination before they are admitted and that they either achieve a certain high school grade average or ranking in the graduating class or that they study certain subjects; eighteen of the twenty schools in the group require College Entrance Examination Board tests. The twenty schools are:[2]

Group V Schools

Babson Institute	Manhattan College
Boston College	New York University
Boston University	Northeastern University
Carnegie Institute of Technology	Northwestern University
Drake University	Pennsylvania, University of
Fordham University	Rhode Island, University of
Georgetown University	Rutgers University
La Salle College	Tulane University
Lehigh University	Villanova College
Long Island University	Western Reserve University

While this group of twenty schools includes some which follow selective admissions policies, a number do not. The mere fact that all applicants take certain examinations is no assurance of high admissions standards; at one of the institutions in this group, nearly 80 per cent of the entire freshman class of 1953 scored under 500 on both the CEEB verbal and mathe-

---

[2] There may be other institutions not included among the 98 schools which belong in this group.

matical aptitude tests.[3] Moreover, even if admissions standards were high at all these schools, they would account for a little less than a fifth of the enrollment in the schools studied.

The evidence seems clear that there is only a bare handful of four-year schools located at universities which carefully screen beginning students. If many students and employers look to schools which maintain high admission standards, this small group of institutions will not begin to meet the demand. As long as present admission practices persist, any school seeking to raise its standards of academic performance is subject to the very serious handicap that there is a hard core of beginning students who do not have the minimum mental equipment to handle more demanding work. In the interests of diversity and greater variety of choice alone, there is pressing need for a good many more schools with high standards of admissions; schools which are obliged to accept all high school graduates have no alternative but to screen students at the end of their sophomore or junior years more carefully.

As indicative of the situation confronting a number of institutions, and the steps that are being considered to deal with it, consider this excerpt from an interview report on a large nonresidential university in an eastern city:

Qualitatively, the student body of the university is thought to be similar to that of any of the larger state universities. The standards for admission of students are not rigid, and although there are many bright students, the average is only fair. However, this situation is likely to improve. The university will become more selective in the admission of students in the future, since it has a great enough demand to permit the rejection of a rather high proportion of its applicants. For example, this year's Freshman class (1957–58) of 1800 students was selected from among about 4800 applicants. All applicants are now required to take the CEEB tests, which is new here. Most of the students at the university come from within a 40 mile radius and most come from homes without college backgrounds. Recent experience has shown that one-quarter of each Freshman class leaves the University at the end of the first year, while about one-half of those who enter eventually graduate.

The students in the school of business administration share, to a considerable extent, the characteristics of the student body as a whole. In general, however, they are students of lower ability than those who go into liberal arts or engineering. This is shown by some figures on the scores achieved by entering Freshmen on the verbal and mathematical sections of the Scholastic Aptitude test of the CEEB. These compare the scores of students who went into the colleges of engineering, liberal arts, business and education. On both verbal and mathematical tests, students in the school of business ranked below those in all three of the other colleges, even education, although the difference between business and education was not great.

At present, in contrast to this school, most of the four-year business schools are located at universities which legally or in fact are committed

[3] The score of 500 is the average score for the total test population.

to accepting any graduate from an accredited high school within a given state or locality. In these schools and universities the only effective way of improving the quality of students is to screen them more intensively at the end of the freshman or sophomore year. Campus interviews at over sixty of these schools in 1957 revealed that very few do so. On the contrary, in many instances the business schools were found to be a good deal more lax than most other branches of the universities visited in setting promotion standards beyond the freshman year, with the consequence that they are serving as a dumping ground for students who cannot make the grade in engineering or some branch of the liberal arts. This need not be the case, as the example of a few of the four-year schools testifies, and the time seems well past when this condition should be allowed to continue.[4]

Schools which admit students as juniors (a few admit them as sophomores) are in a rather different position with respect to admissions-

[4] One very rough test of comparative academic standards is the proportion of students who discontinue their work before graduation, although many other factors such as financial status, interest in college work, etc. affect drop-out rates. For what the figures are worth, unpublished data of the U.S. Office of Education show that a larger proportion of men business students than of other students graduated from the school they entered first in 1954, due to the fact (1) that a larger proportion went beyond the first registration period and (2) that a larger proportion of those entering the fourth year of college went on to graduate. Data were collected on fifty universities representing about one-fifth of total undergraduate enrollments in universities and other institutions of higher education in all parts of the country as part of the study *Retention and Withdrawal of College Students;* however, the data on university business school students only cover 269 students and cannot be considered as representative of the country as a whole. The specific figures are:

PERCENTAGE OF MEN STUDENTS AT FIFTY FOUR-YEAR UNIVERSITIES AND BUSINESS
SCHOOLS WHO WITHDREW IN DIFFERENT PERIODS OF ATTENDANCE
AND WHO GRADUATED IN 1954

Period of attendance	% of all men	% of men in business school
Not beyond 1st registration period...........	11.3	6.7
Beyond 1st registration period, not more than 1 year.................................	13.0	13.8
Beyond 1 year, not more than 2 years........	12.8	14.5
Beyond 2 years, not more than 3 years.......	6.7	5.9
Entered 4th year, not graduated.............	12.1	5.2
Graduated in 1954........................	39.1	47.2
Others...................................	5.0	6.7
Total number of students in this part of study..	3,802	269

SOURCE: U.S. Office of Education, *Retention and Withdrawal of College Students.* 1958. p. 16, and specially prepared statistical material.

promotion standards, so comparisons are hard to draw. The great majority of the thirty-four schools in this category, for which admissions information could be secured, required students to have maintained a C average during their first two years of college, typically a university-wide requirement. While this requirement may or may not be very exacting in a given case, at least these schools are not in the position of the four-year schools which have to cope with huge numbers of inferior beginning students. More important still, business schools which admit students as juniors and even sophomores (the so-called "2-2-" and "1-3-year" schools) have somewhat more leeway in setting entrance requirements at higher levels. In at least five or six instances, admissions standards under these programs are definitely above those for the student body as a whole; this is true at California (both Berkeley and UCLA), Emory, North Carolina, and Wisconsin among others; at four-year schools for which information could be secured, Rutgers was the only example of a business school which requires its students to maintain a somewhat higher grade average after admission than is demanded by the parent university. Other considerations aside, this means that the 2-2- and 1-3-year schools are in a considerably better position to raise standards than the 4-year schools.

Admissions into graduate business programs present a somewhat different picture. Some ten or twelve schools apply quite strict entrance requirements, and eighteen institutions now stipulate that all applicants must take the admission test for graduate study in business. The schools in the latter group are: Carnegie Institute of Technology, Columbia, Cornell, Harvard, Kent State, Massachusetts Institute of Technology, Northwestern, Purdue, Rutgers, Seton Hall, Stanford, Syracuse, Chicago, Michigan, Pennsylvania, Virginia, University of Washington, and Washington University (St. Louis). Most schools in this group use information on undergraduate grades along with the admission test results, since these two criteria taken together have proven the best predictors of academic success.[5]

Almost all the schools offering a graduate business degree stipulate that students must have completed a four-year program at an accredited institution, and often some effort is made to evaluate the quality of the undergraduate school's curriculum. On the other hand, admission to many graduate programs depends merely on the student's providing some kind of a college degree or its equivalent. At these institutions the gap

[5] A study of ten graduate schools of business showed a correlation between first year grades and the two combined criteria of .50 as against .43 for ATGSB scores and .35 for undergraduate grades when used alone; "adjusted" ATGSB scores, however, showed a correlation of .50. Marjorie Olsen, *The Admissions Test for Graduate Study in Business as a Predictor of First Year Grades in Business School*, 1954–1955. Educational Testing Service, Princeton, N.J., 1957, p. 4.

between prevailing standards and what could be reasonably expected is no less great at the graduate than at the undergraduate level.

QUALITY OF BUSINESS STUDENTS

The effects of prevailing admission practices among undergraduate business schools are reflected in the quality of their students as measured by comparative intelligence-test score results. The most authoritative general investigation, *The Report of the Commission on Human Resources and Advanced Training* prepared by Dael Wolfle, found that among twenty undergraduate fields, graduates in business administration on the average ranked sixth from the bottom. The specific rankings are shown in Figure 4-1.[6]

Because of its broad scope and diversity, comparisons between business and other fields of study in terms of median values of intelligence test scores are not too meaningful; of more significance are comparisons based on distributions of students among score rankings by fifths. On this basis, however, the results of the Wolfle study are, if anything, more striking than before. For all graduates, the scale is set in such a way that the students are evenly distributed among the five percentile groups; using this same scale, 72 per cent of the graduates of undergraduate business programs are in the lowest three-fifths and only 12 per cent are in the top fifth. Other fields with a similar distribution are general education, agriculture, home economics, and physical education. Dael Wolfle concludes:[7]

In general, and at both undergraduate and graduate levels, fields which have the reputation of being "hard" get somewhat brighter groups of students than do fields which have the reputation of being easy. This is true whether one thinks of broad areas—for example, science ranks above education and commerce—or of individual fields—chemistry, mathematics, and physics average higher than do biology and geology. Thus the physical sciences, languages, engineering, and law are all fairly close to the top of the lists, while education, business, some of the social sciences, home economics, and physical education are close to the lower end.

[6] Dael Wolfle, *The Report of the Commission on Human Resources and Advanced Training* in *America's Resources of Specialized Talent*, Harper & Brothers, New York, 1954, p. 199. The comparisons are based on the Army General Classification Test, and the sample consisted of over forty "representative" colleges and universities; the methods employed are described on pp. 189–191 and in Appendix I of *America's Resources of Specialized Talent*.

[7] *Ibid.*, p. 202. The Selective Service Qualification Test given to nearly half a million American college men between 1951 and 1953 yielded substantially similar conclusions. Educational Testing Service, *Statistical Studies of Selective Service Testing*, 1951–1953, Educational Testing Service, Princeton, N.J., 1955, p. 5.

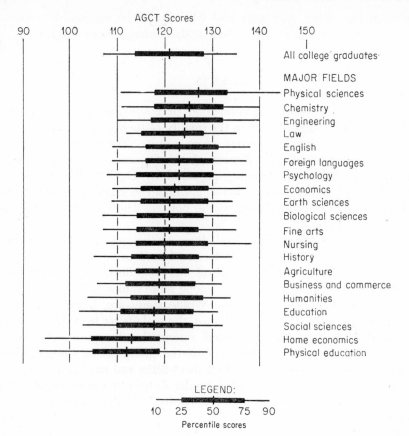

FIG. 4–1. Intelligence-test-score distributions of students graduating with bachelor's degree, by field of specialization. Source: Dael Wolfle, *The Report of the Commission on Human Resources and Advanced Training* in *America's Resources of Specialized Talent,* p. 199.

Rather surprisingly, these rankings even hold in examinations taken by applicants to graduate business schools whose undergraduate work was also in business. The results of the Admission Test for Graduate Study in Business given by twelve graduate schools of business in 1954–1955 showed that these students ranked lowest among five groups studied. The results are summarized in Table 4-2.

Data on recent test score and high school ranking comparisons, secured from individual schools in the course of interview visits, also support the above findings. Detailed figures were only available on seven schools, five with 4-year and two with 2-2- and 1-3-year programs; all were large, nationally known institutions. The data show that the business students scored on the average 5 to 15 percentage points below the median of liberal arts students on admission test scores, or ranked a good deal lower

TABLE 4-2

PERCENTILE RANKS FOR STUDENTS ADMITTED TO GRADUATE STUDY AT TWELVE GRADUATE BUSINESS SCHOOLS, GSB SCORES CLASSIFIED BY UNDERGRADUATE MAJOR, 1954–1955

Percentile rank on GSB score	GSB Admission Test scores				
	Business and accounting	Economics	Engi- neering	Liberal arts	Miscel- laneous
75th percentile....	540	560	610	570	620
Mean............	479	497	550	505	541
25th percentile....	420	435	485	430	490
Number of cases...	369	143	162	233	25

SOURCE: Educational Testing Service, Apr. 9, 1956 (mimeographed). (The 75th and 25th percentile figures were supplied separately.)

relative to liberal arts students in their high school class.[8] For example, in one school 23 per cent of the freshman business students were in the top fifth of their high school class as against 48 per cent of the arts and science freshmen; in another, the percentages were 21 and 42, respectively. At one of the institutions in the 2-2- and 1-3-year group, the figures show that on a proportional basis, the liberal arts school draws about twice as many students scoring in the top 20 per cent on the ACE examination as the business school and, again on a proportional basis, about half as many appreciably-below-average students. At the three universities providing test score or high school ranking comparisons for engineers, the contrast with business students was even more sharp. At the six universities providing comparative data on students in education, two showed them to be above, two below, and two on about a par with business students. The results, wherever given, put students in agriculture and physical education at the same level or below business students.

Reports based on interviews with faculty members of about seventy undergraduate schools lend general support to these findings. On the other hand, the opinion was expressed by both the business and non-business faculty at some schools that the intellectual quality and academic seriousness of the business students were improving, and at a few institutions it was agreed that they were "catching up" or had even gone ahead of some groups in the liberal arts schools. At one well-known Midwestern university, for example, the mean score of business students in the aptitude test given all incoming freshmen rose from 75 to 84 between 1948 and 1953 compared with an increase from 83 to 89 for students in liberal arts. In this instance, as in almost every other where a

[8] The scores were based on the American Council on Education Psychological Examination and the College Entrance Examination Board Scholastic Aptitude Test.

substantial improvement in the academic quality of business students was noted, the program was limited to the last two years.

Recent figures on test scores of graduate business students were not obtainable. In the Wolfle study referred to above, they stood third from the bottom among nineteen graduate groups with a median score on the AGCT examination of 119 against 124 for all graduate students in the sample. In relative terms, this was somewhat lower than the ranking of undergraduate business students. The specific rankings are shown in Fig. 4-2.[9]

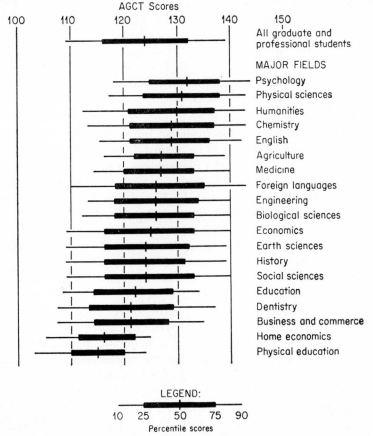

Fig. 4-2. Intelligence-test-score distributions of graduate and professional students specializing in different fields. Source: Dael Wolfle, *The Report of the Commission on Human Resources and Advanced Training* in *America's Resources of Specialized Talent,* p. 200.

Detailed test comparisons in 1945–1947 of twenty-four graduate student groups in eight different subject areas showed that graduate busi-

[9] The sample consisted of 4,500 graduate students from about fifty universities scattered over the country; the results were published in 1954.

ness students rated among the three lowest on the basis of tests in the areas of biology, fine arts, literature, and verbal factor, about midway in the rankings in chemistry, physics, and social studies, and seventh from the top in mathematics; in general they compared favorably with graduate students in economics and other social science subjects with respect to the examination in quantitative and scientific work and unfavorably with respect to the examination in social sciences and humanities.[10] As already noted, a number of schools with graduate business programs have adopted selective admission standards, so a wide gap doubtless exists between these and other schools with respect to the academic quality of students. There is no way of determining how the over-all improvement compares with test scores of graduate students in other areas.

These data underscore the need for a sharper delineation of the academic role of undergraduate and graduate business schools and a general tightening of their admissions standards. The question just how far the schools should attempt to go in this direction is perhaps debatable, but that there is room for considerable improvement seems abundantly clear. The prospective upsurge in enrollments gives special urgency to the problem, but with more students to choose from, more schools should find themselves in a position to take corrective action. It is especially disturbing, judging from individual reports on seventy-five schools in all parts of the country, that there is such a comparatively small number of outstanding students studying in the field of business administration. As the evidence presented in this chapter indicates, these issues appear to be most pressing at the 4-year schools, less so at the 2-2- and 1-3-year schools, and perhaps still less at the graduate level, but the need for corrective action at all three levels is apparent.[11]

[10] *Profile Tests*, 1945–1947, Educational Testing Service, Princeton, N.J., December, 1947, pp. 16–27. Data on comparative class rankings of a sampling of 1,999 graduates from Amherst, Brown, Harvard, Oberlin, and Chicago's lower division who went on to graduate or professional study showed a smaller proportion of students in the top 7½ per cent and a larger proportion of students in the lowest ranking 66 per cent entered graduate work in business administration than in any of the other fields studied (social sciences, mathematics and natural sciences, humanities, law, and medicine). Elbridge Sibley, *The Recruitment, Selection, and Training of Social Scientists*, Social Science Research Council, New York, Bulletin 58, 1948, p. 32. The sample was limited to the classes of 1938 and 1946 in these five institutions.

[11] A spokesman for a large, well-known business school comments on this finding in the following way: "I am inclined to agree with your conclusions on this matter. There can be no doubt that schools of business do not attract the calibre of students they should. . . . Frequently the low calibre of students admitted to the school of business (as far as means or medians go) is the responsibility of university authorities with the passive approval of the school of business. At our school, there have been a number of years when we were requested to admit an additional 50–75 stu-

In assessing the steps which undergraduate and graduate business schools might take to draw more highly qualified students, it is worth asking whether careers in business have as much attraction for the most capable students, academically speaking, as careers in science, medicine, engineering, and law. The difference cannot be measured at all precisely since careers in business are so diverse; to make the comparisons accurate, business would have to be broken down into a number of categories and levels—accountants, brokerage account executives, purchasing officers, office managers, sales directors, and the like. Moreover, business is entered by so many different educational routes—high school, night school, junior college, liberal arts, engineering and business schools, among others—that the sampling problem becomes most difficult.

The approach which comes closest to meeting these difficulties is to study the career plans of high school seniors and college freshmen. although these data are also subject to obvious pitfalls. The results of these studies with respect to the point at issue here are striking. A study

TABLE 4-3

RANKING OF MALE FRESHMEN IN TEXAS COLLEGES AND
UNIVERSITIES BY ACE PSYCHOLOGICAL EXAMINATION SCORES
AND BY OCCUPATIONAL OBJECTIVE, 1950–1951

Occupational objective	Male freshmen		
	Number	Mean	Sigma
Law	193	101.9	23.6
Medicine	273	101.9	23.3
Engineering	979	98.5	22.4
Religious work	171	94.5	26.2
Dentistry	112	93.7	25.1
Undecided	702	92.9	24.6
Business or secretarial	863	90.9	23.0
Teaching	420	85.3	26.1
Farming or ranching	569	81.2	22.3

of 5,278 freshmen in 38 Texas colleges and universities showed that the 863 male students who planned to do business or secretarial work stood seventh from the top among nine major occupational groups on the basis of 1950–1951 ACE Psychological Examination Test Scores. (Presumably

dents to make up for the failure of the College of Liberal Arts to meet its quota. Unfortunately, this number was usually composed of low calibre applicants. The result, of course, has been a reduction in the median scores on college boards. On the other hand, many schools of business have sought to expand their empires and have admitted numbers without regard to ability. These points do not contradict your analysis but shed a rather different light on the subject."

the number of men planning to follow secretarial careers was negligible.) The data for the nine groups are summarized in Table 4-3.[12]

According to a study of mental capacities of 17,141 high school senior men in 516 schools in 45 states conducted by Educational Testing Service during the first quarter of 1955, 10 per cent of the students in the highest of three scoring groups aspired to business supervisory positions and 4 per cent to nonsupervisory jobs as against 25 per cent planning on careers in engineering and 29 per cent in other professions; on the other hand, 10 per cent of the lowest scoring group hoped to become business supervisors and 9 per cent nonsupervisors as against 8 per cent who hoped to become engineers and 12 per cent who were planning on some other professional career.[13] Interestingly enough, there is some evidence to suggest that roughly similar findings hold for England as well.[14]

Comparison of the college curriculum plans of 1,045 Philadelphia high school seniors in the fall of 1956 with aptitude test score results show much the same picture. Using the U.S. Army Air Force standardized scale classifications and treating the mid-point of category 5 as the normal or 100 IQ for the entire population, students planning on pre-professional training were found to have the highest IQ (median IQ expressed in terms of standardized scale categories of 6.09) and those planning on a collegiate school of business course were found to have the lowest (standardized median IQ group of 4.37). The median IQ levels of the other groups in descending order below the preprofessional students were: engineering, science, teaching, music and art, nursing, pretheology, and business. The students planning to take a collegiate business curriculum were the only group whose IQ fell below the general student population norm. These data, it should be noted, throw only an indirect light on the career plans of the students answering the questionnaire, since they were only asked what college curriculum they planned to follow after graduation from high school.[15]

[12] Texas Commission on Coordination in Education, *Report on* 1950–1951 *Testing Program,* Research Bulletin 33, 1951, p. 10.

[13] Educational Testing Service, *Background Factors Relating to College Plans and College Enrollment among Public High School Students,* Educational Testing Service, Princeton, N.J., 1957, p. 51.

[14] A study of 1,374 graduates of Cambridge University in the classes of 1937 and 1938 showed that about 10 per cent received first-class degrees, but that only about 3½ per cent of those taking jobs in commerce were in this academic category; the proportion of first-class men entering medicine, science, government, and the like was considerably higher. The study concluded that "business is not recruiting so high a proportion of the intellectually ablest university men as certain other occupations." Report by a committee appointed by the Cambridge University Appointments Board, *Recruiting Business Leadership,* Cambridge University Press, London, 1945, p. 7.

[15] The data, which are unpublished, were taken from a survey of 17,952 high school seniors in the fall of 1956 as part of a general study, "Higher Education and

The foregoing evidence underscores the difficulties faced by business schools. These schools have come to be rather generally identified with students of limited academic ability. More than this, there is even doubt how much academic work contributes to success in this field. It appears, for example, that the brightest students, academically speaking, may not be the most successful businessmen, although it has been shown that these men were well above average in their studies.[16]

Moreover, even under the most favorable circumstances, the study of business is a relatively undemanding subject or can easily be made so. The upshot is that, barring unusual factors, the pressures to dilute content, reduce standards, and concentrate on practical skills win out. It takes a most exceptional school, possessing bold, imaginative leadership, plus a venturesome, dedicated faculty and strong backing from the parent university to break out of this circle of unfavorable circumstances.

These facts may be interpreted as indicating that the situation is hopeless or, alternatively, that efforts should be redoubled to reverse the natural course of events and raise standards all along the line. The latter seems the only defensible course of action. The fact that serious difficulties stand in the way of raising academic standards at many business schools should not be allowed to determine university policies. Rather, the difficulties should be faced and dealt with as effectively as possible. Later sections of this study set forth a number of proposals designed to further this objective.

STUDENT BACKGROUNDS AND INTERESTS

Another important influence on a business school's program is the background, interests, and motivations of its students. A widely held view is that most students studying business subjects have a rather strong vocational orientation and that to a greater or lesser extent business programs will inevitably be shaped by this fact. According to this view, to

---

the Future of Youth in the Greater Philadelphia Area," prepared under the direction of John F. Adams for the Philadelphia Committee on Higher Educational Opportunities. Only 37 per cent of the students indicated they were interested in going to college after graduating from high school in 1957, and of this group, only 20 per cent indicated the type of curriculum they hoped to follow.

[16] This is the general conclusion of a number of business school alumni surveys, including studies conducted at Harvard, Michigan, and Stanford. It is also confirmed by data on the backgrounds of individual business groups, such as the most successful life insurance salesmen, i.e., members of the Million Dollar Round Table Club. Doubtless, the particular field or line of activity has much to do with the result. This general issue is considered further in the next chapter.

force such students to spend any considerable amount of time studying subjects far removed from their main interest is felt to be largely a waste of time if not actually stultifying; rather, it is said, their college work should be geared closely to their career interests without permitting the latter to become completely dominant.

In assessing this point of view, it should be recognized at the outset that there is comparatively little known about the interests, motivations, and learning capacities or processes of college students, particularly when grouped by programs of major study, so these are not matters which can be discussed with much assurance. This comment may apply somewhat less strongly to students in a well-defined specialty like forestry or accounting and to students concentrating on a specific career objective at the graduate level, but it holds with special force for undergraduates, and even general graduate students, in broad, vaguely defined areas like business administration and the liberal arts. In both cases it seems only plausible to assume, a priori, that the interests and attitudes of the students would be spread out over a rather wide spectrum, with some (presumably a relatively small number) interested in the broader reaches of knowledge, others (presumably a somewhat larger number) interested almost exclusively in some specific vocational objective, and still others (presumably the largest group of all) lacking any clear educational or career purpose.

Of the four groupings of dominant life attitudes (pragmatic, humanistic, political, and lack of purpose and values), into which the students were finally divided, the pragmatic group was found to be the largest (38 per cent) and the humanistic group the smallest (16 per cent).[17] A study of business school students would presumably show a considerably higher proportion in the first category.

It is evident from the Grant Study and similar investigations that a substantial portion of college students, including those in liberal arts programs, think of their college experience primarily in terms of finding a good job and advancing their subsequent careers. This is hardly a surprising result and, particularly for men students, a thoroughly understandable one. The issue is not so much whether undergraduates (business students included) approach their college work in career terms but rather in what sense and to what extent this attitude is dominant during their college going years. The type of career interest, and the approach which students and schools take to it, is really the important issue, since some career interests can be most broadening and others may be very narrowing. The available evidence, while for the most part indirect and sketchy, is reviewed from this point of view.

[17] Clark W. Heath, *What People Are*, Harvard University Press, Cambridge, Mass., 1946, pp. 28–29 and Appendix B.

Income and Family Status

The economic and social backgrounds of students presumably have an important bearing on the approach they take to college work, with those from the lower-income and lower-status groups placing a higher premium on the more immediate vocational aspects of their college experience. In the study already cited, Dael Wolfle found considerable overlapping in the family backgrounds of students majoring in various areas, but he noted that when families of modest income and social standing try to "move up the ladder," they enroll their children in programs not too far above the parents' general occupational level: "The farmer sends his son to agricultural school to learn to be a better farmer; the skilled craftsman sends his son to college to become an engineer; the daughter of a factory worker moves upward by going to college and becoming a school teacher." [18] The analogous relation to business would presumably be the son or daughter of a clerical employee or small shopkeeper going to business school to qualify for some modest managerial post or to help run the family business. While differences in the backgrounds of students in specific areas were not found to be clear-cut, Wolfle discovered a fairly sharp difference when all the fields were classified into two broad categories, liberal arts-sciences against applied fields. [19]

The elaborate study of the college-going plans of 10,000 high school seniors which Elmo Roper made in 1949 for the American Council on Education touches on this same issue. A comparison of family backgrounds showed that 25.6 per cent of the men students planning some kind of business career had fathers who were small business proprietors while 14.6 per cent had fathers who held professional and executive positions. In the case of law and medicine, the relationship was reversed; 14.2 per cent of the men students planning to enter these two professions had fathers who were small businessmen, whereas 22.1 per cent were in professional and executive positions. The sons of white-collar workers, of service trade workers, and of factory workers showed a pattern of occupational choice similar to the sons of small business proprietors, although the proportion going into engineering was relatively greater. Among women high school seniors, teaching replaced engineering as the principal career choice of those coming from working class back-

[18] Dael Wolfle, *op. cit.,* p. 210.

[19] Dael Wolfle, *op. cit.,* p. 210. Another study covering 590 Milwaukee high school graduates found that median parental incomes, ranked in descending order by the students' choice of college curriculum, were: law, medicine and dentistry, liberal arts, journalism, engineering, teaching, commercial (i.e., business), nursing, and industrial trades. Helen B. Goetsch, "Parental Incomes and College Opportunities," *Teachers College Contributions to Education,* No. 795, Bureau of Publications, Teachers College, Columbia University, New York, 1940, p. 93.

grounds, with business the next most frequent choice of girls whose fathers were workers or small business proprietors.[20]

Analysis of family income data of 1,045 Philadelphia high school seniors planning to go to college, referred to earlier, shows a ranking of the different curriculum groups with those planning on a preprofessional program at the top (modal income in the $7,500–$10,000 class interval) and business and pretheology at the bottom ($3,000–$5,000 interval); all the other specific interest groups show modality of family income in the low to middle $5,000 to $7,500 class interval.[21]

An intensive but, on the basis of coverage, rather limited study by Frederiksen and Schrader in 1951 of students in agriculture, business, engineering, and liberal arts at twenty colleges and universities, found that students studying business tend to come from families with somewhat less education and income than those studying liberal arts, but that students in engineering and agriculture have even less-favored backgrounds. When asked whether they were "bothered very much making ends meet financially," 63 per cent of the students studying business answered in the affirmative as against 56 per cent in engineering, 53 per cent in liberal arts, and 46 per cent in agriculture. When asked about their purposes in coming to college, the proportions listing "to prepare for a better-paying job than otherwise available" as the chief reason were as follows:[22]

[20] Elmo Roper, *Factors Affecting the Admission of High School Seniors to College,* American Council on Education, Washington, 1949, Table 9a, pp. 104–105. It should be noted in passing that, according to the Roper study, the proportion of men and women high school seniors heading for business who said they planned to do outside work during college (47.3 per cent) was about the same as those planning careers in law, medicine, and teaching, while the proportion heading for engineering who said they would need outside work was higher (55.4 per cent); the sex factor may explain part of the difference. *Ibid.,* Table 8c, p. 114.

[21] Analysis of unpublished data collected for the Philadelphia Committee on Higher Educational Opportunities, *op. cit.* Professor Adams, who directed this part of the study, notes that the difference in modal income between the "Business" and "Other than business" groups "may be significant and may be attributable to the high proportion of immigrants and first generation Americans in the Philadelphia area, a large proportion of whom expect to enter business."

[22] N. F. Frederiksen and W. B. Schrader, *Adjustment to College,* Educational Testing Service, Princeton, N.J., 1951, Appendix Table, items 10, 43, and 44. This study was based on questionnaire returns from 4,063 veteran and 2,885 nonveteran students at twenty colleges and universities. The numbers in each course program of studies were:

Program	Number of students
Agriculture	240
Business	497
Engineering	1,347
Liberal arts	4,864
Total	6,948

Area	Per cent
Business	69
Engineering	60
Agriculture	38
Liberal arts	36

Practical Course Emphasis

The foregoing data support the view expressed by W. Lloyd Warner that college programs such as those offered by large public institutions in business play a very important part in promoting social mobility for students "from lower positions in the social heap." [23] They also help explain why business schools are tempted to offer a variety of courses of an immediate job-getting value and why it is so difficult to induce students to take work outside the business area. For many students attending these institutions, the pull to keep within the business curriculum, and even within a major subject within this curriculum, seems well-nigh irresistible. The tenor of the interview reports at almost every institution was strikingly uniform on this score—again and again those interviewed said that students were inclined to choose as many courses as possible in the business area, with a heavy emphasis on a given major. Students headed for jobs in accounting were reported as wanting all the accounting work they could get, the future marketing specialists as wanting course after course in marketing, the insurance majors as much insurance as possible, the more specific and practical the better—such was the gist of interviews conducted with deans and course advisers in business schools in all parts of the country. As the assistant dean in a large business school with a four-year program put the issue: "Our students don't see anything to be gained by taking advanced courses in liberal arts. If we didn't lay down the law, I think they'd take almost all their Junior and Senior year in their major."Another dean at an institution with a 2-2-year program stated:

We urge our students to take their "swing" electives outside the business school but it's an uphill fight. In spite of everything we do, I'll bet almost all of their work during the last two years is taken in business subjects and a good deal of that, in one area.

A review of the programs of undergraduate business students at the latter institution, one of the most highly regarded in the country, shows that nearly three-fourths of all the junior and senior students took their entire last two years in business subjects, whereas only a minimum of 42 of the 60 hours was actually required. A review of a large sampling of

[23] W. Lloyd Warner, Robert J. Havighurst, and Martin B. Loeb, *Who Shall Be Educated?* Harper & Brothers, New York, 1944, p. 72.

student transcripts at comparable institutions in other parts of the country modifies these results somewhat. For example, a random sampling of the course programs of fifty-five students majoring in accounting and marketing in six large business schools in the Middle West and South revealed that the great majority of accounting students took five or less courses outside business and economics during their last two years, while most of the marketing students took between six and nine such courses. The outside work consisted mostly of introductory courses in fields like literature, history and sociology, skill courses in report writing, public speaking and practical English, and a miscellany of courses such as Greeks and the Bible, Air Science, Marriage and the Family, and Life Problems. It seems doubtful that much of the latter work played a very vital part in the total educational development of these students. Within the business field, the accounting students tended to concentrate in their field of specialization beyond the minimum required by their departmental major (two-thirds took between ten and twelve courses in accounting whereas only seven to nine were actually required); most of the marketing students, on the other hand, kept fairly close to the minimum five to seven courses required by their departmental regulations.[24]

In another survey of programs taken by undergraduate business students, this one at a nationally known Eastern university, it was found that hardly any work was taken outside business and economics except what was needed to satisfy certain requirements for graduation. The proportion of total student semester credit hours taken during the four-year period in business and economics was found to be 66.4 per cent, of which a little over one-quarter was in specialized business courses. The study notes further that subsequently the students at this institution were given a somewhat wider choice of electives, but that even so, they showed a definite preference for additional work in business rather than in nonbusiness courses, almost all of it being of a rather specialized nature.[25]

In an extensive poll of undergraduate opinion among the business students at this same institution, 48 per cent reported that qualifying for a vocation was a "very important" objective of their college education; "training to think and solve problems" was given a similar rating by 89 per cent of the students, and training in oral and written English by 54 per cent; other objectives, such as fostering habits of contemplation, inquiry and reading, developing an awareness of moral and social values,

[24] The programs of students in liberal arts and other fields appear to follow much the same pattern; the data taken from student transcripts are analyzed in Chap. 8.

[25] Total student semester credit hours in a given course were computed by multiplying the number of semester credits in the course by the number of students taking it. The study was made available on a confidential basis.

and training in the tools of accounting and statistics were rated lower, although in most cases the combined ratings of "very important" and "important" showed little difference in the rankings.

Practical Emphasis Assessed

Viewed in the light of these findings, the natural trend among undergraduate business students appears to be in the direction of greater demand for strictly business subjects and, within the latter, for major specialties of a quite practical, first-job value.[26] This poses the following question: If specific job training is what most of the students want and perhaps are best suited for, what would be gained, other than a certain amount of frustration and lowered morale, from tightening admissions policies, increasing the analytical content of the work, and generally raising standards?

The answer to this query, which is obviously crucial to any assessment of business school programs, turns on five principal considerations. First, it begs the question posed at the outset of this chapter whether there are certain areas of study which constitute the distinctive subject matter of this field. If not, then one program of work is quite as good as any other, and perhaps student appeal is as proper a criterion to apply as any; but from the viewpoint of an educational enterprise, this is certainly an argument of last resort. Student preferences and interests will naturally be reflected in the emphasis given certain parts of a school's program, but responsibility for its general direction and character must rest with the faculty and administrative leaders. After the basic elements have been worked out and the essential subjects agreed upon, rather than before, is the time to consider student motivation, morale, preferences, and the like. This in turn underscores the importance of looking at the programs of business schools in terms of the total career needs of the students, an aspect of the problem which is considered at some length in the next two chapters. Presumably, student demands for certain types of courses reflect their ideas as to what employers want and what successful careers in business require; a careful review of the

[26] A business school professor with long experience in curriculum problems commented on this conclusion as follows: "I wish to take issue with the suggestion that business administration students are interested only in specialized subjects with first-job value. While this is undoubtedly true to a large extent, it should be recognized that the majority of teachers of the basic, multi-section courses in liberal arts, social sciences, and business core courses are inexperienced and often mediocre. The 'stars' teach specialized subjects, including English Literature. At many institutions, the only way to get a professor with a national reputation is to take specialized, advanced courses. Lack of interest or capacity does not adequately explain this motive."

problem from the latter point of view is accordingly very much in order.

Second, the prevailing pattern of student interests and motives is a product of the quality, previous training, and thinking habits of existing student groups at business schools. It would be hazardous to assume that this pattern is fixed and immutable for all time—it is not unheard of for people, even students, to change habitual ways of thinking. If the business schools, either singly or together, concluded that a certain level and type of work had to be mastered, the chances seem reasonably good that many students would respond. Furthermore, at any one institution there is the distinct possibility that higher standards would gradually attract a student body capable of handling the work at a more demanding level, while students who could not hold the pace would look elsewhere. Even before enrollment pressures have become great enough to exert much effect along these lines, a few business schools have already taken a number of steps to tighten admission policies and raise standards generally, a pattern which is increasingly characteristic of such areas as engineering, law, and medicine as well as of a number of other branches of higher education.

Third, it is easy to exaggerate the attitudinal-motivational differences between business students and other undergraduates. Mention has already been made of the strong career emphasis which apparently permeates the thinking of all campus groups, especially those in undergraduate professional schools. In this connection, a faculty committee at Syracuse University conducted a sampling of programs of 1947 graduates in eight undergraduate professional schools (including business administration, engineering, etc.) and found that

. . . two-thirds of the average student's work was primarily specialized, i.e., consisting of course work within the major area, in closely related fields contributing directly to professional competence, or in subjects prerequisite to the major work.

The committee found further that

. . . the typical 1947 graduate from these professional schools left the University having taken, outside his major field, one course in one of the sciences (many left with none at all), two courses in the social sciences (most frequently psychology), and work in the humanities which seldom went beyond freshman English and English literature . . .[27]

Extensive changes in the curriculum at Syracuse University have occurred since 1947, but as a clue to student thinking the findings of this report are important.

[27] C. Robert Pace, "University-Wide Studies in Evaluation of General Education at Syracuse University," p. 5, reprinted from *Evaluation in General Education.* William C. Brown Company, Dubuque, Iowa, 1954.

A recent sampling of undergraduate student programs at the University of California at Berkeley showed that hardly any engineering graduates in the class of 1956 took a single course in language and literature and very few took as much as one semester course in any branch of the social sciences; students in social welfare and public health took considerably more work in the social sciences but hardly more in language and literature, while the journalism students took a good many more courses in both fields. A striking feature of the Berkeley data was the extent to which students outside the professional schools also avoided courses outside their areas of immediate interest; the language and literature students took nearly 50 per cent of their entire four years in their major subject, with almost all of their electives in rather closely related areas; the history students took a little over a fifth of their program in education, English, and political science and over two-fifths in their major; and the economics majors also took about two-fifths of their work in their major and about one-fifth in other social science subjects. In none of these cases was there any significant amount of work done in the sciences or in mathematics, although the economics majors took approximately 4 per cent of their programs in the latter field. While the students in business administration devoted nearly 60 per cent of their program to business courses, they took over 4 per cent of their work in economics and nearly this amount in the other social sciences; the amount of work they did in mathematics and the sciences, however, was negligible.[28] On the whole, their courses of study appeared to be little more career-oriented than those of other students, and the reasons which induced them to specialize were apparently no more compelling than in other fields. The fact that the problem is a well-nigh universal one does not alter the basic issue, but it does put the matter in a rather different light.

Fourth, data on student interests and motivations are not without their ambiguities. Undergraduates in business schools (as in other areas) sign up for a given major and then frequently change their minds—or wish they had! In a recent national study, the U.S. Office of Education reported that of 217 students who indicated an original interest in accounting, only 36 per cent maintained the same interest throughout their undergraduate career or found they had the academic ability to do so; 36 per cent switched to some other subject in business administration, 4 per cent to economics, 3 per cent each to prelaw and engineering, and the balance to a scattering of other subjects. In general, the pattern of change was toward a more general program. The same study shows

[28] It should be noted that considerable changes have been made in course requirements at Berkeley, in both business administration and other fields, since this information was secured.

that of 487 students whose first interest was in some other phase of business administration, 46 per cent maintained their interest in this general area although not necessarily in the same major within this broad field; 8 per cent switched to accounting, 5 per cent to engineering, and no less than 41 per cent to other nonbusiness subjects.[29]

In this connection, mention should be made again of the fact that a very substantial number of undergraduate students seek only general preparation in business, rather than study in a specialized area. This is in part indicated by the heavy enrollments in management and general business majors; in their replies to the Survey Questionnaire the business schools reported that more students in 1956–1957 majored in these two subjects, when considered together, than any other, with even accounting, the traditional leader, slightly eclipsed.[30] Moreover, judging from numerous interviews with students at business schools in different parts of the country, the career interests of even the most practical-minded are frequently vague and subject to change.

The fact that many undergraduate business students come from relatively low-income families has an important bearing on many aspects of the programs of these schools, including the high proportion who work part time to defray expenses. How far this should affect the level and content of a school's curriculum, however, is debatable. Provision should be made for giving students the minimum equipment and skills necessary to gain initial footholds in business, but as developed more fully in the next chapter, the amount of time and effort devoted to this end can easily be exaggerated. The important task, and the one that deserves almost exclusive attention in undergraduate and graduate study, is to help students develop the capabilities they will need throughout their careers. This holds quite as much for students from low-income as from high-income backgrounds. In this connection it is worth noting that intellectual promise among college students appears to be unrelated to family income levels. In the Office of Education study noted earlier, a large sampling of college students were ranked by their position in college placement tests in comparison to estimated family income level. While cautioning that the data do not apply to the general population where selection by college registration does not take place, the study

---

[29] U.S. Office of Education, *op. cit.*, pp. 55–57. An informal sampling of the career plans of thirty-three seniors in the business school and twenty-four seniors in the humanities and social sciences at Temple University, class of 1957, showed that at least half of both groups were "quite unsure" about their career interests.

[30] On the other hand, perhaps many students take the general business major because they think it will be easier to handle or that it will put them in managerial positions more quickly. The difference between management and general business as a major is frequently not too clear; this is discussed further in Chap. 9.

concluded that "the quality of college students as measured by placement tests bears a negligible relationship to family income." [31] A special tabulation limited to students majoring in business yielded substantially similar results; in their case, however, the number was not large enough to serve as a reliable sample of all undergraduates taking work in this field. The two sets of figures are summarized in Table 4-4.

TABLE 4-4

ESTIMATES OF 1953 FAMILY INCOME BY A NATIONAL SAMPLING OF COLLEGE STUDENTS AND BY STUDENTS IN UNDERGRADUATE BUSINESS PROGRAMS, ACCORDING TO RANKING IN COLLEGE PLACEMENT TESTS

Ranking in college placement tests	All students		Business students	
	Number	Estimated family income	Number	Estimated family income
Top tenth.................	827	$5,775	56	$5,555
2nd tenth.................	845	5,855	54	6,400
3rd tenth.................	815	5,858	52	6,000
4th tenth.................	768	5,784	56	7,300
5th tenth.................	715	5,711	62	6,571
6th tenth.................	679	5,701	66	5,923
7th tenth.................	624	5,687	72	5,500
8th tenth.................	582	5,482	48	5,800
9th tenth.................	510	5,613	45	5,688
Bottom tenth.............	375	5,324	44	7,300
Total..................	6,740	$5,713	555	$6,009
Top half................	3,970	5,800	280	6,222
Bottom half.............	2,770	5,590	275	5,869

SOURCE: U.S. Office of Education, *Retention and Withdrawal of College Students*, 1957, p. 61, and specially prepared statistical material.

Considered as a whole, the argument that students attending undergraduate business schools are only pursuing narrow, practical purposes and that their academic work must be designed to match the financial position of the majority does not stand up under analysis. Business schools, in this respect, are essentially in no different position than any other branch of higher education—engineering, law, and medicine included. Without minimizing the difficulties that would be involved, any school which puts more analytical content into its program and raises standards should not lack favorable student response.

Fifth, and last, business schools share with other educational institutions which deal with large aggregates of students the danger of losing

[31] U.S. Office of Education, *op. cit.*, p. 61.

sight of superior minds. One of the most consistent themes running through all the interviews conducted at business schools as part of this survey was that the better students found little challenge in many of the courses. This came not only from the students but from faculty members and, less frequently, from the deans. It would be an oversimplification to attribute this solely to vocational specialism, but courses which deal with practical techniques were more often cited in this connection than any other. Contrariwise, schools which are beginning to attract more academically promising students have gone to considerable lengths to reduce this category of courses to a bare minimum. One of the most baffling questions facing any educational institution is why college going is an exciting and challenging intellectual experience for some and a routine, even aimless, experience for others. Speaking broadly of business schools, the answer appears to depend on where the general goals of a program are set in relation to the interests and abilities of the students. If the main purposes of a program are fixed no higher than what individual students would aspire to in a conventional or nonacademic setting, the life of an institution will begin to atrophy, but if students are part of a program which stretches their powers and holds them to purposes which lie beyond their immediate interests, an intellectually stimulating atmosphere is likely to emerge. The evidence reviewed in this chapter suggests that business schools face rather special problems in designing their work along such lines but that no insuperable difficulties stand in the way of their doing so. Indeed, there are compelling reasons for believing business schools must move in this direction if they are to meet the full range of responsibilities which will confront them in future years.

CHAPTER 5

EMPLOYER REQUIREMENTS

Business careers involve many elements which lie outside the purview of higher education. The principal contribution which business schools can make is to help students apply general knowledge and special abilities to significant business problems. A variety of educational backgrounds is needed at all levels of company organizations but especially at upper management levels. Colleges and universities should concentrate on strengthening the students' powers of imaginative thinking. Business schools should concentrate on helping students apply background knowledge and general-purpose tools to significant business problems.

The problems encountered in running a business organization define the special province of business education while the staffing needs of these organizations determine how graduates of business schools will be employed. Any appraisal of academic work in this area must therefore consider the question of employer requirements for qualified personnel. In turning to the "market" for guidance, however, the business schools confront a welter of opinion. Among some 4¼ million operators of nonfarm companies in this country, of whom over two-thirds hire three employees or less, it would be surprising indeed if anything approaching consensus could be obtained on what business schools should seek to achieve, especially if the views of individuals at different levels of responsibility within firms are given proper weight.

Even with respect to the corporate sector, which includes the most influential companies, extreme care has to be exercised in interpreting employer thinking and practice because of the diversity of their needs, experience, and backgrounds.[1] Few employers and company officers

---

[1] It is worth noting that of approximately 400,000 corporations in the United States, three-quarters hire twenty employees or less. On the other hand, the 200 largest nonfinancial corporations hire about one of every eight employees in the country.

have had the opportunity to give these matters much systematic thought and quite naturally they are inclined to approach such questions in rather personal terms. It is therefore important to relate the discussion of employer viewpoints and experience to the particular industries or groups involved and wherever possible to check their opinions against observed behavior. The various soundings among employers which are attempted in this and the next chapter should be thought of, not as providing any precise guideposts, but as suggesting some general approaches to the field of business education.

In the face of the many diverse purposes which they might serve, a number of business schools have endeavored to center their programs around upper-staff and line positions in industry. Even under the most favorable circumstances there is real question how far students can go in this direction; no ready-made formula exists whereby a school's program can be given a top-management emphasis and thereby achieve solid content. Nevertheless, if this conception of business education were really held to, there is little doubt but what the work in this area would be greatly clarified—study designed to prepare for less complex and less important jobs would be left to other institutions, to on-the-job training, or to the individual studying on his own. The basic difficulty is that, if taken at all seriously, this conception of academic preparation for business would close out most programs now in existence, since there obviously are not enough openings in upper management to satisfy more than a minute fraction of the thousands of students enrolled in these courses. As a consequence, it leads to confusion and even misrepresentation for the great majority of business schools to assert, or imply, that they are preparing students for jobs at this level of responsibility. This applies with particular force to undergraduate business schools, but it bears on many offering graduate work as well.

The fact that even the most promising students cannot hope to assume highly responsible jobs in business for a number of years after graduation raises an issue of critical importance for this branch of higher education. If business schools concentrate on preparing students for work they will be doing twenty or thirty years after graduation, the value of their education will largely be limited to later stages in their careers. On the other hand, to concentrate on the initial stage of the students' working lives by only helping them secure their first jobs would lead to an even more restricted educational result. Neither of these conceptions of the role of business schools appears wholly satisfactory since the full value of the college-going experience can only be realized if it contributes to every stage in a person's development. Knowledge tends to be quickly forgotten unless it is used regularly. If the work which students take at business schools is aimed either at beginning jobs or at some point late in their careers, its chances of achieving meaning for the individual are greatly reduced. In a changing world where many business school students will go to work in jobs and companies not known at the start, knowledge must be *generally* applicable across jobs and companies in order to have any value outside of pedagogy.[2] The need is for knowledge and understanding which will transfer to new situations and for the kinds of abilities which will be useful at all stages of a person's career. A lifelong view of learning would thus appear to be quite as applicable to the work of business schools as to any other branch of higher education.

The foregoing raises the question whether there are elements which are common to a wide range of jobs and careers in business and if so, whether business schools are especially well qualified to prepare for them. If the answer to either part of this question is in the negative, the need for offering special preparation for careers in business as an aspect of a general college or university program largely disappears. Since the greater part of the rationale of the business school movement as it has developed in this country rests on the answer to this question, it is examined at some length below.

ELEMENTS IN BUSINESS CAREERS

Any discussions of the elements which go into different careers in business must start with the admission that there is very little known about this complicated and elusive subject. While the effort to piece together some kind of a general picture seems worth attempting—and from the point of view of the business schools, inescapable—there is no use pretending that the results will be anything but first approximations, subject to numerous qualifications and questions.

Broadly speaking, careers in business which call for special college preparation can be said to consist of three main components: technical skills, general background qualities, and what might be termed "strategic capacities." The first refer to the particular techniques which have to be mastered to achieve competence in any line of work, whether as a stenographer or secretary, bookkeeper or comptroller, foreman or company executive; while there are certain general groupings of such skills, they obviously cover a wide range of positions, and any one school can-

---

[2] For example, according to the work histories of 447 U.S. and Canadian executives sent to the Advanced Management Program at the Harvard Business School, 85 per cent had previously held at least three different types of jobs, i.e., sales, accounting, quality control, investments, etc. other than changes in level of responsibility. Lewis B. Ward, *Executive Performance on Executive Tests,"* unpublished, Graduate School of Business Administration, Harvard University, 1957, p. 23. This part of the discussion has benefited by a number of suggestions made by Mr. Ward.

not hope to include more than a few. The second component refers to background preparation necessary to carry out job responsibilities, such as knowledge of language and literature, ability to handle numerical relations, observance of accepted standards of behavior, and the like. While an essential element in all lines of work, this phase of career preparation does not point to any special role for business schools since it can be satisfied by studies of a rather general nature. The third component refers to the capacity for grasping relationships between jobs, activities, physical magnitudes, and/or human beings in a business environment, and developing out of them a pattern of analysis and a specific course of action. This capacity for creative synthesis, though hard to define and harder still to prepare for in an academic program, can be brought to a wide variety of jobs in business and, by the same token, to every stage in a business career.

Put somewhat more specifically, this last-named capacity has to do with reasoning about business-operating questions with both precision and imagination, seeing the immediate and further removed possibilities in situations, using general principles to illuminate concrete problems, and working through the complexities of specific cases to workable solutions. Put more broadly, this quality has to do with the growth-potential which an employer or administrator always looks for in a subordinate. The capacity for seeing beyond the immediate and routine is, of course, much more important in some positions than in others, and different aspects of this capacity are emphasized in different branches of a business (production, finance, etc.); accordingly, such differences have to be taken into account in developing suitable programs of academic work. The underlying capacity required, however, is potentially useful in all jobs and careers in business, and the prime task of business schools is to foster it in every possible way.

In stressing the element of creative analytical power in the conduct of modern business, Lyndall Urwick writes:[3]

Qualities of character and personality are still of great, even of paramount, importance in management. They can be learned only through practical experience. And such practical experience is still the most vital element in the development of any executive, provided it is practical experience of the right kind. But unless it is accompanied by mental capacity of a high order, the fruit of *continuous* intellectual development, it will be sterile. Everyone knows men of unimpeachable integrity and sterling worth who have remained janitors or mechanics. The difference, the *new* factor, in the total situation is the recognition of the importance of the intellectual factor in the complete picture and of the fact that intellectual growth can occur only as the result of *continuous* education. [Italics in the original]

[3] Lyndall F. Urwick, *Management Education in Business,* American Management Association, New York, 1954, p. 37.

In characterizing the average individual's work in a business organization, Crawford Greenewalt, president of the DuPont Company, observes:[4]

The delegation of authority and the principle of individual laissez-faire extends throughout the organization. At each organizational level, sufficient authority is delegated to enable the individual concerned to discharge adequately the responsibilities associated with his particular post. . . . The responsibility of management in any organization is to provide such conditions as will inspire, among as large a group as possible, the unusual rather than the perfunctory effort.

If the problems confronting business organizations at various levels or in various branches of activity do not require this quality of mind, it is hard to see why any special type of college preparation for business is justified, since the other two components of business jobs can adequately be taken care of by special institutes, liberal arts studies, and other types of educational programs. It is not too much to say that the entire case for business schools rests on the validity of this one idea.

How can business schools strengthen the capacity of students for precise but imaginative reasoning about business situations? The answer, briefly put, would seem to be to give them certain essential tools and knowledge of subject matter which can then be applied to a variety of business issues and problems. Both these aspects of the students' development need to be carried forward together, but preparation in the foundation subjects should be emphasized in the undergraduate years while application of such knowledge to specific business problems should be emphasized at the graduate level. The special province of business schools at both levels of study, however, is to serve as a bridge between these two phases of the students' growth.

The need for persons in business with technical competence in at least one significant area plus a capacity for grasping the broader implications of problems poses a difficult issue for business schools, especially at the undergraduate level. If the schools stress the kind of general preparation associated with executive responsibility, they are accused of preparing students for positions their students will never attain; if they stress specific job preparation, they are accused of providing narrow vocational training. The view suggested here is that there is a wide range of jobs, both in and out of the managerial ranks, for which a broad type of education with very limited specialized training seems altogether appropriate. Simply because a school adopts this approach does not mean that it aims to prepare large numbers of students for top executive positions. Rather it means that essentially the same kind of education appears to be appropriate for a wide range of jobs and careers. This conception of the

---

[4] Crawford H. Greenewalt, *The Uncommon Man*, McGraw-Hill Book Company, Inc., New York, 1959, pp. 13 and 31.

role of business schools has come to be associated with a management or managerial decision-making emphasis, and this terminology is accordingly used in the present study. This way of characterizing the work of business schools, however, should not be interpreted as meaning that all programs should be aimed exclusively at top-management or even upper-management positions.

EVOLVING SOCIAL ENVIRONMENT

The logic of this approach to academic work in business is rooted in certain trends and projected needs of modern society. It would be impossible to identify all of them even if space permitted, but some of the more important can be singled out with a fair degree of confidence. Since every branch of education must be essentially forward-looking in the sense that its principal concern is with the needs of individual students over their lifetimes, the discussion centers on a few general tendencies in American life which promise to have continuing significance for business schools. Any detailed prognostication would doubtless be wide of the mark, but some broad assumptions have to be made about the future if any planning is to be done at all.

One of the continuing influences which will have an important bearing on the future role of business schools is the need for maintaining the growth rate of the American economy. The significant fact is not so much that the long-term rise in the national product has been about 3 per cent per annum but that continued improvement in all phases of living has now become a basic assumption of the society. Since the business system is looked to as the principal source of material progress in this country, responsibility for maintaining economic expansion devolves mainly on the businessman and those working with him. It is up to him to uncover the new products, the cheaper methods, the substitute materials, the improved quality, and the wider distribution of an expanded range of goods which have come to be the hallmark of the American enterprise system. This means in the future, as in the past, continual experimentation, continual searching for the new and untried, continual research of both a formal and informal kind, and continual striving to match and better one's rivals in getting goods to the consumer. This calls for the ability to see the larger dimensions of problems, bring novel insights and methods to bear on familiar issues, and probe situations for new opportunities. The qualities which enter into such decisions relate to every phase of business activity, whether in large firms or in small, and are an absolute essential to the conduct of any successful enterprise. Business school programs designed to help prepare individuals for difficult decisions of this sort would fit well into an academic environment and in fact would contribute vitally to its enrichment. Broadly speaking, business schools could perform no more valued service than to help students develop capacities in this direction.

Another continuing trend deserving attention by business schools is the broadening role that science, technology, and mathematics will play in the business system of tomorrow. The vital point from an educational point of view is not only that scientific research will be the main source of new products and materials, important as this of course will be, or even that mathematical techniques will be increasingly used in many phases of business operations. What is still more significant is that the scientific point of view, or spirit, is becoming increasingly important in dealing with a wide range of business questions. It follows that the person who is familiar with what science can and cannot do and where the methods of science and mathematics do and do not apply will have a marked advantage over those who lack such preparation. This type of study will contain much more relevance for certain operations or industries than others, but most fields (wholesaling, retailing, utilities, and manufacturing) and most jobs (processing, distributing, selling, and general office work) will doubtless be affected by this trend to an increasing degree. Even now, decisions with respect to the best method for handling inventory problems, controlling traffic and flow of materials, recording production data, and analyzing cost or sales information involve a fair degree of sophistication in the use of modern mathematical and statistical concepts. Looking to the future, a company that does not have the personnel with the requisite preparation for handling such problems along scientific lines is likely to suffer serious consequences. How far business students should be expected to go in the direction of scientific and mathematical training is an open question, but that this will be an essential part of their preparation in the future, there seems no doubt.

Another continuing trend in American industry relevant to the development of business education is the increasing complexity of internal operations within firms. If widening the scale and variety of a company's internal activities were simply to require a different kind of top management, the problem would be difficult enough, but the need for balancing and coordinating a diversity of functions reaches down to many lower-level activities as well. An employee coming up through the financial, marketing, or personnel aspects of a business who has the capacity for seeing where his specialized function fits in with the firm's production and distribution requirements is much more likely to make a significant contribution to the company's success than one who does not. The task of detecting all the possible ramifications of a given decision in introducing a new product or changing to a new method of production or shifting the location of an important operation cannot possibly be carried out successfully by one man or even by a small group of men sitting at the apex of a company's structure. The steps leading up to such actions and, even more, their implementation once decided upon, call for insight, inventiveness, and imagination on the part of many staff and line workers. Essentially the same qualities, though in different form, are needed in small firms as well. Those who can recognize the relatedness of business processes and can act on such knowledge, whether in large or small organizations, add a very important dimension to any job in business today.

Another trend in modern business which bears on the work of business schools is the increasing attention paid to the human aspects of internal company operations. If all of management cannot be summed up in the pat phrase "working with people," at least it underscores the extent to which the needs and potentialities of individual employees have become a part of management's concern. Here, clearly, effective action cannot be confined to top leadership, since relations between people in a business organization involve all levels and all jobs. The record of company attempts to improve dealings between employees or between workers and superiors is strewn with examples of elaborate programs which touched face-to-face relationships hardly at all and were dismal failures as a result. How far academic preparation can go in avoiding such errors and in developing more meaningful programs is uncertain, but at least it is clear that these questions are not all going to be settled at the top. Sensitiveness to individual needs, awareness of group loyalties, understanding of status systems, insight into conflict relationships—these are qualities which are needed as much if not more on the foreman and supervisor firing line as in the company board room. In smaller organizations, such problems assume a somewhat different character but in importance they bulk no less large. Many elements in modern life have conspired to put human behavior at the center of all levels of business operations, and this whole area is therefore receiving increasing attention in programs of business education.

Relations between the business enterprise and its external environment mark still another area of increasing complexity and importance. The range of a firm's external stimuli and responses often becomes extremely wide, and the success of a company frequently turns on the ability of its management to foresee opportunities and dangers in time to take appropriate action. To a considerable degree, relations with the outside world must remain the exclusive responsibility of top management, but again the listening-observing-interpreting function cannot be carried out by one or two individuals in an organization. The tasks of probing evolving market situations or following various collective-bargaining patterns or sizing up shifting competitive positions are often too varied and involved to be dealt with by a few top administrators acting on their own. Perhaps even more to the point, it is one thing to blueprint a general strategy and quite another to carry it through to a successful conclusion. Even if policy planning in the face of a continually shifting external environment could be left to a small leader group, which seems doubtful, policy execution requires participation and positive understanding by many others. Just to cite the example of the problems faced by a company which establishes a plant in a new, relatively small community is enough to suggest the importance of this kind of active participation. The capacity to see how relationships to the outside environment can change for a firm and where alternative courses of action can lead is one of the most valuable abilities to be derived from academic work and accordingly should play an important part in the programs of business schools.

A no less important influence shaping the work of business schools is the increasing attention being given to the social responsibilities of business enterprises. Formal standards embodied in law and governmental regulations are but one aspect of this development. Even more pervasive are the informal rules and obligations which the community expects business to meet, whether they involve dealings at national, state, or local levels. No one would argue that there is a clear and precise code of conduct applicable to business in its relations with representatives of government, unions, suppliers, stockholders, rival firms, and the like, but the norms within which employers operate are nonetheless real. The contributions which employers themselves have made to developing standards of socially responsible conduct are also worth noting. Perhaps more than in any other area of business behavior, it is essential that these viewpoints and ideas be widely understood not only within companies but by the public at large. On the other hand, how they can best be dealt with at the educational level is far from clear. A school that cannot make concern for ethical conduct a part of the whole atmosphere of its program through the kind of faculty leadership it provides is unlikely to have much impact on the attitudes of its students.

Finally, this country's business faces a future in which its ties with other countries will become increasingly varied and complex, conditioning many aspects of its activities. In an immediate sense, foreign countries will gain importance as customers, suppliers, and rival producers in relation to American business. In a longer-range sense, the course these countries will follow will largely shape the environment in which this nation's business system will operate. How American business can contribute to the international economy at the same time that it adapts itself to this new international environment poses a baffling range of issues of the greatest importance. Whatever the outcome, it seems safe to say they will not be disposed of by a few top leaders charting a course for all industry to follow; if American business is to find its way in this new international environment, many resourceful, imaginative, and broadly prepared persons will be required. Here our educational institutions, including our business schools, face a heavy responsibility and a magnificent opportunity.

It is evident from this brief review of some of the underlying trends in American society which will have continuing importance for educational policy that business schools face a mounting demand for students who can use powers of independent analysis to help solve business problems. This is the quality which was referred to earlier as the most important element in the work of business schools and the subsequent discussion merely corroborates its strategic importance at many levels of business performance. If the business schools center their attention on developing the ability to apply the principles and methods of certain foundation subjects to a wide range of questions, it would seem apparent that they should concentrate on the basic intellectual equipment of students rather than on the specific techniques applicable to given situations. Just what these prebusiness and business foundation subjects are, how they might best be approached at the undergraduate level, and where the balance between technical and general preparation should be struck, are questions dealt with at length in Part 2. The discussion to this point, however, goes a considerable distance in indicating the general path which business schools might well follow in the future.

Beyond a common emphasis on these foundation subjects and on their application to business problems, there is nothing in the foregoing discussion to suggest that business schools should embrace a common program. The field of business contains too much variety and its future course of development too much uncertainty to justify any detailed blueprinting of the future work of these schools. Efforts by individual institutions to forge new tools and to concentrate on certain unexplored approaches to the subject are to be applauded, but it would certainly be premature for all schools to try to reproduce these experimental programs at this time. It should be noted further that schools which center their attention on the frontier aspects of the field are apt to find themselves concentrating on highly abstruse, technical, or specialized questions, and it becomes no easy matter to decide just when work of this sort is of demonstrable value and when it is so much curricular padding.

EDUCATION FOR DIFFERENT MANAGEMENT POSITIONS

While the tasks of the manager or administrator provide a focus for the programs of a number of business schools, the management function of planning, organizing, motivating, and controlling is itself many-sided and diverse. Graduate work at a few business schools, as already noted, is largely centered on problems of upper management, especially in larger concerns, but as already noted a more realistic definition of management for the great majority of schools would include middle management and lower management, to say nothing of a variety of jobs in small firms.[5] The issues confronting business schools are seen in a clearer light when the nature of the managerial function at different levels of authority is examined in more detail; the duties of professional staff members at comparable levels of responsibility also deserve consideration.

Historically, there has been a slow rise in the managerial class in this country relative to the employed civilian labor force, the rate of increase accelerating since 1940. The United States census category "managers, officials, and proprietors, excluding farm," which consisted of 6.4 million persons in 1955, accounted for 10 per cent of the employed civilian labor force that year as against 7 per cent in 1910. It is expected to rise at about the same rate as the total employed labor force until 1965.[6] This census classification is much too broad for present purposes; if the retail and wholesale trade category, which is made up largely of shop managers and proprietors in very small firms, is excluded, the rate of increase in this more narrowly defined managerial group was twice as fast per annum between 1940 and 1950 as between 1910 and 1940.[7] Moreover, during the forties nearly two-thirds of the increase in this more traditionally defined manager group was accounted for by categories in which the proportion of both college graduates and median salary levels were relatively high, a rough measure of the mounting need for highly trained management personnel.[8]

[5] Most business schools, including even those that are exclusively graduate, report a large percentage of their graduates work for small companies. Among 6,685 Harvard Business School alumni responding to a questionnaire, nearly one-third reported working for companies of 100 employees or less; the percentage among younger graduates, however, was somewhat smaller. More than one-third of the responding graduates were owners-managers. Harvard Business School, *Alumni Bulletin*, Summer, 1956. Among some 2,000 alumni of Stanford's Graduate School of Business, about a quarter reported working in companies of 100 employees or less. Of those graduating between 1927 and 1936, 50 per cent were either chief executives or the first level below. On the other hand, less than 10 per cent of all responding alumni said they supervised more than 100 employees; moreover, 25 per cent of the respondents were at the fourth level of responsibility or less. Graduate School of Business, Stanford University, *Alumni Bulletin*, January, 1959.

[6] Paper delivered by Ewan Clague at the Conference on the Changing Character of American Industry, AFL-CIO, Washington, 1958, pp. 18 and 20.

[7] See Appendix 7.

[8] These categories, seven in number, were those in which both the proportion of college graduates and the median salary level in 1950 were higher than the average for the entire census category of "managers, officials, proprietors, excluding farm."

From an educational point of view, the most important difference between management positions at various levels of responsibility is the ⱱ scope and diversity of the activities involved. Top officers, especially in large concerns, must be prepared to cope with a host of issues and personalities during a typical week, their decisions range from how to entertain an out-of-town customer, pacify an outraged board member, or answer a reporter's questions to whether to buy an electronic computer, fire a plant superintendent or initiate operations in a foreign country. Intensive studies of the duties performed by top management all stress the breadth of viewpoint and range of abilities demanded of corporate executives in order to keep the various functions of an enterprise in proper balance and the organization as a whole moving toward certain predetermined goals. Carroll Shartle's Ohio State Leadership Studies, for example, indicate that over half the time of a "typical" company president is devoted to planning (decisions affecting "the aims of the organization as to volume or quality," etc.), evaluation ("of reports, policies, and standards"), and public relations (to inform and be informed by "outside persons regarding the program and functions of the organization"). Many of the other duties which Shartle found to be part of a company president's job, such as coordinating activities of units or persons within the organization or interpreting directives and regulations, also call for the capacity to see problems in multi-dimensional relationships and to put individual decisions in a larger policy-making setting.[9] Preliminary findings of the Executive Study of the Educational Testing Service suggest that as individuals move up the position hierarchy in a manufacturing enterprise, there is a progressive shifting of emphasis from direct supervision and control of operations through planning and the exercise of broader powers to concerns with the reputation of the company, demands on personal behavior, and preservation of the organization as a going enterprise.[10] Other studies likewise emphasize that executives must combine an ability to analyze complicated situations with a

---

The number employed in these categories was 1.4 million in 1940, or 36 per cent of the entire manager category, and 2.2 million in 1950, or 43 per cent of the category; they accounted for 64 per cent of the increase in the nonfarm manager category as a whole over this ten-year period. These calculations were made from the following sources: *Statistical Abstract of the United States*, 1947, "Detailed Occupation of Persons in the Experienced Labor Force and of Employed Persons (Except on Public Emergency Work), by Sex, 1940," pp. 180–181; U.S. Bureau of the Census, *Census of Population: 1950*, vol. IV, *Special Reports*, Part 1, Chap. B, "Occupational Characteristics," U.S. Government Printing Office, 1956, p. 1B-10.

[9] Carroll L. Shartle, *Executive Performance and Leadership*, Prentice-Hall, Inc., Englewood Cliffs, N.J., 1956, pp. 83–86.

[10] This finding of the Executive Study, which is under the direction of John K. Hemphill and Lewis B. Ward, is still in tentative form.

grasp of the principal consequences which will follow from various courses of action.[11]

Breadth versus Depth

The clear implication of these investigations is that academic preparation, to the extent it is relevant to the work of upper-management personnel, should concentrate on general background education, basic intellectual equipment, and the capacity to apply general principles to new and unfamiliar problems.

Other than their emphasis on the need for breadth and analytical vigor in academic programs these studies admittedly throw little light on the specific subjects which such programs should include. In writing about the responsibilities of managers in the decades ahead, however, Peter Drucker has advanced some definite proposals on this subject. He stresses the importance of intensive preparation in writing and speaking, knowledge of logic and of its analytical and mathematical tools, familiarity with science and scientific method, and understanding of the environment through history, political science, and economics. He adds:[12]

> I do not mean to imply that what the young man needs to prepare himself for management is incompatible with specific business or engineering training. On the contrary, there is no reason why the required general education should not be an integral part of the business school or engineering school curriculum (as is indeed being recognized increasingly by our engineering schools). I also do not mean that there is no value to specific business or engineering subjects. On the contrary, they give a man ability to perform functional work with some degree of workmanship . . . The young man who only acquires functional skills, however, and only learns specific business or engineering subjects, is not being prepared to be a manager. All he is being prepared for is to get his first job.

As is well known, executives in larger firms speak with almost one voice on the need for broad understanding, intellectual imagination, and sensitiveness to values in preparing for positions of corporate leadership. Thus, Albert L. Nickerson, president of the Socony-Mobil Oil Company, states:[13]

> Our business system, indeed our whole scheme of contemporary American life, requires the education of young men and women of moral stamina who

---

[11] See, for example, Ralph C. Davis, *Industrial Organization and Management,* Harper & Brothers, New York, 1949; Peter F. Drucker, *The Practice of Management,* Harper & Brothers, New York, 1954; and William H. Newman, *Administrative Action,* Prentice-Hall Inc., Englewood Cliffs, N.J., 1951.

[12] Peter F. Drucker, *op. cit.,* pp. 375–376.

[13] Albert L. Nickerson, "Climbing the Managerial Ladder," *Saturday Review of Literature,* vol. 36, Nov. 21, 1953, p. 39.

can think and who can discriminate among values. This implies the necessity for the continued extension of a sound liberal education to every American boy and girl with the capacity to assimilate it.

Clarence Randall, formerly president and chairman of the board of Inland Steel Company, says that the abilities needed in responsible management positions are "the lively imagination, the critical survey, and the logical processes of thought." He interprets his own experience in these terms:[14]

Standing as I do on the plateau of retirement and looking over my shoulder at my life, I can see with startling clarity that the greatest asset I have had in business from the point of view of personal preparation was the general education that I received at Harvard. I have no shadow of a doubt that the early selection of a specialty would have been a long-time limitation in my life, even though for a few years I might have earned more money.

James M. Symes, president of the Pennsylvania Railroad, in stressing the need for leaders at all levels of business, concludes:[15]

It has become increasingly clear that an engineer who knows only engineering, a chemist who knows only chemistry, a lawyer who knows only law, is not likely to be much of a leader. . . . His technical skill takes him up to a certain level, but his lack of general education, sound judgment and ability as a leader—his failure to see the company's business except in terms of his particular skill—halts him there. Nor is the tragedy confined to him—the company loses full benefit of a brilliant mind.

After deliberating for many months and preparing a series of individual reports, seventy-three North Carolina businessmen reached the following consensus on the subject of academic preparation for business:[16]

The main goal of a *business education* should be the development of an individual with broad training in both the humanities and principles of business, capable of independent, imaginative, and constructive thought. A business education should help a student—
Acquire a general knowledge of his chosen field
Develop his capacity to reason
Develop a sense of values
Help him communicate more effectively
A business education should also help develop in a student an inquiring, analytical, and searching mind and a code of ethics including honesty, integrity, and an uncompromising respect for the rights of others. [Italics in the original]

Such expressions of employer thinking are hard to translate into specific proposals for existing educational programs. Many of the qualities

[14] *The Randall Lectures,* Fund for Adult Education, White Plains, N.Y., 1957, p. 9.
[15] *Railway Age,* Nov. 21, 1955, p. 7.
[16] Claude S. George, *Business Looks at Business Education,* School of Business Administration, University of North Carolina, Chapel Hill, N.C., 1958, p. 6.

stressed by business leaders—intellectual courage, moral stamina, social responsibility, and understanding of motivations—can hardly be taught in the classroom, at least in any formal or direct manner. Then, too, frequent mention is made of the fact, discussed later, that actual recruiting practice among college graduates does not accord with the pronouncements of top business leaders. From the viewpoint of business schools, however, the general import of top management's thinking on these issues is clear: industry is in great need of persons who have developed a capacity for searching, wide-ranging analysis, and business schools should accordingly set their sights on trying to meet this need.

Educational Requirements Below Top Management

Coming down the management structure, the scope and variety of duties tend to become progressively narrower until a level is reached where the work is almost entirely routine and specialized. Studies of management jobs even immediately below the president level indicate a much greater emphasis on specialized professional functions; for example, Shartle found that company treasurers give much less time than company presidents to planning, coordinating, and public relations—much more time to professional consultation.[17] At middle-management and even more at lower-management levels, the immediate demands of the job within a rather narrow frame of reference are almost always more important. Yet the difference between what might be termed the minimum and maximum qualities relevant to lower-level management positions is enormous. In terms of barely meeting the requirements of such jobs, little in the way of analytical power and intellectual imagination may be necessary, but in terms of making the work fully contributory to an organization's success, many of the same qualities are needed at these as at higher levels. Indeed, in so far as general intellectual qualities are concerned, companies appear to look for much the same attributes in a front-line supervisor as in a top-management man.[18] The distinction between the minimum and maximum requirements of positions would therefore appear to provide an appropriate demarcation between the type of work which does and does not belong in a four-year college or business school program.

Officers in small companies typically perform a wider variety of duties

[17] Carroll L. Shartle, op. cit., p. 86.

[18] Joseph M. Trickett, A Survey of Management Development, American Management Association, New York, 1954, pp. 42–44. At both levels, Trickett found that the most frequently sought for attributes were leadership, character, integrity, ability in human relations, and intelligence; the chief difference was that intelligence was less frequently cited, and operating or technical ability was more frequently cited, in the case of front-line supervisory positions.

than their counterparts in large organizations, since delegation of responsibility is often not feasible. In this sense, the problems facing a given individual may be more complex in small firms than in large. Limited financial resources may also reduce the allowable margin of error, putting a greater premium on competitive daring and imagination. At the same time, competitive pressures may circumscribe the small-firm manager so completely he has little latitude for choice. His operations may be so small that relationships within the organization can be based wholly on rule-of-thumb procedures. He may even operate successfully with little or no understanding of modern accounting methods, credit practices, inventory controls, etc., to say nothing of such occult matters as capital budgeting, operations research, or communications theory. Many of the basic problems facing both small and large firms are, however, similar, and courses confined wholly to the problems of small companies are likely to be unduly narrow. For this reason it seems desirable to analyze such problems as part of the more general courses in marketing, finance, and the other functional areas.

EDUCATIONAL BACKGROUNDS OF MANAGEMENT GROUPS

Comparisons of the educational backgrounds of those now holding responsible jobs in business throw further light on the needs of industry for college-trained talent. Even before 1900 the proportion of business leaders with a college education was well above the population as a whole;[19] since then, despite the rapid rise in the percentage of the population attending college, the disparity has increased. Thus, Mabel Newcomer found that about 39 per cent of the older business executives in 1900 had attended college as against 80 per cent of the younger executives in 1950.[20]

The study conducted by Warner and Abegglen of 8,562 business leaders of the largest firms in the country revealed that college going, while related to occupational status of the parents, was characteristic of all groups of business leaders studied. For example, over half the leaders

[19] Keller found that 35 per cent of the business leaders had some college education in 1870. S. I. Keller, "The Social Origins and Career Lines of American Business Leaders," unpublished doctoral thesis, Columbia University, New York, 1953, p. 73. Mills also found that in still earlier periods, the educational background of business leaders was far above the average for their contemporaries. C. Wright Mills, "The American Business Elite: A Collective Portrait," *Journal of Economic History*, Supplement V, 1945, p. 34; both references are cited in Mabel Newcomer, *The Big Business Executive*, Columbia University Press, New York, 1955, p. 70.

[20] *Ibid.*, pp. 68–70. The Newcomer study was confined to the presidents and board chairmen of the largest railroad, public utility, and industrial corporations; the data for 1950, for example, covered 428 companies and 863 officers.

born to skilled and unskilled laborers attended college. The authors continue:[21]

This proportion increases steadily as one proceeds up the occupational scale; three fourths of the sons of small owners, almost that proportion of the sons of white-collar workers and of farmers, nine of ten of the sons of big business and professional men had some college work or graduated.

Fifty years earlier the proportion of business leaders coming from relatively low income families was considerably smaller, and the proportion of this group attending college was smaller still.[22]

Education of Small Firm Managers

Information on the educational backgrounds of owner-operators and principal officers of small firms is meager. The Taussig and Joslyn study of 1932 concluded that the larger the business, the greater the number of college-educated executives; this relationship was found to hold true through all five of the size groups studied.[23] The great majority of the firms in the Newcomer study fell in Taussig's largest group, but within this rather select category, no clear association between size and level of education was evident. However, it appears from the Newcomer study that a substantially higher proportion of the executives who had not attended college, as against those who had, had organized their own businesses.[24] Warner and Abegglen's earlier study found some tendency for the chief executives of large firms to have more education than their counterparts in smaller firms, but the difference was extremely slight.[25]

Data on the educational backgrounds of the heads of many relatively small firms were secured from the files of the Young Presidents' Organization. In 1955 this group had a membership of 1,300, all of whom were men who had become company presidents before the age of thirty-nine. The median size of the companies was 200 employees; to be eligible, the company must have employed at least 100 employees or, in the case of service companies, at least 50 employees. A questionnaire covering about 60 per cent of the membership revealed that 86 per cent had some col-

[21] W. Lloyd Warner and James Abegglen, *Big Business Leaders in America*, Harper & Brothers, New York, 1955, p. 38.

[22] Mabel Newcomer, *op. cit.*, pp. 75–77.

[23] F. W. Taussig and C. S. Joslyn, *American Business Leaders*, The Macmillan Company, New York, 1932, pp. 181–182. The smallest company group in the Taussig study had gross annual incomes of less than $500,000, and the largest $50,000,000 and over.

[24] Mabel Newcomer, *op. cit.*, pp. 79–81. The proportion of executives included in this study who organized their own companies declined markedly after 1900, but

lege, 50 per cent had graduated from college, and 30 per cent had taken postgraduate work.[26] These results are not too different from the Newcomer and Warner-Abegglen findings, although Newcomer found that the percentage of the 1950 "younger executives" with college degrees was distinctly greater (66 per cent versus 50 per cent).

It seems probable that marked differences would only show up in the case of very small firms; for example, a questionnaire circulated among the principal officers of printing companies in the Philadelphia area showed that only about 25 per cent had graduated from college and an additional 15 per cent had some college.[27]

the decline among those with college degrees was especially sharp. The comparisons for the two periods follow:

Principal factor in obtaining office	All educational levels, per cent	Grammar school education, per cent	First college degree, per cent
1900			
Organizing company............	30	34	24
Working up within company....	18	21	11
Investment and other..........	52	45	65
Total.....................	100	100	1C0
1950			
Organizing company............	6	19	1
Working up within company....	51	50	42
Investment and other..........	43	31	57
Total.....................	100	100	100

[25] Among firms with annual sales of less than $10 million, the smallest category studied, the authors found that 59 per cent of the chief executives had college degrees as against 62 per cent among firms with sales of more than $250 million. W. Lloyd Warner and James C. Abegglen, *Occupational Mobility in American Business and Industry*, 1928–1952, University of Minnesota Press, Minneapolis, 1955, p. 152.

[26] The results of the questionnaire, circulated in 1957–1958, were compiled by Science Research Associates.

[27] This questionnaire was circulated in 1958 in connection with the present survey among approximately 200 printing firms in the Philadelphia area. Five executives were asked to respond from each company and 120 did so; it is believed that a reasonably good cross section of firms was covered. The great majority hire less than 100 mechanical workers; not more than a half dozen employed more than 250, and none more than 2,000 workers. These data, which of course are not directly comparable with the findings of the other studies noted above, were secured with the cooperation of the Printing Industries of Philadelphia through the courtesy of John W. Seybold.

Education of Middle and Lower Management

Information on the educational backgrounds of company officials below the top-executive level is easy to misinterpret because of differences in age levels, parental incomes, type of position, etc. Nonetheless, it is worth noting that members of the management group immediately below the top-management level apparently have as much education as the top executives, if not more. Thus, the Warner and Abegglen study found no appreciable difference between the educational backgrounds of chief executives and vice-presidents, on the one hand, and other officers on the other.[28] Daniel Starch reached similar findings when he compared the educational preparation of a relatively small group of top- and middle-management people, but he found the education of the lower-management group to be much less.[29] A recent report on industrial relations executives in 287 companies, a group of officials somewhat below the top-management level, revealed that 87 per cent of the members of this group had college degrees and 32 per cent had advanced degrees.[30]

Data secured for the present survey on the educational backgrounds of 562 managers in seven industrial companies and sixty firms in various manufacturing and nonmanufacturing lines showed that 61 per cent of top management had graduated from college as against 63 per cent of middle management and 62 per cent of lower management.[31] Similar information gained through a questionnaire circulated as part of this survey among 1,808 leading life insurance salesmen, all members of the Million Dollar Round Table, revealed that 73 per cent attended some college or university as a full-time undergraduate, and of this number 78 per cent

[28] W. Lloyd Warner and James C. Abegglen, *Occupational Mobility in American Business and Industry*, 1928–1952, University of Minnesota Press, Minneapolis, 1955, p. 152.

[29] Daniel Starch, *How to Develop Your Executive Ability*, Harper & Brothers, New York, 1943, p. 22. He found that only 20 per cent of those in lower management had gone to college as against 72 and 76 per cent in top and middle management, respectively. Only fifty persons were included in each group.

[30] *Industrial Relations News, The Industrial Relations Executive*, 1957, p. 2 (mimeographed). The questionnaire consisted of replies from 287 industrial relations directors; about a one-third response was secured.

[31] Unpublished data supplied by Richardson, Bellows, Henry and Co., Inc. The positions studied ranged from company president down to two levels above the first-line supervisor; top management, which represented 18 per cent of the sample, had a mean age of fifty; middle management, which represented 38 per cent of the sample, had a mean age of forty-seven; and lower management, which represented 44 per cent of the sample, had a mean age of forty-four. The seven companies, which accounted for 410 of the 562 cases, were located in the following industries: transportation, oil refining, steel, paper, grain storage, machine tools, and rubber.

earned a degree.[32] On the other hand, differences in the educational backgrounds of various management categories appear to be more marked in the South. An investigation of the educational backgrounds of 319 management and professional personnel in twenty-two companies in Alabama showed that 57 per cent of top management had reached college as against only 48 per cent in middle management and 30 per cent in supervisory positions.[33]

The company interviews conducted for the Ford Foundation survey of business schools included some information on the educational preparation of different management levels in over eighty large, well-known concerns covering a general cross section of manufacturing and nonmanufacturing industries.[34] While complete data were not obtainable, the results indicate that in about half of the companies, 50 per cent or more of the top- and middle-management personnel held college degrees, while in the other companies the proportion was markedly less. In both groups, the educational level of top management tended to be somewhat higher than that of middle management, but the difference was slight; on the other hand, the educational level of lower management in almost all companies was markedly less. Other results of these interviews are analyzed below; it is enough to note here that in almost all the firms, college preparation has become an important element in the background of both top and middle administrators but that in only a few of the firms do college graduates clearly predominate.

It may be inferred from the foregoing that important management and related jobs in larger concerns are today frequently held by college-trained persons and that this level of education will be increasingly expected of anyone aspiring to such positions in the future. To what extent this generalization holds for smaller concerns or for management jobs below the general officer level is less clear, although it is safe to conclude that the facts with respect to existing practice among very small firms and the lowest management levels are considerably different. This broad shift to a college-educated management reflects a variety of changes in the nation's social and economic structure all pointing to greater need by business for administrators with extensive educational preparation.

[32] The data were gathered in 1958 through a questionnaire sent to 2,987 members of the Million Dollar Round Table, which includes the most successful life insurance salesmen in the country; replies were received from 1,808 members, or about 60 per cent of the entire group. The median age of the members of this organization is between forty-five and fifty.

[33] Alabama Business Research Council, *Skills for Progress,* School of Commerce and Business Administration, University of Alabama, University, Ala., 1957, p. 6.

[34] The results of these interviews were made available on a confidential basis through the courtesy of Robert A. Gordon, Director, Ford Foundation Study of Business Education.

MAJOR EDUCATIONAL INTERESTS

Further light on the academic interests and preparation of business managers is gained by reviewing the programs of major study which different management groups selected as college students. A striking feature of the data is the relatively high proportion of college-trained executives who majored in engineering, science, and business-economics. According to *Fortune's* 1952 study of the three highest paid men in each of the 200 biggest industrial companies, 25 biggest railroads, and 25 biggest utilities, these three fields accounted for 76 per cent of the 521 executives who graduated from college.[35] A larger portion majored in engineering and science than in business and economics (46 per cent versus 31 per cent), but for those under fifty years of age, the proportions are reversed, with only 29 per cent in science and engineering and 39 per cent in business and/or economics.[36] Regardless of age, the *Fortune* data indicate that humanities and other liberal arts subjects did not attract a majority following, although the proportion was somewhat higher among the younger executives. The other striking feature of the data is the extent of the shift from science-engineering to business-economics, which accords with general trends in college enrollments noted in Chaps. 1 and 2.

The Warner-Abegglen study of a random sampling of 505 business leaders who had graduated from college found that nearly half had earned Bachelor of Science degrees and about the same number had earned Bachelor of Arts degrees; whether the latter included a heavy percentage of business and economics majors could not be determined, but only nine men reported earning a specialized degree in business. In 1928, before the influence of the rising number of business schools had begun to make itself felt, 71 per cent of the executives studied by Warner and Abegglen had had no formal business preparation, whereas in 1952 the proportion fell to 42 per cent.[37] On the other hand, an extremely small percentage of top executives currently in office have taken enough work in business administration to earn an advanced degree in this subject. This appears to hold true even of younger executives, indicating

[35] Editors of *Fortune, The Executive Life,* Doubleday and Company, Inc., Garden City, N.Y., 1956, p. 36. Of the 900 men included in the survey, 65 per cent went through four or more years of college. The sample is very close to the group covered in the Newcomer study noted above.

[36] *Ibid.,* p. 34.

[37] W. Lloyd Warner and James C. Abegglen, *Occupational Mobility in American Business and Industry,* 1928–1952, University of Minnesota Press, Minneapolis, 1955, p. 112. It should be kept in mind that only about a third of the group graduated from college in 1928 compared with roughly six out of ten in 1952.

how recently this type of work has become important. Finally, both before and after World War II a surprisingly large number of college and noncollege executives reported taking some extra college preparation in business subjects. Warner and Abegglen noted in this connection that college men tend to pursue such studies within formal college programs, whereas noncollege men rely much more on correspondence and proprietary school courses.[38]

Of the 1,300 members of the Young Presidents' Organization, as mentioned above, about 50 per cent graduated from college, and the latter group was divided in roughly equal proportions between business administration, engineering, and liberal arts. Of the 120 Philadelphia printing company officials who submitted answers to the questionnaire referred to earlier, about 25 per cent graduated from a college or university, and of this group, somewhat over two-fifths majored in business administration as undergraduates, about one-third in liberal arts, and one-fifth in natural science or engineering. Among the 1,808 life insurance salesmen belonging to the Million Dollar Round Table who responded to the survey's questionnaire, 73 per cent had been full-time undergraduate students, and of this number 40 per cent had majored in business administration, 40 per cent in liberal arts (including science), and 10 per cent in engineering.

Going below the top-executive level in larger firms, such sketchy evidence as is available indicates that middle and lower management in larger companies include a heavy representation of all three of the principal educational backgrounds—engineering-sciences, humanities-social sciences, and business administration—the exact combination depending on the nature of the firm's product or function, its type of leadership, its most serious management needs, and the like. In the Ford Survey company interviews, public utility and heavy manufacturing concerns reported a higher proportion of engineering-trained management personnel than of the other two types of college preparation; similarly, firms in accounting, insurance, and banking indicated a higher proportion of management personnel in business administration than in the other two fields, while those in advertising and publishing indicated a greater concentration in liberal arts. Some surprising differences between companies in the same industry—including whether management at the different levels had any college preparation at all—were also uncovered, but in a broad way educational backgrounds seemed to fit the characteristics of different industries. Since these differences appear to be closely related to the specific educational requirements of various management and professional positions, they are examined at greater length below.

[38] *Ibid.*, pp. 111–113.

CHANGES IN EDUCATIONAL INTERESTS

As noted earlier, comparisons of the educational preparation of different management levels is complicated by the age factor and by changes over time in the distribution of students among different subject areas or types of college programs. In commenting on this aspect of the educational backgrounds of top management in very large concerns, the *Fortune* editors observed:[39]

During their school days, the younger men [in the group studied] were a degree more interested in the liberal arts and in business and economics, a degree less enthralled by the wonders of science and engineering, than men ten or twenty years their senior. The post World War I Twenties were the occasion for new talk on the campuses about the problems of society, and for new talk in the corporations about the gospel of service and the techniques of selling the flood of new mass-produced goods.

Somewhat similar tendencies doubtless affected the educational preparation of management groups below the top level, although adequate data to test this supposition are not available. One clue is afforded by the survey of industrial relations executives referred to above; according to this study, among those in the over-twenty-years experience group, undergraduate engineering degrees were most frequently cited; in the eleven-to-twenty-years experience group, liberal arts degrees in the humanities held a slight edge; in the five-to-ten years experience group, social science degrees (sociology, psychology, etc.) were most frequently cited; and in the less-than-five-years experience group, business administration was the most common degree held. The report states that the distribution of advanced degrees (noted below) was quite different.[40]

Data made available from the files of Richardson, Bellows, and Henry (also cited earlier) on the educational backgrounds of 562 men at three levels of management in seven relatively large companies, as well as a scattering of management positions in a larger number of concerns, appear to fit this general pattern with respect to undergraduate preparation. Data on 292 men in the group who completed a four-year college program (a little over half of those studied) showed that those receiving liberal arts degrees were the largest category at all three levels, with engineering and science in second place and business administration a poor third; two-thirds of the group were over forty years of age and therefore received their undergraduate degrees before World War II.

[39] *Fortune* Editors, *op. cit.*, p. 38.
[40] *Industrial Relations News, op. cit.*, p. 3; 76 per cent of the respondents were between thirty-six and fifty-five years of age.

The proportion of the top management group receiving degrees in engineering and science, relatively speaking, was considerably higher than the other two.[41]

A much larger group took some college or graduate work prior to their present employment without necessarily earning a degree (399 of the 562 cases), much of the work consisting of courses taken after leaving undergraduate school. Data on the last major studied for this group showed that business and engineering were on a par as the most frequently chosen subjects (about 36 per cent in each) with liberal arts far behind. In this instance, the proportion of the low-management group majoring in engineering, relatively speaking, was considerably higher than the other two.[42] This type of study was in large measure designed to fill gaps in the individual's prior training. While the data summarized above reflect a wide diversity of educational backgrounds and interests, the heavy representation of business administration majors among the groups studied is striking. Foreseeable trends indicate that the proportion of those with this type of preparation will rise markedly over the next ten or twenty years.

[41] The distribution of bachelor degrees among the 292 men completing college was:

Position level	Number in group	Per cent by area				
		Technical or engineering	Ivy league*	Other arts	Business or communications	Miscellaneous
Top.........	56	38	16	36	7	3
Middle.......	114	34	14	44	4	4
Low.........	122	29	9	52	6	4

* Brown, Columbia, Dartmouth, Harvard, Pennsylvania, Princeton, and Yale (the number who studied business was negligible).
SOURCE: Richardson, Bellows, and Henry files on managerial personnel (unpublished).

[42] The distribution of the 399 men who had some college or graduate work by their last major subject was as follows:

Position level	Number in group	Per cent by major		
		Business and economics	Engineering	Other
Top..............	72	39	29	32
Middle...........	154	35	36	29
Low..............	173	32	42	26

SOURCE: Richardson, Bellows, and Henry files on managerial personnel (unpublished).

Importance of Adult Education

Another feature of the educational background of these businessmen is the extent to which they have continued academic work into adulthood. Speaking of top executives in large firms, Warner and Abegglen concluded:[43]

Men who have been ambitious to succeed apparently do not lose this ambition nor their ability to translate it into many forms of self-improvement that continue to enlarge their capacities and increase their skills and abilities. Since the demands made upon a top executive by a large organization are not confined within the company or even the industry but often are ramified by the community, the resources of the business leader may be great, but never enough.

Of the members of the Young Presidents' Organization graduating from college who supplied the necessary information, 30 per cent took academic work beyond their senior year. Among the Philadelphia printing company officials who had college degrees, nearly 60 per cent took additional academic work; among those with "some college" work only, about 83 per cent took one or more evening school courses after completing their formal education; among those with a high school education or less, about 72 per cent took such work. Rarely did the additional training lead to a degree; in fact, of all 120 officials responding to the questionnaire, only five held advanced degrees. Almost all the courses taken were in traditional functional business subjects given at local universities or in practical printing industry subjects taught at trade schools; none was in a traditional liberal arts subject.

Of the industrial relations directors holding undergraduate degrees for whom data could be secured, 32 per cent also held some type of advanced degree; if those who had taken advanced work not leading to degrees had been included, the proportion would doubtless have been considerably larger. The advanced degree holders were concentrated in law, social sciences, business administration, and education in that order; as noted earlier, this was in rather sharp distinction to their undergraduate-graduate work where they tended to concentrate in business administration.

The extent to which adult education programs are providing preparation in practical subjects and related skills in business fields is strikingly illustrated in the case of life insurance salesmen. Of the 1,300 members of the Million Dollar Round Table who took full-time undergraduate work, 46 per cent reported taking additional academic training. Of these, about 27 per cent took between nine and twelve months of such

[43] W. Lloyd Warner and James Abegglen, *Big Business Leaders in America,* Harper & Brothers, New York, 1955, p. 56.

work in addition to their formal undergraduate studies, and another 23 per cent took more than this amount. The additional study was divided in about equal thirds between extra part-time undergraduate work, full-time graduate work, and part-time graduate work, almost all of which was taken at large public or private universities. Approximately one-third of those who took work outside their full-time undergraduate studies reported that half or more of it was taken in evening courses, as against approximately one-half who said that none was taken in nighttime programs.

IMPLICATIONS FOR BUSINESS SCHOOLS

The foregoing discussion of the educational backgrounds of management groups in different periods and industries contains some important implications for the development of business schools. Judging from the data, all major types of educational programs, including engineering, liberal arts, and business administration, have much to contribute to the conduct of business organizations. Perhaps the most striking feature of recent decades has been the increasing relative importance of business school preparation, but it clearly is not a prerequisite to the great majority of management positions, and in most companies a variety of educational preparations will doubtless continue to be desirable.

Judging from the data, persons moving up the managerial hierarchy need different types of educational preparation at different stages in their careers, and appropriate facilities should therefore be available to them as changing need may dictate. The fact that so many kinds of educational programs appear to meet at least the minimum standards required for effective managerial performance underscores the many-sided nature of administrative work. In more responsible positions, the importance of particular subject preparation tends to decline, and the general ability to analyze complex issues and chart suitable courses of action becomes of increasing significance. Since a number of educational paths can be followed in strengthening general qualities of this sort, business schools have ample opportunity to break new ground in developing their programs. In fact, the needs and attitudes of employers with respect to educational requirements for particular careers or responsibilities are far from firmly set. For the most part, then, schools should feel free to develop programs along whatever lines appear educationally most desirable.

VIEWPOINTS OF BUSINESS GROUPS

A number of attempts have been made to sample the thinking of various business groups on these matters through large-scale questionnaires. A few business schools, for example, have tried to sound out alumni opinion on some of these issues, the most ambitious being a long-term study undertaken by the Harvard Business School. For present purposes, such studies are of very limited value because they provide no basis for comparing attitudes and experience of graduates from different institutions. It should be added that the general tone of these alumni surveys is highly complimentary to the schools involved, but how this should be interpreted is not altogether clear.

A few studies which have cut across graduates from different schools (including business versus nonbusiness schools) yield rather ambiguous results. One of the most ambitious was the Havemann and West study, which was based on 9,064 replies collected by *Time* magazine in 1947.[44] Eight per cent of the respondents majored in business as undergraduates and in answer to the question, "Did college help you in your occupation?" 62 per cent of the group answered "Yes, a lot" and 37 per cent answered "Some." On the other hand, those who had taken preprofessional programs (premedical, prelaw, engineering, etc.) rated the occupational value of their college experience consistently higher than the business majors. Moreover, 30 per cent of the business majors wished they had concentrated in another field, engineering being most frequently mentioned; while those who had taken preprofessional programs tended to be a good deal more satisfied.[45] As reported in this survey, general undergraduate preparation largely depended on whether the individual had definite career goals as a student which he subsequently held to. Those who took a general undergraduate program and then went on to advanced work in a professional field reported few serious misgivings about their undergraduate preparation. Those who took only general studies and later found themselves in business jobs, however, often expressed regret that they had not taken a more specialized academic program; in fact, fully half this group stated they wish they had done so. Then, too, there was little or no tendency for those who had taken a specialized course of study to indicate they wished they had taken more general programs—or still more specialized programs either.[46]

The facts in this and other studies suggest that many people holding

[44] Ernest Havemann and Patricia S. West, *They Went to College,* Harcourt, Brace and Company, Inc., New York, 1952.

[45] *Ibid.,* Chap. 11. In another survey of 13,586 college graduates among General Electric employees, about two-thirds of those who had majored in business administration said they would choose the same course if they had it to do over again; this was considerably below the figure for the engineering majors, slightly higher than the figure for various liberal arts majors, and well above the education majors. General Electric Company, *What They Think of Their Higher Education,* January, 1957, p. 22.

[46] Ernest Havemann and Patricia S. West, *op. cit.,* Chap. 12.

business jobs find the need for technical training and that if they could have predicted their careers, they would have taken it. But the kind of specialized training, the amount of it, its relationship to other subjects— these and similar questions yield different answers depending on the individual's situation. Thus, the individual's attitude toward his prior academic experience hinges in large measure on how well he predicted his subsequent career; many persons appear to take business jobs because other career opportunities have not materialized, and for such people, a strictly liberal arts kind of preparation tends to appear inadequate.

Surveys other than the Havemann and West study also stress the contrary theme—that college graduates in business who have had a very narrow, specialized training wish they had taken a broader program.[47] Again, however, the crucial question—how far should general preparation be pushed at the expense of specialized study—tends to remain unanswered.

The present survey endeavored to analyze opinion about the more detailed aspects of these issues among one large but reasonably well-defined business group—life insurance salesmen and office managers who are members of the Million Dollar Round Table Club.[48] Of the 1,320 members of this organization who went to college, about 40 per cent attended a business school, but of the latter, only 12 per cent majored in insurance and 58 per cent did not take any courses in this subject at all. In view of their subsequent career choice, it is therefore not surprising that a large majority (77 per cent) indicated they wished they had taken more work in insurance during their college years. Similarly, only 9 per cent of the members of this organization who went to some institution other than a business school took any work in insurance during college, but again a large majority (77 per cent) wished they had done so.[49]

Whether these successful men would, in fact, have been still more successful if they had studied more insurance in college is an unanswerable question. The fact remains, as mentioned earlier, that a substantial number (41 per cent of the business school and 50 per cent of the non-

---

[47] See, for example, Leonard J. West, *College and the Years After,* Board of Higher Education, New York, 1952. Moreover, those queried in the General Electric survey stressed the desirability of about a four-way equal division of the student's time between science and technical, humanities, social sciences, and business, with the latter somewhat less emphasized than the other three. General Electric Company, *op. cit.,* p. 9.

[48] See footnote 32.

[49] The entire group was asked to evaluate their education on four grading levels ranging from excellent to mediocre in terms of preparation for broader responsibilities in their subsequent careers. Of the business school group, 41 per cent graded their preparation excellent, and 48 per cent, reasonably good; of the nonbusiness school group, the figures were 34 and 44 per cent, respectively.

business school group) took more academic work after leaving college, most of it on a part-time basis. Very few went on to earn master's degrees (5 per cent of the business school and 11 per cent of the nonbusiness school group). Judging from their subsequent careers, it would appear that this part-time type of specialized training at least met their minimum needs.

The evidence on attitudes of business people toward their prior college education, such as has just been cited, does not provide very meaningful guides in planning educational programs. Unless great care is exercised, it is impossible to determine the grounds on which opinions are based, the really serious gaps that may exist in an individual's educational preparation, and whether one kind of program rather than some other would actually have been more appropriate. For example, when the members of the Million Dollar Round Table were asked what courses in insurance they would recommend for a young man planning a career in this area, 25 per cent of the members who had attended business school recommended a course in general insurance, and 25 per cent a general course in life insurance, while none of the more specialized courses was recommended by more than 8 per cent of the respondents; on the other hand, 23 per cent said "Take all available insurance courses." Business schools could hardly derive much guidance from such mixed findings as these. All that can be said is that the schools appear to have ample latitude to chart whatever course they deem most praiseworthy. To go further would require intensive study of the attitudes and experience of a carefully drawn sample of business school and nonbusiness school graduates, presumably by means of personal interviews rather than by mail questionnaire. A trial run of a study along these lines is attempted in the next chapter.

COMPANY HIRING PRACTICES AND ATTITUDES

Attention is now turned to the hiring practices and attitudes of specific companies for whatever light might be thrown on the future role of business schools. As noted earlier, it is often stated that top management stresses the advantage of having a broad educational background for most types of business careers but that company recruiters tend to hire students with specific training to fill specific jobs. Similarly, it is sometimes said that company spokesmen express the desirability of combining undergraduate liberal arts and graduate business preparation, or the latter with undergraduate engineering, but that in actual practice little demand exists for personnel with these combinations of education. Again, it is said that companies claim that marks are of definitely secondary importance in hiring new personnel but that actually grades tend to be crucially important in determining who gets the available openings. These and similar questions call for examination of actual hiring practices of individual companies.

The interviews conducted for the Ford Foundation Study of Business Education among some eighty, mostly large, firms in a wide cross section of manufacturing and nonmanufacturing industries proved illuminating in this connection. As noted earlier, about half the companies interviewed could be said to be actively college-oriented with respect to both the backgrounds of their top- and middle-management personnel and the hiring of new employees for future managerial and general salaried positions; in the other half, the majority of those in management positions at these two levels had not graduated from college, and little or no concerted effort was made to hire such people except for isolated professional positions. Judging from the data on educational backgrounds presented earlier, these latter companies constitute a minority group among firms of comparable size in the United States.

Within the noncollege category, some twelve or fifteen of the firms were found to be rather positively oriented against hiring or promoting college-trained personnel into most management and other positions, while the other twenty-five or twenty-eight companies were passive or more or less neutral on the matter. Among the first group of twelve or fifteen companies, a few hired a limited number of engineers, accountants, and other college-trained persons for highly specific jobs, and a number hired persons with considerable job experience who happened to have college preparation in their backgrounds; but none in this group did any active searching for college personnel, whether at the graduate or undergraduate level, or made any effort to build a managerial staff out of a college trained corps.[50]

At the other extreme, some twelve or fifteen firms in the college-oriented group were found to be especially active in seeking college graduates for a wide variety of positions and for filling future management openings.[51] In these strongly "procollege" concerns, persons with this level of education filled almost all the top-management, and a majority of the middle-management, positions. Recruiting of college personnel was pushed on a large number of campuses and while typically one kind of educational background was especially looked for (usually engineering or science), hiring was extended to quite a number of different student groups. Indeed, besides the high proportion of jobs held by college

[50] One company in this category reported an interest in M.B.A. students for a research position; the others either said M.B.A. students "expect too much" or expressed no opinion.

[51] If more adequate data could have been secured, more companies might well have been put in this same category; these twelve to fifteen companies were the only instances in which enough data were available to assign them to this group with confidence.

graduates, the outstanding characteristic of these companies was the diversity of educational backgrounds of those whom they hired.

A few illustrations should help point up the staffing needs at the three levels of administrative and nonadministrative responsibility among these latter companies. A manufacturing concern reported that at present its staff at the top, middle, and low levels of responsibility was divided about equally among those trained in liberal arts, in business administration, and in engineering and related technical fields. An advertising company reported a roughly equal division between liberal arts and undergraduate business with a "fair number" of graduate business and law school graduates. A utility company said its three levels of personnel were divided into 44 per cent engineering, 32 per cent arts and sciences, 22 per cent business, and 2 per cent other. A bank stated that its 683 member staff, which was 98 per cent college graduates, was well over half business administration, about 17 per cent liberal arts, and the rest scattered through various types of college programs.

Among the "very high college" group of firms, hiring of new employees tended to be quite diversified with respect to type of collegiate training. All the companies in this group hired some undergraduate business students, and almost all hired liberal arts students, though in fewer numbers. Some graduates in both these areas were brought in to take a variety of routine, low-level jobs, but others were recruited with an eye to future advancement. Among the manufacturing firms in this group, technically trained students were taken on in still larger numbers and often at relatively high starting salaries. Students with law degrees, advanced business degrees, or graduate work in other fields were hired much less frequently by both manufacturing and nonmanufacturing companies, usually for rather special assignments requiring professional preparation.

There were few clear-cut differences in the characteristics of the industries represented by the positively "pro" and "anti" college companies, with both representing a fairly broad range of American business. However, there was some tendency for the "very high college" group to cluster in fields which stressed new product research (e.g., pharmaceuticals), complex technology (e.g., electric power), vigorous sales campaigns (e.g., paper products), dealings on a wide public basis (e.g., banking), providing professional services (e.g., accounting), and developing creative ideas (e.g., publishing). In general, they were growing companies, and most could be properly designated as leaders-among-the-leaders in their respective fields. By contrast, the "very low college" companies tended to cluster in fields in which production and selling conditions were either fairly settled or gradually deteriorating. Whether more comprehensive coverage would yield similar results is unclear, although the findings accord with the common-sense view that in some industries companies are free to pursue a variety of approaches in hiring new employees and in developing managerial staffs and that under these circumstances differences in the backgrounds and personal opinions of individual company managements yield widely varying results. In other fields, however, the nature and complexity of the problems which companies face necessitate either a "pro" or "anti" college policy and so lead to only one result; thus, a company operating in a highly technical industry like oil refining would need to have a high proportion of college-trained personnel in its management ranks, whereas a small firm operating in a highly competitive industry like laundry service would find this a "luxury" it could not afford.

The majority of companies in the Ford Foundation Survey interviews fell between these two groups, with of course no clear line dividing borderline cases. These "middle road" companies hired technically trained personnel for a wide variety of jobs and limited important dealings with the public to persons with college degrees, but made no effort to fill the majority of salaried positions with college graduates. In a few of the companies in this middle category, top management consisted almost wholly of persons with college preparation, but in the great majority of cases, the proportion was well under 50 per cent and at lower levels of management substantially less. Most of the company spokesmen interviewed expressed some desire to hire more staff with college training, but reported difficulty in attracting the kinds of persons they really wanted; the clear implication was that among the hiring criteria applied by these companies, college preparation was rather far down the list in the case of most types of salaried positions, including those which would lead ultimately to managerial responsibility.

JOBS REQUIRING ADVANCED PREPARATION

The foregoing suggests some broad patterns of company hiring and staffing needs which carry important implications for educational programs. While individual companies differ, they tend to group themselves into general industry categories, and within the latter, there are certain position groupings which can be identified. The Ford Foundation Survey supplied sufficient data on about forty-five companies to permit such comparisons, but it should be remembered that the interviews were mostly confined to large, rather widely known firms.

From the viewpoint of educational preparation, the positions requiring highly technical preparation are easiest to describe, but the number of careers (as opposed to particular positions) which are limited to a single specialty are comparatively rare. It was evident from the company interviews that an actuary in an insurance company, for example, must have certain preparation in mathematics, or that a corporation tax expert must have certain training in accounting, but that in the course of the individual's career there is every likelihood his responsibilities will change and broaden, calling for skills and abilities of quite a different sort. Thus, an actuary or corporation tax accountant will very likely have to deal with problems coming from the investments, sales, production, legal, or personnel side of the business; a large part of his work will entail communicating with and receiving reports from staff and line personnel outside his own specialty; as his career develops he may well be called upon to assume some administrative responsibilities in which his ability to direct the work of others will be put to the test; even if he is never given such responsibilities, his work is increasingly likely to require an interdepartmental, or even a company-wide, point of view. For such careers, the combination of technical training and broad education that is required means that a good deal of the preparation must come at the graduate level—or even after the student has completed his formal education.

Judging from the company interview reports, however, most of the positions entailing extensive technical training are in the engineering and science area; comparatively few are subjects normally taught in business schools. This appears to hold particularly for firms in light and heavy manufacturing, although many of the companies in these industries stated that they required graduate business training for a limited number of specialized jobs in marketing, finance, and production. Judging from the interview reports, manufacturing companies are more apt to hire students with graduate business background for possible later development as managers, but during their initial years of employment their work is likely to be undifferentiated from that assigned other college-trained recruits. An exception to this, which may prove increasingly important in the future, is the need of companies for students with graduate business preparation who have some background in science and engineering; even though they lack professional competence in these areas themselves, such persons will be needed in increasing numbers to work with technical experts in introducing data-processing machinery and other types of mechanized equipment.

Among railroad and other utility companies covered in the interviews, highly technical jobs requiring graduate school preparation fell almost entirely in the engineering and science rather than in the business administration area. An occasional M.B.A. student was hired for special assignment, but little inclination was found among these firms to hire such students either for technical jobs or as future manager material. Some of the interviews indicated that this emphasis was beginning to shift, but toward nonengineering students in general, not toward graduate business students in particular.

Firms in retail, wholesale, and related branches of the distribution trades covered in the interviews also showed little interest in seeking out students with graduate business preparation (or other kinds of graduate preparation, for that matter) for specialized functions, and they were even less inclined than the manufacturing companies to hire such students on a career basis as future managers. While only one or two expressed actual hostility to hiring graduate business students, the majority expressed either indifference or mild skepticism; at the other extreme, two companies in this group actively sought M.B.A. students for general career purposes.

Among banks, insurance companies, accounting firms, publishing houses, and advertising companies, a wide variety of openings for graduate business students was reported, both in specialized professional jobs and in more general assignments. This accords with common observation. The principal functions of financial institutions and accounting firms fall squarely in the traditional subject-areas of business schools, and students who have done advanced work in these areas have more opportunity to use their specialized skills and abilities directly than in most other industries. Even here, however, there appear to be relatively few openings which are limited just to graduate business students; the main advantage of such students appears to be that they are older, more thoroughly screened, and have broader educational backgrounds. In advertising firms, the principal outlet for specialized talents of graduate business students is in various phases of market research; writing and creative jobs tend to go to students with liberal arts backgrounds. Publishing houses, if anything, lean still further toward hiring liberal arts graduates.

The Ford Foundation Survey company interviews were supplemented by an extensive questionnaire sent to forty-seven college and university placement offices. When asked whether companies prefer a master's degree to an undergraduate major in business, a large majority answered in the negative.[52] Conceivably, this could simply mean that most master's

[52] Ten of the questionnaires were sent to placement offices at liberal arts colleges which were not involved in this question; the results from the questionnaire sent to the other thirty-seven institutions are shown below:

Do Companies Prefer a Master's Degree in Business to an Undergraduate Major in Business?

Answer	Total
Yes	6
No	23
Yes and no	1
No answer	7

SOURCE: Ford Foundation Study of Business Education.

students find jobs through their professors or by other means, not through university placement offices; but on any interpretation, this finding is somewhat puzzling. Substantially more than half said that large firms show a stronger preference for master's degree students than do small firms. The placement offices split about evenly when asked whether companies specify a field of specialization in recruiting graduate business students; the specialized fields most frequently cited in this connection were (1) economic and market research and statistics, (2) accounting, and (3) marketing, in that order. In general, the questionnaire results support the conclusion noted above that specialized professional openings for graduate business students are not too common and that the principal assets of these students, compared with undergraduates, are their broader educational backgrounds and their greater potential for long-term career development.

EDUCATIONAL REQUIREMENTS FOR LOWER-LEVEL POSITIONS

While the Ford Survey company interviews were directed chiefly to upper- and middle-management positions, they contained some evidence on educational requirements for lower-level administrative and non-administrative positions. These constitute almost all the openings for which graduates from business schools and other college programs are eligible immediately after leaving school, but many companies operate general training programs for particularly promising new recruits. The specific skills involved in the first category of jobs are likely to be relatively simple as regards prior academic preparation; the only reason for hiring graduates of four-year college programs for these positions is that they presumably have a broader educational preparation, are better able to adapt to new assignments, are better prepared to deal with the public and other employees, have more potential as future managers, and the like. Thus, the secretary of a top executive might well need little more technical competence than a qualified stenographer but could still put four years of college to very good use if they helped develop some of these abilities. This is in line with the view expressed earlier that business school programs should be centered on developing capacities along these lines, not on relatively simple skills which can be acquired as easily elsewhere.

Even among large companies, such as those covered in the interviews, most nonprofessional salaried jobs and lower supervisory positions do not require a college degree at the present time. Many clerical jobs, whether in factories or offices, are filled with noncollege recruits or by promotion from within. The latter applies particularly to foreman positions. However, there is a clear trend for more college graduates to take jobs even at these levels. This is especially true of companies whose management is college-oriented as a whole. It also tends to be more true of companies in such fields as banking, insurance, advertising, and publishing than of those in retail or wholesale trade, railroads or utilities, and most lines of manufacturing. Among the companies interviewed, jobs in industrial selling, as opposed to retail selling to ultimate consumers, are gradually being turned over to college graduates, since this kind of work requires a fair degree of technical knowledge or general familiarity with a company's products and services. Foremen and other low-level management positions in industries that are technologically highly developed are subject to these same trends.

Judging from the Ford Foundation Survey company interviews, no one academic program prepares best for nonprofessional business jobs of these types. Persons holding such positions may have backgrounds in undergraduate business, undergraduate liberal arts, undergraduate engineering, and occasionally even graduate preparation in some area, suggesting that they have been chosen more with an eye to personal qualities, general character, and long-term promise than to any particular educational background. This applies especially to students hired soon after graduating from college—persons with more experience are usually expected to meet more exacting educational requirements. As the spokesman for one concern put the matter: "We'll use an English major or a history major in our accounting department if they show any promise, but if we hire an experienced man we expect him to have a C.P.A."

For most lower-level, nonprofessional jobs in industry, undergraduate business students appear to have some edge over liberal arts graduates. This generalization applies particularly to the more routine clerical or office-type jobs, much less to work involving general abilities or creative ideas. There appears to be no clear pattern with respect to selling or to jobs which require many varied dealings with people. The answers to the questionnaire circulated among the college and university placement offices are revealing on this score. The offices at liberal arts colleges reported that there were ample opportunities for their graduates in business, but a majority of the centralized university offices (thirteen as against nine) reported that opportunities for liberal arts students were moderately limited. One of the large state university offices answered:

Of course, a lot depends on the personal qualities of the individual. The graduate who is willing to enter a shop or manufacturing plant at the beginning level *and really plug* can often do a better job than the run-of-the-mill specialist in industrial or production management. Retailing and banking are also two fields in which the Liberal Arts graduate stands about as good a chance as the specialist when it comes to getting and keeping a job. [Italics in the original]

Another reported:

Liberal Arts graduates are hired for personal potential rather than for what they took in school; potential in (1) ability to think logically and creatively, (2) ability to communicate well verbally and in writing, (3) ability to deal effectively with people. Estimates are based on grades, extra-curricular activities and work experience.

All agreed that liberal arts graduates had many opportunities in sales and various aspects of marketing, but a number also cited work in insurance and even accounting. This squares with the company interviews, since firms in such fields as advertising, publishing, and banking reported hiring a larger proportion of liberal arts graduates than firms in transportation, heavy machinery, construction, and the like. Even among the latter, recent trends were somewhat in the direction of using more students with liberal arts preparation.

On the other hand, many companies in all the industries represented in the interviews hired large numbers of undergraduate business students who had specialized rather intensively in a given subject. The exact amount of specialization which the companies sought varied somewhat between subjects and between firms. Companies which hired large numbers of college graduates tended to require less specialization for jobs at these levels than those which were less college-oriented. The railroads and the heavy and light manufacturers were rather sharply split, with some in each group requiring relatively little academic specialization for lower level, nonprofessional positions. The utility companies definitely leaned in this direction and so did most of the firms in the distribution field. The companies that were interviewed in finance, accounting, publishing, and advertising were also nearly unanimous in agreeing that they were not looking for graduates with specialized training at this level.

TOP MANAGEMENT VERSUS RECRUITERS

The alleged discrepancy between what top management says it wants and what recruiters actually look for in hiring college graduates showed up in some of the interviews, but as far as lower-level positions are concerned, the difference was not as great as would be expected. It is true that many companies hire graduates with specialized backgrounds for lower-level jobs, but they do not consider specialization beyond three or four courses in a given area as either necessary or desirable. The interviews at the advertising companies, for example, indicated that they hired a number of marketing majors but that they did not want the students to have any substantial number of courses in this area. The banks reported the same with respect to majors in finance, although somewhat less emphatically. In sales work, most concerns did not even specify a major in marketing, much less that the concentration had to be carried very far. This same theme ran through the interviews in other areas.

The answers to the questionnaire circulated among college and university placement offices lend support to these findings. When asked whether employers in a designated group of industries preferred to hire students who had concentrated their studies in these same industries, a surprisingly large number of negatives were reported. In fact only in transportation and advertising was there a clear trend the other way. The detailed findings are given in Table 5-1.

TABLE 5-1

EXTENT TO WHICH INDUSTRIES PREFER BUSINESS SCHOOL GRADUATES WITH SPECIAL
TRAINING IN THEIR PARTICULAR INDUSTRY AREA

Industry	Placement offices reporting*		
	A's	B's	C's
Transportation....................	12	15	4
Other utilities.....................	0	17	11
Insurance........................	2	12	21
Banking..........................	9	15	11
Real estate.......................	3	15	14
Retail trade......................	0	13	22
Advertising and advertising departments of other business.........	16	15	2

A—strong preference for major in related industry area.
B—some preference for major in related industry area.
C—little or no preference for major in related industry area.
* Only answers from business school and centralized university placement offices included; liberal-arts-college placement offices excluded.
SOURCE: Ford Foundation Study of Business Education.

If hiring recruiters look for students with specialized preparation, it clearly is not specialization in a given industry; this finding needs to be kept in mind in determining what major subjects ought to be included in the curriculum.

A listing of broad business functions (accounting, sales, production supervision, personnel, finance, and economic and market research) as opposed to preparation in specific industries yielded quite different replies, however. In almost all cases, the placement offices reported that firms usually wanted the kind of major most closely associated with the job function in question (finance major for jobs in finance, etc.). The most striking deviations were noted in marketing where economic and market research was given considerable emphasis; various backgrounds were also considered appropriate for careers in personnel. Even in the other cases, sufficient diversity was indicated to suggest that the amount of specialization in any one area could quite properly be kept to a minimum and that a student who had, say, three or four semester courses in a subject like marketing or finance stood as good a chance of getting first-job offers as those with six or seven courses. Again, this needs to be kept in mind in planning the work in the various major areas.

CONCLUSIONS

The foregoing review of employer staffing requirements underscores the need of business organizations for personnel at all levels of management, but especially in more responsible positions, with the capaciy for applying imaginative analytical methods of reasoning to the solution of business problems. These problems do not fit into anything approaching a precise mold, and therefore many kinds of academic preparation, as well as many kinds of talents and abilities, will continue to be needed by business.

The minimum educational requirements for nonprofessional staff jobs in industry and for lower levels of supervision tend of course to be less than for positions carrying heavier responsibilities and are also likely to be more specific; as long as the individual's duties remain rather limited, the need for a broad, demanding educational experience is not too great. On the other hand, as soon as a person assumes greater responsibilities, the importance of this latter kind of educational preparation rises commensurately. In the first case, since the question of the breadth and rigor of the student's academic work is not too significant, whether he gets highly specialized training at a junior college, business school, or engineering school is not of much moment. In the second case, however, the breadth and quality of the student's preparation may be of crucial importance in terms of his later career, and for such a person every effort should be made to stretch his powers as much as possible at every stage in his educational experience. Most would probably agree that if the individual's financial position would allow it, four years of liberal arts study and two years of graduate study in business would be desirable. Many students, however, are not in a position to follow this course, and for such students, an undergraduate business program is an altogether logical compromise as long as it is made broad enough and challenging enough to meet their total career needs.

The preceding review of employer staffing requirements has indicated the general lines which business schools might follow in the future, but the schools have wide latitude in deciding what specific elements should go into their programs. The diversity and complexity of purposes served by business schools put chief responsibility on the individual institution to meet its obligations in its own way. Each school should accordingly approach its work in a bold and independent spirit, demonstrating the same qualities of vigorous, imaginative leadership which its graduates will be increasingly called on to display. Prospects for future changes in the country's economy, reflected in trends already well underway, underscore the necessity for a continuing and searching self-appraisal by each school to determine where its distinctive contributions lie and how its highest purposes can be realized.

CHAPTER 6

EDUCATION FOR CAREERS IN MANAGEMENT

Lewis B. Ward

This chapter summarizes the results of an intensive series of interviews among the supervisory personnel of three large companies in an Eastern city. The interviews explored relationships between attitudes, educational backgrounds, and careers in management as a basis for assessing the work of business schools. The data, while limited in scope, raise serious questions about the typical business school curriculum.

INTRODUCTION

The preceding chapters have considered the relationship between career preparation and higher education in general and the special place of business education therein. Student needs and characteristics were discussed in relation to the demands and requirements of business organizations in order to develop basic criteria for a sensible and practical program of business education in the future. In Chap. 5 the question was raised as to whether there were elements in business careers which could properly be the major concern of higher education. This was answered in the affirmative, and it was suggested that the "quality of creative synthesis" required in a wide variety of jobs in business at all stages of a business career should be the central concern of the business schools. It was pointed out that this quality will become even more important on the business scene in the foreseeable future.

The importance of a broad general background and the need for college trained men in industry was documented with comments from observers of the business scene and with data from published studies of business leaders. It was also pointed out, however, that while there clearly is a demand for men with many different types of academic backgrounds, current practices in recruiting of college graduates by industrial concerns are somewhat at variance with the published statements of many business leaders expressing the view that a liberal arts background is superior to any other as preparation for a business career. Not only is there little evidence of any consistent preference for men with liberal arts background, but some state university placement offices report no great demand for men with such preparation.

The discussion in Chap. 5 also cited figures indicative of proportions of college graduates among various groups of executives. Not unexpectedly such figures show wide differences between individual companies, between different types of management jobs, and across industry classifications. In the reports referred to, the range in the percentage of managers who were college graduates is from 25 per cent for a group of small printing firms to 87 per cent in a group of industrial relations executives. Clearly many factors need to be considered in any attempt to reason from information about the educational backgrounds of business leaders in order to arrive at a set of requirements for an ideal program of education for careers in business.

While common sense, current trends in education, opinions of business leaders, and studies of educational backgrounds of various groups of businessmen all indicate that higher education is of growing importance for a career in business, this evidence leaves many questions unanswered. Those who have gone on to college in the past have tended to be men whose families have had the resources to finance such education. Many of these men would have achieved leadership in business concerns without a college education by virtue of ownership or family connections. Nor is it clear from the evidence referred to in previous chapters whether any particular type of preparation has had any advantage in preparing men for business careers. It seemed worth while, therefore, to attempt an intensive analysis of the educational backgrounds and career patterns of a group of business managers, representative in some sense of management within their own companies, to see if further light could be thrown upon factors important in educating young men and women for careers in business. To this end a small study was undertaken in which a sample of college graduates among the managerial personnel in three companies were interviewed to try to uncover some of these factors related to higher education which were important in their business careers.

THE THREE-COMPANY STUDY

Research Objectives

The purpose of the study was to make an intensive analysis of the educational experience and career patterns of college-trained managers in two cross-section samples of the managerial personnel in each of three moderate-sized companies. The focus of this inquiry was on the question, "How effective is business education in preparing individuals for careers in business?" To this end the major comparisons in the study were between those whose major field of study was business or commerce and those with major fields of study in other areas. Additional questions important in the study included the following: Do certain types of careers benefit more than others from business school training? Does graduate business preparation afford special advantages as compared with such training at the undergraduate level? Is there any observable objective relationship between type of education and career progress? What are the attitudes of managers and executives toward their educational experiences in relation to their business careers? It was believed that the reports of executives and managers about their own educational experiences and their opinions as to its influence upon their careers would provide useful material for the formulation of recommendations for improving business education at the college and university level.

Discussion of a number of ways of attempting to get information of the sort required to answer questions such as those stated above led to the conclusion that truly *representative* information could be obtained only through a national probability sample of respondents. Securing such a sample posed a number of practical problems, however. It also was clear that to survey such a sample would require a major outlay of research funds. Rather than seek support at the outset for a venture of this magnitude, it was decided to do a pilot study in a small number of business enterprises (three) and examine the data so obtained before entering upon any larger survey. In the course of such a pilot study, interviewing procedures and methods of analysis could be checked out in actual practice, giving clear indication of the sort of results that might be expected in a more extensive national probability sample.

It is, of course, clear that a study of representative samples of executives and managers in three business concerns will not yield normative information of any general sort. It was hoped, however, that the study might provide evidence of relationships among attitudes, educational backgrounds, and careers in management which would contribute to the over-all objectives of the present inquiry.

Study Procedure

The first step in the special study was to obtain the cooperation of several firms located in a large Eastern city. This was accomplished by writing to the president or other senior officer of each of several companies, outlining the objectives of the study and asking whether it would be possible to interview a substantial number of the supervisory and executive personnel in the company to secure information about their educational backgrounds and business experiences. A number of companies indicated a willingness to participate, and management personnel were interviewed in four of these. In one of these firms the interviewing procedure was developed and standardized. The other three firms provided the data on which this report is based. National Analysts, Inc., an organization experienced in consumer surveys and attitude studies of many types, agreed to assume responsibility for carrying on the study.

In the second step the survey procedure was developed and tested. After careful consideration of the objectives of the study, research personnel of National Analysts, Inc. developed a semistructured interview outline and tested it in interviews with about fifty respondents of administrative or supervisory level in the main offices of one of the companies that had agreed to participate. These interviews were conducted by members of National Analysts' carefully selected staff of interviewers, specially trained and experienced in the use of various psychological and nondirective techniques. After a review of these interviews a more completely structured questionnaire was developed and tested, preparatory to gathering the major data for the pilot study.[1]

The third step involved the gathering of the data of the study. The questionnaire developed in step 2 was used in personal interviews with a sample of administrative and supervisory personnel in:

1. The home office of a life insurance company
2. The general offices and main plant of a light manufacturing company
3. The general offices and a large plant of an electronics manufacturing company

Two samples were drawn in each of these companies. One sample represented the administrative and supervisory employees who had majored in business administration, economics, or related subjects within a school of business. The second sample represented those who majored in fields other than business. In the two manufacturing companies, the "all other" was heavily loaded with engineers, and in the insurance company with lawyers, because of the large number of administrative personnel majoring in these disciplines. In what follows we have used the terms "managers" and "businessmen" to refer to the administrative and supervisory employees who make up the sample of individuals studied.

Altogether 144 interviews were taken—59 with business education majors and 85 with majors in other subjects. In two companies, all administrative personnel with a business education major were interviewed;

[1] Because of its length, the actual questionnaire is not reproduced here; copies are available on request.

however, inasmuch as there were fewer than 25 such respondents in each of the two companies, the total number of business education majors is less than the total of the "all other majors" category.

The final step in the study consisted in an analysis of the replies of this sample of businessmen to the various questions about their educational backgrounds and business careers. Comparisons between the frequencies with which various replies were made by businessmen with business majors in college and by businessmen with other majors provide the raw material for the discussion which follows.

Before reporting specific findings from this study, a word should be said about the significance of particular observations. Leaving aside for the moment the question of representativeness of that sample, there is still the question, "How great must a difference in frequency between different groups be to represent a real difference?" It is obvious that the observed frequencies will rarely be identical. We need to know when we have a difference which could be expected to occur again if we sampled another three companies with the same characteristics in a similar way. Much of the time we will report actual figures (group proportions) for the items in which we are interested. Some of the time, however, we shall just state that one group had a greater frequency for an item than did another group. In all such cases we will be referring to differences which approach the conventional test of significance for a difference between proportions based upon the numbers of individuals in our sample. Whether such differences have any practical significance is an issue which the reader can determine for himself.

THE FINDINGS: GENERAL OBSERVATIONS

The first observation to be made from an examination of the replies of supervisory personnel in the three companies is that there are differences in the educational history and career progress of business education majors as compared with those with majors in other areas. While one cannot safely generalize from such a small sample to the business scene as a whole, there seems to be little reason to suppose that this sample is biased with respect to a number of within-groups comparisons of the sort reported in later paragraphs. Some differences appear consistently in all three company samples. It would be surprising indeed if similar differences failed to appear in other samples of businessmen. In the discussion which follows, the most important of these differences observed between managers with different educational backgrounds will be described in detail, together with some of their implications for business education.

Unfortunately, sample size in the pilot study does not permit detailed comparisons between groups of individuals with many different backgrounds. For the most part we are limited to comparisons between those with business or commerce majors and those with all other types of educational background. In our particular sample the group of "all other majors," however, does have one relatively large subgroup made up of those with an engineering background. For the rest, no particular major field is represented often enough to make any separate analysis possible. Table 6-1 shows the number of individuals classified in these three major

TABLE 6-1

PER CENT OF MANAGERS WITH EDUCATIONAL BACKGROUNDS IN THREE AREAS

Major field of study	Per cent of college-trained managers in	
	Present survey	Harvard Advanced Management Program*
Engineering............................	34	27
Business...............................	40	43
Other (mainly liberal arts and preprofessional)......................	26	30

* These figures are for approximately 500 executives attending the Harvard AMP Program, 1947–1949.

areas of undergraduate study. Also shown in the table are corresponding figures for the educational backgrounds of college graduates in a relatively large management training program to which many companies have sent representatives over the past ten years. These comparative data on the proportions with backgrounds in engineering, business, and other areas are presented here in order to emphasize that while the samples of businessmen in the present study are in no way representative of business as a whole, or even of any one of the three companies, the proportions with educational backgrounds in these areas are not too much out of line with those found in other samples of managers who are college graduates.

Factors Related to the Choice of Training in Business Subjects

In our present study the first and perhaps clearest difference between those with business education backgrounds and those with backgrounds in other major fields lies in the kind of family background from which they came. Twenty-four per cent of the business education majors were sons of *craftsmen, foremen, and kindred workers* while this was true for only 13 per cent of those with other educational backgrounds. Business education majors also were more often the sons of *salesworkers* or of *managers, officials, and proprietors* while other majors were more often the sons of *professional, technical, and kindred workers* or of *operatives and kindred workers*. A related background item is the fact that business education majors more often grew up in a large city or suburbs while

TABLE 6-2

DISTRIBUTION OF ANSWERS TO QUESTION CONCERNING PARENTS' OCCUPATION

("What was your father's occupation? Will you please describe for me, as fully as you can, the nature of his work, his business, or profession'")

Occupation	Total sample*		Business education majors		All other majors	
	No.	%	No.	%	No.	%
Number answering....................	142	100	58	100	84	100
Professional, technical, and kindred workers.............................	34	24	11	19	23	27
Farmers and farm managers...........	2	1	2	3	—	—
Managers, officials, and proprietors, except farm........................	44	31	20	34	24	29
Clerical and kindred workers..........	6	4	1	2	5	6
Salesworkers........................	13	9	7	12	6	7
Craftsmen, foremen, and kindred workers	25	18	14	24	11	13
Operatives and kindred workers.......	13	9	1	2	12	14
Private-household workers............	—	—	—	—	—	—
Service workers, except private-household workers..........................	3	2	2	3	1	1
Farm laborers and foremen...........	—	—	—	—	—	—
Laborers, except farm and mine.......	2	1	—	—	2	2

* In this table, as in most of the tables in this report, the column heading "Total sample" is to be interpreted in a strictly literal sense. The proportions listed under this column are *not* to be interpreted as representative except in rough approximation of administrative personnel in general in the three companies. This is because "business education majors" and "all other majors" respectively represent different proportions of the total administrative population in these companies.

other majors more often grew up in a small town or small city. These results are congruent with the findings of other studies reporting on socioeconomic backgrounds of those entering various types of educational programs.[2] The pertinent data for the present study are given in Table 6-2.

[2] W. Lloyd Warner and James Abegglen, *Big Business Leaders in America,* Harper & Brothers, New York, 1955, p. 54.

The studies referred to above also have called attention to the relation between upward social mobility and choice of certain types of educational training. It is hard to tell how much such attitudes reflect factors important for career progress and how much they reflect the prevailing climate of opinion which is so greatly influenced by the major social events of a period. Attitudes born of the great depression of the thirties undoubtedly colored the educational choices of many in our sample. The data in Table 6-2 suggest that, among those entering on business careers, close family contact with business is a factor leading to a choice of concentration in business subjects. As we shall see later, this difference does not necessarily imply a more favored financial position and may only reflect social rather than economic factors. As a matter of fact, several items of information suggest that those who majored in business education actually faced greater handicaps in securing their higher education than did their associates with majors in other areas. This point will be discussed in greater detail later on.

None of the questions asked the businessmen in the three-company study provides direct information about the socioeconomic level of their parents. Information given in response to three of the questions gives some indirect evidence, however. On all these questions, men who majored in business subjects and those who majored in other areas gave similar patterns of answers. Both groups report about the same frequency and amount of inherited wealth. Both obtained their first positions through relatives and friends equally often. Asked to estimate the position of their parents on a living scale ranging from 1 to 10, the two groups gave distributions of placements that are strikingly similar. We are forced to conclude that neither group started off with any marked financial advantage.

Some light is thrown upon the motivation leading to a choice of business as a major field in our sample by answers to direct questions on this point. Business education majors more often chose this field because they thought it was practical and offered an opportunity or reward (29 per cent). Only 17 per cent of "all other majors" report this reason for choice of their major field. On the other hand, those who majored in other fields most often chose their field (44 per cent) because of its intrinsic appeal or interest. This reason for choice of major field was less common among business majors (36 per cent). The data for these comparisons are given in Table 6-3.

The two points made so far present an obviously oversimplified picture of the kind of population from which business education draws its students. The single item on career motivation cited in the previous paragraph suggests those choosing majors in business subjects have more clearly a single practical motivation to get ahead. While answers to some other questions indicate the situation is one of great complexity, they also point to the importance of this economic motivation. For example, one of these related questions asked respondents to indicate whether or not they felt their careers had followed along pretty much as they had first planned them. Here the business education majors tended to one of two extremes. They felt that their careers had followed pretty much their planning (36 per cent as compared with 29 per cent for "all other majors") or that they had turned out to be very different (42 per cent as compared with 38 per cent for all other majors—which is not a significant

TABLE 6-3

DISTRIBUTION OF ANSWERS TO QUESTION CONCERNING CHOICE OF MAJOR

("Would you think back to the time and tell me as much as you can, please, about what you had in mind at the time which made you decide to major in _____?")

Occupation	Total sample		Business education majors		All other majors	
	No.	%	No.	%	No.	%
Number answering....................	141*	100*	59*	100*	82*	100*
Appeal or interest (in it and no other)...	57	40	21	36	36	44
Had aptitude for it, ability.............	13	9	4	7	9	11
Thought it offered opportunity or reward, practical.........................	30	21	16	27	14	17
Specific goal required course of study; needed it to qualify for job, etc.......	35	25	17	29	18	22
Family or friends encourage; same field as father...........................	22	16	8	14	14	17
Prestige of occupation.................	2	1	1	1	1	1
Other...............................	14	10	4	7	10	12
No major............................	1	1	—	—	1	1

*Multiple answers.

difference, however). "All other majors," on the other hand, more often indicated a "somewhat different" career than planned (35 per cent as compared with 20 per cent for the business education group). It is when we examine the reasons why they thought their careers differed from their plans that the practical motivation of the business education majors again shows up. They more often changed careers because of better opportunities or rewards (50 per cent as compared with 39 per cent for all others) or gave some other specific and concrete goal as a reason for the change (27 per cent as compared with 12 per cent).

Circumstances under Which College Education Was Obtained

In the discussion of possible differences in motivation between those who majored in business and those with majors in other areas, we noted certain differences in background which indicated business courses were drawing students from different socioeconomic backgrounds than other subject areas. This is reflected in a number of other differences between the two groups, including the circumstances under which college education was obtained. Business subject majors more often than others took the major part of their work in night school (24 per cent as compared with 8 per cent). They much more often held a full-time job while obtaining a college education (32 per cent as compared with 12 per cent), while the characteristic pattern for those who majored in other areas was to do part-time work. Both groups contained about the same proportion of individuals who did not work at all while in college (31 and 35 per cent, respectively).

Although we are suggesting that the greater incidence among business majors of full-time work while in college tells something about their motivation to get an education, what this means is not too clear. Perhaps those with majors in other areas found the college work so demanding that full-time work was impossible. Or again, attendance at night school no doubt included many of those who worked full-time. It may have been that, in the communities from which these men came, night school work was not offered except in business subjects. We do not have any information to resolve this point.

In any case it is clear that from a quarter to a third of those with business education majors financed their own education almost entirely by working. The proportion doing so in the group with majors in other areas was much smaller. In view of this, the fact that the business majors reported higher college grades than did majors in other areas is quite remarkable in that these higher grades were achieved in the face of the heavy work burden carried by a sizable proportion of this group. This suggests different standards of grading in business subjects as compared with subjects in other areas, or in night school courses as compared with regular courses.

The responses to still another question bear on the circumstances under which college courses were taken. This question also relates to career motivation and might well have been discussed in that context instead. The question is "When did you decide this was what you wanted to major in?" Not unexpected is the observation that among all other majors many more had made a decision as to type of college course before graduating from high school. The proportions so deciding were 44 and 19 per cent, respectively, among majors in other fields and majors in business. It will be recalled that the group of all other majors contained a sizable proportion of engineers. These individuals would have had to make their decision while in high school in order to enter engineering training without losing time. Those who majored in other areas also more often delayed a decision as to major field until the last two years in college. Business majors tended to decide upon their major field sometime after graduation from high school and before the junior year in college.

One of the current issues in business education is that of the total amount of higher education needed to prepare for a business career. Data from the three-company study provide information as to the amount of higher education actually achieved in this particular sample. Here is a point where age is an important variable in that apparently a significant change is taking place in the business education sample. For individuals thirty-eight years of age and older, the figures are as follows: 37 per cent of business education majors and 64 per cent of majors in other fields have taken additional courses beyond college. Among the younger individuals the picture is different. Sixty-three per cent of the business education majors have taken courses beyond college while the corresponding figure for majors in other areas is 58 per cent. Note, however, that these percentages should not be taken as indicating that many of these men received graduate degrees. Only 20 per cent of business majors and 30 per cent of those with other majors actually have graduate degrees. Nevertheless, these figures do suggest that education beyond the college level is an important feature in business careers.

To the question concerning plans for further education, most of those thirty-eight and older have no such plans. Among those thirty-seven and younger, however, it is clear that many of these individuals consider their education as unfinished business. Again the business majors have greater expectations of additional preparation than those with other majors. Two-thirds of the former as contrasted with half of the latter plan further education.

Taken at face value, the foregoing figures are quite extraordinary. In these three companies nearly two-thirds of their supervisory and management personnel who are college graduates have taken some additional training beyond college. Among those under thirty-eight, half to two-thirds plan to take more. No wonder the demand for graduate education in business subjects is growing by leaps and bounds! At this point, however, it would be well to note again the restricted nature of the sample we are concerned with here—three companies in a large Eastern metropolitan area. In small companies or in companies with headquarters in a different type of community, the pattern might be somewhat different.

Nevertheless, with the current tremendous increase in mobility and speed of communication in this country, any regional or local differences of this sort would seem likely to disappear in the near future.

Educational Background and Career Progress

A prime concern of many young people in deciding first upon a career and secondarily upon training for that career is the question, "How successful will I be?" This is a natural question and does not need to imply any lack of idealism. Nor will it imply a completely selfish and materialistic attitude if we suggest that one of several criteria of this "success" which will be considered important is the level of position which is achieved and the salary which goes with it. Choice of a particular type of education will be influenced greatly by observations that individuals with certain educational backgrounds progress more rapidly than others. Here again in the three-company study the responses of businessmen with college backgrounds of different sorts provide some interesting information.

Before taking up this evidence we need to digress a moment to consider another factor present in our survey which needs to be taken into account in interpreting the results. This is the factor of age. Fifty-nine per cent of those who had majored in business subjects were thirty-eight years of age and older while only 46 per cent of those with majors in other areas were of similar age. This in itself is a rather suggestive finding, particularly in view of the rapid growth of business education in recent years. Hence, in considering the effect of other factors, comparisons need to be made separately for different age groups in order to make sure we do not merely reflect an indirect effect of this age differential.

To return to our question as to the relative career advantages of business education and education in other areas, the first bit of evidence relates to the first full-time position held after leaving college. Thirty-six per cent of those who majored in business subjects started in clerical or kindred work. Only 11 per cent of those with other backgrounds started in such jobs. This pattern is even more striking in the older group where 43 per cent of those with majors in business subjects started in clerical jobs. If one can assume that clerical positions are less desirable than professional, managerial, sales, and operational jobs, which are the other classifications, the business group clearly started at a disadvantage. In light of this, it is rather interesting to find very little difference between the starting salaries of individuals with the two types of educational backgrounds.

With respect to present salary, the financial rewards of those with educational backgrounds in business are seen to lag somewhat behind those for individuals with other types of preparation. The pertinent data are given in Table 6-4. It is rather surprising in view of the equal (actually slightly superior) starting salary of the younger business education majors that their present salaries have already lagged behind those for individuals majoring in other fields.

TABLE 6-4

PRESENT SALARY IN RELATION TO EDUCATIONAL BACKGROUND

Age and degree	Total number	Annual salary					
		$9,999 and under		$10,000–$13,000		$14,000 and over	
		No.	%	No.	%	No.	%
37 years of age and younger:							
Business education majors....	24	19	79	5	21	0	0
All other majors.............	45	27	60	13	29	5	11
38 years of age and older:							
Business education majors....	35	14	40	10	29	11	31
All other majors.............	40	14	35	11	28	15	38

The interpretation to be put upon the above results is complicated by a number of considerations. In Chap. 5 it was pointed out that students majoring in business receive slightly lower scores on tests of general intelligence than do students majoring in most other areas, especially those such as engineering and law from which students are likely to enter business careers.[3] Thus there is a distinct possibility that in the three-company study also, those with business majors are slightly less able than those with majors in other areas. Of course, the important question here would be, "Given equal ability, how do business majors and majors in other fields compare in business careers?" Data from our study provide no evidence on this more precise question. The evidence does suggest, however, that business education has great need either to select students of greater ability or to provide more effective preparation, or both, in order to compete with other types of preparation for business careers.

A related point of a somewhat different sort is raised by the reports of college grades made by individuals in the three-company study. Business education majors report higher grades in college than do those whose majors were in other areas. The proportions reporting mostly A's or mostly A's and B's were 49 and 35 per cent, respectively. Furthermore,

[3] Dael Wolfle, *The Report of the Commission on Human Resources and Advanced Training* in *America's Resources of Specialized Talent*, Harper & Brothers, New York, 1954, p. 199.

this difference is more marked among the younger managers (54 and 33 per cent), who were also shown to have the larger salary differentials in favor of those with majors other than business. Not only do the courses in business apparently draw less able students (as shown by other studies), but if one can believe the individuals in this survey, they give them higher grades as well! Perhaps this state of affairs contributes to the widely held belief in the superiority of liberal arts and science education.

One of the questions in the three-company study asked the respondents to indicate how they secured their first jobs. The men in both groups were roughly evenly divided in their answers to this question. About a quarter secured their first full-time jobs *through relatives or friends in the company,* another quarter *through making a personal application,* and a third quarter obtained their jobs *through their colleges.* Very few secured jobs *by answering want ads* or in other ways. When we compare the answers to this question given by individuals thirty-eight and over with those given by individuals thirty-seven and younger there are some trends indicated. First of all, the college seems to be playing more of a part in placement, especially in the group with majors in other fields than business. The second trend is a reduction in the number who obtained the first job through relatives or friends in the company. The proportion obtaining jobs in this way dropped from 35 per cent in those thirty-eight and over to 13 per cent for the younger group. The same trend showed up in the answers of members of the Harvard Advanced Management Program to a similar question, although these were a somewhat older group. In the Harvard sample, 31 per cent of those forty-five and older obtained their first jobs through family or friends while only 12 per cent of those under forty-five obtained their first job in this way. Such results as these should be encouraging to those who object to special privilege in our society. For what they are worth, these data suggest a reduction is taking place in the part played by family influence in gaining a foothold on the bottom rung of the ladder leading toward management.

The academic grades reported by these men, while incidental to our main interest, throw some interesting light on the answers to the above question. For both those with business majors and those with majors in other fields, it is interesting to see that three-quarters of the ones who got their jobs through relatives and friends were in the lower-grade groups, reporting mostly B's or lower. In this setting, nepotism does not seem to be at all associated with high academic performance! Whether ability level parallels grade level in this group is a question, of course. Those with family ties leading to assured jobs may not be as motivated to work hard on their studies.

As is found in nearly all studies, the most obvious factor related to present salary is age. For this population the correlation between seniority and salary is a substantial .50. This state of affairs makes it much more difficult to tease out relationships between present salary and other information inasmuch as the influence of this seniority factor must first be discounted before we can consider other relationships. For example, there is an intriguing observation in relation to the starting salaries. Those who had the lowest starting salaries are disproportionately represented in the group earning $14,000 or more today. Before one becomes too much concerned with this, however, two other observations need to be kept in mind. First, those thirty-eight and over have most of the higher salaries today. Second, because of inflation over the years, those thirty-eight and over also report lower starting salaries. Thus the apparently incongruous fact that those with lowest starting salaries have today the highest salaries is entirely mediated by inflation and seniority.

Present Attitude toward Educational Experience

One of the questions designed to throw light on the attitudes of the two groups toward their educational experience was the question, "If you knew a high school boy with about the same interests, ability, and financial resources as you had at the same age, what kind of an occupation would you advise him to follow?" Of the business education majors, 46 per cent would advise a career in law, engineering, medicine, or other profession and 61 per cent would advise a business career.[4] The picture is quite different among those with educational backgrounds in other fields than business. Eighty-one per cent would advise getting into a professional career, and only 17 per cent would advise a career in business. Looked at in one way, this is a rather paradoxical finding. Does it mean, for example, that those with majors in other areas are less happy in their business careers and so they would advise young men to avoid business as a career? This hardly seems a likely interpretation in view of the high proportion advising careers in engineering (49 per cent of "all others") since most engineers have careers in business, as we have defined these terms in picking our survey sample. We seem to have here some confounding of "occupation" (which was asked about in the question), type of training, and business career. Many of those working for the three companies probably consider themselves as members of a profession rather than as businessmen. This appears explicitly in answers given by these businessmen to the request to describe their present jobs. The pertinent data are given in Table 6-5. Furthermore, in none of the answers to questions in the three-company study is there a suggestion that those with majors in other areas than business are less satisfied with their

[4] Since these figures include multiple answers, they do not add up to exactly 100 per cent.

TABLE 6-5

DISTRIBUTION OF ANSWERS TO QUESTION CONCERNING PRESENT JOB

("Please describe your present job, duties, and responsibilities.")

Occupation	Total sample		Business education majors		All other majors	
	No.	%	No.	%	No.	%
Number answering....................	144	100	59	100	85	100
Professional, technical, and kindred workers.................................	61	42	15	25	46	54
Managers, officials, and proprietors, except farm.........................	73	51	37	63	36	42
Clerical and kindred workers...........	3	2	1	2	2	2
Salesworkers.........................	4	3	4	7	—	—
Craftsmen, foremen, and kindred workers	2	1	1	2	1	1
Unclassifiable........................	1	1	1	2	—	1

careers than those who majored in business subjects. If anything, the evidence points the other way.

At this point we are touching upon what is a persistent and pervasive problem in relation to programs of business education. At one level of discussion there is the classification of careers in terms of type of institution in which they take place. Thus one can speak of careers in business (firms, companies), in education (schools, colleges), in religious organizations, in government, etc. A different rubric of classification is provided when the emphasis is upon the nature of the activity engaged in. Here one could list machinist, farmer, engineer, accountant, teacher, etc. Because the two classification systems are not entirely independent yet are so very different, much confusion is generated when it is not made clear which type of classification system one is using. When our educational institutions continue to multiply course offerings under both systems of classification (e.g., Retailing—institutional, and Personnel Management— activity) and when the activity may be carried on in a number of types of institutions and also may be a type of institution itself, it is no wonder that people are confused. Lawyers, for example, work for business, government, and others. They also practice law in their own organizations. All of this suggests that the answers to our question, "What occupation would you advise?" do not tell us very clearly what the respondents think of their own careers as members of business firms.

One possible reason that many businessmen would advise some other preparation for a business career than a major in business subjects may be because business education is felt to be inferior in some respects to

other academic training. None of the questions asked in the pilot study
bore directly upon this point. Questions as to which courses had proved
most valuable in helping them get ahead, however, did show marked
differences between those with business education and those with other
backgrounds. Table 6-6 lists the answers to this question. The differences

TABLE 6-6

DISTRIBUTION OF ANSWERS TO QUESTION CONCERNING
MOST INFLUENTIAL FACTOR IN GETTING AHEAD

("Taking into consideration your work experience since you left school, what subject,
course of study, or area of interest during college has done you the most good in getting
ahead?")

Area of interest	Total sample		Business education majors		All other majors	
	No.	%	No.	%	No.	%
Number answering....................	142*	100	58*	100	84*	100
Business subjects......................	51	36	40	69	11	13
Liberal arts and other subjects.........	75	53	14	24	61	73
Engineering..........................	31	22	1	2	30	36
None................................	10	7	5	9	5	6

* Multiple answers.

revealed in the table do suggest that business majors may have found
their courses less valuable in their careers than did those who majored
in other areas. These results, however, are open to question because of
the different exposure of the two groups to various types of courses. Most
business students had taken a number of liberal arts courses, while few
of the "all other majors" had taken business courses. Thus the latter
might have indicated they had received support from business courses
in getting ahead if they had taken more of them. Those who majored in
other areas also gave more multiple answers to this question than did
those who majored in business.

Another question, "What has been of most value to you in the work
you've done—what you learned in college or what you learned on the
job?" gave similar results in the comparison for those thirty-seven years
of age or younger. Among these younger business majors only 21 per
cent answered that what had been learned in college was of most value.
The corresponding percentage among majors in other areas was 38 per
cent. For some reason, in the older groups there was here no difference
between business majors and majors in other areas. Whether the longer
time lapse since their college years is a factor here we do not know.

When one considers the applied nature of so many business courses coupled with greater desire for practical training on the part of those who choose them, one would expect an overwhelming vote in their support. Results such as these raise some question about how well many business or commerce courses actually prepare students for their chosen careers.

Respondents in the three-company study were also asked which of the subjects they had taken in college they liked most and which least. While the differences between those with business majors and those with majors in other areas were striking in terms of the subjects they liked most, these differences paralleled almost exactly the differences in subjects actually taken, thus revealing nothing significant beyond this fact. Interpretation of these figures and similar figures for the subjects liked least is complicated by the fact that exposure to various subjects differed so markedly in the two groups. No general conclusion seems possible, therefore, on the basis of these data.

The actual courses taken by those majoring in business subjects and in other areas are of some interest. First of all, exposure to English, biological sciences, public speaking, and psychology was about the same in both groups. The business majors, however, clearly had more courses in history than did those who majored in other fields (58 per cent as compared with 42 per cent had taken two or more courses in history). Not unexpectedly, the vast majority of those with majors in other areas had two or more courses in mathematics (89 per cent) while a little over half (59 per cent) of the business majors had this much work in mathematics. An even more marked difference existed in physical sciences with percentages of 79 and 29, respectively, for those with majors in other areas and those with majors in business subjects. In accounting, the difference between the two groups was the most extreme of all, this time in the other direction. Seventy-six per cent of the business majors had two or more courses in accounting while only 12 per cent of those with majors in other areas had more than one course in accounting. Nearly three-quarters of them had had no accounting at all! Finally, 90 per cent of the business majors took two or more courses in economics, while 49 per cent of those with other majors took as many economics courses as this.

Considering the above figures, one cannot claim that there is much evidence of any greater degree of narrow specialization in either of the main groups compared in the three-company study. Here is where it would be interesting to examine a larger sample so that comparisons might be made among three or four groups, i.e., business majors, engineers, liberal arts majors, for example. If, as we have suggested, those with majors in other fields have had some slight career advantage, this cannot be ascribed to any greater breadth in their academic preparation.

Businessmen in the three-company study were also asked whether they think now that they had too many, too few, or about the right number of courses in various subjects. Both groups pretty well agreed that about the right number of courses had been taken in biological sciences, physical sciences, and history. Both groups also agreed (61 per cent) that they had had about the right amount of mathematics, but a minority of 30 per cent or more in both groups felt that what they had was not enough. The view of both groups with respect to psychology was similar, but they were split about evenly between those feeling the number of courses was about right and those feeling that too few courses in psychology had been taken. Finally, more than half of both groups felt they had not had enough public speaking, with somewhat more of those with majors in other areas reporting they felt this way.

In English, those with majors in business subjects split about evenly between those satisfied with their English experience and those wishing they had had more English courses. Among those with majors in other areas, the proportion was nearly two-thirds satisfied to one-third desiring additional English. With respect to economics, more than half of both groups were satisfied with the number of courses taken but a sizable minority of 42 per cent of those with majors in other areas felt they had too little economics. Only 27 per cent of those with majors in business felt this way. The last subject to be considered here is accounting, and here again there are marked differences between those who majored in business subjects and those who majored in other areas. Nearly half of the latter (48 per cent) felt that they had had too few courses in accounting. This may not be too surprising since three-quarters of them had not had any accounting. Only 15 per cent of those who majored in business felt that they had had too little accounting.

If one can accept the testimony of practitioners, the foregoing would suggest that, regardless of major field, those planning on business careers should take more courses in psychology and public speaking. There is some suggestion that more English and mathematics would be desirable, especially for those with business majors. For those who major in areas other than business, a strong case can be made for providing more courses in economics and especially some training in accounting. This reinforces the point of view that business education has an important contribution to make to those whose major field of interest is in some other area, particularly if a career in business is a possibility.

General Attitudes or Values

A number of questions were asked to get some picture of the system of values held by the businessmen in the three-company study. One of these was, "Would you describe the best way of life for yourself?" Such questions as this yield answers which must be categorized according to some rubric or classification, the choice of which is to a large extent up to the researcher, for there is no single classification of such matters which is clearly better than others. The categories used in the three-company study were chosen because they have been found useful in other surveys and because they do seem to fit the answers of our sample.

The first observation here is that frequency of choice in the three-company sample among various alternative values does differ in relation to a number of factors. First of all, those thirty-seven years of age and younger tended to place a higher value upon *occupational satisfaction* than did the older group (75 per cent versus 54 per cent). Because of the effect of the seniority factor in the salary figures mentioned earlier, we need to take account of the above relation between *age* and *occupational satisfaction* before we see the influence of salary upon the latter. Actually both age groups show similar results. It will come as no surprise that those with higher salaries choose occupational satisfaction as a value more often than those with lower salaries.

Another value examined was that of a belief in the importance of *material possessions*. This showed little relation to age or to any other factor except present salary. Here rather surprisingly we find those with lower salaries more often refer to this value. The differences are small, however, and not much should be made of this point. The importance of *income sufficient for one's needs* was selected as a value more often by the younger individuals in the business major group and equally often among both the younger and older businessmen with majors in other areas. Three-quarters of the younger business majors seem to be preoccupied with this question. This is interesting in the light of the fact that their present salaries are somewhat less than those of nonbusiness majors in the younger group.

The three-company study checks out with common sense when we find with both business majors and other majors and at all ages that the importance of *education, books, and self-improvement* is greater among those whose grades were mostly A's, or mostly A's and B's, than it is among those with lower grades. The 30 per cent of this group who checked this value are contrasted with 7 per cent of those with lower grades who gave this as an important value. To the extent that belief in the importance of books and literature is considered the mark of a well-rounded citizen in modern society, these rather low figures do not give one much comfort.

The importance of *moral standards* is recognized more by those who are thirty-eight or older (36 versus 17 per cent), and this is about equally true for business and other majors. One is tempted to relate this to "preaching" by the older generation—a phenomenon which has been remarked on from time immemorial.

Interestingly enough, *financial security* was rarely mentioned as an important value by any group. Satisfaction with *community, leisure, and vocational interests; need for social contacts; personal happiness; travel; satisfaction with present way of life; fulfilling responsibility to children; ability to make a worth-while contribution to society;* and *freedom* all received a small amount of attention. Group differences did not seem large or significant enough to be reported here and most of these items were referred to less than 20 per cent of the time.

One item that does deserve some mention is *participation in community activities.* This is considered more important by those in the older groups and by those with majors other than business. In the latter group, this value appears more often in those with higher salaries. From what we know of the demands of higher-level executive positions, this finding makes some sense. It also appears that those with business administration background are not as community-minded as their associates with other backgrounds. This may be related to the fact that they more often grew up in large cities where the community may tend to be impersonal and beyond the influence of the individual.

Miscellaneous Observations

Where did the businessmen in the three-company sample receive their college education? The answer is in many different institutions, although clearly the largest representation is from local institutions. There is also a difference here between those who majored in business subjects and those with majors in other areas. Fifty-nine per cent of those with business majors came from either one of two local colleges. The remainder represent a total of twenty-six different colleges. For those with majors in other areas, 25 per cent came from either one of two local colleges (one of the same, one different from the two represented by the business majors) while the rest came from forty-eight different colleges.

We have already referred to some other related information. Those with business majors frequently took their college work at night or while working full time. They also were brought up in larger cities and towns. Since our sample is taken from a large metropolitan area, it is perhaps not surprising that there is such a strong local flavor to the group that majored in business subjects.

The important part played by local institutions in staffing local companies probably needs no special mention. This does seem to be more important with respect to business education than with respect to other fields. It suggests the possibility of capitalizing upon these local ties through providing direct experience in the business setting for students in business courses. Much of this is already done, no doubt. Conversely, it suggests that companies such as these have a real stake in the quality of preparation offered locally in business education. A more active interest in the local colleges on the part of company executives might well pay dividends in many ways.

IMPLICATIONS FOR BUSINESS EDUCATION

In a democratic society holding the often-expressed ideal of equal opportunity for all, higher education has come to have a very special significance. To many people, education is the means whereby the ideal can be translated into reality. Indeed, a college education is a prerequisite to many types of careers, and it is rapidly becoming a requirement for an administrative career in business. The question then is, what kind of a college education should it be for a business career? In this chapter, the experiences and opinions of a group of consumers of college education in the past have been examined for evidence bearing on this question.

Any survey of individuals currently engaged in a particular type of career is likely to yield information with a definite bias in at least one respect. These individuals are likely to reflect mainly successful outcomes in the career area in question. We rarely encounter a career failure in such surveys because these have long since moved into something else. In our three-company study, our population was made up of college graduates who are now in administrative positions in their companies. Presumably they are all relatively effective performers in their jobs. What we do not know is how much attrition there has been in the group of prospective administrators of which these individuals were a part at the time of graduation from college. Such attrition information for various types of college training would provide the most convincing evidence for evaluating types of training as preparation for careers in business management.

Lacking information about those who fell by the wayside, there are nevertheless some useful observations to be made of those who have made the grade into business management. Their opinions and attitudes toward their own educational backgrounds in the light of their business experiences are a valuable source of evidence to confirm or raise questions about propositions relating to business education arrived at in other ways. We should not expect too much, however, from these observations of the business scene itself.

From the data obtained in the three-company study, it is clear that a substantial number of the businessmen trained in business subjects accomplished their preparation while carrying a full-time job. Apparently business education more than any other kind of education made college preparation possible for some of these businessmen who might otherwise never have achieved it. One question this study raises then is whether in the ideal program of training for business careers there will be adequate provision for night school and part-time students. No doubt most will agree that from the point of view of educational objectives, such arrangements are less satisfactory than others. From the viewpoint of the greatest good to all, however, should there not be adequate opportunity for those who cannot afford full-time study in a regular undergraduate program? The fact that a number of administrators in the three-company study might have been barred from, or at least handicapped in, their business careers without the opportunity to study while working makes this question a pertinent one.

Perhaps one answer is to make full-time college education generally available to all who qualify for it in terms of ability and desire. Recent developments in government support of loans for college study and the possible development of massive Federal scholarship programs may make it less important to provide special opportunities for college preparation at night or on a part-time basis. Thus the issue we have raised here may be out of date by the time a more ideal program of business education can be implemented.

Observations from the three-company study also provide us with some evaluation of business education in comparison to other avenues of training. First of all, the salary information from the study reflects unfavorably on the face of it upon work in business subjects. Although those majoring in business start at about the same salary level as those prepared in other areas, their salaries fall behind rather quickly. As was pointed out in the discussion, what this means is not too clear. It could mean that those trained in business subjects do not perform as well on the job and hence are not promoted as rapidly as others. Other explanations are possible, however. Nevertheless, in the absence of evidence to the contrary, the observation as to salaries suggests that business education needs to upgrade its product. Whether this is to be accomplished through more discriminating selection or through improved programs is not the issue here. Both would seem to be desirable under the circumstances.

Attitudes revealed in alumni surveys and other inquiries about past education usually turn up strongly favorable opinions in retrospect. Most people, when asked what kind of training they would take if they had it to do over again, pick the kind of education they actually had. Thus any study such as was made of businessmen in the three companies starts with an expectation of a favorable report on the education actually received. What proportion of negative reactions constitutes a significant departure from such expectations is hard to say. Also, even if one finds a significant vote of disaffection, there will still be the question how much this may be due to a commonly held prestige stereotype operating in favor of some other type of program and how much it represents well-reasoned judgments as to the value of different programs. For these reasons we would not want to make too much of the fact that only 61 per cent of those with business preparation would advise such a course of study for a young person starting off on a business career. This proportion can be contrasted with reports from several hundred graduates of a graduate business school program,[5] in which more than 90 per cent said that if they had it to do over again they would prepare themselves for business in the same way. It is apparently possible to get a nearly unanimous vote in favor of a business education program at the graduate level. The much lower figure actually obtained for business majors in the three-company study suggests that considerable improvement is both possible and needed in the undergraduate programs attended by these businessmen.

The same conclusion is supported by the observation that the businessmen with business majors less frequently than those with majors in other areas reported that they found their college training was of more value in getting ahead than was experience on the job. This was true in spite of the fact that business majors more often than others had chosen their major field of study because of its "practical" value. Business education apparently has not fulfilled expectations in this respect, at least not as well as engineering and other areas of study.

Comments made by businessmen in the three-company study as to the need for preparation offered by particular courses support some of the recommendations as to business curricula in later chapters. For example, many administrators in the three companies felt that additional training beyond what they had themselves received was needed in English, public speaking, and mathematics. It is interesting that these three subjects should have been mentioned more often than others and by both those who had majored in business subjects and those who had majored in other areas. These courses can all be classed as bearing upon skill in communication. This suggests not only that courses in these areas are needed but that actual practice in communication in situations similar to administrative situations in business might prove even more valuable. The case discussion method may derive much of its effectiveness from the fact that it does provide practice in communication.

Comments by those who had not majored in business subjects on the need for preparation in economics and accounting support the view that these subjects occupy a special and central position in preparation for

[5] *Harvard Business School Alumni Bulletin,* Autumn, 1949, p. 137.

a business career. Schools of business can here make an important contribution to professional training in other areas, such as engineering, and to liberal arts programs, many graduates of which will enter upon careers in business. This potential service to the college as a whole needs to be kept in mind in planning a program of business education.

Finally the picture of management seen in the three companies suggests that in the competition for places on the management team there is going to be room for individuals with many different types of background. Quite properly the focus of the present inquiry has been on business education. Granted its importance in contributing to tomorrow's management, however, this does not mean that business education needs to take sole responsibility in the matter. Engineers and lawyers will continue to fill a large share of top-management positions, and they will help to meet the coming shortage in administrative personnel. Some attention to the unique contribution that can be made by academic work in business may therefore contribute more than attempts to outline some one program that will meet all management needs in the future.

CHAPTER 7

FOUNDATIONS OF EDUCATION FOR BUSINESS

Preparation for careers in business has a legitimate place in undergraduate and graduate education. Whether a particular school's program does so depends on whether the work is maintained at a sufficiently high analytical level.

Some of the more important implications of the preceding chapters can be brought together at this point to provide a framework for the review of existing business school programs in Part 2. Chapter 2 examined the relationship between career preparation and higher education in a number of fields and from a variety of viewpoints. Seen in the light of this discussion, the issue confronting colleges and universities is not whether they should offer such preparation but rather the form and direction it should take.

The chief purpose of any institution of higher education is to help the individual student achieve the highest intellectual and personal development of which he is capable. Career needs are certainly an integral part of the individual's growth just as are his responsibilities as a citizen and his potentialities as a person. Career preparation presents no problem in the undergraduate or graduate curriculum as long as it is conceived in broad terms, is related closely to the student's general studies, and contains considerable analytical content. Difficulties arise when education is offered for careers which do not require extended academic study or which entail knowledge of a highly detailed, technical nature. In the first case, the work tends to be little above the high school level and, as an intellectual experience, adds little or nothing to the student's total development. In the second, the work may be quite intellectually demanding but nonetheless narrowing, tending to cut the student off from important learning experiences. Unless kept under severe control, both types of preparation can prevent the student from achieving his maximum potential.

As fields of activity like medicine and law have moved toward complete professional status, the pressure on the student's time has increased

149

and the need for him to concentrate on underlying principles rather than on practical techniques has become correspondingly greater. In such fields the subjects themselves have become broader and more complex, and the importance of certain preprofessional subjects has become greater. A more comprehensive and more rigorous kind of educational preparation has therefore become necessary. At the same time, the super-structure of specialized knowledge and skills in these areas has expanded and become more elaborate. Subareas have emerged with principles and specialties of their own, and what were once simple skills have become highly refined techniques requiring exacting training. The result is that as career areas develop, the period of learning is lengthened, the scope of the educational experience is broadened, the extent and variety of specialized knowledge is increased, and the intellectual rigor of the training is enhanced. These tendencies become still more pronounced as the public responsibilities and ethical standards of professions become more clearly defined and more widely accepted.

Thus, the trend in the more highly developed areas is toward limiting direct professional training to graduate instruction while the undergraduate years are devoted to general background education and training in certain preprofessional subjects. There appears to be no simple method for determining what should be included at the undergraduate or graduate stage of the student's preparation, but three elements seem to be common to all the highly developed professions. First, the tendency to lose sight of the general background and preprofessional subjects poses a serious danger at every stage of the student's preparation. Second, education is largely self-education and if it is to have any enduring meaning for the individual, must be continued throughout life. Third, emphasis should not be placed on mastering the detailed aspects of a given subject but on developing the abilities and methods needed for meeting problems in later life. These elements of the student's preparation complement one another and in terms of educational planning point in the same direction.

These findings have an important bearing on academic study for business. If this type of career preparation is to have a legitimate place in graduate, and even more, undergraduate education, it never should be carried to a point where it warps the student's growth as a citizen and as an individual. Both of the latter are not only of supreme importance in their own right but are essential to fully successful and responsible careers in business as well. If career preparation becomes an end in itself to the point where mastery of a particular job or type of activity is made all-important, the most precious element in the college or university experience is likely to be lost. Only those aspects of business life which have close ties with the student's broader range of studies and contribute significantly to them can be said to warrant serious attention at this level of education.

The discussion of career preparation in other fields underscores the view that institutions of higher education should concentrate their efforts on strengthening the individual's intellectual powers through work in a number of underlying or related fields of study. Career preparation for business should have a similar focus. To this end the students should be challenged to undertake the most broadening and demanding programs of which they are capable. Every safeguard should be taken to insure that superior students will be given work commensurate with their abilities, and every opportunity should be given all students to explore untried paths and look for new relations between subjects.

The educational experience in business just as much as in other fields should as much as possible be a venture for the individual, opening up areas of knowledge and ways of knowing which would otherwise be closed to him. There should be no room in a college or university program for pedestrian, trivial, or frivolous subject matter. There should be no piling up of repetitive detail in which students take course after course at much the same level of analytical difficulty. There should be a minimum of rote learning of extensive factual matter having to do with the minutiae of a particular field. College going should be one of the summits in the individual's experience, giving him a view of what life in its richest sense can mean and helping him develop the capacities for bringing this vision into being.

This view of business education is not only supported by experience in other areas of career preparation; it also accords with the kinds of responsibilities which are becoming increasingly important in different branches of business as well. The review of employer requirements and career patterns in Chaps. 5 and 6 showed that in the business field it is quite impossible to segment the individual's training into its career, citizen, and personal-development components, since all three are so much a part of business responsibilities. Nor does the chief value of college or university work for business careers lie in any specific subject matter which may have been learned, since the rate of obsolescence of such knowledge over the individual's lifetime tends to be extremely high. Rather it lies in developing those qualities of mind which can be used to resolve difficult problems in different contexts and at different levels of a firm's operations. A business school should accordingly concentrate its energies on strengthening the student's basic intellectual equipment and on helping him learn to work with methods of analysis which are appropriate to various types of business situations. No more than in any other branch of higher education should attention be given to subjects which have little relation to broader or more basic fields of knowledge.

Each course should provide an opportunity to bring a wide range of methods and insights to bear on a significant group of issues, the work centering around elements of learning which have career-long value and broad applicability.

What has been said about undue emphasis on career preparation in higher education applies to specialized study as well. The two go hand in hand but are not the same. Specialized work can be of a very high order, as when it contributes to original research or permits a student to follow out some new line of investigation on his own. But it can be wholly sterile too as when it becomes ensnared in the rituals of modern scholarship. This is to say that specialized study need not be made up of pretentious pedantry any more than career preparation need consist of memorizing recipes out of a practitioner's cookbook. On the contrary, specialized study and career preparation can contribute a vital element to the individual's intellectual development and are in fact essential to it. The outcome clearly depends on the nature of the work, how it is related to the rest of the student's program, and where it comes in his studies. Graduate work, for example, can permit a degree of concentration in a student's program which might well be inappropriate during the under-graduate years, much depending on the ability of the student and in-structor to put a given topic in its proper setting. The continuing task of any institution of higher education is to keep asking itself what, when, and how can specialized study and career preparation contribute to the individual's intellectual growth and thus to his total development. This question should be in the forefront of every discussion of business edu-cation, since the way it is answered largely determines the character and direction of a school's entire program.

Chapter 3, which contrasted the historical patterns of different types of schools, throws considerable light on this range of issues. Programs which concentrated on preparing for specific business careers, and espe-cially on the less-demanding aspects of such careers, became overlaid with specialized courses that were hardly above the high school level. Only those schools which kept close ties with broad areas of learning outside business, and emphasized analytical methods of study in dealing with complex business problems, were able to offer challenging pro-grams.

Judging from the historical record, the path of least resistance for most institutions to follow during the years preceding World War II was to add courses and major specialties as faculty preferences and opportuni-ties for expansion permitted. Most observers of the academic scene, in-cluding many actively involved in business school programs, decried this trend, but the process of course proliferation apparently developed a momentum of its own which proved impervious to criticism and control.

This outcome was a compound of the number, diversity, and general quality of students admitted to the programs, the demand for academic recognition by various employer groups, the interests and ambitions of the faculty members and deans most immediately involved, and the passive or disinterested attitude of other faculty and university administration spokesmen. Its main impetus was centered in the accounting departments, an area in which highly specialized instruction was perhaps more justified than any other, but the same pattern of instruction became generalized as departmental recognition was won for other subjects. As a consequence, most business schools during the interwar years cut themselves off from other branches of learning, largely emptying their programs of serious intellectual content.

Some schools, mostly at the graduate level, stoutly resisted this trend. A very few, notably Chicago, attempted to establish more demanding programs by emphasizing the relationships between the study of business and various branches of the social sciences, but these experiments encountered serious difficulties. Others, led by Harvard, put decision making in simulated business situations (i.e., business cases) at the center of their programs. The students were made to grapple with specific policy questions on their own, rather than absorb textbook versions of general principles, and this proved both intellectually stimulating and demanding. Moreover, case instruction obliged students to consider aspects of policy making which lay outside any one of the business specialties or indeed outside business itself as normally defined. This opened the business studies to influences from nonbusiness fields at the same time that it precluded the excessive specialization found at many schools. As conceived at Harvard, students preferably came to the case method after a broad undergraduate preparation, the cases providing a variety of opportunities for them to draw upon their general background knowledge. At the same time, the relation between the business and nonbusiness subjects was deliberately left on a flexible, rather vague basis, and formal academic work of a systematic or "scientific" nature was carefully avoided. Even under the case method, preparation for business as a serious discipline remained in a confused state.

The intellectual qualities, social backgrounds, and range of interests of students attending business schools discussed in Chap. 4 have an important bearing on the foregoing issues. Intelligence test results reveal that business students (both graduate and undergraduate) tend to be among the lowest-scoring academic groups, suggesting that the programs described in the historical chapter have served to attract the less academically able. This outcome is also in good part a result of the low admissions standards prevailing at the great majority of institutions. Among the four-year undergraduate schools, hardly any make even a pretense of admissions screening; at a few of the schools which admit at the junior year, however, and at an even larger number of graduate schools, students enter on a selective basis. Unlike the more highly developed professions, such as medicine or engineering, the subject of business administration does not have sufficient content to screen students automatically, making the need for selective admissions standards all the greater. Neither the academic quality of a school's student body or the academic content of its program can be raised very far alone, however; both must be pulled up together.

One of the perplexing issues in this field is whether the general run of students headed for business careers would either be interested in or capable of participating in rigorous academic programs. The general conclusion reached in Chap. 4 was that they doubtless would be if the work could be given meaning for the individual student and were taught in an imaginative manner. Obviously, to require a course in mathematical statistics, for example, just because it involves difficult subject matter would not be defensible, but if work in this subject were shown to be a vital part of the student's intellectual equipment, a quite different result might well follow. The arguments that most business students have a strong vocational bias, that their social backgrounds preclude serious academic work, that at present they do not have the intelligence to handle such work—these and similar contentions are for the most part quite beside the point. If demanding intellectual effort is helpful in business careers and if programs of business studies can be developed which require such effort, the colleges and universities should take whatever steps are necessary to put the programs into effect. Indeed, the danger is not that too few superior students would be available to do the work but that too few qualified faculty members could be found to teach it.

As to possible steps that might be taken to put the study of business administration on a sound academic footing, some of the trends in professional education in other areas reviewed in Chap. 2 are again worth noting. In certain of these areas, notably architecture, medicine, and engineering, there is a reasonably well-defined body of principles or basic subject matter which has to be mastered. In these fields, as already noted, the critical issue becomes one of deciding how much of the subject can be contained within four years of undergraduate, or two or more years of graduate, work. In many professional areas, however, such as law and teaching, no such clearly demarcated subject matter exists, and the problem of defining the nature and content of these fields presents the same difficulty as in business administration. While there is a clear tendency in all of these fields to limit professional training to the post-bachelor years, there is considerable controversy in almost all branches of professional training concerning the proper balance between general and professional education, the extent to which specific skills or specialized study should be emphasized, and the content of the student's work in general or liberal arts education. These issues are difficult enough in all fields but especially so where the subject itself remains ill-defined or lacks any sharp analytical focus. The latter appears to be the source of most of the difficulties besetting business administration as an area of academic study.

A common element in the criticisms raised in different branches of professional education is the view that general or liberal arts subjects should receive more emphasis, not only in preprofessional programs but perhaps in the years of professional training as well. A logical next step is to argue that some substantial percentage of the student's work as an undergraduate, and even as a graduate, should consist of general courses which will provide the breadth and rigor he needs. This crucial step, however, raises serious difficulties. The liberal arts studies do not form a clear, well-defined body of knowledge. Rather, they embrace some subjects which are intellectually very demanding and others which are much less so; some which can be reduced to theoretical principles and others which defy abstract reasoning; some (if the sciences are included) which require exact laboratory testing and others which do not lend themselves to any kind of controlled experiments; some which take human values as given and others which are addressed to ultimate questions of existence. Out of this vast range of subject matter, it is simply not possible to specify in some over-all, universal sense what is central and what is peripheral, what is part of the main tradition and what is not. Each age, each institution, and each group must discover for itself what it means by the liberal arts studies, a venture which is likely to yield its highest rewards in the doing, not in the finishing of the task.

There is another and even more disturbing reason why the relation between the liberal arts and professional studies can not be approached in any mechanical or uniform manner. By now the view has been given wide currency that many of the liberal arts courses at many institutions are patently vocational in orientation while others which purport to adhere to a broad, liberalizing point of view are in fact narrowly specialized. This is held to impose special hardships on students whose major interests and career plans lie in other fields, e.g., the engineering student who is required to take an English literature course, but one wonders whether this conception of education even serves the needs of the student taking work in his own major. As in most branches of higher education there is the additional difficulty that the quality of faculty members and the resulting instruction varies enormously between institutions, between subjects, and between individuals in the same department of the same school. In an area as diverse as the liberal arts, it is perhaps not surprising that course labels and descriptions mean very little, but the extreme unevenness of the work certainly makes any sweeping proposals for reform of professional education more than merely suspect.

These considerations have a direct bearing on business administration programs. Few would deny that a background in the liberal arts studies is desirable as preparation for business careers, but the grounds for singling out one subject for special emphasis rather than some other are none too clear. The difficulty can be attributed in considerable measure to the inchoate state of business administration as a field of academic study, but it results at least as much from the parlous condition of the liberal arts studies themselves. The need therefore is, first, to define as precisely as possible the elements which should go into the business studies proper and, second, to determine what aspects of liberal arts work are of special importance to pursuing such studies. This, of course, is not something which can be put into a master blueprint and applied at once to all schools for all time to come. Of necessity, considerable latitude must be left to the individual institution to make its own way; more than this, the undertaking must in a real sense be a never-ending one. Nonetheless, if these two basic steps cannot be agreed upon at least in broad outline, further progress in business education would hardly seem possible.

It might be assumed that at the graduate level, business schools would not be obliged to cope with these issues, but such is not the case. On the one hand, graduate work quite as much as undergraduate work faces the danger of excessive specialism, though the need for introducing materials and ideas from nonbusiness fields expresses itself in a rather different manner. On the other hand, there is no simple formula for fulfilling this latter need even if the emphasis on specialized professional training is reduced to a bare minimum. As at the undergraduate level, the outcome all depends on the particular fields drawn upon, the way they are introduced into the business program, and the quality and enthusiasm of the faculty which is responsible for the work. These considerations help explain why the relationship between graduate and undergraduate study in business administration raises so many perplexing issues.

What are the concrete steps which a school might take to develop workable answers to these issues? What is the general direction of thinking which gives greatest promise of yielding worth-while results? Again, the review of employer requirements and business career patterns in Chaps. 5 and 6 hardly provide specific answers, but they indicate fairly clearly the general road which undergraduate and graduate business schools might well follow in the future. First, an important element in most forward-moving careers in business is the capacity to use basic communication skills—written, oral, and numerical—in solving business problems. Another is the capacity to use the methods of the humanist in approaching business issues, especially in developing sensitivity to human aspirations and an imaginative awareness of the value elements in business situations. Another is sufficient familiarity with the work of mathematicians and scientists to be able to understand their language and to use at least some of their more important methods in tackling business problems. Still another is the capacity to see the relevance of the various social sciences to business affairs and to draw upon these subjects in whatever manner may be indicated in specific business situations. Finally, there is need in most careers in this field to master the underlying principles of at least one broad area of business policy (accounting, finance, marketing, etc.) and to gain an appreciation of the contributions which a given specialty can make to managerial policy making.

These are some of the guidelines used in reviewing current practice among business schools in the next part of the study. However, they chiefly relate to certain intellectual qualities which are by no means the only capacities needed at different levels of business responsibility. Perhaps they are even of a second order of importance compared with such attributes as a high degree of physical and nervous energy, emotional balance, outgoing traits of personality, the skills of the diplomat or politician, perseverance, and integrity. The fact remains these latter qualities can hardly be taught in any direct manner at the college level. The special province of higher education is to strengthen the individual's capacity to think for himself. In the context of business situations, this capacity involves the ability to relate basic skills and general knowledge to specific business decisions and the capacity to approach particular problems in an imaginatively intellectual manner. Both of these capacities are greatly prized at all levels of business, they are wholly in keeping with the highest traditions of college and university work, and they mark out an area in which business schools, working in close collaboration with various nonbusiness disciplines as well as with business organizations themselves, can assume a leadership role of the greatest importance.

A design for work in business administration along these lines would place much more stress on developing methods of analysis than on knowledge of specific subject matter. A grasp of the basic institutional facts and essential elements of the various functional business areas would of course be necessary, but much greater attention would be centered on applying different analytical methods to resolving specific business problems. The functional areas would then simply serve as a convenient way to organize the material and to highlight the issues in an orderly, logical manner, not to demarcate boundaries between subjects in any rigid or formal way. A similar approach would be taken to the study of business as a whole in relation to other fields, with certain nonbusiness subjects providing the principal tools for analyzing business problems. The distinction between undergraduate and graduate preparation would rest largely on the greater emphasis placed on broad background preparation at the undergraduate level and the greater emphasis placed on the uses of knowledge to solve management problems at the graduate level.

This view of the role of business schools would have far-reaching implications for many aspects of their programs, including the kinds of students they would attract, the subjects they would offer as major concentrations, the number and type of courses they would give, the character of faculties they would seek to develop, and many others, but its bearing on the role of research deserves special comment. It is worth noting that, even in the highly developed professions, emphasis on research varies enormously from one field to another, and there is no little controversy over the kind of research which should be encouraged. As in other branches of education concerned with preparing students for a life of action, business schools continuously face the danger of slighting their research efforts. The danger is all the greater in business where the results of research, other than those coming out of science and technology, are not too tangible and tend to yield indirect benefits at best.

In their very efforts to achieve immediate and concrete results from research, business schools expose themselves to the most serious danger of all—a type of research which comes to little more than nose counting and which employers can quite as efficiently do for themselves. A design for business education which centers attention, not on the minutiae of business practice, but on the contributions of a variety of fields to the solution of complex business problems would call for research of an equally broad and demanding nature. Since the development of this kind of an educational program lies mostly in the future, a lot of intensive, imaginative work by many first-rate minds will be required. Continuing research designed to explore the frontiers of this emerging area will therefore be needed to give this conception of business education real content and solid grounding; teaching programs and research efforts should accordingly go hand in hand, each supporting and contributing to the other. Beyond this is the responsibility of business schools to serve as a source of new materials and path-breaking ideas for business, for other branches of education, and for the community at large. Not until these schools have developed programs which put the study of business in a broad, academic setting and relate it to the most demanding kind of research can they hope to achieve any considerable degree of influence, much less positions of genuine leadership.

Little emphasis has been given in this discussion to the wide differences in qualities and interests which exist between student groups, faculty members, and the schools themselves. It is obvious that these differences, especially between undergraduate and graduate instruction, will have to be taken into account, if for no other reason than the constraints imposed by the various institutions' budgets. At the same time, every business school is part of a great university tradition, and regardless of location, size, or wealth, each school has an obligation to maintain that tradition, offering the highest standards of academic achievement of which it is capable. There is no school so poor it cannot set its sights on doing a more effective job, just as there is no school so successful it cannot improve its existing program. The particular lines along which schools develop will probably be quite different, and quite properly so. It is also to be expected that the actual level of academic performance attained by individual schools will continue to vary considerably. The broad direction in which all the schools move, however, could well be the same.

It is appropriate to conclude this brief review of the role of business schools by stressing again that many other facilities exist to provide mass education in all the techniques of business practice. Some of the more important of these other facilities are company training programs, evening schools, junior and community colleges, special institutes, and the like. As developed in detail in Part 4 of this study, they need to be greatly strengthened and utilized much more fully than at present if the prospective upswing in enrollments is not to demoralize standards completely. Despite the pressures to the contrary (and they are admittedly formidable), there is no compelling reason why undergraduate and graduate business schools need prostrate themselves in their efforts to duplicate all the types of training provided by these other institutions. Rather, the business schools should concentrate their energies on developing the most demanding programs of which they are capable, providing the kind of intellectual leadership for students, business, and the community which they alone can give.

PART TWO

THE AMERICAN BUSINESS SCHOOL

CHAPTER 8

UNDERGRADUATE GENERAL STUDIES

Undergraduate preparation for business necessarily rests on a number of subjects in the liberal arts area. The work in these subjects should be pursued beyond the first-year introductory level. The student should be given every opportunity to transfer general knowledge to applications in the business area. This requires active cooperation on the part of both the nonbusiness and business faculties.

The curriculum of the undergraduate business school provides a logical starting point for a detailed examination of what these schools are doing. After a brief review of some of the more important elements common to almost all programs, the discussion centers on principal points of difference among the schools. This chapter is chiefly concerned with courses in the traditional liberal arts area, and the next chapter with courses in the business curriculum itself.

Typically, business students are required to take either one or two years of introductory work in each of the three liberal arts areas—humanities, social sciences, and sciences—a standard program consisting of a series of one-year courses in composition, English literature, history, economics, another social science and a science, a one-half-year course in mathematics, and two years of courses (but at reduced credit) in military science and physical education.

These requirements, including those in the last two subjects, are for the most part set by the university and are the same for all students. Occasionally the business school will specify one or two additional courses in one or more of these areas, and typically students can elect at least two or three courses more. The work in liberal arts (or "arts and sciences") accounts for the greater part of the freshman and sophomore years while the business studies make up most of the junior and senior years; only the beginning-year courses in economics and accounting are usually required in the lower division.

In addition to the work in these two last areas, the required business

163

courses, or business core, generally consist of a series of introductory courses dealing with the major functions of the business enterprise: business law, finance, management, marketing, personnel administration, and/or industrial relations, production, statistics, and sometimes two or three other more narrowly defined fields. The business core generally accounts for at least three-fourths of the student's work in the junior year but for not more than one- or two-semester courses in the senior year. The bulk of the remaining time is devoted to work in the student's major, with a few courses taken in business subjects closely related to the student's specialty on either a required or elective basis.

Thus, the student's four years are divided into three categories—about 40 per cent in liberal arts background subjects, about 40 per cent in required business and economics subjects, and about 20 per cent in some business specialty.[1] For the most part, these categories are laid on top of one another, the liberal arts courses predominating in the first two years, the required core of business-economics courses in the third year, and courses in the business major in the fourth.

Interviews conducted in 1957 and 1958 at approximately seventy undergraduate schools in all parts of the country threw considerable light on the relationship between liberal arts and business courses prevailing at most institutions.[2] Typically, the work which students do in liberal arts subjects appears to have little relation to their studies in business and economics and not infrequently consists of a certain number of courses to be gotten out of the way as quickly and painlessly as possible.

A number of those interviewed felt that the basic difficulty was that these courses were chiefly designed for future majors in the various liberal arts areas and that the business students tended to find them either incomprehensible or uninteresting, or both. A few liberal arts faculty members agreed with this explanation, and some were enthusiastic about developing special "integrated" courses for business and perhaps other nonliberal arts students. The great majority, however, held that many other factors were involved, including the academic abilities and interests of large numbers of business students, the business schools' "nonacademic approach" to university education, and the failure of the

[1] Because of the intimate ties between the two fields, economics is treated as part of the business studies in the discussion that follows. Depending on how it is approached, economics can just as well be considered part of the liberal arts curriculum; the relation between economics and business courses poses an important issue and is considered at length in Chap. 10.

[2] A description of the interview methods and a list of the schools visited will be found in Appendix 6; in addition, the interviews conducted in conjunction with the Ford Foundation Study of Business Education were made available through the courtesy of Robert A. Gordon.

business courses to build on the liberal arts subjects. Specific evidence was not available to test these views, since the factors underlying this problem stem from complex causes. The fact remains, and this is all but universally admitted, the liberal arts courses mean little or nothing to a very large number of undergraduate business students.

While the broad division of subject matter between liberal arts and business courses was found to be fairly uniform among schools, our interviews revealed no clear basis for the prevailing 40–40–20 division of the student's time. Typical of the answers we got to questions along this line among deans and faculty members were the following:

"This seems to come closest to satisfying everyone."

"The AACSB rules require it."

"It's as good as any other arrangement which has been suggested."

"I personally think a roughly 50–50 division between business and nonbusiness makes sense."

"We've sort of grown into it without too much thought one way or the other."

Almost without exception those interviewed agreed there could be considerable variation in the distribution of the student's time without doing serious violence to the essential subject matter that should be covered.[3] Fairly general support was given to the desirability of expanding the nonbusiness portion of the curriculum, subject to resolving some of the more important difficulties noted above. Not one of the hundreds of persons questioned expressed a fear that the students were being exposed to too little business course matter; conversely, a surprisingly large number expressed the opposite concern. Comments such as the following were typical:

"There is no doubt but what there's a lot of padding in our intermediate business courses."

"We would be quite willing to cut down on the number of courses our students take in marketing if the other departments would do the same."

"If we could convince the liberal arts people to change some of their courses, we'd be glad to have business students take more nonbusiness subjects."

"I suppose when you come right down to it, nobody needs more than three or four semester courses in any one of our majors."

These sentiments of course do no more than support the presumption that greater emphasis should be placed on work in liberal arts subjects. Talk of the need for greater breadth appears to have become almost as fashionable in academic circles as in the upper ranks of management. The

---

[3] The one exception to this was found in accounting; as noted in Chaps. 9 and 14, the needs of undergraduate students in this field call for rather special treatment.

fact remains that this view is widely held among persons most immediately concerned with the business curriculum and is therefore especially deserving of consideration.

A common feature of these programs is that the work in different areas
of the liberal arts all carry about the same weight. As noted above, the
student is required to take a number of introductory courses in various
liberal arts subjects, with provision for a few electives if he so desires.
Each unit of work tends to remain isolated from all the others and, what
is still more serious, to have little carry-over value into the student's business studies. Responsibility for this outcome must be shared by faculty
members in the two areas; unless both groups make careful provision for
such a transfer of knowledge, the chances of its happening seem slight
indeed. One possibility, developed more fully below, is to mark off certain liberal arts courses as essential to training for careers in business and
to see to it that students continue their work in one or more of these areas
beyond the introductory survey level.

Another hardly less common tendency is for each department in a
business school to require enough work of its majors to justify a full
departmental staff and a substantial portion of the student's time. Judging from the interviews, the indiscriminate piling up of departmental
requirements and offerings is the most serious weakness of American
undergraduate business schools, an observation that may apply to most
other branches of higher education as well. Here, as an example chosen
at random, are the courses which a student majoring in real estate at a
well known Midwestern university is required to take: real estate principles, real estate finance, real estate appraisals, real estate development
and management, and real estate brokerage. A student in marketing at
this same institution must take the following five courses in his specialty:
marketing principles, retailing, wholesaling, sales management, and principles of advertising. In addition, both departments require six other
courses in closely related subjects, for a total of about one-third of the
student's entire program.[4] While drawing anything like a precise line is
difficult, the most casual inspection of course offerings shows that many
undergraduate business schools have gone well beyond the point where
education at the college level stops and mere busy-work begins.

THE LIBERAL ARTS STUDIES

For purposes of this discussion, the studies outside and inside the
business-economics area are considered as but two parts of a single pro-

[4] Schools differ considerably with respect to major requirements; detailed comparisons are given below.

gram; as already indicated, most or all of the courses in the former category are required for graduation under general university regulations, but from the viewpoint of the individual business student, the distinction is not (or should not be) important.

While a substantial majority of the business school spokesmen interviewed stressed the importance of the work done in subjects other than business and economics, sharp differences in opinion existed over the form it should take. A substantial number (certainly over half) felt that at least 50 per cent of the student's program should consist of subjects outside this area, while a surprisingly large minority believed it should be over 60 per cent. There was a definite tendency among those interviewed to stress the need for more work in mathematics, psychology, and sociology—nonbusiness subjects which bear closely on certain new developments in the field of business administration. Emphasis was also placed on the desirability of more attention to improving the student's oral and written skills. Other nonbusiness subjects—the sciences, literature, philosophy, history, the "other" social sciences—received less support. The study of foreign language, if mentioned at all, was usually referred to in indifferent or even slighting terms. Regarding other proposals, no consensus was discernible.

While the discussion in Part 1, and the preceding chapter which summarized its results, provide some general guidelines for appraising the programs of business schools, difficulties quickly multiply when they are applied to concrete issues. The question, how much of the student's time should be devoted to subjects outside the business-economics area and what such work should include, is a case in point. The most that can be hoped for is to lay out the broad alternatives which schools confront in dealing with this issue, using the principles outlined earlier to indicate the general direction that future developments might take. The recommendations advanced in this and succeeding chapters have to be cast in rather specific terms if their meaning is to be made clear, but detailed proposals inevitably generate argument. The details, of course, are far less important than the general view of business education which lies behind them. It would be unfortunate if attention immediately centered on matters of specific application while their underlying import slipped from view. Indeed, one of the main findings of Part 1 was that the schools should be much more bold than in the past in experimenting on their own. While in broad outline the conception of business education developed in this study seems applicable to all schools, the spirit underlying it would be lost if individual institutions were not to exercise independent leadership in planning for the future.

As a first step toward appraising the liberal arts part of these programs, the approaches of representative schools are compared. The programs of two urban schools, the first nonresidential and the second residential, provide an appropriate starting point for such a review. Of 60 credit hours in the freshman and sophomore years, the first of these schools requires business students to take the following work in academic subjects outside business and economics:

Subject	Semester hours required outside business and economics
English Communication	6
Man and Civilization	6
American Civilization and Institutions	5
Problems of Human Behavior	3
Business Mathematics (Mathematics department)	3
Total	23

In addition, students may choose the equivalent of one elective during this period. In the last two years, students are required to take almost all their work in business, with a few of the fourteen major sequences requiring a course in English and/or one other nonbusiness subject, and most permitting one elective per semester.[5] The proportion of their total work which all students must take in liberal arts subjects comes to about 25 per cent.

Students preparing for business careers at this institution are not required to take any work whatsoever in any of the sciences, in psychology, sociology, or political science, in any of the foreign languages, or in fine arts, music, or philosophy. Two semester courses are normally required in mathematics; one is mathematics of finance, taught in the business school, while the other, business mathematics, need not be taken if the student has had two years of high school algebra. In place of work in the liberal arts area, the students take a variety of business courses which even in the first two years take up by far the greatest portion of the student's time. Because of this early concentration on business subjects, it is more difficult for a student who wishes to change his field of interest during his first two years to do so. Without inquiring into the content of the courses, the previous discussion leads to no conclusion but that a curriculum built along these lines falls far short of meeting the minimum requirements of work in liberal arts.

The second school, Emory University, has a common program for all undergraduates for the first two years, with students planning to study business required to take the following nonbusiness subjects:

[5] In the case of the major in general business administration, it is recommended that three of the electives be taken outside the school of business.

Subject	Semester hours required outside business and economics
English	10
History (Western and American Civilization)	7
Bible	3
Mathematics	3
Foreign language (in one language)	10
One of the social sciences*	7
Two of biology, geology, and physics	13
Total	53

* Includes economics, sociology, political science, philosophy, and psychology.

This leaves 7 hours of electives in academic subjects in the first two years which the business school recommends be taken in accounting and economics. In the last two years, no liberal arts subjects are required, but the students have 14 semester hours to be chosen on an elective basis. The minimum amount of work which all business students at Emory must take outside business and economics comes to about 45 per cent of their four years of study.

In contrast to the first school's program, Emory gives its business students an opportunity to lay a broad foundation in all the major areas of learning—science, mathematics, English and foreign language, history and the social sciences. The student who decides to go into another field at the end of his sophomore year is in a relatively good position to do so; if he decides to continue his work in business he has a satisfactory basis on which to build his later work. The contrast between these two schools in the way they approach the relation between business and nonbusiness subjects could hardly be more sharp.

Replies to the Survey Questionnaire dealing with the division of the student's time between liberal arts and business studies give some notion of how the programs at other institutions compare with these two schools. Since their curriculum planning problems are rather different, the answers were summarized separately for the four-year schools and for those that admit students after two years, or more rarely one year, in a general education program (the so-called 2-2- and 1-3-year schools).[6] Table 8-1, which presents the data for ninety-eight 4-year schools by size of enrollment, shows that the great majority fall between the two types of programs just outlined, with only four schools requiring less than 25 per cent of the work outside business and economics, and fifteen requir-

[6] This grouping of schools was followed in summarizing all the results of the Survey Questionnaire. Usable data were secured from 132 of the country's 157 undergraduate business schools; these 132 schools accounted for over 90 per cent of the undergraduate degrees granted by business schools in 1955–1956.

ing 45 per cent or more. Among the 2-2- and 1-3-year schools replying to the questionnaire (thirty-four in number), Table 8-2 shows that only three programs are in the less than 30 per cent category and eight are

TABLE 8-1

PER CENT OF TOTAL SEMESTER HOURS REQUIRED OUTSIDE BUSINESS AND ECONOMICS BY 98 BUSINESS SCHOOLS WITH FOUR-YEAR PROGRAMS, BY SIZE OF ENROLLMENT, 1955–1956

Total business enrollment	No. of schools by % of semester hours required outside business and economics								Total
	Under 20%	20– 24%	25– 29%	30– 34%	35– 39%	40– 44%	45– 49%	50% and over	
4,000–4,199			1						1
3,800									
3,600									
3,400			1						1
3,200									
3,000			1						1
2,800									
2,600									
2,400						1			1
2,200		1				1			2
2,000				2					2
1,800									
1,600			1	2					3
1,400		1		4	2	2	1		10
1,200			1	7	5		1		14
1,000			2	2	1				5
800		1	1	1	4		2		9
600	1	1	2	2	6		3	2	17
400			2	6	5		2		15
200				5	3	4	2	1	15
0–199								1	1
				1*					1*
Total.........	1	3	11	34	26	8	11	4	98

* Enrollment data not given.

SOURCE: Questionnaire sent in March, 1957, to all undergraduate business schools at accredited institutions; referred to as the Survey Questionnaire throughout the present study.

in the more than 45 per cent class. As a group, these schools tend to concentrate in the 35–39 per cent range, whereas the four-year schools cluster toward the lower end of the 30–39 per cent interval; however,

TABLE 8-2

PER CENT OF TOTAL SEMESTER HOURS REQUIRED OUTSIDE BUSINESS AND ECONOMICS BY 34 BUSINESS SCHOOLS WITH 2-2- AND 1-3-YEAR PROGRAMS, BY SIZE OF ENROLLMENT, 1955–1956

Total business enrollment	No. of schools by % of semester hours required outside business and economics							Total
	Under 25%	25–29%	30–34%	35–39%	40–44%	45–49%	50% and over	
1,800				1				1
1,600								
1,400		1	1					2
1,200			1	1				2
1,000				1				1
800								
600			1	3		2	1	7
400	1	1	1	2	3			8
200			1	2		1	1	5
0–199				3	1	1	2	7
					1*			1*
Total.........	1	2	5	13	5	4	4	34

* Enrollment data not given.
SOURCE: Survey Questionnaire.

the difference between the two groups when judged in the light of these data appears to be slight.[7]

Considered on the basis of size of enrollment, Table 8-1 indicates that the 4-year schools requiring the most work outside business and economics (45 per cent or more) tend to be in the relatively small-size category (enrollments below 1,400); on the other hand, those requiring the least work in nonbusiness areas are in this relatively small-size group, too. About half of the largest schools, those with enrollments of 1,400 or more, fall within the 30–34 per cent range. Among the 2-2- and 1-3-year schools, there is a somewhat clearer tendency for those which require the most work outside business-economics subjects to be relatively small in

[7] The percentages in this and succeeding tables are figured on the basis of 120 credit hours, or the equivalent, as the total required for four years of work in academic subjects; courses in physical education, military science, etc., which often bring the required total above 120 hours, were excluded. If work in the latter subjects is required, many institutions increase the number of hours needed for graduation beyond the usual 120 hours; even where this is done, the latter figure would remain the appropriate one to use in computing total requirements in academic subjects.

size, but there are not enough schools in the group as a whole to attach much weight to this finding.[8]

Tables 8-3 and 8-4 make the same comparisons for the two groups of

TABLE 8-3

PER CENT OF TOTAL SEMESTER HOURS REQUIRED OUTSIDE BUSINESS AND ECONOMICS BY 98 BUSINESS SCHOOLS WITH FOUR-YEAR PROGRAMS, BY TYPE OF CONTROL, 1955–1956

% of semester hours required outside business and economics	Public institutions		Private institutions		
	State	City	Catholic	Other	Totals
50% and over		1		3	4
45–49%	2		8	1	11
40–44%	2	1	4	1	8
35–39%	11		4	11	26
30–34%	16	2	6	8	32
25–29%	10	2		1	13
20–24%	1			2	3
Under 20%		1			1
Total..........................	42	7	22	27	98

SOURCE: Survey Questionnaire.

TABLE 8-4

PER CENT OF TOTAL SEMESTER HOURS REQUIRED OUTSIDE BUSINESS AND ECONOMICS BY 34 BUSINESS SCHOOLS WITH 2-2- AND 1-3-YEAR PROGRAMS, BY TYPE OF CONTROL, 1955–1956

% of semester hours required outside business and economics	Public institutions		Private institutions		
	State	City	Catholic	Other	Totals
50% and over	1	1	1	1	4
45–49%	3			1	4
40–44%	3			2	5
35–39%	9	2		2	13
30–34%	4			1	5
25–29%	1			1	2
20–24%	1				1
Total..........................	22	3	1	8	34

SOURCE: Survey Questionnaire.

schools by type of administrative control. Among the four-year schools there is some tendency for the public institutions (state and city) to require less work outside business and economics than those in the pri-

[8] The four-year schools, of course, generally have larger business enrollments.

vate category (Catholic and other). Only six of the public-supported schools require more than 40 per cent of such work, whereas seventeen of the private schools do so. Of the latter, twelve are affiliated with the Catholic Church; the other private schools show a pattern not too different from the public group, with a median percentage requirement of about 34 per cent (as against 32 per cent for the public institutions) and a somewhat greater spread above and below this amount.

TABLE 8-5

PER CENT OF TOTAL SEMESTER HOURS REQUIRED OUTSIDE BUSINESS AND ECONOMICS BY 98 BUSINESS SCHOOLS WITH FOUR-YEAR PROGRAMS, BY MEMBERSHIP IN AACSB, 1955–1956

% of semester hours required outside business and economics	Members of AACSB	Nonmembers of AACSB	Total
50% and over		4	4
45–49%	1	10	11
40–44%	5	3	8
35–39%	14	12	26
30–34%	16	18	34
25–29%	6	5	11
20–24%	3		3
Under 20%		1	1
Total..............	45	53	98

SOURCE: Survey Questionnaire.

TABLE 8-6

PER CENT OF TOTAL SEMESTER HOURS REQUIRED OUTSIDE BUSINESS AND ECONOMICS BY 34 BUSINESS SCHOOLS WITH 2-2- AND 1-3-YEAR PROGRAMS, BY MEMBERSHIP IN AACSB, 1955–1956

% of semester hours required outside business and economics	Members of AACSB	Nonmembers of AACSB	Total
50% and over	1	3	4
45–49%	4	0	4
40–44%	4	1	5
35–39%	9	4	13
30–34%	3	2	5
25–29%		2	2
20–24%	1		1
Total..............	22	12	34

SOURCE: Survey Questionnaire.

Tables 8-5 and 8-6 group the schools by membership in the American Association of Collegiate Schools of Business. Somewhat surprisingly, the median percentage of work required by the four-year schools is much the same for nonmembers as for members (about 34 and 33 per cent, respectively), but it should be mentioned that fourteen of the Catholic-affiliated schools (as against eight which belong) are not in this organization. Among the 2-2- and 1-3-year schools, comparison shows little material difference between members and nonmembers either. As noted earlier, the Association's admissions standards stipulate that in order to join, a school must require students to take at least 40 per cent of their work in nonbusiness subjects. However, the definition of what may be included in the latter is slightly different from the one used here, since the association permits schools to include courses in economic principles and economic history in the nonbusiness category. Allowing for this distinction, it appears that a little under one-half of the four-year member schools did not meet the association standard at the time the Survey Questionnaire was circulated; on the other hand, only four of the 2-2- and 1-3-year schools were found to be in this category. These facts have already received considerable attention by the association, and steps are being taken to deal with the issue.[9]

Broadly speaking, the proportion of the student's time devoted to subjects outside business and economics at most undergraduate business schools appears unduly low. In more than seven out of ten cases, the schools require less than 40 per cent of the work to be taken in these subjects. Judged against the principles developed in Part 1, this proportion certainly is not enough. It is also worth noting that the great majority of faculty members and other business school spokesmen who were interviewed in the course of the survey expressed serious reservations about the way in which the student's time is allocated at present. The results of such programs in terms of specific subjects which students study are even more revealing in this regard; these findings are summarized below.

The courses which undergraduate business students take outside business and economics can be conveniently grouped into six areas: English, other humanities, science, mathematics, history, and social sciences other than economics. In the great majority of business schools, as already noted, these subjects take something less than 45 of the 120 semester credit hours typically required for graduation. The way these courses are distributed at most schools is as follows:

[9] If courses in nonacademic subjects like physical education are included, they should also be added to the 120 credit hours required for graduation; if this is done, the proportion of work in nonbusiness subjects in relation to the total would be unchanged.

	Required courses outside business and economics	*Range of semester hours required*
English and composition		9–12
Other humanities		3–6
Science		3–6
Mathematics (or business mathematics)		3–6
History (or civilization course)		6
Social science (or integrated course)		6–9
Other "arts and science" electives		3–9
Approximate total		33–54

Roughly 75 per cent of the undergraduate schools responding to the Survey Questionnaire fall within the limits indicated (see Tables 8-1 and 8-2), with a substantial majority skirting closer to the lower than the upper figures shown. In specific areas, individual schools occasionally require more, e.g., English, or less, e.g., science, than the amounts listed above.

English and the Humanities

Every institution required some work in the humanities area, but the amount varies rather considerably from school to school and subject to

TABLE 8-7

SEMESTER HOURS REQUIRED IN ENGLISH, FOREIGN LANGUAGE, AND OTHER HUMANITIES BY 98 BUSINESS SCHOOLS WITH FOUR-YEAR PROGRAMS, 1955–1956

Semester hours required	Number of schools requiring		
	English*	Foreign language†	Other humanities
3–5	—	—	13
6–8	24	4	17
9–11	16	—	4
12–14	35	6	5
15–17	17	—	1
18–20	6	—	5
21–23	—	—	2
24–26	—	—	2
27 and over	—	—	8
Total	98	10	57
% of schools requiring	100	10	58
% not requiring	0	90	42

* Literature is specified as part of the English requirement at 20 of the 98 schools.
† Other courses may be substituted for foreign language at 10 additional schools.
SOURCE: Survey Questionnaire.

subject. The requirements in English, foreign language, and other humanities are shown for the four-year schools in Table 8-7 and for the 2-2- and 1-3-year schools in Table 8-8.

TABLE 8-8

SEMESTER HOURS REQUIRED IN ENGLISH, FOREIGN LANGUAGE, AND OTHER HUMANITIES
BY 34 BUSINESS SCHOOLS WITH 2-2- AND 1-3-YEAR PROGRAMS, 1955–1956

Semester hours required	Number of schools requiring		
	English*	Foreign language	Other humanities
3–5	2	1	3
6–8	9	3	12
9–11	8	2	2
12–14	9	2	4
15 and over	3	1	—
Total..................	31	9	21
% of schools requiring.....	91	27	62
% not requiring..........	9	73	38

* Three additional schools include English as part of a required survey course. Literature is specified as part of the English requirement at 7 of the 34 schools.
SOURCE: Survey Questionnaire.

The data show that, without exception, all undergraduate business schools make work in English obligatory, with the great majority requiring students to take two or four semester courses. This clearly testifies to the importance in which work of this sort is held by business schools and by college faculties generally. However, it should be noted that at many business schools the English requirement consists wholly of work in composition; in fact, at only 27 of the 132 schools answering the Survey Questionnaire is the study of literature specified as part of the English requirement. Interviews conducted at approximately 70 of these schools indicate that in almost all cases, composition courses are hardly above a high school level of instruction.

There is no denying the importance of providing remedial training of this sort. Indeed, the criticism which employers make of college graduates (not just business students) more frequently than any other is their inability to write a clear sentence or a well-phrased report and to handle an oral presentation effectively. Similarly, there may be much merit in the remedy employers tend to recommend—old-fashioned drill courses in English grammar and speech with plenty of practice in handling both skills by every student.

This, however, is only a small part of what students heading for business careers should gain from the study of English. As developed more fully in Chaps. 5 and 6, human values play an increasingly important part in all aspects and at all levels of business affairs. Appreciation of the beauties of the best in prose and poetry, development of the critical abilities that come from intensive study of creative writing, awareness of the vision of man's aspirations as voiced by the leading literary figures of different lands and epochs—these are qualities which have relevance for conduct in business as in other aspects of life. The need in business, as elsewhere, is not so much for greater mastery of communication techniques as for a conception of the human situation that is itself worth communicating. Lacking keen sensitivity to the goals and ideals of different groups and societies as reflected in the world's literature, the administration of business affairs tends at best to be mechanical and at worst antisocial.

Having said this it must also be noted that serious difficulties stand in the way of achieving anything like an adequate teaching program either in composition or in literature at most institutions. Two difficulties deserve special mention. The first is the strong tradition of research specialization among faculty members of English departments. The surest way for a young English instructor to achieve success is to choose some narrow area or "lesser" figure (often growing out of a Ph.D. thesis interest), spend five to ten years writing up the results of his investigations and become an expert in this small sector of the field. More than this, the main interest in teaching tends to become centered on training students who expect to do this kind of highly specialized research themselves. It is impossible to say exactly how far this thinking has permeated the work of English departments at most colleges and universities, but judging from our interviews among business and liberal arts faculties, it appears to be widespread enough, particularly at larger institutions, to pose a serious problem for students in fields such as business administration.

At the great majority of the big universities we visited, most of the first-year work in literature and almost all of the work in composition were taught by graduate students or instructors who had just earned their degrees. The exceptions were certain literature courses in which senior faculty members lectured in classes ranging in size from 50 to 500. Thus, at a typical large university, upwards of 2,000 students would have to be accommodated in composition courses alone. Under the circumstances, it is hardly surprising that the bulk of the work with beginning students is left to the youngest and least experienced members of the faculty.

The other complicating factor is the relatively low interest and low aptitude level of most business students for work in English literature—

and perhaps in English composition, too. Judging from our interviews, this opinion is widely held among academic circles, although conclusive evidence to test its validity is lacking. Measures of comparative interest levels are especially hard to apply to specific subjects. The intensive studies carried on at Syracuse University under the direction of C. Robert Pace, cited in Chap. 4, indicate that male undergraduate business students tend to put "developing an understanding and enjoyment of literature" further down among the various goals which college might help students achieve than do male undergraduates in liberal arts-science, social science, or humanities, though slightly higher than male majors in applied science and forestry; a similar pattern was found with respect to the importance attached to developing an understanding and enjoyment of art and music. Of 125 Syracuse business students answering the poll, only 6 stated that college had given them much knowledge, skill, or understanding in either of these two areas.

A survey of student attitudes at another business school in the East indicated that they assigned considerable importance to the school's "fostering habits of contemplation, inquiry, reading," etc. but that performance in realizing this goal was on the whole unsatisfactory.[10] It seems plausible that the principal interests of business students would tend to preclude much incentive to pursue literary studies and the other humanities and that the general atmosphere surrounding such work is therefore likely to be unfavorable.

The data on test scores reviewed in Chap. 4 point to relatively low performance among undergraduate business students in the literature studies. To cite one example, among twenty-four groups of student majors taking Graduate Record Examination profile tests, the business majors rated third from the bottom in the literature test, ranking only above students with majors in engineering and agriculture; in the verbal factor test, the business students stood at the bottom.[11] Even under the most effective type of program, these facts indicate that many difficulties in teaching English to business students would remain.

As noted earlier, almost all business schools require work in composition and speech, often at a level not much above a good high school course. Fewer schools require students to take a course in literature appreciation and literary criticism. At most of the institutions visited in connection with the interviews, the work in both composition and literature was handled in sections by junior members of English departments whose

[10] 870 students, or 43 per cent of all undergraduates, enrolled in this school responded to the questionnaire which was circulated in the spring of 1957; this material was made available on a confidential basis.

[11] Graduate Record Office, *The Performance of Accepted Graduate Students on the Profile Tests,* 1945–47, New York, 1947, pp. 16–17. The mean of scaled scores for all groups in literature was 408 and for students with a major business, 357.

main interests lay elsewhere. Except for what the students might derive in the way of writing skills or literary insights as an incidental feature of courses in other departments, this appears to be the only exposure to the study of English which at least four-fifths of undergraduate business students experience throughout their college careers. In fact, judging from a sampling of the transcripts of every tenth senior in the class of 1957 at ten well-known business schools in different parts of the country, no more than a bare handful take any advanced work whatsoever in this area.[12] The outcome is as predictable as it is deplorable—large numbers of business students graduate with little or no familiarity with English, considered either as a basic skill or as a major area of knowledge. A college or university that is really determined to provide thorough preparation for business might well start right here.

Assuming an institution assigns a high priority to this problem, what steps might it take? Considering work in composition and speaking skills first, it does not seem practical to expect the English department to carry this work beyond the first- or second-semester level, at least within existing budgetary and staffing constraints. There is even question whether most of the work in composition and speech deserves to be counted as credit toward graduation; speech courses are especially likely to be at the subcollege level and therefore probably should not be included in the formal requirements.

The underlying need is to make the beginning course in this area something more than a perfunctory review of materials and rules which should have been mastered in high school. The course should combine analysis of ideas and training in language skills which the student develops in frequent themes and oral presentations which in turn are carefully evaluated and discussed by the instructor and other members of the class. There is no need to confine the student's attention to topics directly related to his future career or, on the other hand, to topics which are completely outside his field of interest. The students should be required to write, and perhaps to speak, on issues of both personal and general significance—they should be obliged to do some outside reading and study on whatever topics are selected, and above all they should be held to high standards of individual effort both in terms of style and content. Perhaps, as one English professor observed during an interview, any course which is centered on language as a skill is doomed to be pretty much of a failure, but one along these lines should certainly prove of some value to business students and to students with other backgrounds as well.

Beyond the beginning course, it is up to the business schools to see that students continue to improve their writing and speaking skills. This

---

[12] The total number of student transcripts sampled came to 250.

seems indicated not only on grounds of a reasonable division of labor, but also because the basic problem is to help students carry over what they learn in English courses to their field of major interest, making these skills a part of their everyday working equipment. While not precluding the use of English department staffs as circumstances permit, this means that the business schools should assume main responsibility for bringing this type of study into their own programs. Each school, of course, will have to meet this important need in its own way, but some examples will serve to illustrate the possibilities and the difficulties that are involved.

The institution which has gone further in this direction than any other is the Harvard Business School. While exclusively graduate, its work in this regard is directly applicable to all business schools and therefore deserves attention. According to Melvin Copeland's history, the need for this type of preparation was recognized from the start, but it was not until employers voiced widespread criticism that a really serious program was undertaken. Under a system begun in 1914 and broadened considerably in the early twenties, instructors assigned written reports to students in the first-year courses as a regular part of their work, usually in connection with the student's analysis of cases. In addition to customary evaluation on the basis of content, these reports were turned over to a staff of "women graders" who marked the reports on the basis of grammar and style; at the present time, students may be asked to rewrite reports, and if they are still below standard, the grade is reduced one level. Finally, training in written expression was given a definite place in the curriculum, with Written Analysis of Cases a required two-credit course for every first-year student, supplementing the practice in written work normally assigned in other first- and second-year courses.[13]

The business school at the University of California at Berkeley has also placed considerable emphasis on this part of the student's preparation, in this instance at the undergraduate level. Students taking one of the required courses (Business Economics) are assigned to one of four teaching assistants who read and evaluate all written work, including examinations, and consult with students individually about their style, organization of material, and general mode of expression. At present the four teaching assistants are English Ph.D. candidates who are on the business school staff on a part-time basis. After some experience, it was decided that the work in composition would not be for credit but could reduce the course grade by one letter if the student does not cooperate with the teaching assistant and if his style of writing does not improve. A student may spend on the average about fifteen minutes a week in con-

[13] Melvin T. Copeland, *And Mark an Era*, Little, Brown & Company, Boston, 1958, Chap. 11.

ference with the teaching assistant; under this system, no additional time is involved on the part of the regular course instructor.

The School of Commerce at New York University has gone a considerable way toward making the study of writing and speech a required part of each year's work and relating it as closely as possible to analytical issues, not to matters of technique alone. The first-year course, Fundamentals of Effective English, exposes the student to a wide range of readings bearing directly or indirectly on business problems at the same time that it provides intensive training in writing skills. In the second-year course, also required of everyone, the student is obliged to relate his work in written expression to various aspects of business administration, including reports on a number of case situations; also in his second year, every student is required to take a survey course, Great Western Literary Heritage. In each of the last two years it is contemplated that report writing will be made an important part of a required course such as Business Policy, in which case reports are widely used. Ultimately, it is hoped that an adequate staff can be developed to supervise the student's work in writing over his entire four years. Rather special problems arise in an institution such as New York University where the business school has traditionally maintained its own staff in fields such as this, but its determination to put training in writing on a continuing and demanding basis is noteworthy.

These illustrations of the approaches of three rather different schools indicate that there is no panacea for dealing with the problem of inadequate writing skills among business students; indeed, all three schools would promptly concede that they have no short-cut formula to offer and that little improvement can be expected unless such work is made a part of almost all courses. The value of these examples is in showing how work of this sort can be tied in with a school's regular program, a step that is essential to making language skills a part of the student's working equipment.

Whether further steps should be taken to increase the proportion of the business student's time now devoted to the study of English as literature is more debatable and can best be considered in connection with the work in the humanities as a whole. As a preliminary to that broader discussion, only a few observations need be made here. First, on balance it seems advisable to keep the work in literature in the hands of the English faculty; similarly, the content of the courses, the standards applied, and the methods of instruction should generally be the same for business students as for all other groups of students. Some gains would, of course, be derived from specially designed courses in terms of greater student interest, but the quality of the work would almost certainly suffer. This comment applies particularly to "integrated" courses which endeavor to link the work in English, history, and social movements together for the benefit of business students or try to tie the study of literature more closely to business situations and problems. In the hands of extraordinarily gifted teachers who are prepared to give great amounts of time to this kind of instruction, such courses can be wholly successful, but in most cases they lack any enduring substance.

Second, a year's course in English literature is hardly enough, except under the most unusual circumstances, to give students a real grasp of the values which can be derived from literary studies. The background, interests, and abilities of business students are only a part of the reason for this. Nor can the unsatisfactory outcome be laid wholly to the English faculty's distaste for teaching literature at the elementary level to nonmajors. Basically, it is a result of trying to apply mass education methods to a subject in which they are peculiarly inappropriate. Very occasionally, a gifted lecturer can hold the attention of a large class without frequent resort to charlatanism and trickery, but such lecturers stand out only because of their extreme rarity. Barring a major upheaval in the beginning course work, the only hope seems to be to get more business students to take work in literature beyond the first-year level. By this means, at least a few might get far enough into the material to make it really come alive.

Third, from the viewpoint of nonmajor students, such as business students, English literature is not the only route to the study of the humanities. As noted below, the way should be left open for students with the necessary background, ability, and interest to do serious work in foreign literature, fine arts, music, philosophy, or religion; this would allow in some measure for differences in student aptitudes and in faculty quality or "appeal" in different schools, while giving all students more than a perfunctory exposure to the humanities.

These observations underscore the need for assigning a higher priority, qualitatively speaking, to work in English composition and literature than is true at most schools of business at the present time. Particular circumstances at a given institution may call for special treatment, but in general there is need for putting more of the "best" faculty's time and effort into the foundation humanities courses. Too often the beginning course is treated as a stepchild to be taught by inexperienced instructors as an unpleasant chore. Too often the nonspecialist student is unable to find suitable courses midway between the introductory and very advanced levels of instruction. It is up to the business schools and the various professional schools to push the case for the general, nonmajor student, but it remains for the English and other humanities faculties to see that the needs of these students are more fully met. Efforts along these lines, which have already received considerable attention, deserve vigorous support.

Foreign Languages and Other Humanities

A striking feature of most undergraduate business programs is the paucity of work which students take, on either a required or elective basis, in such fields as the foreign languages, philosophy, or fine arts. Referring to Tables 8-7 and 8-8 above, only 19 of the 132 schools answering the Survey Questionnaire required any foreign language work. About three-fifths of the schools required some study in one of the other humanities, of which about half stipulated three semester courses or less. Judging from the ten-school sampling of student transcripts referred to earlier, most of the courses taken in these areas consist of beginning instruction in French or Spanish and an introductory course in either one or two of the following: philosophy, religion, and art history. It is a very rare business student who carries his interest in any of these subjects beyond the bare beginning level.

The flight away from the humanities is a reflection of widely prevailing attitudes among both students and other groups which are unlikely to change in the foreseeable future. The business student, perhaps because of an unsatisfactory high school experience or simply because of unfamiliarity with what these subjects involve, resists taking work in these areas even more than in English. Employers, possibly for much the same reasons, appear not to rate work in these particular branches of the humanities very highly either. Nor do these subjects enjoy the same prestige on many campuses as some of those taught by big departments, a fact which unfortunately can be crucial when the infighting becomes bitter. A fuller analysis would call for detailed examination of college admissions standards, the work in secondary schools, and many broad cultural and institutional influences which cannot be undertaken here. The overall result, however, is clear—at most institutions no strong voices are raised for intensive study by all students in these areas, and if some work has to be cut out, which sometimes seems inescapable, these are the first areas to feel the knife.

Before the leaders of our business schools and universities turn their backs completely on these branches of educational preparation for business, it would be well for them to spend a few hours, as has been done in connection with this investigation—and at length—comparing the detailed outlines of courses in these subjects with those offered in traditional business areas. On the face of it, courses in advertising, insurance, or real estate seem more germane to preparing for careers in business than courses in Proust and Gide, Renaissance painters, or modern philosophy, but a step-by-step review of what the two groups of courses at most institutions actually contain might well lead to a different conclusion.

Often the issue comes down to this: should a student be required to take a sixth course in a subject like marketing instead of a basic course in logic, or will a fifth course in finance be more valuable either in personal or career terms than a course in German literature? Business courses at their best can match any work taken in liberal arts, but the latter subjects cover a far wider and more diversified terrain, so the chances of the students opening up wholly new vistas of learning are correspondingly greater. The contrast becomes doubly sharp when the business course is taken on top of many others in the same functional area.

Of all the subjects in the undergraduate curriculum, foreign languages present the most baffling range of issues. The great majority of students entering business schools are unable to pass a reasonably difficult reading knowledge examination in any foreign language, so where this is a graduation requirement, business students must take at least a one-year grammar course in a foreign language after entering college. There are good grounds for arguing that if this is all their work in foreign languages amounts to, their time could better be spent elsewhere and that therefore the requirement should either be abolished or the work developed to a point where more students would be able to study a foreign language as literature, not as grammar.

Again, this raises a question about the type of work being done at the secondary school level—as long as students coming to college have only the barest training in foreign languages, the problem seems insoluble. On the other hand, the view is widely held that familiarity with a foreign language should be part of the equipment of every educated person, so this would hardly be an appropriate time for the business schools to accelerate the drift away from such work. If the business schools, along with colleges generally, remove all foreign language requirements, the secondary schools can hardly be expected to strengthen their programs in this area. Nor is it sound educational policy for the business schools to ask for special treatment in this regard. On a number of campuses, students seek admission to business schools in part because they require no foreign language proficiency, hardly a suitable basis for choosing one's course of study. The needs of business students in the foreign language area are essentially no different from those of students in other fields—the amount of work, if any, which should be required in foreign languages is a college-wide problem and should be approached accordingly. Translated into specific terms, this means that the same standards which a college or university applies to undergraduates generally in the humanities field should apply to business students as well.

The interview reports did not reveal the same degree of dissatisfaction with teaching methods in these areas as in the case of English, perhaps because they involve subjects with which business faculties and students have had little direct contact. One factor is very much in favor of those who feel that business students should take more work in languages and the other humanities—the faculty members handling these courses are typically less overwhelmed with students than, say, the English or other departments. The possibility of devising courses which are beyond the grammar or elementary level, but are not extremely specialized, is accordingly likelier. It would be heretical, for example, to suggest that more foreign literature courses should be offered in English translation, but on a number of campuses, work of this nature has proved both solid and stimulating.

The conclusion suggested by the foregoing is that the present status of the foreign language requirement at most institutions is thoroughly unsatisfactory from the viewpoint of business education and that steps should be taken to require, as a condition for graduation, ability to read the literature of at least one foreign language with proficiency. If, on the other hand, an institution is not prepared to establish this standard on a campus-wide basis, the foreign language requirement should be eliminated altogether for business students and perhaps for others as well. The time seems long past for perpetuating the kind of curricular window dressing in this area that is found on most campuses today.

There are branches of philosophy, such as ethics, social philosophy, and aesthetics, the study of which would also serve business students in good stead since such courses can do much to develop a student's capacity for critical insight and appreciation of human values. The same can be said of certain courses in art history, music appreciation, and the like if sufficient effort and imagination go into their planning and teaching. In developing this part of the business program, the particular subject studied is less important than the level within a given area which is reached. A foreign language, seriously pursued, can satisfy many of the needs met by work in English. Philosophy, art, and music, as well as literature, can give breadth and dimension to the student's studies. There is value in permitting students as much flexibility and scope as possible in the choice of such courses, as long as he pushes his interest in this broad area of knowledge far enough to appreciate its significance and gain some grasp of its underlying meanings. In practical terms, this would require a student to take one or two semester courses in one branch of the humanities beyond the introductory level. A semester's course in composition on a demanding enough level to warrant college credit, a year's course in English literature, and a year's course in one of the other areas of the humanities (either a foreign language or philosophy, etc.) would provide reasonably adequate preparation for taking one or two advanced courses in one of these subjects. On top of the five basic courses, this additional work would bring the total to six or seven semester courses, but the advanced electives could well prove more valuable than all the rest of the work combined in helping the student make his study of the humanities a vital part of his experience. Given sufficient cooperation and imagination on the part of both the business and humanities faculties, greater emphasis on this area should raise the general level of business education materially.

Mathematics and Natural Science

The increasingly important role of technology in modern industry, as shown in Chap. 5 of this investigation, is directing considerable attention to the mathematics, science, and engineering aspects of business school programs. The traditional area of the curriculum in which work of this sort has been largely concentrated is factory production management, but it is now assuming greater prominence in such areas as marketing, finance, and general management. Looking to the future, it seems clear that these subjects will command still greater attention.

The chief difficulty posed by this development is that the great majority of undergraduate business school students (and undergraduates in most other fields as well) are not equipped to go very far in the mathematics-science area, and yet to limit their work to one or two introductory courses will hardly meet their needs. One thing that is perfectly clear is that a student who wants to gain enough competence in mathematics and/or the sciences to be able to use his knowledge with facility and confidence later in his business career should go to an undergraduate liberal arts or engineering school, not to a business school. Moreover, the further the mathematics-science trend in business education is carried, the stronger the case becomes for limiting academic preparation for business to the graduate level. The principal reason for this is that a student cannot hope to get an adequate foundation in these subjects without devoting several years to studying them, and if he does not lay such a foundation as an undergraduate, the chances of his ever doing so are slim.

At the same time, many students who have neither the interest nor the ability to achieve this degree of competence could at least take enough work in mathematics and science to grasp some of the more important implications of these subjects for business policy and to appreciate the different kinds of contributions which experts in these fields can make to a business enterprise. Employers in a position to have an informed judgment on this matter stress the need for giving students a framework for conceptualizing mathematically and for grasping quantitative, statistical relationships. Next to their weakness in written expression, employers appear more critical of college students' preparation in mathematics and statistics than in any other area. This squares with the general findings reached in Part 1 of the present study. If business schools made sure that their students had a reasonably good working knowledge of calculus or its equivalent, there is little question but that their graduates would have an advantage over those with more general preparation in many lines of endeavor.

By contrast, the amount and quality of work which undergraduate business schools require in this area seems woefully weak. The facts on prevailing practice at the ninety-eight and thirty-four reporting schools with 4-year, 2-2-year and 1-3-year programs, respectively, are summarized in Table 8-9. The data show that about one-third of the reporting schools

TABLE 8-9

SEMESTER HOURS REQUIRED IN MATHEMATICS AND NATURAL SCIENCE BY 98 BUSINESS SCHOOLS WITH FOUR-YEAR PROGRAMS AND 34 BUSINESS SCHOOLS WITH 2-2-YEAR AND 1-3-YEAR PROGRAMS, 1955–1956

Semester hours required	No. of 4-year schools requiring		No. of 2-2-year and 1-3-year schools requiring	
	Mathematics	Natural science	Mathematics	Natural science
1–2	—	1	—	—
3–5	20	8	15	3
6–8	36	42	13	15
9–11	7	6	2	3
12 and over	—	9	—	5
Total......................	63	66	30	26
% of schools requiring.......	64	67	88	77
% not requiring............	36	33	12	23

SOURCE: Survey Questionnaire.

with 4-year programs require no work in either mathematics or natural science, with a somewhat larger group requiring one semester or less in either field. The schools with 2-2-year and 1-3-year programs have their students do more work in these subjects, with nearly 90 per cent stipulating a semester or more in mathematics, and over three-fourths a semester

or more in natural science. In both groups, the number of schools requiring more than an introductory or basic year course in either area
is negligible.

Reports based on interviews at individual schools raise serious questions about the general quality of these basic courses, especially in
mathematics. In a substantial portion of the cases, work in the latter area
is confined to business mathematics or mathematics of finance. Courses
of the first type are typically designed for students with one year of high
school algebra and are usually aimed at explaining how to handle relatively simple calculations used in everyday business dealings—operating
ratios, proportions, percentages, logarithms, and the like. Courses in the
mathematics of finance, for which the sole prerequisite is usually the
course in business mathematics, tend to be constructed along similar
lines, with principal attention being given to the figuring of compound
interest, installment payments, valuation of bonds, depreciation, amor-
tization sinking funds, and elementary probability calculations relating
to pension plans and insurance reserves.[14] In none of the interviews was
the opinion expressed that this type of instruction met the needs of
students in this area, although some felt, given the limited faculty resources and poor secondary school preparation of most of the students,
that this was all that could be done. Several business school spokesmen
took strong exception to the latter view, arguing that all too frequently
courses of this sort could be passed with a modicum of effort, even by the
more indifferent students. Compared to the work required in statistics,
economics, or some of the functional business areas, these spokesmen
considered the mathematics courses to be distinctly weak.

The sampling of the course programs of every tenth senior at ten well-
known business schools, referred to above, revealed many instances in
which business students took no mathematics at all. Of those who did,
hardly any went beyond an elementary level equivalent to a solid, third-
year high school course. In fact, of the 250 course programs examined,
only six students took work as advanced as calculus, and of these, three
were enrolled in a combined engineering-business program. Whether
some kind of advanced mathematics should be required of all undergraduate business students is perhaps debatable, but that only a bare
handful of graduates from a number of the country's leading schools took
any serious work in this area seems indefensible from almost any point
of view.

In considerable measure, the type of mathematics that can reasonably
be required of business students will depend on the entrance require-

[14] These topics were taken from descriptions of these two courses secured during
interviews at a large number of schools.

ments of the particular school or university. In Chap. 4, it was indicated that three years of high school work in algebra, geometry, and trigonometry should be the minimum required, and this amount of preparation is assumed in the following discussion. Judging from reports from some of the schools which have gone furthest in this direction (University of California at both Berkeley and Los Angeles, Tulane, Carnegie Tech., and M.I.T.), a school faces one, or some combination, of two choices—require either a year or two of traditional college mathematics through an introduction to the calculus, or a year or two of specially designed courses which would give business and perhaps other social science students a grasp of mathematical principles particularly relevant to their field of interest.

The rationale of the first approach is that at this stage in the development of business education, the principal need of students is to gain a clear understanding of underlying mathematical principles, and specially designed courses almost inevitably involve short cuts or a general watering-down of the material. The second approach rests on the assumption that traditional college mathematics courses cover many topics far removed from possible use in a business setting, with the result that the student never gets to the work which would be of most help to him. Some of the basic subjects in mathematics of particular relevance to analysis of business problems are probability theory, vectors, determinants, matrices, difference, and differential equations. Finite mathematics includes a number of topics of general applicability to business decisions, and it is likely that a semester or year course which gives fundamental grounding in this area would be the best practical solution. While a full year's course in calculus would hardly be necessary to understanding the work in finite mathematics, a semester's course would seem to be an absolute minimum, in which case the next semester could center on finite mathematics.

At the present time, there is room for considerable experimentation along the lines indicated by these two schools of thought. Mixed reports have thus far been received on the finite mathematics courses, but further efforts to design special programs of mathematical study for business and other social science students deserve support. Except for schools of technology, Tulane University has apparently gone further than any other business school in pushing work in this area. At present it requires a two-semester freshman course, the first in calculus and analytical geometry and the second in finite mathematics; in addition, it plans to require another year course covering selected aspects of advanced calculus, matrix algebra, and probability analysis. Without attempting to pass on the detailed features of the Tulane experiment, its underlying purpose and general design are to be applauded. As already noted, a number of other schools are also taking vigorous steps in this same direction.

Despite the risks involved, a specially designed sequence of mathematics courses appears to hold great promise for business and other students in the social sciences. Some rather far-reaching changes are beginning to occur in secondary school teaching of mathematics; in addition to the more traditional work in intermediate algebra, geometry, and trigonometry, high schools may begin to introduce third- and fourth-year students to functions, probability theory, and statistical inference.[15] Business schools should build on these recent and prospective developments as much as possible by requiring a year's work in topics having special relevance to the social sciences; some of these topics might be sets and functions, polynomials and rational functions, exponents, trigonometric functions, and introduction to certain aspects of the calculus. It would be essential to make use of this preparation in the various business subjects—production and finance particularly; otherwise it would be quickly forgotten.[16] A semester's work in finite mathematics beyond the course outlined above would help toward this end. Students wanting more advanced preparation in linear programming, theory of games, systems analysis, and the like should be encouraged to take it, but at the undergraduate level it would probably be advisable to limit the major in this area to statistics.

In establishing a minimum requirement in mathematics, there is no denying that, even if business schools limited admissions to students with three years of high school preparation, the vast majority could not go immediately into a course in calculus. This means that they would have to take a college-level course covering algebra, trigonometry, and geometry first; students who have had four years of high school mathematics could presumably start immediately with calculus.

Perhaps because of the complexity of the materials, business schools have made few efforts to relate studies in natural science or engineering to their programs. This does not hold for institutes of technology and, as shown in Chap. 19, a number of engineering schools, either on their own or in conjunction with business schools, have developed rather broad programs in industrial administration. The initiative in almost all cases,

[15] See, for example, the recommendations of the Commission on Mathematics of the College Entrance Examination Board; these proposals are reviewed briefly in "Teaching Math in the Twentieth Century," *The Carnegie Corporation of New York Quarterly*, April, 1958.

[16] This follows the general approach being developed by the School of Business at Indiana University, though the work is being required of only a few majors at this institution at present. See, for example, Committee on Mathematical Training of Social Scientists of the Social Science Research Council, *SSRC Items*, June, 1955.

however, has come from the engineering schools, and the resulting programs have had more significance for their students than for the business students. Despite the serious difficulties involved, the time has come for similar efforts to be made for the benefit of students in business schools.

Table 8-9 summarizes the science requirements applicable to business students. Under present arrangements, at about one-third of the undergraduate schools with 4-year programs and about one-quarter of the 2-2-year and 1-3-year schools, no work of any sort is required in the sciences; in all but a small fraction of the remainder, no more than a basic year's work is stipulated. In the sampling of student programs at ten of the better-known business schools, it was found that the great majority of the students took a one-year course in a variety of fields, the most popular being geology, geography and, less frequently, astronomy. At a number of institutions, the work consisted of an interdepartmental course which integrated materials from several areas. Except for three students in joint business-engineering programs, none included in the ten-school sample took any courses in engineering. These facts lend strong support to the individual school interview findings that at most institutions the work which business students do in the sciences tends to be perfunctory and quite unrelated to the rest of their programs.

The inability to make science a meaningful subject of study is just as much of a problem for other nonscience students as for business students, and the issue is receiving increasing attention at many institutions. As in the case of mathematics, various approaches and experiments seem worth trying since the difficulties to be overcome are indeed formidable. One device that has been attempted at a number of institutions is to require nonscience students to take an integrated, interdepartmental science course. This approach has much to recommend it, chiefly as a means of getting away from excessive compartmentalization of subject matter, but frequently this means giving up all laboratory work, an essential part of beginning work in this field. An even more serious difficulty with integrated courses of this sort is that at present most science departments do not permit such courses to serve as a basis for advanced work. From the viewpoint of at least some business students, this is a serious weakness, since a single, composite-type course is likely to have little carry-over value into their main field of interest. As in other areas, such a transfer is more likely to occur if students carry their studies in at least one science beyond the elementary level, and every opportunity should be given for them to do so. If a year's work in mathematics and another in a laboratory science are required, it would be desirable to require one or two additional semesters in either of these areas, depending on the student's interests and career plans.

Social Sciences Other Than Economics

Traditionally, academic preparation for business careers has been considered an aspect of the study of economics. Even today, economic principles provide the main theoretical framework of this field, so much so that it is best to treat the two subjects together. In recent years, however, the other social sciences have come very much to the fore in the business studies. As brought out in Part 1, business processes and policies are coming to be increasingly interwoven with broad social tendencies in which historical, political, and human behavior influences are no less important than more strictly economic factors. The findings reached in Part 1 indicate further that these social and behavioral influences reach to all levels of management and professional staff responsibility, although they of course have their greatest impact at upper-management and staff levels. In today's, and probably even more in tomorrow's, world considerable familiarity with the work of social scientists would seem essential to anyone who is engaged in the serious study of business problems.

Tables 8-10 and 8-11 summarize present requirements in these areas

TABLE 8-10

SEMESTER HOURS REQUIRED IN SOCIAL SCIENCES OTHER THAN ECONOMICS
BY 98 BUSINESS SCHOOLS WITH FOUR-YEAR PROGRAMS, 1955–1956

Semester hours required	Number of schools requiring			
	History	Political science	Psychology	Other social science
1–2	—	1	1	1
3–5	12	24	20	14
6–8	35	19	12	28
9–11	3	—	—	10
12 and over	4	—	—	10
Total..................	54	44	33	63
% of schools requiring.......	55	45	34	64
% not requiring...........	45	55	66	36

SOURCE: Survey Questionnaire.

among the 4-year schools and the 2-2- and 1-3-year group of schools, respectively. Outside of economics, history is made a requirement at more undergraduate schools than any other social science subject, with a two-semester survey of European history being fairly typical. Political

TABLE 8-11

SEMESTER HOURS REQUIRED IN SOCIAL SCIENCES OTHER THAN ECONOMICS
BY 34 BUSINESS SCHOOLS WITH 2-2- AND 1-3-YEAR PROGRAMS, 1955–1956

Semester hours required	Number of schools requiring			
	History	Political science	Psychology	Other social science
1–2	—	—	—	—
3–5	7	7	3	3
6–8	11	2	1	9
9 and over	—	—	—	5
Total......................	18	9	4	17
% of schools requiring........	53	27	12	50
% not requiring............	47	73	88	50

SOURCE: Survey Questionnaire.

science is less emphasized and psychology still less so. Of the other social
sciences, sociology is the chief subject included as a requirement. With
the possible exception of history, the amount of work business students
are required to do in these areas seems unduly limited. Even with respect
to history, nearly half the schools do not require any work at all, and the
number of students who are required to go beyond the introductory level
is negligible. On the other hand, at some schools business students occasionally elect to take as many as three or four courses in one of these
subjects. For example, at three of the ten institutions at which a sampling
of individual transcripts was made, a few students took as many as three
courses in history, political science, or psychology. The prevailing pattern,
however, is to keep this type of work to a bare minimum, with economics
serving as the major area of study in the social sciences.

While the general case for building up the social science branch of
the business studies seems strong, a number of approaches deserve consideration. A principal objective of this part of the work is for business
students to go far enough in the social sciences to be able to use the skills
and methods of at least one of these disciplines under a variety of circumstances and to sense when and how a given specialty can be fitted
into the complex patterns of actual business situations. To achieve this
objective it would seem necessary to require at least six semesters of study
(two in history, two in political science, and two in psychology-sociology) plus one or two more semester courses at an advanced level in an
area of the student's own choice.

The increasing emphasis which is being placed on psychology and sociology by modern management would make it highly desirable for students to lay a foundation in this area (sometimes referred to as the "behavioral sciences"), and therefore a year of required study in either of these subjects, or one semester of each, seems particularly appropriate. The purpose of the limited-choice social science elective would be to help students carry their work beyond the elementary level in at least one of these areas, thus increasing the likelihood that it will become a meaningful part of their intellectual equipment. A course in social psychology or industrial sociology might well serve this purpose. As in the humanities and mathematics-sciences, there is certainly room for flexibility and experimentation among institutions in their efforts to strengthen this part of their programs, both in the content of individual courses and in the way they are taught.

The interviews at individual schools yielded fewer criticisms among business school faculties about the quality and general direction of the work in social science courses than in either the humanities or sciences. A more frequently expressed complaint came from the social scientists themselves, that "business hardly ever sends any of its students over here." Doubtless, this opinion would be less often heard if the beginning courses were designed for nonmajors and if attention were given to implications for business policy, but there appears to be even greater need in these areas than in the humanities and sciences for intermediate courses which would have somewhat more relevance to the business student's interest. Every branch of the social sciences contains a wealth of ideas and materials which are germane to the problems business administrators will face in the course of their careers, but the number of departments of history, political science, psychology, and sociology which offer courses touching on such problems is disturbingly small. The contributions which psychologists and sociologists can make to a fuller understanding of management problems is especially great, and lack of any serious work by business students in these two subjects seems particularly deplorable.

A number of business schools are becoming increasingly aware of the importance of these social science subjects for their own programs, chiefly in connection with graduate courses. At the latter level there is perhaps room for both the business schools and the social science departments to offer work in closely related areas, but at the undergraduate level, emphasis needs to be kept on training in fundamental principles; accordingly, it seems less appropriate for the business schools to offer such work on their own. In discussing the work which business students should be required to take in English literature, the conclusion was reached that the instruction should be left in the hands of the departments involved. The same conclusion is quite as applicable to all the other nonbusiness subjects which business students may be asked to study. At the same time, this puts a heavy obligation on the various liberal arts departments to make sure that at least some of the special interests of business students are met.

PROPORTION OF NONBUSINESS COURSES

If the main findings of the foregoing discussion are accepted, the proportion of undergraduate work outside business and economics at most schools would be raised materially. It will be remembered that at present over 70 per cent of the 132 schools answering the Survey Questionnaire require less than 40 per cent of the student's four years to be taken in these subjects. The suggested program developed above would increase this to between 50 and 55 per cent of the 120 credit hours in academic subjects normally required for graduation.

Whether programs along these general lines would leave adequate scope for work in business and economics is discussed in the next chapter. It goes without saying that the suggestions are to be regarded as no more than rough guides to some of the principal issues confronting business schools; as emphasized earlier in the discussion, room should be left for variation (and disagreement!) at many points. The important consideration is the broad purpose and direction of the recommendations. If the business and liberal arts faculties are not prepared to accept the general educational objectives implicit in these recommendations, no changes of a formal nature in the curriculum will have any lasting significance. On the side of the business faculties, this means giving more explicit attention to the contributions which humanists, scientists, and social scientists can make to the solution of business problems. On the side of the liberal arts faculties, it means greater awareness of the dangers of excessive specialism in their own province and more willingness to adapt their work to the needs of the general student. There are doubtless numerous paths leading toward this common end.

CHAPTER 9

UNDERGRADUATE BUSINESS STUDIES

There is considerable evidence that the business curriculum has expanded beyond justifiable limits at most undergraduate business schools. There is need for a general tightening of standards in terms of the scope of the core studies, the variety of majors, the number of courses that can be taken in a major, and the kind of electives students can choose. If students were obliged to concentrate on basic aspects of the business subjects, the way would be cleared for them to devote more attention to certain subjects in the liberal arts area.

Unlike the courses discussed in the last chapter, the student's work in business and economics is largely a matter for the business schools to handle as they choose.[1] Subject to budgetary limitations and, in a more general sense, to presidential participation in faculty appointments and promotions, the schools are for the most part free to change majors, add or eliminate courses, and tighten or loosen requirements in the business-economics part of the program. On occasion, a proposed change may clearly raise the issue of a duplication of offerings, and the university's top administration may then be drawn into the matter, but usually such issues are sufficiently blurred to avoid presidential intervention. As long as no direct duplication is involved, business schools, like other instructional units, are largely free to work out their own destinies.

An analogous relation exists between a business school and its own departments although there is considerably greater variation in practice. In some institutions the departments have a great deal of latitude in developing courses as they see fit, but in others, rather close control is exercised. The budget, however, puts a pretty effective check on the individual department in many situations. For example, any revision of a department's offerings is likely to involve additions to staff, thus involv-

[1] Where economics is in the liberal arts school, this, of course, would only be true of the business subjects. Since the work in economics and business is closely interwoven in many institutions, they are dealt with together in this discussion.

ing the dean in a very direct way. Hirings and promotions are inextricably linked to the way programs are developed, and in these matters, the dean's voice is important, if not decisive. Where issues of hiring, promotion, and the budget are not involved, the chief influences determining departmental latitude appear to be, roughly in the order named: the personality, leadership, and educational philosophy of the dean, departmental relations or rivalries, size and diversity of student body, and a school's historical tradition or main line of development. The last influence can be all-important where a strong, well-defined tradition, such as preparation for upper management, has been built up. More often no such dominant tradition exists, a school's historic role being itself somewhat amorphous and subject to change.

The relations between a school and its departments are brought into sharp focus in determining how much of the business-economics curriculum should be uniform for all students, how much required by different majors, and how much left to the student's own choice. Thus, each school confronts the same issue which a university must deal with at a different level: what should be (1) the common core required of all students, (2) the requirements of the special areas, and (3) the freely chosen electives. At both the business school and university level, the answers to these three questions go a long way toward determining the general character of an institution's program.

In summarizing existing practice among undergraduate business schools with respect to these three questions, the over-all relation between the business-economics studies and nonbusiness studies needs to be kept in mind. In the last chapter it was found that the great majority of schools require less than 40 per cent of the student's time in academic subjects be taken outside the business and economics areas and that even if additional nonbusiness electives are included, the actual programs followed by students should not depart widely from this general pattern. This means that at most schools more than 60 per cent of the student's four years is devoted to business and economics studies. If the general conclusions reached in the preceding chapter are accepted, the percentage devoted to business and economics subjects would come to only about 45 or 50 per cent of the total. Whether this reduction in the proportion of the work devoted to these subjects is desirable or even tolerable is examined in this chapter.

TYPES OF BUSINESS-ECONOMICS PROGRAMS

In line with the earlier comparisons of courses taken in the nonbusiness areas, the business-economics programs tend to exhibit three general patterns. One important group of schools requires all students to study a long list of such subjects and in addition stipulates about the same number of courses in the student's major. Typical of this group are the core requirements found at a well-known Midwest business school; referring to courses carrying two credits or more, these requirements are:

	Semester hours required
Introduction to Business	3
Modern Economic Society	3
Elementary and Intermediate Accounting	10
Principles of Economics	6
Business Law	2
Corporation Finance and Money and Banking	6
Elementary Statistics	3
Marketing	3
Outlines of Public Finance	3
Principles of Insurance	2
Principles of Management	2
Problems of Labor	2
Total core requirements	45

Beyond the core, a student must take a substantial number of courses in whatever major he chooses in his last two years. For example, an advertising major must take the following:

	Semester hours
Business Communications	2
Industrial Organization and Management	2
Marketing Research	2
Retailing	3
Wholesaling	3
Sales Management	3
Principles of Advertising	3
Advertising Copy and Layout	2
Broadcast Advertising Media	2
Retail Sales Promotion	3
Total major requirements	25

Since 117 semester credit hours (exclusive of required courses in air science and physical education) are needed for graduation, an advertising major at this institution must take about 60 per cent of his four years in the business-economics area. One or two of the majors require slightly less than this but most, substantially more. The number of electives which a business student can choose during his four years is negligible or nonexistent.

Another, though considerably smaller, group of schools requires substantially less work in business and economics subjects, some putting the minimum as low as 40 per cent of the student's four years. Typical of this group is the core program found at the School of Business at the University of Colorado which consists of the following:

	Semester hours required
Introduction to Business Statistics	3
Accounting Principles and Procedures	6
Principles of Economics	6
Business Law	6
Business Finance	6
Principles of Management	3
Personnel Management and Labor Relations	3
Principles of Marketing	3
Total core requirements	36

Students can choose among nine majors which typically specify that eighteen credit hours must be taken in each, of which three or four are chosen on an elective basis. This means that slightly over 40 per cent of the student's four years must be in business and economics subjects, since 120 semester credits exclusive of physical education and military training are necessary for graduation.

Still a third group of schools requires somewhat over 50 per cent of the student's academic work to be in these subjects, about midway between the two examples just cited. In addition to the core courses found at the University of Colorado, the schools in this middle group typically require an additional semester course in marketing, either a semester in production or an additional semester in management, and either a semester in one of the more specialized fields, like insurance, transportation, real estate, or utilities, or an additional semester in economics. Students must also take two or three courses to satisfy their major requirements and may elect as many more, bringing the total amount of work in business and economics to about 50 per cent of the student's four years.

The standards for membership in the American Association of Collegiate Schools of Business permit schools considerable latitude in deciding how much of the student's four years should be confined to business-economics subjects and in what ways this time should be allocated between a universally required core program and courses taken in a particular major. Standard 3 provides:

At least forty per cent of the total hours required for the bachelor's degree must be taken in business and economics subjects; the major portion of the courses in this group shall be in business administration.

Standard 4 reads:[2]

[2] Both excerpts are from the "Standards for Membership in the Association," as amended Apr. 27, 1957.

As the foundation for training in business administration, instruction shall be offered in the fields of economics, accounting, statistics, business law, finance, marketing, and management. (Management is here used to denote Industrial or Production Management, or an integrating course in organization and management or a business policy course. Finance is used as a generic term to describe courses in Money and Banking, Business Finance and Investments.) In general, candidates for the undergraduate degree shall receive basic instruction in each of these fields. Opportunities beyond the basic course shall be available in at least three of the above fields. However, a proliferation of courses which might serve to diminish the effectiveness of the staff in meeting its obligations toward fundamental areas of training is not to be encouraged.

The latter provision lists the seven specific areas which the business schools' official body considers most important in preparing students for business careers. However, as the statement enclosed in parenthesis suggests, the schools are given considerable leeway in deciding how each of the core subjects should be approached. Moreover, there is ample latitude for schools to add core requirements of their own choice on top of those set forth in the association's standards, and very broad limits are imposed on the extent to which students can specialize in a given major area.

Judging from the replies to the Survey Questionnaire, business schools differ widely in the number of courses they include as core requirements, with the highest reporting twenty-six, and the lowest, five (expressed in 3-semester credit units). The answers for the responding undergraduate schools with 4-year programs, as well as for schools with 2-2- and 1-3-year programs, are summarized in Table 9-1. The median number of core

TABLE 9-1

SEMESTER HOURS REQUIRED IN BUSINESS AND ECONOMICS BY 98
BUSINESS SCHOOLS WITH FOUR-YEAR PROGRAMS AND 34 BUSINESS
SCHOOLS WITH 2-2- AND 1-3-YEAR PROGRAMS, 1955–1956

Semester hours required in business and economics	Number of 4-year schools	Number of 2-2- and 1-3-year schools
Under 30	8	6
30–35	17	11
36–41	22	10
42–47	21	3
48–53	22	4
Over 54	8	—
Total................	98	34

SOURCE: Survey Questionnaire.

courses among the first group of schools comes to 42 semester hours (35 per cent of the total) and among the second, to 36 hours (30 per cent of the total). While a complete appraisal would entail examining each individual core course, it is difficult to believe that some reduction in the number would cost much in terms of essential educational preparation. If the alternative were simply to add routine or highly specialized courses in either business or nonbusiness subjects, more might well be lost than gained, but the preceding chapter indicated a number of areas outside traditional business subjects which would add considerable strength to the required studies.

A related question concerns the number of majors which a school should offer and the extent to which students should be permitted to specialize in any one area. Again, a full discussion would require examination of each major, but rather obvious dangers are run when the subjects for concentration are multiplied much beyond, say, five or six areas. Often, the majors are little differentiated from one another, students in advertising, for example, taking much the same work as those in marketing. Where this is true, the issue is a good deal less serious, but it is nonetheless part of a general approach to business education which seems highly questionable. In terms of existing practice, the range among schools is wide (zero to twenty-seven), with the median school offering eight majors. The replies of the 4-year schools and the 2-2- and 1-3-year schools are summarized in Table 9-2. These data, of course, should not be interpreted as demonstrating that many schools could eliminate portions

TABLE 9-2

NUMBER OF MAJORS OFFERED BY 98 BUSINESS SCHOOLS WITH FOUR-YEAR PROGRAMS AND BY 34 BUSINESS SCHOOLS WITH 2-2- AND 1-3-YEAR PROGRAMS, 1955–1956

Number of majors	Number of 4-year schools	Number of 2-2- and 1-3-year schools
Less than 4	6	3
4–5	16	3
6–7	27	9
8–9	17	7
10–11	11	3
12–13	6	4
14–15	4	2
16–17	7	2
Over 17	4	1
Total..................	98	34

SOURCE: Survey Questionnaire.

of their programs without serious loss, but the findings at least establish the presumption that some shift away from business-economics subjects in the direction indicated in the preceding chapter would be likely to give students sounder preparation for careers in business. Whether this is the future path which business schools should in fact follow and, if so, what specific areas they should include in their core and major programs are discussed in the next sections.

THE CORE PROGRAM

In a field as new, academically speaking, and as diversified as business, it is hardly surprising that, despite the leadership provided by the American Association of Collegiate Schools of Business, many differences of opinion persist over the subject's core elements. Even today there is no little controversy over what constitutes the essential core of such long-established fields as engineering, law, and medicine. Differences of opinion are, of course, even more likely in deciding what are the central subjects in as diversified a field as business.

TABLE 9-3

NUMBER AND PER CENT OF SCHOOLS REQUIRING BUSINESS AND ECONOMICS STUDIES,
98 BUSINESS SCHOOLS WITH FOUR-YEAR PROGRAMS AND 34 BUSINESS SCHOOLS
WITH 2-2- AND 1-3-YEAR PROGRAMS, 1955–1956

Required subjects	4-year schools		2-2- and 1-3-year schools	
	Number	Per cent	Number	Per cent
Accounting................	96	98.0	33	97.0
Finance-banking............	93	94.9	31	91.2
Business Law..............	87	88.8	32	94.1
Economics.................	86	87.8	32	94.1
Marketing.................	86	87.8	31	91.2
Statistics.................	82	83.7	26	76.5
Management...............	54	55.1	21	61.8
Production................	41	41.8	18	52.9
Communications...........	32	32.7	10	29.4
Introduction to Business.....	30	30.6	4	11.8
Personnel.................	19	19.4	7	20.6

SOURCE: Survey Questionnaire.

The replies to the Survey Questionnaire reflect the schools' attitudes toward what should be designated as the core studies. Table 9-3 lists these subjects on the basis of the number of schools requiring them. The data show that three-quarters or more of the schools require all students to take work in the following six areas: accounting, finance, business law, economics, marketing, and statistics. Between roughly two-fifths and three-fifths of the schools require courses to be taken in the general management-business policy area and in production or industrial management; these two last-named subjects figured hardly at all in the schools' core requirements thirty years ago.[3] In terms of prevailing practice among schools, these eight areas can be said to comprise the core of the field. A substantially smaller proportion of the schools at the present time require work in other areas, communications-business writing, introduction to business, personnel administration, and the like. However, there are twenty-two different core areas in which the 4-year schools as a group require students to take work, while those in the 2-2- and 1-3-year group stipulate work in seventeen different subjects.

Appraisal of Core Programs

To appraise prevailing practice among business schools with respect to the areas they designate as core subjects, the principles developed in Part 1 of the study give a useful frame of reference. The following are propositions derived from the earlier discussion which bear particularly on this aspect of the business school curriculum.

1. A school's core program should maintain as close ties as possible with a number of disciplines outside business and economics, notably literature, psychology, history, political science, and mathematics-science. The required courses should help the student transfer what he has learned from these other disciplines to his career interests and, ultimately, to his daily work, showing wherever possible how the insights and methods of the humanities, social sciences, and sciences can be used to analyze and illuminate the problems of business. It would be absurd to argue that every part of a core course should perform this "bridging" function, but it is a perfectly reasonable test to apply to most of the required courses, and certainly to the core program considered as a whole.

2. The core program should possess enough internal cohesion for the student to see the major functions of business enterprises and the business system in the round. Similarly, each of the core courses should either deal with a pervasive aspect of the business world or provide a tool which can be used in a wide range of business situations. The more scattered the required courses become, the further they negate the purpose of a central body of required work. On the other hand, unity and comprehensiveness for their own sake are not desiderata either, if they are carried to a point where essential issues are slurred over. Rather, the touchstone of an effective core program is to help students develop a funda-

---

[3] James H. S. Bossard and J. Frederic Dewhurst, *University Education for Business,* University of Pennsylvania Press, Philadelphia, 1931, p. 303.

mental point of view, a way of approaching business situations, and a capacity for tackling different problems. This is not to suggest that the core should be a kind of philosophical mish-mash of various ideas and experiences—there is every reason to stress rigor in most if not all the required courses. Yet the overriding objective is to assist students to gain perspective on the world of business and their place in it and to aid them in fashioning the tools they will need to carry on their lifework. This is admittedly an exalted view of academic preparation for business careers, but a university cannot remain true to its traditions and attempt anything less.

3. In keeping with the two foregoing principles, the core program should give students a variety of opportunities to put their general knowledge and abilities to concrete use. A besetting weakness of much of higher education is a tendency to fill student's programs with so many introductory or survey courses, they have little time or incentive to work with what they learn; yet it is precisely at this point that the educational experience is most likely to come alive. Business schools, even at the undergraduate level and even at the core course level, are under special obligation to see that students use their academic equipment to work out concrete situations or problems on their own. Again, this is not something which needs to hold true of every part of every required course but it surely deserves repeated emphasis in the core program as a whole.

4. As a closely related principle, the core courses should expose students to some of the more important findings and methods of modern research, help them to master some of the rudimentary tools which are needed to interpret such research, and provide them with opportunities to put such tools to at least limited use. This aspect of the student's experience can be carried further in connection with his major concentration (presumably in his senior year), but it is not too early to start laying the groundwork in his core courses. As to the general place of research in undergraduate work, it is a curious commentary on higher education that research is relegated wholly to the graduate level, while undergraduate work is supposed to remain vigorous and up-to-date without it. Yet much of the basic preparation of students who later must be depended on to do research occurs during the four undergraduate years. Even more important, research is a necessary part of any vigorous academic environment. Indeed, unless the results of research are continuously being worked into a teaching program, whether graduate or undergraduate, the learning process will sooner or later become routine and pedestrian. A school must be research-minded, or at least research-results-minded, if it is to keep the faculty alive, and to keep the students alive as well, since it is the continuous grappling with new ideas that spells the difference between growth and deterioration for both. As the

central feature of the student's four years, the core program should reflect this same conception of academic work.

5. Similarly, the core program should make sure that the individual student is challenged to the highest level of his intellectual capacities. This is not something that can safely be deferred until work in the major field is begun—it needs to be kept to the forefront in every course and in every part of the program. The danger in the very idea of a uniform sequence of courses is that the work becomes too standardized, especially if extensive coverage is attempted. Any effort to group students by type or level of academic proficiency, to identify and stimulate intellectually gifted students, and to put greater responsibility on the individual deserves most careful attention. These considerations relate to methods as much as to content of instruction, but they should be worked into the construction of the required courses wherever possible.

6. Finally, a school should aim to put its core program on a par with the most demanding work offered anywhere in the university and to insist that every one of the required courses meet a similarly high intellectual standard. The core sets the tone, and largely shapes the objectives, of the work in all the business studies. If this part of the student's experience lacks breadth and substance, the rest is likely to be no less deficient. Where courses which lack either scope or content have gotten into the core, they should be eliminated or reorganized. Where the core as a whole is devoid of the kind of intellectual rigor which earns the respect of first-rate students and keeps its faculty growing, it too is due for an overhauling. The very fact that the core is central to the entire program makes these conclusions inescapable.

Implications for the Curriculum

These six principles, which perhaps are as applicable to other fields as they are to business, will not give ready-made answers to what belongs or does not belong in the undergraduate core. It is even conceivable that some conflict with others (e.g., the first and second appear to aim in rather different directions), although for the most part they appear consistent. Yet the foregoing principles provide a reasonably clear point of reference for discussing the development of the core studies. Since as guidelines they are more germane to deciding what to exclude from the core than what to put into it, their negative implications will be noted first.

Judged against these six propositions, there appears to be little room in core programs for courses which are limited to specific industries or skills. Work of this sort is out of step with a number of the principles discussed above but especially with the second which emphasizes the

need for developing as much unity as possible among the courses constituting the core. Barring the most unusual kind of instruction, such courses
tend to focus on the special features and problems of a particular trade
or vocation, and once a school begins to move down this road, there
seems to be no end to the number and variety of offerings it will provide.
For the most part, work in banking (treated as an industry or enterprise),
insurance, real estate, retail store operations, transportation, or such specific office skills as secretarial training, would fall into this category. As
usually taught, none of these subjects meets the criteria for the core developed above.

Actually, relatively few schools require all students to take courses in
any one of these areas, and where this is true it may well be a holdover
from an earlier period. A check among the 132 undergraduate schools
responding to the Survey Questionnaire reveals that 15 require work in
insurance, 12 require work in office and secretarial skills, 7 work in transportation, and only a few work in such areas as real estate, advertising,
and salesmanship techniques.

In a similar category are courses going under such titles as Introduction to Business, American Industry, Commercial Areas, and the like
which beginning business students are sometimes required to take their
freshman or sophomore year. Table 9-3 shows that 31 per cent of the 4-
year schools and 12 per cent of the 2-2- and 1-3-year schools include such
courses in their core programs. According to the individual school interview reports, survey type courses of this sort are almost without exception thin and superficial. The job is formidable enough in a subject which
has a well-defined theoretical framework, but where, as in business, this
is not the case, the task becomes all but impossible. With the enrollment
pressures to which business schools are already subject, such courses
cannot be defended as a necessary device to attract students. As an
alternative to a basic course in business organization or management,
given perhaps at the beginning of the junior year, these courses cannot
go deeply enough into critical issues to be of much value. Instead of
making the student's initial experience in the field a significant one, these
courses tend to accent the subject's weaker academic qualifications.

Similar questions can be raised about courses which center almost
completely around description rather than theory and are almost exclusively informational rather than analytical in character. It would obviously be incorrect to say that all courses of a certain type fall into
this category, but the interviews at individual schools indicated that
the introductory courses in business law and production (among others)
were rather frequently in this group. The basic difficulty is that the great
majority of students do not have the background and experience neces-

sary to put the introductory work in such areas on a demanding level, so almost perforce attention tends to be concentrated on matters of procedure and detail. The issues raised by these two courses are of considerable importance, since they figure prominently in the core programs of many schools. Of the 98 schools with four-year programs responding to the Survey Questionnaire, 89 per cent included business law and 42 per cent included production or industrial management; of the 34 schools with 2-2-year and 1-3-year programs, the figures were 94 per cent and 53 per cent, respectively. In view of this, the work in these two areas is considered more fully later in this chapter. It is enough to point out here that these courses, as taught at most schools at the present time, probably do not deserve a place in the core program.

In translating these general considerations into specific core program recommendations, the findings of the preceding chapter also need to be kept in mind. There the conclusion was reached that business as an academic discipline rests on the following broad foundations: human-social values (literature and the other humanities), quantitative-scientific methods and principles (mathematics-sciences), and human-social behavior (history, political science, psychology, and sociology). Since study of these three areas was held to be vital to an understanding of business, considerable emphasis was placed on these aspects of the student's work. The chief purpose of the core program is to bring the student's studies in each of these areas more directly to bear on types of situations he will face in his business career. This calls for thorough grounding in those aspects of the foundation subjects which are closely related to business problems and for frequent application of the skills and knowledge thus acquired to issues of business policy.

Humanities Core Subjects

The first foundation area, human and social values, is the most difficult of the three to deal with, not only because value judgments as they relate to business behavior tend to be rather vague, but also because they enter business decisions at such a variety of points. Much, if not all, of the benefit of such work would be lost if it were studied apart from the various functional subjects and the student's major, yet there is danger of ethical and value considerations being slighted or lost sight of altogether if they are treated as but one aspect of traditional business subjects. Some schools that have given considerable thought to this problem have made this area the special concern of the business policy course, usually taken near the end of the student's four years. The senior-year course in Competition of Ideas in a Business Society at Northwestern's

School of Business is an interesting example of such work.[4] It is centered around controversial issues in which there are competing ideas about goals of individuals or groups and in which there is an important degree of business involvement. In successive units of the course, the student's attention is directed to the political, economic, and moral aspects of different conflict areas, which are approached as cases to be analyzed and for which proposals for action must be weighed; however, heavy emphasis is placed on assigned essays, selected chapters from such books as Heilbroner's *The Worldly Philosophers*, Northcote Parkinson's *Parkinson's Law*, Hansen's *The American Economy*, and current magazine or newspaper articles. Some of the unit headings are: Ends, Means, and Value Judgments; Information, Propaganda, and Advertising; Individual Freedoms and the Business Man (property rights, rights of minorities); Corporate Power; The Business Man and the National Economy; and The Business Man and the World Community. The course is taught by a small group of faculty members drawn from several departments in the business school. The problem of adequate staffing of such courses is particularly difficult, but their role in helping students see all four years of their work in perspective can be invaluable.

Another issue faced by business schools is how far they should go in preparing students in composition and speech. Most schools, as noted in the preceding chapter, limit formal work in this area to a single course in the first two years, given by the English department. A few go beyond this and either require all students to take an additional course in written and oral reporting in the business school or make it a specific part of one or more of the other required courses. This latter "compromise" solution may well be the most satisfactory approach for most schools to take. Unless some formal provision is made, training in written and oral skills is likely to be neglected, but an advanced course which is limited to this area alone is likely to be rather thin and quite isolated from the rest of the student's main subject interest. As developed more fully in the previous chapter, there is no reason why work in this area cannot be given separate recognition in the business curriculum and yet be closely tied in with one or more of the regular courses.

Quantitative Core Subjects

The next foundation area, mathematics-sciences, presents a rather different range of issues in terms of what to include in the core of business studies. Certain aspects of modern management have become so closely identified with the use of mathematical and engineering concepts they

[4] At present it is not required of all undergraduates but it was introduced as part of a general revision of the undergraduate business program some four years ago.

can best be approached through courses offered in these departments. Some of the more important topics which this work would include are linear programming, game theory, set theory, combinatorics, and various uses of probability theory and the calculus. One of the purposes of the mathematics requirement described in the last chapter was to give students the necessary background to pursue studies along these lines; the limited-choice elective in the mathematics-science area would give them a further opportunity to take such work. As brought out in Chap. 19, the industrial engineering department might offer courses suitable for business students who desire more intensive preparation in these aspects of modern management. Depending on faculty backgrounds and interests, perhaps on some campuses the business schools should offer one or two of these latter courses themselves, but on balance this seems undesirable. In any event, the teaching staff in courses of this sort should be trained primarily in mathematics and the sciences and only secondarily in business administration.

The application of quantitative methods to business problems has traditionally been approached through courses in accounting and statistics. In both areas, business school faculties have played an important role; in fact, the development of business schools was for many years closely bound up with the development of accounting. A rather elaborate structure of principles and techniques has gradually been built up in both these fields, and in the case of accounting, the licensing regulations for the C.P.A. in various states (notably New York) have put still more course barriers in the way of students seeking to enter this profession.

Considered from the viewpoint of core program requirements, there appears to be almost universal agreement that all students should take work in both accounting and statistics; the point where controversy arises is in determining the approach best designed to meet the needs of nonmajor as well as major students in the two areas. Judging from the school interviews, the core courses in accounting and statistics all too often stress elementary techniques in handling records, preparing reports, and answering day-to-day operating questions. In the first-year accounting course, for example, considerable attention is often given to working out bookkeeping procedures and to discussing the techniques and records employed in recording, classifying, and summarizing simple business transactions. The basic work in statistics often includes a survey-type introduction to data collection, tabular and graphic methods, measures of central tendency and dispersion, times series analysis, index numbers, and an elementary treatment of correlation analysis. It should be noted in passing that almost all of the 98 schools with 4-year programs which answered the Survey Questionnaire required at least two semesters of accounting while 52 required more than this amount; the same pattern held for the 34 responding schools with 2-2- and 1-3-year programs, although in their case only 12 required more than two semesters. Eighty-two of the 98 schools required all students to take at least one semester of statistics, but of these only 9 required more than one semester; of the 34 schools, 26 required at least one semester in this area, and 7 required more than this.

Presumably, introductory courses in accounting and statistics developed along these lines are thought to provide the best preparation for students who want to do more intensive work in these two areas, though even from the viewpoint of future majors such courses are being increasingly questioned. From the point of view of nonmajors, however, there seems little doubt that the emphasis on mechanics and techniques is a serious mistake. Indeed, attention ought to be centered on accounting and statistics as aids to management in reaching decisions, with special reference to their uses as tools for coordinating different aspects of management decision making. Viewed in this light, accounting becomes an extremely important instrument for analyzing sales policy questions, pricing problems, capital expenditures programs, debt-financing methods, etc. Statistical analysis likewise can provide management with a sensitive "listening-seeing" device for surveying markets, controlling inventories, analyzing supply sources, forecasting sales prospects, and the like. There is no denying that to give accounting and statistics a strong managerial emphasis at the undergraduate level raises serious difficulties, not only because beginning students lack minimal technical preparation in these two subjects, but also because they have little or no familiarity with general management problems.

It appears that the beginning work in both these subjects is beset by the danger that too much attention is given either to their mechanical and procedural aspects or to their broad implications for business policy making. Both dangers can be avoided, or at least minimized, if the beginning courses are limited to underlying principles, with sparing use made of bookkeeping assignments, on the one hand, and management or business-policy case materials, on the other. After this groundwork has been laid, the students can be given whatever preparation in technical procedures and/or in managerial uses of these two subjects which seems appropriate; at this point the nonmajors would presumably concentrate more exclusively on the latter aspects of the work than the majors, but ultimately both groups of students should attempt to acquire a working knowledge of the managerial uses of one or both these two tool subjects. An approach to accounting and statistics along these lines should do much to reconcile the needs of major and nonmajor students, at the same time tying both areas more closely to the rest of their business studies.

A promising development in this part of the core curriculum is the introduction of courses in quantitative methods which combine work in accounting and statistics into a unified one-year program. Harvard pioneered this change at the graduate level, but a few schools have followed a similar path in their undergraduate programs. Northwestern, for example, has developed a required year course, Quantitative Controls in Business, which seeks to introduce students to the managerial uses of accounting, statistical, and related financial methods of analysis. The first part of the course deals with the development of financial statements and the use of such information in reaching operating decisions. The second part deals with the nature of cost accounting and what it can contribute to controlling cost components and quality of the product, as well as to controlling over-all operations. This section introduces some basic statistical concepts, such as dispersion, probability distributions, analysis of variance, and correlation analysis. The section of the course dealing with control of over-all operations is built around an analysis of operating budgets, uses of financial ratios, fund flows, and cash budget forecasting. The last part of the course approaches the problem of managerial decision making through the use of statistical forecasting methods. As in the "parent" course at Harvard, heavy use is made of cases at a number of points in the course.

The question can be asked whether a course along these lines, especially for students in their sophomore year, should be aimed at such broad objectives. It is worth noting that, in fact, much the greater part of the course deals with accounting principles. The significance of this experiment is that it departs sharply from traditional beginning courses in accounting and statistics and relates both subjects much more closely to the decision-making function of management.[5]

Economics and Social Science Core Subjects

The social sciences are the third and most important field underlying academic preparation for business. Indeed, economics as one branch of the social sciences has traditionally provided the only theoretical framework for the study of business, and even today the two fields are so closely related they can hardly be discussed separately. It follows that every business student should go far enough in economics to be able to use the subject with a fair degree of confidence and facility. This means requiring a considerable amount of work beyond the introductory year level, a practice which is fairly common among undergraduate schools—specifically, at 50 of the 98 schools with 4-year programs and at 12 of the

[5] Some further observations about the work of accounting majors in connection with C.P.A. examination requirements are developed later in this chapter; the general position of accounting in the business school curriculum is discussed in Chap. 14.

34 schools with 2-2- and 1-3-year programs. Judging from the interviews with members of the economics and business faculties, there appears to be general agreement that this advanced work should emphasize micro-economics (or theory of the firm) and macroeconomics (theory of income and employment), as both relate to the determination of business policies. The study of microeconomics, especially as it has developed in courses in managerial economics, can be a valuable part of the student's equipment, but even if the work is put on a fairly high level, it probably can be handled adequately in a single semester.

On the other hand, the course in macroeconomics should give considerable attention to such topics as the determinants of the demand and supply of money, the behavior of credit, the role of banking and monetary policy, as well as the more usual analysis of the determinants of national income, the causes of economic instability, and the role of fiscal policy. To secure a working knowledge of these matters and to see how they impinge on various decisions of the firm can hardly be achieved in less than two semesters, making five semesters of required work in economics in all. Even this would exclude a number of subjects often regarded as essential to an understanding of business processes and policies, notably international economics and public finance. While it perhaps would not be feasible to include any of these areas in the undergraduate core, students should be given every opportunity to study some of these subjects on their own election. Certain other issues, such as the relations between undergraduate and graduate work in economics and the location of the economics department, can best be deferred until the next chapter.[6]

The increasingly important role which government plays in economic life and the complex relations which now exist between business enterprises and the legal-political-social environment make further work in this branch of the social sciences mandatory. These environmental factors could be approached historically or in terms of political and governmental influences or from the viewpoint of the role of law in business affairs. There is need for considerable experimentation in this general area, though the tendency to skim over too much ground in too little time is an ever-present danger. If approached broadly and imaginatively, the relation of law to business could provide an excellent focus for such a course, helping the student carry forward the work he did earlier in

[6] For a comprehensive review of the teaching of economics see Report of the Committee on the Undergraduate Teaching of Economics, American Economic Association, "The Teaching of Undergraduate Economics," *American Economic Review,* vol. 40, no. 5, December, 1950, part 2 (supplement). The findings of the committee with respect to the relation of economics to the undergraduate business curriculum generally parallel those reached in this study (see pp. 107–124 and 129–138 of the committee's report).

history and political science. Such a course would deal with technical details of contract, agency, employment, etc. only to the extent necessary to show some of the ways the living law enters into specific business situations. How society pursues its varied purposes through law, how the great themes in the development of jurisprudence parallel and fuse with the changing position of business in society, how the role of law in business can be illumined by inquiry into the nature of legal reasoning, how the relationship between private law (business law) and public law (antitrust or public control law) has come to assume its present form— these are some of the questions which might well be given prime attention. Since much of the province and function of law can be taught with cases and other materials concerned primarily with business, the work would be particularly useful in developing the student's capacity for analytical investigation and for responsible action in a social setting.[7] A course in business and legal institutions along these lines would be particularly useful in helping students bridge the gap between their non-business and business studies.

Ideally, the person who gives this course should have preparation in law (especially constitutional law), political science (especially political theory), and problems of business organization and management. The difficulty of finding faculty members with this background, especially at the undergraduate level, is indeed formidable, and as a practical matter the scope of the course would have to be adapted to the interests and training of whatever persons could be found to teach it. In some cases it might be possible to get a practicing lawyer with an academic or philosophical bent to handle the work; in others, a member of the political science department; in still others, the member of the business school who previously taught the course in business law. The important consideration is not where such a course is located (e.g., in the political science department or business school), but whether the person offering it is prepared to make a sharp break with the past and deal with significant issues in the relationship between business and the law.

The last broad area of the social sciences which underlies academic preparation for business is the study of individual and group behavior. In the preceding chapter it was recommended that business students be required to take a full year of work in psychology and/or sociology; room was also left for them to take additional instruction in this area if they desired. It is highly important for students to carry this work forward into their business studies although it is an open question how this can best be done.

<hr/>

[7] The foregoing reflects the thinking of a number of persons conversant with this field, especially the views of Leland Hazard of Carnegie Tech. and Jacob Weissman of the University of Chicago.

Considerable progress has been made of late in applying the findings and methods of social psychology and industrial sociology to problems of business organization, and a carefully planned course in this area could be a valuable part of a school's core program. Harvard's course in human relations (Administrative Practices) is used as a springboard at this institution to a review of many aspects of management decision making; undergraduate schools might well consider a similar approach, with perhaps certain modifications to bring the work somewhat closer to traditional courses in business organization. Perhaps the most perplexing aspect of the entire management field has to do with questions of motivations, social systems, group loyalties, emotional responses, and the like, and there is therefore much to be said for introducing the student to these problems early in his career.[8] If the full contributions of the so-called behavioral sciences to this field are to be made, it is no less important that the instructors in such areas as marketing, personnel, finance, and production introduce these materials wherever possible. As in other expanding phases of the curriculum, the problem is primarily one of finding faculty members who have developed a double identification with an applied business field and an underlying human behavior field. As persons with the requisite preparation in the latter area are drawn into business school programs, the behavioral science approach can be worked into the business curriculum at a number of points and in a variety of ways; some suggestions for doing so are discussed below.

The Functional Core Subjects

A program of study which followed the lines outlined in this and the preceding chapter would account for 87 to 93 of the 120 semester-credit hours customarily required for graduation, leaving only 27 to 33 credit hours (23 to 28 per cent of the total, respectively) for work in the functional business subjects and the area of the student's major interest. The question which remains to be considered is whether this leaves sufficient scope for these two important steps in the student's preparation. As noted earlier in this chapter, prevailing practice at most business schools points to a negative answer, since at the great majority of schools the business subjects (exclusive of economics, accounting, statistics, and business law) account for 42 to 48 hours (35 to 40 per cent) of the total. The earlier discussion indicated that not all this time was necessary, or even desirable, but just how much could be eliminated was left unsettled.

In light of the principles outlined in Part 1, every effort should be

---

[8] Judging from a review of some of the current textbooks and general treatises in this field, the subject of human relations seems to lack solid content; on the other hand, a number of first-rate research reports and monographs have been prepared.

made to keep the functional business areas included in the core to a bare minimum. Otherwise, emphasis would almost inevitably shift to matters of detailed business practice lacking substantial analytical content. If the main objectives of the core program are to be realized, it is especially important to omit courses which bear on only one or two industries or have only limited applicability to the rest of the student's work. For purposes of academic work, activities of a business enterprise can be grouped into four principal areas: production, finance, marketing, and personnel. Management which directs and coordinates these activities cannot be studied apart from any one of these, but neither can it be wholly subsumed under them; consequently, even at the risk of some overlapping, it requires separate attention, which would mean that study of the functions of business would be limited to these five broad subjects. While the work in these and certain other business areas is examined at length in later chapters, a few observations are needed to show how their treatment would fit into the four-year program as a whole.

Each of the five areas contains a substantial body of factual and analytical materials which warrant careful study. Indeed, the danger is that the basic courses will become so overloaded with details and refinements that underlying principles and critical issues will be submerged. Rather than trying to give equal attention to all facets of each subject, attention might better be concentrated on a relatively few topics of critical importance. Here, the contributions of the general and business foundation subjects may be found to hold the key. If the functional business subjects are cut off from their underlying disciplines, as often tends to be the case, they are likely to become pedestrian and narrow, but if they are studied as integral parts of broader fields, they can become both challenging and meaningful. Naturally, these interfield relationships vary, depending on the subject matter involved. Thus, the study of production should keep particularly close ties with mathematics, engineering, and the sciences; the study of finance, with the "parent" disciplines of economics, accounting, and mathematics; the study of marketing, with economics, psychology, and sociology; and the study of personnel administration, with law, economics, psychology, and sociology. Similarly, attention in each of these areas should be given to the economic, political, and social environment surrounding business organizations. Especially in the case of finance, marketing, and personnel, it is necessary to consider influences that are external to the firm. How much of this emphasis can be worked into the basic course also varies from subject to subject; in production, for example, there may be less room for this kind of material than in the other areas. Nonetheless, the growing edge of each of these areas appears to center at just such intersection points.

The various functions of a business enterprise can also be approached in terms of their own interrelationships, and here lies another important key to enriching the core program and the entire business school curriculum. The duties of a production engineer, marketing director, finance officer, or industrial relations director are part and parcel of a single undertaking, and the methods and activities of each need to be continuously compared, checked, and synchronized with the others. Thus, the study of these four functions must take account of how they mesh, where dangers of breakdown are greatest, how failures of communication can be avoided, and what principles of analysis emerge. These aspects of business operations are not only fascinating in their own right; they raise issues of increasing urgency as firms become larger and organizational structures more elaborate. At the same time, how much of this material is appropriate at a first-course level can well be debated. The student could probably be given some appreciation of these relationships even in the core course, but he would not be likely to gain much in the way of understanding until later—perhaps much later.

The third element which study in these five areas should include is problem solving and case analysis. Herein lies the distinctive feature of work in business administration, and it is not too early even in their undergraduate days for students to gain some experience in analyzing concrete situations. Obviously, not much time can be devoted to this before students gain some familiarity with essential facts and principles in the several areas, especially in the beginning course, but the sooner the student begins to apply background information and broad principles to specific decision-making situations the better. This becomes all the more true if the work in each of the functional areas stresses relationships with general (i.e., nonbusiness) and business foundation subjects and with the other functional areas.[9]

The Management Area

The program of study suggested above will be readily recognized as a managerial approach to each of the functional business subjects. The modern manager needs to have some grasp of the relationships between his area of special responsibility, on the one hand, and the general and business foundation subjects, the external environment, and the various functional areas on the other. Above all, he needs to develop the capacity for making decisions in light of this broad conception of his managerial role, and the higher up in the hierarchy he stands, the more important these qualities and understandings become. This raises the question whether the management function should be studied separately from the other four areas or treated as an integral part of each. Somewhat over

[9] The matter of teaching methods is examined at greater length in Chap. 11.

half of the 132 schools responding to the Survey Questionnaire reported that they required all students to take a one-semester course in management or business policy; only a very few required an additional semester (see Table 9-3). Slightly under half offered management as a separate area of major concentration (see Table 9-4).

As the diversity in practice suggests, this issue can be argued either way, and to do it justice would require another full-scale survey.[10] One view, apparently somewhat in the minority, is that courses in management either duplicate the work in the other functional areas or deal in vague generalities of a rather common-sense nature. The opposite view is that the management role cannot be broken up into separate functional subjects and that the study of decision making from an interfunctional (i.e., managerial) viewpoint provides a valuable focus for the student's entire academic experience.

The arguments against treating management as a separate undergraduate major seem on balance the more persuasive. To teach a managerial approach to business problems is a formidable undertaking even with students who have had considerable job experience; to essay it with young, inexperienced students becomes doubly hazardous. A major course of study is generally assumed to mean that the student has achieved a fair degree of competence in a given area which in this case is simply not possible. More than this, a major inevitably tends to become a self-contained subject, separate in varying degrees from related areas. But management can hardly be divorced from the various functions which make up the business enterprise; if it is studied apart from them it is likely to be emptied of the greater part of its content. On balance, then, in spite of its increasing popularity as a field of concentration, it does not seem wise to treat management as a major in its own right.

As for including some work in management in the core program, rather different considerations are involved. Despite certain difficulties and dangers, there are real advantages in having all students take a basic management course in which the students gain some familiarity with structural characteristics and functional relationships of business organizations, some comprehension (admittedly limited) of the kinds of issues involved in setting up and operating a business enterprise, and some "feel" for the problems encountered in coordinating internal-firm functions, and in adapting to change in the external-firm environment. This work might come toward the beginning of the core program or toward

---

[10] The literature on the managerial function is already extensive, although much of it has but an indirect bearing on the question considered here. A recent study on the teaching of management at American business schools is Charles E. Summer, Jr., *Factors in Effective Administration,* Graduate School of Business, Columbia University, New York, 1956.

the end, or it might be divided between the first and last semesters. If all students take a course in organization and human behavior in their junior year and if the courses in the four functional areas have a management emphasis, it would seem logical to put this work in a business policy course at the end of the student's academic career. To give it the depth and scope it deserves, the course should probably cover two semesters and give considerable attention to the social responsibilities, as well as to the key policy issues, of the business enterprise. To strengthen the student's powers of independent analysis, considerable emphasis on case materials and report writing would also seem desirable.

These observations raise again the question touched on in Chaps. 4 and 5—whether undergraduate students can hope to make any serious start toward understanding the managerial point of view or whether this type of work should be limited wholly to graduate instruction. If emphasis is placed on background preparation and on basic analytical tools, the answer appears to be that undergraduates can make some headway in this direction. It would be a serious mistake, however, to imply even by indirection that they can make more than a bare beginning or that the students' work is pointed toward careers in top management. As stressed earlier, the emphasis in undergraduate programs needs to be kept on those underlying elements in the students' preparation which are common to a wide variety of forward-moving careers in business. It is only in this sense that a managerial approach seems appropriate at the undergraduate level.

THE MAJOR SUBJECTS

In addition to deciding whether a major in management should be offered, business schools must determine in what other areas undergraduates should be permitted to concentrate. Earlier in the chapter it was tentatively concluded that a school need offer no more than six or seven subjects for specialization and that no more than four- or, at the most, five-semester courses need be taken in any one area of concentration. The latter issue is examined in the chapters dealing with different areas of the curriculum, so only passing reference is made to it here.

The 132 schools answering the Survey Questionnaire, as noted earlier, showed wide diversity in their major offerings, with the median offering eight majors but with some providing upwards of seventeen and others less than four. Table 9-4 summarizes the replies on major subject offerings of the four-year schools as well as of the 2-2- and 1-3-year schools. Only three subjects are offered by three-fourths or more of the schools (accounting, marketing, and finance-banking), but about half provide

TABLE 9-4

NUMBER AND PER CENT OF UNDERGRADUATE BUSINESS SCHOOLS OFFERING DIFFERENT
MAJORS, 98 SCHOOLS WITH FOUR-YEAR PROGRAMS AND 34 SCHOOLS WITH 2-2- AND
1-3-YEAR PROGRAMS, 1955–1956

Major subject	4-year schools offering		2-2- and 1-3-year schools offering	
	Number	Per cent	Number	Per cent
Accounting	93	94.9	31	91.2
Marketing	83	84.7	28	82.4
Finance-banking	74	75.5	27	79.4
Administration–general business	63	64.3	23	67.6
Economics	48	49.0	15	44.1
Management	46	46.9	17	50.0
Secretarial	46	46.9	17	50.0
Production	41	41.8	13	38.2
Personnel–industrial relations	35	35.7	15	44.1
Insurance	29	29.6	15	44.1
Retailing	28	28.6	7	20.6
Business education	28	28.6	9	26.5
Transportation	24	24.5	8	23.5
Real estate	22	22.4	7	20.6
Miscellaneous nonbusiness	22	22.4	7	20.6
Statistics	20	20.4	11	32.4
Business law	19	19.4	6	17.6
Advertising	18	18.4	5	14.7
Foreign trade	18	18.4	4	11.8
Public administration	14	14.3	4	11.8
Office administration	9	9.2	7	20.6
Salesmanship	5	5.1	2	5.9
Public utilities	2	2.0	3	8.8

majors in both general business and management. Other majors offered by a third or more of the schools are economics, secretarial science, production, and personnel-industrial relations.

Everyone looking into this phase of the business school curriculum has his favorite examples of absurd major offerings; the ones noted here are a thirteen-course major at a well-known Western institution (36 semester hours) in hotel and restaurant administration which includes a course in hotel front-office procedures ("physical layout of the hotel front office, procedure used in registering guests, keeping records and accounts") and an eight-course major at a large Southern university in baking science and management which includes courses in Principles of Baking: Bread and Rolls; Principles of Baking: Cakes and Variety Products (both two-semester courses); Bread and Roll Production—Practical Shop Opera-

tion; and finally Cake and Sweet Baked Products—Practical Shop Operation.[11] Actually, majors which are as clearly vocational as these tend to
be isolated from the rest of the programs and often are vestigial remnants
of some earlier "historical accident." This is sometimes even true of more
widely offered majors with strong trade ties, such as retail merchandising,
insurance, and secretarial science. The importance of these often-cited
examples is that they reflect a tendency which, if allowed to spread, will
convert a school's entire program into mere vocationalism.

Evaluation of Major Subjects

With some modifications, the schema developed for appraising core
programs can be used to evaluate major offerings as well. Opportunities
for major specialization should be sufficiently diversified to allow for
the more important, general differences in student interests and career
requirements. Certainly, provision should be made for variation among
schools, depending on faculty resources and interests, and to a much
more limited degree, regional or industry requirements. However, a
prime purpose of the major is to help students carry their earlier work
forward by giving them the opportunity to use their previous training
in one area of study. If the area is narrow, lacks challenging analytical
issues, is unrelated to subjects studied previously, and does not itself
lead logically to a higher level of study—in short, gives no opportunity
for the student to develop his thinking powers—it has no place in a four-
year college program. It is difficult to be more specific than this, since
under certain conditions the most unpromising sequence of courses can
become a demanding intellectual experience, but if the work centers
either on a particular industry or trade skill or on descriptive aspects of
business practice, the strong presumption is that it lacks sufficient content. The same would hold if the major subdivides a subject to a point
where considerable overlapping occurs or any analysis of underlying
principles is largely removed (e.g., advertising as distinguished from
marketing, or investments from finance). Broadly speaking, these are the
same considerations which were held to be applicable to core programs.

A tentative listing of the major subjects which would avoid these
pitfalls would certainly include accounting, finance, marketing, personnel-industrial relations, and production—also economics where it is given

[11] The catalog of the first school states that its "complete curricula are planned
for students who eventually expect to become business executives or to assume
positions of research or administrative responsibility in private or governmental
organizations." The second school's catalog states that its program will help students
"secure the broad vision of economic affairs and the understanding of fundamental
economic courses which are today essential for successful business leadership."

by business schools.[12] About two-thirds of the schools answering the Survey Questionnaire reported offering a major in general business or administration which is designed for students who want a broad preparation in business rather than specialized training in one area. At many institutions at the present time, this major fills a real need, and while it may run the risk of being something of a potpourri, it deserves a place in the curriculum. On the other hand, if schools broaden their core requirements and their individual major offerings along the lines advocated in this report, this need would be largely met. The interviews at individual institutions revealed no compelling necessity for adding more areas to this group of six or seven majors—on the contrary, they raised serious doubts about doing so.

If the major areas were held to these subjects, the question whether students could secure the necessary preparation to enter fields like advertising, banking, foreign trade, insurance, retailing, real estate, and transportation would have to be faced. The principal reason for offering majors of this sort is that employers reputedly prefer to hire students who have specialized along one of these lines. The data on employer-hiring attitudes and practices reviewed in Chaps. 5 and 6, while by no means unequivocal, throw serious doubt on this view. The gist of those two chapters was that students and schools have considerable latitude in determining how much intensive specialization is needed to prepare for first jobs—that employers are not nearly so definite in their own minds as is commonly supposed about what amounts of preparation in what directions are needed to secure initial job footholds. It seems perfectly clear that if schools of business, as a group, moved away from highly specialized majors, most employers would accept their action at least passively and, more likely, enthusiastically.

Whether all *courses* of this sort, as distinguished from *majors*, should be eliminated raises a quite different question. A basic course or two in subjects like insurance, real estate, and transportation can be put on a demanding analytical level where six or seven courses in any one of these fields probably cannot. There is reason to believe (see the chapters on employer requirements) that companies are not looking for students who have had a long list of courses in a given area as much as they are for capable individuals who have had some basic grounding in a particular field of work. Aside from a few highly technical lines of endeavor (cost accountancy, actuarial science, etc.), two carefully planned courses would usually be sufficient for this purpose in any one of these areas. The question of how work of this sort could be geared in with the offerings

[12] A major in statistics might also be included, but the work in this area requires a thorough grounding in mathematics; if it is offered in the business school, joint arrangements should be worked out with the mathematics department.

of one of the broader departments like finance or marketing could pose difficult questions for some schools, though these problems should not prove insurmountable. The effects on faculty members handling courses which should be consolidated or eliminated raise far more important issues and are therefore discussed in Chap. 11.

Specialization in a Major

Assuming an area qualifies as an undergraduate major, how many courses should be required or permitted? To answer this question, consideration must be given to the kind of preparation needed in each subject, a task undertaken in Part 3. However, the broad findings of the discussion to this point put the burden of proof squarely on those who argue for more than four- or five-semester courses in any one subject. To go beyond this exposes the student's work to the kind of narrow, stultifying instruction which hardly accords with the educational objectives set forth earlier in this study. It should be emphasized that this conclusion stands quite apart from the need discussed in the preceding chapter for more courses outside the business-economics area. By reducing the number of courses which students take in a given specialty, the work outside business can be correspondingly increased.

Some notion of prevailing practice in this regard can be gleaned from minimum and maximum hour standards in selected major areas at individual schools. Table 9-5 summarizes this information for two important majors, accounting and marketing, at schools with four-year programs; the maximum hours which students are permitted to take at different schools are shown as additions to the minimum hours required of students majoring in these two areas.

The table shows that among the 71 schools for which data on accounting major hours were available, about 60 per cent required a minimum of between eight- and eleven-semester courses, and of this latter group, about one-half permitted students to take upwards of three-semester courses more. Among the 67 schools for which data on marketing major hours could be secured, about 66 per cent required a minimum of seven- to ten-semester courses, and of this latter group, over half permitted students to take upwards of three-semester courses more. These figures should be compared with the 120 total semester credit-hours, or 40-semester courses, in academic subjects normally required for graduation. Thus, it is not at all unusual for accounting majors to be permitted to take as much as one-third, and marketing majors one-fourth, of their entire four years in their specialty, while departmental regulations typically require accounting majors to take as a minimum over one-quarter, and

TABLE 9-5

MINIMUM AND MAXIMUM SEMESTER-HOUR STANDARDS FOR ACCOUNTING (71 SCHOOLS) AND MARKETING MAJORS (67 SCHOOLS) IN UNDERGRADUATE BUSINESS SCHOOLS WITH FOUR-YEAR PROGRAMS, 1955–1956

Minimum semester hours required	Major in accounting					Major in marketing*				
	Maximum additional semester hours permitted					Maximum additional semester hours permitted				
	0–9	10–19	20–29	30 or more	Total	0–9	10–19	20–29	30 or more	Total
	(Number of schools)					(Number of schools)				
Less than 20	1	1	—	—	2	3	8	2	—	13
20–24	6	3	—	1	10	11	9	4	2	26
25–29	6	8	2	—	16	8	8	2	—	18
30–34	14	9	3	1	27	3	2	1	1	7
35–39	8	1	1	—	10	2	—	—	—	2
More than 40	6	—	—	—	6	1	—	—	—	1
Total.............	41	22	6	2	71	28	27	9	3	67

* In a few schools in which no marketing majors were offered, minimum and maximum hours in the management major were substituted.

SOURCE: Survey Questionnaire and school catalogs.

marketing majors nearly one-fifth, of their entire program in these two fields.[13]

A limited sampling of courses which students actually take indicates that there is some tendency for them to specialize as much as the regulations permit, but that there is considerable difference between accounting and other fields. A random check of thirty-two accounting students' programs at six large institutions in different parts of the country showed that two-thirds took between ten and twelve courses in their specialty against seven to nine required as a minimum; by contrast, a sampling of twenty-three marketing students' programs at these same schools showed that two-thirds took between five and seven courses in their specialty, not too different from the minimum course requirements of their major department.[14] The programs of students majoring in other business

[13] As elsewhere in this study, course credits are converted to a semester-hours basis, and total hours required for graduation exclude such nonacademic subjects as physical education and military science. The sample of schools covered by Robert G. Cox in discussing accounting in Chap. 14 shows a somewhat lower concentration in terms of minimum hour requirements for majors in this subject.

[14] The number of students covered is, of course, too small to serve as a scientific sample.

studies also showed a consistently different pattern from that in accounting.

Part 3 of this study examines individual course offerings in these subjects in detail. In no instance, other than accounting, are more than four required courses recommended, and even in this subject only five courses are considered essential for an undergraduate major. The principal reason for requiring more work than this in accounting is to meet the licensing requirements for the C.P.A. in a number of states, notably New York. There is no denying that these requirements pose a genuine dilemma for any school that is seeking to put its undergraduate program as a whole on a high academic level, since under present arrangements a certain amount of work in basic subjects has to be sacrificed if students must devote more than four- or five-semester courses to the study of any one subject area.

The issue posed by New York C.P.A. licensing requirements is laid bare in the following excerpt from a letter received from a faculty member of a large, Eastern institution:

We have a curriculum leading to a B.S. (major in accounting). In New York State, the content of that curriculum is governed in good part by a State Board of Examiners in accounting. This Board reflects in clearest form the professional vested interests of the C.P.A.'s. At any rate, this Board refused to grant credit toward fulfillment of the academic requirements for admission to the state C.P.A. examinations for any courses creditable as well toward our B.A. degree. This latter degree, whose curricular content is not controlled by the C.P.A.'s, allows a maximum of only 12 credit-hours in accounting.

We were satisfied with our B.A. degree and its accounting limitation. However, our school decided as a matter of community policy to bow to the State Board so as not to place some of our students, interested in a professional career in accounting, at a disadvantage in preparing for the State C.P.A. examinations. This meant that we registered the aforementioned B.S. degree with the State Board. . . . Its minimum requirements for aspiring C.P.A. candidates are:

24	credit	hours	in accounting
8	"	"	in business law
8	"	"	in finance
6	"	"	in economic theory
14	"	"	in "other business subjects"

These constitute 60 credits of specialized work which we consider acceptable, together with the basic 68 aforementioned credits of liberal arts courses, for our special B.S. degree, thus duly registered with the State Board.

For many schools these standards mark a real advance over prior practice, but for schools striving to put their work on a still broader basis, C.P.A. licensing requirements constitute a serious strait jacket. Looking to the future, much more of the work preparatory to the C.P.A. examinations should be taken at the graduate level. Students who are not in a position to complete their training by this route would then be obliged to supplement their undergraduate preparation by attending special summer sessions, night school, or separate accounting institutes. Meanwhile, the schools face a genuine dilemma which cannot readily be resolved. Their sole effective course of action would appear to be to shift to a graduate emphasis just as rapidly as possible.

In modified form, the same issues face business schools in the other areas of major concentration, and a similar outcome seems indicated. Students who desire a thorough grounding in such areas as finance or marketing will find it increasingly necessary to take further graduate study. Those who desire highly specialized preparation will need to supplement their undergraduate work by attending night schools, special institutes, and the like. The undergraduate business schools as well as the liberal arts schools can then give chief attention to the preparation of students in the broad foundation subjects.

FOUR-YEAR VERSUS 2-2-YEAR PROGRAMS

An issue which has received considerable attention from time to time is whether it is desirable to confine all undergraduate work in business and economics to the last two years or to spread it out over three or four years. Considered in the light of the foregoing discussion, this issue does not seem too momentous. Since there is need for devoting half or more of the student's four years to work outside the business and economics area, some nonbusiness courses would have to be taken in the junior or senior years in any event, especially if one or two of the basic business subjects (economics and quantitative methods) were taken during the first two years. Actually, this is the general pattern followed at most schools, whether on a 4-, 2-2- or 1-3-year basis. From a curricular point of view, the basic differences between schools occur over the proportion of work done outside business and economics and over the type and amount of specialization permitted in a given area; there is no compelling reason why these two issues should be approached differently under these two kinds of programs.

There is some evidence to indicate, however, that the 2-2- and 1-3-year schools have established broader programs than the 4-year schools (see especially Table 9-1). This is hardly surprising since presumably the liberal arts tradition is strongest at institutions which require a common program of general education in the freshman or freshman-sophomore years. The difference between the two groups of schools show up more in qualitative than in quantitative measures. According to the interview reports, almost all the schools which have pioneered in broadening programs, introducing stiffer requirements, emphasizing problem solving or case analysis, and unifying the student's work as a whole have embraced the 2-2- and 1-3-year pattern; relatively few of the four-year schools are in the vanguard of this movement. Many factors, such as the financial resources and prestige of the parent institution, teaching loads, quality of the faculty, and the like, lie behind this difference in the two groups of schools; as emphasized in Chap. 4, perhaps the outstanding difference between these schools is that the 4-year institutions pursue relatively lax admissions policies. Whatever the explanatory factors may be, it is noteworthy that schools with broader and more rigorous standards have generally chosen the 2-2- and 1-3-year pattern of instruction.

The likelihood of developing new and broader interests on the part of students is perhaps somewhat greater if they are enrolled in a general university-wide program than in a professional school during their first two years, although again much depends on what the latter conceives its role to be. In some fields, such as medicine and engineering, the subject matter puts heavy pressure on students to choose their major early and to concentrate on a comparatively narrow range of courses. The subject matter of business administration (save for the possible exception of accounting) does not require such a narrowing focus early in the student's career. In fact, all the evidence reviewed in Part 1 of this study points in the opposite direction. Universities with four-year business programs might well find it advantageous to shift to a 1-3- or, better still, a 2-2-year basis.

A SUGGESTED CURRICULUM

The recommendations advanced in this and the preceding chapter are summarized in the proposed curriculum in Table 9-6. The purpose of presenting them in this form is to point up the issues as sharply as possible and to indicate the general direction in which business schools might move in the years ahead. It would be presumptuous indeed even to suggest that the schools should follow a rigid pattern of development along these lines—rather, as indicated earlier, variation within rather broad limits is to be encouraged. Hence, a range of requirements is indicated at a number of points in the suggested curriculum. Even this device does not suggest the extent to which schools should be urged to experiment on their own, a consideration which was emphasized repeatedly in the earlier discussion.

ELECTIVE COURSES

A possible criticism of the general approach to business education sketched out here is that it does not leave sufficient room for free elec-

TABLE 9.6

SUGGESTED UNDERGRADUATE CURRICULUM

Required subjects and limited-choice electives	Number of semester hours

General foundation subjects:

Humanities

English literature and composition*...............................	9
One or two other humanities (e.g., either in foreign language or in philosophy, etc.)...	6
Advanced elective in one of above................................	3 or 6

Mathematics-Science

College algebra-trigonometry-geometry............................	6
Calculus and finite mathematics...................................	6
Laboratory science (physics, chemistry, etc.)......................	6
Advanced elective in one of above†...............................	3 or 6

Social Sciences (excluding economics)

History..	6
Political science...	6
Behavioral science (psychology, sociology, etc.)...................	6
Advanced elective in one of above................................	3
Total semester hours outside business and economics...............	60–66

Business foundation subjects:

Principles of economics...	6
Economics of the firm (microanalysis).............................	3
Economics of money and income (macroanalysis)....................	6
Quantitative methods (accounting-statistics)......................	6
Advanced elective in quantitative methods†.......................	0–3
Political and legal factors in business............................	3
Organization and human behavior.................................	3

Functional business subjects:

Personnel management..	3
Production management...	3
Finance management..	3
Marketing management..	3
Business policy and social responsibilities........................	6
Studies in major subject (exclusive of work in business foundation and functional subjects)...	9
Electives (no more than one in major subject).....................	0–6
Total semester hours in business and economics....................	54–60
Total semester hours required for graduation......................	120

* If the work in composition is not at a level for which college credit can be given, additional work in English or foreign language would be required.

† An advanced elective in mathematics-science or in quantitative methods could be substituted for each other.

tives. Students should be encouraged to follow up their own interests as long as the courses they select meet appropriate academic standards. Too wide latitude can lead to abuse, especially where there are large numbers of students and many courses of varying quality from which to choose. In the suggested curriculum, the type of electives open to the students is rather circumscribed, and it could be argued that more freedom would be desirable. It would be wholly in keeping with the spirit of the proposed program if these limited-choice electives were increased still further; for example, students might not be required to take the course in personnel management or one of the semesters in business policy, especially if the faculty's strength does not happen to lie in either of these directions. For qualified students who are particularly interested in the border areas between business and liberal arts, the work in the functional business subjects might be cut down even more.[15] Flexibility of this sort is all to the good if it is not used to undercut standards of performance; in fact, if skillfully administered, it should have quite the opposite effect. In this and other respects the schools themselves need freedom of choice in deciding where the best interests of their students lie.

[15] Still more limited-choice electives could be made available to students who can satisfy the composition and first-year mathematics requirement.

CHAPTER 10

MASTER'S PROGRAMS IN BUSINESS

> The emphasis on managerial decision making is more appropriate at the graduate than at the undergraduate level. Even this approach, however, does not differentiate the two levels of study sharply. The difference between graduate and undergraduate work in business largely depends on the quality of the faculty and students involved. This suggests that business schools should not endeavor to offer advanced degree programs unless they have the resources needed for high-quality work.

The historical discussion in Chap. 3 pointed to the increasing importance of graduate work in business administration. As a result of developments which have chiefly occurred since World War II, there are today 12 separate graduate schools of business and 146 other schools and departments of business which offer general graduate programs in this field. In 1955–1956, these institutions awarded approximately 4,500 master's degrees and 158 doctor's degrees in business; in 1939–1940, the number of second- and third-level professional degrees in business as defined by the U.S. Office of Education totaled only 689.[1]

In the coming decades there is every likelihood that graduate programs, certainly in terms of total enrollments and probably in relation to undergraduate work, will become still more important. At many of the older schools this shift in emphasis is already well under way, as new

[1] Estimates for 1955–1956 based on data from the Survey Questionnaire. Contrary to the classification method employed by the U.S. Office of Education, all work for which a master's degree is granted is usually referred to as graduate study in this field even though many of the students have taken their undergraduate work in nonbusiness subjects; this usage is followed here. The data on graduate business degrees contained in this chapter and in the reports of the U.S. Office of Education are not comparable since the latter groups graduate and undergraduate degrees together if the "graduate" degree is the first the student has earned in the field of business. In 1955–1956, for example, the U.S. Office of Education reported only 3,106 master's or second professional degrees in business. *Earned Degrees Conferred by Higher Educational Institutions,* 1955–1956, U.S. Office of Education Circular 499, p. 6.

schools have come into the undergraduate field. At five institutions which offer both graduate and undergraduate work—Carnegie Tech., M.I.T., Michigan, Northwestern, and Rutgers—the proportion of master's to undergraduate business degrees granted in 1955–1956 came to 60 per cent; at three institutions—American University, New York University, and Pennsylvania's Wharton School—the proportion of master's to undergraduate business degrees came to between 45 and 50 per cent that year; and at eight other schools the proportion came to between 20 and 35 per cent.

Of seventy-six schools with graduate programs which supplied the necessary data, fifty-three estimated that their graduate enrollment would increase twice or more by 1970, while thirty-one projected an increase of three times or more. Projections of undergraduate and graduate enrollments to 1970 at schools offering work at both levels indicate that graduate enrollment will increase more than twice as fast.[2] At present, however, graduate work is largely concentrated at a small group of institutions, with nine schools granting 57 per cent of all master's degrees and 50 per cent of all doctoral degrees;[3] of the schools answering the Survey Questionnaire, twenty-nine schools reported awarding doctoral degrees in business that year.

While graduate work has only recently achieved quantitative importance, educational leadership has long centered at this level. The boldest program to emerge before World War II was at Harvard's Graduate School of Business Administration. Some of the other graduate programs in the prewar period which received widespread attention and enjoyed considerable prestige were developed at Chicago, Stanford, and the Tuck School at Dartmouth, although then as now the last-named school accepted students in their senior year. All these schools were at privately endowed institutions. Michigan, a publicly supported institution, should also be included in this group; in the prewar period its program was exclusively graduate, but since World War II it has also offered undergraduate preparation beginning in the junior year. The main efforts to improve standards at many other schools during this period—for example, Columbia, Minnesota, Pennsylvania's Wharton School, and Wiscon-

---

[2] Estimates supplied by schools in answer to the Survey Questionnaire (see Appendix 3, Table 6); it should be kept in mind that the percentage projections of graduate business enrollments are figured on a smaller base than the undergraduate projections.

[3] These nine schools are: Chicago, Columbia, Harvard, Indiana, Michigan, Northwestern, New York University, Stanford, and Wharton. If four more of the schools which gave doctoral degrees in business are included (Minnesota, State University of Iowa, Ohio State, and University of Texas), the group accounted for 76 per cent of all doctor's degrees in 1955–1956. The data on graduate enrollments and degrees were derived from the Survey Questionnaire.

sin—were also largely centered on the graduate phase of their programs. If the past serves as any sort of guide, the major changes in the future will continue to come first at the graduate level, though the need for pioneering work is every bit as great at the undergraduate level.[4]

EVALUATION CRITERIA

The general principles developed in Part 1 and applied to undergraduate business programs are appropriate to graduate business education as well. While at a higher and more demanding level, graduate work should help carry forward the self-education which the student begins as an undergraduate. The underlying issues are therefore the same: Where should the balance be struck between education in breadth and in depth? What should go into the work designed to achieve these two goals? How much of the student's program should be required, how much left to individual choice? How much of the required work should be in traditional tool and functional business areas, how much in non-business areas? What should go into the student's program in his major? What research should be undertaken, and how can it be related to the teaching program?

Graduate work in business, as in other fields, has some inherent advantages over its counterpart at the undergraduate level. The number of students at a given school is, of course, considerably smaller; their undergraduate record provides a reasonably good test of their academic abilities; their interest in the business studies is presumably on a firmer basis; many have had a broad undergraduate preparation; and in general they are more prepared to undertake serious study.

Similarly, it can be assumed that graduate work in business attracts a better quality of faculty; as in other areas, graduate teaching in business carries more prestige, gives the instructor more freedom, provides a generally better atmosphere for both teaching and research, and quite often yields higher pay. The entire program for both students and faculty centers more completely on study and investigation—the distractions associated with undergraduate campus life, discipline questions, personal adjustment problems of undergraduates, and the like are less likely to obtrude. While difficult to attribute to any specific causes, there can be

---

[4] Of the twelve separate graduate business schools, six are at institutions at which there are no undergraduate business programs: Chicago, Columbia, Cornell, Harvard, Stanford, and Tuck; the others are separate from the undergraduate programs: Carnegie Tech., University of California (Berkeley), University of California (Los Angeles), M.I.T., New York University, and University of Virginia. Since 1956, graduate business schools have been established at other universities, including Purdue and Washington University (St. Louis).

no doubt that the atmosphere of graduate work is generally more conducive to serious intellectual effort.

Graduate study in business also has the advantage that it can be focused more completely on the problems of upper management. At the undergraduate level, as shown earlier, there is a strong tendency for the programs to stress either broad background preparation appropriate for almost any kind of career in business (and many other fields for that matter) or intensive training in rather specialized skills. Some weight, of course, can be given to preparation for management or for comparable administrative work of a professional nature, but the age, interests, experience, and numbers of students tend to prevent this emphasis from being carried very far. At graduate schools of business, especially if the students have had some work experience after leaving college, preparation for executive leadership and top professional responsibilities becomes a more realistic objective, and almost all the graduate business programs have at least some of this flavor.

The problems posed by specialized study are also somewhat easier to handle at the graduate level. In undergraduate schools the specialized skills are likely to be rather rudimentary and unrelated to the rest of the student's work. Graduate schools can confine specialized study to advanced subjects which build on prior preparation, which possess high analytical content, and which test the student's grasp of general principles. In areas like insurance and real estate, for example, undergraduate instruction is almost inevitably pedestrian, but this need not be so at the graduate level. This suggests that the second main test to apply in appraising graduate study is the success of the schools in giving students competence in one or more important areas of business and in relating this competence to their understanding of managerial decision making.

It would appear from the above that there is a fairly clear road ahead for graduate instruction in this field. Unfortunately, such is not the case. Two principal difficulties, both stemming from the same source, plague graduate business schools. The first is that there is no clear distinction between the undergraduate and graduate studies. Direct duplication is, of course, likeliest where students have already had extensive undergraduate business preparation; but in terms of the analytical content and level of the work, the problem of adequate progression applies to students with other backgrounds as well. Students from the stronger liberal arts schools (and from some of the undergraduate business schools as well) report that graduate business study tends to be no more difficult and is often even less demanding than the work they took as undergraduates. This is not uncharacteristic of student attitudes in other fields, but the opinion is too widely and too vigorously held to be disregarded.

The second difficulty is that there is no clear direction which schools can follow in putting business studies on a genuine graduate level even if they are determined to do so. To be sure there are some promising beginnings and worth-while experiments, as discussed later, but whether they can be transplanted successfully and emulated on a wide scale is far from certain. It is very easy in a field such as this to capture the form and lose the substance of a particular method or approach. Concepts or phrases like decision making, problem solving, policy making, and the like can mean much or little depending on the instructor's competence and imagination and the students' preparation and abilities. Principles of management, management science, organization theory—these can be significant or meaningless approaches to the subject depending on how they are used. At the present time these ideas largely restate rather than alter the essential problems which advanced work in business confronts, and there should be no illusions about the extent to which they will clarify such work in the future.

These two quite different difficulties stem from the same source— business administration is a vague, shifting, rather formless subject in which neither the foundations at the undergraduate level nor the super-structure at the graduate level can be sharply defined. The two preceding chapters suggested a general approach to the former, and this chapter suggests an approach to the latter, which go some way in the direction of meeting this basic problem, but the proposals mark hardly more than a beginning. For the foreseeable future, a good deal of variation and experimentation seems inevitable.

What has been said above underscores the importance of creating conditions at the graduate level under which faculty members and students can explore different areas together. This is an ideal toward which all graduate study should aim, but it is especially needed when the subject is as elusive and ill-defined as this one. Under these circumstances, provision for small seminar discussions, joint investigations, report writing, term projects, and the like become all the more important. The students should have frequent access to members of the faculty, and an important part of the work should be on a collaborative basis. Above all, the faculty and student body should be of high enough quality to carry through advanced study along these lines. Here lies a school's main defense against offering work of less than graduate stature; lacking this defense, a graduate program should not be attempted.

It is apparent from the foregoing that a graduate program in business which is worthy of the name entails a heavy expenditure of money. Salaries have to be high enough to attract capable faculty members and to free them for serious intellectual activity. Teaching loads have to be light and leaves of absence frequent, so that faculty members can pursue their varied interests. The faculty needs to work in an atmosphere of free inquiry and continual exploration which in turn requires adequate provision for research, library facilities, research materials, and clerical assistance. A program of this sort also requires attracting the right kind of students—fellowships have to be provided, recruitment activities have to be undertaken, adequate living facilities for students, some of whom will be married, have to be established. The ratio of faculty to students has to be high enough to permit reasonable teaching loads and personal dealings between student and teacher. It seems obvious that a program of this sort cannot be wholly financed out of tuitions. The choice appears to lie between substantial outside financial help and work at less than graduate quality.

These observations bear on certain general conditions requisite to graduate instruction in business. They tell little, except by indirection, what might go into the programs themselves, a task which is undertaken next.

GUIDES TO GRADUATE BUSINESS EDUCATION

First, minimum competence in a specialty is an altogether proper objective of graduate business work, especially if the student already has had broad undergraduate preparation. Anyone looking forward to a career in management needs a base in at least one subject from which to start and on which to build. Academic study is especially well designed to help the individual achieve just such a single-area foundation for further building.

As noted in the case of undergraduate programs, the danger is that specialized study will dominate the student's and faculty member's work, crowding out other no less important aspects of career preparation. A related danger is that the specialized work will be in some skill or subject which could quite as easily have been mastered earlier, or on a part-time study basis, or later on the job; or that it is treated as an end in itself without any meaningful relation to the rest of the student's academic preparation. Just as at the undergraduate level, graduate students in business should only be permitted to specialize within definite constraints; if the work commands an inordinate amount of the student's time, or requires little in the way of prior academic preparation, or bears little relation to the student's other more general studies, it should not be included in a graduate business program. If these dangers are avoided, specialized work cannot only be a valuable adjunct to the student's preparation but may well be absolutely essential to it.

There is some justification for arguing that graduate students should be permitted to pursue their particular interests much more intensively than would be appropriate at the undergraduate level. A certain flexibility is to be encouraged for the unusual student or faculty group to develop some subjects intensively, but it is very doubtful whether there is any area in this field (with the possible exception of accounting) which would justify more than four or five semester courses of study. Graduate work should start at a higher level of analysis than undergraduate and move ahead a good deal more rapidly, so that the same number of courses should cover much more ground. A limitation of four or five semester courses, with perhaps a still lower limit in some areas, would leave ample room for advanced seminars, research projects, and the like.

Second, understanding of mutual relations between relevant areas of knowledge is an appropriate goal of graduate work in management. Management in today's society is a complex process and many disciplines can make contributions to it. The traditional functional subjects—finance, marketing, personnel, production, etc.—should be kept open to these interfield influences and the student aided in every way to assimilate them. Needless to say, a high degree of selectivity is called for, as well as experimentation, in helping students grasp relationships between subjects which bear on managerial responsibilities. Graduate work in business should entail a good deal of exploratory study along these lines with students and faculty as partners in the enterprise.

Third, graduate business education even more than undergraduate should help students apply their specialized and general knowledge to significant issues of business policy. Mastery of a given subject or group of subjects, such as the theory of the firm, the theory of probability, or the theory of cost accounting, is essential—but not enough. A graduate student should be able to work with the ideas and tools which his advanced study provides. This in turn goes beyond mere intellectual exercises in manipulating formulae or simplified models. To a considerable extent it means that the individual student should assume responsibility for his own educational development. He should be required to analyze complex and what for him are new situations, weigh the human and material aspects of proposed courses of action, bring out the hidden dimensions in conflict relationships, trace the consequences of alternative policies in environments of rapid change, and, finally, recommend specific courses of action. Without suggesting that the classroom can ever duplicate conditions found in actual business situations, graduate students should demonstrate some capacity for transferring academic learning to specific operating problems.

Fourth, and last, graduate work can flourish best in an atmosphere where there is widespread and continuing interest in research. True, the bulk of the students are headed for a life of action in which research of any serious or demanding sort will play little direct part; and it may not be reasonable to expect graduate students to do any extensive research as part of their work for an M.B.A. On the other hand, graduate instruction in specialized areas, in the relationships between areas, and in applications of knowledge to specific situations is most likely to be kept alive and forward-moving if it is continually enriched by new ideas from research. The need for research most assuredly does not stand or fall on this ground alone—quite aside from their instructional responsibilities, the graduate schools have a special obligation to provide the breadth of viewpoint and leadership which can only come through the discovery and testing of new ideas. The point is that not even the teaching of practitioners can be kept vigorous and challenging if it is cut off from the wellsprings of research endeavors.

More important than the quantity of research is its quality. In the field of management, as elsewhere, there are the counterpulls of pure and applied research. In terms of contributing to the stock of knowledge, the former is much the more important and at least in the long run, the more vital to good teaching as well. If the discovery of new truths of enduring significance is the special province of graduate study, both intellectual imagination of a high order and capacity for meticulous investigation are called for. To carry forward such undertakings, bold leadership is needed, but the help of many supporting workers is also required. Viewing the matter realistically, the number of persons in any field capable of formulating and setting in motion a piece of truly fundamental research is extremely small; the contribution of most workers, and perhaps most schools, must be at a much more modest level. Yet the end result—the enlargement of knowledge—must ever be kept in view. This is as essential to the teaching of future practitioners as to the advancement of the scientific study of management.

In this schema, the long-standing conflict between general and specialized business education is seen in clearer perspective. The work in the major gives students the opportunity to apply basic principles and general background knowledge to a specific area, and in this sense, specialized study should play a larger role in graduate than undergraduate programs. However, the work in specific areas should be on a correspondingly higher level, too, requiring more in the way of technical and general background and demanding more in the way of independent analysis. Applying this distinction in a given case is not easy, but as shown below, there are some reasonably clear guides for determining when specialized study is an appropriate and vital element in graduate work.

Schools which develop along these lines may still be faced with the problem of differentiating their work sufficiently from undergraduate instruction, especially if the latter moves in the direction recommended in the last two chapters. The outcome will largely turn on the quality of faculty and students which a given school can attract. The question of assuring a clear progression from undergraduate to graduate study is not one which can be resolved by some simple curriculum change. It is largely due to the nature of the subject itself. This same issue is faced at a certain stage in the development of every field and when this stage is reached, no quick solution can be expected.

PATTERNS OF MASTER'S PROGRAMS

When set against the foregoing framework of principles, there are only a bare handful of graduate schools, perhaps no more than four or five, which can be said to have achieved a significant progression beyond work done at a high-caliber undergraduate school. Even among this select group, the distinction appears to rest almost wholly on the quality of the faculty and student body, the method of instruction employed, and the general spirit in which the work is carried on—not on the content of the programs as such. Thus, while the promise of an emerging discipline seems real enough, it remains a promise for all of that.

In contrasting the graduate work of different schools, attention will be centered on the two-year master's programs (usually leading to the M.B.A. degree), since they account for the great majority of students pursuing advanced study. On first examination many of the two-year programs appear to be similar, with the great majority requiring graduate students to study the same group of core subjects as undergraduates during their first year (accounting, statistics, economics, marketing, finance, business law, personnel, and production) and during the second year to take some type of management or general administration integrating course, plus a major concentration in one of the core subjects or related areas. As already noted, students who have had the requisite courses in business and economics as undergraduates can normally start with the second year's work, completing the requirements for the master's degree in two semesters or three quarters.

Closer study of the programs, however, shows that there is wide variation among the schools when judged on the basis of abilities and interests of students and faculty, methods of instruction, content of curricula, and underlying educational philosophies. As to the last two aspects of graduate work, the topics with which this chapter is primarily concerned, differences among schools are reflected in the nature of the core programs, types of majors, degree of specialization required or permitted in major subjects, the extent of the student's work taken in undergraduate courses, and the like. The evidence on these aspects of graduate business programs reflects the decisions of the schools to center their work almost completely either on careers involving broad administrative responsibilities or on training in specific techniques. Many schools seek to do both, but over time there appears to be a tendency for one or the other of these two conceptions of business education to gain dominance.

Specialized Schools

A review of two-year graduate business programs shows that the schools tend to fall into three groups—those which concentrate (1) on the specialized studies, (2) on combining specialized and general studies, and (3) on general studies in business administration alone. In the first group of schools, students are permitted to specialize more intensively in one area, but otherwise graduate and undergraduate work is largely indistinguishable. In fact, the more specialized courses in areas like marketing, production, and sometimes even accounting, tend to be on a lower analytical level than the elementary courses which students take as undergraduates. This result occurs wherever greater specialization leads to repetitious treatment or concentration on the minutiae of business practice.

In the programs in this group, students who did not have prior undergraduate business preparation are required to take a series of undergraduate courses covering the usual functional areas; an effort is often made to give graduate students in such courses additional work, but the general level of instruction is clearly of nongraduate caliber. In the second year, which is the only year taken by students who have had a full complement of undergraduate business courses, the bulk of the work is limited to graduate students only, but frequently three or four (sometimes, many more) are regular undergraduate courses. At almost all of these schools, the undergraduate and graduate business faculties are also intermingled, with the individual instructor giving the greater part of his time to undergraduate teaching.

Because the prime objective of these programs is to give students an opportunity to specialize in a particular area, little effort is made to relate all their work to some central theme. An important beginning toward unifying the individual courses is found at the schools in this group which require all students to take a course or seminar in business policy, but the clear intent of most of these programs is to provide training in specific skills for specific lines of work. Frequently, a substantial portion of the students hold part-time or even full-time jobs, and sometimes the entire graduate program is confined to night classes; under these circumstances business schools are in effect assuming responsibilities normally carried by night schools.

A large urban school, which is fairly typical of this group, requires all graduate students to satisfy its core curriculum in seven areas and then choose a specialized curriculum from one of the following subjects: business administration, finance, industrial management, marketing, personnel and industrial relations, retailing, real estate, and accounting. The student must take ten or twelve courses in his major or some closely related area; thus, in retailing the year's work consists of the following:

Name of course	Semester units
Marketing Research ⎫	
Advanced Marketing Research ⎭	2
Economic Basis of Retailing....................	2
Problems in Retailing (2 semesters).............	4
Marketing Problems...........................	2
Merchandise Planning and Control.............	2
Trends in Retailing...........................	2
Seminar in Retailing.........................	2
Thesis (2 semesters)..........................	4
Electives approved by department.............	8
Total.....................................	28

The thesis, which is required in all majors except accounting at this school, is written under the supervision of a faculty committee appointed by the chairman of the student's major department; in accounting, a comprehensive examination takes the place of the thesis requirement. According to the catalog of this institution:

Graduate classes are at present scheduled chiefly during the evening hours, so that students may combine full-time employment with a limited schedule of course work and so that training programs in business may be integrated with graduate courses. Students employed in full-time positions should not enroll for more than 8 units during any one semester.

Many of the schools in this group simply require two semesters of work beyond the bachelor's degree, but a minimum proportion must be "strictly graduate in character," and a few specific courses in addition to those in the usual functional areas must be taken. At one of the larger schools offering graduate work, the student must take at least eighteen of the thirty hours required for the M.B.A. in his major and half of the latter may be in undergraduate courses. However, the catalog of this school states:

"All thirty semester-hours may be taken in the major department if it offers sufficient work to meet the requirements for the master's degree." Every student must submit a thesis "in a subject germane to his major courses of study"; after the thesis is submitted and approved, the student must pass an oral examination.

The conclusion seems clear that graduate work in business at such institutions is for the most part indistinguishable from undergraduate and in many cases is below it. All that was said earlier about the proliferation of courses in undergraduate programs applies here. Students who take ten or twelve courses in any one field, whether it is finance, marketing, retailing, or any other, will inevitably spend a good deal of time on work of nongraduate stature. If business schools expect to win, and hold, the confidence of students, employers, and the general academic community, programs of this type should be represented for what they are—vocational training in trade techniques to prepare students for specific job openings. If such work has any place in higher education, it belongs in night schools, extension schools, and junior or two-year community colleges. It certainly should not qualify for the M.B.A. degree or for an advanced degree of any sort. To call such work "advanced" can only result in confusion, if not outright misrepresentation.

Multipurpose Schools

The second group of schools pursues a wide variety of aims in their master's work, ranging from specialized training in practical skills to systematic or detailed analysis of complex management problems. These multipurpose programs, typically found at large institutions, place considerable emphasis on the viewpoint of upper management, but room is also left for quite intensive study in a variety of major subjects. Similarly, preparation for the master's degree at these institutions ranges from undergraduate to nearly graduate quality. Students who have not had prior business training are generally required to take the same core courses as undergraduates, but many of the other courses are definitely at a higher intellectual level. The group also includes a very small number of schools which do not give credit for prior undergraduate work in business except under unusual circumstances, but whose programs are nonetheless indistinguishable from those offered at any "good" undergraduate school.

The record of research output at this second group of institutions is decidedly mixed; most have a few faculty members whose primary interests lie in this direction, with a much larger group whose activities lie more in consulting, teaching, and community service. The range of abilities and interests of faculty members, and of students as well, at one of these schools tends to be extremely wide. The boundary lines which set off this group of schools become blurred at the edges since, ultimately, the level of work at a school rests on such intangible but all-important elements as quality of faculty, analytical content of individual courses, and general breadth or philosophical undertone of the program.

Many of the state universities with long-established business schools are in this second group. A typical master's program at one of these schools requires work in nine foundation business and functional areas: principles of economics and accounting (two semesters each), statistics, money and banking, business law, industrial management, personnel, marketing, and corporation finance; students who have not done work in these areas earlier (about 80 per cent of the total at this school) meet these requirements by taking sophomore–junior-year courses in company with undergraduates. Seven of the ten remaining courses in the M.B.A. program must be at the purely graduate level, with three of the ten consisting of managerial economics, business research and report writing, and business policy. This institution requires a written and oral comprehensive examination, but no thesis and no foreign language proficiency.

The feature of the school's program which puts it in a rather different category from those in the first group is the limited specialization permitted M.B.A. students. Of the seven semester courses not included in the core, no more than three can be selected from any one area; moreover, the seven must be distributed over a minimum of four areas of business study. The latter include the usual eight business subjects (exclusive of economics) plus insurance and transportation. The specialized area courses are apparently not related to the core program in any close or meaningful way, but a fairly even balance is maintained between the student's work in his major and in the core.

Most of the other schools in this group have gone somewhat further in permitting students to concentrate in a single area; also, the variety of areas from which students choose their majors is usually greater, with some schools offering such fields as real estate and general management. As a somewhat different pattern, a few have relied heavily on seminar work in the last year of the M.B.A., with the students reading widely in some advanced area, like land utilization and regional planning, and/or investigating some subject of their own choice under the supervision of one or more faculty members. Similarly, a few of the schools in this group have gone further in making each major, and indeed each course, subordinate to a central curriculum theme. Just where the grouping shades off at either end of the spectrum is open to question, but all these schools have achieved a roughly even balance in their programs between an undergraduate versus graduate emphasis, as well as between a specialized major versus a broadly unifying core.

By way of general evaluation, these programs can be said to mark a serious start toward genuine graduate study while falling short of this goal by a considerable margin. They all go some way toward putting their work above the undergraduate level, but the distinction is not clear-cut and, for as much as half of the student's work, is openly disregarded. Each has a unifying core of studies which helps give some sense of direction to both the first and second year's work, but the student's major is still viewed as an essentially self-contained subject, bearing little relation to his program as a whole. Each school sets some bounds to the variety of majors (usually eight or nine) and the number of courses within a major (usually six or seven) which students may take, but the limits are broad enough to permit more specialization than seems defensible. Each school's faculty numbers at least a few who are engaged in research of a significant nature, but this is not a dominant or even principal interest of the faculty as a whole, nor does the typical course reflect a research emphasis.

Management-centered Schools

Finally, the third group consists of a small number of schools, perhaps no more than ten, which relate all the student's work to managerial decision making. One of the external characteristics common to their programs is that all students, regardless of prior preparation, are, with few exceptions, required to take two full years of graduate study. This has the natural result of discouraging students who had undergraduate business preparation from attending. Another common external characteristic is that they preclude work in highly specialized majors or courses. The general view underlying the programs of these schools is that every course should contribute to the student's understanding of the decision-making process. To this end all the schools endeavor to keep their entire programs, including both the work in the core and in the major, centered on issues facing upper management, usually in larger firms.

Given this orientation, the various specialties, such as accounting, finance, and marketing tend to be studied not as self-contained bodies of knowledge but as supporting branches of a broader subject—management. As a consequence, the student is in a better position to weigh the advantages and disadvantages of concentrating on a single subject and to decide for himself how far specialized study is worth pursuing. Similarly, his work in individual courses is more likely to have a unifying rationale than in programs built around traditional major areas.

The management emphasis is of special value in directing the student's attention to the external relations of the firm, including the relations between business and government. In this part of the program, major emphasis is sometimes placed on legislative and other legal controls over business (as at Chicago), sometimes on the social responsibilities which business is being increasingly asked to assume (as at Harvard). All the schools in this group, however, stress the broad role which firms must play in today's world, an outcome following directly from the managerial focus of their programs. In a few instances, such as the course in Business and Society at Dartmouth's Tuck School, this has led to studying the ethical bases of business policies; in others, as at Columbia, to increasing interest in the historical and philosophical background of business; in still others, as at Carnegie Tech., to analysis of the relations between ideas and social change. By these and other attempts to put the business enterprise in a wider social setting, the schools in this group are contributing to the development of a philosophy of management and to a code of professional ethics.

Another common characteristic of this third group of schools is the extent to which they build their work on the foundation subjects of mathematics and the sciences, the social sciences, and, to a limited extent, the humanities. Again, to the degree that breadth of viewpoint is associated with business executives' jobs, this is a logical outgrowth of the emphasis which these schools put on upper management. In their endeavor to apply the methods and findings of the background foundation subjects to problems of management, the students are obliged to draw on their prior preparation to a much greater extent than under more traditional business programs. This tends to put the entire level of the work on a more demanding basis than would otherwise obtain.

As another common characteristic, the focus on upper management has led these schools to concentrate on critical policy decisions of the firm. It is at the top of an organization where all considerations which go into important actions interlock. By putting the student, figuratively speaking, behind an executive's desk, he is helped to see the many sides of a particular course of action. By this means, much of the learning process becomes the responsibility of the individual student. The all-important task of bringing separate skills and understandings together and applying them to particular problems is put where it belongs—on the student himself. It is hard to imagine a more effective pedagogical device for making the student's general academic experience a vital part of his working equipment.

Another salient feature of the programs at these schools is the increasing attention they are giving to research, although the results to date are decidedly mixed. Some of those which have received wide attention are studies in capital budgeting, applications of mathematical statistics to inventory control policies, applications of psychological concepts to consumer and worker behavior, and economic analysis of the effects of tax policy on corporate investment decisions. While the research of these schools is of an applied character, some of it is of very high quality. In certain respects, the business schools have an advantage over older branches of universities in their research activities—they have fewer academic vested interests with which to cope, it is easier for them to undertake studies of an interdisciplinary character, and they have natural access to highly useful data. If they can resist the pressure to be pushed into primarily practical, descriptive investigations, schools such as these should become increasingly important as centers of research.

Quite aside from the specific content of their programs—and it should be stressed they vary considerably—the schools with a heavy management emphasis have put the business studies on a definitely stronger basis than before. The students are obliged to deal with concrete problems from a variety of viewpoints; they are required to engage in independent analysis; they must exercise a certain degree of ingenuity and judgment in their work; they must be prepared to meet questions and criticisms on their written and oral presentations; they gain some feel, at least, for the complexities and difficulties of decision making in a business setting; and they gain some appreciation of the interrelationships between business processes within the firm and between the firm and its external environment.

There are some dangers, however, in the managerial emphasis. Students may be deluded into thinking that the work will in some way assure them positions of executive responsibility. They may be left unprepared either technically or temperamentally to cope with routine responsibilities on the ground that they have been groomed only for decision making in the grand manner. The work may be so high-flown as to have little relevance to anything the student may do in his later career. There is even the danger that in the zeal to avoid undue specialization, a kind of overgeneralism may result. Certain aspects of the work in this field, especially having to do with human relations, organization theory, and management principles, seem rather thin. When some of these newer approaches are worked into the traditional functional subjects, such as marketing, personnel, and production, they can add real substance to the work, but standing alone they can be quite superficial. These dangers are not inescapable but are simply risks to be avoided. They loom especially large, of course, wherever the quality of the faculty and students is low.

Chicago and Harvard Programs

While all the schools just discussed concentrate their attention on questions of management policy, their work varies considerably in a number of significant respects. These differences, which raise a number of important issues, can be grasped more readily when put in the context of particular schools.

The Chicago and Harvard programs represent two approaches to managerial decision making which warrant closer consideration. The work at Chicago has only recently been reorganized, while Harvard's program is being intensively reexamined at the present time; it would hardly be appropriate, therefore, to compare the two programs in any detail. There are some general features which stand out, however, and which indicate the direction the two schools are taking. The program at Carnegie Institute of Technology is an example of still another approach with a rather different emphasis, and it is accordingly reviewed in Chap. 13.

The points of similarity and dissimilarity between the Chicago and Harvard programs are reflected in the courses required of all students at the two schools as shown in Table 10-1.

TABLE 10-1

COURSES REQUIRED OF ALL M.B.A. STUDENTS AT THE CHICAGO AND
HARVARD BUSINESS SCHOOLS, 1957–1958

Chicago	*Harvard*
Managerial Accounting (accounting measures of use to management)	Administrative Practices (working with people)
Statistics (introduction to concepts for organizing and interpreting data)	Business Responsibilities in the American Society (social aspects of competition and economic stability)
Economics of the Firm (the structure of American industry and effects of changes in the composition of the economy)	Control ("imaginative" use of accounting, statistics, and other figure procedures in management situations)
Economics of the Economy (analyzing and forecasting fluctuations in income, employment, and prices)	Finance (problems in handling working capital and long-range financing operations)
Public Policy and Business Law (public control of business and role of law in business)	Marketing (decisions with respect to consumer behavior, sales promotion and organization, and price policies)
Introduction to the Behavioral Sciences (review of findings of selected parts of psychology, anthropology, and sociology)*	Production (more concerned with methods of supervision and execution than with policy formulation)
Financial Management (the monetary system, flow of funds, capital and cash budgeting, etc.)	Written Analysis of Cases (to understand the interrelation of functional areas and skills by providing experience in thinking and writing about specific business cases)
Marketing Management (application of modern tools to fundamental marketing problems)	Business Policy (a "capstone" analysis of business situations from the viewpoint of the chief executive)
Personnel Management (organization, direction, and control of personnel in the firm)	
Production (survey of manufacturing processes, inventory policies, statistical quality controls, etc.)	
Business Policy (top-management decisions in a variety of case situations)*	

* These two courses are to be added to the core requirements in 1959–1960.

The required courses in both programs all have a heavy managerial policy-making emphasis. In general, the same broad tool and functional subjects are covered—accounting and statistics, finance, marketing, and production. Both have a capstone course in business policy centered on the decisions and problems of top management. Beyond the required courses, the amount of specialization in any one area is severely limited at both schools; in most instances, no more than four semester courses can be taken in one subject. The main safeguard, however, against undue specialization at Chicago and Harvard lies in the restricted number of total course offerings available to the students, in the design of each course in the different sequences, and in the counseling of individual students.

On other counts these two schools differ rather sharply. As some of the course titles suggest, the Chicago program puts more stress on preparing students in the basic business disciplines—accounting, statistics, economics, and law. The Harvard program, on the other hand, starts from the viewpoint of the administrator who faces difficult policy choices, asking the question in each case: What information, considerations, goals, etc., need to be reviewed and weighed to reach the best possible decision? The work in economics is indicative of the difference in the educational philosophy of the two schools. Put directly, study of economic theory is taken a good deal more seriously at Chicago than at Harvard; two courses are devoted to a quite sophisticated review of major economic concepts as they relate to various aspects of business policy, whereas at Harvard these concepts are mostly brought in as part of the discussion of cases in the Business Responsibilities course. Much the same holds true of the work at the two institutions in accounting, statistics, law, and the public regulation of business.

According to the Chicago view, the best academic preparation for business is to give students a thorough grounding in these basic subjects. The application of this knowledge to specific business problems is not to be ignored—indeed, is considered essential to gaining a minimum competence in these fields—but the prime responsibility of graduate business education is to equip students with certain analytical tools. Nor does the Chicago view suggest that the element of discriminating judgment can be disregarded in dealing with specific situations—only that this is a quality which is acquired primarily as a result of on-the-job experience and that the special role of the university is to provide the essential equipment needed to make the most of such experience. As Dean Wallis of the Chicago Business School puts the issue:[5]

> Social science training in school is the optimum way of hastening, stimulating, and making more profound that education which is acquired on the job. It raises pertinent questions, increases sensitivity to relevant phenomena, and provides a coherent frame of reference into which the individual can assimilate his complex and occasionally untidy vocational experience.

The Harvard view puts quite as much stress on helping the student develop a coherent frame of reference, but the method of doing so is considerably different. Under the Harvard program the student works his way through about 1,000 cases during his two years of study. While

[5] In a staff memorandum for private circulation.

varying in complexity and completeness, these cases are simulated business situations, with many of the shadings, ramifications, and contradictions which the student will face later in dealing with concrete business problems. Formal study in economics, statistics, psychology, etc., is reduced to very much of a supporting role in the student's work, while practice in how to balance a host of considerations and in how to single out the crucial elements in a given situation is brought very much to the fore. The former, in the Harvard view, relates to skills born of knowledge —the latter, to skills born of judgment.

To probe beyond these obvious and somewhat superficial differences raises difficult questions of fact and interpretation. The Harvard approach appears to be centered somewhat more on the immediate and practical circumstances surrounding particular business situations, the student being required to thread his way through to specific policy recommendations as best he can. The Chicago approach tends to center attention rather more on general causal factors often of a highly theoretical nature. The students at Harvard are asked, "How can a given case be effectively resolved?" while the students at Chicago are asked, "Why did a given problem arise?" In this sense, there is more analysis of an *ad hoc* nature at Harvard and more analysis of a conceptual, systematic nature at Chicago.

There is some tendency at Harvard to look at issues from within the firm much as they would be seen by a practicing administrator. At Chicago, the viewpoint tends to be more external to the firm with less emphasis on how matters look from the position of the operating executive most immediately involved. Harvard, however, puts rather heavy emphasis on the business manager's responsibilities to society while Chicago gives little overt attention to this aspect of the work. At the same time, systematic analysis of public policy issues in such areas as legal factors in business, antitrust, and the like tends to bulk larger at Chicago.

A rather sharp difference is evident in the approaches of the two schools to teaching, research, faculty recruitment, and perhaps even to student selection. Harvard places great weight on the collection of detailed case materials for classroom use, intensive analysis by the student of such materials, oral and written case discussions in both large and small groups, the faculty members in all these situations serving primarily as questioners and critics. Chicago follows a good deal more diversified approach to the teaching function ranging from straight lecture to individual student investigation, with case instruction introduced on a selective basis. In general, Chicago appears to be less teaching-oriented and more research-oriented than Harvard. Moreover, the research at Chicago tends to range more widely than at Harvard and to stress issues of a more purely theoretical nature. Some of the best-known research work at Harvard has little connection with case analysis, but the greater part of it has a heavy case emphasis. While both schools have striven to attract a balanced staff, faculty recruitment at the two institutions reflects similar differences; there is more of a tendency at Chicago to appoint persons for their research interests and abilities, while Harvard puts somewhat more emphasis on their experience in responsible business jobs and on their promise as teachers. It is debatable whether admissions practices of the two schools differ along the above lines, although there is probably some tendency for Chicago to attract more academically minded, and Harvard more business operations minded, students.

Despite these differences, it appears that both schools are introducing elements of the other's philosophy and methods. It should be noted that neither school treats management in terms of a single set of principles or as an area of specialization separate from the functional aspects of the firm. Both center their attention on certain issues of business policy approached from a broad, interdisciplinary point of view. In this connection, the work at Chicago clearly bears the impact of Harvard's use of cases in bringing out the critical elements in different business situations. At both schools, for example, the course in business policy is built almost entirely around case analysis. There are increasing indications, on the other hand, that Harvard is broadening its research interests considerably and that in the future its teaching program will have a somewhat greater academic emphasis than in the past. The following excerpt from a recent speech by Dean Teele suggests that there may be some rather important changes in this direction in the near future.[6]

I believe that all of us would readily agree that top management is a mixture of art and science. My own view is that it is overwhelmingly more art than science, but that the element of science will increase notably during the next generation. To be brash indeed and put out specific numbers to provoke discussion, I would say that today top business management is 90% art and 10% science and that in another generation a tremendous increase in attention to scientific aspects might make the ratio 80% art and 20% science. Obviously what I have in mind particularly here is the growing attention on the one hand to mathematical-statistical theories and on the other hand to the electronic data processing equipment which may make those new mathematical-statistical theories and methods usable in the day-to-day and year-to-year operation of a large and complex enterprise.

Other schools seeking to strengthen their graduate offerings will doubtless be affected by these same trends.

[6] "The Fourth Dimension in Management," speech delivered by Dean Stanley F. Teele, Graduate School of Business Administration, Harvard University, May 25, 1956, before the American Management Association, New York.

PROPOSED AREAS OF GRADUATE STUDY

While the above discussion suggests the general direction which graduate work in business might well take in the future, some definite proposals are needed to point up the issues now confronting these schools. At the graduate level even more than at the undergraduate, it would be unwise for all the schools to follow the same pattern of development; one of the central features of any strong graduate program is the provision made for individual faculty and student differences. It would therefore not be profitable to work out a recommended graduate program in great detail, especially since the different branches of the curriculum are examined more intensively in Part 3. To avoid repetition, the discussion will center largely on the aspects of the business studies which might differentiate graduate from undergraduate studies.

As in the upper division portion of the proposed undergraduate curriculum, a two-year master's program in business administration may be divided into five parts: courses in (1) the contributions of quantitative methods to management (accounting, statistics, and applied mathematics), (2) the contributions of economics, psychology-sociology, and law to management (theory of the firm, theory of the economy, individual and group behavior, legal institutions and public policy), (3) the contributions of these disciplines to the principal business functions (finance, marketing, personnel, production) and to policy making for the firm (business policy), (4) choice of one area of management for special study (not exceeding three or four semester courses beyond the basic course level), and (5) choice of free electives inside or outside the business school.

Under the first two parts of the curriculum, the student would develop the tools of analysis useful to management and would begin to use them in dealing with major issues of business policy; in the next two parts he would shift his emphasis more completely to problems of application; finally, the free electives would permit him to pursue interests of his own choice.

The principal aim of the program would be to help students dig into certain disciplines (quantitative methods, economics, psychology-sociology, law, and public policy) of most relevance to management and apply them to a wide variety of management problems or situations in the different functional areas. At every step, specific issues would be related to the over-all administration of the firm, with the final course or seminar in business policy addressed solely to the "internal-external" coordinating function of top management. Inevitably, there would be a considerable amount of systematic reading and exposition in some of the work, the extent depending on the background and ability of the students; but in the greatest measure possible they would be obliged to work through questions independently, thus assuming chief responsibility for their own education.

Variations among schools would have to be allowed for, due not so much to differences in underlying viewpoints as in the backgrounds and abilities of students, and, to a lesser extent, of faculty members. This becomes especially important in the two areas of quantitative methods and psychology-sociology. Some schools are in a position to make work in calculus and in the major concepts of finite mathematics a condition of admission, in which case the student can be introduced almost immediately to some of the more advanced aspects of mathematics which are applicable to management problems—for example, linear programming and game theory.

Work along the latter lines, however, probably should not be required of all students; instead, emphasis in the core program would better be put on more intensive work in statistics and mathematical statistics. Judging from the company interviews summarized in Chaps. 5 and 6, advanced work in statistics has wider application in business situations than advanced work in mathematics. A student who combines graduate-level study in statistics through probability theory, sampling theory, correlation analysis, estimation, and hypothesis testing with undergraduate work in mathematics through calculus will be able to use his academic equipment to advantage in any number of business situations. Important advantages are also derived from tying the work in statistics and accounting together, but again the benefits are maximized if the student has already had a solid grounding in mathematics; the possibility of fusing these two subjects together in the basic undergraduate course was touched on briefly in the preceding chapter and is examined at greater length with respect to both undergraduate and graduate instruction in Chaps. 13 and 14. Where this is not the case, there is no recourse but to put the courses in quantitative methods one notch lower and one step further removed from application to management decision making; presumably, this would mean initial instruction in mathematics and/or statistics at an undergraduate-level equivalent.

These same considerations apply, though with less force, to graduate studies in the psychology-sociology area. If students are required on admission to have had a full year of either of these subjects, the emphasis in the basic graduate course can be focused more immediately on applications to business problems, e.g., organization theory, industrial sociology, human relations, employee motivation, and the like. Where this is the case, a one-semester requirement in human behavior and management would probably provide an adequate basis for later work; otherwise, a two-semester requirement would be the minimum needed. If the course is used as a broad introduction to the whole field of management, two semesters would probably be required.

Even more than in the mathematics-science area, the relation between the basic and applied aspects of these subjects presents difficulties from the viewpoint of graduate business schools. If they concentrate too much on the foundation subjects of psychology and sociology, any discernible relevance to business problems may disappear; if they concentrate too much on their applied aspects, the work may lack any underlying theory or perhaps any long-range significance. Even among the small group of schools doing serious work in this area, there is little consensus on this issue. Most, however, are attempting to add one or two faculty members who are primarily trained in psychology and sociology and who have only a secondary interest in business administration as such. At the same time, these institutions are taking steps to help faculty members in the more traditional business subjects develop greater competence in these areas. In addition to the work in management or business policy, the subjects most affected by these developments to date are marketing and personnel management. A few schools are considering making the behavioral sciences or organization theory a separate major, but in view of the present inchoate state of this area, to say nothing of the difficulty of securing properly trained faculty members, the schools are understandably hesitant about doing so.

The matter of specific prior preparation has less effect still on graduate work done in the area of law and public policy. Other than the desirability of a good general background in the social sciences, it does not appear to be an issue of great importance whether students have taken philosophy, for example, rather than psychology, or mathematics rather than English literature. The schools in the third group are in complete agreement that graduate business students cannot hope to master the rules and procedures in the field of business law or the detailed regulations of public law. Increasingly, emphasis is being placed on work in law and public policy as an essential part of the general environment in which employers operate, serving to highlight the varied and changing relations between society and business management. This work introduces students to some of the ends a society seeks in its relations with business enterprises and some of the means (through law) which it has devised to carry out these purposes. As in the suggested undergraduate studies in this area, the work is designed to help students develop a broader perspective on problems of management by analyzing certain issues or concepts in spheres where private and public interests overlap.

Given this emphasis, it is not surprising that the specific topics covered by these courses show little similarity. The focus of some (as at Chicago) is on the legal and economic principles underlying the public control of business; of others (as at Carnegie Tech.) on legal institutions and procedures emerging from broad industrial and social changes. In summarizing the latter course, entitled Ideas and Social Change, Professor Leland Hazard states:[7]

Obviously it was not within the scope of our course on Ideas and Social Change to teach rules of law. Nevertheless it was important to examine, as we did, a few cases. They were selected to point up that most difficult, and at the same time most illuminating, situation in which one of two equally innocent persons must suffer. . . . We spent some time on the necessity for procedure in law. . . .

The employment of several novels in the course was not a pretense at literary criticism. . . . Neither was there a pretense at history, philosophy, or theology. Of course it was necessary to skirt these fields in order to develop the proposition that law arises not in mystery but rather in the ebb and flow, in the very flux, of life.

It would have been more convenient to teach such a course out of a book. It would have been preferable—possibly preferable—to have avoided a considerable amount of non-chronological treatment of the materials. But life is not always neat. The world has been somewhat disorderly in every century, our own not the least. In any case I made an effort to avoid teaching answers.

In such a course, the development of legal principles is not viewed as an end in itself but as a way of looking at the business enterprise and at the society of which it is a part.

Finally, and perhaps most important, graduate business students should develop a good working knowledge of economics.[8] In the earlier discussion of undergraduate business programs, it was concluded that economics was essential both as a background subject and as a tool subject and that, therefore, undergraduate business students should have a minimum of five semester courses in this area, including a year of introductory economics and intermediate courses in money, theory of the firm, and theory of income and employment. In addition, it was concluded that economics should be given considerable attention in the functional area courses—marketing, finance, production, etc.—and that students should be encouraged to elect economics courses in such subjects as public finance, government and business, and international economics. The purpose of the recommendations was to give undergraduate business students enough economics to be able to use the subject in dealing with

[7] Leland Hazard, Summary Comments at Closing Meeting of Class, Jan. 21, 1958 (mimeographed).

[8] The general status of graduate education in economics is surveyed by Howard R. Bowen, "Graduate Education in Economics," American Economic Review, vol. 43, no. 4, part 2, September, 1953; see also "A Report on Panel Discussion at Yale," Graduate Training in Economics, Yale University Press, New Haven, Conn., 1956.

concrete situations as well as to provide them with essential background for their future roles as administrators and citizens.

If the broad findings of the present chapter are accepted, graduate business education should also include a considerable amount of economics, but the emphasis would shift to advanced analysis relating more specifically to internal and external problems of the firm. Thus, the students would be adding to their knowledge of one of the foundation business subjects while at the same time developing skill and judgment in applying this knowledge to a variety of business situations. As in the area of quantitative methods and behavioral sciences, the starting point of the students' work would depend on how much economics they had had as undergraduates.

In this connection, two areas in economics which deserve particular attention in graduate business programs are the theory of the firm and the theory of income and employment. The work should be on a considerably higher analytical level than comparable courses in undergraduate business programs. Accordingly, it ought to be taught by persons whose graduate preparation was mainly in economics, chiefly theoretical economics. The instructors should of course be able to relate the work to actual business problems, and therefore some interest and experience in applied areas would be essential; but their main task would be to help students master the tools of economic analysis. If the choice has to be made—and it almost always does—the instructor should be an economic theorist first and a business economist or "management-expert" second.

The respective approaches of graduate and undergraduate work can be illustrated in terms of one area, the theory of the firm. At the graduate business level, this course might well stress problem solving rather than problem formulation, pricing under complex rather than highly simplified market conditions, cost analysis in multiproduct rather than in single-product firms, production problems in multiplant rather than in single-plant operations, etc. More important, the students should be required to do much more in the way of putting their analytical tools to work, in thinking through on their own the limitations, as well as the contributions, of economic analysis, and in applying theoretical concepts to empirical data. In an area as broad and difficult as the theory of the firm, the problem of overlapping between undergraduate and graduate work need not be serious—in fact, some duplication would seem desirable from the viewpoint of most students. A similar distinction can be drawn, although perhaps less sharply, between graduate and undergraduate work in the area of income and employment theory.

Also, graduate programs should go considerably further than undergraduate in relating economics to the other tool courses as well to the courses in the functional business areas. Accountants, statisticians, market analysts, or financial officers can easily become mere technicians if they are unable to relate their specialties to a general theory of the internal and external relations of the business enterprise. Economics can contribute materially to helping the student develop such a frame of reference, but only if the applied business courses contain a considerable amount of economic analysis as well. Unless the student finds that his economic tools are usable in the various business areas, they will quickly be put to one side and forgotten; especially at the graduate level, it is important to see that this does not happen.

Location of Graduate and Undergraduate Economics

This raises the thorny question whether the faculty which handles the economics part of the graduate and undergraduate business curriculum should be on the staff of the business school or the college of arts and sciences. In any case, it can be assumed that courses having heavy economic content ought to be taught by persons with predominantly economics graduate training, but it is a matter of some moment whether business schools should assume responsibility for staffing these areas.

According to the Survey Questionnaire, in 50 per cent of the graduate programs and 52 per cent of the undergraduate programs, economics is located in the business school (see Appendix 3, Table 9). There is a tendency for the two groups to be separate at larger institutions, i.e., at universities with enrollments exceeding 15,000.[9] This is almost universally the case where the economics department offers a graduate program of national repute, although there are a few well-known institutions where this is not true.

If economics is to be made an integral part of both graduate and undergraduate business programs, the closest possible ties should exist between the members of the economics and business faculties. On first consideration, this would appear to argue for keeping both in the business school, but the interviews uncovered a number of instances where close administrative ties have seemed to widen, rather than narrow, the gulf between the two groups. The matter is complicated by the fact that the interests of economists extend well beyond the business sphere, while the same holds true of the interests of business faculties in relation to economics. On some campuses, the fact that the business program is rapidly expanding in terms of student popularity while student enrollments in economics are either static, or even contracting, exacerbates an already difficult situation.

So many elements enter into a relationship of this sort in a given case,

[9] Howard Cutler, "Organization of Collegiate Schools of Business," *Collegiate News and Views*, vol. 7, October, 1953, pp. 1–8.

it is hard to go beyond the most obvious generalizations. It would seem rather evident that the economics faculty should teach courses which emphasize economic theory and public policy and that the business faculty should teach applied courses dealing mostly with the individual firm or industry. Some of the borderline courses, like economics of the firm (sometimes called managerial economics), corporation finance, and labor are not easy to categorize, and here the interests and backgrounds of the various faculty members should be taken into account. On some campuses one gets the impression that the economists regard all these courses as their exclusive domain and that if they are not taught in the economics department they are hardly worth teaching at all. At other institutions, exclusive ownership of such courses is sought through somewhat similar reasoning by the business faculty.

On most campuses where the two groups are independent, almost all the work in the border fields has gravitated to the business schools. This is hard to avoid in view of the relatively rapid rise in their enrollments, but it can have the unfortunate result of unduly restricting the economic content of the instruction in these fields. It also seriously undercuts the offerings of the economics departments, tending to limit them to courses in introductory principles and pure theory. Unless the undergraduate and graduate enrollments are very high and the two faculty groups of most unusual quality, it would seem educationally desirable to keep the basic course offerings in the three border areas—economics of the firm, labor, and corporation finance—in the economics departments, with both groups offering advanced work in these areas if resources permit. The economics faculty would have to be prepared to give more attention, perhaps, to the applied or institutional aspects of these subjects, but even if this were not done to the complete satisfaction of the business school, any losses in this direction would be more than made up for in the increased analytical economic content of the work. At earlier points in the discussion, as well as in the later chapters on individual areas of the curriculum, the need for more emphasis in this direction is clearly indicated.

From the viewpoint of a university's total undergraduate and graduate program in the social sciences, it is important to keep the economics department independent of the business school and to maintain it on a vigorous, well-balanced basis. This is as essential to the programs in business as in other areas of the social sciences. The fact that economics may be administratively within the business school should not be permitted to limit its role to a principles course plus a few offerings in advanced theory. In those schools where the economics faculty has withdrawn into their private domain and the business faculty into theirs, the result has usually proven educationally preposterous and administratively unwieldy. Initially when this occurs, most of the students are likely to go over to the business program while most of the analytical content is apt to stay in the economics program. The next step is for the business school to add economists to its own staff in order to strengthen and broaden its offerings, and they in turn begin to offer courses with a heavy economics emphasis. The upshot is that some universities now have two economics faculties offering more or less the same courses, though with different titles and somewhat different emphases. In other universities with two groups of economists of about equal size and stature, the business school economists have concentrated chiefly on policy issues in the individual firm, and where this has occurred, the resulting division of labor has proven mutually beneficial. As is so often the case, the fact that relations are distant at one institution and close at another is much more the result of personalities than of any formal division of responsibility.

Other Core and Major Subjects in M.B.A. Programs

The foregoing review of graduate business work in the general foundation subjects has stressed the importance of adding to the student's equipment in certain areas while at the same time showing him how this equipment can be used to help management reach decisions on significant issues. The functional fields in the graduate core program and the majors in graduate business subjects should give the student the opportunity to carry forward these two aspects of his preparation, but especially the second. This means that the same principles which were found to be applicable to the undergraduate core of functional business subjects and the major specialties apply to graduate programs as well. The essential difference is that the latter should permit students to develop a firmer theoretical grounding, including a better grasp of inter-subject relationships, and more facility in applying analytical methods to concrete business situations. Since the considerations which should govern this aspect of graduate and undergraduate instruction are essentially the same, the following discussion can be brief.

Considering first the functional areas to be included in the required core of graduate programs, most schools specify the same subjects as in the undergraduate business core; in fact, as already noted, graduate students who have not had undergraduate business preparation are frequently required to take the same business courses as undergraduates. Even among the third group of graduate schools with a heavy managerial emphasis, the core areas are substantially the same as in undergraduate programs, but a real effort is made to put the quality of work on a definitely higher level. Some of these schools (Carnegie Tech., Chicago,

Harvard, and M.I.T., among others) require students to take the first year's courses, or equivalent work, even if they have completed a full undergraduate business program. While it would hardly be appropriate to ask students to repeat a nearly identical course, it is not too much to require them to fill gaps in their preparation in nonbusiness areas. For most students, a beginning graduate-level course in fields like finance or marketing need not involve serious repetition in any case, the outcome largely depending on the way the material is approached.

In general, there appear to be no clear grounds for making the functional areas in the graduate core different from the undergraduate core. However, the graduate core courses in the four functional business areas (production, personnel, finance, and marketing) can assume that students have considerably more background in mathematics, psychology-sociology, and economics than in the case of undergraduate programs—especially if the latter move in the direction recommended in the last two chapters! Likewise, less time can be given to straightforward description or discussion of elementary principles in these four areas, so that the core courses in graduate programs can begin much sooner to explore advanced topics. In the core course in production, this can mean early emphasis on problem solving, laboratory work, and the like; in marketing and personnel, on the contributions of economics and psychology; and in finance, on the uses of mathematics, accounting, and economics in analysis of important issues. If the student chooses to major in one of these subjects —or any other subject, for that matter—his later studies would go further in these same directions, helping him develop his abilities for analyzing and dealing with a variety of business-type situations. The chapters in Part 3 of the study on individual areas of the curriculum explore these matters in greater detail.

It is evident from the discussion that if certain dangers are guarded against, the work at the graduate level should be more closely geared to the managerial viewpoint than the undergraduate studies. This would be a natural concomitant, for reasons touched on earlier, of any move to strengthen a school's graduate offerings. From this it follows that both the core and advanced courses in the functional areas should stress the role of management in coordinating internal operations and in adapting to change in the external environment. This also means giving more attention to general administrative theory and action, at both the beginning and end of the student's two years, the two courses in management or business policy serving even more as a focus for the student's entire studies than at the undergraduate level. Similarly, the further the student proceeds in his work, the greater should be the reliance put on problem solving and case analysis. Whether incorporated in the capstone course in business policy or treated separately, it is also important to require as much report writing and independent investigation of cases in the latter part of the student's graduate career as circumstances permit.

Graduate Major Subjects

Centering graduate work around the management viewpoint precludes offering a long list of specialized majors or permitting students to take as many as six or seven (certainly not eight or ten) courses in a single area. The schools in the third group show some diversity in this regard, including an occasional major offering in such fields as transportation, insurance, and retailing. The clear trend within the group as a whole, however, is to limit the fields of concentration to five or six broad subjects which cut across specific industries and specialized functions. A composite list of the majors at these schools would be limited to the following fields: accounting, finance, marketing, personnel-industrial relations, and production; in some cases, students may concentrate in business economics, statistics, or quantitative methods, and where this is so, a good deal of the advanced work can be done elsewhere in the university. It is indicative of the general approach of this group of schools that some do not offer majors as such at all and that each has tried to reduce departmental autonomy to a minimum. Similarly, students at these schools are usually limited to four or five courses in any one area of concentration.

With few exceptions, the schools which concentrate their attention on the decision-making process do not offer management as a separate major. The latter issue is somewhat more complicated than at the undergraduate level, because the students are more mature and better able to assimilate the work in management. However, the very fact that their entire programs have a managerial emphasis largely eliminates the necessity for offering a separate major in this area in these schools.

Looking beyond this small group of about ten institutions, a rather different picture emerges with respect to major offerings. Among 64 schools offering M.B.A. degrees in 1955–1956 (of 66 institutions known to have such programs), 12 offered no majors as such or only one general major; of the 52 other schools, 28 offered 7 majors or more, and 15 offered 10 or more. Table 10-2 presents information on specific fields of major study at the 64 schools granting M.B.A. degrees; in terms of the areas covered, the results generally conform to the data on major studies at undergraduate schools (Table 9-4) but it should be noted that the median undergraduate business school offered eight instead of five majors.

Because most M.B.A. programs have been established since World War II, it seems likely that unless counteracting steps are taken the number of graduate majors available at these schools will increase still

TABLE 10-2

NUMBER AND PER CENT OF GRADUATE BUSINESS SCHOOLS
OFFERING DIFFERENT MAJORS AMONG 64 SCHOOLS
GRANTING M.B.A. DEGREES, 1955–1956

Major subjects*	M.B.A. schools offering	
	Number	Per cent
Accounting	48	75
Marketing	47	73
Finance-banking	45	70
Production	28	44
Economics	24	38
Management	24	38
Personnel–industrial relations	23	36
Statistics	20	31
Transportation	20	31
Insurance	15	23
Administration–general business	14	22
Real Estate	13	20
Advertising	8	13
Business education	8	13
Foreign trade	8	13
Public administration	6	9
Retailing	5	8
Business law	3	5
Public utilities	3	5
Salesmanship	2	3
Miscellaneous	2	3
Secretarial	1	2

* Some schools offer majors in subdivisions of the subjects shown.
SOURCE: Survey Questionnaire.

more over the next five or ten years. The issues raised by this trend, if it occurs, are basically the same as those faced in undergraduate programs, and the strictures set forth in the discussion of those programs need not be repeated here.

This is not to deny that provision should be made for intensive work in especially difficult subject matter or along the frontiers of a given field. As noted earlier, this kind of high-level specialization is perhaps more appropriate in research undertakings or as part of doctoral programs, but it would not do to foreclose all such work at the master's or even undergraduate level. Under proper conditions, this is the very type of study which the ablest students are most likely to find most challenging, and despite the risks involved, the opportunity for promising students to follow their varied interests just as far as their capacities will allow should be preserved at all costs. Somewhat similar considerations apply to faculty members as well. Not infrequently their research interests become closely identified with particular courses which on first consideration might seem unduly limited, but, in fact, may prove unusually challenging. It is especially desirable for this reason to keep graduate offerings rather flexible, bearing in mind that the best safeguard lies not in any rules about course offerings but in the quality of new appointments to the faculty. There is no need, however, for such intensive work to be cut up into different majors, each with its own faculty, requirements, and series of course offerings. Indeed, the exploring student and faculty member appear to be more often inhibited than helped by departmental barriers and traditions. The problem is not one of offering an occasional course or seminar in some recently developed area or in a field of special interest to certain students or faculty members; rather it is one of expanding and rigidifying offerings into full-blown departmental major programs.

The work which some business schools have undertaken, or are contemplating, in the international field affords a good illustration of the issues involved. Prospective trends in the American economy, as noted in Chap. 5, point to the increasing need for study and research in this area. Emphasis in such work, however, should be placed as much, if not more, on international economics, international relations, and perhaps anthropology, as on foreign-trade practices and opportunities of American business. It would therefore appear to be a serious mistake to establish departments and majors in international business at this time, whereas a single, well-designed course or seminar for advanced students would seem wholly desirable. Somewhat similar considerations might well guide the development or reorganization of work in other special areas like insurance, real estate, and transportation.

M.B.A. Thesis and Comprehensive Examination

Despite the increasing importance attached to written reports and independent projects by students, surprisingly few schools require a thesis for the M.B.A. degree. Of the 64 reporting schools granting this degree, only 24 definitely required a thesis while 13 made it an option with some other requirement. Even among the group of schools which concentrated most of their attention on managerial decision making, a thesis was hardly ever a rigid condition. In the interviews, most faculty members expressed the opinion that a thesis requirement would strengthen the academic content of the programs considerably, but that there would not be enough faculty manpower to administer it effectively. A substantial number (and this included most of the deans interviewed) held that the M.B.A. was not and should not be a research degree, while all agreed that to make such a requirement of any real value to the student, an enormous amount of faculty time and effort would have to go into the undertaking.

A thesis requirement would be in keeping with the general pattern of graduate work outlined earlier, although it can be argued that a research investigation in the traditional academic sense might prove to be wide of the mark. Hence, if there is any way a school can handle the added work load, some type of thesis requirement would be worth including as part of an M.B.A. program. Short of this, it becomes doubly important for a school to emphasize report writing and independent investigation on the part of every student in one or more of the required courses. The discussion of the Written Analysis of Cases course at Harvard and similar programs at other schools in Chap. 8 is again worth noting. Moreover, supervisory responsibility should be fixed in such a way that the written work cannot be shortchanged or disposed of in a routine manner. If it becomes no more than a formal requirement, lacking any real intellectual content, its value is completely lost.

In lieu of a thesis, some schools are experimenting with shorter types of investigations in which students are required to analyze and report on perhaps three or four carefully delimited issues in the course of a single academic year. Where this is done, emphasis can be placed on giving every student the experience of doing at least a few pieces of analysis and reporting superbly well. Another variant is followed by the business school at the University of California at Berkeley. In place of a thesis, every M.B.A. student is required to carry out an independent investigation of some business problem, the work being equivalent to 3 to 6 semester-credit hours. It has become rather common for the students at Berkeley to work on their independent projects under the joint guidance of a business executive and a faculty member. These experiments have a lot of educational merit, to say nothing of easing the placement problem for some students.

According to the replies to the Survey Questionnaire, the number of schools requiring some kind of written and/or oral examination in M.B.A. programs is also quite small (twenty-four and thirty-eight, respectively). This may well be misleading since many schools require an integrating course (usually in the business policy area), and any examination on this work would serve much the same function as a comprehensive. Where this is not the case, serious consideration ought to be given to remedying the deficiency, since the students (and perhaps the faculty) need this spur to tie the different parts of their work together.

Schools seeking to broaden and strengthen their graduate programs have used the M.B.A. comprehensive examination as an important enabling device. At the business school at Indiana, for example, the morning examination entails answering general questions based on a hypothetical case situation; sometimes students are given the case an hour or even a day in advance. Two hours are allotted for writing the morning examination and a half-hour for editing. The student's specialized examination in the afternoon is limited to his major area and takes three hours; however, the examination given general business students, an important M.B.A. major at Indiana, emphasizes finance, methods of business research, and business economics. By dint of effort and imagination, the faculty has made the comprehensive a genuine capstone of the entire M.B.A. program at this institution.

UNDERGRADUATE PREPARATION FOR
GRADUATE WORK IN BUSINESS

It is worth noting that a liberal arts undergraduate education is probably the best preparation for the kind of graduate business program outlined here. The student who has a thorough grounding in the general, and in at least one or two of the business, foundation subjects will find himself rather better prepared for work along the lines outlined in this chapter than if he centered the greater part of his attention as an undergraduate on the functional business areas. If undergraduate business schools move in the direction indicated in the two preceding chapters, the issue will not be so sharply drawn, but if they do not, students hoping to go on to graduate study would be well advised to take as much work in the foundation subjects in their undergraduate years as possible. A certain amount of catching up in such areas as mathematics, economics, psychology, and even literature is possible at the graduate level, but the more of this that has to be done, the greater the likelihood that short cuts will have to be resorted to. In this connection, mention should be made again of the fact that students who have taken their undergraduate work in economics, engineering, and liberal arts tend to score better in the Admission Test for Graduate Study in Business than those who have majored as undergraduates in accounting and business (see Table 4-2).

A comparison of the educational background of students attending individual graduate business schools tends on balance to support this conclusion. A substantial majority of the third-group schools—those with a heavy managerial emphasis—draw a quarter or less of their students from undergraduate business programs, the balance coming from liberal arts and engineering backgrounds. In the incoming class of 1956–1957 at the Chicago School of Business, for example, students from business schools accounted for 22 per cent of the total, while at Harvard they accounted for 18 per cent; at several other schools in this group, the proportion was considerably less. In the case of Stanford it is now a matter of record that the school will not accept students with undergraduate business preparation except under the most unusual circumstances; in the class admitted in 1958, there were only three students with this background. The increasing importance of students with undergraduate engineering preparation is a particularly notable feature of admissions practice at these schools in recent years.

It is, of course, difficult to distinguish between different types of undergraduate programs and the quality of the instruction; in fact, it may simply be that abler students tend toward engineering and liberal arts undergraduate preparation. Data on the performance of graduate business students at the University of California (Berkeley), for example, indicate that students with engineering training do better than either those with liberal arts or business administration backgrounds, but such comparisons have little meaning divorced from the intelligence level of the students, the particular schools involved, etc. All that can be said with assurance is that at the present time, undergraduate preparation in business tends to provide too narrow a background for students going on to graduate work in this field. Reports from eighty-six business schools with graduate programs indicate that in about three-fifths of the cases 50 per cent or more of the incoming class in 1955–1956 had their undergraduate training in business, and in about one-third of the cases the proportion was three-fourths or more.[10] For these students, a broader kind of preparation would almost certainly have been preferable.

3-2-YEAR PROGRAMS

An interesting variant of graduate work in business is exemplified by the Tuck School program at Dartmouth College in which students take three years of undergraduate work in liberal arts, and two years of work in business, beginning in their senior year. The basic issue posed by such programs is whether the year of liberal arts study which the students lose is too high a price to pay for the time saved. As a compromise between undergraduate and graduate programs, there is much to be said for the 3-2 approach; indeed, it could be fitted in rather easily with the undergraduate and graduate programs recommended in the present study.

On the other hand, there appear to be important advantages in keeping undergraduate and graduate business education at most institutions within the conventional framework of the four-year undergraduate and the two-year postbachelor graduate program. The end of the senior year is a widely accepted cutoff point in the education of many students. The difficulties encountered in dovetailing the first three years of work

[10] Source: Survey Questionnaire.

at a variety of undergraduate institutions into the requirements of a business administration program at a particular institution are not easily resolved. Undergraduate schools (and undergraduate departments for that matter) can hardly be blamed for shrinking at the prospect of losing large numbers of students at the end of their junior year. Since students typically choose their major at the end of their sophomore year, the 3-2 arrangement would tend to put their next year (i.e., the junior year) in a kind of limbo. For many students, the senior year is the high point of their undergraduate experience, so the prospects of transferring to another school at the end of their junior year is likely to have little appeal for them either. As a consequence, it is not surprising that this pattern has not been widely followed and that where it has, it has been largely limited to students already at the institution introducing it.

There are equally strong doubts about this plan of study from the viewpoint of graduate business education. If the standards of preparation for graduate work in business rise, as they certainly should, it will become increasingly difficult to satisfy them within four years, much less three years, of undergraduate study. Then too, looking ahead, it is important to put graduate instruction in this field on its own feet. There are subtle but nonetheless powerful influences which may quickly destroy the "graduate school" quality of a program where half or more of the students are undergraduates. While a matter of degree, there is no gainsaying that under these circumstances standards will be below what could reasonably be required of somewhat older, more broadly prepared students. Difficulties may also be encountered with respect to student morale if graduates of four-year schools are mixed with seniors in the first year of a program, especially if many of the undergraduates continue active in local campus affairs. The issue of including seniors is of course not serious where, as is sometimes done at law and medical schools, a few students in this category are admitted on a highly selective basis to the first year of the program, but it becomes quite otherwise where a substantial portion of the first-year graduate students are undergraduates.[11]

To sum up, the 3-2 type of business program meets most of the standards set forth earlier in this report; at least as a transitional arrangement, schools offering both undergraduate and graduate work may want to give it serious consideration. Under conditions prevailing at most schools

[11] All the conditions requisite to the success of a 3-2 program are present in the case of the Tuck School—a nationally known parent institution, adequate financial backing, an extremely careful, double-screening of students at the freshman and senior years, etc.—yet it is worth noting that during the past four years, the proportion of men with A.B. degrees has been increased to about 35 per cent of the entering class, and active consideration is now being given to raising this to 50 or 60 per cent of the total. Letter from Dean Karl A. Hill, July 8, 1958.

today, there is no reason why a student should not be permitted to start his business studies his senior year, earning an M.B.A. degree in two years' time. However, for a school that cannot count on attracting a large group of outstanding first-year students from its own campus, a 3-2 plan would run serious dangers, since almost inevitably it tends to be a locally oriented program. By the same token, a school that wishes to establish a graduate program with nation-wide drawing power should think twice before adopting this approach. Looking well beyond the present to a time when graduate business work generally is put on a more demanding basis than it is now, there will be increasingly less justification for the 3-2 pattern of instruction.

ONE-YEAR VERSUS TWO-YEAR PROGRAMS

This raises the more general question of the length of time required to complete a graduate business program of the sort recommended here. Prior to World War II, most graduate programs in business consisted of one year of specialized study which students took after undergraduate preparation in business, the year of study leading to an M.S. or M.A. degree. It is still possible to earn this degree in one year at about 100 institutions which have schools and departments of business; in 1955–1956, however, these institutions only awarded about 600 such degrees.[12] The M.B.A. is now much the more important degree, but most schools are fairly liberal in granting credit for undergraduate courses in business and economics, so the change is not too important.[13]

It could be argued that one year of specialization is a perfectly proper program for students who have already had broad preparation in business and nonbusiness subjects and want to prepare in some one line of work, such as accounting. Not all students are in a position to take two full years to earn an advanced degree, and many could not really put the preparation to good use even if they were in a financial position to do so. Then, too, it could be argued that the year of specialized work could be kept to a high analytical level, quite as high as the second year in any M.B.A. program.

Given proper safeguards, this viewpoint may be defensible. However, it is to be hoped that many more schools offering graduate work will make it demanding enough to require two full academic years of study

[12] The figures are based on replies to the Survey Questionnaire; 30 of the 158 schools and departments offering graduate work did not reply to the questionnaire so estimates had to be used.

[13] For example, about half the students receiving the M.B.A. at Indiana, Washington University (St. Louis), and the Wharton School in recent years have earned the degree within one calendar year; the proportion of M.B.A. students who take two academic years to earn a degree at these and most other schools is very small.

of all students. The most promising development in this entire field is the emphasis on managerial decision making. A student cannot hope to make much headway in this direction in nine or twelve months' time. If his undergraduate preparation was in business, he will doubtless need further preparation in certain nonbusiness subjects; if it was in liberal arts, he will need general preparation in the functional business areas. In either case, two academic years would seem the minimum necessary to gain some comprehension of the management point of view.

There are very few areas in business which justify a full year of specialization beyond the work done in a typical undergraduate business school. If this is all graduate work amounts to, it might well be taken in night school or learned on the job. The one exception, as shown in Chap. 14, may be accounting, although even in this area advanced specialization which neglects the managerial viewpoint and the contributions of other subjects is likely to prove unsatisfactory. In keeping with the pattern of the highly developed professions, it seems likely that in the future more schools will require two years of study for an advanced degree in business. This trend deserves support.

SUMMARY OF FINDINGS

To highlight the principal findings and recommendations of this discussion, a suggested M.B.A. program is presented in Table 10-3. The first four groups of courses deal with the foundation business subjects and the tools of analysis which the student will need in his later work. They will give him some of the basic equipment he will need in the next three groups of courses: functional areas of decision making, managerial policy making, and the major concentration.

Even more than in the case of the proposed undergraduate curriculum, these suggestions can no more than indicate the general direction of the schools' future development. The proposed program places heavy weight on preparation in the four foundation areas—quantitative methods, economics, law and public policy, and psychology-sociology. The work in the four functional business subjects and in the area of the student's major is designed to give him minimum competence in a broadly defined specialty; it is also designed to give him frequent opportunity to apply the general principles studied in the four foundation subjects to specific problems in decision making. The policy-making course is aimed at helping the student integrate his studies in the different areas, thus carrying forward the theme emphasized from the outset. Finally, considerable latitude is left to the individual student and the individual school in the weight that seems best to give to electives outside the major.

The whole intent of these recommendations would be lost if they were

TABLE 10-3

SUGGESTED M.B.A. CURRICULUM

Required and elective subjects	Number of semester hours
Quantitative methods:	
Accounting and mathematical-statistical tools of management	9–12
Economics:	
Microeconomics and management	3
Macroeconomics and management	3
Law and public policy:	
Legal institutions and business policy	3
Public control of business	3
Psychology-sociology:	
Human behavior and management	3–6
Functional areas of decision making:	
Production	3
Finance	3
Marketing	3
Personnel	3
Managerial policy making:	
Business policy	3
Major concentration	9–12
Free electives (outside the major)	3–12
Total semester hours required for M.B.A. degree	60

construed in a rigid, uniform manner. To be worthy of the name, graduate work must be a common exploration on the part of teacher and student. This cannot be achieved through any master curriculum design. In fact, no sequence of courses can substitute for the joint venturing of two minds dedicated to finding the truth in whatever context the quest is carried on. The significance of any educational enterprise ultimately turns on the nature of the relationship between teacher and student.

CHAPTER 11

FACULTY AND TEACHING METHODS

The most precious resource which any business school can possess is a highly qualified and highly motivated faculty. The schools, however, suffer from a number of handicaps in their efforts to attract top-flight staffs. The search for talent will have to be pushed in many directions, and present faculty members will need help in continuing their own development. The steps which are taken to strengthen faculties also carry important implications for standards of employment and methods of teaching in this field.

One of the striking features of the interviews conducted at business schools in all parts of the country was the difference in general atmosphere found among these institutions. At some schools the work was approached in a rather mechanical or even listless manner; each part of the program was largely isolated from the rest; instruction was continuing much as it had for many years before and few proposals for change were under discussion; little opportunity existed for group consideration of new ideas, and morale appeared to be at a low ebb. At other schools departmental barriers were kept to a minimum, and the work in each area contributed to the program as a whole; there was frequent opportunity for the exchange of ideas, and a spirit of experimentation and exploration prevailed; the result was an enthusiasm and esprit de corps which quickened every phase of the work and gave life to the learning process.

Many elements doubtless contributed to these differences among the schools but the critical factor appeared to be the quality and motivation of the faculties. In the first group of schools, teaching was largely a means of livelihood—instructors met their classes, gave examinations at the proper time, turned in grades in the appropriate form, but the teaching function largely ended there. In the second group, teaching was a continuing exploration—the staff was committed to making the students' experience just as meaningful as possible and to adding new dimensions to the subject itself. To a considerable extent, the differences in atmos-

268

phere reflected the fact that some faculties regarded serious academic work as a part-time or perfunctory interest, while others put it at the very center of their lives.

The crux of all the problems confronting business schools lies here. No proposal for strengthening their programs will come to anything if the faculties are not prepared to accept them or if they lack the capacity to put them into effect. Improvements in this as in any other field of education must proceed hand in hand with faculty development; in fact, the quality of a school's program and of its faculty are largely one and the same thing. It follows that building a faculty must be the central concern of every forward-moving school.

What are the qualities which a top-flight business faculty should possess? To a considerable degree they are, of course, the same as in any other field. Some of the more important are personal and professional integrity, a sense of community responsibility, intellectual imagination, genuine interest in students, capacity to communicate ideas effectively in oral and/or written form, thorough grounding in at least one broad area of learning, understanding of background subjects most relevant to the individual's area of special competence, and close familiarity with and active participation in current research developments. Perhaps the most important single characteristic of a vigorous and effective faculty is that it is still learning, still growing. Without this quality, teaching can easily become a humdrum performance; with it, the element of discovery and excitement will never be wholly lost.

Beyond these general attributes which would be highly prized in every faculty group, business schools should look for certain distinctive qualities in their staffs. According to the prior discussion of undergraduate and graduate programs in this field, education for careers in business should fuse certain of the basic academic disciplines with a study of managerial responsibilities. It follows that the faculties of business schools should be made up of broadly educated scholars who are applying general knowledge and scientific methods to important issues in decision making. The business faculties should be neither wholly business-oriented nor wholly nonbusiness-oriented, but both. They should be neither solely functional-area specialists nor solely cross-area generalists, but both. They should approach the study of business as an area of the greatest importance in the nation's life, fully worthy of meticulous investigation and profound study. They should be committed to helping students carry over general education to career preparation, giving them the materials and inspiration to continue this kind of learning after graduation. They should be dedicated to uncovering new insights and new ideas in this broad field of study—the kind of exploration by which all branches of knowledge progress.

The field stands athwart a number of important areas, so the schools' faculties need to do likewise. The field includes a number of tool and functional subjects, so the faculties should possess competence in each. Since the central problems lie in the relationships between certain non-business and business subjects as they in turn relate to decision making within the individual firm, the test of any faculty is how effectively it deals with these same relationships. The earlier discussion stressed the double aspect of successful careers in business—the need for imaginative analytical abilities and for putting such abilities to effective use in concrete situations. This same combination of qualities should inhere in a business school's faculty as well.

According to the evidence adduced in previous chapters, business schools have weighted the scales unduly on the side of applied as opposed to general knowledge, command of facts rather than mastery of methology, *ad hoc* practice rather than systematic analysis, specific techniques rather than widely applicable abilities, elementary skills rather than advanced analysis of subject matter, separatism between the functional business subjects rather than relatedness between broad areas, refinements in matters of practice rather than key elements in managerial decision making. Some schools, as noted earlier, have shifted the scales in the other direction, and it is hoped more will do likewise in the future. It follows that faculty building plans should be developed with this realignment of the schools' work in mind.

The qualities identified with the traditional pattern of business education—close familiarity with practice in a particular industry or area and interest in descriptive treatment of the techniques of business performance—should accordingly be ranked much lower than has been true in the past, while the qualities associated with the newer pattern—application of general knowledge to complex problems of business behavior and the development of new approaches to critically important issues of business policy—should be ranked much higher. This shift in the ranking of desired qualities need not be an either-or matter, but rather a shift in emphasis only. At the same time, such a change would have far-reaching consequences and there is no denying that many difficulties would have to be surmounted in order to put it into effect.

FACULTY INTEREST AREAS

The most important interest areas of a business faculty cannot be specified too rigidly, but some fairly definite guides as to desirable lines of development can be gleaned from the preceding discussion. First, a faculty needs to have sufficient familiarity with broad background subjects and the tools of the major disciplines in the humanities, sciences, and social sciences to be able to work with them effectively in different contexts. More than this, the faculty needs to be genuinely interested in applications of one or more of these underlying disciplines to business problems. It is especially important that a business faculty should include at least one person thoroughly steeped in each of the key foundation areas—English literature or philosophy, mathematics, engineering or science, law or political science, and psychology or sociology. As noted in Chap. 8, it does not seem generally desirable for business schools to handle instruction in these related subjects themselves, but much is gained if members of the business faculty can approach their teaching from the viewpoint of the various underlying disciplines.

Second, the faculties should include persons who have a thorough grounding in the basic business subjects—accounting, statistics, and economics—and be actively engaged in using one or more of these subjects in analyzing significant questions of managerial policy. As indicated in the curriculum chapters, business schools have generally built up their faculties in accounting far more than in statistics. If, as was recommended earlier, schools concentrate on the managerial uses of these quantitative tools, the accounting staffs at many institutions could be reduced while additions would seem indicated in the statistics area. The recommendations with respect to economics, on the other hand, would require a number of faculty members trained in this subject.

Third, there is need for persons with a special competence in the four broad functional areas—finance, marketing, personnel, and production—who, in addition, have enough familiarity with business practice to be able to identify central problems and enough academic background to put such problems in an analytical framework. As noted in earlier chapters, the competence needed is not a mastery of detailed techniques but a grasp of central issues and major principles. A business school hardly needs faculty members versed in more specialized areas than the four just mentioned except as more specialized work is essential to their research.

Fourth, the faculties should be versed in managerial decision making and actively engaged in relating the different areas to the decision process. This calls for faculty members with an imaginative awareness of the managerial implications of particular situations, an ability to use different tools and subjects in analyzing managerial decisions, and a capacity for balancing a variety of considerations in recommending different lines of action. Needless to say, this is a rarely found quality, and no one faculty member can hope to possess it in full degree—and remain for long outside the executive's ranks! Everyone on the teaching staff, however, should be able to make some contribution to understanding management's responsibilities and serve as an active contributor to this central concern of a school's work.

Since, ideally, each faculty member's interests and abilities would cut across several areas, it is impossible to say how large a staff would be required to handle all phases of the work. Its total size would largely be determined, of course, by the number of students. As to a faculty's composition, the important consideration is to maintain the general distribution of backgrounds and interests described above. Additions to a teaching staff should not be allowed to skew the course offerings along unduly narrow lines. The specialized interests of the faculty should largely be reflected in a school's research activities and perhaps in certain advanced seminars, not for the most part in the regular course offerings. Though it may be difficult to avoid, the necessity for building a large staff should not be permitted to lead to a proliferation of courses in a variety of business subjects; it is a matter of the utmost importance that every appointment to the faculty should be made with this danger in mind.

Interests and Backgrounds of Present Faculties

Once having set up targets of faculty development, business schools need to consider ways and means of achieving them. Every school must work within more or less severe budgetary restraints. Every school is also confronted by a serious scarcity of highly qualified faculty personnel. These two circumstances make it all the more important for the schools to help existing faculties continue their intellectual growth and to explore all possible sources of qualified new personnel. There are a number of considerations which a school needs to keep in mind in pushing along these two lines.

One is the composition and general quality of the existing faculty. Schools differ greatly on this score, and each must decide for itself where its greatest needs lie and how best to work with its present staff. If the schools make any serious effort to implement the program proposals set forth in this study, a substantial majority of faculty members should presumably hold doctor's degrees. It goes without saying that this degree carries no automatic guarantee of effective academic performance, but it is generally associated with standards of scholarship which business schools should strive to attain; a high proportion of degree holders is therefore an important first step.[1] At present, somewhat less than half of

[1] The standards for membership in the American Association of Collegiate Schools of Business (1957) provide: "It is expected that at least 50 per cent of the teaching credit hours on either the Junior-Senior level or on an over-all basis will be taught by full-time faculty members having terminal degrees." The latter include the doctoral degree in economics or business; in the case of accounting, the master's degree in economics or business together with the C.P.A. certificate is considered terminal, while in business law the professional degree of LL.B is also considered terminal.

the regular, full-time faculty members have the doctorate; in 1955–1956 the proportion was about 45 per cent.[2] The prospect for the future is that the proportion will drop substantially. According to one estimate, business schools will need about 5,400 new degree holders by 1970 to maintain the present ratio of those holding the doctorate to the total full-time teaching staffs; in 1956 there were about 2,600 such degree holders. If prior trends are any guide, not more than half of the new appointees will be in this category.[3] These estimates put business schools close to the national average. In 1956, the proportion of full-time faculty members in the nation's colleges and universities who held doctor's degrees has been estimated at about 40 per cent; by 1970 it may well fall to half this amount.[4]

Comparisons by individual fields are virtually nonexistent. The only data uncovered were contained in a study of faculty backgrounds in a variety of academic and professional fields in twenty-five large public universities in the north central states in 1952–1953; according to this study, business administration ranked ninth among the eighteen fields covered in percentage of full-time faculty members who held the doctorate, above such fields as engineering, social service, and home economics but below forestry, agriculture, and pharmacy.[5]

While it is hardly surprising that the percentage of business faculties holding doctor's degrees in these schools was substantially below the percentage in long-established academic fields like history, it is a matter

[2] Survey Questionnaire. For comparisons among schools of different size, see Appendix 3, Table 3.

[3] American Association of Collegiate Schools of Business, *Faculty Requirements and Standards in Collegiate Schools of Business,* AACSB, New York, 1956, pp. 55, 58. The estimates were prepared by John P. Lewis.

[4] *Teachers for Tomorrow,* Fund for the Advancement of Education, Bull. 2, 1955, pp. 25 and 62. In 1957 only 23 per cent of all new full-time college and university teachers held doctor's degrees, a decline of 8 per cent from the proportion among new appointments in 1953; conversely, in the same period the number of new full-time teachers holding less than a master's degree rose from 10 to 23 per cent. National Education Association, Association for Higher Education, *College and University Bulletin,* vol. 10, no. 15, 1957, pp. 1–3, cited in John S. Brubacher and Willis Rudy, *Higher Education in Transition,* Harper & Brothers, New York, 1958, p. 212.

[5] The faculties in history and biology had the highest proportion of doctorates in the fields and schools included in this study (87 and 79 per cent, respectively) while those in architecture and nursing had the lowest (0 and 1 per cent, respectively). All the established fields in the liberal arts such as sociology and English ranked well above business administration; data, however, were not available on doctorates in economics and political science. The proportion of business faculty holding the doctorate in these schools was 34 per cent. Manning M. Pattillo and Allan O. Pfnister, "Faculty Training and Salaries in Institutions of Higher Education," *North Central Association Quarterly,* vol. 29, no. 4, April, 1955, p. 387.

of concern that the proportion was less than in a number of the relatively undeveloped professions. The findings in general underscore the importance of doing everything possible to increase the number of academically promising students who continue advanced study in business and to recruit new faculty personnel from other areas of graduate study relevant to this field.

Two developments call for special comment in this connection. The first is that, if the study of business is put on a serious academic footing, more first-rate scholars will be attracted to this field. This is the clear lesson to be learned from those schools (e.g. Carnegie Tech., Chicago, and M.I.T.) which have gone furthest in this direction. Heretofore, the most promising academic students in graduate economics have tended to shy away from business school appointments; relatively few such appointments existed for graduate students who had done their work in fields other than economics. Lacking well-developed doctoral programs of their own, these schools also failed to attract academically oriented students to take graduate work in business. Generally speaking, superior students viewed their success at graduate business schools as a start up the ladder of business, not academic, attainment. The same pattern may hold even if strong doctoral programs are established in business schools. The salary differential will still propel the better students into business rather than teaching; more important, by temperament and general outlook business students are oriented toward a life of action, not of study and research. Stronger academic programs, however, would certainly tend to attract students of a more academic turn of mind.

At the three schools referred to above, this pattern has undergone considerable change. By stressing the scientific aspects of the field and establishing close ties with various basic disciplines, they have been able to attract a number of nationally recognized scholars as faculty members. This, in turn, has drawn students of higher academic ability. The merits of this approach are not at issue here, though it is worth noting that simply bringing together a group of scholars from different disciplines and telling them to study business scientifically does not add up to a program. The fact remains that this general orientation has aided these schools immensely in their efforts to attract faculties and students of real academic distinction.

If business schools generally move in this direction, the character of their faculties would have to change materially. The possible effects on their present fields of interests have already been indicated. Their prior training would also be affected. At present the background of a typical school's faculty is heavily weighted on the side of practical business experience, graduate work in economics, and advanced study in various business subjects, especially accounting. In the future, it will be impor-

TABLE 11-1

FACULTY MEMBERS WITH C.P.A. CERTIFICATES AND DOCTOR'S DEGREES IN 61 BUSINESS SCHOOLS OFFERING M.B.A. DEGREES, 1956–1957

Type of school with M.B.A. program	No. of schools	Total regular faculty	Total C.P.A.*	Faculty with doctor's degree					Type of Economics Ph.D.	
				Total†	D.B.A. or D.C.S.	Ph.D. Business Administration	Ph.D. Economics		Economic theory	Applied economics
4-year school............	42	1,739	159	763	29	225	418		260	158
2-2-year school............	14	524	37	315	27	81	178		84	94
Exclusively grad. school...	5	180	6	105	30	19	41		17	24
Total................	61	2,443	202	1,183	86	325	637		361	276

* Does not include faculty members who have both C.P.A. certificates and Ph.D. degrees.
† Total includes doctor's degrees outside business and economics; subtotals include doctor's degrees in business and economics only.
SOURCE: Survey Questionnaire.

tant to place increased emphasis on training in other areas of graduate study as well as on raising the total percentage of business faculty members who hold doctor's degrees. Information on faculty members with degrees beyond the master's level (Table 11-1) shows a heavy preponderance in economics and business, but a considerable number in accounting also. The data, which are limited to 61 schools offering M.B.A. degrees, show that nearly 90 per cent of the faculty members with the doctorate held their advanced degree in economics or business. Because of their recent origin, relatively few held D.B.A. or D.C.S. degrees and most of them were concentrated in a few schools.[6] If, however, it is assumed that the degrees in applied economics were in business subjects, the number in the business area comes to nearly 60 per cent of the total. In addition to the members of the teaching staffs of these schools who held doctor's degrees, about 8 per cent of the entire group (a total of 202) held C.P.A. certificates.

While it is important to recruit faculty members whose graduate work was in such fields as mathematics, statistics, psychology, and sociology, they need to be persons who are prepared to make the study of business a major intellectual interest. This raises a serious difficulty because these persons need to keep close ties with their original fields. The task of finding such individuals and helping them maintain a double identification of this sort is, to say the least, not easy. Whether this can be done on any wide scale seems doubtful, though much depends on how business as an area of serious academic study develops in the future.[7]

The other development which may change the character of business faculties materially is the increasing emphasis some of the schools are

[6] Of the 61 schools, only 27 had faculty members with a D.B.A. or D.C.S. degree and of these, only 13 had more than one person holding such a degree; the total number of faculty members in this category came to 86, of which 42 were on the staff of just two schools—Harvard and Indiana.

[7] The business school at Chicago has reorganized its program extensively in recent years. In the fall of 1959–1960 the major areas of graduate training of its regular faculty members were as follows:

Areas of graduate training	Number of faculty members
Accounting	7
Behavioral science (psychology, sociology, anthropology, and political science)	6
Business administration	6
Economics	22
Industrial engineering	1
Law	3
Mathematics	3
Statistics	3
Total	51

giving to their own doctoral programs. The difficulty is that, while this will help solve the problem of quantity, it may contribute little or nothing to solving the problem of quality. Looking to the future, the pressing need of business schools will be for faculty in greater numbers and greater ability. Simply putting large groups of students through greatly expanded doctoral programs will not be enough. Indeed, the net result may be to duplicate at the doctoral level what is all too characteristic of the work of business schools at lower levels now. This raises the broad question of the direction and content of doctoral programs in business, a subject which is best deferred to the next chapter.

Faculty Consulting and Businessmen Teachers

One of the difficult issues confronting business schools is how much emphasis they should put on part-time teaching, practical experience, and faculty consulting work. It would seem to follow logically from the general approach of this study that business schools should hold part-time teaching within very severe bounds.[8] Admittedly, some flexibility is needed because of the scarcity of qualified personnel and the positive contribution which part-time teachers can make. Nevertheless, a strong academic program demands the full energies of a teacher, and where the proportion of part-time to full-time faculty comes to any substantial amount (perhaps 10 per cent or more) a school's program is almost bound to suffer.[9]

The results of the Survey Questionnaire show that the ratio of part-time to full-time teachers exclusive of evening and extension faculties runs rather high at most schools. The average among 138 institutions answering this question came to 30 per cent, with schools in the smallest and middle-size category reporting about 40 per cent.[10] Again, the outlook is for this proportion to rise still higher in the future.

The issue of part-time teaching is related to two other questions about which it is even more difficult to generalize—the importance of practical business experience as background for teaching in a business school and the desirability of consulting work to keep abreast of changes in business thinking and practice. Both can contribute significantly to the kind of program recommended in this study but they can also detract from it if carried too far. Schools which emphasize specific job training and de-

[8] It is well to note that if the data on doctor's degree holders in business administration referred to above included part-time faculty, the proportion would be considerably less than shown.

[9] The standards of membership of the AACSB (1957) provide that "the majority of members of the teaching staff shall give the greater part of their time to instruction and research."

[10] Appendix 3, Table 10.

tailed techniques naturally stress the value of practical business experience and consulting activity rather more than schools with a broader managerial emphasis, although almost all schools have at least a few faculty members who have had active careers in business.

The desired quality seems to be more a matter of temperament than of specific experience. Some scholars could doubtless work for years in industry and never achieve a genuine sense of what is relevant to an employer's needs; others have a sixth sense for business operating problems which requires only the briefest kind of contact to activate. While some academicians of unquestioned ability who lacked business experience have not been too successful as teachers, others who were equally innocent of any direct administrative experience have been striking successes. A feel for the feasible and the relevant in a business environment is a highly desirable quality—in fact, is essential for effective performance—but it is unlikely that there is any simple means of determining its existence.

The opposite danger is probably the more serious. Institutions of higher education which prepare for careers in a particular field always court the risk of becoming mere followers of the particular group they serve. In their zeal to please, i.e., to be realistic and practical, they may fail to provide any leadership. In the case of business, employers are hardly in need of the practical kind of advice they can derive from their own experience and immediate associates. Business school faculties should strive to break new ground for business, playing the role of informed questioners and constructive critics. This emphasis on independent investigation through formal or informal research calls for faculty members who are ready to challenge widely accepted ideas; this is an absolutely essential quality at the graduate level, but a highly desirable one at the undergraduate level too. Thus, a sense of the practical is desirable only if it does not crowd out the element of originality, the very quality which is the hallmark of first-rate academic work. The interviews among the schools indicate that the emphasis on the practical appears to have had this result on many campuses.

The opposite side of the question is whether business schools should seek to add more businessmen to their faculties. The benefits to be derived from frequent contacts with operating executives are clearly evident but whether many businessmen have the background and interests necessary for effective teaching and research is less certain. Most of the larger schools, judging from the campus interviews, have one or two outstanding businessmen-faculty members but many disappointing experiences were also reported in the course of the school visits. The schools should accordingly continue their efforts to find men of practical experience who are ready and able to make teaching their chief interest, but it seems doubtful that their principal faculty needs can be much aided from this source.

These observations indicate the part that consulting activities should have in the work of a business school faculty. At many institutions, especially large schools in urban areas, teaching and research have become pretty much of a side line, while work for industry has become the main focus of the faculty members' interests and means of livelihood. Carried to this degree, consulting cuts the student off from easy access to his teacher and can even block the latter's intellectual growth as well. Essentially the same questions should be asked about consulting work as about a school's program as a whole. Does it open up new approaches to business as a field of study? Does it have general applicability beyond the immediate situation? Does it entail analytical work which an employer could not do just as well on his own? Does it add elements to a school's teaching-research activities which would otherwise be lacking?

There may well be some rules of thumb which can help to keep such work on a productive level. The convention of limiting consulting to one day a week, for example, seems an appropriate one to apply in most cases. Limiting this type of activity to new issues as opposed to the familiar and repetitive is another useful criterion to keep in mind. The ultimate safeguard, however, must lie in the kind of faculty these schools attract and the general direction their programs take. Abuses in this area are attributable to the attitudes of the faculty members themselves and to the way in which their interests have developed. Salary levels which prevail in academic fields have also led to excessive consulting activity. The very conception of the schools' central mission as reflected in the views and actions of their deans and leading faculty spokesmen has sometimes invited abuse in this regard. If a school can deal effectively with these causal influences, the consulting problem will pretty largely take care of itself.

RESPONSE OF PRESENT FACULTIES

One of the key questions facing any business school seeking to strengthen its staff and general program along the lines outlined in this study is how the present faculty would respond. If the more influential professors or the majority of the faculty as a whole are determined to maintain the traditional pattern of work, effective action is virtually impossible. The natural presumption is that business faculties, like most academic groups, would resist extensive change. Depending on circumstances, however, this may not be true of business schools today, for reasons noted below.

First, faculty sentiment as reported in many of the school interviews tended to favor the approach to business education outlined in this study. No systematic polling proved possible but widespread dissatisfaction with important features of existing programs was frequently found among faculty members (see especially Chap. 8). Sometimes it appeared that a faculty was ready to move if only a clear, forward-looking program could be presented. Opposition to innovation, quite understandably, centered among a relatively few influential older men at the different schools. The younger and newer staff members tended to be more receptive to proposals for change, and at many schools the majority of the faculty seemed similarly minded. Sometimes it appeared that the faculty was quite ready to consider suggestions for change but that certain department chairmen or administrative spokesmen prevented effective action.

Second, the very effort required to think through a school's objectives and prospects seems to engender an atmosphere conducive to change.[11] The chances of acceptance are greatly increased if respected spokesmen for the faculty are actively involved in reviewing the work, although outside consultants can serve a useful function as catalytic agents. Whatever the procedure, it is absolutely essential that the faculty as a whole be given full opportunity to express its views effectively. Sweeping proposals for change are unlikely to be accepted unless they are worked out after careful study, long debate, and a clear understanding by all concerned of how the new program will work in practice. Where the need for extensive change has been demonstrated and a specific program of action developed, faculty groups have generally evidenced a willingness to go along.

While planning should be on a school-wide basis, implementation might possibly begin in departments where the chances for immediate success are greatest. This might mean introducing further changes in the offerings of a department that has already moved in the desired direction, or it might mean making a new appointment to round out the work in an already well-developed area. Departments known to be most resistant to change can be tackled later. Occasionally the opportunity to move comes first where it is needed most and such an opportunity should, of course, be exploited to the full. In most situations, however, these are the very areas where resistance to change is the most uncompromising. Judging from the experience of a number of institutions, the top ad-

[11] As one dean whose school has recently tightened its offerings observed: "The pressures for attacking the proliferation of courses across the board came mostly from the very conscientious review of our objectives and our program, a concurrent feeling at the University that students' independent work should be increased through a lessening of required classroom hours (concurrent with other things to make sure the students put the released hours to use), plus the whole atmosphere of change."

ministration of a university can play a crucial role in winning over a faculty group. Any school seeking to strengthen its work significantly needs to keep the top leaders of the university fully informed of its plans and to secure their vigorous support.

Third, the fear that change will eliminate jobs and block promotions must be squarely faced. In some schools or departments little can be done on this score until retirements make new appointments possible. Usually a number of approaches are open. Thus, the pressure of increasing enrollments often means that course programs can be reorganized without endangering jobs. The general outlook is for a serious deficiency in the number of qualified teachers, not a surplus, so a tightening of course offerings may be indicated on the grounds of both educational philosophy and more efficient utilization of existing staffs. Moreover, a number of business schools are endeavoring to introduce graduate work, management development programs, research activities, etc., for the first time or to increase their emphasis in these areas. Some of the energies expended on particular courses in the existing program might therefore be shifted to these other activities. Then, too, there may be hitherto neglected aspects of traditional business subjects which would fit in well with a realignment of the work. The principal contributions of subjects like accounting and statistics to managerial controls, for example, still lie in the future. There are challenging theoretical issues in such fields as land economics and transportation which have hardly begun to be explored. Faculty members who have been plowing one end of a particular field may be more than glad to shift to a related phase of their specialty. More than one school has found its faculty in accounting, marketing, finance, etc., quite ready to consider new approaches to their fields if only they are given a fair opportunity and some incentive to redirect their interests. It need hardly be added that any program which threatens many jobs might as well be forgotten immediately; in most situations firm assurances can be given that this will not happen.

Fourth, any plan to alter the essential elements of an established program must show in realistic terms what the present faculty will have to do in order to keep pace with it, and provide effective means for their doing so. This is not just a matter of justice—it is absolutely essential to the success of the proposed program itself. Every effort should be made to further the development of each member of the faculty, but particularly of those who might be adversely affected by the new plan. This might entail something as simple as looking into new reading materials or as extensive as going back to graduate school on a year's sabbatical. Attendance at one of the institutes and summer seminar programs already established through foundation support in such areas as marketing, production, and quantitative controls can be of real help in this connection if the experience is followed up effectively. There are any number of ways new opportunities can be opened up for faculty members of these schools. Someone must explain tactfully but clearly how important these opportunities are from the viewpoint of the development of individual faculty members and of the school as a whole. Often these are matters which faculty groups or departments can work out themselves, once the general direction of a school's work has been agreed upon.

Fifth, any extensive alterations in a school's program should, if possible, be coupled with improvements in salary scales, teaching loads, sabbatical leaves, research opportunities, and the other conditions of employment. If, for example, teaching hours can be reduced from 12 to 9 per week, or from 9 to 6 per week for at least some teachers, the way may be cleared to cut back some of the highly specialized offerings. If more released time can be arranged for research purposes, faculty members will be more receptive to a reorganization of their courses. Such moves can prove costly, thereby requiring the approval and active cooperation of the university's top administration. On some campuses, the business schools have been operated on a maximum-revenue–minimum-expenditure basis, leading to a kind of bargain-basement educational policy. It would be disastrous if universities allocated budgets solely on the basis of comparative enrollments but it seems equally indefensible to use some schools as a source of profit. If universities ever hope to put the study of business administration on a solid basis, they must make sure that these schools have the means for doing so.

Sixth, and last, faculty members can be expected to accept a proposed program only if it seems worth the adjustments and risks involved. There is little to be said in favor of change for change's sake. The goals of a school's efforts and the broad direction of its planning must justify general faculty support. This is why bold thinking may prove to be the most practical way to proceed. There are many approaches to stepping up the morale of a teaching staff but perhaps none is so effective as to pioneer a new road to learning. There is an unmistakable *élan* in a faculty group that feels it is breaking fresh ground. Old rivalries and fears begin to fade; convictions about teaching methods start to loosen; departmental aggressions tend to subside; minds become more open to different combinations of materials and subjects; in short, a true community of scholars begins to emerge. Nothing quite captures the imagination of an academic group like the belief that their school is moving ahead and that they are part of a significant educational venture. This is the "leader-role" view of education mentioned earlier at a number of points. There seems little doubt that the quality of a faculty's morale largely turns on whether a school accepts or rejects this conception of its destiny.

TEACHING CONDITIONS

Mention has already been made of the importance of providing favorable teaching conditions if business schools are to attract and hold first-rate faculties. The need for higher salaries and better standards of employment for faculties generally has been discussed in many other studies so only a summary of the essential facts as they pertain to business schools is necessary here. These facts provide a rough measure of the distance business schools will have to go to establish suitable conditions of employment.

In 1956–1957, the majority of the 135 schools which supplied salary data in response to the Survey Questionnaire reported paying full professors between $6,000 and $8,000 per academic year; at the lower end, 7 schools reported paying less than $6,000; and at the upper end, 32 schools reported paying $8,000 or more. The overwhelming majority of the schools had raised salaries of full professors during the preceding five years by 10 to 39 per cent, and the median institution had increased annual rates by 24 per cent.[12] Since 1956–1957, it seems safe to assume, salaries have risen at a comparable rate.

Nearly 50 per cent of the reporting schools stated that salaries in the business and liberal arts schools were the same, but about 40 per cent said the former exceeded the latter by $250 per annum or more. Doubtless the advantage of business faculties would show up more sharply if allowance were made for speed of promotions, extent of outside consulting income, and the like.[13]

Information on teaching loads is difficult to interpret since, in addition to his regular class-meeting hours, a teacher's job is affected by the number of preparations he must handle per week, the size of his classes, night school assignments, theses supervision, and various administrative duties. Data on standard-class-hour loads per week are nonetheless indicative of the principal duties of a school's faculty and give a fair indication of the amount of time available for research and other non-teaching activities. As shown in Table 11-2, nearly two-thirds of the undergraduate and

[12] Survey Questionnaire (see Appendix 3, Tables 4 and 5). The percentage of private schools reporting salaries for full professors below $6,500 was somewhat greater than the percentage of publicly supported schools; otherwise the distributions were the same.

[13] Salary data for 1952–1953 covering all full-time faculty in 27 liberal arts and professional fields in 25 large public universities in the North Central states showed business close to the middle (ranking 12th among the 27 fields covered with a mean salary of $5,480). The three highest fields were law, medicine, and chemistry, and the three lowest were physical education, English and literature, and home economics. Manning M. Pattillo and Allan O. Pfnister, *op. cit.*, p. 398.

TABLE 11-2

STANDARD WORKLOADS OF BUSINESS FACULTY,
UNDERGRADUATE AND GRADUATE
BUSINESS SCHOOLS, 1956–1957

Hours per week	Number of institutions
Over 15	2
15	12
12–15	5
12	53
9–12	19
9	10
Under 9	13
Total	114
Not given	24
Total	138

SOURCE: Survey Questionnaire.

graduate schools answering this question in the Survey Questionnaire reported a standard work load of 12 hours per week or more. While this is probably not out of line with prevailing practice in other branches of higher education, it is obvious that faculty members would have little opportunity under these circumstances to pursue their own research interests and would even find keeping abreast of current developments difficult.

A not altogether successful attempt was made to analyze teaching loads in terms of the ratios of students to faculty. The schools were asked to report the number of full-time and part-time students taking business courses and the number of faculty members teaching such courses in the fall of 1956.[14] Of 112 institutions supplying data, 92 reported a student-faculty ratio of 20 to 1 or more, and 40 reported a ratio of 30 to 1 or more (see Table 11-3). Taken together with the information on standard work loads, it appears that business faculties at most schools must be hard pressed to keep up with their teaching responsibilities. Prospective enrollment trends will of course raise student-faculty ratios still more unless the rate of new appointments is increased.

Crude as these indicators are, they tell a good deal about the working conditions found at most business schools. Typically, the ratio of students to total resources as measured by a school's budget is so high that teaching conditions are necessarily adverse.[15] Judging from the interviews

[14] The schools were asked to convert part-time faculty and students to fractions of full-time.

[15] Some notion of comparative business school budgets can be derived from Appendix 3, Table 2.

TABLE 11-3

STUDENT-FACULTY RATIOS, UNDERGRADUATE AND
GRADUATE BUSINESS SCHOOLS, 1956–1957

Number of institutions

Less than 10:1....................	1
10:1 to 19:1......................	19
20:1 to 24:1......................	22
25:1 to 29:1......................	30
30:1 to 34:1......................	21
35:1 to 39:1......................	8
40:1 or more.....................	11
Total.........................	112
Not given......................	26
	138

SOURCE: Survey Questionnaire.

on numerous campuses, most schools have had to squeeze one or more aspects of their programs severely in order to include all the things they feel called upon to do. At state universities and other large institutions, this often means extensive reliance on graduate students and young instructors to handle much of the undergraduate teaching. Smaller institutions frequently require faculty members to handle three or more separate preparations in the course of a single week. Many institutions, whether large or small, rely heavily on part-time teachers who may or may not be fully qualified but who are less of a burden budget-wise.[16] Expensive educational ventures such as seminar work, closely supervised investigations, carefully evaluated written reports, etc., are conspicuous by their absence. In a number of cases, it is understood that faculty members will supplement their meager salaries by outside consulting work. In others, it is taken for granted that the faculty will make both ends meet by teaching night classes, summer work, etc. Sabbatical leaves, clerical assistance, and other aids to research are generally kept to a minimum. The size of classes is often allowed to creep up; through the use of loud-speaker systems, television, and other devices, some schools are handling groups of 500 or more at a time.[17]

These are all means to the same end—to stretch the educational dollar

[16] See Appendix 3, Table 10.

[17] The relevant standards for membership of the American Association of Collegiate Schools of Business (1957) read:

"No instructor should, at any one time, offer instruction in more than two of the core fields . . . members of the instructional staff should not teach undergraduate courses in excess of twelve credit hours per week, nor more than ten hours per week of graduate work."

just as far as humanly possible. Until the country is prepared to give a higher priority to college and university work in general, perhaps no other approach to business education is possible. The earlier discussion in this and other chapters, however, showed that there is much that business schools can do to strengthen their faculties and programs with no substantial increase in budgetary outlays. Money may not be far removed from the root of all educational progress, but the life force of a school really lies in the ideas of its faculty. Judging from the interview reports, there are hardly any undergraduate schools, and surprisingly few graduate schools, wholeheartedly committed to developing programs of first-rate academic quality. Here, rather than any marked deficiency in funds, lies the great need in business education today.

On the other hand, for many publicly supported institutions and many others as well, an academic program of such high quality could hardly be more than an ideal toward which a school should strive. Even if this ideal were in some sense realizable, other obligations would have to be met. Initially, for these institutions it may be feasible to establish high academic standards in only one or two subjects and then perhaps only for a relatively small group of students. Presumably these "islands of excellence" would vary from school to school, depending on the backgrounds and interests of particular faculty and student groups. Some might concentrate first on raising standards in the quantitative aspects of the field, others in the behavioral or organizational areas, and still others in the economic; or main attention in the early stages might be centered on some one feature of the graduate or undergraduate programs such as the comprehensive examination. There is also much to be said for concentrating all available funds and energies on a few strategic faculty appointments; the addition of even one or two really first-rate persons can add immeasurably to a school's program as well as help attract other qualified personnel. Admitting the difficulties to be many and formidable, there is no school that cannot raise standards in some important aspect of its work—and relatively quickly.

TEACHING METHODS

Much of the quality of a school's program depends on the manner in which the faculty approaches its teaching responsibilities. By the same token, the method of instruction is largely shaped by the educational objective of the individual school. The lecture method with heavy reliance on textbook recitations tends to predominate where the emphasis is on training for particular jobs. This method is often supplemented by quiz-section meetings of smaller groups, but even under these circumstances the tendency is to stress exposition by the instructor, not active participation by the student. Except for classes in accounting, students do little laboratory work or other types of independent analysis at schools of this sort. Emphasis on reports or essay writing is kept to a minimum, especially among the larger schools in this category. Course offerings and study materials are usually limited to the traditional business subjects.

Schools stressing the managerial approach or preparation for general careers in business tend to put more emphasis on participation, discussion, and investigation by the individual student. Assignments are less likely to be drawn from textbooks and more likely to come from firsthand reports and outside readings. Considerable attention is given to background subjects and to nonbusiness areas like psychology and mathematical statistics. Care is taken to work materials from these areas into the regular business courses. There is a somewhat greater effort at these schools to draw on current research and an even more pronounced tendency to emphasize questions which cut across different business areas. To a considerable extent, the difference between these two groups of schools is bound up with their methods of teaching, not with subject content as such.

These differences in teaching approach show up more sharply in upper- rather than lower-division undergraduate courses and in graduate rather than undergraduate work. The introductory or basic courses in the main undergraduate subjects tend to be handled in much the same manner at all schools, with considerable emphasis on systematic exposition and textbook recitation at most institutions. The major differences among undergraduate schools come at the intermediate and advanced levels. Among graduate schools differences in teaching approach are found throughout the programs, the contrasts at the general survey level being particularly marked. These differences may be as much a result of variations in student and faculty ability or background as in the extent to which a managerial viewpoint is emphasized.

The Case Method

The teaching method which has exerted more widespread influence than any other in this field is the case method developed at Harvard. Chapter 3 showed that, historically, the introduction of this method did more to invigorate academic preparation for business than any other one development. This method of study may be characterized in the following terms:[18]

"The student is placed in the position of the businessman who must

[18] Malcolm P. McNair, ed., *The Case Method at the Harvard Business School*, McGraw-Hill Book Company, Inc., New York, 1954, in Foreword by Donald K. David, p. viii.

act, who must before he acts weigh the bearing on his problem of a variety of different considerations, both short-run and long-run in character, but who must in any event make a decision and implement it."

A business case normally involves a diversified array of facts and considerations calling for action by an employer or his spokesman. No one solution can be said to be right and all others wrong. Every case requires the student to exercise his own judgment in arriving at a defensible course of action. But the specific method of analysis employed is crucial; there must be a mastery of the particular facts in the case, a logical but imaginative balancing of the various elements involved in it, and a reasoned reconciliation of such elements leading to a recommended course of action. It is admittedly difficult to evaluate the work of students under the case method, but it is quite erroneous to assume that they cannot be held to objective standards of performance. It is also erroneous to assume that generalized principles cannot be developed by this method of study. In the hands of capable users, cases can provide widely applicable conclusions even though the method of reaching them tends to be laborious and time-consuming.[19]

The school interviews yielded a rather mixed picture of the value of this method of study. Almost everyone with whom the matter was discussed felt that some areas lend themselves to the case method much better than others. For example, it was almost universally agreed that case analysis can accomplish a good deal in personnel management, human relations, and business policy making, whereas in accounting, statistics, and economics exclusive reliance on the case approach tends to impede the student's development. The outcome, it was felt, largely depends on the amount of systematic knowledge already available and the amount which students have to master. In the human relations area, case analysis is apparently the most effective way to get at the principal issues involved. It seems quite otherwise in such an area as modern statistics. The difference lies in the fact that the formal content of the first subject is relatively small, whereas it is relatively large for the second.

The special value of the case method, judging from the individual campus interviews, is the experience students get in balancing a variety of considerations in controversial situations. True, this can lead to rather superficial, undisciplined thinking unless the students and faculty possess considerable intellectual capacity and broad educational back-

[19] Much has been written on the case method. In addition to the foregoing reference, see Kenneth R. Andrews, ed., *The Case Method of Teaching Human Relations and Administration*, Harvard University Press, Cambridge, Mass., 1955 and Pearson Hunt, "The Case Method of Instruction," *Harvard Educational Review*, Summer, 1957, pp. 175–192.

grounds. This suggests that the case method is better adapted to older students who have had considerable work experience.[20]

The case method is the logical counterpart of the managerial approach to business education. In fact, until recently, the one has hardly been distinguishable from the other. Cases can bring the varied elements in different decisions into sharp focus, providing a valuable type of interdisciplinary analysis. It is precisely at this point, however, that difficulties with the case method begin to arise. If much systematic knowledge of the different disciplines is necessary and if a step-by-step, cumulative analysis has to be followed in applying such knowledge to business problems, the case emphasis is likely to be rather unsatisfactory. As long as the issues confronting businessmen can be grasped more or less intuitively and a good general background gives students all the formal knowledge they need, no serious problems arise. This method of study, however, becomes much less appropriate where a high degree of academic sophistication is needed. Recent advances in the application of quantitative methods to management decisions, for example, are difficult to handle by this method; the same is true of some of the more recent developments in finance and marketing. The prospect is for these aspects of the subject to loom more importantly in the future, with the case method playing a somewhat more modest role than in the past.

Heavy reliance on cases seems especially questionable at the undergraduate level. Concentration on the specifics of business situations can lead to unfortunate results where students lack broad preparation and general maturity. It is true that carefully selected cases can do much to sharpen issues and challenge interest even in undergraduate courses. Some subjects toward the end of the undergraduate program may also lend themselves to the case approach. Moreover, as a device for shaking up conventional teaching methods and breaking away from a straight lecture-textbook emphasis, the case method has much to recommend it even at the undergraduate level.[21] As at the graduate level, its main value lies in forcing the student to pick out crucial issues from a welter of facts and to be an active participant in deciding upon a course of action. This is not something which can be carried very far, however, until the stu-

[20] Whether cases should be widely used in management training programs, however, is debatable; as one dean put the matter, many executives who come back to school want the work to move forward quickly and at a high theoretical level. See also Professor Timms's discussion of the use of cases in Chap. 18.

[21] Introducing cases in schools where they have been little used can be extremely effective in broadening the interests of faculty members and strengthening teaching methods; on this score alone, the decision by the AACSB and the Ford Foundation to establish an Intercollegiate Case Clearing House for the pooling and dissemination of cases is to be applauded.

dent develops the mental tools and general background needed to do this kind of work. The same question arises concerning the relative emphasis on the managerial viewpoint in undergraduate as opposed to graduate work and essentially the same answer seems indicated.

Other Teaching Methods

There are many variations on the case method which also can be useful in helping schools get away from excessive emphasis on lectures and textbooks. A device used at Columbia and a number of other schools is for a business executive to present some issue which his firm has faced and later make a return visit to hear the students' analysis and recommendations.[22] Another variation is for students (either singly or in groups) to work on some one problem referred to them by a corporation which requires on-the-spot investigation and a sustained piece of analysis; reports are then prepared and presented to officials of the company, as well as to the students' professor and fellow classmates, for their criticisms.[23] Many schools invite corporate officials to participate in classroom sessions and to discuss current policy questions, but this is rather different from the case emphasis in that student reports are not required. The same applies to field trips or other less formal contacts with business organizations.

Some schools stress problems in the sense of exercises rather than cases. This reflects a quite different point of view since problems, thus defined, involve the application of certain principles and presumably yield determinate solutions. They are, of course, most appropriate in accounting and statistics, but many schools use them in courses in economics, finance, and production as well; they figure less prominently in marketing, personnel, or general management courses. Another rather different emphasis involves the use of incidents or short cases which sometimes entail role playing or team presentations. Still another is the use of business games in which students operate rival "firms" under certain assumed production, distribution, and marketing conditions; decisions are fed into a computer machine and the results are used to guide future strategies of the decision makers. Game playing can be a stimulating learning experience if carefully planned, though it requires a degree of maturity and sophistication which tends to make it inappropriate for undergraduate students.

Despite the close ties which many undergraduate and graduate busi-

[22] This, for example, is the approach of the course in Problems in Business Policy at Columbia.

[23] This is the general plan of the course in Creative Marketing Strategy at the Harvard Business School.

ness schools have with employers, few have attempted to establish cooperative or internship relationships with firms. Some of the better
known are the alternating work-study arrangements at Cincinnati,
Drexel, and Northeastern.[24] The advantages of tying the student's academic and job experience more closely together would seem rather
obvious. Why, then, have not more schools moved in this direction?

Administratively, of course, cooperative programs are extremely difficult to maintain. The road of least resistance is to let students take jobs
with employers who can get the most from their services, even though
educationally such jobs are likely to be quite useless. A careful screening
of firms and positions is therefore necessary, but this is not easy to do on
a continuing basis for large groups of students. The underlying difficulty
is that there are very few openings of much educational value in business
which young, inexperienced people can fill on a temporary basis. This
appears to be the case even if it is granted that conventional standards
of educational achievement are not applicable to on-the-job experience.
For most students and most schools, this would not appear to be an
appropriate pattern to follow.

It would be most unfortunate, however, if the matter were allowed to
rest here. The basic idea of bringing work and study more closely together is too valuable to lose hold of altogether. Surely ways can be
found to use it in a form that would avoid the dangers just cited. In this
regard business schools have proved to be rather unimaginative. There
is no reason why special internship arrangements could not be worked
out with certain carefully chosen companies for particularly qualified
students. Most schools have been quite aggressive in finding bread-and-
butter jobs for their students in summer and on a part-time basis during
the school year. Job experiences that would tie in more closely with the
academic program should be sought for at least certain students just as
vigorously. This is an area in which business schools (and engineering
schools too) have a natural advantage over most other branches of universities. They should use it more effectively than in the past.

INDEPENDENT STUDY AND THE SUPERIOR STUDENT

The main purpose of all these approaches to business education is to
put more responsibility on the student to learn for himself. The business
schools are dealing with a field which lends itself to this kind of learning,
perhaps more than most other fields. It is important, therefore, that they
exploit this advantage to the full. The difficulty is that self-learning can-

---

[24] Some schools, such as at CCNY, permit certain advanced students to participate
in company training programs. This work, which is under joint school-employer
control, is given a small amount of course credit.

not be relied on very extensively if the students are of mediocre academic quality, a point frequently emphasized earlier in this study. Another difficulty is one of sheer numbers. It is extremely hard to get students to carry forward their own education when they meet in very large classes or divide up in numerous sections under the aegis of relatively inexperienced instructors. This raises again the dilemma posed in Chap. 1, how the schools can provide mass education and at the same time give superior students an adequate learning experience.

There doubtless are various ways for conserving the time of the best equipped and most effective faculty members. Many professors devote a good deal of energy to purely routine matters—preparing class lists, recording grades, checking on books, filling out forms of one kind or another. Many scatter their energies over a wide spectrum of activities, ranging from a hurried conference over a senior's thesis to helping prepare a client's income tax return. The most serious waste of faculty resources results from the wide variety of course offerings found at many schools. Merely reducing the number of subjects taught would not resolve the problem, since provision would still have to be made for the same number of students. However, fewer separate preparations could represent a real time saving for many faculty members and a more even distribution of teaching loads. It should be added that, if the schools follow the general curriculum recommendations outlined in Chaps. 8 to 10, a substantial portion of the teaching would be handled by faculties outside the traditional business area, thereby spreading the teaching load still more evenly.

Despite these and similar efforts, a number of schools will have to resort to more extreme measures to conserve faculty time. The blunt fact for many institutions is that their staffs cannot begin to cope adequately with the number of students enrolling in their programs. For these institutions the choice seems to be either mass lecture methods or recruiting large staffs of young, relatively inexperienced instructors to handle section meetings. Indeed, the great majority of large undergraduate business schools are moving rapidly along both these lines. There is a praiseworthy effort at most of the latter schools to keep the sections in basic courses below 40 students, but whether this yields the best results in view of the caliber of the teaching is by no means clear. If the sections or classes go much above 40 or 50, it is hard to see why the students could not be quite as well handled in groups of 500 or more.

A few business schools are experimenting with television but to date the results have been mixed. Penn State University, for example, has used this device in various business and nonbusiness courses over the past four years; among the business school courses taught by this means are accounting (a basic course and a course in cost accounting), introductory economics, business law, and transportation. Each classroom is proctored and is equipped to handle questions from the students. While some subjects appear to be more adaptable to this kind of instruction than others, the main differences lie in the abilities of the teachers. The planning and cost involved in educational television are extremely great and the instructors have to be chosen and trained with considerable care.[25] Despite all these reservations, this method of teaching shows much promise and further experimentation should be encouraged.

If the schools resort to such extreme methods, the need for offsetting measures to make sure that students are treated as individuals and challenged to their best performance will become all the greater. Every step toward mass education should be offset by a move toward more individualized education; otherwise quantity rather than quality standards will come to prevail. Superior students have a special claim in this regard and every effort should be made to identify them early and give them abundant opportunity to develop their talents.

Undergraduate business schools almost without exception fail to challenge the more promising students. This was one of the most important conclusions to emerge from the interviews conducted in 1957–1958 in all parts of the country. Many factors explain this, as previous chapters have tried to show, but the schools have been singularly lax in doing anything about it. Aside from the curriculum reforms outlined earlier, there are many steps the schools can take to meet this problem. One is to strengthen the advising system to help students follow programs more commensurate with their abilities. Another is to waive requirements for students of special ability and training in areas where the work would be repetitious or too elementary. Still another is to give students who have the inclination and capacity to do so particularly rigorous work in certain subjects or to permit them to do much more in the way of individual investigation and report writing. Still another is to establish advanced seminars in especially challenging areas or to allow certain students to study by the seminar method altogether.

Many colleges and universities have established honors programs for superior students, usually in the liberal arts subjects. These programs are designed to get away from lecture-textbook courses and often involve seminar study in broad fields, interdisciplinary areas, or newly developed subjects. A lower-division honors program typically permits superior students to move ahead at a relatively more rapid rate or to take specially designed courses in addition to their regular work. An upper-division

---

[25] Judging from the Penn State experience, college teaching by television is not feasible economically unless there are at least 200 students in the group. This institution is also planning to use television more widely in its branch centers in different parts of Pennsylvania.

program usually consists of a wholly separate sequence with emphasis on group discussions of weekly papers, independent reading, and a final set of examinations leading to an honors degree.

Professional schools apparently have done very little along such lines, although the need is especially great for their students.[26] In the seventy-five campus interviews only a bare handful of schools were found to have taken any serious steps in this direction. Some permit their more promising students to participate in special courses or seminars, set up on a campuswide basis; a few have established such arrangements on their own initiative.[27] The great majority, however, evince no genuine concern over the plight of the abler student or any disposition to do anything constructive on his behalf. The reasons most often cited are the high cost of such instruction and the scarcity of qualified personnel; these can be real limitations but they need not bar every approach to this aspect of higher education.[28]

CONCLUSIONS

The picture which emerges from this brief review of faculty requirements, teaching conditions, and teaching methods in business schools is cause for concern, all the more so since rising enrollments will doubtless bring further deterioration in teaching standards in the future. In large measure the difficulties which business schools face in staffing their programs are shared with other branches of higher education, and until the country is prepared to allocate substantially more resources to strengthening its colleges and universities, these difficulties can be expected to continue.

There is much, however, which the business schools themselves can do under existing conditions. Their prime obligation is to formulate programs of study which will command general respect and confidence.

[26] "Honors programs are least often found where they are most needed—in the professional schools that train young people for specialized careers in such fields as engineering, business administration, education, law, and medicine." Fred H. Harrington, "What About Professional Schools?" *The Superior Student*, Newsletter of the Inter-University Committee on the Superior Student, vol. 2, no. 1, February, 1959, p. 2.

[27] The College of Business Administration at the University of Washington provides special offerings in interdisciplinary areas taught by business and nonbusiness faculty members; the work is open to superior junior and senior business administration students and each offering is equivalent to 5 hours credit on a quarter basis. *The Superior Student*, Newsletter of the Inter-University Committee on the Superior Student, vol. 2, no. 1, February, 1959, p. 15.

[28] This issue is a good deal more acute at the undergraduate level; students have a better notion of their abilities and career interests at the graduate level so abler students are more likely to find work that will challenge them.

Without this as a rallying point, any moves toward improvement are likely to be haphazard and short-lived. The faculty of each school should therefore undertake a broad reexamination of its work; every opportunity should be utilized to assist faculty members to continue their own intellectual growth. Wherever possible, teaching conditions should be altered to give greater scope to the scholarly interests of faculty members. The various activities in which business faculties now engage should be reviewed from this same point of view. Only by making the scientific study of business their central interest can faculty members win the influence which should be theirs.

The most heartening aspect of this field is the interest which many schools are showing in new approaches to education for business. A number of institutions have already pioneered new programs and others are in process of restudying their work. On many campuses, as noted earlier, the faculties seem ready to move forward if only strong leadership can be provided. True, there is an atmosphere of uncertainty and perhaps even of frustration in many cases, but the underlying tone is one of willingness to explore and innovate. Here is where the hope for higher standards mainly lies, and the schools should capitalize on it to the full.

CHAPTER 12

DOCTORAL PROGRAMS AND RESEARCH

Business schools are giving increased attention to doctoral programs and research. This attests to the improved academic status and new responsibilities of these schools. The approaches of the different institutions to both their doctoral and research programs reflect the historical development of the field as a whole. The principal issue is how these programs can be greatly expanded at the same time that their general quality is improved.

The next major development in education for business will come at the doctoral level. This seems inescapable if business schools are going to meet the anticipated increase in demand for faculty, research workers, and technical business specialists described in previous chapters. Doubtless other branches of graduate education will also figure prominently in meeting this demand, but even if their part is materially increased, a shortage of qualified personnel will still remain. Business schools therefore have no alternative but to enter this area themselves.

The difficulties and dangers to be faced in building such programs are essentially those already discussed at the undergraduate and master's levels. The question in all three cases is whether the subject possesses sufficient content to justify full academic status. The dangers at the doctoral level are particularly great since it is generally assumed that work for the doctorate will be rather highly specialized. Earlier chapters showed, however, that specialization in the business studies can lead to unsatisfactory results. Great care has to be exercised to make sure that this does not happen at the most advanced level of instruction.

In business administration, perhaps to a greater degree than in more fully developed fields, the outcome largely depends on the breadth and imagination of the faculties and students. There is no escaping the fact that the doctorate entails a considerable measure of specialization, but the context within which the specialization takes place is all-important. Previous chapters constructed a framework for the study of business out of certain nonbusiness subjects, the business functional areas, and the decision-making process. This same framework can also be used in developing doctoral studies of solid academic content. The important consideration is to make sure that doctoral programs, including the dissertation requirement, are kept in this broad framework. As long as this is done, specialization will assume its proper role as a constructive educational experience.

It is evident that the development of doctoral programs along these lines must be a slow and laborious process. In the first place, it would require heavy financial outlays to attract the necessary personnel and to give them the facilities and time they would need for such an undertaking. Second, even with adequate funds, the problem of finding persons qualified to carry out such programs would continue to be extremely serious. Third, and most important, the field itself is in considerable ferment, and doctoral programs are in a similar transitional state.

These are sobering considerations, enough at least to cast doubt on any easy formulas or quick-success proposals. A few schools, however, have already gone some distance toward building strong doctoral programs and others are laying plans which give real promise. Whatever the difficulties, the task of preparing more doctoral candidates in business must be undertaken. The supply of teaching personnel, the quality of instruction in business schools generally, and the scientific advance of the field itself all depend on the outcome. Looking to the future, this part of the work of business schools deserves more attention and support than any other.

PRESENT PROGRAMS

There are now about twenty-five business schools with active doctor's degree programs.[1] Before being admitted to candidacy, a student generally must have taken the core courses required for the master's degree or their equivalent. In addition, the student usually is required to take written examinations in three or more fields and often must pass a foreign language requirement set by the graduate school. After being accepted for candidacy, the student selects a topic for independent research approved by his doctoral adviser and/or committee and then prepares a doctoral dissertation which is subsequently defended in an oral examination. This is essentially the same procedure found in most fields of graduate study. Widespread criticisms have been voiced about this gen-

[1] Twenty-eight schools, plus one institution with a department of business, reported awarding doctor's degrees in business in 1955–1956; the total of such degrees was 158 in that year. Several of the programs, however, were on paper only. The top ten schools ranked on the basis of number of doctor's degrees granted in 1955–1956 were N.Y.U., Harvard, Indiana, Ohio State, State University of Iowa, Minnesota, Texas, Michigan, Chicago, and Columbia; these ten schools awarded 74 per cent of the total. These data were derived from the Survey Questionnaire.

eral pattern of education; these will not be taken up here;[2] attention instead will be centered on the distinctive features of doctoral programs in business.

The differing status of these programs at individual institutions reflects the prior stages of development of business schools described in Chap. 3 and elsewhere in this study. The formative period when business courses were but one aspect of the work of economics departments is clearly evident in almost all these programs. Typically, the schools require students to study and take qualifying examinations in one or more branches of economics, usually economic theory. As noted below, however, even the work in the latter area is taking on more of an operational emphasis; if present trends continue, economics departments (where they are located outside the business schools) may be excluded from the doctoral programs in business altogether.

In the next important stage in the development of business schools, the work centered almost completely around certain functions of the firm, such as accounting and statistical controls, marketing, insurance, etc. Current doctoral programs bear the impact of this emphasis, again in varying degrees and with varying results. Usually doctoral candidates are required to have taken the first year M.B.A. courses dealing with the functional subjects. Usually, too, the candidates can present two to four of these subjects as fields for the qualifying examinations. In most cases the doctoral requirements do not specify that students choose one of the functional areas as a major; this distinction is not too important since most doctoral candidates will already have concentrated in some area as part of their work under a master's program. Moreover, after passing their qualifying examinations, students must focus their interests sharply in connection with their thesis projects.

The third major development in the work of business schools was the introduction of the case method and the change to a managerial point of view. This entailed a shift from the functional subjects considered as separate specialties to company-wide relationships between the functional areas. At least initially, emphasis centered primarily on decision making as affected by interarea (or interfunctional) relationships within the individual firm, although some attention necessarily had to be given to broader, extrafirm influences. Viewed historically, the most important feature of this development was the change in the position of the functional specialties.

---

[2] The principal criticisms leveled against doctoral programs are set forth in Committee of Fifteen, *The Graduate School Today and Tomorrow*, Fund for the Advancement of Education, New York, 1955; for an earlier but more detailed discussion, see E. V. Hollis, *Toward Improving Ph.D. Programs*, American Council on Education, Washington, D.C., 1945.

The present day doctoral programs reflect in various ways this third major development. At some schools, considerable emphasis is placed on case analysis; at Harvard, for example, both the course program and the dissertation have a heavy case emphasis.[3] Most schools use other means as well as case analysis to give the doctoral studies a managerial focus, their field requirements and dissertation ground rules being rather flexible. It is characteristic of these schools as well as those with a case emphasis not to require doctoral candidates to concentrate on a single functional area in connection with their qualifying examinations.

In a few schools there appears to be little stress on the managerial viewpoint in the doctoral program, chief weight still being given to the functional areas as self-contained specialties. It is typical of these schools to require students to major in one of these areas in much the same way as under an M.B.A. program. In their case the managerial emphasis, to the extent it is introduced at all, is chiefly limited to the student's prior work in the master's program.

Some business schools have reached a fourth phase of development in which managerial decision making is emphasized from an extrafirm, quite as much as from an intrafirm, point of view. Attention thus tends to center on the contributions of a number of basic disciplines (notably mathematics and psychology-sociology) to analysis of the administrative process, and emphasis has shifted from a case-by-case approach to more direct use of the basic disciplines in analyzing business decisions in a complex environment. While for the most part of recent origin, this orientation has already had considerable effect on the doctoral programs of most business schools. Some, such as Chicago, now require students to take a qualifying examination in one of the basic disciplines—economics, mathematics, or psychology-sociology—and others introduce these materials into the field examinations in the more traditional business areas; most schools make an effort to have doctoral candidates take work outside the business schools' own programs, sometimes in connection with the minor requirement, but few students appear to avail themselves of the opportunity.[4]

A SUGGESTED FRAMEWORK

The issue presented by doctoral programs in business is how these elements can best be combined and what differences among the schools

---

[3] In recent years, however, Harvard's doctoral program has moved somewhat away from this orientation.

[4] For further details on the current status of doctoral programs in business, see George P. Baker and David B. Tyack, American Association of Collegiate Schools of Business, *Faculty Requirements in Collegiate Schools of Business, op. cit.*, Chap. 4.

seem desirable. The findings and recommendations of previous chapters suggest the general direction the schools might follow in this regard. At the same time there needs to be considerable variation among the schools and considerable flexibility within each school's program to keep the work fresh, responsive to new approaches, and adaptable to the interests of individual students and faculty members. The propositions derived from earlier chapters which bear on doctoral programs are set forth briefly below.

First, the prime objective of doctoral programs is to make sure that holders of the doctorate have the necessary equipment to analyze significant problems in managerial decision making in a scientific manner and to present the conclusions of such analysis in effective oral and written form. Just as the M.B.A. degree points to a life of action, so the doctor's degree points to a life of scholarship or special technical competence. There is no denying that many aspects of the decision-making process defy precise scientific analysis. Doctoral programs in business must be addressed to a diverse range of activities in which the element of unpredictable human behavior bulks large. This, however, should not be permitted to alter the underlying purpose of such programs, which is to give advanced students the equipment they will need for careers of academic or professional service.

Second, the work for the doctorate in business should make sure that the student has sufficient command of the basic disciplines underlying the field and its principal analytical tools—accounting, economics, legal and political institutions, mathematics-statistics, and psychology-sociology— so he will be able to draw on these underlying fields as a teacher, research worker, and staff specialist. The relevance of these subjects to academic preparation for active careers in business has been repeatedly stressed in previous chapters, and their importance for scholarly careers in this area would seem even more evident. Some students may have rather serious gaps in their backgrounds which will have to be filled; others may merely have to carry forward studies in which they are already well along. Students who have taken most of their prior preparation in business subjects would presumably place greater stress on the basic disciplines, while those who have taken most of their earlier work in nonbusiness fields would emphasize the business subjects. The sequence of study would accordingly have to be tailored to the needs of the individual, and the closest kind of ties established with other branches of graduate work.

Third, the student's area or areas of special competence should afford him the opportunity to apply his knowledge of other subjects to significant aspects of business behavior. Presumably emphasis would be placed on the various functional areas, but even more than under a master's program, the work needs to be put in a broad academic context. A Ph.D. candidate in accounting, for example, should not simply specialize more intensively in refined techniques of accountancy but should approach the subject from new and broader vantage points such as its relation to modern statistical methods, to important issues in financial administration, and the like. While in general this suggests a managerial decision-making emphasis, it may be unwise to delimit the approach of the various schools even to this degree.

Fourth, a doctoral program in business must necessarily have both a practitioner and a scholarly orientation, but the latter deserves much the greater emphasis. The central subject matter—the nature of the decision-making process in a business environment—cannot be understood without looking at it from the viewpoint of active participants. On the other hand, if much of a practitioner emphasis comes into the doctoral program, the outcome would almost necessarily be a more specialized M.B.A. degree. The principal test to apply is whether a candidate for the doctorate has shown a capacity for scholarly analytical work as a potential teacher, research worker, or business staff specialist. The dissertation is important for this purpose but so is the student's performance in individual courses and in the field examinations.

Much of the work for the M.B.A. degree would accordingly be appropriate for students planning to go on to the doctorate, but certain important differences would need to be recognized. Theoretical principles underlying the business and nonbusiness subjects would have to be examined intensively; sources of primary and secondary materials would have to be covered systematically; the proper methods of scientific investigation would have to be mastered; and critical research issues would have to be explored. It seems obvious that, even though the precise differences cannot be easily identified, a good portion of the doctoral program would have to be distinguished from the work done for the M.B.A. degree.

As shown below, this conception of the doctorate in business contains important implications for various aspects of these programs. Its chief significance, however, lies in the general emphasis it would give such programs. Scholarship, research, and advanced analysis would be put at the center of the work, making this part of the schools a true community of scholars. Students earning doctor's degrees under these programs would presumably bring a good deal of this same orientation into their later work. Gradually over the years the quality of academic performance at all levels in business schools could be expected to rise.

At the beginning of this chapter, reference was made to the danger that doctoral programs in business might degenerate into narrow specialism. The view suggested here would leave ample room for study in depth but would keep it part of a general framework. This should provide a fair measure of protection against the blighting effects of specialization. The only real safeguard lies, however, in the kind of backgrounds and interests which faculty members and students bring to their work—a consideration which applies to other fields quite as much as to business administration.

AREAS OF COMPETENCE

Given this framework for appraising the doctoral studies, what are the subjects in which students should be required to show general competence before taking their field examinations? At most schools these subjects are the same as those required for the M.B.A. degree, doctoral and M.B.A. candidates taking identical courses. Since both groups need broad preparation in the principal business subjects and many students decide to go on for the doctorate after they are well along in the master's program, this procedure seems only sensible. If the M.B.A. program requires a number of highly specialized courses or emphasizes practical techniques, the work would hardly be suitable for potential doctoral candidates, but in the case of schools which develop along the general lines recommended in Chap. 10 the difference in orientation of the two programs would not be unduly sharp. Since Chap. 10 set forth in some detail the required areas that might be included in an M.B.A. program, there is no need to review this aspect of the doctoral program further.

The schools, however, should not stop here. Most of the first year's graduate work and perhaps as much as one-half of the second might well be the same under both programs, but in both years doctoral candidates should place more stress on research methods and the more purely scholarly aspects of the field than M.B.A. candidates. Contrariwise, they would require somewhat less emphasis on the functional business areas studied from the viewpoint of the operating executive. There are a number of ways these differing requirements can be met, and even within a given school considerable flexibility would have to be exercised in order to allow for differences in student backgrounds and faculty interests. Special competency in one of the basic disciplines underlying the business field or familiarity with modern research methods in one of the social sciences or some evidence of promise along lines of research and scholarship might be required. As to the level of competency required in economics, many schools, perhaps a majority, require doctoral candidates to go beyond the level stipulated in the M.B.A. program. There is much merit in this, especially if the students are required to take an advanced course in economic theory offered by the graduate school's economics department. These matters bear closely on the choice of fields to be covered in the qualifying examinations and are discussed below more fully.

It would not seem practical to require all students to decide between an M.B.A. and a doctor's degree before the end of their first graduate year, but they should be given the opportunity to do special work for the latter degree even during their first year of graduate study if they should choose to do so. These special doctoral requirements would be considerably increased during the next year, with a corresponding reduction in some of the more specialized courses the student would have taken if he had stayed in the M.B.A. program.

Recent changes in the doctoral program at Harvard illustrate one approach to this range of problems. Before 1957–1958, doctoral candidates took the same courses as M.B.A. students and the only essential difference was the work done in the third year on a dissertation topic. Since then, students can choose four courses in the second semester of their second year from the following offerings specially designed for doctoral candidates: Advanced Economic Analysis, Business History, Concepts and Research Methods of the Behavioral Sciences, Statistical Methodology, and one of the special field reading seminars.[5] In addition, two additional seminars in research and its presentation and in teaching by the case method can also be taken; it should be noted that neither of these two seminars counts for credit toward the M.B.A. degree. This part of the Harvard doctoral program is kept on a flexible basis and is adapted to the needs of each student; of the courses or seminars listed above, only the one in research and its presentation is explicitly required of all candidates.[6] Whether specific features of this part of Harvard's doctoral program will stand the test of experience is still an open question. It could be argued that the program does not utilize the resources of the regular graduate school nearly enough or that the student's work in research methodology cannot be divorced from specific research activities in which the student is currently engaged. More effort might also be made to introduce some work for the doctorate in the first year. Nonetheless, the move toward a more systematic treatment of the behavioral sciences, as well as more emphasis on economics and statistics, appears altogether sound.

THE FIELD EXAMINATIONS

After giving evidence of competency in certain areas, the doctoral candidate takes examinations in a few broad fields of special importance.

[5] Except for the special field reading seminar, all these courses are open to M.B.A. candidates too, but they are especially designed for students in the doctoral program.

[6] See Memorandum on Proposals in Regard to the Doctoral Program, Approved by the Doctoral Board, Harvard Business School, January 25, 1957.

The fields specified and type of examinations given are a distinctive feature of the work for the doctorate and largely determine the quality of the program as a whole. The place of economics in these examinations is a case in point. A majority of schools specify that economics must be one of the fields, but some stipulate that the examination shall be in economic theory given by the graduate school's economics department; others require an examination in business economics or economic analysis given by the business school. A minority of the schools place little stress on economic analysis of any kind. Among some of the schools in the first group (e.g., Wisconsin), the emphasis of the entire doctoral program is placed on economics.[7] In schools in the second group, there is a tendency to require a rather wide scattering of fields much as in the M.B.A. program; Stanford, for example, requires doctoral candidates to take the M.B.A. core courses, field examinations in four business areas chosen from a list of nine, and a minor in a nonbusiness area.

A few schools take what appears to be a middle position on the importance of economic theory and other branches of economics in the doctoral programs, but they may well represent the prevailing pattern in the future. At Indiana, for example, doctoral students were formerly required to take a field examination in economic theory based on courses in microanalysis and macroanalysis and in the history of economic thought given in the graduate school's economics department. Beginning in the fall of 1956, students were given the alternative of substituting a course in economic and business analysis taught in the business school in place of the history of doctrine course; the examination which students choosing this alternative take in economic theory is administered by the business school. However, they must still take the economic theory course given in the economics department, and the chairman of the economics department (though not the professor in charge of the course) must pass on the examination in this field. The other fields may be taken in either business or economics but the thesis field must be in business; the student can also substitute a fifth field for the former language requirements.

The tendency among business schools to provide their own courses and examinations in economic theory for doctoral candidates ought to be resisted. Almost inevitably this means a dilution of standards and a move toward less rather than more use of economic analysis in the business program. Conceivably this need not happen if a school has developed a

---

[7] North Carolina also has a heavy economics orientation; it requires all Ph.D. students to concentrate in economic theory and to choose four other areas from accounting, econometrics, economic history, international economics, labor, management, marketing, monetary theory, private finance, public finance, public policy, and statistics.

strong economics staff of its own. Moreover, it seems clear that business students should not be held responsible for abstruse aspects of the subject which have little bearing on their field of interest. Business students, nonetheless, need exposure to nonbusiness subjects taught by the most capable persons available. The programs of both the business schools and the economics departments in the graduate schools would benefit by maintaining the closest possible ties. It would therefore seem highly desirable for the two groups to make such adjustments as would be necessary to keep the doctoral work in economic theory in the hands of the economics departments; only as a last resort should it be taken over by the business schools. While less important, it would also be desirable for doctoral candidates to take at least one other field in economics; whether the work is offered in or out of the business school would depend on the particular circumstances, personalities, etc., in a given case.[8]

A few schools, as already noted, require doctoral students to take a field examination in some other nonbusiness area, e.g., mathematics, mathematical-statistics, political-legal institutions, or the behavioral sciences. The same question regarding the handling of the field examinations arises in these areas as in economics, but the circumstances are rather different.[9] These areas are not nearly so close to business, at least by tradition, as is economics, and with the possible exception of the field of political and legal institutions, there are very few persons who are familiar with the business applications of these basic disciplines. Perhaps in time these circumstances will change; if so, it would be desirable to follow the procedure recommended in economic theory. It also is vitally important for students preparing for a field examination in one of these disciplines to take work in the graduate school department involved. However, it hardly seems practical to have these departments handle the examinations at the present time.

A more important issue is whether such disciplines, insofar as they relate to the business area, deserve a place in the field examinations at all. Using the principles set forth earlier in this study, the answer would appear to be in the affirmative. This aspect of the business curriculum is relatively new, however, and the schools should move carefully in adding any of these areas to the field examinations. The question of finding qualified faculty—and keeping them—to handle this part of the program seems especially serious. Nor is it clear as yet how the basic disciplines

[8] The relationship between the business schools and economics departments was discussed at some length in Chap. 9. Potentially the competition for students between the two groups seems more serious at the doctoral level than at either the undergraduate or the master's levels.

[9] Most schools only attempt to introduce materials of this sort as part of the field examinations in the conventional business subjects; sometimes students may choose to minor in an area outside business or economics.

can best be related to the business studies at the doctoral level. Thus experimentation needs to be encouraged, with the schools developing different patterns of work.[10]

Finally, almost all the schools require field examinations in one or more of the traditional business areas, but judging from a perusal of the questions asked of doctoral candidates at a number of schools, there are wide differences in practice. Some of the schools concentrate on analysis of a particular business case, others on principles of a given subject, still others on relationships between the functional areas and managerial decision making. These approaches need not be mutually exclusive and in fact most schools endeavor to keep them in some kind of balance. As suggested earlier, a decision-making approach seems the most promising one to follow, though a clear understanding of what this approach entails is still to be achieved. Such questions as whether management decision making should be treated as a separate field or made a part of the functional areas were discussed in previous chapters, and the earlier findings seem applicable here.[11]

FOREIGN LANGUAGE REQUIREMENT

The schools are rather seriously split on whether doctoral candidates should be required to meet a foreign language requirement. Where the programs are still subject to control by graduate schools, a reading knowledge of one or more foreign language is usually required, but where they are not, this requirement is often waived. Sometimes students can petition to substitute another field for this requirement.

In the discussion of this issue at the undergraduate level, the foreign language requirement was approached in terms of the general background equipment which students will need in the business world. At the doctoral level, the principal issue is whether this requirement is needed for careers in teaching, research, and professional staff work in business. Viewed in these terms, the foreign language requirement seems less essential for doctoral candidates than for other types of preparation. Some doctoral students might well find it to their advantage to round out their training in a foreign language and they, of course, should be encouraged to do so. The requirement hardly seems appropriate, however, for those

[10] The business school at Chicago now requires doctoral candidates to take a field examination in one of the three following disciplines: economics, behavioral science, and the algebra and analysis branches of mathematics. The examinations are administered by the business school but students are encouraged to take a good deal of work in the graduate departments involved.

[11] Further observations on these aspects of the doctoral programs will be found in Part 3 of this study, especially Chap. 13.

who begin their doctoral work with little or no language preparation. For the latter students another option should be available, preferably in a research-tool subject. The graduate schools might well consider some such change as this rather than see the business schools establish autonomous doctoral programs. As indicated earlier, there is much to be said for making the doctorate in business an academic degree, but if the schools move toward autonomy, the degree will almost certainly become more professional in character.[12]

DISSERTATION AND RESEARCH PREPARATION

While doctoral programs in business, as indicated, can be differentiated from M.B.A. programs in certain respects, it must be admitted that the differences cannot be too great. The principal distinction must come in the final step, the writing of the dissertation. Here the student is obliged to stake out an area of independent investigation and carry through a piece of sustained research to a successful conclusion. This is a formidable requirement but it can hardly be anything else if its purpose is to be achieved. There doubtless are ways of modifying the requirements for the dissertation without subverting its essential purpose. In many fields other than business, it appears that the trappings, rather than the substance, of the thesis requirement have come to receive prime attention. Few would quarrel with the basic idea of the dissertation, however, or with the general method it embodies for testing a student's capacity for scholarly work.

This is hardly the place to assess the place of the dissertation in American higher education, although the question may be asked in passing whether this much maligned feature of graduate work, even in its present form, is quite as valueless as some of its critics would make it appear. The need is to determine where the strengths and weaknesses of thesis projects in particular fields lie. In the case of business administration, this issue cannot be divorced from the development of the field as a whole, since the quality of the students' dissertations is not likely to rise much above the quality of a school's general program.

Put briefly, students should regard the dissertation as an opportunity to use modern analytical tools in investigating significant problems in a broad business setting. It would hardly seem advisable to limit all dissertations to a business-case orientation, although case investigation may be wholly suitable under certain circumstances. In view of the impor-

[12] Whether the degree is called a D.B.A. or Ph.D. is perhaps immaterial in itself, but whether it is primarily a professional or academic degree is a matter of first importance; for reasons developed earlier, an academic type of degree seems preferable.

tance of the basic disciplines in this field, it might not even be proper to limit the student's focus to managerial decision making, although again this would be a fruitful area for many. At the same time, diversity of subject matter does not mean flexibility of criteria. The test is whether a student can put the tools of research to productive ends; there are many ways this requirement can be satisfied but the test itself is exacting in the extreme. It is not something which can be measured in terms of number of pages written, footnotes cited, or facts accumulated. It is nothing less than a measure of the student's capacity to use what he has learned to carry out a scientific investigation on his own. Unless the purpose of the thesis requirement is more or less completely negated, this test is bound to be an arduous intellectual experience.

It is difficult to say how closely the dissertations in the business field approach this ideal. An attempt was made to sample a number of theses in this area, but how they compared with dissertations in other areas (a dubious criterion at best) could not be determined. Judging from the campus interviews, business dissertations are not held in high regard; often the comment was made that they chiefly involved description of business practice and required little use of sophisticated methods of analysis. Much diversity in the quality of the work doubtless exists but the general impression derived from the interviews is that many of the dissertations in the business field do not meet the test set forth above.

There are many considerations, including the way in which the field itself has developed, which bear on this outcome, but one calling for special mention is that doctoral candidates in business often do not have the preparation necessary to carry through a piece of research. In many instances the students have had the barest kind of exposure to the methods used in scientific investigations or to the tools needed in such undertakings. Frequently they have had no experience in following out the steps of a specific research study—defining the nature of a problem, formulating an hypothesis, assembling the relevant data, and interpreting the results. The recommendations made in earlier chapters, as well as the general approach to doctoral programs suggested in this chapter, would go part way toward meeting this deficiency. In addition, however, explicit provision needs to be made for doctoral candidates to get this kind of preparation. Seminars or workshops might be established, for example, in which each student would work on a limited type of research project under close faculty supervision. It would be important for doctoral candidates to get some comprehension of research methodology through systematic discussion and reading, but it is doubtful whether this kind of instruction would have much meaning unless it were put to use in specific application. The schools need to push this aspect of the work much more vigorously than they have in the past.

SUMMARY OF DOCTORAL RECOMMENDATIONS

This discussion has emphasized that doctoral programs need to be kept flexible to allow for considerable diversity in the backgrounds and interests of students. Those with good general preparation or particular ability might well be able to take their field examinations within two academic years from the time they get their B.A. degree; others might require two and a half years. Since the emphasis in doctoral programs is quite properly on mastery of certain fields, it would be dangerous to establish requirements which might be misinterpreted as referring to individual courses. The summary presented here, therefore, is presented in terms of general fields, and the references to particular courses are merely made to indicate the level of work and the amount of time involved.

Assuming that a student has reasonably good general undergraduate preparation, it should be possible for him to take his qualifying examinations by the end of his second year of graduate work. Other students would have to take at least an additional semester of study. In the first year most students would be enrolled in the M.B.A. program, but even if they were aiming for a doctorate from the outset, the work would largely be the same. In the approach to the M.B.A. program summarized at the end of Chap. 10, it will be remembered that there was ample room left for students to pursue additional studies in the basic disciplines. Provision could therefore be made for those with doctoral ambitions to take a specially designed course or seminar in economics, mathematics-statistics, legal-political institutions, or psychology-sociology in their first graduate year. Alternatively, such work might be taken in the graduate school departments involved. Similarly, it might be possible for such students to take a special seminar in research methods in the second semester of their first year. Even though many would not have made definite plans so soon, the opportunity ought to be made available to those who have.

By the end of the first year, students would need to know whether they wished to go on to the doctorate so that they could take the work specially designed for them in the second year. They still presumably would take the core courses required of M.B.A. students but in addition they would need work in the other basic disciplines noted above. It would also be important for them to participate in a seminar designed to give them concrete experience in research methodology, and they would need to satisfy the foreign language requirement or other conditions specified by a particular institution. Even with the latitude provided in the suggested M.B.A. program, it seems likely that one or two of the course requirements in the latter program would have to be waived.

This might best be done in the area of the student's major concentration.

With this broad preparation, the student would be in a position to take his qualifying examinations at the end of his second year. Since their purpose is to test mastery of a broad field, it is doubtful whether the student should be required to take more than three (or at the most four) field examinations: one chosen from the basic disciplines of economics, quantitative methods, legal-political institutions, and psychology-sociology and two from the broad functional areas. Some schools might well want to experiment with two field examinations in the basic disciplines. Finally, the dissertation requirements could be developed along the lines suggested above, requiring about another year of full-time work to complete.

It seems unwise to develop more precise recommendations than the above, especially in view of the unsettled state of this part of business school programs. However, it is hoped that enough has been said to indicate how the schools might approach their responsibilities in the doctoral area. Clearly, a program along the lines recommended here could not be established without a highly trained, diversified faculty and strong financial backing. It would be very doubtful, for example, if programs of this sort could be developed outside major universities. Even at the risk of limiting the number of doctorates, therefore, these programs should be concentrated in a small number of the most strongly established schools.

RESEARCH PROGRAMS

Greater stress on the research role of business schools is a logical corollary to the increased attention being placed on doctoral programs in this field. By their very nature, doctoral programs have a heavy research orientation and are largely shaped by a school's conception of its research function. Harvard's emphasis on case collection and analysis as a type of research, for example, has had a profound effect on its approach to the doctoral program. Similarly, schools which concentrate on specific industry or locality research tend to develop doctoral programs of a like orientation. This parallelism is of course most marked at the dissertation level but it is also evident in the general preparation which doctoral candidates receive before starting their thesis projects. Thus the quality of the training which future teachers and professional staff personnel in business receive is intimately related to the way in which the schools approach their research responsibilities.

Far more than the content and quality of the doctoral programs, however, is at stake. Research, or the lack thereof, sets the whole tone and direction of a field. It is the contribution which each generation of scholars makes to the work of those who have gone on before. It in turn provides the new base on which the next generation of scholars will build. The direction which any field of learning takes is thus the sum of the contributions of successive groups of investigators and depends on the intellectual leadership each group can provide. In no other way is it possible for a field to gain in strength and influence. It is quite appropriate, then, that a general review of the work of business schools should end with this summit question.

Unfortunately, this means that the discussion must close on a negative note. From every side—judging from the comments of university leaders, faculty members in other fields, business executives and other company spokesmen, business faculty members, and even the deans themselves—comes the common complaint that business schools have seriously underrated the importance of research.[13] Specific evidence, much of which was touched on in earlier parts of this study, could be cited in support of this well-nigh universal opinion, e.g., data on the time business faculties give to research, the proportion of a typical school's budget allocated to this purpose, the extent to which business looks to business schools for significant research ideas, the types of activities and publications which the schools define as research, the research training and equipment of business faculty members, and the like. However, since this opinion is so widely accepted, it seems more important to consider the factors that lie behind this outcome and the steps that might be taken for dealing with it.

Three sets of factors appear to be primarily responsible, the first of which has to do with career preparation in all fields. Schools which train students for any line of work—whether for agriculture, architecture, engineering, law, or even medicine—inevitably have a strong practitioner emphasis. In some career areas the gulf between study and doing, between inquiry and action, is narrow and in others it is broad, but it is there in any case. A few schools in such fields (and several come to mind in engineering, law, and medicine) can put a great deal of emphasis on research, but for most, research activities must be a subsidiary interest, supplementing the main program in practitioner training.[14] Moreover, such research as is done is likely to have an applied character and to be closely related to the problems that practitioners will face in their later careers. In almost all schools there is a strong pull away from research of a fundamental, long-range character.

[13] Regarding the views of businessmen, it would be more accurate to say that company spokesmen are largely oblivious of any research being done at business schools.

[14] Because of the widely known work of a few schools it is sometimes assumed that there is a great deal of research carried on by professional schools in most fields; this, however, is far from the case. Chapter 2 considered this issue at somewhat greater length.

The second set of factors has to do with the particular field in which business schools operate. Careers in business are scattered; the duties of businessmen, even managers, cannot be readily catalogued, much less reduced to teachable terms; the body of knowledge on which business skills rest is loosely formed, ill-tested, and lacking in generality. Thus the relation between systematic study and on-the-job performance in business tends at best to be general and indirect, and the significance of research for individual careers or for specific business operations is likely to be even more obscure. Little wonder, under these circumstances, that the schools have tended to regard research as less important than some of their other responsibilities.

The third and probably most important set of factors has to do with the institutional status and background of business schools. Most of the work has traditionally centered in undergraduate schools, graduate programs largely being a postwar development. The rapid rise in enrollments, the diverse interests and abilities of students attending these schools, the spread of course offerings, and the multiplication of new programs have all tended to crowd out research. Both on the campus and off, it has come to be accepted that business schools are not a significant source of new ideas or important centers of newly discovered truths. The emergence of graduate programs has modified this image somewhat but has not essentially altered it. Today, even in the eyes of their own faculties and leaders, business schools are almost wholly concerned with transmitting knowledge for use in business careers, rather than creating knowledge in a major area of learning.[15]

These three sets of factors provide a measure of the difficulties business schools face in developing research programs of any genuine promise. They also indicate the kind of steps that will have to be taken. Most discussions of this problem center on the last-named group of factors and quite appropriately so. Until the schools are prepared to devote much more of their time and resources to serious scientific investigations than they now do, not even the beginning steps toward serious research can be taken. Since this same theme has run through previous sections of this study, it need not be elaborated further here.

Assuming a school has both the will and the resources to develop a vigorous research program, what can it do? Where should it concentrate its efforts? Or should it simply hire the best faculty members possible and support their research in any direction they want to go? What are the steps which a school can take to bring about the most useful results? These are the kinds of questions for which no ready answers are of course

[15] These observations are based on earlier sections of this study, especially Chaps. 3 and 10.

possible but which have to be resolved somehow if the schools are going to take effective action in this area.[16]

OBJECTIVES AND AREAS OF BUSINESS RESEARCH

The broad purpose of business research may be said to be to increase the fund of scientific knowledge about the operations of the individual firm. To this end business schools need to concentrate on developing a body of widely applicable generalizations which have been scientifically tested and can be used in developing still further knowledge in this area. The significance of any given piece of research depends on how much it contributes to this objective. Other things being equal, a project that bears on a broad aspect of business behavior is to be preferred to one that does not. Even if the odds against success are high, the risk may well be worth taking, although obviously a line has to be drawn somewhere in assessing the prospects for success.

To be widely applicable, research findings must go beyond description to analysis. Both hypothesis forming and hypothesis testing are essential. Finding out how businessmen behave under various circumstances and what practices exist in different areas is an important step but is not research in any serious sense of the term. Not until the data are embodied in principles or generalizations which can be said to "explain the facts" can research attain general significance. Research in an applied field, as in any field, must consider why, not simply how, events occur.

These observations may seem painfully obvious but they have received scant attention among business schools. Much of the research at these institutions is heavily weighted on the side of description; much of it centers on particular companies or local trade groups; much of it is undertaken because of its practical usefulness; very rarely is emphasis placed on developing analytical findings which can be fitted into a general system of principles and tested in a scientific manner. This misplaced emphasis is almost as serious as the dearth of research itself.[17]

[16] Carnegie Tech. has emphasized research more than any other business school; for a discussion of its approach to this subject, see Chap. 13.

[17] In response to an inquiry about the status of research at business schools, a number of deans expressed the view that much of it was on an elementary level. As one well-known dean expressed the matter in a letter to the writer: "In my own opinion, one of the greatest defects of American business schools today is the comparatively meager amount of research that is going on within them, and the low level of much of the present activity that passes for research. Part of the trouble has been that in many institutions, the business school is regarded as a producer of revenue to finance other parts of the university, and its faculty are chosen primarily for teaching ability, and are not given the financial and other incentives and equipment to do good research. This is a regrettable situation and surely ought to be corrected in the future."

Within this general framework of research thinking, business schools need to consider what types of investigations they are particularly qualified to undertake successfully. It would hardly seem appropriate for these schools to devote much time and effort to studies which other agencies— government, business, or other branches of universities—could carry out as well or better. The discussion of the direction in which this field is moving contained in Chaps. 8 to 10 is relevant to this question. The critical task of business schools, judging from that discussion, is to utilize the methods and findings of economics, mathematics-statistics, and psychology-sociology in analyzing the functional aspects of the firm as these functions in turn relate to the managerial process. Business schools are the logical centers for path-breaking research along these lines, the basic disciplines being drawn upon to illuminate the problems of the individual firm. Properly developed, the findings of the schools will enrich the other disciplines as well and become a part of broader systems of knowledge. It follows that no rigid boundaries should be established between business schools and other branches of universities and that a fair degree of overlap is in fact to be welcomed.

One is tempted to endeavor to spell out areas for further research in more detail, but the scope and nature of such work need to be broadly defined and allowed to evolve in a variety of directions. The framework suggested here is wide enough to encompass investigations of many types and this is as it should be. The schools need to be given ample scope to develop studies of their own and to break away from the cramping influences (sometimes self-imposed) which have limited their research activities in the past. The fact that a few schools are doing so is the single most encouraging development that has occurred in this field in the last twenty-five or thirty years.

IMPLEMENTING RESEARCH OBJECTIVES

In carrying out a philosophy of research of the sort just described, a school has to set up a priority of needs. For most schools, the most pressing requirements are personnel and money; therefore the first tasks are to try to find one or more faculty members who have the capacity for serious research and to unearth the funds to enable the work to be done. Faculty recruitment, promotions, teaching loads, sabbaticals, etc., are of great importance in this connection; unless the schools can secure improvements in these employment conditions, research can hardly get beyond the talking stage. Considered in the light of the last chapter, there is no use minimizing the difficulties which the schools face in this regard. The scarcity of qualified personnel and the heavy costs involved mean that most research must center in a few graduate schools, though it would seem perfectly possible and certainly desirable for smaller institutions and undergraduate schools to foster some research too. The graduate schools which are now putting heavy emphasis on research (such as Carnegie Tech., Chicago, and the University of California at Los Angeles) allocate roughly a half or more of their instructional budgets, or well over $100,000 per year, to this purpose; a number of state universities allocate as much as 20 per cent. These sums could not be made available unless other parts of the schools' budgets were large enough to cover the cost of the regular teaching program.

Beyond these basic tasks, the schools will need to establish more specific targets and procedures for helping faculty members carry out research undertakings. At this level, however, little can be said by way of generalization, since the particular needs of the schools differ so greatly. A number have found it useful to establish a bureau of research to serve as a clearinghouse for information on projects, to provide clerical assistance to faculty members, and even to screen requests for funds;[18] others have dealt with these matters on a more informal basis. Some have appointed a director of research to handle these activities and to work as closely as possible with faculty members in developing their research plans; others have found little need to designate any one person to assume these responsibilities. A few schools, notably Carnegie Tech., have endeavored to build their research around a common theme, but most have given faculty members wide scope to pursue their individual interests. Some have concentrated their energies on one aspect of the field; for some, the purchase of expensive computing equipment has been a dominant factor in developing their research activities;[19] for others much of the work revolves around the interests and leadership of a single faculty member or very small faculty groups. These differences are healthy and need to be encouraged as long as they are kept within the broad philosophical framework for research planning outlined above.

[18] Most of the research bureaus at business schools are heavily involved in surveys of local economic conditions or in special investigations for local employer groups; whether this kind of work should be referred to as research is debatable but it is not scientific study in the sense that the term is used here.

[19] In this connection, the dean of a well-known business school comments: "In our case the impact of this giant computer we have obtained causes drastic rethinking of our research role. With this facility we will be one of the few places where certain kinds of work can be done. . . . Hence we will undoubtedly be doing some work which is not 'pure' simply because with this equipment we can do it where no one else can. Secondly, universities seem more and more to be getting into the position of contracting time on such equipment as a part of the process of financing it. This too may be unavoidable though we are trying to hold the line on principle. Technological requirements are, I rather suspect, breaking down the distinction between what might formerly have been regarded as 'appropriate' research for universities and that which might have been regarded as best done by non-academic groups."

One aspect of research calling for attention by all schools, however, is the importance of fostering close ties with other branches of academic study. This has been repeatedly emphasized in the earlier discussion so the necessity for implementing this need requires no underscoring here. The responsibility of a school's top leaders is especially great in this connection since without their active support nothing probably will be done. A number of possibilities deserve consideration:

Joint appointments with nonbusiness departments, particularly if they are tied in with some joint research interest.

Participation by business faculty members in interdisciplinary research undertakings or institutes. Advanced seminars in which doctoral students in business can study with faculty members both in business and non-business departments.

Dissertation topics which cut across fields and require active participation by faculty members in different areas.

Research projects calling for close planning and implementation by members of different department staffs.

There are innumerable opportunities open to an imaginative faculty group along such lines, although there is some danger that such work will be treated as an isolated endeavor and not be made a part of a school's main stream of activities. To get undertakings of this nature started and to relate them to other aspects of a school's program in a meaningful way requires strong support from the top.

These brief observations about the role of research at business schools follow logically from the general conception of their work developed elsewhere in this study. The emphasis on research will serve to improve the school's teaching programs, strengthen their faculties, and attract better students. The schools, however, will need to move ahead on all these fronts simultaneously if permanent gains are to be won on any one of them. Part 3 of the study spells out the implications of this view, first, for a school's entire program, and second, for different areas of the business curriculum. This part as well as the one following were written by individuals actively engaged in the areas they were asked to discuss.

PART THREE

DEVELOPING THE CURRICULUM

CHAPTER 13

MANAGERIAL DECISION MAKING AS AN ORGANIZING CONCEPT

George Leland Bach

Education for business needs to be focused on the world of tomorrow, not on the world of the 1950's. Making managerial decisions and getting them carried out effectively is the core of the manager's job. This should provide the primary focus for educational activities looking to the future. It implies greater emphasis on the development of fundamental analytical tools and on the use of these tools in identifying, solving, and implementing decisions on managerial problems. Fundamental tools will be provided especially by the behavioral sciences, economics, and quantitative methods (including the use of mathematics). The "applied" fields of business (marketing, production, finance, and so on) should, at least now, be viewed primarily as important problem areas in which solutions depend heavily on the effective application of such fundamental tools. This approach implies equally the need for new types of doctoral programs to train the teachers of tomorrow and for far more intensive fundamental research than is now found in the business schools.

Managerial decision making as a central concept in education for business is not new. From the beginning, many business schools have sought to train men who would look toward managerial posts. The major emphasis on learning to make informed judgments through the "case method" at the Harvard Business School, which has exerted so great an influence on business education during the past quarter century, has focused central emphasis on managerial decision making. Other universities have stressed the same notion broadly and in particular areas— for example, in the development of "managerial accounting" in place of more traditional C.P.A.-oriented accounting.

But while emphasis on managerial decision making as a central educational focus has had advocates, for the most part business education has moved along quite different lines. Emphasis on specialization within fairly narrow fields of business and upon detailed information, technique, and "how-to-do-it" has been widespread. Educational methods that emphasize the teacher as the teller and the student as the sponge appear to have marked the majority of American business schools over the past half century.

During the past decade there has been an upsurge of fresh ideas and approaches. These build on the past, but they well justify separate attention here, for they may mark the most significant development of this quarter century in business education. It is this development to which the present chapter is devoted, a development I have connoted by the words "managerial decision making."

I shall mean by this phrase a somewhat wider range of activities than is sometimes conveyed by the term. Specifically, I mean by managerial decision making the entire three-part process of: (1) deciding what decisions ought to be made, i.e., what problems need managerial decisions; (2) making decisions (operating decisions, plans, or policies) concerning those problems; and (3) getting the decisions implemented effectively. Exclusive emphasis on the second stage of this process—actually reaching a decision after the problem has been isolated and defined, without concern for getting the decision carried out—is clearly an overnarrow view of the managerial function and is equally an overnarrow focus for education aimed at training men for management. Some may prefer to substitute the broader term "managerial behavior" for what I term "managerial decision making."

UNDERLYING PRESUMPTIONS

Increasing focus on managerial decision making in business education arises from many factors. Different individuals and different institutions reflect different backgrounds and interests and are moving along different lines. Thus it is not possible to state sharply the foundations upon which this approach rests. But some underlying presumptions seem so important as to merit special attention, even though they have already been noted earlier in this volume.

The Pervasiveness and Rapidity of Change

To be useful, management training must look to the future, not to the present. It will be 1970 before most of our undergraduate students of today begin, as they enter their thirties, to assume significant managerial responsibility. It will be 1980 (some twenty years hence) before they begin, in their early forties, to reach general management responsibility. And it will be perhaps 1990 before those few, in their early fifties, who will finally reach the top as presidents and general executives have much chance of getting there. Thus a rough target of 1985, a quarter century hence, may be appropriate in thinking of the world for which we are training business school students today. Many of them will still be active businessmen in the year 2000.

What will 1985 be like, and what will be the role of business management then? No one knows. But one thing seems sure. The business world, and the rest of the world, will change greatly in the next quarter century. The complexity of modern life has increased at an amazing rate. Our knowledge of the physical universe has grown as much in the past century, it is said, as it has during all the previous recorded history of mankind, and the rate is increasing. Today there is evidence of the beginning of a great upsurge of our knowledge about man himself, as an individual and as a social being, paralleling, perhaps, the development that has taken place in the physical sciences over the past century.

Given the certainty of change and the uncertainty as to its direction and outcome, the argument is strong that we must place central importance in university training—for business as elsewhere—on students' thought processes and not on the particularized subject matter of the present. In such a world, emphasis on flexibility of mind, openness and receptivity to new and changing ideas, habitually orderly thought processes, skill in learning for one's self, and other such mental characteristics must promise more to the individual and to society over the quarter century of change ahead than would comparable emphasis on descriptive information about today's institutions and today's best business practice. This outlook also suggests that insofar as we build in analytical tools, we must continually reach for those tools of broad and general applicability, emphasizing how to use them effectively in widely varying situations, rather than concentrate on detailed, particular skills and techniques. Never was it truer that college "commencement" must mark the beginning of learning for oneself. Training the student to learn for himself after graduation may be the most crucial of all university teaching objectives.

Increasingly Analytical, Rational Nature of Management

Over the quarter century ahead, management will almost certainly become persistently more analytical, more rational. The role of "hunch" and even of "informed judgment" will become smaller as the years go by. At the extreme, this will mean increasing use of such fairly elaborate analytical approaches as mathematical programming. To focus too heavily on these, however, would be a serious mistake. The critical change will be the increase in the clarification of variables that need to be considered in making decisions, the increase in the use of carefully obtained quantitative information concerning these variables, and the increase in rigorous analysis weighting and combining the variables involved. We all know that in some vague intuitive way this is what we must be doing when we make decisions now. The change I am predicting is, therefore, one of clarifying and of bringing to the surface the variables and implicit logical models our minds must be using now in decision making, and of persistently improving the logic of these models. Long steps have been taken in this direction over the past quarter century, resulting in some of the changes described in earlier chapters.

The implication of this argument parallels the implication of the pervasiveness and uncertainty of change. It points toward training in independent problem solving, toward a firm grasp of fundamental analytical tools which will have general usefulness over the years ahead, and toward development of ability to continue to learn new analytical tools and methods after leaving school. For we can be sure that not only the managerial problems but also the methods of handling those problems will be different in 1980 than they are today.

Developing Role of Management and "Professional" Managers

The need for effective administration per se has been widely emphasized in recent years. It is related to the growing size and complexity of business in all its elements, to the greater need for conscious planning and control, to the growing difficulties of communication in large and complex organizations, and so on. Management must make decisions, but even more of its time and energy must go into getting the decisions (plans and policies) carried out effectively. With this growing awareness of the importance of the job of management per se, it is safe to forecast less and less willingness to assume that good managers are just born and there is nothing to do about it except let them develop as they will.

Unless recent trends are drastically reversed, the status of the manager will become increasingly that of a coordinator of diverse interests and "pulls" in the modern firm and in modern society, rather than that of "the boss," responsible only to the stockholders. This will mean a different framework for management decision making and decision implementation. It will mean new types of decisions and new ways of weighting the variables in making decisions and getting them implemented.

This argument strengthens the general implications for training outlined in the preceding sections. But it stresses also, and especially, the need for a deep understanding of the administrative and organizational processes, for it is through these that decisions must largely be made and implemented. Human behavior—in face-to-face relationships, in small groups, in the corporation, in the community, everywhere—is at the center of management decision making. It is central to the problem of what the important decisions are, to the choice of the best decision, and to getting the decision carried out effectively. Training for the manager of tomorrow must cope with this fact.

Increasing Social Responsibility of the Corporation

It is likely that the social responsibility of the corporation and of the businessman in it will continue to bulk larger in the day-to-day life of most business firms. In contrast to any simple emphasis on short-run profit maximization, explicit interest in "the public good" as a legitimate and important goal of business behavior will continue to grow. Business will participate in a conscious fashion to an increasing extent in the social-economic processes of our democratic society. Business will be judged increasingly by the community according to the way it participates in these processes as well as by the older criteria of production and price. The role of the manager, therefore, will be more and more that of a man with many masters, and it will behoove him to be sensitive to the pulse of the whole community, not merely to what goes on inside his factory walls. Here again this prospect is merely a continuation of the forces that have been strongly at work over the past half century.

Again, this argument reinforces the implications outlined under the preceding three points. It adds to them heavy emphasis on the need for the manager of tomorrow to understand, and be sensitive to, the entire economic, political, and social environment in which he will live and in which his business will operate and be judged. No one can predict in detail what this environment will be two or three decades hence. But the successful businessman, and the useful civic leader, will be one who senses the processes of change and who moves with or ahead of them— or who at least understands them thoroughly if he chooses to oppose them.

THE FOCUS ON MANAGERIAL DECISION MAKING

Considerations like these point strongly toward educational focus on the development of individual abilities to think, to adjust, and to learn independently in a world of change after leaving the campus. Certainly for men who will rise to real management positions, they emphasize the importance of becoming prepared to make and implement decisions on unknown problems with unknown, yet-to-be-developed, analytical tools. They emphasize, rather than the teaching of today's best prevailing business practice, capacities like the following:

1. Development of orderly, rational, problem-solving ability

2. Development and repeated use of basic analytical concepts—development of tools and comprehension of their effective use in handling problems

3. Development of the individual's ability to learn from experience and to grow in understanding in a changing world

4. Development of ability to deal effectively with others, both in person and through written communication

5. Development of an understanding of the role of business in the entire environment and of sensitivity to the processes of social change

6. Development of a personal philosophy or ethical foundation for business life and for making decisions in it

Broadly summed up, they point toward emphasis on training for effective managerial decision making in the rapidly changing world of tomorrow.

How can such a focus on managerial decision making be implemented? How can the business schools best prepare men for such careers, whether the careers lead toward the presidency of General Motors, to a lower-management responsibility in a small local firm, or to a job as staff assistant in a large corporation? The answer must consider the problem of the appropriate curriculum, the range of problems for which the decision maker must be reasonably equipped, the best teaching methods, the kinds of teachers needed, and the problem of variation depending on student quality and the range of student objectives. The next two sections deal with these problems for M.B.A. and undergraduate business students respectively. The two concluding sections deal with the related responsibilities of graduate schools for training teachers equipped to teach in such programs (the doctoral program) and for research programs looking toward tomorrow.

THE M.B.A. PROGRAM

What do these considerations suggest concerning what to teach and how to teach it in business schools today? There is little doubt that the business schools' largest problem lies with the huge mass of undergraduate students looming ahead. But it is useful to begin by considering the M.B.A. problem, because here it is possible to isolate the "professional training" aspects of the problem on the assumption that undergraduate education has already provided the general citizenship component that is widely emphasized as an undergraduate educational objective.

Although the focus on management decision making leads to no one best answer as to what to teach and how to teach it, I propose to spell out in some detail one type of suggestive curriculum and to supplement it with specific comments on teaching approach and types of teachers. This is not because this is necessarily the best approach, but because it presents clearly some of the issues involved and thus may provide the most stimulating basis for further thought about the problem. It is important to recognize that among the institutions emphasizing this general type of approach, there is far from complete agreement on curriculum building or teaching method. On the other hand, the program outlined below is representative enough of the thinking at a number of prominent graduate schools to picture some important trends now discernible in graduate business education.[1]

Assume a school for graduate students who have little or no undergraduate training in business but who come with good undergraduate training in, say, the liberal arts or in engineering. These are good-quality people, say in the upper third of their undergraduate classes. It is reasonable to expect that most of them will end up with *bona fide* management jobs, ranging from middle management in both large and small concerns to top-management jobs. Assume two years in which to provide a master's-level program, leading, say, to the M.B.A.[2]

[1] The program described is largely that which was introduced in the Graduate School of Industrial Administration at Carnegie Institute of Technology in the early 1950s. I have been asked to use it primarily because it was a pioneering program in several major aspects. There is no intention to imply that Carnegie is the only school that has adopted this point of view or that it has been a pioneer in all the areas covered. Among the schools which have introduced, or have announced plans to introduce, programs incorporating in varying degrees this approach are California (Berkeley and Los Angeles), Chicago, Columbia, Dartmouth, Harvard, Kansas, M.I.T., Michigan State, North Carolina, and Tulane. Numerous others, of course, emphasize the managerial decision approach in particular areas. But so far as I know, the program outlined is not currently in operation at any other school, and strong support for this type of program is currently found at only a few schools, all focused primarily on the graduate level.

Carnegie's program is specifically designed to provide graduate training in management for men with prior training in engineering or science who look toward managerial careers in industry where backgrounds combining engineering and management will be especially useful. Because the interest of most readers will be on general business education, this description omits certain special Carnegie courses and approaches designed especially to build on this type of student background, particularly in the areas of quantitative methods, production, and combined engineering-economic analysis.

[2] The confusion in terminology for degrees is considerable. In general, the M.B.A. refers to a management-oriented program, while the M.S. refers to an academic or specialist-oriented program. On the other hand, some of the programs most strongly oriented toward general management (for example, those at M.I.T. and Carnegie Tech.) give the M.S. degree.

It is convenient to begin with the curriculum, though it is essential to remember that the objectives outlined above focus not on subject matter but on qualities of mind and methods of approach.

Curriculum—First Year

In pursuit of the objectives above, the first-year program would include three major foundation stems, plus a set of applied foundation "core areas," with a strong focus on orderly problem-solving processes throughout.

1. *Foundation Stem in "the Administrative Process and Organizational Behavior."* It is trite but true that little is accomplished in management except with and through people. The definition of nearly every managerial problem, the best decision on it, and the most effective ways of getting the decision carried out all involve human behavior. Often human behavior poses the most difficult aspects of managerial problems.

This foundation, or "tool," stem would look in detail at the firm as a going organization and at the behavior of human beings as individuals and as groups in it and in other organizations. Toward understanding these processes, it would draw heavily on the analytical concepts and approaches of the "behavioral sciences," as well as upon what is beginning to be built up in the theory of administration and organization. This stem would be concerned, not merely with the traditional descriptive aspects of typical business firms (formal organization, departmental functions, and so forth), but more fundamentally with analytical concepts, hypotheses, and models designed to help understand and analyze human and organizational behavior. Motivation, influence, communication, organizational equilibrium, group cohesiveness—these are examples of the kinds of analytical concepts that promise to be of greatest general usefulness in understanding human behavior in organizations; these contrast with primary focus on prevailing practices in line-staff arrangements, optimal spans of control, best types of working committees, and so on in particular companies. There is much we do *not* know about human behavior in organizations; the well-equipped student needs to know what he does not know as well as what he does and the inadequate bases on which current real-world business decisions often are made. The stem would suggest hypotheses concerning human behavior under varying conditions, with suggestions on how to assess evidence on such hypotheses as it is presented by day-to-day life and by research over the years ahead. It would sensitize students to the major problem areas in understanding and dealing with major problems of human behavior.

Basically this would be a "tool" stem, with the hope that the analytical tools emphasized would be useful in understanding a wide range of situations as the student moves into the business world. This approach thus also implies heavy emphasis on the processes of *using* such analytical tools effectively as aids in analyzing particular situations faced in later life. It denies the usefulness of giving "answers" to problems as a primary teaching device. It recognizes equally the danger (to be fought against continually) that students may use analytical hypotheses, or "models," as rigid guides to thinking, or as substitutes for individual thinking on particular problems.

Thus the emphasis would be on the development of the analytical tools of the behavioral sciences, but with related stress on practice in using these tools. Case materials are helpful for this purpose. So are role playing, projects, and live "demonstrations," especially of sorts that involve students in situations more "real" and less far-fetched than many of the role-playing situations casually introduced in many human relations classes. Fundamental analytical concepts, which are by their nature abstract, are both powerful and dangerous, in this area as in others. The goal of the stem would be to help the student build up an inventory of such fundamental concepts, hypotheses, and models and to help him gain experience in using them effectively for himself in a variety of situations.

The behavioral sciences as they now stand do not provide a large reservoir of immediately useful analytical concepts and models. All workers in the field agree that there is a big job ahead in cooperation between business schools and behavioral science faculty members to reforge many of the tools of the behavioral sciences and to build new ones in order to develop this stem from the modest level at which it must now operate to the crucial position it will surely have as the years go by.

It is important to recognize the inadequacy of present knowledge, but it is important also to recognize the considerable body of theoretical and empirical work rapidly developing in the behavioral sciences. There is a growing, though still seriously inadequate, supply of useful teaching and reading materials.[3] Case and problem materials in the field are now widely used.[4] In addition, especially in the areas of face-to-face behavior in two-person or small-group situations, successful use has been made of special approaches to role playing and student-participative classroom "demonstrations" which involve and reinforce use of the analytical concepts for guiding personal behavior.

Many of the applications and examples in the stem are within the

[3] Merely to provide concreteness for readers not acquainted with the field, a few widely used, typical readings may be listed: Gardner and Moore's *Human Relations in Industry;* Simon's *Administrative Behavior;* Haire's *Psychology in Industry;* Leavitt's *Managerial Psychology;* and Knox's *Sociology of Industrial Relations.*

[4] Glover and Hower's *The Administrator* is a typical, published example.

business firm and involve different functional activities. But some examples completely outside business firms are chosen, plus some involving relationships between business firms and other individuals and organizations. Thus the stem shares the responsibility of providing tools that will be useful to the student after graduation in understanding interactions outside the firm as well as within it.

2. *Foundation Stem in "Economic Analysis."* A parallel foundation stem would develop the tools provided by economic analysis. Here, too, the stem would look both inward and outward—at the analytical concepts, hypotheses, and models useful in understanding and operating more effectively within the firm and at those useful in understanding the place of the firm and its policies in the total economy, at both the "micro" and "macro" levels. Here again the goal would be to train men as future managers, not as professional economists (just as the goal in the behavioral sciences stem is to help train managers, not behavioral scientists). The student should obtain a good grasp of the central analytical concepts of modern economics. He should get some experience in using them in thinking through diverse problems of making managerial decisions within the firm. Equally or more important, he should use them in considering the behavior of the firm as an individual unit in the market economy, the over-all processes of economic growth and fluctuations, and the public policy issues related to business behavior in these areas.

As in the behavioral science stem, the emphasis would be on tool building and tool using. Again, analytical concepts, hypotheses, and models would be developed, with stress on getting the student to use them in thinking through *for himself* problems presented in the course, looking toward similar use following graduation. Here again both the potential usefulness and the dangers of misusing such abstract tools would be emphasized.

Such fundamental concepts as opportunity cost, comparison of alternatives at the margin, income, capital accumulation, and elasticity of demand are obviously useful in analyzing the behavior of a market economic system, in understanding interactions between the individual firm and the outside economy, and in thinking through public policy problems. They can be equally useful in managerial decision making within the firm. Economic analysis until recently has not been greatly concerned with decision making within the firm. But in recent years considerable attention has been given here, and it has rapidly become "respectable" for economists to work seriously on intrafirm decision problems.[5]

---

[5] Little teaching material specifically applying economic analysis to managerial problems is yet available. Dean's *Managerial Economics*, Spencer and Siegelman's *Managerial Economics*, and Colberg, Bradford, and Alt's *Business Economics* are examples. Some master's programs use parts of texts on "engineering economics."

The balance between managerial and extrafirm applications might vary depending on preferences, but the larger objective would be to focus on the functioning of the market economy, the interactions between the firm and the total economy, and major public policy problems, such as economic stabilization and growth, antitrust policy, and the distribution of income. Happily, some emphasis on managerial use of these analytical tools clearly strengthens student understanding of the more traditional areas of economics, such as product pricing, capital investment decisions, and inventory policy. For example, requiring a student to make one or more price policy decisions in "real world" business cases certainly helps deepen his understanding of, say, oligopoly pricing. Similarly, requiring him to make an investment decision in a "real world" business situation surely helps his understanding of the purely abstract investment curve he sees in most macroeconomics texts. There is no reason such teaching should occur in the traditional isolation from economics courses.

This presumably could be an intermediate-level stem, since a preceding course in elementary economics could reasonably be assumed, though probably one without much analytical focus of the sort outlined here. Before enrolling, students could reasonably be expected to study for themselves one of the leading basic economic texts, if they lack the relevant undergraduate course.

3. *Foundation Stem in "Quantitative Method."* The third foundation stem would deal with the use of figures in business decision making and control. It would center around the use of accounting and statistical procedures for obtaining and processing information that management needs to make and implement wise decisions. But again, the primary emphasis would be on *managerial* accounting and on *managerial* statistics. The tools would be forged with a view to being useful in making and carrying out managerial decisions, not in training traditional accountants or statisticians. On the other hand, effective managerial uses of figures in business require some understanding of the way those figures were produced and processed, as seen by the producers of the data (accountants, statisticians, budget officers, and so forth).

This stem would, thus, place relatively little emphasis on the detailed procedural aspects of accounting that might be important in training C.P.A.s. Instead, it would generally ask: what kinds of information are important for managerial decision making; how can this information be obtained; how should it be processed to be most useful; and how can it,

---

Grant's *Principles of Engineering Economy* and Thuesen's *Engineering Economy* are examples. But journal literature is growing rapidly. In the more traditional areas of market, price, and distribution analysis, plus related questions of public policy, texts have long been abundant, though generally not strongly focused on independent student problem-solving approaches.

or related information, help most in carrying out the decisions made? Close interaction with some of the questions raised in the economic analysis stem would be obviously fruitful—on cost and pricing problems, on make-or-buy decisions, on income determination, and on historical versus opportunity costs. Joint cases and problems between the courses have proved useful in emphasizing these interrelations.[6]

In the same way, statistical tools would be developed, giving strong attention to their use in managerial or general economic analysis. For example, statistical decision theory might provide one useful focus for much of the statistical material. Probability, tests of hypotheses, sampling theory, and other such central statistical concepts would be faced as fundamentally as is consistent with the time available and the quantitative and mathematical aptitudes of the students.

Statistical analysis is an area in which different schools do, and probably will continue to, differ substantially on their approaches. But if the central notions of statistics are to be useful as management tools, work going beyond the traditional, descriptive business statistics textbooks seems essential, even for students without formal mathematics. Teaching materials providing this emphasis are beginning to appear.[7] The danger that emphasis on technique as such will overshadow basic objectives is perhaps greater here than anywhere else in the program. Here perhaps more than anywhere else, there probably must be a substantial element of pure tool learning, involving sheer drill. Problems can be posed to make the statistical tools seem more relevant, and the tools once learned can be *used* in handling managerial problems. But real understanding of substantial elements of statistical analysis appears to require strict, hard study of the reasoning involved per se. Combining such technique training with focus on managerial decision making requires highly skilled teaching. Happily, the problem with the accounting tools is a less serious one.

This approach to quantitative method is feasible for students with or without college mathematics. On the accounting tools, there is little evidence that mathematics training helps perceptibly—though high quanti-

---

[6] "Managerial accounting" texts and supplies of local mimeographed cases and problems have begun to appear in recent years, though they are still the small minority. Anthony's *Management Accounting* and Robnett, Hill, and Backett's *Accounting: A Management Approach* are examples.

[7] For example, Wallis and Roberts' *Statistics* and Schlaifer's more advanced *Probability and Statistics for Business Decisions*. For students who have college mathematics, texts like Wilks, *Elementary Statistical Analysis* may be feasible; though more fundamental, such texts are also more dangerous, since they need strong instructor supplementation to focus emphasis on application rather than on statistical technique per se.

tative aptitude certainly does. In statistical analysis there is no doubt that deeper understanding is possible for students with at least a year or two of college mathematics, even though many of the central concepts can be grasped with nothing beyond high school algebra. Emphasis on statistical *reasoning* (rather than on detailed technique) is, in this approach, the prime objective.

A few graduate schools now require mathematics through calculus as part of the general college background for entrance. Perhaps this will be common if undergraduate standards of rigor improve, but this prerequisite seems unlikely for most graduate business schools in the near future. Given this deficiency, there is considerable doubt that the graduate business school should take time to try to replace two years of college mathematics, useful as the tool might be. If it does allocate time to building up mathematical competence, the case is strong for a special course focused on developing the particular mathematical tools and approaches most useful for managerial problems, rather than for taking time to plow through the standard undergraduate math sequence. Such special courses have been developed with reasonable success in a few institutions (see the following section on the undergraduate program).[8]

4. *Foundation Analysis of the "Functional Fields" of Business.* Students cannot learn to make decisions and carry them out in a vacuum. They cannot learn to use analytical tools effectively without using them. In the world of business, the so-called functional fields (e.g., marketing and production) provide the major problem areas, short of general management, for the exercise of decision-making and tool-using abilities. It is important that students get acquainted with these major problem areas of business for their own sake. It is equally important that they see them as problem areas calling for the application of orderly decision-making processes and involving the application of the analytical tools being developed in the other foundation stems.

The operating world of business can be sliced up in any number of ways, depending on the degree of specialization and detail desired. If the major emphasis is on managerial decision making, as defined above, there is a presumption against either an elaborate division of the fields of business into many compartments or primary emphasis on any one of these compartments as the sole exercise in managerial decision making. There is some agreement among schools with a strong management decision-making emphasis that division into three major areas—marketing, production, and finance—may be a reasonable subdivision of the operating areas of business. Some would add "personnel," though this appears

[8] Here, too, more appropriate texts are beginning to appear, for example, Kemeny, Snell, and Thompson's *Introduction to Finite Mathematics.*

somewhat less commonly, especially where there is substantial emphasis on the behavioral sciences as a major *general* tool stem for managerial training.

Each of these three fields—marketing, production, and finance—would thus be viewed as an applied problem area. Consider the area of marketing as an illustration. In the marketing area the student should get a good exposure to some of the major types of problems faced by modern business in the whole process of selling or distribution. In looking at these selected major problems, he would pick up a good deal of institutional information about marketing in the modern business world. But the main emphasis of the course would be as an exercise in analysis of problems in the various subareas of marketing, bringing to bear the tools being learned in the rest of the first-year curriculum, with repeated emphasis on the importance of orderly problem-solving behavior. There is not yet in the marketing area, or in other functional areas, a highly developed, cohesive body of analysis and organized knowledge. Thus, for at least some years ahead, most of the really analytical material being taught in the marketing area will reach back to the three foundation stems outlined above for its concepts and, in considerable part at least, for its way of using them.

For example, a problem in market research almost inevitably uses the tools of statistics and of the behavioral sciences if a good job is to be done. A problem in sales organization requires the same general analytical tools as one in any other type of organization planning—tools drawn from the foundation of the behavioral sciences for the most part, if the problem is to be fundamentally understood. A problem of new-product analysis should be handled by the use of tools from economics, the behavioral sciences, and quantitative methods. In nearly every marketing problem, both intrafirm and extrafirm (market, public relations, etc.) aspects appear. A good analysis of such problems would of course recognize both as relevant and interacting in each situation. Each of the three underlying tool areas would help in dealing with both aspects.

This is not to say that there is nothing of value to be taught in marketing per se. But the course would emphasize problem solving in the area and the importance of reaching back to fundamental tools for thorough understanding, rather than the descriptive aspects and stress on the best-prevailing current business practice that dominate many of the current texts and courses. Here again, unfortunately, the underlying stems do not provide all the analytical tools needed to do a first-class job on many marketing problems. But this is no reason for retreating from an analytical approach that uses the best tools we have available.

The functional areas of production and finance would be treated in much the same way, though the field of production, on the one hand, probably has less developed, organized knowledge than does marketing and that of finance probably has more. In all three, presumably the body of systematic, organized knowledge will grow steadily over the years. As this occurs, the focus of the functional areas stem will need to be reconsidered.

In the first-year curriculum, these three functional areas together would get only about one-fourth of the total time available—that is, an amount roughly equal to any one of the three foundation tool stems indicated above. This would mean perhaps the equivalent of about a one-semester course in each of the three major functional areas.

In summary, the first year would be devoted to foundation- and tool-building, with strong emphasis on the methods of orderly problem solving, and to an introduction to the major functional areas of business, largely through repetitive problem solving, involving integrated use of the analytical tools and methods being learned concurrently. The year would have a strong managerial orientation. But there would be a good deal of emphasis, especially in the economic analysis stem, on the total environment within which the business firm operates and on the extra-firm uses of many of the analytical tools being developed—broadly on the place of the firm in the economy and on the kind of environment provided by the modern economic-social system.

Curriculum—Second-year Program

The second year would build on the first-year foundation. In the second year, each student would be required to take two full-year sequences, which might represent half or two-fifths of the total program, depending on how many courses are included in a normal program. The balance of his time would be open for electives, with the restrictions indicated below.

1. *One Full-year Required Course Would Be in Administration and Business Policy.* This course would be what the title implies—a more advanced, integrating approach to a wide variety of business policy and administrative problems, mainly at the upper-management level. Stress would be on integrated use of *both* the analytical tools from the three major foundation areas *and* knowledge from the various functional fields of business, in making company-wide policy decisions and getting these decisions carred out effectively. Depending on one's taste, the course might include a good deal beyond the first-year stem of the newly developing theory of organization and administration, or it might concentrate heavily on developing more effective use of the tools already developed in the program. Preferably, it would place considerable emphasis on both.

Both cases and formal reading materials on planning, organization, and administration would be used heavily in the course. Cases would provide a major device for developing integrated analyses of problems, using whatever tools and functional background might be relevant. Projects in industry might be useful. Detailed reports by business executives on particular decisions, together with intensive class cross-examinations, have been used effectively. To overcome the serious disadvantage of most case materials in not involving the sequential process of living with one's decisions that is so central to actual policy making and administration, some use might be made of the newly developed "business games" utilizing electronic computers. These games, while still elementary, do provide (highly simplified) experience in making repeated decisions over a sequence of many time periods and in having to live with and adjust to the consequences of such decisions in simulated marketplace environments. More elaborate games now being devised promise to increase greatly the realism of these situations and thus to supplement importantly the more traditional case-teaching approach to business policy.

2. *The Second Full-year Required Course Would Be on the Place of Business and the Businessman in the Economic, Political, Legal, and Social Environment.* This stems from the propositions above concerning the likely future role of business and businessmen in a democratic society. It would include attention to problems of government and business, not in the narrow sense of how to beat the antitrust laws, but in the broader sense of trying to understand the reasons for government intervention in and regulation of business. It would look intensively at the political and legal processes in democratic industrialized societies and at the role of business and businessmen in relation to other organized groups. It would look at the reasons for development of power groups in society, e.g., labor unions, and at processes of interaction among such groups. It would try to force students to think through thoroughly problems of business ethics and social responsibility and their own systems of social values.[9] In all of this, it would have the strong

---

[9] Most schools prefer to approach this objective through separate courses in government and business, labor economics, business law, and so on. Neither approach seems clearly preferable in principle, so long as the broad objectives are the same. But there is a danger that individual courses will become particularized and specialized on narrow problems and techniques. For example, most business law courses clearly do not fit into the pattern outlined here. At Carnegie, at least half the year is devoted to an analysis of the interaction of ideas and societal change. This course uses major historical or current problems or developments as case studies in socio-economic-political change, stressing the interacting roles of "ideas" and "practical affairs" in the continuing process of change.

"outside-the-firm" analysis in economics and the behavioral sciences from the first year to build on.

The analytical tools of the first year would be used whenever they are helpful, just as they would be used in the required course on business policy and its administration. While many of the first-year tools would be pointed definitely toward "internal" management decision making, many would also be useful in understanding broader economic, political, and social issues, and some would be developed specifically for this purpose, especially in the economics area. The course would emphasize the necessity for the student to understand the broader social forces at work in shaping his environment and the need for equally careful, objective problem-solving processes in extra- and intra-firm decisions. Management decision making tomorrow will need to pay increasing attention to the impact of external affairs on the firm and of the firm on the economy, if business is to prosper in a democratic society.

3. *The Rest of the Second-year Curriculum Would Be Elective.* Two special comments on this elective area are important.

First, there would be a restriction that no student could take more than one full year of advanced second-year work in any one of the special functional areas—marketing, production, or finance.

This much specialization (about a year and a half of course work in any one functional area) appears to be quite sufficient to get the man ready for the work he will be required to do immediately after he leaves graduate school. Emphasis on building more fundamental and general tools, rather than on accumulating more particularized knowledge in specialized fields, appears to be the preferable alternative, looking toward long-range management growth. Emphasis on managerial decision making, with only moderate emphasis on any particular functional field, provides men who, at least in the experience of some schools using this approach, readily match the performance of more highly specialized men in their own areas after only a few months of catching up on the details of the particular job situation.

In the marketing area, for example, to continue the illustration used above, there might be offered two one-semester electives. One might be a course emphasizing "management science" applications to marketing problems—market research, analysis of consumer behavior, application of statistical analyses to marketing data, and so on. A second semester might focus particularly on marketing policy, perhaps as generally seen from the level of the vice-president for marketing. Here policy problems involving new-product development, sales organization, and such other operating areas might be emphasized, in contrast to the lower-level, information-providing processes emphasized in the first semester.

Many marketing specialists argue that this is insufficient training for the man who wants a career in the marketing area. There are two answers. First, this curriculum is primarily aimed at training men to move up in management in whatever functional area they may find themselves —not to produce area specialists. But second, it would aim to provide more fundamental training even for the man who will stay largely within the marketing area than would a more highly specialized program which inevitably would leave out many of the nonmarketing elements of this curriculum. A more complete analysis of the problem of specialization is included below.

Similarly in the other functional fields of production and finance, two one-semester courses might be organized, one devoted especially to a "management science" information-gathering, -organizing, and -using focus and the second to managerial policy and upper-level operating problems in the field.

Second, there would be a number of elective courses dealing with further tool development as well as with more traditional areas, to replace numerous detailed courses in the traditional functional areas. Intensive advanced courses on communication processes, managerial mathematics, managerial economics, advanced statistical methods, and small-group behavior, for example, might be offered. Similarly, limited electives in areas like union policies and labor-management relations would be appropriate.

At the end of the second year, the graduate should have a sound foundation not only for long-range advancement in management but also for taking and doing a job promptly on entering industry (more comments on this below). Most important, he would have the tools and the training to learn for himself in adapting to a changing world and in facing different problems as he moves from functional field to functional field and from firm to firm over the next half century.

Teaching Methods

How teaching is done is at least as important as what courses are taught. Teaching method would be of dominant importance in the type of program outlined above.

It is important to remember that the basic objectives of this program are qualities of mind rather than detailed subject matter and that the subject matter taught would be focused largely on the development of fundamental analytical tools and their use. Thus first emphasis in day-to-day teaching would be not on the detailed subject matter of the courses but on the development of orderly analytical problem-solving ability, on development and use of basic analytical concepts, on student learning from experience, on effective communication, and on the development of independence of thought and maturity of judgment.

The implications of the above argument for teaching method are clearly eclectic. A good teaching method is one that accomplishes the particular objectives at hand. Some methods are better for some purposes, and others for others. Use of cases, for example, is excellent for many purposes—for integration, for emphasis on orderly problem solving, for experience in the application of analytical concepts. On the other hand, cases may not be very useful where the primary emphasis is on development of sharp analytical concepts or models. Student-participative demonstrations and role playing may be of special usefulness in the behavioral science areas and applications, especially when carefully arranged situations are used to maximize the realism and to develop situations in which particular preplanned concepts and hypotheses are illuminated. More traditional lectures and student-teacher question-and-answer techniques may be most helpful where good reading materials are not available and where a highly developed discipline is involved— for example, in statistical analysis and some phases of economic analysis. Group projects involving "real world" situations in industry are useful, both in the foundation area courses and in the more advanced second-year work. Use of "business games" involving electronic computers to simulate business situations, both internally and involving market interactions, promises to become a valuable teaching device, as suggested above, where the time dimension of living with one's decisions is an important teaching objective. Over the two years, the primary goals would shift from time to time, and teaching methods would be adjusted to the particular subject matter and goals at hand, with careful teaching attention throughout to which method is most useful at which point.

It may be useful to compare and contrast this approach to managerial decision making with one that places primary emphasis on the "case method." [10] The basic objective in both is the same—to develop in the student the ability to make good managerial decisions in a world where

[10] The comparison is not intended to be with the program of any particular school. The "case method" no longer has a simple, agreed connotation, since increasingly the use of any type of teaching material intended to stimulate student participation in examining problems of managerial behavior has been termed "case teaching." Nor does any school, so far as I know, now teach solely by the "case method," in the older, narrower use of the term indicated in the following paragraph. I mean by the case method here teaching that uses predominantly written business problem or case situations as teaching materials; that emphasizes student participation (in the class and outside it) in searching for "good" managerial solutions to these cases; and that largely or completely shuns formal, systematic abstractions, theories, or generalizations as teaching devices, whether provided by readings or the professor or developed by the students.

problems will be unclear and, in considerable part, unforeseeable at the time he is in business school. They agree on a major point of educational philosophy—that the focus should be on student learning rather than on teacher telling and that active student participation in the learning process is essential. They differ strongly on the importance attached to explicit analytical concepts, hypotheses, and models, both in the teaching process and in the handling of problems in the post-business school world.

The approach outlined here rests on the presumption that such explicit analytical concepts, hypotheses, and models can be of value in helping students to handle problems effectively—indeed, that an inventory of such analytical tools is one of the most valuable possessions the potential manager can have as he moves into the world of unknown and unsolved managerial problem areas. The case method, in its traditional form, places entire emphasis on repetitive, guided problem solving in a wide variety of cases but without the formal development or use of specific analytical concepts or models (theories). Indeed, many advocates of the case method fear that such precise analytical concepts or models may do more harm than good, because the student will believe that in them he has a pat answer to any problem that comes along and that the model may stand in the way of independent thinking rather than aid it. Others doubt that there are precise analytical concepts or models yet developed that are of any appreciable help in making managerial decisions.

An oversimple analogy may help to clarify the point. Suppose we want to train a carpenter. One approach would be to spend our time getting the man thoroughly acquainted with the tools. This is a hammer; you use it for the following purposes. This is a saw. This is a blueprint. And so on. At the end, we could send the man out saying: Now you have all the basic knowledge you need. You can readily adjust your knowledge to the particular job you get, say building a garage. In revolt against this extreme of academic abstraction, another approach (the "pure" case method) would be to begin the first day by saying: I want a window frame; build me one. The man would then struggle through and somehow produce something like a window frame, making hordes of mistakes but, hopefully, learning in the process. Next time we might say: All right, now I want a doghouse. And so on, never pointing out explicitly the lessons being learned or the usefulness of various tools for various particular purposes. The presumption would be that the man could learn the tools needed on his own, looking for a hammer here, a set of blueprints there, and adapting them to each job as it came along.

A third approach, roughly that argued here, accepts both as valid learning devices and emphasizes their combination. It says: Begin with an explicit introduction both to tools and to their use in simple situations.

Make the student learn for himself in considerable part but recognize the value of making explicit the main facts we know about what tools are best for what purposes and what some of the major pitfalls are. But in the end, be sure the main test is whether the student can *use* the tools he has been learning—in building a garage or in making managerial decisions.

It would thus be a mistake to overemphasize the differences between the two methods. The example states in extreme form the "traditional" approach to the case method. But the educational differences are real. The approach outlined here places much greater emphasis on explicit reliance on the development of systematic and organized knowledge and on the role of "theory" and explicit analytical concepts as a guide to effective and orderly independent thinking. In this respect it is much more in the tradition of the sciences, even though it recognizes that the body of organized knowledge and tested theory is far too small to do more than provide a partial set of aids to managerial decision making. It agrees wholeheartedly with many "case method" advocates that analytical concepts and models can easily be so misused as to do more harm than good—whenever they become the master of the student's thinking as he tackles a new problem rather than a set of tools to help him organize and deal with the problem.

The Teachers

Such a program, focused on the development of managerial decision-making abilities, requires teachers who are more interested in what goes on inside the student's mind than in what comes out of their own mouths. It requires persistent emphasis on method, on analytical tools, and on looking across the various functional fields of business. While subject-matter-oriented faculty members can usefully teach in such a program, they cannot do so if the subject matter itself becomes the prime object. "Strutting one's stuff" is a cardinal sin for a teacher in such a program, yet the symbol of status in many teaching situations is the ability to sound more learned and to display greater erudition on the detailed niceties of the subject than anyone else.

The program outlined above would require, in most business schools, a considerable number of new teachers, probably in part from the behavioral sciences, mathematics, statistics, and other related disciplines. Most business schools do not have on their present faculties enough men with sufficient understanding of the basic tool areas to do the complete job themselves. On the other hand, it is clear that mere introduction of a man from the psychology department or the sociology department or the mathematics department does not necessarily solve any problems.

Traditional departments in the behavioral sciences are as far from being tooled up to work effectively with business problems as are business schools from being tooled up to work effectively on basic problems of psychology or sociology. Experience with importing faculty members from mathematics departments has been far from uniformly happy.

If business schools are to gain from importing members from other departments, it is likely that they must do so on a basis whereby the new men become thoroughly engrossed in the problems of business teaching and have a large commitment of time and energy to learning about business and business education. Without this, they are unlikely to understand the problems sufficiently to be very useful. Their analytical concepts, their ways of thinking, their frameworks of reference, are not generally applicable without considerable readjustment to the problems the business schools face. Merely borrowing a faculty member on a temporary basis from outside the business school, or inviting him to teach a special course in the business school while his main allegiance remains elsewhere, offers only dubious promise on the basis of reasonable expectation and experience.[11]

A large amount of tolerance, patience, and hard work is required from both the business school and the "outside" faculties if the attempt to draw in resources from other fields is to pay its largest dividend. The long-run pay-off appears to be large, and the business schools badly need this kind of importation. But to pretend that the import is there ready to be had for a semester's salary may be a very bad mistake indeed.

Another approach is for business school faculties to tool themselves up to do the job. Surely this must be part of the solution. But it is doubtful that it is enough in most cases. A large amount of hard work is required ahead to develop out of the behavioral sciences, mathematics, and so on the new analytical tools that will be operationally useful for the areas of business. To accomplish this combined reconversion and new development requires a depth of understanding that is hard to come by in a brief period of time for any business school faculty member not firmly grounded in those disciplines, just as the behavioral science outsider alone is unlikely to be successful in doing the job without extensive interaction with present business school faculty members.

Generally, the kind of program outlined above requires closer faculty group planning and interaction than is present in most business school programs now. Integrated focus on managerial decision making requires throughout, and especially in the functional areas and in the business policy course of the second year, a thorough-going emphasis on the basic goals of student learning, plus a high degree of faculty competence at

[11] And, as a psychologist who has lived through this experience feelingly points out, it may create major problems of adjustment for him.

doing the tool-using and integrating job himself. The assumption that the student will put together in his mind what the faculty cannot accomplish in theirs seems a dangerous assumption indeed. Careful cross-planning of the use of the tools in the various functional areas, and the use of good instances and examples in the foundation-tool areas, is essential to this type of program if the student is to receive maximum help toward the objective. It is reasonable to predict that many present faculty members will have a hard time keeping up with the graduate students currently being trained in programs like this as these younger men enter business school teaching.

THE UNDERGRADUATE PROGRAM

The case for managerial decision making as the focus of undergraduate training for business is much the same as at the graduate level. The pervasiveness of change, the uncertainty as to the problems of the future, the increasingly rational nature of management, the changing role of the manager, and the increased interaction between business and its environment—all loom large in the future whatever level of education we consider. But very few undergraduate business schools have moved strongly in the direction outlined above. Even where this focus is accepted on the graduate level, two main objections are raised against it for undergraduates:

1. The lower average ability of undergraduate students in the mass, and hence the smaller likelihood that they will end up doing a real management job at the middle or upper levels.

2. The need for more specialization in training and for more detailed techniques so that undergraduates can get jobs and do them satisfactorily when they leave school.

Both these objections have been widely stated. They need careful consideration. It is useful, however, first to consider the curriculum and teaching method this emphasis would imply at the undergraduate level and then to consider the objections posed.

Curriculum

At the undergraduate level, assume the availability of about two full academic years for training in the business area—about the same as in the graduate program outlined above but not necessarily concentrated in the last two years of the undergraduate program. This is somewhat less than the time generally given to business subjects in undergraduate business schools. It would thus, happily, increase the time available for "preprofessional" or nonbusiness teaching in the liberal arts and sciences. But the general education (liberal arts) portion of the collegiate objective, critically important as it must be in any first-rate undergraduate business school program, lies mainly outside the scope of this chapter. The "business" program proposed rests on the presumption that this objective is largely met in the remainder of the curriculum, although it is important to recognize the strong component of liberal arts (i.e., non-specifically management) focus in the "business" part of the curriculum, for example, in the behavioral sciences and the public policy portions of economics.

With this amount of time for the business program, a strong case can be made for much the same curriculum outline as for the graduate program above, with the expectation that the man receiving his bachelor's degree will view this as a terminal degree. This would mean emphasis on the three foundation-tool stems in the junior or, possibly, sophomore-junior years. It would mean required foundation functional area courses in marketing, finance, and production not earlier than the junior year. It would mean an approach in the senior year to integration along business policy lines and avoidance of specialization in any one of the particular fields of business beyond a very modest level. It would mean parallel attention to business' economic, social, legal, and political environment throughout and to the pervasive interaction between business and its environment. It would mean a managerial decision-making focus in teaching method and teaching materials—one aimed at active student participation, at getting students to understand the fundamental tools, and at gaining experience in making independent, reasoned judgments with the help of these tools.[12]

But although the course names might look much the same as in the graduate program, there should, and inescapably would, be important differences:

1. Undergraduate students are, on the average, less competent intellectually and less highly motivated than graduate students. The pace would thus need to be much slower at the undergraduate level, and a larger proportion of the time would need to be diverted to the foundation areas of the first year of the graduate program. These might well get more than half the total time. In this slower pace there would be throughout more explicit stress on showing how applications of the analytical concepts could be made in business situations. Use of abstractions does not come easily to many undergraduate students, especially those who select business. Thus the analytical tools would be simpler and

---

[12] All this assumes the presence of a faculty competent to teach such a program—unfortunately a reasonable assumption today for only a small minority of undergraduate business schools. Change will necessarily come more slowly here than in the graduate schools.

the emphasis on application relatively greater. As intellectual aptitude declines, the danger becomes greater that the abstract concept or model will be used blindly and unthinkingly—that it will be taken as an answer rather than as a flexible tool.

2. Undergraduate teaching method would include more exposition and less use of cases and problems, especially in the early stages of the program. The evidence seems clear that student self-teaching from case-and-problem materials works well with mature able students and much less well with immature, lower-ability students. The self-education that is so effective for highly selected graduate students cannot be counted on to anything like the same extent for the average undergraduate. The undergraduate program would recognize the fact, especially where classes are large, that exposition by the teacher still has an important role to play. But the lectures would focus on helping the student to understand the process of using analytical tools in making judgments for himself.

Evidence is not yet available to indicate where along the intelligence scale we need to give up hope that the students will develop substantial understanding and sophistication in the use of analytical concepts in making decisions for themselves. Perhaps in some of the business schools which accept large numbers of low-ability students the problem would be very great. On the other hand, there is every reason to suppose this is a workable approach for many of the better undergraduate business schools, certainly if they are willing to put harder intellectual pressure on their students and are willing to see some of the laziest and least able fall by the wayside.

3. Less time would be allocated in the senior year to the advanced tool courses (such as organization and administrative theory, managerial mathematics, managerial economics, and so on) than in the second year of the graduate program. This difference would be especially important for the run-of-the-mill students, who probably can better use their time in getting a firmer grasp of elementary concepts and more experience in using them under guidance. On the other hand, some advanced tool courses would be appropriate for top-notch undergraduate students. Not all the best students wind up in the graduate schools, and the case is strong for giving these superior seniors the fundamental tools they need to keep on learning and working for themselves, plus guided experience in applying these tools imaginatively. Limited experience suggests that top-notch students tend to take these advanced tool courses, while the ordinary students generally choose their electives in the traditional functional fields where they get more emphasis on the application of the simpler tools.

The Problem of Low Ability and Low Managerial Promise

It is widely argued that the typical undergraduate is so much lower in ability and in promise of managerial advancement that this would be simply the wrong kind of program for him.

Accept for the moment the proposition that the undergraduate's ability is much lower and that he is unlikely to become president of General Motors, or probably of anything else. Suppose that, on the average, he will be doing well if he gets up to a minor managerial responsibility in either a large or a small firm. Does it then follow that managerial problem solving is the wrong focus for the business component of his education?

A strong argument can be made that something like the above is still the best focus, recognizing the drastic modifications that need to be made in moving from the graduate level. The rate of obsolescence of particularized knowledge and of particularized training is so great that the more fundamental type of training may still be better for the undergraduate, even though he gets less out of it than does the more advanced, higher-quality student. A curriculum emphasizing detailed descriptive and technical material that will be largely out of date in a few years and which, from all the studies that we have, will be largely forgotten in a few years anyhow is hard to defend. If the student does remember the detailed information and the "answers," the information he has memorized today is likely to be wrong for the problems of tomorrow, whether they are answers on how to set market quotas, schedule production, or organize an accounting department.

Thus, even after drastically scaling down the graduate aspiration level, emphasis on independent problem solving (managerial decision making) still appears to offer more for the undergraduate than does the accumulation of particularized knowledge and know-how. If our business school students are so poor that nothing can be done to train them to think independently on managerial problems, do they deserve a place in the university? If such low-ability candidates are to be university students, surely a larger relative allocation of time to general citizenship training deserves serious consideration as an alternative to descriptive, trade-school-level "business" courses.

It is important to remember that not all the most promising students go on to graduate school. The undergraduate program needs to be devised with due attention to the promise of the better men as well as to the needs of the lower half. Too, it is often hard to tell at that stage of a man's career how far he will go in management. Often the student who seems only average may turn out to be the president of tomorrow who can best use the kind of managerial problem-solving training argued for above. To forego the chance of providing a fundamental education for those students who will move furthest ahead in management is a heavy price to pay in order to gear the program to the supposed low-level needs of the many.

The Problem of Specialization versus General Management

The second general criticism of this kind of program for the undergraduate is that he will probably be something of a specialist all his life and ought, therefore, to be trained in more detail in some speciality so that he can at least be a good specialist. It is true that most business school undergraduates will never achieve general management positions. Many of them will end up being "specialists" all their lives—though, as indicated above, I am doubtful that we can always pick out the ones who will move up from the ones who will not. Moreover, even the specialists often move around a good deal in modern industry.

The managerial decision-making focus is appropriate for the training of either a specialist or a man looking toward general management. Surely a man who has any managerial promise in modern industry needs to know something of the general functional activities of the modern business world. Surely he needs a managerial way of thinking about, and acting on, the problems he faces in his special field. The negative considerations against specialization are equally important. First, the evidence is clear that the student who starts out for a specialist's career in one area often ends up being a specialist in something quite different. This fact casts great doubt upon highly specialized training. Second, and more fundamental, highly specialized training is seldom the most useful training even for the specialist. The world changes, new problems appear, and human knowledge advances at an amazing rate. A rereading of some of the textbooks in specialized areas of business from about twenty-five years ago provides impressive evidence. Most of the contents were institutional description and detailed rule of thumb and know-how that would be of dubious value, if not of positive harm, if the material were remembered today. We cannot be sure that the detailed techniques and know-how of today will not be of lasting value, but the history of newly developing fields like management suggests great caution in reaching this conclusion. As argued in earlier chapters, history constitutes a firm testimonial to fundamental and generalized, as contrasted to highly specialized, college training—in business as elsewhere.

The major in "industrial management" found in many undergraduate business programs merits attention in connection with the problem of specialization. In a few instances, it connotes a program aimed at training for general management. In most, however, it connotes one focused on "personnel management" or "production management," or both. Course content varies widely. It often emphasizes the techniques of personnel administration, sometimes those of elementary production (time and motion study, methods study, plant layout, and so on). There is often an introductory course in "industrial organization and management," or a similar title, which includes a survey of the functions of business with some emphasis on business organization, personnel methods, and especially the areas of production.

Present programs under this title are often as specialized in technical training in personnel and production management as are the programs in marketing, finance, accounting, or other fields in their particular areas. The treatment of business organization is generally largely descriptive and seldom reaches back to underlying analytical concepts. While the name "industrial management" is a legitimate one, it appears that a program truly aimed at training men for management in industry, or in any other business area, might better be focused along the broader and more fundamental lines outlined above as a managerial foundation. The argument here is that the word "management" should be considered a part of the training for managerial performance in all areas of business enterprise, not reserved especially for special options with the word "management" attached to a special field title, whether it be production management, personnel management, sales management, industrial management, or another such combination. In any case, it is important to distinguish between the actual content and focus of such programs and the breadth and analytical managerial emphasis connoted by the name used.

DOCTORAL PROGRAMS

Doctoral programs in business schools have generally been of two types. While titles have varied, the Ph.D. has generally been a highly specialized program involving intensive graduate-level course work in a particular area (e.g., personnel management, finance, or accounting), followed by a traditional thesis with the avowed goal of adding to the stock of human knowledge. In most cases, these theses have either been descriptions of current business-operating practice in the field or investigations (library and field) of some particular aspect of the area not yet thoroughly written up. As in many other fields, most of the dissertations have not represented a significant contribution to human knowledge, nor have many shown evidence of student knowledge of modern research methods.

The other doctoral program, usually leading to the D.B.A. or some comparable degree, has stressed the "professional" nature of the doctoral degree. It has departed from many of the traditional requirements for the Ph.D., placing little emphasis on modern research techniques or on the usual university requirements for doctoral dissertations. Instead, the dissertation has often been a case study, or a group of case studies. Emphasis on training for research or teaching has not been large. The hope has often been that the degree will serve equally well to equip men for industry or for academic life. This degree appears to have been most prevalent where schools have focused their master's program on relatively general management training.

The first type of traditional program produces a man too narrowly specialized in his own functional area to do the kind of teaching required in a managerial problem-solving curriculum aiming toward general management, unless he is prepared to learn the breadth required on his own after leaving graduate school. The second type produces a man all too often insufficiently equipped with an understanding of the role of disciplined and organized knowledge, including theory, to understand and teach effectively in a program that makes strong use of such analytical tools in managerial problem solving. These are, of course, oversimplified generalizations, but they help to point up the nature of the problem.

Business schools of tomorrow will need teachers of many sorts. They will undoubtedly draw their faculties in part from men trained in traditional business school doctoral programs. Many will also want to draw from the related disciplines and professions—the behavioral sciences, economics (the principal source of business school teachers to date), statistics, mathematics, engineering, and others. But they will also need, and need badly, a new type of faculty member, equipped to play a central role in the type of business program spelled out in the preceding sections.

A new type of doctoral program, focused on training teachers and researchers for programs oriented around managerial decision making, has appeared in a few institutions. As at the M.B.A. and undergraduate levels, it grows out of the past and draws heavily upon it. But it is significantly different. In general, such "new looks" in the doctoral programs have appeared at the same schools that are pushing along managerial decision-making lines at the master's level. The number of men trained in such new doctoral programs is still extremely small, but with the help of new fellowship and faculty-development funds it is increasing.

What should a doctoral program provide for the man who is to become a key teacher in the business school of tomorrow, oriented toward management decision making? The need is for a remarkably well and broadly trained man. He should be well equipped in all the basic-tool areas outlined above and well grounded in the operating side (functional fields) of modern business; sophisticated in the use of analytical concepts and models as aids to managerial problem solving; especially competent in one field or set of tools involved in his major, dissertation area; and thoroughly trained in the use of research in the development of fundamental new knowledge and its application.

This is a large assignment—for the graduate school that does the teaching and for the graduate student who does the learning. Nevertheless, it is being tried, with apparent success, in at least one doctoral program; somewhat similar experiments, with varying specific objectives and methods, are under way in a few other graduate schools. Again, to provide concreteness, a brief description of a specific doctoral program may be useful.[13]

Assume that the student arrives at graduate school with substantially no background in the field of business but with a high intellectual aptitude and strong motivation. Assume, moreover, that he has a good liberal arts or engineering-science training, involving at least a little experience in economics, the behavioral sciences, and mathematics—for example, at least a year's college work in each of these areas—but that none of this training has been focused along the lines described above.

The course work is pointed toward the doctoral qualifying examinations, usually taken in the spring of the third year of graduate study. Something like half of the student's first two years is taken in common with the master's program described in the M.B.A. section above. This includes basic-tool courses in the behavioral sciences, economic analysis, and quantitative method, plus usually the foundation courses in the functional fields. The student, however, begins midway through the first year to move into more research- and theory-oriented seminars along with his basic training in the master's program. Depending on the primary interests of the individual, he begins a more advanced, special doctoral sequence in the behavioral sciences or in economic analysis, and he generally moves into a special three-semester sequence in advanced applied statistics in lieu of the latter portion of the basic quantitative-method stem for the master's candidates.

In the second year, he normally takes part or all of the master's program course in administration and business policy. Depending on his background, he takes a good deal or little of the work in the economic-social environment of business. He also continues the more advanced doctoral sequences in quantitative method, the behavioral sciences (built especially from social and individual psychology, industrial sociology, and the theory of organization and administration), and possibly in economic theory. In this year, he may take a special mathematics-for-management science course, or he may have included it in the first year.

[13] Continuing the master's-level example above, Carnegie Tech.'s doctoral program is used for the same reasons as before.

Depending on his primary interests, he may take some or none of the advanced functional field courses for the master's students. Most students do take further functional area work, especially when their special interest lies toward applied problems rather than in basic tool-building (say in the behavioral sciences or quantitative method). Some of these courses carry over into the third year for nearly all students.

Beyond the second year, and to some extent during it, students are encouraged to form quasi-tutorial relationships with faculty members, related to faculty research projects under way. These arrangements often lead to special "reading" and "project" courses, looking toward both the doctoral qualifying examinations and dissertation plans. Considerable freedom is given students to "read" in any of the areas involved, especially at the more advanced levels, where careful discussion and individual experience suggest that this is a more efficient use of student time than formal classwork. The main responsibility is on the student to prepare for the written doctoral qualifying examinations. If he wants to receive the master's degree en route, he must complete substantially the required master's course program and take the master's comprehensive examination.

The written doctoral qualifying examination is usually taken in the spring of the third year of graduate study, though it may be taken earlier or later. The examination covers four major areas: administration and organizational behavior; business and economic institutions and policies; quantitative methods; and advanced economic analysis, psychology, or some other related field. The student must "major" in either the first or second of these areas and write a six-hour examination in that area, compared with four hours in the other areas. He is required to take the first three fields but has an option among advanced economic analysis, psychology, or other related fields for his fourth area. Nearly all students choose either advanced economics or psychology.

The level of competence required in each of the four fields is that expected of the master's student at the end of two years, plus greater sophistication and skill in the use of formal analytical concepts and models, plus much greater understanding of research techniques and developments (including quantitative method), plus high-level competence in the area chosen for the major. For example, the doctoral student has normally taken a three-semester sequence in advanced applied statistics, as an operating and research tool. He has taken, or read, at least an additional year's seminar in the theory of administration and organization—plus at least another year of behavioral science if administration is his major. If he elects business institutions and policies as his major, he is expected to have completed the advanced functional area courses in that portion of the area he emphasizes, plus seminar or tutorial work and reading in it, preferably looking toward a dissertation subject in the area. If he chooses the minor in economic analysis, he normally takes part or all of the three-semester doctoral sequence in advanced economic analysis beyond the M.B.A. economic analysis stem (which is required for the institutions and policy area in any case); a similar pattern prevails for the area of psychology as a minor.[14]

An appreciable portion of doctoral candidates come from regular master's classes—men who originally set out for managerial careers. The man who first completes the two-year master's program and then goes on for his Ph.D. has a richer background in the areas of operating managerial behavior but also generally needs three full years of course work before taking the qualifying examination. He can thus still complete the Ph.D. in four years, but he works on a narrower time margin in doing so than does the man headed for a doctor's degree from the outset.

Upon this background of competence, as measured by success in the qualifying examination, the candidate is permitted wide choice as to a dissertation subject. The goal of the dissertation is primarily training in research on a quasi-tutorial basis, and considerable specialization is expected. Candidates may work in the foundation areas or in the applied functional fields. In the former, topics may range into fundamental areas, such as organization theory and human problem-solving, as well as into more closely business-oriented questions. In the latter, major emphasis is placed on development and application of new tools to problems of business operation rather than on mere description of existing industrial practice. Thesis subjects thus far have been roughly divided between work in the foundation areas (behavioral sciences, economic analysis, and quantitative method) and applications (in production, marketing, and financial controls).[15]

In his fourth year, while writing his dissertation, the student is encouraged to teach one section of an undergraduate course (in a combined

[14] Some business schools offer separate Ph.D.s in economics; this is more common than the Ph.D. in business administration. Carnegie offers separate but closely related Ph.D. programs in economics and psychology in which students may take some or all of the first three qualifying examination areas indicated above for their own doctoral qualifying programs. In these separate degrees, however, the candidate is expected to show more advanced competence in his own major field of economics or psychology, using the industrial administration areas as minors.

[15] Carnegie and a few other institutions substitute competence in mathematics for managerial applications for one of the foreign languages traditionally required by universities for the Ph.D. At Carnegie, which has a more advanced requirement than most others, this is competence approximately at the level of calculus plus a special one-year course in mathematical foundations for management science, involving some linear algebra, matrices, and differential equations. Most schools do not have any mathematics requirement. Some have neither mathematics nor foreign language requirements.

engineering-management B.S. program at Carnegie) roughly corresponding to the subject areas of the first-year master's program. He is generally assigned to a course where he is helped by a senior faculty member, wherever possible to a multisection course shared with a regular faculty member. Since the student normally has begun his thesis work before the fourth year, this teaching is consistent with devoting a full academic year to the thesis while providing some teaching experience with informal coaching somewhat comparable to the coaching received on research methods.

Such a doctoral program, if successful, should produce useful academicians for the business school of tomorrow, well trained to participate in programs oriented toward managerial decision making and to contribute significant knowledge for the textbooks of the next generation. On the other hand, the program is open to legitimate question as to whether it may not risk becoming a superficial survey across an impressive range of subject matter but not containing enough depth in any area to make the man a thorough scholar and teacher. This is a real danger with such demanding objectives. However, experience indicates that the objectives are realistic ones for top-notch students.

The program is then open to the criticism that it is not feasible for any except unusually competent students. This is probably true, though it may not be a telling criticism since presumably the business schools need to draw into their future teaching ranks men of superior intellectual quality. Limited experience at the schools emphasizing this general approach suggests that it is feasible for students of good quality short of genius but that it requires major effort by the faculty and by the students concerned.

RESEARCH

History suggests that there is no one "best" method of research. Increases in human knowledge and understanding have come through many channels and will undoubtedly continue to do so. The direction of business education outlined above suggests emphasis, however, on some types of research not commonly found in the business schools. And some new approaches to research have begun to appear over the past decade to supplement those already being pursued. The focus outlined in this chapter calls for research along several lines.

First, more research is badly needed in the foundation-tool areas themselves to provide the analytical concepts, working hypotheses, and models needed to give better guidance in managerial decision making. All three tool areas (with the exception of mathematics, in so far as it may be included in quantitative method) are relatively new in the history of human knowledge. Statistics has undergone major revolutions in the past few decades as it has mushroomed. Economic analysis has long dealt with public policy issues but until recently has given little attention to managerial problem solving. The behavioral sciences are only beginning to come of age, and few of the leading practitioners have given careful attention to the problems of making the working tools of the field useful for managerial purposes. Mathematics itself is moving forward rapidly, and mathematicians have begun to display some interest in developing concepts especially useful for handling the problems of the behavioral and social sciences and management science. Research, cooperatively between business school faculty members and men from the other disciplines involved, needs to be encouraged in every way.

If the business schools leave such research to the other disciplines, the lag in relevance to business problems may be great. Most behavioral scientists, economists, mathematicians, statisticians, and so on have little direct interest in management problems—indeed are not aware of what the problems are. Close involvement of such outside experts in the business area can help bring their powerful talents to bear on business problems. Traditionally trained business school faculty members alone can seldom hope to carry out fundamental tool research, because their training has not provided the foundations for it. But together, business school researchers and those from other disciplines can bring combined talents to bear on building up more fundamental and directly useful tools for the management of tomorrow. If doctoral programs like that suggested above become prevalent, more researchers will be available who combine such talents within single individuals.

Such fundamental research is often "impractical," with little obvious direct usefulness. Such research, this approach suggests, is entirely appropriate for the business schools to undertake. For example, fundamental research is now under way on human higher-learning and problem-solving processes, using large electronic computers to simulate the human mind. The prime objective is to understand how the human mind must work, say, in learning formal mathematics or in playing chess well, as examples of human problem solving. This is far removed from most business school research. Yet the results promise to throw major light on how better to teach managerial decision making and, indeed, on how operating managers can learn to make better managerial decisions. Comparable examples can be found in other fundamental-tool areas, for example, statistical decision theory. They may prove to be the most important research being done in the entire business area or in the foundation areas related to business, even though today they seem at first far from the world of practical business.

Second, more thorough understanding of prevailing business and managerial behavior in all its aspects is needed—not merely at the level of particular descriptions or case studies but in looking toward more useful generalizations. Such generalizations are few indeed in the current state of knowledge. They will come only slowly and with careful observation and research, well planned and oriented toward the development of such generalizations, if indeed the regularities exist to be found.

This type of research is not new to the business schools. It presumes, however, a much stronger focus on the search for generalizations and a much greater concern for careful research methodology than has characterized most business school research. Mere description of business institutions or practices may be useful research, but it is unlikely to lead toward more general understanding unless it is done with painstaking care to obtain and preserve objective data and with forethought as to how the description may fit into later attempts at generalization. Case collection to obtain teaching materials is thus unlikely to contribute substantially to constructing a larger body of discipline-tested knowledge of business behavior, because it is seldom planned to fit into broader research objectives and because the search for teachable materials almost inevitably colors and biases what the collector sees and writes up in the case. Much of the information of greatest value to the later researcher is likely to be lost. (This observation in no way, of course, detracts from the importance of case-collection activities to obtain teaching materials and to help educate faculty members who have had limited contact with business operations.)

Third, more fundamental research needs to be done on the development of normative aids and guides to managerial decision making in the functional fields and indeed in all aspects of management. This is research at the "applied" level. For example, the standard rules of thumb on production scheduling and inventory control, representing accumulated know-how, have clearly in the last few years been surpassed by more formal "decision rules" developed through the application of careful (mathematical) reasoning and measurement to these problems. Similar progress has been made in the analysis of consumer behavior and capital budgeting, to cite only two other cases. Comparable applied research is needed in all areas of management. There is no likelihood it will completely replace informed business judgment. But there is every reason to suppose it can increasingly aid such judgments and in many areas, especially in the middle-management range, effectively replace current rules of thumb and traditional operating practices which have not been carefully analyzed.

Research along all these lines has blossomed rapidly at a very few leading schools over the past few years. Interaction between business school faculty members and distinguished researchers from the allied fields of behavioral sciences, economics, mathematics, and statistics has moved rapidly and encouragingly, though still in only a few centers. Much of the most significant research is still being done outside the business schools—in departments of the behavioral sciences, economics, and mathematics, and in special institutes.[16] Research results, though modest, are encouraging. Such research may not be feasible for most business schools over the decades immediately ahead. But its rapid recent growth suggests it will spread steadily and will play an increasingly important role in supporting the teaching activities of the business schools of the future.

[16] Research being done outside business schools thus may have more influence on the business teaching of tomorrow than that being done in most business schools. (This would be comparable to the relationship between most medical schools and underlying work in the biological sciences outside medical schools.) The Bureau of Applied Social Research at Columbia, the Survey Research Center at Michigan, the School of Industrial and Labor Relations at Cornell, and the Industrial Relations Section at M.I.T. are examples of sources of such research.

CHAPTER 14

ACCOUNTING

Robert G. Cox

Programs in accounting, at both the undergraduate and graduate levels, have been dominated by professional accounting requirements to the neglect of management aspects of the subject. Professionally oriented courses have, for the most part, been narrowly slanted with emphasis placed upon techniques and procedures. The problems and decisions that face the public accountant and the accountant in private industry require broad education in functional areas of business and government, an understanding of the human aspects of business, and an awareness of the responsibilities of business to society, as well as competence in accounting. Excessive specialization reduces the extent to which these requirements can be met.

Joseph Wharton, in the deed of gift which made the Wharton School of Finance and Commerce at the University of Pennsylvania in 1881 the first school of business in the United States, specified that the staff should include "One Professor or Instructor of Accounting or Bookkeeping, to teach the simplest and most practical forms of bookkeeping for housekeepers, for private individuals, for commercial and banking firms, for manufacturing establishments and for banks. . . ." During the rapid growth of collegiate business schools after the turn of the century, every new school, without exception, provided instruction in accounting. Thus from the earliest college-level program to the present, a course in accounting has been included in business school curricula, usually as part of the core course work.

The field of accounting is much like that of engineering, with several distinct areas which serve many different objectives. Our business schools today graduate large numbers of men and women trained in accounting who find employment in many different fields, including:

1. Public accounting
   a. Auditing

  b. Tax service
  c. Management service
2. Governmental accounting
  a. Regulatory commissions (ICC, SEC, etc.)
  b. Tax and fiscal agencies (Department of Internal Revenue, General Accounting Office, etc.)
  c. Services and other governmental agencies (Department of Agriculture, Post Office, etc.)
3. Industrial accounting
  a. Financial institutions
  b. Trading companies
  c. Manufacturing organizations
  d. Service organizations
4. Nonaccounting positions in which a knowledge of accounting is desirable, such as:
  a. Financial analysis
  b. Production planning
  c. Statistical analysis
  d. Marketing research

In view of the many vocational possibilities available to those who have studied accounting at the college level, it is not surprising that a variety of courses in accounting have appeared in the curriculum to serve these different objectives. A number of leading colleges offer from twelve to twenty different courses in the subject, many as specialized as retail store accounting and accounting for the petroleum industry. Accounting courses leading to a major in the field are more widely offered than any other subject in business school curricula. It is not uncommon to find in the catalogs of even small liberal arts colleges four or five courses in accounting, frequently taught by the same person.

As indicated in Chap. 9, over 90 per cent of the undergraduate schools of business offer a major in accounting, usually complete enough to satisfy educational requirements of state boards of examiners for certified public accountants. Generally the accounting courses are incorporated in the regular degree program in business administration in accordance with one of three common arrangements: (1) A two-year course of study in business administration is preceded by a two-year course of study in liberal arts. It should be noted that almost all students who are accounting majors under this arrangement take elementary accounting, principles of economics, and business law, or another course in business administration, during the first two years. (2) A three-year course of study in business administration is preceded by one year of general studies in the liberal arts college. (3) A four-year course of study in business administration is integrated with a concurrent program of selected and elective liberal arts subjects. Although a few programs of the latter type are flexible enough to permit the student to take as much as 60 or 65 per cent of his work outside of the business-economics field, requirements in core courses and in the major field are so rigid at the large majority of such schools that it is seldom possible for the student to elect more than 50 per cent of his course work in nonbusiness subjects. In practice, business administration students tend to choose something less than 40 per cent of their studies from subjects other than business and economics. Unfortunately, all too often a high proportion of the courses in non-business subjects which the student chooses under free-elective or restricted-elective arrangements are less challenging and less broadening than might be desirable and beneficial. In addition, too frequently the elective subjects selected in business and economics are too narrow and factual to be intellectually stimulating.

A number of institutions which have offered degrees in business administration only at the graduate level have attempted to meet the demand for undergraduate accounting education by creating "institutes of accounting." These programs are usually based on one year of general studies followed by three years of accounting and other business subjects, and thus are similar to the second arrangement mentioned above. A Bachelor of Science degree is conferred upon candidates completing such program requirements. The programs are not unique in themselves, but are worthy of note since they represent the only undergraduate programs in business at schools concentrating on graduate work in business administration.

Many universities offer majors in accounting as part of the degree of Master of Business Administration, including those which also offer a major in accounting at the undergraduate level. Recently, a few institutions have offered specialized programs leading to the degree of Master of Professional Accountancy. Other universities which offer graduate instruction in business administration at the master's level but not majors in accounting usually require a basic course in accounting as part of the core course work.

A smaller number of institutions offer majors in accounting as part of the work leading to the degree of Doctor of Business Administration or Doctor of Philosophy. Several large universities offer the Ph.D. in accountancy.

In addition to those students following regular programs leading to degrees in accounting, an even larger number study accounting in evening and extension classes at universities, institutes, and commercial schools which do not offer degrees and through correspondence courses. At these different levels of instruction, emphasis within the accounting courses may be professional, managerial, or conceptual in character. Therefore, it is essential to distinguish among the many purposes of accounting courses, the levels at which they are given, and the objectives of the over-all program of which they form a part.

THE DEVELOPMENT OF ACCOUNTING EDUCATION

The rapid growth of accounting as a profession and as a function within the business firm is an outgrowth of economic, social, and legal developments which have occurred in the United States since the latter part of the nineteenth century. Directly and indirectly these developments have influenced the nature of education in accounting at the college level.

The Growth of the Corporate Form of Organization

Prior to the late 1800s most business enterprises in the United States were organized as sole proprietorships, and their accounting needs were limited to internal analysis and record keeping desired by the owner-manager. As the economy of the United States developed, the corporate form of organization became increasingly more popular until today it is the dominant form of business organization engaged in interstate commerce. According to estimates by the New York Stock Exchange, approximately 11 million individuals own shares in publicly owned corporations. Very few of this number participate actively in the operation of the businesses in which they have invested. Instead, management is delegated to hired executives who serve as trustees for the owners. This separation of ownership and management has led to a need for authoritative and reliable standards of financial reporting.

The Federal Income Tax Act

Adoption of the Sixteenth Amendment on March 1, 1913, giving Congress power to levy taxes on income, led to Federal income tax legislation. Although tax rates in the Revenue Act of 1913 were low and the tax base excluded a large majority of individuals and businesses, the act required each taxpayer to keep accounting records that would enable him to make a proper return. This requirement changed preexisting conditions considerably. Thus, those individuals and business firms who formerly maintained accounting records solely for their own use or to meet obligations to shareholders and creditors were compelled to keep accounting records for another purpose.

More than forty different revenue acts and enabling laws have been passed by Congress since 1913. Exemptions have been steadily reduced and rates increased until today the large majority of individuals and corporations are taxed. Tax laws have, in addition, become more and more complex. Today so many business decisions have tax implications of one kind or another that successful management must be informed of these implications. As a result, demands for the services of public accountants and others familiar with tax accounting have grown at an astounding rate.

Regulatory and Fiscal Legislation of the 1930s and Early 1940s

Partly to offset the effects of the depression and partly to recognize vitally needed social changes, many significant legislative acts came into existence between 1930 and 1945. The Federal Securities and Exchange Commission was given broad authority to establish accounting procedures and reporting methods in an effort to prevent publication of misleading or fraudulent financial data. Many contributions to accounting standards had their origin in regulations issued by this agency. Social security acts, wage and hour acts, and similar legislation also contributed to the need for accounting services. To payroll accounting, formerly a problem primarily of determining wages owed to individuals, has now been added the need to determine the number of hours worked by individuals and a variety of tax deductions; also, in 1943 the problems of payroll accounting were increased by the passage of "pay-as-you-go" income tax legislation.

Personnel Movement and Union Expansion

The spread of the personnel movement in the twenties led to greater awareness on the part of many companies of the interests of employees in their companies' income reports and prospects. Expansion of labor organizations in the late thirties and through the war years also led to the development of new and large groups with a recognized interest in corporate reports. Analysis of annual reports of corporations during this period reveals a definite attempt on the part of large business to use annual reports as a means of conveying information to employees as well as to investors. Related to the growth of unions has been the need for accounting records setting forth pension obligations, checkoff dues, and other voluntary and involuntary employee deductions.

Recognition of the Social Responsibilities of Business

Along with legislative changes, development of the personnel movement, growth of labor unions, and diversification of ownership in large corporations there has been increasing recognition of the obligations of business to society. Accounting reports reflect the change in business attitudes. Large corporations devote much space in both the financial and promotional sections of their annual reports to activities of a social and civic nature.

THE SEARCH FOR ACCOUNTING CONCEPTS AND STANDARDS

The great increase in demand for the services of accountants, in both public practice and industry, unfortunately was not matched by rapid growth in the development of acceptable accounting standards of reporting. Prior to the mid-1930s, development of theory and practice in the art of accounting was based largely upon expediency. The standards that did exist stemmed mostly from early textbooks which placed great emphasis on the form of financial statements and very little upon their content and significance. Early authors, attempting to develop "principles of accounting," drifted in diverse directions. The ideas of a few whose textbooks were successful commercially were copied and established patterns for the many textbooks that followed. Thus, in the early stages, contributions to the development of accounting theory reflected individual rather than group effort. The theory which evolved was neither uniform nor consistent. Procedures and technical aspects of accounting were stressed while basic concepts were neglected. It is not surprising, in view of this emphasis upon techniques, that students of accounting prior to the mid-thirties became masters in "how-to-do-it" with limited understanding of the "why" behind accounting processes. Unfortunately this is all too often the case at many institutions today. Greater interest in principles on the part of professional and academic societies in the field of accounting since the mid-thirties has contributed much to the development of accounting standards and toward bridging the gap between procedures on the one hand and concepts on the other. The process of creating a generally accepted body of accounting theory, however, is still in the evolutionary stage.

The American Accounting Association

In 1936 the American Accounting Association, formed in 1918 as the American Association of University Instructors in Accounting, issued a statement setting forth twenty principles of accounting having general applicability to published financial reports. In its statement, the association expressed concern over the variations existing in the application of accounting principles to items appearing in annual reports and suggested as a guide a "set of principles" that was intended to become the pattern for a mandatory set of regulations. The statement of principles has since been revised four times. The latest was issued by the Association's Committee on Accounting Concepts and Standards in 1957.

The favorable reception received by the tentative statement of principles clearly endorsed the need for standards of accounting by which corporate reporting could be judged. Under the auspices of the A.A.A., W. A. Paton of the University of Michigan and A. C. Littleton of the University of Illinois prepared a monograph, *An Introduction to Corporate Accounting Standards.* The monograph attempted to replace with a "coherent, coordinated, consistent body of doctrine" the expediencies and inconsistencies which existed in corporate reports. To this day, the Paton and Littleton monograph is recognized by many as the most significant contribution to the field of accounting theory that has yet been made. While it has caused much controversy, with readers being either very enthusiastic or highly critical, it has contributed more to the development of a logical explanation of accounting than any other single work. In addition, the monograph has caused many to look again at the "folklore" of accounting and the lack of significance in many of the accountant's most prized tools.

According to Paton and Littleton, "Standards are conceived as gauges by which to measure departures, when and if departure is necessary and clearly justifiable. Standards, therefore, should not prescribe procedures or rigidly confine practices; rather standards should serve as guideposts to the best in accounting reports." Unfortunately *An Introduction to Corporate Accounting Standards* was less well received during the 1940s than might have been expected. Its release during the early stages of World War II came at a time when the accounting profession and business in general were more concerned with the problems of producing war materials and meeting the exigencies of wartime taxation and financial restrictions than with accounting theory. Although it is difficult to say exactly when the monograph became widely recognized, it is interesting to note that seven printings have been needed since 1950.

The Work of the American Institute of Certified Public Accountants

In 1939 the Committee on Accounting Procedures of the American Institute of Certified Public Accountants (formerly the American Institute of Accountants) issued the first of a series of accounting research bulletins now numbering fifty. The early bulletins were valuable contributions to the understanding of accounting procedures and reports in their attempt to achieve uniformity in the treatment of special items. The general rules set forth in the bulletins may be subject to exception and thus are not binding upon practicing accountants. The committee noted, however, in the first bulletin that "the burden of proof is upon the accountant clearly to bring out the exceptional procedure and the circumstances which render it necessary." Although the work of the committee has been outstanding, its pronouncements have not produced a body of generally accepted accounting principles. Through the years, the efforts of the committee have been devoted largely to solving pressing current problems. For example, Research Bulletin 19, entitled *Accounting under Cost-plus-fixed-fee Contracts,* issued in December, 1942, was specifically designed to aid in defensework accounting. Similarly, *Renegotiations Liability* in 1942 and *Contract Termination* in 1945 were highly specialized topics. Unfortunately the distinction between accounting procedures (ways of doing things) and accounting principles (underlying reasons for doing them) was seldom recognized by the committee. In fact, procedures and principles were quite often confused, so that it is not surprising to discover that even now among well-informed practicing accountants a clear distinction between procedure and principle is often not understood.

The need for a new approach to the development of an authoritative set of coordinated accounting principles was recognized by the AICPA in December, 1957, with the formation of a Special Committee on Research Program. The committee's report, submitted in December, 1958, recommended the creation of an Accounting Principles Board to be the sole group in the institute having authority to make pronouncements on accounting principles. The Committee suggested that the board give its attention to four levels of financial accounting: first, postulates; second, principles; third, rules or other guides for the application of principles in specific situations; and fourth, research.[1] The governing council of the AICPA accepted the report on April 22, 1959. The efforts of the AAA and AICPA, on both coordinated and independent bases, should contribute much to accounting education through research activities and by stimulating thinking in the area of accounting principles.

Securities and Exchange Commission

The Securities and Exchange Commission, through publication of *Regulations S-X,* has contributed significantly to the accountant's search for concepts and standards. The SEC is primarily concerned with the failure of companies to utilize generally accepted accounting principles in preparing the financial statements submitted to it in conjunction with registration of securities offered to the public on an organized exchange. By publishing opinions of the chief accountant of the SEC and any ob-

[1] Report to Council of the Special Committee on Research Program, *Journal of Accountancy,* vol. 106, no. 6, December, 1958.

jections raised to statements submitted to him, the SEC has influenced the attitude of practicing accountants substantially. Through publication of the regulations and SEC releases, the profession became conscious of a "doctrine of full disclosure," "principle of materiality," "doctrine of consistency," and "independence." The chief accountant of the SEC and the Committee on Accounting Procedures of the AICPA have cooperated closely since 1939. As a result, the recommendations of the AICPA and the opinions of the SEC are for the most part similar and consistent.

Federal Income Tax Regulations and the Development of Accounting Theory

Academicians argue that Federal income tax legislation should have little influence upon the development of accounting principles devoted primarily to the measurement of income for the purpose of reporting to shareholders and other interested groups. This position is reinforced when it is realized that Federal income tax legislation is designed to do substantially more than tax income. Among the many nonrevenue objectives which Congress may attain through income tax legislation are:

1. Economic stimuli to specialized industries
2. Economic penalties against other industries or activities
3. Encouragement of international trade
4. Redistribution of national income
5. Control of inflation or deflation
6. Encouragement of defense production
7. Subsidies which may be practical though not economic in nature

Because so many different objectives are served by income tax legislation, and because the definition of income is subject to legislative fiat, the tax code has not established a distinct, consistent definition of income or a body of cohesive concepts to determine income.

Unfortunately, as a result of the impact of tax legislation upon accounting, the expression "generally accepted accounting principles" is more often than not a fine-sounding but meaningless phrase. The term should refer to a body of cohesive principles, but too often it refers to contradictory concepts or widely differing procedures.

The Gap Between "Theory and Practice"

It has already been indicated that to many C.P.A.s, "principles of accounting" often mean solutions to the pressing problems of the moment. Teachers frequently hear from many of their acquaintances in public accounting such expressions as, "It may be good theory, but it won't work in practice." Such statements are based upon false reasoning, for the theory and practice of accounting are part of the same body of knowledge. More emphasis, therefore, must be placed upon the reasons behind accounting procedures and upon the need for accounting standards. The so-called "gap" between accounting theory and practice is in reality no gap at all but rather a convenient phrase used by those who have lost sight of the significance of accounting and who have bogged down in procedures and problems. If accounting is to provide management and other groups with financial data from which intelligent decisions may be made, it must be based upon a sound foundation. Furthermore, accountants must recognize that what is good accounting for tax purposes may be very bad accounting for internal management of a firm and for reporting to shareholders and other interested groups.

Development of Accounting Curricula in Business Schools from 1930 to 1950

Changes in accounting programs during the 1930s and 1940s largely reflected improvements in techniques. Such important problems as business liquidation, reorganization, renegotiation, and termination were accompanied by additions to advanced courses in accounting. Great strides were made in cost accounting as cost procedures received wider acceptance. The developing of auditing standards reflected recognition of advances in the methods already in existence. As these areas of specialized problems, cost accounting, and auditing developed, they led to greater specialization and proliferation of courses in accounting programs. Mention has already been made of the large number of specialized courses in accounting which exist at some schools of business. It appears that such proliferation has resulted from improved techniques, not from advances in theory.

To a considerable extent the teaching of accounting has been directly influenced by certification requirements of different states. New York, for example, has established rigid quantitative educational requirements which include twenty-four semester credits in accounting courses, eight semester credits in business law, eight semester credits in finance, six semester credits in economics, etc. Through strict interpretation of the law, the New York State Board of Examiners has, on occasion, determined that seminar courses are not acceptable in meeting the accounting requirement and that courses in money, credit, and banking do not meet the finance requirement. In addition, the board has not seen fit to distinguish between quantity and quality. In one case known to the writer, a student who had received a master's degree in business administration with a major in accounting was not able to obtain permission to sit for the New York State examination because he had taken only twenty-two semester credits in accounting at the graduate level. The caliber and content of the courses taken by this student and the reputation of the institution which granted the degree indicate that the twenty-two graduate credits were qualitatively equivalent to as many as thirty-three semester credits at the undergraduate level at most institutions. To overcome this "defect," this student repeated the elementary course in accounting at an evening school—apparently satisfying the New York State Board, for he was later given permission to sit for the examination. In a second instance, a partner of a national public accounting firm, holding certificates in two Eastern states, found it necessary to take a four-semester credit course in intermediate accounting at an evening school in order to qualify for a reciprocal certificate from New York.

The requirements of the New York State certified public accounting law are singled out, not because that state is alone in setting rigid requirements, but because of the influence that New York has had upon accounting curricula along the Eastern seaboard. Requirements in other states have had similar effects.

It was mentioned earlier that the demand for accountants has grown substantially during the past twenty years. Demands upon our universities to provide training in accounting at the college level have increased at a similar pace. In order to meet the "needs" of expanding student bodies during this period, accounting programs at most business schools were designed to make it possible for graduates to meet the requirements of the local C.P.A. laws and also those of important neighboring states.[2]

It is not implied that the impact of such C.P.A. requirements upon the development of accounting courses in our universities has not had some helpful results. The writer has observed, as a student adviser, that students majoring in accounting are, as a group, inclined to add as many technical courses to their programs as possible. Unrestricted, many would ignore subjects in liberal arts in order to enroll in every accounting course available. The student who may some day wish to sit for the C.P.A. examination in New York or New Jersey must exert care in selecting optional courses to complete his program. To make sure he will meet the educational requirements, he must balance sufficient courses in eco-

---

[2] The law in Pennsylvania covering C.P.A.s has been relatively lenient over the years. Even today Pennsylvania does not require the candidate to have a college degree or to complete specific courses. It would appear that accounting programs in this state could develop unhindered by restrictive C.P.A. educational requirements. Schools of business in Pennsylvania, however, are acutely aware of the requirements in New York, New Jersey, and Ohio—areas from which large numbers of students are attracted. Consequently, accounting programs throughout business schools in Pennsylvania have been strongly influenced by the laws of these three states. This same condition exists elsewhere.

nomics, finance, business law, and other business areas with courses in the liberal arts.

The AICPA in April, 1959 adopted the report of a special committee recommending that "each state consider revising its laws to set up the following qualifications for admission to practice as a certified public accountant:

1. College graduation, with about one half of the time devoted to study in the humanities and social sciences, one fourth in accounting, and one fourth in other business subjects.

2. Postgraduate professional study, as soon as it is feasible, devoted principally to accountancy and business administration.

3. As education is extended beyond the undergraduate degree, a minimum of one year's experience in public practice under the guidance of a CPA, some of which should be in the area of reliance by bankers and other third parties on the financial reports of CPA's clients." [3]

EVALUATION OF EXISTING ACCOUNTING PROGRAMS

Because program objectives, the quality of students and faculty, and the content of courses vary considerably at different levels, evaluation of existing programs in accounting will be segregated into three categories: undergraduate, graduate, and evening or extension programs. Programs offered by noncollegiate institutions or by executive development groups are not considered in this chapter.

The Major in Accounting

The curriculum for an undergraduate student majoring in accounting is composed of three basic areas, each containing required and elective courses as follows:

1. Liberal, cultural, and other nonbusiness subjects
2. General business subjects
3. Accounting studies

Although most schools of business seem to adhere, at least in appearance, if not in fact, to the basic requirements of the American Association of Collegiate Schools of Business, many variations in programs exist. Because of these differences, evaluation of all programs would be an impossible task. Instead, it is wiser to examine a program that is typical of a large number of institutions which have been accredited by the American Association of Collegiate Schools of Business. Comments per-

[3] News release, American Institute of Certified Public Accountants, Department of Public Relations, New York, April 22, 1959.

TABLE 14-1

THE TYPICAL ACCOUNTING PROGRAM

1. *Nonbusiness subjects*   *Semester credits*

Required courses:
Composition...	6
Economic principles..	6
English literature...	6
Social science, other than economics.........................	6
History..	3–6
Mathematics...	3–6
Science..	3–6
Other humanities..	3–6
Required electives...	0–9
Range...	36–51

2. *General business subjects*

Required courses:
Business law...	6
Corporation finance..	3
Industrial management or production..........................	3–6
Principles of marketing.......................................	3–6
Money and banking...	3–6
Statistics..	3–6
Others, including insurance, survey of business, mathematics of finance, and/or industrial relations...........................	0–6
Range...	30–36

3. *Accounting studies*

Required courses:
Elementary accounting principles.............................	6
Intermediate accounting principles...........................	6
Advanced accounting principles...............................	0–6
Cost accounting...	3–6
Auditing principles and procedures...........................	3–6
Income tax accounting.......................................	6
Range...	24–30

4. *Elective courses*

Generally free electives......................................	12–20
Total in program..	120–128

Note: Where ranges of semester credits are listed, consistency among programs studied did not exist; the totals shown mark the limits within which almost all the schools fall, not the sums of the two columns.

taining to other programs, including those of unaccredited institutions and those containing special features, will be made in a later section. Although the quality of the accounting program is influenced considerably by the content of the curriculum which surrounds it, only indirect attention can be given in this chapter to the nonbusiness and general business segments of the accounting program.

It might be noted how closely the "typical program" for accounting majors corresponds with the requirements of the New York State Board of Certified Public Accountant Examiners whose specifications are given in Table 14-2.

TABLE 14-2

NEW YORK STATE EDUCATIONAL REQUIREMENTS
CERTIFIED PUBLIC ACCOUNTANCY

	Semester hours of credit
Liberal arts.....................................	48
Accounting*....................................	24
Law (business law).............................	8
Finance (excluding money and credit)..............	8
Economics......................................	6
Other business subjects.........................	14
Electives......................................	12
Total......................................	120

* Seminar courses in accounting have not, on occasion, been accepted by the board.

The requirements of the state of New Jersey are similar to those of New York, except that thirty semester credits of accounting are required.

The Basic Course

Accounting serves a dual role in most schools of business. A basic course in accounting is required of all students at institutions accredited by the American Association of Collegiate Schools of Business, and usually at nonmember schools as well. In addition, the beginning course is usually designed as an introduction to the field as the first in a sequence of courses in accounting.

In recent years attempts have been made to expand the basic course to survey the main areas within the field of accounting. For example, two of the leading textbooks in elementary accounting, which are used by an estimated 60 per cent of all students taking the basic course, include fragments of cost accounting, income tax accounting, consolidated statements, budgeting, and installment sales in addition to the more traditional coverage of principles and procedures generally applicable to corporations and partnerships. Literature accompanying one of these textbooks describes the book as being designed for students intending to major in accounting, for business administration students not intending to major in accounting, and for liberal arts students who are not taking other business administration courses. Unfortunately, an elementary course in accounting may not serve these three separate objectives equally well; there is some doubt that it is achieving even two of these objectives at present.

Too much attention has been paid to introducing the student who intends to major in accounting to the field and too little to equipping the business administration student with a knowledge of underlying concepts, basic processes, and the role of accounting in the business world. Students who have been exposed to the typical basic course as part of their preparation in business administration are too often unaware of the limitations of corporate reports. While it is important that those majoring in accounting should become aware through the basic course of the underlying assumptions of accounting and the limitations of quantitative financial data, it is even more necessary that those who take only a single course in accounting should gain this knowledge. Students who continue in accounting will eventually become familiar with concepts and limitations through exposure to advanced principles, cost accounting, and specialized courses. Those who have mastered the techniques of elementary accounting but who have not acquired an understanding of concepts and standards as well as of the uses and limitations of accounting information will find themselves using financial statement data improperly later on.

For example, correlation of net income over time with measures of output—analyses frequently made by statisticians and economists—may be meaningless unless defects and inconsistencies in net income figures are removed. Similarly, the student attempting to analyze securities of corporations may unknowingly base his conclusions upon ratios containing defects or limitations of which he is unaware. Since efficiency of effort is measured throughout the field of business by accounting methods and since the tools of accounting are essential to control of men and materials, more attention should be paid in the basic course to uses and limitations of accounting and less to techniques.

At present several obstacles make this approach difficult. First, as already noted, programs have been indirectly dominated by C.P.A. requirements. Consequently, textbooks have been slanted toward professional aspects of accounting, emphasizing the techniques and procedures of accounting practice. Second, authors who have departed from the "traditional" have encountered resistance. Many teachers of elementary accounting have not been convinced that change is either necessary or desirable. Third, the basic course is commonly taken by first-year or second-year students. (Even in 2-2-year programs where elementary accounting is listed as a third-year course, it is usually taken in the sophomore year by students intending to transfer from liberal arts to the business school.) Many instructors feel beginning students are not sufficiently mature to accept a more thought-provoking approach to basic accounting. Finally, the more experienced staff members who are best equipped to adopt and present a broader and more liberal approach to elementary accounting are seldom available to handle sections of the course. When assigned to the basic course, more mature staff members have tended to "resent the waste of their talents" on beginners.

A few institutions have established two basic courses in accounting, one for those who intend to major in accounting and the other for those who do not. Although this plan is not without some merit as an attempt to deal with a difficult problem, there are certain objections. First, it requires the student, before he has been exposed to accounting, to determine whether he will select that field as a major. Second, it assumes that the background in accounting for business administration students who will not take additional work in accounting should be different from that of students who will. Generally the separate course for nonmajors deemphasizes some of the specialized techniques and requires the students to solve fewer practice problems. The time saved by these omissions is sometimes used for survey topics, such as elements of cost accounting, budgeting, and tax accounting which are not covered in the regular course. In other instances, the material is covered at a more leisurely pace, with the result that nonmajors devote the same number of class hours to the subject but cover only two-thirds as much. In a smaller number of instances, the course for nonmajors has been developed along the lines suggested earlier, i.e., with greater emphasis upon uses and limitations of accounting and less upon techniques. In at least one institution where this occurred, the staff decided that the nonmajor course was superior to that required of students intending to major. As a result, the broader course is now required of all students, including accounting majors.

Widespread adoption of a more useful elementary course in accounting is not likely to take place in the immediate future. First, there must be a change in attitude on the part of those responsible for establishing curriculum policy within the schools of business. There appears today to be ever greater recognition of "managerial accounting" as contrasted to "professional accounting." Whether this recognition constitutes a movement or is just a ripple only time will tell. Second, young inexperienced teachers are apt to "stick close to the book." Until such time as elementary textbooks adopt a new viewpoint, classroom teaching will be determined by textbook content. The problem may be alleviated somewhat by having mature, experienced teachers lecture to multi-section groups on general topics, such as accounting concepts and standards, uses and limitations of accounting, and the relationship of accounting to other fields of activity. Such lectures could account for one-fourth to one-third of the time allotted to the course. The remaining time could be handled by younger staff members in small quiz sections and in laboratory sections. Proper integration of broader aspects of accounting with fundamental processes is vital. Where the lecture-and-quiz system has been used, integration has been achieved to a very limited extent, with the result that students tended to apply themselves to the materials for which they felt they would be held in examinations.

Other Courses

Intermediate Accounting Principles. This course, which is required of all accounting majors and which, in whole or in part, is required of all business administration students at many institutions, usually examines at greater depth the general area covered by the second part of the elementary course. Accordingly, balance-sheet categories, such as cash, investments, plant and equipment, etc., are examined from three different viewpoints, namely, (1) nature and content of the asset or equity category, (2) accounting transactions giving rise to changes in the category, with emphasis upon income statement effects, and (3) special analytical problems or situations related to the item. In addition, other topics, not previously introduced in the basic course, are covered, such as, Statement of Funds, Analysis of Changes in Profit, and Statements from Incomplete Records. In most instances, materials covered in the first course and duplicated in the second course are examined in greater depth and breadth.

Although authors of intermediate accounting textbooks have tried to incorporate more theory into their books in recent years, their attempts have not been altogether successful. Unfortunately, the term "accounting theory" has come to mean different things to different persons. To some it means a body of accounting concepts woven through all accounting courses and representing an important (if not the most important) part of materials presented to the student. To others it represents an isolated course in the field or a chapter in a book related to other accounting subjects but treated as an independent area. Another group believes accounting theory consists of articles or collections of readings covering different aspects of the field of accounting in general. For example, a widely used reference book bearing the words "accounting theory" in its title is a collection of essays on different aspects of accounting, covering such topics as government influence upon accounting, asset cost and expiration, responsibilities of the internal auditor, and the future of accounting. The book, which might better be entitled *Readings in Accounting*, introduces basic concepts and their applications to business problems but does little more than scratch the surface. It does not present a body of logic, nor is the "theory" consistent throughout.

In general, few undergraduate courses in intermediate accounting have done more than give lip service to integrating concepts with procedures. The majority of intermediate courses today concentrate upon accounting exercises. In this regard most are useful to the student looking forward to the C.P.A. examination.

However, many excellent courses with high standards exist in intermediate accounting. In general, this course is not a "snap course." Defects in most courses in intermediate accounting are associated with unnecessary duplication, inadequate attention to concepts and standards, and overemphasis upon technical aspects.

Adoption of changes in elementary accounting along the lines discussed earlier would contribute much to improving the second course. Emphasis upon underlying concepts and fundamental processes and concentration upon managerial uses of accounting data in the elementary course could well lead to improved integration of theory and practice in the second course. In addition, complete revision of the second half of the elementary course would eliminate the undesirable duplication of subject matter in both courses.

Advanced Accounting Principles. This course, sometimes called Advanced Accounting or Advanced Accounting Problems, deals with specialized technical problems in the area of general accounting. Such topics as partnership admissions and liquidations, consolidated statements, specialized statements prepared for companies in financial difficulties, fiduciary accounting, and installment sales are usually included in the course. The term "general accounting" is applicable to this course, since the subjects discussed are broadly applicable to different segments of industry, including manufacturing, retail establishments, wholesale distributors, and service institutions. The term "specialized accounting" is also appropriate, since the problems presented are highly technical and are not usually encountered on a recurring basis.

Advanced Accounting Principles is commonly offered on a one- or two-semester basis, carrying from three to six credits. It is required of all accounting majors at many schools and is recommended for majors as an elective at other schools. As in the case of intermediate accounting, the nature and content of the course have been patterned after advanced accounting textbooks, which are generally quite similar. While sections of books in the area seem to be organized along logical lines covering broad areas of partnerships, consolidations, fiduciary accounting, actuarial science, etc., the topics covered do not follow a common theme. Historically, the introduction of new subjects has appeared to follow by one year the inclusion of such subjects in the C.P.A. examination given by the American Institute of Certified Public Accountants.

The course would probably be improved considerably if it were restricted to valuation of the firm under conditions of continuity, reorganization or combination, and liquidation. With this as a common denominator, actuarial or compound interest computations would be treated as part of the problems of valuation and not as an isolated topic, and consolidated statements would be but one part of the larger problem of business combinations. (One leading advanced accounting textbook devotes eleven chapters covering 250 pages to the highly technical subject of parent and subsidiary accounting, approached in a rather mechanical manner.) Further improvements could be gained by transferring certain materials, such as installment sales and long-term contracts, from the advanced course to the intermediate course. These topics are part of the broader topic of revenue measurement and recognition, generally considered essential to intermediate accounting.

Cost Accounting. Cost accounting broadly covers the determination and control of costs in manufacturing and service enterprises. It differs from manufacturing accounting mainly in degree. The latter determines over-all costs of production during a specified period. The former makes it possible to compute and account for costs by departments, job lots, production processes, etc. Materials presented in cost accounting courses stem from the general principles covered in basic accounting, but branch out into a separate area. In large part the principles and procedures discussed are general in nature, although more specialized topics are included in the course.

Emphasis in the typical cost accounting course has been placed upon methodology, with insufficient attention paid to the inadequacies of cost-determining procedures. For example, many classroom and study hours are devoted to computations of unit costs of producing products in a department during a specific period of time. End results are carried out to six or more decimal places. The student is often unaware of the assumptions upon which costs were initially determined and, consequently, fails to recognize the many limitations that tend to make his computations less meaningful. Similarly, much time is spent in calculating favorable and unfavorable variances from standards, and little time is spent in evaluating the variances and determining what corrective action might be taken. While the content of cost accounting courses has changed in the past ten years, with greater emphasis placed upon cost analysis, this improvement has come largely from refinements in techniques.

Currently, the typical accounting program requires of all majors from three to six semester credits of cost accounting. Schools requiring the smaller number of credits usually cover only cost determination and job order cost accounting—two topics which are mainly procedural. Schools requiring additional cost accounting cover process costs and standard costs and, occasionally, cost analysis. Some duplication in topics exists between the general courses in accounting and cost analysis. For example, analysis of profits, including break-even analysis, is found in elementary or intermediate accounting. The same topic is covered in cost accounting. Similarly, inventory costing methods and the mechanics of computing charges to production are discussed in general accounting and covered in greater detail in cost accounting. Through improved coordination between the three courses in principles and cost accounting, and with less emphasis upon procedures, materials in cost accounting essential to a major could be covered in three or four semester credits. These materials would include cost accumulation, job-order and process costs and standard costs and analysis pertaining to the manufacturing company. Eliminating practice sets which take a long time to solve and provide doubtful benefits would help to bring this course within reasonable bounds.

Auditing. This course is devoted primarily to the application of auditing standards and procedures to the examination of financial statements by the independent public accountant. The course is designed primarily for those intending to become certified public accountants, although a knowledge of auditing principles is important to the internal auditor and to the comptroller of a company and benefits accounting students who do not intend to pursue careers in public accounting.

In 1947 the Committee on Auditing Procedure of the American Institute of Certified Public Accountants issued its first tentative statement on auditing standards. In 1954 this report was augmented by a statement entitled "Generally Accepted Auditing Standards—Their Significance and Scope." The work of the AICPA in developing auditing standards contributed much to the improvement of courses in auditing during the past ten years.

A significant part of the auditing course at most schools is a case or practice set designed to acquaint the student with auditing procedures and reports similar to those for which he will be responsible in public practice. Use of such practice sets may duplicate procedures in the training courses provided for new employees by the large national public accounting firms. On the other hand, the small firms which employ a large number of accounting graduates usually do not provide their own training programs and expect the auditing course to provide this background. In any event, the effectiveness of the cases is debatable.

In recent years, particularly since World War II, public accountants have been called upon to provide many types of special services other than those of examinations of accounting records and reports. These services include development and modification of organization plans, assistance in the installation of data-processing equipment, preparation of capital budgets and other forecasts, assistance in management incentives and pension programs, economy studies, and other analyses not ordinarily considered part of the year-end audit program. Managements have looked to the public accounting firms to provide such services because of their high professional standing in the business community. Courses which heretofore have been oriented toward technical aspects of auditing should be broadened in the future. A greater degree of coordination between accounting courses and elective courses in finance and management could contribute materially to better understanding of the wide range of problems which are faced by the public accountant.

Many of the basic principles of auditing applied by independent public accountants to examinations also pertain to internal auditing and internal control, both important aspects of the comptrollership function. Similarly, the accounting or financial officer within the firm may be called upon frequently to deal with the management problems mentioned above for which the services of public accountants are sometimes used. It is quite likely that auditing principles and procedures essential to industrial or governmental accounting will be very similar to those considered applicable to public accounting. It is doubtful that the differences will be great enough to merit two separate courses.

Income Tax Accounting. Although the number of semester credits assigned to required work in income tax accounting varies greatly (from two to six) and the topics covered range from an introduction to individual income taxes to corporate taxes and tax planning and saving, a course in income tax accounting is almost always required of accounting majors. Nearly every major business decision made today is affected by tax considerations. Because tax regulations permit alternative methods of computing taxable income under different circumstances, it is the executive's responsibility to make decisions which will maximize both the short-run and long-run return to the shareholders. Many of these decisions will be made by the comptroller; others will be made by other members of the management team with assistance and advice from accountants. Thus the accountant needs more than the ability to prepare tax returns if he is to serve this function well; he needs in addition to have a conceptual approach to tax accounting—to understand the "why" of tax accounting as well as the "how."

Currently, the content of the income tax course is largely determined by the coverage found in textbooks prepared and published by Prentice-

Hall, Inc., and Commerce Clearing House. These two tax books are used by over 90 per cent of all institutions offering a basic income tax course. Although both these companies gather opinions of accounting staffs at many colleges and seek assistance from consulting editors, the organization, content, and method of presentation are determined by the companies themselves. As income tax regulations have become more and more complex, new subjects have been added to the tax course and existing topics have been expanded, with the result that many schools have found it necessary to increase the time allotted to income tax accounting.

It is the writer's opinion that required work in taxation is as essential to the accounting curriculum as advanced accounting and cost accounting. Coverage should be limited to the basic principles of income taxes as they pertain to individuals and corporations. Every effort should be made by teachers to explain the logic or reasoning behind certain tax regulations and the effects of these provisions upon the business entity and the economy. Topics currently found in the two widely used textbooks, such as installment and deferred payment sales, estates and trusts, corporate reorganizations, personal holding companies, social security taxes, and many rarely encountered refinements of other matters should not be included in the required course. Many of these topics will have been discussed in preceding accounting courses, although admittedly they will have treated tax aspects only to a limited extent.

The goal is to provide the accounting student with an understanding of the major features of income tax regulations, their application to business situations, the reasoning behind these provisions, and their impact upon the business firm. Although the student will be expected to deal with tax problems of varied types, he will not be an "expert" tax accountant upon completion of the course. Rather he will have a broad understanding of the importance of income taxes in the business world and will be in a better position to recognize the impact of tax regulations upon his future decisions as a manager.

Elective Courses. A wide variety of courses is offered the accounting student on an elective basis in the schools whose composite accounting curriculum was presented earlier. Among those which appear with some regularity are Advanced Tax Accounting, Cost Analysis, System Design and Installation, Budgeting, Governmental Accounting, and C.P.A. Review. Other courses, such as Data Processing, Specialized Accounting Systems, Retail Accounting, Accounting for Public Utilities, Cost Systems, Standard Cost Accounting, Accounting Theory, and Accounting Seminar are offered but on a less common basis.

Elective courses add materially to a program by permitting students to delve more deeply into a subject in which they have a special interest.

It was noted earlier that the subject of accounting may be subdivided into areas such as cost accounting and analysis, auditing and control, financial accounting, etc. Opportunities in the field may also be divided into careers in industrial accounting, governmental accounting, public accounting, etc. As is true in other professions and in other fields of endeavor, some specialization is justified in the accounting program. The point at which desirable specialization changes to undesirable proliferation of courses is difficult to determine. As a general guide, elective courses should cover broad areas examined in depth. In these courses, underlying principles should be given primary consideration, although technical aspects not considered necessary in required courses may be covered.

Of greater importance than the number of elective courses available to all accounting students are the number and type that a single student will be able to include in his program. Graduation requirements and major specifications are very misleading in this regard. In all too many universities, catalog specifications indicate that the student will receive broad preparation in the humanities, in general business subjects, and in the field of concentration. Actually, the student is permitted to take every course offered in his field of concentration to satisfy elective credits, thus limiting exposure to nonbusiness courses to the bare minimum. Requirements in the humanities and fields outside the major are often so loosely established that the student is able to avoid courses which would benefit him but which have a reputation of being more difficult than others.

For example, at one institution six semester credits covering the broad areas of laboratory science, mathematics, or foreign language are required of all business administration students. Over 90 per cent of all students at this school select a general course in psychology to satisfy the requirement. Less than one-tenth of 1 per cent choose natural science and less than 2 per cent elect a foreign language. At this same institution, it has been observed that a large number of students deliberately choose "snap" courses for electives to be filled from courses outside their major fields.[4] The writer does not pretend to judge the value of many of the elective courses outside the business field (or within it) whose popularity appears to be in direct proportion to the high grades given and to the lack of homework. The student may receive much benefit from, say, Clog Dancing 102. If, however, a sizable number of students suddenly develop an interest in two or three clog dancing courses and include them in their programs, one may be justified in suspecting their motives.

[4] Judging from the data reviewed in Chap. 8, the situation at this institution is typical of many schools.

A Recommended Undergraduate Program

Managerial Accounting. Reference has been made in different sections of this chapter to "managerial accounting." The term needs clarifying because, with its popularity increasing in the past few years, it has been used in many different ways. To some, for example, "managerial accounting" means narrowly the subject content of textbooks bearing such a title. Topics in these books include analysis of financial statements, profit planning, budgeting, break-even analysis, funds statements, elements of consolidated statements, etc. Although no discernible pattern has as yet emerged, all textbooks in this relatively new area emphasize uses of accounting data for managerial purposes. Some are designed as substitutes for an introductory course in accounting principles; others are more advanced and require knowledge of basic concepts. "Managerial accounting" is sometimes used as a new name for an abbreviated course in cost accounting designed for students who want a basic course in cost control and cost analysis but do not wish to take the courses required of accounting majors. Occasionally the term is used to refer to all accounting not oriented toward public practice. To still others, "managerial accounting" represents a point of view, not a course or group of courses. The name assumes an attitude toward the functions of accounting regardless of the student's intent to be a public accountant or an industrial accountant or to follow another career in which knowledge of accounting is vital. It is in this latter meaning of the term that "managerial accounting" is used here.

A growing number of leaders in the field of accounting education are concerned over the tendency of the curriculum to become more and more technical, with excessive emphasis upon a narrow concept of public accountancy. Many believe that the accountant of tomorrow must be more broadly trained, capable of handling problems far afield from those encountered by the accountant of yesteryear. The man going into public practice must be equipped to recognize and solve problems of reorganization, valuation, forecasting, fixed- and variable-cost analyses, and other perplexing issues of the business world. Auditing will be only a small part of his work. As new and fantastically rapid electronic equipment is produced, he will be called upon to assist business organizations in selecting and installing units which will economically and adequately serve their needs. He will be called upon to manage professional engagements, branches, and districts. To deal with such problems, the accountant must be capable of making business decisions or providing data which are needed for such decisions. His training must, of necessity, include all elements of "decision making" as well as an accounting background. The profession of public accountancy can ill afford to accept an educational program for students intending to go into public practice which is lower in quality and more narrowly oriented than that designed for students who will seek employment as accountants with industrial organizations.

A program designed for business schools which desire to provide the broad type of training discussed above within a limitation of fifteen semester credits is presented in Table 14-3. Those schools which wish to

TABLE 14-3

RECOMMENDED PROGRAM ORIENTATION IN ACCOUNTING

Semester credits

Required foundation courses:

Accounting Fundamentals..	3	
Applications of Accounting Data to the Administrative Process...........	2	
Total...		5

Required advanced accounting courses:

Concepts and Procedures of Financial Accounting......................	6	
Administrative Controls and Analyses................................	4	
Total...		10
Total required in accounting..		15

Recommended as related course:

Taxation and Business Policy..	3	
Total...		18

prepare undergraduate students for immediate careers in public accounting will find it necessary to provide elective courses in addition to those suggested in the program. Although four or five specialized courses might be established, the student should not be permitted to select more than two such courses. The recommended program envisages a fresh approach to the teaching of accounting. Although existing accounting materials can be used, reorganization of traditional sequences of elementary, intermediate, and advanced principles would seem desirable.

Accounting Fundamentals. The objective of this course is to introduce the student to the basic concepts and procedures essential to an understanding of the accounting functions of collecting, summarizing, and presenting financial information of the business organization. Record-keeping procedures should be minimized but not eliminated, since an adequate knowledge of how transactions originate and are recorded is necessary to an understanding of the uses and limitations of accounting. Problem assignments and short reports should be used. However, lengthy repetitive practice sets should be replaced by shorter cases designed to emphasize principles and their applications to accounting situations.

Application of Accounting Data to the Administrative Process. A second foundation course emphasizes the uses of accounting reports and analytical tools. It is designed to acquaint students, whether they plan to continue accounting studies or not, with the contributions accounting makes to the operation and management of the business. Elementary analysis of financial statements, break-even analysis, evaluation of inventory methods, depreciation procedures, budgetary control, fund statements, and similar subjects illustrate the types of topics which should be presented in this course. Problems involving computations and preparation of financial statements and reports should be assigned, but emphasis should be placed upon discussion of the significance, uses, and limitations of each statement or tool.

Concepts and Procedures of Financial Accounting. This course, covering two semesters, continues with the examination of concepts and procedures introduced in the foundation courses. As the title indicates, theory and practice of financial accounting are combined so that each supplements the other. Emphasis should be directed toward the determination of income and financial position of the business organization. Consideration should be given to such topics as price-level adjustments, revenue recognition, allocation of applicable costs, expansion and contraction of the firm, and similar problems which deal with the relationship of management to contributors of capital and other interested parties. Cases and problems may be included as an important part of the course, but should not be emphasized to the exclusion of written reports and analyses.

Administrative Controls and Analyses. This course deals with the role of accounting in the internal management of the firm. The staff function of providing information for the use of line executives is emphasized. Fixed and variable relationships, accumulation and presentation of data under job-order and process-cost systems, use of standards, direct costing, differential costs, and similar topics should be covered. Content of the course will deal largely, but not exclusively, with manufacturing companies. Technical details of cost calculations should be minimized. Although practice sets are not necessary, cases should be used extensively.

Taxation and Business Policy. This course is recommended as an advanced course available to all students, but is especially designed for those taking the accounting program. Depending upon the organization of the school, it could be taught by members of the finance department, by members of the accounting department, or on an integrated basis by members of several departments. It is not intended to be a course in income tax accounting, but rather a broad examination of the major taxes imposed by Federal and state governments, the impact of these taxes upon business decisions, and economic reasons for the ways in which taxes are imposed, calculated, and assessed. Major issues such as taxation of capital gains, percentage depletion, small business provisions of tax regulations, and use of tax legislation to accomplish governmental objectives other than raising of revenue should be discussed.

ACCOUNTING EDUCATION AT THE GRADUATE LEVEL

An earlier chapter noted that the growth in business education at the master's level has been accompanied by the development of programs whose "trademarks" are associated with specific schools. Thus one finds such expressions as "the case method," "decision making," "management school," and "science of administration." In most instances the programs of these schools are sufficiently atypical to merit some special identification. In some cases, however, it must be admitted the program is quite ordinary, although a glorified name leads prospective students to believe otherwise.

The same is true of accounting programs at the graduate level. Such identifications as "graduate school of professional accountancy," "M.B.A. in accounting," and "management accounting" are commonly encountered.

The Master's Program in Accounting

In 1956 the Task Committee on Standards of Accounting Instruction of the American Accounting Association conducted a survey of American universities offering master's degrees in business administration or management.[5] Of 133 schools which responded to the questionnaire, 86 offered a master's degree with concentration in accounting. The master's program at 76 of these was designed for students with undergraduate degrees in business administration. Twenty-five schools offered a master's program which required little or no prior study of business subjects. (It should be noted that at least fifteen schools offered master's degrees in accounting to both groups of students.)

Thus two master's programs in accounting exist: (1) those designed for students who have had several accounting courses at the undergraduate level and (2) those emphasizing accounting but designed primarily

[5] "Preliminary Master's Degree Curriculum," Report of the Task Committee, *Accounting Review*, American Accounting Association, vol. 32, no. 3, July, 1957, pp. 362–368.

for students without prior training in accounting. There are variations of these basic plans. In addition, both types may be offered within the framework of the master's degree program. For example, a student with an undergraduate degree in business administration including several courses in accounting may receive waivers for similar courses at the graduate level, including core courses. He would then be able to complete requirements for the master's degree in two semesters. On the other hand, the student with an undergraduate degree in liberal arts, engineering, or other nonbusiness fields may find it necessary to take four semesters of work to complete the requirements.

Master's Programs of the First Category

These programs are generally oriented toward professional accountancy. The student, having completed several accounting courses at the undergraduate level, is exposed to specialized, advanced courses, such as Advanced Tax Accounting, Tax Planning and Tax Savings, Advanced Auditing Theory, Comptrollership, etc. In addition, he may be required to take one or two core courses, such as Management Concepts or Business Policy, for which waivers for undergraduate equivalents are not granted.

At more than a few institutions, the type of master's program described above is in reality a fifth year of undergraduate-level work in which specialized courses are taken. Programs of this type are more often found at institutions having an undergraduate program in business administration to which students are admitted after they complete two years of liberal arts. In order to complete a sufficient number of courses at an advanced level to qualify for professional examinations and practice, students occasionally find it necessary to enroll in a fifth year of accounting, during which time it is also convenient to obtain an M.B.A. or M.S. degree. Although standards of admission to graduate programs are generally high and may be expected to be higher in the future, many students of average or less than average ability have been admitted to "fifth-year M.B.A. programs" in the past as an automatic process.

Occasionally it is difficult to distinguish between graduate and undergraduate courses in programs leading to master's degrees in accounting under the fifth-year arrangement. At some institutions combined sections of advanced undergraduates and graduate students are tolerated for budgetary reasons. In others the practice is common. At one school with an excellent reputation in business education, fifteen courses open to both undergraduates and graduates are offered in accounting. One cannot help but wonder toward which group the courses are addressed!

Master's Programs of the Second Category

These programs are designed primarily for students without prior background in business administration. They tend to include fewer specialized accounting courses. Core courses in other business subjects are generally integrated into the over-all master's program and are approached from a broad or liberal point of view.

Accounting courses in these programs generally are different in nature and quality from courses serving similar purposes at the undergraduate level. More emphasis is placed upon managerial uses of accounting data in courses in principles. Because the amount of time in which a master's candidate must acquire a thorough knowledge of accounting is limited to four semesters, the usual sequence of subjects common to undergraduate and five-year programs must be modified considerably. Thus it is necessary to develop courses to meet the needs of graduate students instead of fitting graduate students into existing courses. In many respects, courses within programs in the second category are more truly of graduate level than many of those in the programs designed for students with undergraduate business administration training. On the other hand, the student who has had accounting training will be eligible to take more advanced and specialized courses than those available to the student without prior training.

It should be noted that, regardless of the type of program emphasized, the quality of the offerings in accounting is either strengthened or weakened by the quality of the core courses in the M.B.A. program and by the degree of integration and coordination between functional areas.

Curriculum—M.B.A. in Accounting

Accounting courses at the master's level must meet three demands—a course or courses for all candidates for the degree, courses required of students concentrating in accounting but available to students majoring in other areas, and courses available only to accounting students.

Accounting Courses Required of All M.B.A. Students. The primary purpose of work in accounting required of all master's candidates is to provide them with a thorough understanding of the uses and limitations of accounting data, whether they intend to concentrate in accounting or in another field. M.B.A. students should be thoroughly familiar with the assumptions upon which accounting standards are based. In addition, they must understand the processes by which accounting data are collected, tabulated, summarized, and presented. Through dealings with these processes, the student will be capable of recognizing the limitations of accounting. The objectives summarized above can be adequately presented in a one-semester three-credit course.

A second course is designed to assist the M.B.A. student in developing skill in the proper use of accounting data and reports for management purposes. From this course, he should be able to recognize the purposes for which general-purpose statements, such as the balance sheet and the income statement, may and may not be used. He should become familiar with the construction, content, and use of special-purpose reports to management, including price-level statements, funds statements, manufacturing statements, and appraisals of performance. He should study broad issues in accounting, such as replacement cost and historical cost controversies, inventory methods, conflicting concepts of net income, and impact of tax regulations upon the determination of income. Emphasis in the second course should be upon interpretation and analysis of accounting data and the utility of accounting to management. From two to three credit hours will be required for one semester to achieve these goals.

A third course (one semester, two credits) dealing with the place of information flow in decision making should also be required of all M.B.A. students. This course should deal with data processing, including uses of electronic equipment. Emphasis should be placed upon economic and human problems of adapting computers to business and not upon "hardware" or techniques. In many institutions the course in Information Flow and Data Processing would be taught by members of the accounting staff. In others it could be handled by representatives of the management, statistics, or finance departments. In still others it could be taught on an integrated basis by several departments. The latter approach is highly desirable inasmuch as the subject matter of this course calls for the talents of several functional areas.

Accounting Courses Required of Majors and Open to Nonmajors. Knowledge derived from the study of advanced principles courses or from selected specialized accounting courses is of particular use to students concentrating in functional fields. For example, a student majoring in production will find Cost Accounting or Cost Control an excellent addition to his studies. Similarly, a student majoring in finance is better equipped to understand his field through study of Concepts and Procedures of Financial Accounting.

Courses Required of Accounting Majors. Advanced courses in accounting required of all students majoring in this subject should be limited to those dealing with principles of financial accounting and administrative accounting. The programs within the accounting major should be sufficiently flexible to permit the student's adviser to recommend other courses in accounting and other fields to fit the student's needs and background. The three courses required of all accounting majors would be:

1. *Concepts and procedures of financial accounting.* This course is an extension of the basic courses required of all candidates for the degree. It deals with analysis of concepts and standards and their application to income determination, statement preparation, and interpretation and to similar major problems of financial accounting. Contrasts between income tax methods of determining income and those acceptable for use in the preparation of reports to contributors of capital should be explored. Theory and practice should be merged without treating either one as a separate segment of the course. In addition to assigned readings and cases, students should study pronouncements, controversial issues, and current topics published by accounting societies, regulatory bodies, and accounting periodicals.

2. *Problems of valuation.* This course deals with the complex accounting problems of valuation encountered when the entity is dissolved, reorganized, or expanded. The emphasis should not be on specialized topics but on the application of concepts and standards to such general subjects as price level adjustments, foreign exchange, and productivity analyses.

3. *Administrative controls and analyses.* This course emphasizes the use of accounting as a tool in the internal management of the firm. Concepts of cost accumulation and presentation, application and analysis of standards, fixed and variable relationships, and special cost reports as they pertain to job-order and process-cost systems should be considered. It should also include specialized analysis devices not covered in other courses required of all students, such as differential costs, budgeting, and profit-control measures.

Elective Courses. Other accounting courses available to majors will undoubtedly vary from school to school. Those most essential to prepare students for both professional and industrial accounting would include: Auditing, Tax Accounting, and Comptrollership. Although additional courses, such as System Design and Installation, Distribution Cost Analysis, Tax Planning, C.P.A. Problems, Governmental Accounting, and Machine Accounting, undoubtedly make important contributions to the field of accounting, a single graduate school of business should not attempt to include more than two or three such courses in its program. Those included should be carefully coordinated with the more general courses of the program to avoid unnecessary duplication. Proliferation of courses should be avoided, since it does not strengthen a program; it weakens it.

The curriculum suggested for accounting majors in the master's program is designed to fit the needs of those who intend to enter public

accounting as well as those who look forward to careers with private industry. The suggested course of study is concerned first of all with the
development of a sound educational program designed to enable the
student to handle management responsibilities in future years. The program is only secondarily concerned with professional requirements of the
different states. Progress in accounting education, particularly at the
graduate level, has been hindered by the rigid C.P.A. requirements of
several states. It may be hoped that these states will recognize the utility
of graduate programs developed to produce well-rounded persons with
management potential and, therefore, will introduce a greater degree of
flexibility into their requirements. Until this occurs, it will undoubtedly
be necessary, under the recommended program, for students who intend
to sit for the C.P.A. examination to take additional specialized courses in
accounting, business law, and finance at an evening or extension school
after graduation. Under the suggested curriculum, a student seeking to
sit for the C.P.A. examination in New Jersey would lack from eight to
twelve semester credits in accounting, five credits in business law, and
from three to five credits in finance.

TABLE 14-4

RECOMMENDED M.B.A. PROGRAM—MAJOR IN ACCOUNTING

Semester credits

Required of all M.B.A. students:

Fundamentals of Accounting	3
Managerial Uses of Accounting	2–3
Information Flow and Data Processing	2
Total	7–8

Required of all accounting majors:

Concepts and Procedures of Financial Accounting	3
Accounting Problems of Valuation	3
Administrative Controls and Analyses	3
Total	9

Optional courses (two to be selected):

Auditing Standards and Procedures	3
Tax Accounting	2
Advanced Tax Accounting	2
Accounting Systems Design	2
Comptrollership	2
Total	4–5

The program recommended for master's candidates majoring in accounting and that proposed for undergraduates are similar in many respects. The primary objective of each program is to provide the student with broad understanding of both conceptual and technical aspects of accounting. The programs are oriented toward managerial uses of accounting but at the same time are designed to equip the student with ability to excel in professional, private, or governmental positions in accounting or related fields.

The programs differ mainly in the degree to which the individual student is expected to undertake independent investigation and in the depth of analysis required. Because high-quality, mature students with broad undergraduate training are admitted to the M.B.A. program on a selective basis, a high proportion of these students may expect to end up with bona fide management positions—a goal which will be achieved by a smaller percentage of undergraduates.

Graduate Programs of Professional Accountancy

In 1956 the Commission on Standards of Education and Experience for Certified Public Accountants sponsored by the AICPA and other professional and educational societies published its report setting forth recommendations pertaining to the education of accountants intending to go into public practice.[6] The commission recommended the development of a type of curriculum which would be new in accounting but which had long been tested in other professions. It did not advocate the mere addition of a fifth year of academic study or completion of existing master's degree programs. In this connection the report recommended "establishment of professional (post graduate) programs, designed to follow an undergraduate curriculum with a major in accounting. . . . It is anticipated that the accounting curricula at the undergraduate level could be restricted to basic courses in principles, leaving to the postgraduate professional program the specialized and professional aspects of preparation for public accountancy." [7]

As might be expected, this recommendation was followed by programs designed to conform with the commission's basic idea. As of the present time, however, no single program has come into existence which adheres to the recommendation precisely. Several universities offering M.B.A. programs of the first category have expanded their course offerings to make it possible for graduate students to take additional specialized

---

[6] *Standards of Education and Experience for Certified Public Accountants,* Bureau of Business Research, University of Michigan Press, Ann Arbor, Michigan, 1956.

[7] *Ibid.,* p. 131.

courses over and above those taken in undergraduate programs. Other schools have introduced new programs which permit greater specialization. For example, a Midwestern university which had previously offered only a master's degree oriented toward management principles and practices introduced an "M.B.A. in accounting."

Unless the professional programs suggested by the commission are developed with care, the dangers of overspecialization and proliferation of courses exist. The accounting profession needs well-rounded young people who will be capable of dealing with broad business problems. It is true that these people will need sound training in accounting principles and practices, but requiring or even encouraging the student to take a large number of narrow, technical courses will not provide this training.

"Postgraduate professional accounting programs," if established, should be developed within the framework of high-quality master's programs, thus making it possible for "professional accounting" to draw upon the courses in Policy Making, Decision Making, Concepts of Administration, and other management courses forming the core of the master's program. The professional accounting programs should not be created as isolated institutes or evening-school programs, unless practitioners and educators are willing to tolerate narrowly trained technicians.

The issues involved may be noted at an Eastern university with a moderate-sized undergraduate school of business which established a "Graduate School of Professional Accountancy" in 1956. Unlike the program recommended by the commission, which called for studies in professional accountancy at the graduate level to follow an undergraduate major in accounting, the program was designed primarily for students with liberal arts backgrounds. On paper the curriculum calls for sufficient courses in accounting and other business subjects to qualify graduates to sit for the C.P.A. examination in the state in which the university is located.

The program has not been in existence sufficiently long nor have enough students graduated and entered practice for a fair evaluation to be made. As the program has been created, however, it contains basic defects which may or may not be corrected in time. For example, required business and accounting courses are waived if the student has had similar courses at the undergraduate level. Nonaccounting business courses required for graduation are sandwiched in at convenient intervals throughout the year. To illustrate, a course in principles of marketing may be taken between the spring and summer sessions, or at any other time it can be squeezed in. At the present time the courses offered are not, in truth, graduate-level courses. In fact, because of lack of integration of materials, lack of coordination between courses, widespread waiver of required courses, and the elementary character of the courses, the program cannot be considered a contribution to accounting education, at least as it is currently offered.

The Doctorate Program in Accounting

There are several different types of doctorate programs with concentration in accounting. For example, a Ph.D. in economics with a major in accounting is a common arrangement. Frequently, applied fields, in addition to accounting, form part of the program. The Ph.D. in accounting is of more recent vintage, having become popular in the past ten years. Most common of all is the Ph.D. in business administration or the doctorate in business administration (D.B.A.) which provides for a major in accounting.

The quality of programs within these plans varies greatly. A few of the Ph.D. or D.B.A. programs in accounting are little more than glorified master's programs. Others are high-level programs comparable to the finest doctorate programs in other fields.

As with the master's degree, the quality of the doctorate program in accounting depends as much upon the nature of requirements outside the field of accounting as it does upon the accounting courses. In fact, few, if any, formal accounting courses should be needed for the student who has completed the master's program. Emphasis should be placed instead upon seminar discussions and research.

Seminars in the Doctorate Program. Financial accounting concepts and developments and managerial accounting concepts and developments are two broad areas which lend themselves to seminar discussions. These topics cut across all segments of accounting and, at the same time, form the basis for integration of accounting and other functional areas of business. Current developments in accounting theory and practice should form an important part of each seminar.

The Thesis in the Doctorate Program. Interdisciplinary topics of research are highly desirable in the doctorate program in accounting. In the first place, accounting principles and procedures deal with business transactions and reports which arise from different segments of the firm. Secondly, the contributions which can be made toward improved understanding of the functional areas of business through accounting analysis are unlimited. In general, while the requirements of the Ph.D. or D.B.A. program must govern the thesis, it should be analytical in nature and must contribute to a better understanding of accounting and the impact of accounting upon business activities. Mere reporting of current practices or description of existing accounting systems should not be acceptable.

The Role of Evening Courses in Accounting

As will be noted in Chap. 22, many students attend evening courses in business administration. Among evening and extension school offerings, accounting often exceeds any other functional area or subject in both the number of courses offered and the number of students enrolled. In evening programs in some metropolitan areas, as much as 50 per cent of total student hours is in accounting.

Although a high proportion of the evening programs in accounting offer degree programs, it must be recognized that only a small percentage of students obtain degrees. Those who are familiar with evening school programs are aware that a sizable number of students in evening programs, perhaps a majority, enroll in order to take isolated courses which will better equip them for their jobs, but have no intention of taking the degree program.

Accounting courses in evening programs serve these two objectives in several ways. Elementary and intermediate courses in the evening school are substantially similar to those offered in the regular day program. Others, including retail accounting, accounting systems, and tax accounting, are vocationally oriented. Because teachers and administrators in evening programs are aware that students are strongly motivated by employment benefits obtained from their studies, the content of many courses, methods of teaching, and standards are often changed considerably from day-program equivalents. At some institutions, evening courses are added if there is a demand and dropped if enrollment is small. At one university, for example, a course in dairy accounting was offered for credit for several years because local industries supported it financially.

Few evening courses in accounting are staffed by full-time experienced teachers. Sections are commonly taught by practicing accountants. Although most of these part-time teachers know their subjects well, many lack the ability to teach and the time to devote to their students and courses. Pressures of population increases upon the universities in the coming years will undoubtedly result in expansion of evening programs. The problems that are faced today will be magnified in the future. It would seem desirable now and in the future to distinguish between those courses which are an integral part of a degree program and those special courses which are vocationally oriented and which are offered as a community service. While practicing accountants can make valuable contributions to evening courses, they should be given limited responsibility for course development and teaching.

Evening school courses which are part of a degree program should be established and taught on the same basis as regular day courses. The role of accounting in evening programs, however, should be sufficiently flexible to permit creation of noncredit courses to meet the vocational needs of the community.

THE FUTURE ROLE OF ACCOUNTING IN BUSINESS EDUCATION

The foregoing analysis of accounting in schools of business as it has developed to the present has been critical of many existing practices and conditions. This has been necessary in order to point out weaknesses in accounting courses and to examine areas in which improvement is desirable. It would be unjust not to recognize that the content of accounting courses, teaching requirements, caliber of students, and coordination of accounting with other disciplines have steadily improved over the years. Generally speaking, those who teach and those who practice accounting may be proud of the contributions they have made toward improving accounting as a profession and as a field of study. Room for additional improvement exists.

The domination of accounting courses and curricula by C.P.A. requirements will probably continue for some time in varying degrees. It is not likely that the heavily populated states will revise educational certification requirements to make them more flexible and less specific in the near future, particularly if a large number of schools continue to design accounting programs to fit the most restrictive C.P.A. requirements. The creation of new programs combining the merits of professional, managerial, and financial aspects of accounting will have to originate in a few business schools that recognize the necessity of developing accounting curricula on a sound academic basis, even if this means ignoring state C.P.A. requirements.

CHAPTER 15

FINANCE

John A. Griswold

The typical finance curriculum (banking, corporation finance, and investments), which has already gone through the period of course proliferation that still exists in several other business fields, needs no further consolidation. Principal needs in the finance field are (1) improved student background in mathematics, economic theory, and behavioral studies, (2) application of these and other subjects to the dynamic aspects of financial administration, and (3) provision for the preparation of additional and more realistic teaching materials.

This report on the teaching of finance in collegiate schools of business is an analytic study of the content, principles, and approaches used in the presentation of the subject. It is not a statistical study. The material derives from analysis of catalog information of one hundred collegiate schools of business, from personal visits to twenty-three leading business schools of different types in various parts of the country, and from interviews at these schools with some seventy teachers of finance subjects. The first part of this discussion traces the development of the content and structure of the present finance curricula. Then certain weaknesses are analyzed and a curriculum suggested, undergraduate and graduate, which is designed to help correct the faults. Finally the problems of integration and instructional materials are discussed.

The term "finance" as applied to a field of study is somewhat more limited in scope than common usage implies. Finance has been limited by the American Association of Collegiate Schools of Business (Standards of Membership, No. 4) to include courses in or derived from money and banking, business finance, corporation finance, and investment. The following section on the history of the field will show why some subjects having the word "finance" as part of the title, "public finance" for example, are not included in this discussion.

HISTORY OF THE FIELD OF FINANCE

Finance as a field of study separate from political economy, later called economics, began to develop in the latter part of the nineteenth century. Since then it has first moved away from the parent discipline to emphasize technical specialties and then moved back again to a more general economic approach. The latter trend, occurring largely after 1929 and accelerated in recent years, was accomplished by new combinations of subject matter within the field, by returning to an emphasis on economic theory, and by integration with other related fields. The programs of finance study to be discussed here are representative course offerings at the different periods; they do not reflect the finance curriculum of any one school but rather illustrate or characterize the common practice.

Finance had always been an integral part of the body of economic theory but it did not appear as a separate field until the latter part of the last century. By that time the growing complexity of the American business system brought a need for better understanding of detailed financial problems and processes. One answer to this need was the establishment of business schools at existing colleges and universities.

Finance was one of the first of the specialty studies to be differentiated from the all-inclusive subject of political economy. This is understandable in view of the fact that the first business schools were founded by international financiers and bankers. It was logical that the first "finance" courses to emerge from the background of political economy were in international finance, comparative European financial systems, and public finance. At the time financiers were interested in the financial "solvency" of each world power. The system of taxation was an important element in this solvency.

FIG. 15–1. Finance curriculum of the late nineteenth century.

Figure 15-1 shows the finance courses that had derived from political economy by the end of the nineteenth century. From these beginnings the number of courses multiplied during the first third of the twentieth century with the ten years before 1929 showing the greatest growth and proliferation (see Fig. 15-2). During this decade also, finance became a separate department in many business schools and was less often subordinate to economics departments. Enrollment in finance reached a peak in 1929 and 1930 but declined steadily after the stock market crash.

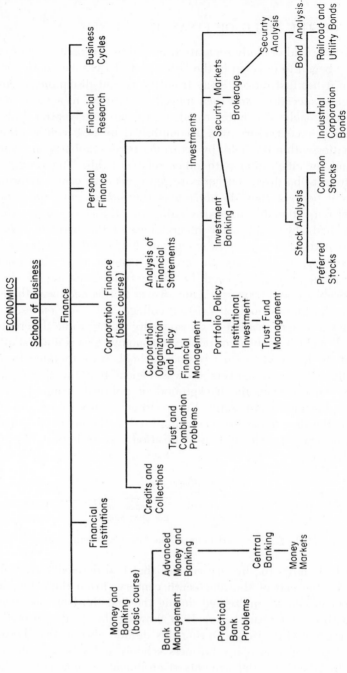

FIG. 15-2. Combined finance undergraduate and graduate curricula, 1922, to 1939.

With some exceptions, the current period since 1946 has been one of consolidation and combination of finance courses, together with a turn toward more reliance on economic theory and rejection of specialized technical training. The reasons for the trend toward consolidation in finance lie first in the naturally close relationship between economics and finance; second, in the special impact on the finance field of the 1929–1933 experience; third, in a shift in the philosophy of business education; and finally, in a shortage of finance teachers. Most finance subjects grew logically from political economy, although in the mushrooming of investment specialties the connection with economics became quite tenuous. But this proliferation into technical and detailed aspects met an automatic cutback, not experienced in the same degree by other business fields, when disillusionment with overspecialized investment training reduced student demand during the early thirties. The unnecessary "skill" courses were weeded out because they did not meet the practical needs they purported to serve. Demand for "advanced" or technical courses dropped, except in some night schools. Thus through the economic influences of the thirties, the efforts of finance instructors became to quite a large extent concentrated in the fewer and still popular service courses. The postwar period brought increased pressure from educators, the foundations, and sometimes from business leaders toward providing general education rather than specific training. This philosophy of business education, reflected in newly stated objectives of most business schools, reinforced the depression trend in finance against developing a variety of specialized courses.

A final condition that influenced the field of finance was the great postwar influx of students. It was no longer felt necessary or desirable to engage in the practice that most, if not all, schools had followed to some extent of attracting students by "window dressing" in the form of practical courses. After 1929 finance could no longer be considered a "bread-and-butter" field, and since World War II the sheer weight of numbers combined with a shortage of finance teachers has discouraged the development of new courses. Not only did finance share the increased business school enrollment, but the recent return of the field to popularity as a subject of study has kept its instructors exceptionally busy on the courses offered. In a number of schools finance now ranks first from point of view of total enrollment and of majors, surpassing the traditionally popular subjects of accounting, marketing, and administration.

Figure 15-3 illustrates the effect on finance curricula of these influences and shows how subjects formerly offered by finance departments became parts of the economics curriculum. As would be expected, this picture of common practice has a number of exceptions, the finance program varying from school to school through influences of the institution's history,

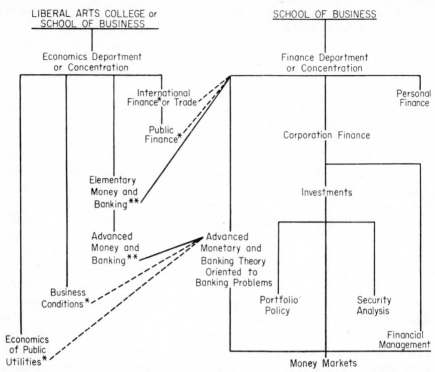

FIG. 15–3. Combined finance undergraduate and graduate curricula, 1946 to 1958. * Economics courses generally accepted toward finance concentration. ** Courses generally listed in finance curriculum and sometimes given in finance department.

location, purpose, and special faculty interests. Regrettably some schools still have the proliferated program of past years. In others, the thinking is in the direction of consolidating courses, but this is not yet reflected in curriculum changes. But Fig. 15-13 shows in general the current trend of thinking and reflects finance course offerings in about three out of four schools. Personal finance is sometimes offered as a service course for nonfinance majors, but it has not played any role in the development of the finance curriculum.

Some business schools whose programs can be said to be within this general pattern, but of course not corresponding in detail, are: University of California (Berkeley and Los Angeles), Carnegie Institute of Technology, University of Chicago, University of Cincinnati, Dartmouth College, Harvard University, Indiana University, Massachusetts Institute of Technology, University of Michigan, University of Minnesota, University of North Carolina, University of Notre Dame, University of San Francisco, Stanford University, University of Virginia (McIntire School and Graduate School of Business Administration).

Currently, corporation finance continues its two lines of development in investments and financial management. Investments material has been quite concentrated compared with the numerous courses offered earlier. Financial management has grown immensely in importance through enrichment of content, a type of development not evident in the illustration, and is given major emphasis in most schools by their stated aim of preparing business executives. In fact, it might be said that gradually the emphasis on management decision making is broadening the field of corporation finance and turning it away from the traditional legalistic-descriptive method of teaching.

The change in money and banking offerings is one of the most marked in the current period, with the elementary course almost always being given in the economics department or taught by an economist. Only in advanced banking is it felt that business-problem orientation should be emphasized. Even so, banking theory courses given by economics departments are generally accepted toward a degree in finance and in many instances are recommended to the student.

PRESENT COURSE CONTENT

The content of elementary finance courses is reasonably uniform in all schools. As courses become more advanced, and particularly at the graduate level, titles become less descriptive and content more varied as the individuality of different instructors and the circumstances of different schools are given expression.

The elementary money and banking work usually covers the following topics: the nature of money and theories of value; the American banking system; elementary theory dealing mainly with the role of the individual bank and of the system in the expansion and contraction of credit; and a simple treatment of the influence of monetary, banking, and fiscal policy on the price level. The first course in corporation finance, sometimes rather illogically called Business Finance, includes a description of: the nature of the corporation and of the securities constituting its capital structure; methods of both long- and short-term financing; management of income; expansion, reorganization, and dissolution.

Advanced work in money and banking usually covers the impact of monetary, banking, and fiscal policies on the economic system, with some forecasting of future trends. Some courses develop these topics analytically on an abstract level while others, given in business schools rather than in economics departments, orient the material at some point in the course toward such problems of bank operation and management as investment, credit analysis, and credit policy. It is the exception rather than the rule for a school to offer courses solely on the internal characteristics and problems of bank organization and management.

One course in capital markets, sometimes appearing in the more specific form of security markets, is related both to money and banking and to corporation finance, with the difference in titles reflecting the range of material emphasized. The capital markets course includes application of finance principles to the money and capital markets, the operations of private financing institutions in the market, and the effect of government regulation. The main emphasis is on economic analysis. In the security markets course, analysis is directed more specifically to the structure of the stock and bond markets and to the organization and operation of the exchanges, with some discussion of price behavior of the market and of specific securities. Where no course in money markets is given, the material is absorbed by other related subjects.

Advanced corporation finance courses take the form of both investments and financial management. A typical first course in investments includes the following: a study of investment risk; institutional and individual investment policies; selection of investment media; and an elementary analysis of securities. The more advanced course in portfolio policy includes detailed analysis of institutional and investment policy, a study of the theory of risks, tax problems, problems of business cycles, timing and investment, performance of different industries, and types of securities. The securities analysis course is more detailed, dealing with methods of analyzing specific securities, both corporate and government, and with the appraisal of industries and companies.

The other line of corporation finance development, financial management, is the study of the financial administration of a business, with usually, though not always, some attention being given to cash-flow. Specific subjects commonly covered are financial planning and capital structure, the use of sources of both short- and long-term funds, management of earnings, problems of growth, and mergers and consolidations. The teaching approach takes a management point of view, analytical in nature; materials used are problems and cases.

Variations from Common Practice

While the trend in finance curricula is toward the Fig. 15-3 pattern covering subjects just outlined, there remain, as mentioned above, a number of differences among schools. Some schools still offer a great diversity of specialized finance courses, sometimes over twenty in number, reminiscent of past generations of finance education. Other schools depart from the trend by having more specialization only in certain areas of the curriculum. In other cases, courses offered show variations in lines of thought from typical practice.

The greatest specialization in current curricula occurs in banking, partly because of its having been one of the earliest branches from the stem of political economy and partly because several schools by long tradition have been closely associated with and influenced by their banking communities. A roster of banking courses in various schools includes, beyond the elementary course, such subjects as bank organization and management (two terms), bank credits, international banking, investment banking, and mortgage banking. Organization, management, and credits obviously stress the practical phases of the subject. International banking is carried over from the original international finance course and while quite within the finance tradition, is now generally the responsibility of economics departments. Investment banking is a pre-World War II holdover; in most schools the material has been absorbed by other courses. Where mortgage banking is offered, it is obviously a specialty of the school or of a particular instructor.

One variant in a number of curricula is the offering of a course in financial institutions, sometimes as a preliminary to all other work but in one or two cases as an advanced course. It describes the development and current organization of the important financial institutions of the country (investment houses, banks, trust companies, commercial credit companies and factors, real estate financing organizations, and consumer credit groups) and usually makes some analysis of their functioning. The thoroughness of coverage and analysis depends upon the level at which the .course is offered. Where it is a preliminary course, the later work in money and banking and in corporation finance starts at a higher level than otherwise.

Variants from the corporation finance line of development include courses in corporation finance problems and in trust and combination problems. The former is an advanced course in financial management devoted to intensive study of managerial decision making. Where such material is not given in a separate course but is included in financial management, the latter may run a year rather than the equivalent of a semester. A course in trust and combination problems remains in a few curricula as a vestige of early developments in the teaching of finance. In most schools this subject matter has been absorbed in economics or financial management.

Another variant appearing in several curricula has derived from the early credits and collections course. In its most practical form it has been relegated to night programs. If given in day classes it sometimes appears as Consumer Credit, being given a strong economic orientation. In other cases it is an expanded course in financial statement analysis with emphasis on credit practices and their effect on the financial position of a company. In this type of course, where generalizations or patterns are developed that represent practice or experience of an entire industry, economic analysis is important.

The Undergraduate Major

In schools where undergraduate majors in finance are offered, the same rules apply that govern business school majors generally, as discussed elsewhere in this book. Briefly, the number of hours permitted for a major varies from 9 to 25, the trend being toward the lower number, usually between 9 and 15 hours. These hours are in addition to the basic courses in money and banking and corporation finance commonly required of all business students.

Basic courses in finance are most often given in the junior year although a minority of schools still require them in the sophomore year. In no case are they offered in the first year. The trend toward moving beginning finance courses to the junior year is in keeping with increased emphasis on liberal arts and with the probable eventual change to two-year business schools, away from the traditional four-year program.

The finance major may differ in two ways from other business majors. One variation sometimes occurring is the division of the field into three subfields—banking, investment, and business finance—in each of which the major is offered. Often the division is more apparent than real since there is a difference between the three majors of only a course or two. It is claimed that the aim in specifying the major is that of establishing a student's special interest for purposes of placement. Another variation occurs in a few schools where the finance major is eliminated as such and merged with business administration. By this arrangement a student may concentrate in finance under a business administration major. Where this plan exists, majors other than business administration are also offered, such as accounting, marketing, production, and industrial relations.

The Graduate Programs

The nature of advanced work in finance is such that a certain background in the field is necessary before a student can begin graduate work. In most cases submission of credits for the elementary courses will permit a student to enter graduate study. Where admission requirements are not met in this way, survey courses in the graduate school may be provided which aim to give a mature presentation of undergraduate material compressed into a shorter time. Other graduate business schools require students to take a year of core courses, whatever the entering background. Finance is usually one of these core courses.

Graduate school requirements governing advanced degrees permit considerable freedom to the particular field both in setting up its own graduate program and in recommending related courses. A comment needs to be made about the indefinite line between undergraduate and graduate work. A number of schools designate a set of courses as "advanced undergraduate and graduate." Such advanced courses, as well as exclusively graduate work in these and other schools, fall in the categories of portfolio policy, security analysis, financial management, and advanced money and banking. Unless special attention is given to graduate students in such courses, often not the case, the result of giving graduate credit for undergraduate work is a weakening of the entire finance curriculum.

Further flexibility in the graduate curriculum is possible, because in addition to the formal courses yielding part of the prescribed hours for advanced degrees, seminars are offered, especially in the doctoral program. Where, as is often the case, a master's program is emphasized, the orientation of the school toward management preparation rather than academic and research work, determines the relative balance between prescribed courses and the more academic seminar. The variety of subjects offered in finance seminars reflects the interests of particular teachers or the special relationship of a school to its business community. One school may offer the greatest number of seminars in banking where another offers aspects of investment and another emphasizes financial management. Some seminar subjects are: banking problems, money and employment, money markets, administrative controls, financial institutions, financial management, and investment management. In some instances a student may pursue individual research under the direction of a faculty member. General finance seminars are sometimes given in which students have a chance to gain an integrated knowledge of the entire field.

A second way in which the graduate program in finance shows individuality is in designating related courses and in encouraging students to take these courses. The most common of the related subjects, some phase of which is recommended for graduate finance study, are:

I. Economics:
   1. International trade and finance
   2. Public finance
   3. Theory of income and prices
   4. Advanced money and credit theory
   5. Business conditions

II. Accounting:
   1. Advanced accounting
   2. Managerial accounting
   3. Auditing
III. Other:
   1. Production
   2. Law

The election of these related business courses leaves little room for nonbusiness work in most graduate programs although some catalog descriptions of the master's degree indicate that students are encouraged to take a very limited number of courses outside the business school. It is the rare student who consciously seeks an interdisciplinary education, and it must be acknowledged that the limits of time in the existing schedule of requirements discourage it. Doctoral programs have a more interdisciplinary character, at least on their surface. Subjects outside the field of doctoral study are customarily accepted if they have logical relatedness, and it seems to be a growing practice to require that at least one field of study be outside the business school.

Weaknesses of the Current Finance Curriculum

The history and recent development of the finance curriculum have been described from the viewpoint of current practice. Before making proposals that could direct future development and reinforce desirable trends of thought already at work in the field, certain weaknesses in the present curriculum should be pointed out. The standards accepted in viewing these faults and failures are the general principles for business education set forth in Part 1 and other sections of this survey.

Money and Banking. Money and banking, one of the earliest special fields under the finance heading, is closely related to economics and in many schools is almost purely an economics course. This close tie to the parent field has had both advantages and disadvantages. The commendable theoretical development in money and banking compares favorably to the situation in corporation finance where little contact has developed with economic theory. Practical and operational aspects of money and banking have declined in teaching importance. When the development is stated in this way, the intellectual prestige of money and banking at first seems academically admirable. But if the question is asked whether the education of business executives has been advanced, the answer must be in the negative.

All will agree that the operation of the banking system, and the effect of policies enunciated by the central bank and applied by constituent banks, should be understood by every business executive and especially by every finance executive. But regrettably this is not the case. Although there is no objective measure of this knowledge, qualified judges have found in working with business executives that there is an inadequate understanding of the influence on business of banking policy. Even more astonishing is the judgment that many bank officials, though excellent operating men, also do not have this basic understanding. In short, the theoretical learning of economists has not been transmitted to operating business executives and bankers by existing money and banking courses. This is certainly a major failure of finance education.

Several causes contribute to this failure. First, elementary money and banking is often studied in the sophomore or the first part of the junior year, a level at which most students cannot be expected to appreciate the significance of banking theory for the business life which still lies several years ahead. Moreover, the student may come into money and banking directly from a dull and poorly taught elementary economics course, in which case he reacts emotionally against the necessarily somewhat theoretical treatment of parts of money and banking.

Second, comprehension of a subject like banking theory can be acquired only by frequent later reviews of the concepts through integrating them with material in other courses. Yet in the present course structure, seldom after the initial money and banking course is there opportunity for reacquaintance with banking concepts until late in the program, if at all. This explains how it is possible for a future executive to graduate with credits in a money and banking course but without an understanding of the field adequate for his coming responsibilities.

Another weakness of the money and banking field is the failure to carry theory over into operating problems and decisions in a way that is interesting and useful for the average student. This may be one of the disadvantages of the close tie to economics and of the fact that economists are basically more interested in broad considerations than in business operation. A full development of education in this management side of banking would perhaps have paralleled the theoretical development of the field had it not been inhibited by criticisms concerning the excessively practical emphasis in business schools. But it is surely a legitimate teaching concern to bridge the gap between theory and practice. Under the present curriculum and content, future executives graduate without this knowledge and future teachers continue their interest in theory, making few attempts to develop teaching aids. To be specific, no new case-problem book that would be of help in carrying banking theory over into operational practice has been published in the last twenty years.

Corporation Finance. In contrast to money and banking, corporation finance, instead of being related to economic forces, has been descriptively taught, largely from legal and accounting viewpoints, ever since the earliest courses in 1905 to 1910 and since the first textbooks. Some attempts to introduce economic analysis through texts with broader orientations have not been successful. Recently, with the appearance of collections of simple problems and a casebook, corporation finance has taken on a more analytical approach, but the basic character of the course has not changed. It is an interesting question why the field has taken this turn over the years whereas money and banking turned toward economic theory. Apparently the first teachers and texts set the trend. The preface of one of the earliest texts states: " 'Corporation Finance' aims to explain and illustrate the methods employed in the promotion, capitalization, financial management, consolidation and reorganization of business corporations."[1] The same author in the following year, 1911, showed his prevailing interest by publishing a text in investments. A second text written by a successful New York lawyer reinforced the trend in the field. His preface stated that he would deal "especially with two topics, the distribution of corporate securities and the financial side of corporate reorganization." This author felt that it was "the duty of anyone undertaking a presentation of any aspect of the subject to steer a course between the legal and the accounting sides of corporate business."[2]

These quotations from prototype texts reveal the early trend toward the descriptive approach in the course. Since corporation finance was soon overshadowed by growth of investment courses for which a descriptive knowledge of the nature of the corporation was adequate, it is not surprising that teaching in the field continued its early character to the present. Today prefaces of texts usually state that the management point of view is used, but the material continues to be statically descriptive rather than suggestive of the corporation as a functioning unit. Comparison of a widely used modern text with an early one shows that over 60 per cent of the textual material in both is devoted to description of the following topics: promotion, incorporation, characteristics of securities, management of earnings, expansion, reorganization, and investment banking. The newer books describe additional topics, such as short-term financing (a major omission of the early texts), financing patterns of different industries, and social responsibilities. But with two exceptions, economic analysis and the dynamic nature of the corporation have little emphasis in most current texts. It is not the object here to be unduly critical of modern corporation finance texts, for they are up-to-date in

[1] Edward S. Mead, *Corporation Finance*, D. Appleton & Company, Inc., New York, 1910, p. viii.

[2] Hastings Lyon, *Corporation Finance*, Houghton Mifflin Company, Boston, 1912, p. i.

facts, thorough in coverage, and in most cases well written. But despite statements showing awareness of need for a new approach, they perpetuate the lack of a theoretical framework. Both future executives and future teachers would benefit from a more dynamic and analytical approach.

Corporation finance is usually required of all students in either the sophomore or junior year. The early place of corporation finance in the curriculum does not involve the same handicaps as beset money and banking. The subject matter is not as abstract, and whereas banking theory is not integrated with later work, the nature and characteristics of the corporation constantly reappear in other courses, so frequently, in fact, that by graduation the alert student could know the salient financial features of corporations whether he has had an advanced course in corporation finance or not.

Satisfactory as this corporation finance integration with other work is compared with money and banking, there still remains a basic problem. A student may well understand the corporation as a static unit without being able to appreciate, first, its functioning in the economic system and, second, the impact upon it of economic situations and the effect on its financial policies of internal departmental decisions. Since 1946 a new development in the field has been the growth of an advanced course in financial management, which does give a dynamic view of the corporation. But its development has been hindered by lack of teaching and textual materials, and until recently each teacher has had to attempt the difficult if not impossible task of providing his own materials, a problem to be discussed later. As a result, this course which is the growing end of the field has not had the development it merits.

Investments. Investments was unusual among finance subjects in its early proliferation into courses almost vocational in character. While these technical aspects of the subject have since been cut back, there remain today, in addition to the parent course, the courses in security analysis and in portfolio policy, usually offered for graduates but in some cases also for advanced undergraduates.

In most undergraduate investment courses the analysis of securities plays an important part and is popular with students. The data upon which this analysis must be based come from published financial statements. The validity of this approach may be challenged. Professional analysts today base their judgments primarily on analysis of such factors as quality of management, quality of the research program, and the market for the products, before giving weight to financial analysis. But data on which to base these judgments are not available to the general public, including the graduate student and the teacher in finance. The public relations documents known as "annual reports," where a firm is putting its best foot forward, must be considered the weakest body of data for analysis purposes. Even detailed financial statements are not useful unless the analyst is acquainted with such factors as each firm's accounting valuation process. This key information can often be inferred from published financial data only by expert accountants.

These characteristics of the materials mean that the average student does not have the data, skill, and judgment to arrive at useful conclusions, and the resulting unfortunate tendency is that interest develops on a speculative rather than on an analytical basis. In a few schools the undergraduate investments course has had the misfortune to be given a small fund of money to be managed by the class. While this may appear superficially to be a good teaching technique, it in fact interferes seriously with the educational process. Such a sum can hardly be large enough to embrace a sufficient variety of investments to give a broad view of the field, and with interest narrowed to the few securities that can be purchased, the principles of risk and ability to carry risk are likely to be neglected. Also, attention is focused on individual investment problems solely, and other types of investment policies are likely to be forgotten. Finally, far too much class thought and discussion are given over to noneducational debate on what specific securities to buy and sell. This device could be useful, however, in a small graduate seminar where a careful scientific approach would be possible.

Another criticism of the investment field is the narrowness of the subject matter. Traditionally, only industrial and governmental securities have been covered. Yet other types of investment play important roles in our economy. For example, real estate investment is seldom included, perhaps because of the problem of limiting discussion to investment without becoming involved in the whole real estate field. Insurance policies and annuities as investments are slighted in most courses as are investment in banks and in securities of insurance companies.

However, broadening the undergraduate course to include these neglected topics still leaves unsolved a basic question. If security analysis is eliminated from the course as unsuitable for undergraduate work, there remain the problems of risk and risk bearing and of portfolio policy. Analysis of these subjects requires an understanding of economic forces that is probably beyond the background and maturity of average undergraduates. Consequently, it appears that the subject of investment with all its subtleties and ramifications should be reserved for the graduate curriculum. In short, the traditional undergraduate course in investments may encourage false confidence and careless investment rather than give sound instruction in handling funds.

Courses in capital or money markets are usually sufficiently broad, but security markets courses are often too narrow in scope. Where content is limited solely to security markets, only the highly specialized student will find it valuable, in which case a seminar might be more suitable. Though offered as Security Markets, the course often goes into too-detailed consideration of market movements and of the process of speculation. It is questioned here whether this content has any place in the regular finance curriculum and whether it would not be a more suitable field for special studies by interested students.

Weaknesses of Integration. While integration in the field of finance has been carried on satisfactorily in terms of organizing general courses from a number of more specialized courses, another type of integration has not always been provided whereby the student may assemble and coordinate his knowledge about the field of finance and its role in business and society. Part of this lack exists, not through unawareness of a need for pulling together the various lines of development in finance, but because it is assumed by finance departments that the school provides an over-all coordinated picture in a course often titled General Management and required of all students. But finance education would be more complete if a student could be given some aid in coordinating the knowledge gained from finance courses taken over a period of two or three years. As the situation exists, the financial knowledge of the graduate may be too segmented to be fully useful.

Finance seems to be quite well integrated with other business school work and with economics, judging by the department-recommended courses outside finance and by the diversification of requirements in most business schools. The exception, as pointed out, is that corporation finance might well be more oriented toward economics to bring out the effect of external conditions and of internal decisions upon financial policies. The most serious weakness in integration occurs between finance and nonbusiness subjects. Although master's requirements accept any reasonable nonbusiness course and catalog statements encourage such elections, elective fields are not named. Apparently little advantage is taken of this opportunity, occasionally for reasons of difficulty in scheduling and lack of cordial interdepartmental relationships, but more commonly because students and often instructors oriented toward business lack interest in and awareness of the supporting and enriching value of work in nonbusiness subjects.

Lack of this type of integration is especially discouraging at the doctoral level, although some courses outside business schools are required. Of theses now in preparation, interdisciplinary interest is reflected in only six titles: sociology in three, law in two, and mathematics in one.[3] Psychology and engineering, where one might look for profitable integration with finance, are not represented in thesis topics. When inter-

---

[3] Derived from "Fifty-fourth List of Doctoral Dissertations in Political Economy in American Universities," *The American Economic Review,* September, 1957.

disciplinary influences are rare in current doctoral research, it seems reasonable to think that integration with other fields is one of the weak points of the finance curriculum.

A SUGGESTED FINANCE CURRICULUM

Following the plan of the historical section where common practice was diagrammed and most frequent variations enumerated, in suggesting an improved curriculum to eliminate the weaknesses discussed, a basic program will be outlined and the possible variations described. The important point must be kept in mind that the suggested program is not an absolute but that variations in application are to be expected. Indeed, within broad limits, experimentation by individual schools should be given every encouragement. Accordingly, the specific proposals advanced here are designed as a means of pointing up the issues in this branch of the business school curriculum. While some subjectivism is inevitable when one individual surveys a field, it should be recognized that these proposals are offered as a guide to the kind of development that one person, after thorough study of facts, much discussion with others in the field, and earnest thought, believes will improve education in the field of finance.

The suggested curriculum, undergraduate and graduate, is based on four principles or conclusions accepted by the writer after consultation with many other teachers of finance. First is the assumption generally made but not yet objectively proved that a liberal arts background is the best foundation for business education. However, the ideal program based on this assumption, namely four years of liberal arts followed by specialized graduate work in business, is not the common practice and is perhaps not practical financially or intellectually for the mass of students. Therefore some business subjects are justifiably given and must be included in recommendations for the undergraduate level, provided liberal arts work is embraced by the program. As in any field, the contribution of liberal arts will depend on how successfully it is taught. From the viewpoint of finance, it is hoped that a maximum proportion of liberal arts background will provide a more adequately prepared student than it does at present and that liberal arts subjects will be presented so that the student will at least have learned to express himself adequately, use mathematical tools readily, appreciate the relevance of economic theory, and understand the concepts presented by the behavioral studies. The maturity, mental discipline, and breadth of interest derived from any of the range of liberal arts fields will of course be beneficial to the business student.

The second principle is that, in order to permit this full development of a liberal arts background and to allow the student time to gain the necessary maturity and academic experience, finance work should not be offered before the junior year. This is made all the more necessary by the growing dependence of the field, corporation finance included, upon an understanding of economic forces.

Third, undergraduate finance courses ought to be broad and comprehensive, avoiding vocational emphasis. This does not mean that problems and elementary cases should not be used. On the contrary, such specific materials are exactly what is needed to catch the student's interest and to avoid or offset the abstractness which quite possibly characterized his elementary economics course. But there should be a minimum of undergraduate emphasis on the techniques involved in such fields as banking organization and management and security analysis.

Finally, the suggested curriculum is proposed in the belief that the average undergraduate, because of his lack of maturity and experience, cannot profitably be educated in financial decision making or managerial techniques. A controversy over this point is in progress in some schools, one side arguing that the very reason for a business school's existence is to train managers and the other side that actually the great majority of business undergraduates will never reach the level of making managerial decisions, particularly in finance.[4] Since it cannot be predicted what fields or what levels of business activity students will go into, it seems best to offer the most comprehensive undergraduate finance curriculum possible as a foundation for later experience whether in graduate managerial studies, in middle management, or in top management.

An Undergraduate Finance Curriculum

Figure 15-4 illustrates a course plan for finance on a two-year liberal arts base. Business work would begin in the junior year with four basic courses two of which, Accounting (or Finance and Accounting) and

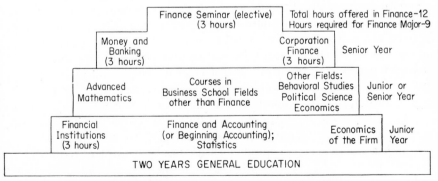

Fig. 15–4. Suggested undergraduate finance program.

[4] This issue is discussed at some length in Chaps. 8 and 9.

Statistics, would presumably be required for any business major. The finance major would take also one finance course, Financial Institutions, and one economics course, Economics of the Firm. The remainder of the junior-year schedule would be chosen from the second level of the table. Economics of the Firm would teach the character of a business enterprise, including such topics as the nature of demand for products, problems of cost and production, competition and markets, the relation of size and efficiency, and simple problems of finance. These topics ought to be related as far as possible to general economic principles. It is assumed that this course would make use of elementary mathematics already studied at the lower-class level.

A beginning course in finance, here called Financial Institutions, is suggested at this point to provide the student, whether a finance major or not, with an understanding and appreciation of the process of capital formation and the dynamic nature of our financial system. The process of saving and the functioning of credit policy and of fiscal policy are so basic to our current financial world that the first principles underlying production, consumption, and our banking system should become an ingrained part of every student's thinking. The functioning of financial institutions in addition to commercial banks (such as commercial finance companies, factors, savings banks, savings and loan associations, trust companies, investment banks) and the process of individual investment should be viewed in the perspective of an operating, not a static, financial system. This course ought to give a working knowledge of the financial world adequate for immediately succeeding courses. Use of simple cases and problems relating business financial needs to institutional sources of funds would make this course more dynamic than the usual, merely descriptive survey.

Dropping the traditional beginning corporation finance course may seem to present a problem of supplying necessary background. But it is contemplated that the economics of the firm course and beginning accounting, especially if combined with finance, would provide enough working knowledge until a more mature corporation finance course could later be given. The ideal situation for supplying this working knowledge in corporation finance would be in combination with an accounting course that takes the point of view of asset development. Such a course in finance and accounting would supply the essential content for corporation finance and also demonstrate its integral relationship with accounting. For example, in the beginning accounting course at the Tuck School, called Finance and Accounting, almost half of the course is devoted to the subjects of: assets as capital, securities as sources of capital, allocation of capital, and the relation between business transactions and financial statements. The introduction to the course states:

Accounting is in no sense an isolated field, for its significance is lost unless it is approached in the light of the business practices with which it is associated. If the study of accounting is to progress smoothly and rapidly, the forms of business organization, the various types of business activity, and the relation of accounting to the individual enterprise are topics which must be understood. Once the reasons for, and the purposes of making, the records are fully appreciated, the methods and procedures of making them are readily learned.[5]

Omitting the beginning money and banking course moves even further from traditional practice than omitting beginning corporation finance. The question was raised earlier whether money and banking as a beginning course meets current needs. It is suggested that the more concrete material of Economics of the Firm and Financial Institutions would be a better bridge from economics to advanced business work. A money and banking course for more mature students could analyze the ultimate bearing of banking policy on economic life at a time in the curriculum when the student could better appreciate the import of the material and integrate it with his other business work.

Among courses in nonbusiness subjects appearing in Fig. 15-4, some advanced mathematics is vital because of its ever-increasing importance in the business and finance world. The very nature of the subject of finance would seem to call for special mathematics requirements, but in fact finance majors have been no better prepared in this field than other business majors. As developed more fully in Part 2 of this study, the role that mathematics should play in entrance requirements and in the curriculum is a matter of debate in many business schools today and is discussed here only in relation to finance. Mathematics through advanced algebra and preferably through calculus should be required of every finance major. Technical developments, such as computers, and broadening concepts of the function of the corporation's finance department in its participation in decisions with other departments make an understanding of mathematical concepts more important than ever before.

The mathematics requirement would facilitate teaching advanced work. For example, with the recommended amount of mathematics, corporation finance in the suggested curriculum could be much more effectively taught. In the past, important areas of the field have had to be omitted which certain mathematical concepts could help clarify. One result has been a continuously perpetuated lack of breadth in outlook on the part of finance people in business, since their schooling was oriented largely to the accounting side of corporation finance and the broader mathematical approach could hardly be acquired by experience alone.

Behavioral studies are suggested in this curriculum, not only for their

[5] Louis O. Foster, "Syllabus for Course in Beginning Accounting," Amos Tuck School, Dartmouth College, 1957.

general educational value, but because their relevance to the field of finance has been too long neglected. Of these, psychology is probably the most germane, though sociology is also important in some problems. A firm's financial department is often called upon to analyze proposals for new projects where there may be psychological and sociological overtones of which the financial executive should be aware. For example, he may have to decide on a large capital expenditure for a safety device on which no financial rate of return can be calculated. Or in another case, calculations may show that moving a firm from a long-established location to a new one will be profitable, but there will be serious sociological and psychological problems which the financial executive should understand.

Courses in economics are obviously valuable in the finance curriculum because of the close relationship of the two fields. Certain economics subjects tie in particularly closely with banking and corporation finance. One of these is business conditions or business cycles, which can be related either to investments or to the problems of financing a single business. Other examples are public utility economics, international finance, public finance, and the economic philosophies.

Finally at the top of the pyramid come the advanced courses for which the groundwork has been laid, namely, corporation finance, money and banking, and a finance seminar. The corporation finance course assumes that the student will have learned something concerning the nature of the corporation in accounting and in the course on economics of the firm. Further descriptive material could readily be obtained through reading without class discussion. The course would be devoted mainly to examining the corporation as a functioning unit under such topics as cash-flow, short-term financing, capital expenditures, and sources of funds. Problems and some carefully chosen cases could be presented to lead the student to recognition and understanding of major forces both inside and outside the business that affect financing.

The course in money and banking could include descriptive material now given in survey courses, provided it did not duplicate that presented in Financial Institutions. But the course should mainly develop principles of banking and credit and fiscal policy, demonstrating their influence on both the national economy and the financing of the individual business. Some of the problems and cases used for corporation finance could again be used here to help students integrate their knowledge of finance.

The final course in the suggested finance-major pyramid, the seminar, should be reserved for the best students who are interested in and capable of some independent work. At the undergraduate level, one seminar in finance where participants could report on and discuss a variety of topics should be sufficient. Attempts at highly specialized projects would hardly be advisable. The goal should be some experience in independent research and an opportunity for the student to begin integration of his knowledge toward a specific project.

Graduate Work in Finance

The suggested undergraduate program described above should give a liberal educational background and a general knowledge of the finance field, its basic principles and major issues and problems. In addition, it should provide both for the student entering graduate work in finance and for the student going immediately into business an acquaintance with the useful tools and analytic methods in the fields of accounting, statistics, mathematics, economics, and behavioral science. Some simple cases and problems relating such tools and methods to financial principles would be used in the undergraduate finance work. On this groundwork the graduate program suggested below aims to provide, in the M.B.A. work, an application of principles, tools, and methods to managerial problems of financial decision making and, in the doctoral work, an opportunity for investigation of theory leading to research in finance and to interdisciplinary studies.

The aim of the M.B.A. work suggested here is to focus the basic principles and issues studied in the undergraduate years and, by applying them through extensive use of typical and specific decision-making cases, to give the student who goes into business an understanding of the kind of problems he will meet. The student who goes on to further academic work would carry over into the more theoretical doctoral studies a comprehension of and sympathy for the managerial viewpoint. The importance of emphasizing the managerial function at some point in the finance doctoral work is not always recognized. Failure of the research worker and the theoretician to understand practical business situations is evident in many current studies, particularly in those that are mathematical in nature, where theoretical conclusions that are of interest and importance appear to the business manager to have little relevance to actual situations and thus are not productively exploited. With the accrual of M.B.A. case-study experience in managerial problems, the doctoral work, in broadening to consider financial and economic theory and interdisciplinary relationships, would prove more worth while to society and to the student.

A Suggested M.B.A. Program in Finance

Table 15-1 shows a recommended graduate program including both M.B.A. and doctoral work. The M.B.A. work suggested assumes the usual

Table 15-1

A Suggested Graduate Program in Finance

Semester hours
or equivalent

I. Required finance courses:
   Banking and Credit.............................. 3
   Financial Management........................... 3
   Investment..................................... 3
                                                  –
                                                  9

II. Other required courses:
    Engineering Economy or Managerial Accounting (not a
      controls course)............................... 3
    Business Conditions.............................. 3
                                                    –
                                                    6

III. Finance electives:
     Capital and money markets seminar or course......... 3
     Banking seminar.................................. 3
     Financial management seminar..................... 3
     Investment seminar............................... 3

IV. Other elective fields recommended:
    Business fields: Fitting into the student's plans and
      interests
    Nonbusiness fields: Economics, mathematics, psychol-
      ogy, sociology, political science

first-year core requirements in business subjects, permitting students to enter advanced courses with a knowledge of fundamentals. It is recognized that schools may differ in these requirements and that in each case the graduate finance program must conform to these variations. The M.B.A. candidate would normally take the required courses under headings I and II of Table 15-1. If he were planning future doctoral study, he should elect one of the seminars under heading III. The remainder of his M.B.A. work would probably come in other business fields under heading IV.

The following lines of thought are suggested for the content of courses listed under I and II of Table 15-1. These graduate courses should provide opportunity for penetrating analysis of financial problems. Where issues and principles familiar from undergraduate study are reconsidered, the managerial approach would now be taken, using more numerous and more complex cases and requiring advanced reading.

Banking and Credit. This course could include a historical study of the theories of money and credit as well as analysis of credit theory, monetary and fiscal policy, forces affecting the level of production and prices, and the interest rate. The use of complex cases and problems should lead the student not only to an understanding of credit theory but also to the application of theory to financial decision making.

Financial Management. An advanced course in financial management ought to emphasize the role of finance in the operating entity of the firm from the viewpoint of financial decision making. The course should recognize the fact that financial decisions can no longer be directed simply toward maintaining in the business a technically "sound" financial position; they must be made in the milieu of an increasingly dynamic world. One part of the course could develop principles of effective cash-flow management, showing the effects of operating policies on the movement of funds within the business. Another part could relate cash-flow and obtaining funds from outside the firm to credit and fiscal policies, money and capital markets, general business conditions, and economic and social changes. Throughout the course, cases involving decision making should be used to make clear the interaction of internal policies with external financial and economic conditions.

Investment. In contrast to courses in corporation finance, investment courses have long dealt with the dynamic problems of their part of the field. They should continue to deal with portfolio policy and its application by several types of investors; the nature and problems of risk; the relation of investment policy to money market structure; effects of economic changes; timing of investment; and influence of taxes on investment decisions.

One topic usually included in graduate investment courses but omitted from the list above is security analysis. As already stated, this topic presents a problem to the instructor, because only part of the necessary data is available and some of this may be misleading. A feasible teaching device based on broader concepts than most now in general use has yet to be developed. A new approach might involve thorough industry studies, as often made now, but with an attempt to observe patterns in financial data and to relate them to economic factors. Mathematical and statistical processes might come into play here as well as psychological interpretations.

A suggestion often made and one proposed here concerning the teaching of investment is that the course should not be narrowed to security investment alone. For example, as noted earlier, real estate which absorbs large amounts of capital is an important field that is neglected in investment teaching. The problem of introducing real estate in the limited time available is complicated by the necessity of analyzing data in an area where the student does not have considerable background knowledge. It is possible that by beginning the analysis with acceptance of certain valuations and not becoming involved in the appraisal process, real estate could be included in the course. Other neglected fields of investment already suggested are investment in banks, in insurance policies and annuities, and in insurance companies themselves.

Seminars. Suggested seminars would fall within three phases of finance: banking, corporation finance, and investments. These courses could be useful both as an opportunity for a student to pursue some specialty under faculty guidance and as a means of integrating financial knowledge through discussion and criticism among the members of the seminar in their several presentations. Only one seminar could probably be chosen by the M.B.A. candidate; the others would be offered to complete the doctoral program. But anyone intending to work toward a doctorate should include a seminar in his master's program.

Other Required Courses. A word should be said about the purpose of other required graduate courses suggested and about the content that would best fulfill the need of the graduate student in finance. Required courses in engineering economy or managerial accounting and in business conditions are suggested because of the necessity for better communication between financial executives, accountants, engineers, and economists. Many terms are used in common in accounting, engineering, and economics but with a different emphasis or meaning in each field. More important, financial officers need to know how experts in these three areas analyze problems and to learn what contribution the financial officer can make to integrating the areas and resolving general policy issues. Several large businesses have special educational projects attempting to develop understanding of such common terms and common problems. The suggested required courses could help lay the groundwork for this education of the student before he enters business.

A required course in engineering economy is proposed because it includes such subjects as the theory of interest, optimum use of capital, alternative investment, equipment replacement, choice of equipment, quality control, obsolescence and innovation, and industry economy studies. An equally satisfactory alternative requirement would be one type of managerial accounting course. As constituted in some schools, this course would fulfill the requirement because it stresses the analytical use of accounting, engineering, and economic data in decision making. The fields covered are similar to those included in engineering economy, with the possible exception of economy studies. The appearance of a course entitled Managerial Accounting in a curriculum may, however, be misleading. If it presents simply the recording of financial events and the use of accounting data by management, or if it is simply a course in controls, it would not meet the needs of the future financial executive and would not fulfill the requirements of the suggested graduate program.

A required course in business conditions is proposed to give the future financial executive knowledge of the economic approach to business problems by acquainting him with the terminology and methods of economic analysis and especially with problems of business cycles. Usually included in this course are the structure and operation of the economic system and the analysis and forecasting of business fluctuations. Since this work is most often given in economics departments, economic analysis and forecasts are not likely to be related to business decisions, and this integration will have to be made by the student in his business school courses.

In the program shown in Table 15-1, 12 to 15 hours of electives beyond the core and finance-major requirements would be available for other business and nonbusiness subjects. It would be necessary for the holder of a master's degree to have some advanced business work beyond the field of his concentration, elected according to his interests and plans but desirably including additional work in advanced accounting and statistics. These business subjects would absorb most of his elective hours, but it seems advisable to reserve at least 3 to 6 hours, if possible, for study in a nonbusiness field rather than attempt to sample all business subjects. An M.B.A. candidate who anticipates doing doctoral work could use some of his elective hours to get started in economic theory.

A Suggested Doctoral Program in Finance

The usual doctoral requirement of 30 hours of course work beyond the master's degree is assumed. It is apparent in Table 15-1 that, having completed his M.B.A. work, the doctoral candidate's formal course work would come largely from headings III and IV, namely, finance seminars and advanced work in economic theory and in related fields leading to interdisciplinary studies. However, doctoral candidates in finance who had not acquired the managerial background of the M.B.A. work suggested here should be required to take two decision-making courses. The further doctoral study in finance would be directed toward comprehensive examinations and thesis research under direction of a faculty member. The candidate's study in other fields should include economic theory and history of economic thought. In fact, because of the close relationship of the fields, the doctoral candidate might devote the same amount of time to economic theory whether his concentration is in finance or in economics.

The further choice of courses or seminars in other fields, whether business or nonbusiness, should be the province of the faculty adviser and the candidate. It is recommended, however, that the adviser encourage interest in one or more pertinent nonbusiness fields. As pointed out, although most doctoral requirements permit or require some work in outside fields, current titles of doctoral theses in preparation and abstracts of accepted theses show little influence of an interdisciplinary nature. On the contrary, the thesis subjects show a sort of inward turning to technical or historical financial problems rather than a moving into interdisciplinary areas which in the history of many fields of thought have proved so fertile.

INTEGRATION

Curriculum planning can provide for some aspects of integration, but teaching and research carry the responsibility for others. Integration has two aspects in its relation to teaching. One is the subjective integration of knowledge within the mind of the student. The other is integration of subject matter between fields, both business and nonbusiness. Research also has a role in the latter aspect of integration.

As for integration within the field, the history of finance has shown that the proliferation of courses characteristic of one period was checked and subject matter was consolidated within the boundaries of a relatively small number of courses. These courses and their titles have fortunately developed in such a way as to permit the teacher to organize the material of the field around certain themes. Experiments in attempting to combine current courses and the opinions of many finance teachers indicate that further consolidation should not take place in schools where broad-gauged finance courses already exist. In other words, the basic separation of money and banking, corporation finance, and investment should be continued. This does not mean that teachers of these subjects should not introduce correlations with other courses, but it does mean that further combination of finance courses is not advisable in many schools.

The process of combining different facets of finance within the mind of the student is a difficult problem of teaching. It is a common tendency to compartmentalize knowledge under course titles. The movement toward less specific courses in finance has helped to prevent this tendency. Other aids are the teaching techniques of requiring written reports and using problems and cases involving issues from different phases of finance Comprehensive examinations and the seminar also help the student integrate material, especially the latter in its discussion of a wide variety of individual reports. Student finance discussion groups sponsored by the American Finance Association are another useful device for promoting integration of knowledge. But probably the most effective integrating force is the individual teacher. The finance teacher has an opportunity to lead class discussion of a topic, case, or problem into various parts of the field of finance, into other business subjects—accounting, for example—and into areas further afield, if his experience and resourcefulness permit. Because of this vital role of the teacher, integration in the mind of the student will be forwarded by improvements in materials, methods, and conditions of teaching.

Integration of finance with other business fields should offer no serious problem to the teacher. Finance materials are frequently drawn from marketing, production, and sometimes from labor relations. In fact, nearly all problems in finance impinge upon other business subjects. The skill of the teacher and the availability of materials are the only limitations on this type of integration. The need for better integration with several significant nonbusiness subjects has been pointed out in discussing both undergraduate and graduate curricula. It is to be hoped that as some schools oriented toward research become more interested in interdisciplinary projects, studies will be produced that will aid in broadening financial concepts.

Integration between finance and economics has particular significance, especially as it relates to the doctoral program. The desirable relationship between the two subjects is clearly implied in a statement made by Dean Neil Jacoby of the University of California (Los Angeles):

> The relationship between the business school and the economics department is analogous in many ways to the relation between the medical school and the department of biochemistry; or to the relation between the engineering school and the department of physics. Each of these professional schools necessarily utilizes in its curricula principles and theories drawn from those academic disciplines that are basic to its field of professional practice.[6]

The development of finance subjects shows a need both to be based on economic theory and yet to be independent of it. Corporation finance, as we have seen, developed descriptively without much reference to economic analysis and became a somewhat sterile field. At the other extreme, money and banking became virtually a branch of economics and failed to communicate its theory in a practical and understandable way, leaving a blind spot in the education of executives. Of all business subjects, finance most needs to be soundly rooted in economics, but it also needs to keep itself realistic and independent of the abstractions of theory.

TEACHING EFFECTIVENESS AND INSTRUCTIONAL MATERIALS

While curriculum and course planning can bring many improvements, the effectiveness of finance education also depends heavily on the quality of teaching. This in turn depends on the supply of teachers, the time they have free from routine duties, and the supply of up-to-date texts and

[6] Address before the American Economic Association, "Economics in the Curricula of Schools of Business," *American Economic Review*, May, 1956.

teaching materials. The best use of a teacher's time is a pressing problem today, particularly in a field as shorthanded as finance. Efficiency in teaching would be a nearly impossible concept to define if one tried to take into account the intangibles in the instruction process, such as unique and successful personal styles and methods. But there are certain areas in which immediate action can be taken to aid teaching efficiency in finance. These are: (1) provision of adequate clerical and grading help; (2) acceptance of the necessity for larger classes at beginning and even at somewhat advanced levels; (3) provision of financed opportunity for interdisciplinary study by teachers; (4) clarification of the relative emphasis placed by administrations on quality of teaching and on research work when promotions and salary increases are made; and (5) provision of support for developing better texts, teaching aids, and cases. Space is not available here to discuss all the aspects of teaching effectiveness in finance; they are common to other fields and are dealt with elsewhere in this survey. However, the problem of teaching aids is of critical importance in the field of finance and is closely related to the time spent by finance teachers on research.

Effective use of a teacher's time should be viewed in connection with both instruction and research, because in finance, as in other fields, both functions are vital to education. As this report has pointed out, research is needed in many areas within finance and in areas relating it to other disciplines. At the same time, the need for timely teaching aids must be met to relieve finance teachers from individually preparing their own materials.

Many schools today have an unresolved conflict about the relative importance of teaching and research, and they show a resulting ambiguity about which activity merits the greater reward. As the matter stands today, too often the faculty member is thinking on the one hand about the administration's promotion and salary policy if research is emphasized and is trying on the other hand to satisfy his own conscience as a teacher with the result that his time and effort are too thinly spread over both instruction and research. Some administrators have intensified the quandary of faculty members by making much in public of a school's educational opportunities, which are commonly interpreted to mean academic instruction, when the internal policy of the school is actually to reward research effort rather than teaching. Some institutions might wish to state forthrightly their major emphasis on one area or the other; such a clear statement of policy would permit teachers to find a position where the direction of their major interest would fit in with school policy.

It is interesting to note one dean's statement that faculty most capable of research is most capable of good teaching and to observe that he heads a well-financed school where faculty has small teaching loads, adequate clerical help, a complete library, and office privacy. In such circumstances, research and pedagogy could perhaps go hand in hand if a school is well enough financed to obtain the services of the few individuals who are equally gifted in both activities. But the danger of such a statement from an exceptional school is that it will be unrealistically accepted as the combination of talents to which all teachers should attempt to conform. It will be generally agreed that competence in teaching and competence in research work are neither mutually exclusive nor mutually inclusive categories. There should be room on most faculties for the instructor whose skill and range of viewpoint make him primarily an accomplished teacher and who does some research, just as there should be room for the instructor who is especially able in research and who teaches only advanced students successfully. In any case, the finance teacher with the usual class load, especially if it includes advanced work, has a problem keeping his teaching approach and materials adequately up to date. Without neglecting this work, he can rarely find time to engage in research unless he has a period of leave to do so.

Yet the impression is general that most administrators venerate research and that the pressure of promotions and salary increases is directed toward this end. While this report proclaims the need for research in finance, it would like to point out that the inadequacy of instructional aids is encouraged by preference and reward for research projects, of whatever value, rather than for preparation of texts and teaching materials. It is suggested that a better way to encourage worthwhile research, especially in a field as pressed for personnel as finance, would be the indirect method of freeing the individual teacher of the time-consuming task of supplementing inadequate instructional materials.

The preparation of teaching aids receives little support. It should be remembered that in finance, as in any other field, the textbook is a basic teaching device and that it can give the student an attitude toward the field later reflected in much of the rest of his business work. This is true not only in schools where heavy enrollment is a problem but also where smaller classes permit the text to be used as a point of departure for more advanced work. The teacher who feels he would have a contribution to make in undertaking the writing of a finance text is not encouraged. Although a few texts have phenomenal success, the risks of not succeeding financially are great. Sometimes a progressive and worth-while text appears before the time is ripe for its acceptance or pecuniary success. The author assumes the risk of having his ideas work out successfully, whereas the research project financed by a grant may or may not be fruitful. A most useful aid to teaching and one that would free more faculty time for constructive research in the long run would be provision of grants for teachers who propose to write much-needed progressive texts in finance, just as grants are made for proposed research projects.

The same needs and the same arguments for support apply to the case-problem material needed in finance. A certain number of case problems are desirable in undergraduate work to lend interest and concreteness. In the M.B.A. work, where the orientation is toward executive decisions, such materials are essential. The one or two schools that organize their programs around cases have been generous in releasing them for use elsewhere. But the number of finance cases is not adequate, and many available are adapted to an integrated school-wide program and lose their effectiveness when used under other educational circumstances. If those borrowed cases or the few published ones are not used, a teacher of advanced finance must develop his own. Often funds are not available for the necessary travel to collect data and for the clerical work to adapt it. The task of disguising case data is an acute problem in finance.

Actual figures must be changed to conceal the identity of the source, but at the same time the complicated relationships between figures must be retained to preserve the significance of the case. To improve the flow of case materials to finance teachers, it is suggested that the American Finance Association work in close liaison with the Intercollegiate Bibliography of Cases in Business Administration which is a clearing house for cases in all fields. It might be feasible for these two organizations to develop a standard format to report key data for cases, thus simplifying reporting of data and enabling the teacher who borrows a case to write it up in the form most useful to him. If only one case or set of cases were provided yearly by even half the business schools, a more than adequate pool of up-to-date cases and problems would be available.

In short, encouragement by administrators and foundations for the writing of new texts and active support from the American Finance Association for a pool of case materials would improve teaching effectiveness and eventually free much time for finance teachers to do needed research in their field.

CHAPTER 16

MARKETING

Schuyler F. Otteson

The marketing curriculum is being subjected to careful scrutiny and important experimentation. New directions suggest less vocationalism, less concentrated narrow specialization, and study directed more along the lines of marketing management. Special attention in the future will be directed to such matters as market measurement and consumer behavior and to the interrelated play of these and other factors in an effective marketing program. Public policy issues with which marketing is concerned are likely to be treated within this framework and from the viewpoint of enlightened management.

HISTORICAL PERSPECTIVE

Of the major functional areas in business, marketing is one of the more recent fields to receive a place in the organized curricula of our universities. The first courses in marketing—and it is no doubt stretching a point to label them as marketing courses—appeared about 1902. A scattering of courses was added in the years that followed, but not until after World War I did the study of marketing gain a firm foothold in our business curriculum.

The 1920s

The early pioneers in marketing were few in number but extremely influential in laying the conceptual framework for our present marketing curriculum. They were also responsible for founding the predecessor of the American Marketing Association, the major professional organization in the field, and for initiating the research upon which our current understanding of marketing relies heavily.

Three of today's leading textbooks for the general or "principles" course in marketing appeared as first editions in the 1920s. Fred Clark mimeographed a text that was used in 1921 and 1922; this was published in 1922. Since the author was an economist by training and had been influenced strongly by literature from agricultural marketing, this book, through its several editions, showed the leanings and interests of an economist and carried heavy emphasis on agricultural products. While the content had been revised and updated, it is interesting to observe that the 1942 edition (which was the best-selling marketing text in the following year or two) did not differ substantially in organization from the 1922 version.

In 1921 Professor P. D. Converse published his first volume of *Marketing, Methods and Policies,* which preceded *The Elements of Marketing,* the first edition of which was published in 1930. Today this book is in its sixth edition; it is now authored by Converse, Huegy, and Mitchell and is one of the leading books in the field. In 1927 the Maynard, Weidler, and Beckman book, *Principles of Marketing,* was first published. The subsequent editions were revised, updated, and improved, but the general approach is substantially the same as that of the 1920s. The Harvard case materials on marketing, published in book form for use in both an introductory problems course and in an advanced course, were also available to the professor of the 1920s.

Thus the present basic book in marketing—its general structure, purpose, and type of coverage—first took shape in the 1920s, when introductory courses in marketing were also molded. Of course, other books have appeared since then, some following similar patterns and some with different approaches. But those cited above are now among the leading texts, except for the Clark book, which has not been revised since 1942 (Professor Clark died in 1948). Recently there has been some shift in emphasis from the "general economics" of marketing to marketing management. More will be said about this later.

In the writing that went on within major areas of marketing—namely, sales management, advertising, retailing, wholesaling, credits and collections, and marketing research—many earmarks of the writers in the 1920s may again be observed. Tosdal's *Problems in Sales Management* was published in 1921; Paul Nystrom's *The Economics of Retailing* came out in 1915; the first edition of *Credits and Collections in Theory and Practice* by T. N. Beckman appeared in 1924; and *Wholesaling,* also by Beckman, was published in 1926. Although the textbooks on marketing research came out at a later date, the books on commercial research published in the early 1920s laid much of the foundation for the better-known books that were to follow.

These publications are merely a few examples—surely the list is far from complete—to show what teaching materials were made available for the new course areas in marketing and what courses, now traditional, came into being during that era.

The training of these early authors was often in the field of economics. However, in a few instances, such as that of Walter Dill Scott, psychologists added to the literature, especially on the subjects of advertising and selling.

Turning from texts to courses, one observes that the course offerings in marketing in the mid-1920s bear close resemblance to the offerings in many schools of today. A proliferation of courses occurred in the following decade, but the major basic offerings—at least according to course titles and descriptions and other currently available information—often did not vary greatly from then until now.

The basic "principles of marketing" course was firmly established as a requirement for the undergraduate business major. The core of advanced work included sales management, advertising, and retailing. It was not uncommon to find two or three courses in each of these areas, and there were some schools where a student could take at least seven courses in advertising, majoring in that area. Other offerings frequently found were salesmanship, credits and collections, and foreign trade.

Proliferation of Courses in the 1930s

More courses and more types of majors made their appearance during the period of the 1930s. The expansion in course offerings took several forms. Sometimes two courses were created where one existed before. More often, courses were added that permitted greater specialization and at times somewhat greater vocational emphasis. The marketing major came into being at some institutions, and additional majors were created in advertising, retailing or merchandising, and sales. The format of the 1920s was not changed, but it was greatly enlarged. In the process of expanding courses, the general educational objective was somewhat changed by shifting the emphasis (often, I suspect, without plan or preconceived intent) from education for general business management to education for skill in a subarea of marketing.[1]

Marketing research, as an organized study, was finding its way into the curriculum on a more general scale by the late 1930s. Two books, one by Lyndon O. Brown and another edited by a committee in the American Marketing Association, appeared in 1937. These books helped

[1] I wish to emphasize that this generalization, along with others in the descriptive part of the chapter, describes general trends but not the situation at all schools. Such subjects as salesmanship received considerable play in a few schools in the very early 1920s, but on the other hand other institutions have held to the general management objective throughout the years.

provide necessary text materials for courses on this subject. The great popularization of marketing research was not evident until after World War II, but by 1940 it had found its place, at least in a minor way, in most marketing curricula.

War and the Immediate Postwar Situation

Needless to say, in the period from 1941 to 1946 little attention was paid to the curriculum, and especially to the work in marketing. Because of scarcities, allocations, and consumer goods rationing, marketing was viewed as an unnecessay area of study, even by the small group of students and professors that remained in the schools of business during the war period.

The prewar marketing curriculum remained basically unchanged during the years immediately following the war. Several factors may explain this situation. The flood of students and the shortage of teachers forced most schools to spend their efforts in keeping the shop running rather than in making major innovations in curriculum. Doctoral programs dried up during the war, contributing to a dearth of professors, and private business opportunities siphoned off another group of marketing men who had the training for academic work. While this generally was a problem for schools of business, it may have been a bit more acute in marketing since the supply of professors of marketing in immediate prewar days was surely never more than adequate.

The principal development in the curriculum at this time was the increased emphasis on marketing research, which by 1950 stood beside sales management, advertising, and retailing as a major study area in marketing. Not only academic halls but the American Marketing Association blossomed out in this direction—to the extent that it was criticized by some for being a society for marketing research. Research departments mushroomed, and the number of job opportunities in the area greatly encouraged growth and interest in all phases of research work.

In the 1940s critical analyses of marketing thought began to appear. In 1941, for instance, Robert Bartels presented as a doctoral dissertation a study of "Marketing Literature—Development and Appraisal." His inquiry into the status and tendencies of marketing knowledge appeared in articles in the *Journal of Marketing*.[2]

Questions about the development of marketing thought grew into scattered grumblings for change from the general orthodoxy. The noises may have seemed faint, but they heralded movements leading to many

[2] "Marketing Principles" (October, 1944); "Can Marketing Be a Science?" (January, 1951); and "Influences Affecting the Early Development of Marketing Thought, 1900–1923" (July, 1951).

present-day experiments and innovations. A few people expressed an interest in marketing theory; others showed an interest in marketing management. Illustrative of this "unorthodoxy" was the book *Theory in Marketing* (1950), edited by Cox and Alderson and sponsored by the American Marketing Association. Other writings of this type were also appearing. But the mills of the gods grind slowly. While these were significant portents of change, they were slow to be incorporated into the marketing curriculum of the vast majority of schools of business across the land.

THE MARKETING CURRICULUM OF TODAY

As this brief historical synopsis has suggested, the typical marketing curriculum of 1958 was structured in very great measure during the 1920s. A proliferation of offerings occurred in the 1930s, and a *status quo ante bellum* existed in the decade that ended in 1950.

Some schools that had been slow in expanding their marketing offerings during earlier periods did so during the postwar era. Furthermore, in very recent years a few schools have been experimenting with quite different programs, and in so doing they have been reconsidering the objective of the marketing curriculum, course content, and even the training and qualifications of the marketing professor himself. Considerably more will be said about this in a later part of this chapter; discussion at this point is limited to the more conventional marketing programs of today.

The Introductory Course in Marketing

A basic marketing course is generally required in both the undergraduate and the master's program of schools of business. Its over-all objective may lie in one of two directions. The first is to acquaint students with the general nature of marketing, its role and functioning in the American economy. In its broadest sense, a course limited to this objective might well be located in an economics department and considered as part of the liberal arts education for business students.

A second objective of the general course in marketing is to develop talents of potential managers or administrators. Here marketing problems of the firm are discussed, often by the case method, and the student is expected to develop his managerial capacities through such exercises.

Some schools attempt to accomplish both of these broad ends—the general and the managerial. Emphasis on the two goals varies from school to school.

The "marketing in the economy" approach has come in for criticism on the grounds that it is too descriptive, nonanalytical, repetitious, and susceptible to undue memorization by rote of names, pros and cons, characteristics, and numbers (usually percentages). A general, unifying theory that could make the work more meaningful is lacking. Attention is paid to the consumer, to the businesses engaged in marketing, the functions performed in marketing, marketing policies, legislation, price, and costs. Several of these categories are not subclassifications but cover the entire field, albeit each from a different perspective. Adding to the number of ways the field is covered in the one course, time is also usually allotted to covering the field by commodities—consumer goods, industrial goods, and agricultural products. Casual attention is often given to "price." This is difficult to explain since marketing authors and marketing teachers are usually trained in economics and have been exposed to heavy emphasis on price and its central role in equilibrium theory. Yet literature as well as class discussions of such matters have often been limited to a brief discussion of simple and semivocational pricing techniques, including the computation of markup.

The management-oriented introductory course has also come in for a certain amount of "carping," especially at the undergraduate level. The problem is in part one of pedagogy. Students taking the course are often too immature or lack adequate background to work intelligently with complex case materials in which they are expected to solve marketing problems too complicated for the vice-president of marketing in a multimillion-dollar firm. The charge is made that, while the student gets good exercise and may improve his artistry in dealing with a few selected problems, he fails to understand the over-all marketing function in a firm. These criticisms have been aimed principally at the basic course in the undergraduate program; perhaps the fundamental quarrel is with teaching materials and pedagogy rather than with the management emphasis. Attempts to train managers and develop social scientists in the same introductory course have met with mixed reaction. In short, there is at present a widespread uneasiness that neither of these goals is accomplished well and that our attempts to meet both of them leave much to be desired.

The Undergraduate Marketing Major[3]

The advanced course work in the undergraduate and master's programs tends to be built around job opportunities in marketing. Offerings

[3] Limitations of space and obvious problems of duplication require that this discussion as well as that for the graduate programs be limited primarily to the work done within the marketing area. The present discussion also emphasizes conventional patterns, since the newer experimental developments are considered in connection with patterns suggested for the future.

emphasize training the student for such assignments as sales (management or salesmanship), marketing research, advertising, and retailing. For each there is a general course and usually additional courses (sometimes as many as ten), frequently offered on an elective basis. Other job areas for which courses exist, though perhaps not quite so commonly as for the areas mentioned above, include wholesaling, credit work, and foreign trade.

This matter of specialization is handled by either (1) having a general marketing major and encouraging or allowing students to select sufficient electives to give them a specialty, or (2) having majors for each subgrouping, usually for advertising, sales, and retailing or merchandising. On the surface, it would appear that the latter arrangement leads to greater specialization, but this is not ordinarily the case. Students may think that they are being made into greater specialists when the catalogs list such majors, but the course requirements in the one case vary little from courses taken in the other. In one institution, for example, an advertising major requires three advertising courses as such, a sales-management major requires two courses on the subject, and the retailing major requires two retailing courses plus a seminar. For each major a pattern of work is also required from other parts of the marketing department and from other areas of the school of business and the university. The chief difference in these two directions seems to be this: in the one case the work is formalized and promoted as a specialty, and in the other case similar programs are worked out under the umbrella of the general marketing major. But regardless of these facts, students in compartmentalized specialties are more inclined to *think* that they are getting a complete program of specialization. The recent trend has been to shift from a major in one of several specialties to a general marketing major. Growing emphasis upon management and increasing criticism of vocationalism or overspecialization may account for this.

Schools vary widely in the amount of work permitted (or required) in marketing as such and as to whether general objectives are vocational or technical or managerial. This study's Survey Questionnaire revealed that of 67 schools with four-year programs, the *required* work in marketing for majors was as follows:

Number of schools	Minimum requirement in marketing subjects (semester hours)
13	19 and under
44	20–29
10	30 or more
——	
67	

Of the 44 schools requiring 20 to 29 semester hours in marketing, the students were permitted to take additional *electives* in marketing as follows:

Number of schools	Maximum marketing electives permitted beyond required courses (semester hours)
19	0–9
17	10–19
8	20 or more
——	
44	

The announced objective is to prepare students for managerial positions in the different areas. But the actual practice in some schools is to emphasize training of a vocational nature, possibly for jobs that students will be filling upon graduation. Such courses as salesmanship, advertising copy writing, and advertising layout are usually not aimed at the person planning to head a major functional division of a firm.

Master's Marketing Major

In a great many schools, especially in the smaller ones, graduate work comprises a small part of the entire program, and the work in such functional areas as marketing is basically a "souped-up" undergraduate arrangement. Students take senior and even junior courses and write term papers in them to make them respectable for graduate credit. A thesis is generally required, and a seminar may be available to give the work some distinction from the undergraduate program. Often a course in economics is required; in more recent times a course in management may be on the "must" list. Students may have considerable opportunity to take such specialized work as is available in undergraduate marketing courses. Since this is merely an extension of the undergraduate program, with the same courses and objectives, no more need be said about it here.

The M.B.A. degree is, of course, the principal degree at the master's level, but a few schools continue to offer the M.S. degree as well. Since marketing is a highly diversified field and requires a variety of staff specialists, the M.S. degree is offered as a means of providing the training for such specialists without disrupting the management-oriented M.B.A. program. The argument is that a high level of professional technical competency is needed in marketing research and in advertising. Undergraduate programs do not and should not provide such training, and thus a place is provided for it in the master's program.

M.B.A. programs differ substantially as to whether their goals should be preparation for general management or specialized training. At one extreme are schools like the University of Minnesota, which states, concerning its new M.B.A. program, "This degree is offered for students who desire unspecialized training for top-level business leadership." [4] The program at Carnegie Institute of Technology is similar in that the work in marketing is primarily a part of the training for general management. No marketing major is offered, and a student is specifically limited in the amount of marketing that he can take.

Certain advocates of the general management M.B.A. (not referring to the schools cited above) even claim that marketing is not a field of study, that it has no body of knowledge of its own, and that anything known about marketing has been transplanted from economics, statistics, and the behavioral sciences. If this is so, then how can even one course be justified? Yet many of those who take this position attempt to justify limited course work in marketing. The usual justification is that certain problems which are marketing-oriented are best studied under such an umbrella! The logic of such an argument is a bit difficult to follow.

At the opposite extreme are the graduate schools of retailing and the schools offering full-fledged majors in retailing or merchandising and in advertising. Even if their objective were to prepare general managers, such managers would be trained exclusively in one function or type of enterprise. A look at course offerings suggests that some of the work in such schools is aimed below the top functional management level.

Between these extremes are the many institutions that provide for a major in marketing, with considerable variation within the major as to the nature and amount of work suggested or required. One group, including the University of Chicago and the Amos Tuck School, has a unified program with a small number of courses designated to cover the field. The basic master's program at Chicago, for example, consists of:

Price Policy and Market Organization
Marketing Research
Market Communication
Theory and Analysis of Consumer Markets

Marketing majors are required to take three of these four courses; they may take as electives a course in marketing management, a seminar in marketing, or one of several courses offered in the departments of psychology, sociology, statistics, or economics.

Some schools offer a limited opportunity to pick and choose in what is perhaps a more traditional framework. Typical of this category is a well-

[4] *Bulletin of the University of Minnesota Graduate School*, 1956–1958, p. 67. It should be noted that the University of Minnesota offers the M.S. degree for those who wish to specialize.

known school where a student must select four courses from the following group:

Retail Store Management
Advertising
Sales Management
Marketing Policies
International Trade
Advertising Policies

In still another group of schools an even greater assortment of courses is offered, and still greater flexibility is afforded in developing an individualized program for each student.

The general trend in these programs is toward a management approach as opposed to the "social science of marketing" objective detectable in the master's program of yesteryear when the master's was an intermediary degree leading to the doctorate rather than a terminal professional degree. The distinction between undergraduate and graduate programs is becoming more apparent, with some schools moving toward strictly graduate offerings for master's candidates.

One fundamental issue is raised when comparing the small, unified marketing program with the one offering many courses on a pick-and-choose basis: to what extent should all marketing majors be given a unified coverage of the field and to what extent should the program offer flexibility and allow for adaptation to the individual interests of the students?

Doctoral Program in Marketing

Most schools that offer doctoral work in business include marketing as a field that may be chosen as a major or as one of the minors. But they differ in what they expect of the student. Passing an M.B.A. examination for a marketing major is an acceptable demonstration of competency in some places. At the other extreme are schools that require nearly every marketing course in the catalog for a marketing major—and such offerings are usually numerous. The major in such institutions is limited for all practical purposes to students who were undergraduates and/or master's majors in the subject.

A few institutions, such as The Ohio State University and Indiana University, have set up separate courses in marketing for doctoral candidates. At Ohio State this includes work cutting across the entire field of marketing and a study of the history of marketing thought as well as of contemporary marketing thought. Indiana University has a theory course exclusively for doctoral candidates. Doctoral seminars are prevalent in many places and commonly give attention to contemporary marketing problems, new developments in theory, and general questions relating to the role of marketing in the economic order. Since the objective is primarily that of preparing teachers rather than practitioners, the broad implications of marketing are emphasized while less attention is devoted to managerial problems. The nature of the doctoral degree, whether it is a Ph.D. or a D.B.A., has no discernible bearing upon requirements for a doctoral field in marketing.

It is currently highly fashionable to question and study graduate programs in business, especially the work done in marketing. Special committees are busy in schools everywhere. It would be surprising if the teachers' meetings of the A.M.A. as well as the regional meetings of marketing-teacher groups omitted from the agenda the matter of graduate curriculum. But with all this study and talk, most faculty members admit that little action has been taken in their own schools even though some changes, often fairly drastic, are deemed in order. Nevertheless, the climate is now conducive to making substantial changes where they are believed needed to improve the marketing curriculum.

THE MARKETING CURRICULUM OF THE FUTURE

Seemingly endless demands are made upon the time of the college student; this is to be expected, since he is preparing himself for the entire venture of life. The university has the responsibility of contributing to this preparation in whatever ways are most helpful to the student. Part of an individual's training to become a "whole man" must, of course, come from a wide assortment of places, including his home. For future business executives, an important part of it must be acquired through on-the-job experience and through study programs carried along with work experience.

However, there are many things that can best be learned or acquired through a college curriculum and climate. Adequate opportunities exist for development of cultural traits, for gaining an appreciation of those arts and sciences that enable the individual to appreciate fully the finer things of life. In addition, the development of the "whole man" requires exposure to literature, languages, art, history, philosophy, mathematics, psychology, sociology, government, and geography. Formal collegiate education can fulfill the needs in such areas very well. However, the professional schools, including schools of business, also have their role to play in developing competent contributors to society. Demands on the student's time for work in the traditional liberal arts program are unquestionably proper but must be kept in line. Each professor in each discipline can see good reasons why a student needs more work in his particular area if he is to be well educated. This is as it should be, and the value to a university of a professor lacking such enthusiasm and conviction for his work would surely be subject to question. But, even distilled to a minimum, the highly essential work in the liberal arts heavily restricts the amount of time that a student can spend in the study of business subjects.

Then, within the school of business, and including the work in economics, a broad base of study is undoubtedly essential if the student is to acquire a well-rounded understanding of the internal managerial and decision-making processes of a firm and comprehend the relationships of the firm to the social order (governmental as well as economic). This means that the time available for any attempt at mastery of a functional phase of business, such as marketing, is necessarily very limited and will always be subject to close scrutiny and to keen competition from other areas offering the myriad of courses that a university lists in its catalogs.

At the graduate level the assumption can be made that the student already has his liberal arts preparation. But the competition for scarce time from other parts of the business school program still exists.

Thus in planning a major field of concentration in marketing for the student of tomorrow, it behooves us to ask ourselves this: what are the minimum essentials that a student must receive in the marketing curriculum as such to achieve an understanding and some mastery of this field? Several steps might be taken to reduce this problem to manageable proportions:

First, identify those areas of understanding which a student should acquire in a university but which can perhaps be gained in either the liberal arts courses or other courses in business. Areas of broad general applicability need not be chopped up and departmentalized; if they were, one could figure out ways for including the entire university program in a marketing curriculum. Using some absurd examples to illustrate this point, courses in marketing English, marketing mathematics, and marketing statistics would certainly be unwise.

Second, identify the knowledge and skills that are important but that can perhaps be better taught in an on-the-job training program or a study program taken after the individual selects his specific line of work. True, our country is faced with a severe shortage of highly competent, vocationally trained people, and we would do well to encourage good training programs for shoe salesmen, credit analysts, receiving-room clerks, and persons holding down the other thousands of vocational or semiprofessional positions in marketing. But in terms of opportunity costs and basic educational objectives, the university curriculum is not the place for this, and classwork aimed at such ends should be pruned from our college offerings.

Third, eliminate the purely descriptive aspects of our work, especially those describing business and business problems and methods of yesteryear. The student is preparing himself for the next fifteen- to thirty-year period in his career. Methods and concepts that are sure to be outmoded by then may just as well be eliminated from classroom instruction. Memorization by rote of all provisions of the NRA will contribute little to the future business executive's ability to solve business problems in the 1980s.

However, even after these steps have been taken, further knotty problems present themselves to be resolved before a specific curriculum for a marketing major can be crystallized.

What is marketing? This sounds like an elementary question, but it is not. According to some of the broadest definitions, marketing encompasses most economic and business activities except those associated with the creation of form utility. On the other extreme, there are those who look upon marketing and selling as identical. In university curricula, the boundaries have fallen somewhere between these two extremes, with segments of work going outside or inside depending often upon the specific interests of the instructors.

The Committee on Definitions of the American Marketing Association defines marketing as "those business activities involved in the flow of goods and services from production to consumption." This carries a connotation that production is limited strictly to the creation of form utility; such a narrow conception of production is simply unsound. According to another standard definition, "marketing covers all business activities necessary to effect transfers in the ownership of goods and services and to provide for their physical distribution." Here again one gets a sense of what is meant by marketing, but the boundaries are nebulous.

The main purpose of this chapter, however, is not to spin all the neat ramifications of semantics, important as they may be, so let us identify the elements that lie at the heart of marketing. They include: (1) the market, (2) the product's want-fulfilling qualities, (3) price—the system of rationing products to markets, (4) marketing channels—the business structure designed for the exchange of goods, and (5) promotion—involving communication and stimulation essential to exchange. These elements may not comprise the entire study of marketing, but they identify the problems with which marketing is basically concerned.

Should the program be tailor-made to the interests and aptitudes of the individual marketing students, or should everyone selecting marketing as a major be held accountable for a common core of work? The purpose of a collegiate curriculum is to develop the individual. This being so, one might argue that programs should be individualized and tailor-made for each student. But every student majoring in business presumably is headed for some sort of a business career. A block of work in the school of business is designed for basic preparation and should be helpful to all business students. Thus it would seem proper to require certain general work of all students in the school. Furthermore, certain basic preparation is desirable for all those who plan to work in or up through the marketing phases of a business. There is good reason why all marketing students should master this basic common core of marketing work. Regardless of a student's interests or aims, a sizable share of the marketing curriculum should be useful and helpful. Of course the program must be individualized to correct weaknesses in the background of a given student. Furthermore, we would be remiss to use a student's valuable time on materials that he has already covered. Proficiency examinations could be used freely, and when minimum standards are met, a student might be excused from certain parts of the basic required work. Whether it is a matter of deficiencies or proficiencies, the problem is more likely to arise for the M.B.A. candidate than it is for the undergraduate since greater heterogeneity is found in the backgrounds of graduate students.

Extreme care should be taken in allowing a student to follow a program along a narrow path or toward too specific a professional objective. Experience has shown it is highly probable that students will change their minds and follow quite different objectives, thus making narrow, specific work rather meaningless. Even if a student continues to follow a given line, he needs the breadth and depth that the basic general part of the program provides. Thus a core of work in general business administration and another core of work in basic marketing might be required of all students majoring in marketing. Since a little specialized work may help provide motivation and give perspective to the rest of a student's program, a small amount of elective work in marketing might be justified.

Should the marketing curriculum be oriented toward management or toward public policy? A look at the end product will suggest an answer to this question. The M.B.A. candidate is preparing himself professionally for business management. The goal may be a line assignment, but many students will end up in staff positions. In either case, the goal is business management or operations. Thus logic would dictate that the M.B.A. program follow a management perspective. Each student is also expected to perform as a responsible citizen of his business community. Therefore public policy issues are important and should be given careful consideration. This can be done within a management-oriented decision-making framework.

The same general position might apply to the undergraduate major in marketing. The undergraduate program has more responsibility for a general education; to the extent that this is so, the emphasis may be less strictly management-oriented, and more attention may be given to broad economic and public policy issues.

The doctoral program has quite a different objective, namely, that of preparing individuals for a career in teaching and, for a few, a career in research. As much as possible, the programs for such individuals should be oriented to develop proficiency along these lines.

Are the problems of marketing consumer goods, industrial goods, and agricultural products so dissimilar that separate courses on each are essential? Some might argue for a detailed study of marketing by commodity grouping, since a more accurate and specific understanding of the economic system would result. But the shortage of time is not likely to permit such a luxury. Contrasts and similarities can be brought out in standard marketing courses, and this is about as far as typical schools of business can be permitted to go in the required core of the curriculum. Compelling arguments might be made for exceptions where programs are designed for agricultural students or for engineers. Also, an elective in industrial marketing might be appropriate, especially at the M.B.A. level. But fundamental research must be encouraged along commodity lines. Some marketing problems are difficult to analyze deeply and critically in any other way.

Is special attention required for each of the traditional functions of marketing—buying, selling, risk taking, market finance, standardization, grading, storage, and market information? A valid argument might be developed that a student does not achieve complete understanding of marketing without an orderly study of each of its functions. Yet the stop watch shows us that a 3-hour course in each of the eight major functions means 24 hours of work, which still fails to allow for course work directed toward over-all integration. Nor does it include time to study the consumer, the price system, and the business structure of marketing. Add these, plus a little specialization, and the student has a marketing program of 30 to 40 semester hours. Competition for time for the bare essentials in the remainder of the program makes a marketing requirement of this magnitude prohibitive. Parts of such a program would more than likely tend toward detailed techniques and vocationalism and could be severely criticized on such grounds. Thus it would seem that much of the work in the traditional functional areas of marketing must be woven into a curriculum ordered along other lines.

Should a course in research methods be incorporated within the marketing curriculum? A healthy interest in the scientific method and analytical approach has prompted most schools to include a course in marketing research in the curriculum, often on a required basis. To quarrel with such a worthy goal is much like arguing for sin. But why should a course in research methods be individualized for the marketing curriculum? Analytical methods pertaining directly to marketing problems, such as those pertaining to market measurement, might be taught in the substantive marketing courses. Indeed, development of new and better analytical methods should be encouraged strongly and incorporated in both classwork and research work wherever appropriate. The *general* methods of research and quantitative analysis could then be taught on a broader basis for all students in the school of business.

Should a course in "management methods" be incorporated within the marketing curriculum? The reasoning applied to courses in research methods also applies to the setting up of courses on "management methods" as part of the marketing curriculum. The general theory of management or administration, including decision-making theory, should be of interest to all business students. The applications to marketing problems are not overly difficult for the marketing major to make, even though the name of his major may be omitted from the prefix of the course.

An argument for departmentalizing general materials is that students are better motivated, study harder, and learn more when such things are directly applied to problems of greatest interest to them. On the other hand, there are advantages to having specialists teach and do research in complex areas. The marketing professor certainly cannot be highly competent in every facet of intellectual endeavor, and spreading his talents over too many areas could lead to some watering down in both teaching and research programs.

Should the marketing curriculum have courses on how to run a retail store, a wholesale house, and so forth? General principles of organization and operation apply to marketing enterprises as well as to other kinds of businesses. To the extent that these principles exist and are taught, duplication would occur if a series of "How to Run . . ." courses were offered. Besides, some of the present how-to-do-it literature suggests strong vocational emphasis—the type of thing that may be very proper for an on-the-job training program. Much of this material can be covered by individual reading without the expense or distraction of a professor and fellow students.

Are separate courses needed for international marketing and marketing within foreign lands? A course in foreign trade is now quite common, and economics departments usually have additional theoretical work in international economics. Aside from this, a school is indeed unusual if it includes international considerations in the regular marketing program. Comparative marketing systems are almost completely ignored. The increasing importance of international business, and business within foreign lands, behooves us to incorporate such considerations wherever proper in courses throughout the regular marketing curriculum. However, this may not be enough. Such integration may be slow and difficult and, in certain aspects, hard to effect. Thus a separate course might be justified, perhaps on an elective basis. But the license for such a course should clearly exclude the detailed how-to-do-it type of thing and should require a solid body of analytical and theoretical material. Perhaps present courses in foreign trade can be remodeled along such lines.

Concern is often expressed about cutting back the multiplicity of course offerings lest research in the many aspects of marketing be impeded or discouraged. Such a danger is very real, since there is a tendency for professors to be hired to teach courses; in turn they are inclined to direct their research along the lines of such courses. The research program in such a highly heterogeneous field as marketing must be developed along lines other than those established for the teaching curriculum. The interdisciplinary nature of many problems that are marketing-oriented makes this position even more compelling.

M.B.A. Major

The head of a marketing function in a business enterprise finds himself playing the role of both the rigorous analyst and the clever artist. Carefully ordered empirical evidence forms a satisfactory basis for coping with some problems; it is in this connection that analytical skills are especially essential. But marketing plans and strategy also require daring imagination, visualization of what might be, and a creative attitude toward developing new products and new methods for the future. The need for developing the two rather different types of talents must be considered in planning both course content and teaching methods. Attention to the analytical side of a student's development may quite often be observed in the curriculum of today. Among the more interesting experiments on the creative side is the work done in a class at Harvard University on creative marketing strategy. As the course description suggests, "the word creative is used in the course title because the emphasis in the course is on innovation." [5]

[5] *Official Register of Harvard University, Graduate School of Business Administration*, LV, Cambridge, Mass., May, 1958, p. 120. An exciting experiment with similar goals involves the use of business games and is now being carried on at the University of Pittsburgh. Two quarters of time are simulated each week, and the decisions are fed into an IBM 650 computer. Students work in five teams with eight or nine men to a team. After they have played enough quarters to determine some of the consequences on sales due to manipulating price, promotion, and research, they attempt to articulate and justify the strategy that their team is using. At this stage, the administrative or "human relations" problems begin to be mentioned prominently. Frictions within the team increase when the members are forced to articulate and agree upon the strategy that integrates not only the entire marketing operation but also the marketing operation with the rest of the company. The clear-cut criterion of success that has been established is rate of return on investment.

An uncritical acceptance of so-called marketing principles, with an acceptance of the fund-of-knowledge concept of marketing as a science, can easily stifle creativity. Piling up a group of generalizations and treating them as a kit of tools, revering them as eternal verities, can easily lead to a closed system of reasoning that impedes or prevents the adventurous exploring of new possibilities and the abandoning of outmoded notions or customs. If marketing is to be considered a science as well as an art, then we would do well to accept the dynamic concept of science expressed by James Conant in *On Understanding Science,* in which he places emphasis upon method and the search for truth and not upon findings. The marketing manager would find more opportunity to try his proverbial artist's wings in such an intellectual atmosphere. These ideas may not have direct and specific applicability to a marketing curriculum, but they are fundamental in creating a climate for the study as well as for the practice of marketing management.

The following suggestions are in no way intended to reflect a wholesale condemnation of the work now being done. Rather, some new patterns are suggested for the future because the broad and diversified field of marketing has been growing and expanding; in the process, a degree of maturity has been reached and the time has arrived when a new assessment of goals and methods is in order. It is the considered judgment of many marketing scholars that review and reappraisal are both healthy and essential. Suggestions throughout the chapter are offered in this spirit.

These are suggestions for what might be done, not predictions of what will happen. The latter would be difficult indeed, since development patterns of individual schools vary substantially due to differences in tradition, the nature of the student body, interests of faculty, financial wherewithal, and genuine differences in educational philosophy. Any suggestions would require modification and adaptation for particular institutions, since marketing is only a part of the total curriculum and its offerings may vary to mesh with the nature and content of the other courses.

The following courses are, therefore, set forth as a suggested basis for establishing minimum requirements for the marketing major of tomorrow. The proposals are based upon an M.B.A. program of two academic years, with a 15-hour maximum semester load.

Basic work in each of the major functional areas of business plus accounting and statistics in some form (quantitative methods) would be a part of the program for all M.B.A.s. When students have covered the areas as undergraduates, some of the work might be waived through proficiency examinations or other means. As an experiment, marketing majors might be excused from taking the basic marketing course even

Semester hours

The Consumer and Markets (Macro and Micro) 3
Marketing Management, including: 8
    The Product
    Channels and the Business Structure of Marketing
    Promotion
    Price
    Integrated Marketing Program
Elective in one of the following:* 3–4
    Retail Management
    Sales Management
    Advertising Management
    Foreign Trade
    Credits and Collections
    Wholesaling
    Honors or Research Seminar

* This list of possible electives is intended to be illustrative only. Fewer courses, and possibly different courses, might be appropriate. In any event, each course must meet the rigorous tests of scholarly work before it is approved.

though they enter the program with no background in this subject. If this were done, the student would, of course, be expected to do some carefully selected reading to gain orientation to the field.

Work outside the marketing department should also include the following courses; it would be helpful if the work in economics could precede that suggested in marketing:

Economics of the Firm
Macroeconomic Analysis
Management or Organization Theory
Research Methods
Business Policy
Government–Business Relations

These courses are designed primarily to sharpen and improve decision-making ability; the last course in the list emphasizes problems or issues facing the firm in our broad social order. Titles for all these courses will vary somewhat, especially for the last course listed, since it may be christened with a different and perhaps broader socioeconomic name. Remedial work in the behavioral sciences may be necessary for some students. Those who have taken some of the required business courses as undergraduates may be asked to substitute work in such "outside areas" as mathematics and the behavioral sciences.

Now let us take a more detailed look at suggestions for the content of courses outlined for the marketing concentration.

Consumer and Markets.[6] Perhaps no facet of business is more closely consumer-oriented than marketing. Successful programs of marketing require an astute discovery of consumer wants (existing or potential), consumer behavior, and consumer motivation. Also, market planning requires forecasts and measurements of prospective demand (and sales), in aggregate and by components of the market. Several of these considerations are now included in the traditional course in marketing research. But with the exception of the brief coverage in the introductory "principles" course, a number of important aspects receive scant attention.

Major sources from which subject matter for such a course could be drawn include psychology, sociology, economics, and statistics. The psychologist has the most to offer in the micro phases dealing with the individual. Helpful ideas for aggregate analysis might come from sociologists, social psychologists, anthropologists, and statisticians of the variety working with the U.S. Bureau of Labor Statistics or the University of Michigan Survey Research Center. Some of the work in macroeconomic analysis would also be applicable.

Interesting experiments with work in this area are already under way. A course at the University of Chicago in theory and analysis of consumer markets attempts to give the student "a review of theories of consumer demand with special reference to their significance for market analysis. Appraisal of historical factors influencing changes in consumer behavior, such as changes in level and distribution of income, balance sheet position, population growth, and consumer attitudes and expectations. Examination of changes over time in important representative consumer markets and of factors affecting rate of acceptance of any new products."[7]

Columbia University currently offers a course in consumer market behavior described as follows: "The economic bases of consumption, such as incomes, consumer requirements, availability of consumer goods, advances in the prices of consumer goods, patterns of expenditures, and the effects of social pressure, as modified by managing ability and skills in the arts of consumption. The effects of changes in these bases. Each student makes a special study of the principles and patterns of the consumption of a selected commodity of wide use."[8]

---

[6] The title suggested here may be somewhat nebulous. Perhaps a name including such description as "The buyer and market analysis, measurement, and segmentation" may communicate the nature of the contents more effectively. The course would *not* place central emphasis upon the competitive structure, as the suggested title could imply.

[7] *The University of Chicago, Announcements, The School of Business,* LVIII, Chicago, May 15, 1958, p. 25.

[8] *Columbia University Bulletin, Graduate School of Business,* 1958–1959, ser. 58, no. 10, New York, March 8, 1958, p. 56.

Current offerings are concerned primarily with the ultimate consumer, but the scope for such a course might well be expanded to cover considerations in the industrial goods market.

Marketing Management. A good argument can be made for splitting the work suggested for this course into several separate courses, each carrying a small amount of credit, yet with the total credit amounting to about 8 semester hours. The curriculum would be easier to explain, easier to promote, and in some instances teaching assignments would be simplified. Some schools would undoubtedly find separate courses desirable. But there are also good reasons for teaching these materials as one unit. First, the amount of time needed for each unit is not the same; some segments such as "the product" may not justify over an hour of credit and perhaps less. Thus a separate course on the separate subjects would be administratively unwieldy. Second, segmentation detracts from an attempt to develop integration, and the so-called "marketing mix" requires considerable integration when a marketing program in its entirety is under consideration. The interplay of product, price, and promotion might be difficult to teach effectively if there were separate courses, and the over-all integrating concept would of necessity be required to follow a study of the units.

Product.[9] The marketing manager considers the thing he has to sell, not as a material physical object, but as a bundle of services that are incorporated in a so-called "product," which in itself may be an intangible. These service-rendering qualities, together with physical attributes, are important to designing marketing strategy. A recent yet growing interest is being shown in this matter of the product and its marketing implications. A few schools have gone so far as to add a complete marketing course on the subject, while several others have included product considerations in the general treatment of marketing. Some of the associated problems are manufacturing-oriented, while others are marketing-oriented. In its broader sense, product innovation is recognized as an important factor in economic progress.

Work in this area requires close liaison with production management, and therefore the development of ideas might come in part through close cooperation between production and marketing people. Engineers and fashion artists would undoubtedly have valuable ideas to contribute.

Channels and the Business Structure of Marketing. A detailed description, and nothing more, of each type of business that engages in marketing can scarcely be justified in a collegiate business curriculum. But the rationale for our business system, the basic fundamentals explaining alternate channels and the roles played by various business firms, con-

---

[9] The term "merchandising" is often used to indicate this segment of marketing activity.

tributes importantly to an understanding of marketing problems. The evolution of business structures, reasons for change, and business patterns projected for the future would be vital to this course. An approach of the type suggested would give the student a meaningful understanding of wholesalers and retailers and not merely a description by rote of their names and numbers.

This is a segment of marketing in which the marketing profession must draw heavily from its own resources. A little help might be forthcoming from organization theory people, and the microanalysts from economics could make important contributions. Some explanation of the homeostasis of the structure could also come from sociology and anthropology.

Promotion.[10] The two basic activities associated with promotion are communication and stimulation. Facts about product characteristics (using the term broadly to include all associated services) and consumer demand must be disseminated throughout market channels. Since such information may not in itself lead to action, stimulation toward action (sales action) is essential.

This facet of marketing has been approached traditionally through courses in salesmanship and advertising techniques. But an approach of this sort does not accomplish the real objective of marketing management. Emphasis has often been placed upon vocational, how-to-do-it techniques rather than upon fundamental considerations for the over-all marketing program.

An interesting experiment in dealing with one part of the problem is the course in market communication at the University of Chicago, recently taught by a social psychologist. In some of the more traditional curricula, experiments along similar lines are taking place in the regular advertising or sales management course.

Price and Competition. There are two ways in which price becomes an important matter to the marketing manager in making intelligent decisions for his firm.

First, as an administrative consideration, pricing strategy is part of the over-all strategy in selling. It is one of the major variables affecting sales volume and profits. Problems relating to elasticity of demand, cost curves, marginal analysis, and competitive price behavior under different forms of competition all focus upon this aspect of strategy.

A second set of problems, centering around competition and price, is of a broader, public-policy nature and includes fair trade acts, price discrimination, and antitrust regulations. These are problems requiring decisions and action at the firm level; thus an understanding of them is essential for internal management reasons. Knowledge in this area is also

---

[10] This may not be the best choice of a name. For purposes of immediate discussion, the proposed content is considered more important than the title.

important for the purposes of public policy if the business executive is to assume his social responsibilities in an enlightened manner. To understand fully the analytical tools, the fundamental problems, and the consequences of alternative forms of action relating to competition and price, a prospective marketing executive must comprehend the central role of price in our economy.

Preparation in economics, and especially in micro theory, is essential for careful work in this area. A study of government-business relations should prove helpful as a basis for understanding public policy issues of competition and price. The price system is central to our marketing system, and therefore the marketing area can make many meaningful contributions in its own right.

Other Important Functions and Activities. There may be considerable debate as to whether or not other important functions and activities should be singled out for special consideration in this "umbrella" course in marketing management. Many major aspects, such as marketing finance, market risk, and physical distribution, might deserve exclusive attention. But each of these might also be treated in connection with the topics mentioned earlier. One of the major elements of market risk, for example, is the risk of price change; that might be considered along with pricing. To illustrate further, in the case of physical distribution, pertinent matters might be considered in connection with the product, channels, and the pricing part that deals with the nature and form of competition. Perhaps even more meaning and significance can be derived from the study of physical considerations if viewed in this way.

Integration. When covering individual topics in the sequence suggested, whether as separate courses or within one "umbrella" unit, attempts should obviously be made to relate the parts to the whole marketing program. But a crucial part of a general marketing program requires the interrelating of all parts—product considerations, promotion, channels, and pricing—into one integrated plan. Such integration must follow a treatment of the parts. It could be done in a separate seminar. This might be workable for schools on a quarter system. However, the semester system would present problems of timing with the final integrating seminar, since the core work would very likely be taken throughout the second year.

Matters of standards, control, and appraisal could be considered throughout the course as they pertain to various segments. Such matters also pertain to the over-all marketing program, which would justify treatment in this final integrating unit.

One way of accomplishing this final coordination would be through the use of cases covering complete marketing programs. Problems relating to public policy and social responsibility might be isolated for treatment on some other bases. An overview of marketing in the economic order might also be presented outside a firm-oriented approach.

Electives. The marketing major could be allowed considerable leeway in planning a small but important part of his program. This can be accomplished through careful selection of an elective.

The role of such an elective is twofold. First, it gives the student an opportunity to sink a shaft deeply and critically into one aspect of marketing. An opportunity for more penetrating analytical work is thus afforded. Second, an elective in an area of greatest interest may serve to motivate students and to give gifted students a special opportunity to assert themselves to a maximum. One of the electives might be a course reserved exclusively for outstanding individuals.

While an elective is important to give the student an opportunity for intensive study in some area, it is also equally important that each elective be intellectually challenging. Careful scrutiny of each course is in order at each school. Such inquiries should result in leavening or pruning whenever conditions require such action. There is surely nothing sacrosanct about the illustrative list of electives shown in this chapter.

Doctoral Field in Marketing

The primary purpose of the doctoral program is to provide men and women with advanced preparation for the college teaching profession, or, in the case of a few, for research assignments. Typically, a business student is expected to demonstrate a high level of competency in a number of fields, one of which might be marketing. Ideally, a field in marketing at this level would be based upon the general ground covered in the M.B.A. program, but from a different perspective. Greater emphasis would be placed upon research, upon teaching methods and materials, upon advanced theory, and upon the broader social significance of various issues. Attention to developing the *art* of administration would be deemphasized and considered only to the extent necessary to prepare future professors for handling such matters in the classroom.

But this ideal solution for covering master's-level subject matter in the doctoral program may not be realistic for most schools. Students who enter the doctoral program are likely to have widely varied backgrounds. Some will have taken an M.B.A. major of the type described above, some will have covered a limited amount of work in the field, and a few may have no previous exposure to the subject. Those with little or no work in marketing are likely to be so few in number that separate courses could not be justified. Competition for valuable time would rule out the idea of having students repeat work, albeit with a different emphasis. Thus doctoral programs will require much individualized planning.

Formal course work might be supplemented generously with independent reading programs.

If a student entered the doctoral program with an M.B.A. major in marketing, having taken a program similar to the one already discussed, an additional seminar plus carefully planned independent reading should provide adequate preparation for the examination in this field.

The prospective doctoral candidate with no previous work in marketing and desiring a field in that area might gain the basic work in one of several ways. Considering the maturity and quality expected in such individuals, a carefully designed program of reading and consultation might suffice to provide the background up to the doctoral seminar. In some instances an audit of the M.B.A. work plus independent reading might prove satisfactory. As suggested earlier, if there were a large enough number of students to make such a practice feasible, a separate doctoral course covering this ground in marketing management on an accelerated scale, and exclusively for doctoral candidates, might provide a preferable solution. Such a course would afford an opportunity to explore new theoretical concepts and ideas involving greater abstraction than could be considered in the professionally oriented M.B.A. class.

A doctoral seminar in marketing, perhaps 3 to 6 hours of credit,[11] might be offered as a final capstone for all students choosing marketing as one of their fields. It would be oriented basically to the future academician. Coverage might include a brief history of the development of marketing ideas, an appraisal of literature in the field, a discussion of leading marketing men and their contributions, special problems and new ideas on the horizon relating to teaching this subject, and new developments in subject matter as well as in curriculum.

Undergraduate Major in Marketing

This discussion will not carry a debate on the pros and cons of having an undergraduate major in marketing, since that issue is considered in its broader perspective in other parts of the report. Nor will an attempt be made to suggest a complete and detailed 120-hour program for students interested in marketing. Rather, it is assumed that there will be an undergraduate marketing major. The remarks here are limited to a consideration of the marketing curriculum, plus closely related suggested work.

With some modification, the core courses in marketing suggested for the M.B.A. program would be appropriate in the undergraduate program.

[11] The ideal number of credit hours could not be determined without considerable experimentation and without prior consideration of the entire program of a particular school.

The work may be different in the following respects: less rigorous work might be expected; orientation may slant somewhat more toward social considerations and a bit less toward the straight professional, firm-oriented point of view. The need for flexibility in the offerings and the greater number of semesters available to cover the material might be a strong argument for dividing the general marketing management into separate courses—keeping total hours about the same. This need not be the case, however; some schools may find that the course "packages" outlined for the M.B.A. might be acceptable for the undergraduate program. The introductory course could be taken by majors as well as by nonmajors. Thus the marketing core might be somewhat as follows:

	Semester hours
Consumer and Markets	3
Channels and the Business Structure of Marketing	2–3
Products and Promotion	2–3
Competition and Price	2
Integrating Seminar on Marketing Management	2
	11–13

Suggested coverage in these courses would follow the pattern outlined for the marketing management course in the M.B.A. program. There may be one significant difference. The seminar might be used to a much fuller extent to isolate and give special attention to the gifted student. Similarly, as with the M.B.A.s, one of the electives could be specially designed for this purpose.

In addition to this required base, a student may choose as an elective one of the traditional courses, such as retail management, sales management, et cetera. There is considerable merit in separating the undergraduate and the graduate sections rather than commingling students at both levels in the same course. This is not to imply that a student taking one of these courses as an undergraduate should be permitted to repeat the same course in the graduate curriculum.

If the following courses were not included in the general requirements, the marketing major should be strongly urged or required to take them:

Economics of the Firm
Macroeconomic Analysis
Psychology—especially Social Psychology
Sociology
Geography
Government–Business Relations

The basic course in each of the major functional areas, plus accounting and statistics (or quantitative methods) and possibly business policy, would be a part of the program for all students in business.

TEACHING AND RESEARCH: OPPORTUNITY AND CHALLENGE

Some people in university circles believe that an unduly high percentage of mediocre students are attracted to a marketing curriculum. Possibly the critics are overly impressed with the stereotyped movie version of the drummer; possibly there is some truth in their accusations. Whatever the truth may be, the academic marketing profession must set and maintain rigorous standards and must give special attention to developing gifted students. Special classes, possibly seminars, have been suggested as a means of accomplishing the latter at both the undergraduate and the master's level. Serious thought and attention will no doubt bring about additional and improved methods for developing the gifted few.

Some interesting experiments now taking place offer possibilities for making the teaching of marketing more exciting and more meaningful. To cite but two illustrations: The marketing department at Northwestern University is making tape recordings of interviews with marketing executives and using this and other means to bring actual case situations into the classroom. Every attempt is made throughout the teaching program to involve the student directly in the actual business situation, and recordings are but one means of simulating this realistic situation.

In one of the courses at Harvard University the class is divided into competitive teams. Executives are called in to outline to the teams the salient facts of major marketing problems. Spirited competition then prevails; consultations with executives continue, field work is done, and each team grubs through library materials in order to marshal all available information pertinent to the problem. Finally, each team formulates recommendations and makes an independent and competitive presentation to top officers of the firm. Efforts along these lines should prove helpful in developing the artistry of business management.

The possibility of more "team teaching" may deserve further experimentation. Carried to its extreme, the faculty member who is especially interested in an area such as price, for example, might handle this part of the work in the basic course and in the advanced course at both the undergraduate and the graduate level. Each student would thus be exposed to the thinking of a larger portion of the faculty, and the various phases of the work presumably would be handled by the most competent members of the staff. Such a program would require careful integration if the results were to be something more than a package of fragments, but possible benefits may justify a try.

These illustrations are cited not so much for their value in their own right—important as this might be—but as examples of the many things that could be done if a concerted effort were made toward experimentation and innovation in the classroom.

In addition to improving the effectiveness of our teaching, further efforts are needed to develop both a more professional and a more scholarly attitude among marketing students. The flood of job offers facing the post-World War II student, on the one hand, and the competition in some schools for larger numbers of students, on the other, has encouraged a sophomoric student attitude that is neither becoming to the individual nor wholesome for the school. This problem is not confined to marketing and must be dealt with on a much broader basis.

Marketing cannot be studied as an isolated area. Its problems include considerations of finance, personnel, control, and all other aspects of business. Some ideas about marketing are self-contained, but others must come through contact with philosophy, mathematics, the behavioral sciences, and any other intellectual sources that might have something to contribute. Perhaps marketing can follow the trend of such older professions as medicine, in which allied basic sciences continue to contribute in a major way to both teaching and research while the profession itself has moved forward to evolve a body of fundamental doctrine of its own. Similarly, the marketing student of tomorrow must continue to look to the appropriate areas around the university for his "basics." Adding a marketing prefix to the titles of general business courses, and indeed to general university courses, is not the way to achieve this.

In addition to requiring a broad basic foundation for the study of marketing, we must make every effort to work into the marketing courses themselves the many contributions from other fields, especially the social sciences. This might be accomplished by borrowing, integrating, and applying as Wroe Alderson has so ably done in his book *Marketing Behavior and Executive Action* (1957). But very few faculty members are adequately versed in the literature of the many fields to do this type of thing. Another approach might be to call upon faculty members from various departments and schools to deliver guest lectures or to handle a portion of the teaching assignment in a course. In fact, some schools have added behavioral scientists and mathematicians to their business school staffs on a permanent basis. As an example of still another approach, Columbia University is coordinating a program in which printed materials on marketing topics are prepared by authorities in various disciplines and made available for teaching purposes. A possibility relatively unexplored as yet is that of hiring for brief periods of time faculty members from other disciplines as consultants to advise and assist with teaching and to participate in research projects. Such arrangements would make it possible for them to retain their departmental identity.

Need for an interdisciplinary approach is perhaps greatest when it comes to *research* in marketing. Various avenues of opportunity present themselves for the future. In view of the current emphasis upon quantification, we might do well to go back, with the help of philosophers, and reexamine the fundamental philosophical assumptions that underlie measurement and prediction. Surely the central issue of free will versus determinism, with its implications for prediction of human behavior in the market place, has been largely ignored. Excellent progress is already being made in refining our methods of observation and in sharpening our tools of quantitative analysis. Further progress can be expected along these lines.

In our attempt to become more scientific in marketing there is grave danger that we will unwittingly contribute to the training of human robots rather than of responsible citizens for tomorrow's business community. Exercises in working out narrowly conceived problems—the type, for example, in which highly advanced mathematical problem-solving techniques are easily illustrated and applied—can ignore the really important problem of which quantification is only a minor aspect. I am referring of course to the broad fundamental problem of identifying and selecting personal and social goals and values, the problem of selecting systems for accomplishing desired ends, the problem of harmonizing marketing decisions with their broader implications. By striving to gain breadth and deeper understanding, we run the risk of relying too heavily upon technical specialists who lack the perspective to project, visualize, and comprehend the role of their narrow problem-solving activity in its broader meaningful context. Yet many of the same people who are highly enthusiastic about using technical specialists from various branches of the university in business schools, especially in marketing work, seem to ignore completely, or show only faint interest in, what might be contributed by the philosopher and the broad social scientist. The extent to which this problem must be considered in the marketing curriculum depends in great measure upon what is done about it in other parts of a school's business program.

CHAPTER 17

PERSONNEL MANAGEMENT
AND INDUSTRIAL RELATIONS

George P. Shultz

The field of personnel management and industrial relations, since it involves the relationship of business problems to the changing social, economic, and legislative environment of our times, should be approached as an application of social science. The emphasis in present programs at the undergraduate and master's levels varies from training for job skills to training for general understanding of the problems characteristic of the field. Suggestions are made here for moving the emphasis in the direction of general understanding. At the doctoral level, more emphasis should be given to the basic intellectual disciplines underlying this field and to research.

The field of personnel management and industrial relations has grown tremendously over the past few decades in complexity, claims on public attention, and importance to management. A large volume of material about concepts, practices, legislation, institutions, and other matters related to the field has appeared. Combined with the prominence given to labor relations problems and labor disputes particularly in the years just following World War II, this material has led some people to regard the field almost as a distinct intellectual discipline. Such a view, which would lead to study of the field's content directly and in its own terms, is not justified. Though the field has much substantive content of its own, its fundamental analytic content is drawn from various disciplines within the social sciences and from the law. Exposure to, if not mastery of, these areas must be an integral part of an intellectually ambitious personnel curriculum. In fact, the nature, richness, and vitality of materials available and almost constantly coming to hand offer the teacher a fine opportunity to present this field as an application of social science and as a study in the relationship of business problems to the changing social, economic, and legislative environment of our times. The recommendations offered here represent an effort to capitalize on this opportunity.

We will deal first with the dimensions of the field and with objectives and priorities in curriculum design. Discussions of the variety of programs now available in business schools will follow, together with suggested programs for the undergraduate, the master's, and the doctoral levels. Finally, we will take up briefly a number of special problems.

DIMENSIONS OF THE FIELD

The dimensions of "personnel management and industrial relations" may be portrayed in three ways: as problem areas or functions to be performed by management, as applications of various social science disciplines and the law, and as a flow of problems over time, with shifting emphases and growing knowledge within the field. We may learn something about curriculum design by examining each of these portrayals.

Personnel as a Management Function

The direct functions of management are customarily taken to be the production and sale of goods and services and the raising of money to conduct these operations; thus the traditional functional fields of business study are production, marketing, and finance. But if it is trite to say that management gets results through the efforts of *people* in its employ, that is nevertheless true. The growth of personnel departments in businesses, the formalization of "personnel" as a field of study within the program of many business schools, and the almost universal requirement of some course work in this area all reflect recognition of this fact. Nevertheless, the nature of "personnel" as a management function is somewhat different from that of the traditional fields. As an indirect rather than direct function, it is at once more limited and more pervasive than the others. On the one hand, the specialized functions of personnel departments can be handled by a relatively small number of people, even though the specialty may be regarded as of major importance; on the other hand, every member of the management organization has personnel responsibilities that are of major significance to his effectiveness as a manager. We must keep this dual role of the personnel area (staff specialty and universal responsibility) before us constantly as we examine the scope of this field in terms of management tasks and, later, as we examine curricular alternatives.

The management functions that fall within the "personnel" field range over a broad area. Employees must be recruited to the firm and selected for and placed in particular jobs. At various stages in their employment, training must be accomplished. Decisions must be made about a myriad of issues surrounding allocation of labor within the firm and involving transfers, promotions, demotions, layoffs, work schedules, and changes in work assignments. Another set of issues arises in discipline and discharge cases, and these cases often dramatize the need for some method to hear and resolve employee grievances. Management must create an environment and a set of face-to-face relationships that promote effort toward the objectives of the firm. The question of proper wages is an important and complicated one, including problems of wage level, wage structure, and wage incentives. In recent years especially, employee compensation has expanded to a variety of "fringe" areas such as pensions, paid vacations and holidays, employee services of one kind or another, and insurance against the risks of injury, sickness, death, and unemployment. All these "fringe" benefits present analytic, technical, and practical problems to management.

Particularly in manufacturing, mining, construction, and the transportation and communication industries, management deals with its wage-roll employees through collective rather than individual bargaining. The resultant problems of labor relations are of vital importance to management. The formulation and administration of policies in this area has become a major part of the "personnel" task in many firms.

There are many areas in which the employment relationship is affected by legislation, both state and Federal. Employer rights and responsibilities during a union organizing campaign and in the collective bargaining process, as well as the legality of various union tactics, are subjects about which management must be well informed. Unemployment compensation, workmen's compensation, and other forms of social insurance must be taken into account by management in its operations. In addition, management has a stake in the determination of these and other public policies toward the labor market.

Finally, in discussing the scope of this field as it appears to the firm, we should note the growing numbers and proportions of people in technical, professional, and managerial jobs. Most of the problems suggested above are as important and sometimes as troublesome in relation to these "white-collar" workers as for their "blue-collar" counterparts. In fact, as one looks to the future in the personnel management field, one must surely conclude that the white-collar area is due, perhaps overdue, for an increase in emphasis.

Roots in the Social Sciences and Law

Every discipline in the social sciences is represented among students of the field of personnel management and industrial relations, and questions of public policy in this area have been argued for a very long time. The result of all this experience and trained observation is a vast body of analytic and descriptive knowledge, much of it readily available for use in the classroom.

Economists have always had strong interests in the aspects of this field related more or less directly to wage and employment questions. Economic theory, though it leaves many important questions unanswered, provides a useful way of thinking about problems of the labor market and a framework for research. Important data about such matters as the structure of employment, unemployment, and wage rates have been collected over a considerable period of time and subjected to analysis by economists. In addition, economists, increasingly with help from those trained in other social science disciplines, have studied intensively institutions in the labor market—the union, the firm, employment services—as well as the impact of various public measures like unemployment insurance and minimum-wage legislation. This and much other material based on economics is of obvious importance to the personnel field.

The other social sciences have not had the long history of preoccupation with matters related to this field that has been true of economics but, particularly over the past two decades, the amount of relevant research and writing by psychologists, sociologists, political scientists, and anthropologists has been impressive. This material has enriched understanding of many personnel problems, such as those related to training, selection, organizational arrangements, analysis of union behavior, the operation of small groups, restrictive practices, worker behavior in the labor market, and communication systems.

All this suggests that study of the social sciences will be an important part of any personnel curriculum and that considerable material is available about personnel problems and derived from social science research. In fact, this area appears to be a natural meeting ground for all the social sciences. Thus a wage problem in a plant is often more than an economic problem. It may involve individual status, intergroup relationships, political maneuvering within management and union organizations, and may have some legal implications as well.

We should note, however, and perhaps underline the point, that social scientists cannot presume to have answers to many personnel problems. Their work is helpful in posing questions, developing useful data, and generally in working toward answers to a variety of troublesome problems. But this field contains, and one suspects it will always contain, a large measure of artistry, common sense, wisdom, or whatever it is that talented men develop out of their experience. If it is important to expose students to the contributions of social science in this field, it is imperative to develop the limitations as well and, by discussion of cases and other means, to develop an attitude of respect for experience and what can be learned from it.

Evolution of Content and Emphasis

Like any area of business study, this one reflects today and has reflected in earlier times the flow of environmental forces. But perhaps more than most, "the labor problem" has played a central part in the political, social, and economic history of the Western world. The process of industrialization involves the development of an industrial labor force with the necessity for organizational discipline and a web of rules by which to operate large units. Issues and institutions arise which have a lineage running from present-day arrangements in the United States back to the early days of the Industrial Revolution. Even cursory knowledge of this history will sharpen the student's understanding of the problem of his day and his ability to appraise future relationships between personnel and industrial relations problems of business and the general setting in which these arise.

For our purposes here it will be useful to identify some prominent developments of the past three or four decades, since these will help identify the dimensions of an appropriate business curriculum. First of all, we must note sweeping changes in the labor market. The waves of immigration that characterized our early history were checked during and after World War I, in effect separating the United States labor market from those of other countries. The educational level of the labor force has risen, and the structure of demand for labor has shifted, with higher skills receiving more emphasis. Unskilled labor now makes up only a very small portion of the total. Cultural changes have brought women into the labor market in great numbers. And, of course, we have experienced a dramatic shift from almost a decade of large-scale unemployment, which gave rise to important labor market legislation, to almost twenty years of generally sustained high-level employment.

The Federal government's role in the field of industrial relations has shifted dramatically over the past thirty years. The role of the states has become a subordinate one in many important areas within the field. The growth of unions has been encouraged and, in the post-World War II period, their actions have been regulated by Federal statute. The minimum wage has been specified for many industries by Federal and state legislation, and normal hours of work have been significantly affected by requirement of time and one-half rates of pay for over forty hours' work in a week. And the sweep of public policy has added to state legislation on compensation for on-the-job injury, the Federal-state system of unemployment compensation, and the Federal system of old-age and survivors' insurance.

Along with developments in the labor market and changes in public policy has come the rise in importance of unions. Twenty-five years ago wages and working conditions throughout American industry were set predominantly by individual bargaining between employers and employees. Today this vital process is conducted typically by collective bargaining, with rights and responsibilities of the parties specified in a contract. Such a sweeping institutional change naturally changes as well the problems of supervision at all levels of the management organization and poses many questions to be worked out by staff specialists.

One would expect important environmental developments such as those outlined above to be accompanied by an increase in knowledge about personnel and industrial relations, if only because the developments call attention to the area's importance in a dramatic way. We have already noted the attention paid by social scientists to this area, but we should also note the growth in consciously developed knowledge within business organizations. The evidence has grown that wide variation is possible in the quality of the job done by management in the personnel area and that alternative courses of action often can be identified and evaluated systematically. With the shift in management's attitude toward the importance of this field has come a shift in the quality of personnel staff assistance and a broadening of the functions associated with the more professional and talented men involved. Thus management has been able to learn more effectively from its expanded and sometimes bitter and costly experiences. In areas such as training, selection, administration of wage systems, and union-management relationships a body of conscious experience has developed that is at once useful to management and to those teaching in this field.

OBJECTIVES AND PRIORITIES IN CURRICULUM DESIGN

Our brief summary of the scope of the personnel and industrial relations area suggests several threads that should run through our consideration of curriculum design. As in other areas of business study, our design problem is a problem of choice, since there is obviously a tremendous amount of material that could be covered.

Among the variables affecting this choice must certainly be the objectives and reasonable career expectations of the students involved. Here our earlier analysis of "personnel" as a management function should help us. It suggests that, while most students taking the basic courses will have their primary functions in other fields of business, they must all assume some responsibility for personnel management—but general responsibility, not that of a specialist. They will not be concerned with highly specific and perhaps technical aspects of the field nor in any detailed way with operations of the personnel department. But they will profit from general exposure to the basic ideas and sweep of problems in this field and from some knowledge about what may be expected from the specialist in personnel management. Further, those men who do seek careers in personnel management must build any specialized knowledge they acquire on a general understanding of the field. The dual role of "personnel" as a specialized function and a universal responsibility, then, suggests an emphasis in the curriculum away from technical knowledge and toward broader and more general problem areas.

We have already noticed that the disciplines of economics and the behavioral sciences have much to offer as guides toward learning about personnel management and industrial relations. This suggests that specific courses in these disciplines should be included in the curriculum, as is recommended as a general proposition in the undergraduate and master's programs outlined in Chaps. 8 to 10. But these disciplines cannot be left to the specific courses that are given in them. They must be put to work explicitly in analysis of the labor market and of the problems of administering men in task-oriented organizations. To be most effective, then, the courses in disciplines should precede those which seek to apply these disciplines to specific problems.

We have also emphasized earlier that the content of this field has changed with dramatic force during the past few decades and, in fact, tends to reflect central themes of our social and economic history. These developments appear most clearly when we look at changes in the composition and size of the labor force, the ebb and flow of trade unionism, the growth of the personnel function within management, and the evolution of public policies in the field of industrial relations. Thus, while these subjects are important in themselves, they may be treated in the curriculum so as to show clearly the historical sweep of problems in this field. Further, since each of these areas is still very much in evolution, such a treatment of them will help the student stay abreast of the field in the years following his graduation.

If the emphasis in the curriculum should properly be a broad one, if analytical concepts may be derived from the social sciences, and if the evolution of the field is a critical part of its content, the essence of personnel management and industrial relations lies in the vast experience and extensive practical knowledge of the subject that has been accumulated in this and other countries. The issues involved have been and remain controversial ones, so that rich and varied material easily comes to hand. It would be a great mistake to keep the curriculum on such a general and abstract level that students did not come to grips with the real world in a detailed way. We must distinguish here between highly vocational specialization and intense and specialized work on a subject of relevance to the general subject matter. Detailed knowledge in a few areas is certainly as necessary to general understanding as are abstract though useful principles. If this detailed work can be made useful in a vocational sense, so much the better; but its rewards will probably be greater if its primary objectives are broad in nature.

One final point may be noted about the use of various types of case material to illustrate and deepen the student's understanding of general propositions. This material often springs from controversy and is interesting to instructors and students alike. Certainly part of the problem of curriculum design is to present material in such a way as to capture student enthusiasm and stimulate student effort. Well-selected and well-presented case material will almost always do this. The instructor must be careful to develop points of general value out of the case material, but, properly used, this material can enliven and enrich almost all the course offerings in personnel management and industrial relations.

Summary Statements

Before turning to specific discussion of the curriculum, we may appropriately summarize the main points made so far.

1. Students may be presumed to vary widely in occupational goals and possibly even more widely in their subsequent occupations. Time is bound to be at a premium in any well-developed curriculum, and the general material in this area is voluminous and demanding. There will be little room in the curriculum for courses designed to equip the student with a specific skill immediately applicable to a prospective job.

2. The content of this field may be characterized as an exercise in the application of economics and behavioral science to a vast and controversial area of subject matter. It follows that the curriculum in the area of personnel management and industrial relations should build on prior study of these disciplines and should weave these disciplines into the course offerings.

3. The field has also been characterized by change. The student may gain in understanding of the present and enhance his feeling for the future by being exposed to the sweep of problems as they have arisen in the past.

4. The field is blessed with a tremendous amount of publicly available

data, and well-publicized industrial relations events occur almost daily. Reality-oriented case material should be used throughout the curriculum, since it can enrich the student's understanding and provoke his interest.

OBSERVATIONS ON PRESENT UNDERGRADUATE AND M.B.A. PROGRAMS

The comments which follow are based on close inspection of the catalogs of forty schools of business. The schools were selected from a complete listing of accredited colleges and universities conferring business degrees and represent various parts of the country, great diversity in size, and both private and state-supported schools. The catalog survey was supplemented by discussions of varying length with men from ten schools. This survey suggests some general tendencies and the principal variations from them.

The basic issue that characterizes differences between programs is, "Should the orientation of training be toward fairly specific job skills or toward broad understanding of the problems characteristic of this field?" In general, variations in orientation were associated with the size of the school, its source of support, and its general nature. Thus, large schools are apparently able to support large numbers of courses in a given area, and these courses often seem oriented to particular job skills, such as the administration of employment tests or plans for job evaluation. Schools with smaller student bodies, perhaps only because their enrollment would not support a large number of specialized course offerings, tend to have a more limited number of more general courses. A skill orientation was also more prevalent among schools drawing their support from public funds or their student body from the adult working population of a large city. This orientation may be explained, on the one hand, by the demands of employers for a supply of labor trained for specific tasks and, on the other, by the desire of employed persons to acquire skills for jobs closely related to their own or for jobs to which they aspire. Finally, those business schools associated either directly or indirectly with engineering schools tended to parallel in the personnel curriculum the job-skill orientation often found in the engineering curriculum. These are, of course, general tendencies, and exceptions to them are not hard to find.

The most common pattern of courses for both undergraduate and M.B.A. programs in the personnel and industrial relations area included a beginning course called "Personnel Administration" or "Personnel Management," often required of all business school students. A typical course description might run as follows:

A study of the methods and techniques of organized personnel work. Stress is laid upon scientific procedures and instruments, and the course covers such areas as employee selection, testing, training, motivation, and compensation, as well as the organization and functions of the personnel department.

For those who choose to emphasize this field, there are usually two or possibly three further required courses. One of these almost invariably deals with the labor movement and collective bargaining. Most often this is supplemented by a course in wage administration, particularly when there is a close association with an engineering school. Typical course descriptions are:

Unions and Collective Bargaining. A study of modern unionism and collective bargaining, with emphasis on analysis of the methods and techniques of collective bargaining as currently applied in the relations between labor and management.

Wage Administration. This course examines the need for wage rationalization as a tool of management, gives instruction in the technique of rationalizing wage structure, and analyzes some of the outstanding considerations which may be taken into account in installing and administering such programs.

The content of the fourth course varies widely from one which emphasizes analysis of personnel or labor relations cases to one on labor law or a topic such as employee selection and placement. The number of additional courses from which students may select electives varies from zero to forty-one and includes a very wide range of topics.

The content of courses offered is clearly not nearly so uniform as are the course titles. A course on wages, for example, can include heavy emphasis on economic analysis or can be completely devoted to problems of internal wage administration. A course on selection may include a heavy dose of psychological analysis of personality or be dominated by study of particular tests and how these may be administered. Courses can be found at either end of this general-to-applied spectrum, but the general impression emerging from the curriculum survey is that most courses fall well over toward the applied end.

The curricula also appear to vary substantially in the extent to which the students are exposed to the research process. About half the schools surveyed required or strongly encouraged student research at the master's level, either in the form of a thesis requirement or an option for better students or in the form of an explicit course dealing with the research process. It is almost impossible to tell from course descriptions how much the student is exposed to the research process and methodology as part of his regular work. Apparently, field work on term papers or on class projects of one sort or another is not uncommon, though that work may fulfill more of an exposure than research-method function.

The comments made so far relate exclusively to the undergraduate and master's level curriculum. Work for the doctorate will be discussed later, in conjunction with program recommendations. There is one problem, however, that involves all three levels of work and appears to be a troublesome one for many schools. The problem springs from the existence side by side of programs at two or three of these levels, where the number of students involved is much greater at one level than at the other. The problem is compounded by the fact that the larger number of students is usually at the lower level. Stated from the point of view of the doctoral program the issue is, "Will the need for processing a large volume of undergraduates and/or master's candidates so inundate the faculty that the doctoral program, while perhaps contributing to the quality of the other two, is diluted into something less demanding than it should be?" The same general issue exists as between the master's and undergraduate levels of work. Methods of dealing with this problem will be discussed later, but its existence should be noted as part of the description of current practice and associated problems.

We see, then, at the undergraduate and master's levels a rather similar structure of courses, though often more extensive and specialized at the master's level. Typically, there is a course in personnel administration required of all business majors and two or three additional required courses for those who specialize in personnel management and industrial relations. Additional electives are usually available, sometimes in overwhelming quantity. The orientation of the whole personnel program and of individual courses within it seems to vary rather widely in objectives from school to school. In some cases the emphasis is on training for specific job skills and in others on general understanding of problems, developments, and methods of analysis. In almost every program, students are apparently exposed to problems of the real world either through cases, research courses, term papers, or field projects of one sort or another.

PROPOSALS FOR THE M.B.A. CURRICULUM

The M.B.A. program will be discussed first, since much that may be said about it applies, though with some modifications, to the undergraduate program. While the M.B.A. and undergraduate programs thus differ in degree, the Ph.D. program recommended here differs in kind from the other two and so will be discussed last.

A few assumptions must precede any discussion of an appropriate program. First of all, the students to whom the program is addressed are assumed to be seeking careers in business organizations, primarily as operating officials. Most of them do not intend to be specialists in the personnel and industrial relations area, though some have career interests in this field. It is also assumed that students must take the required subjects in the suggested M.B.A. curriculum that appears in Chap. 10. It may be noted that this required program includes two courses in economics and one or two in behavioral science. The program also provides for three or four courses in a field of concentration and at least three limited-choice elective courses. Finally, a course in the general personnel area is required of all students.

Given these assumptions, two somewhat separate problems face us. The first is, "What should be included in the personnel course required of all students?" and the second, "What is an appropriate program for those who wish to concentrate in this subject?"

Course in Personnel Management Required of All Students

The course required of everyone must obviously be looked on as a terminal rather than an introductory course. It presents two types of issue to us. First, we have already noted that this course is now typically one in the function of personnel administration, with emphasis placed on such traditional subjects as recruitment, selection, placement, training, personnel appraisal, wage administration, and so on. But we have also noted earlier that the scope of this field is far broader than that. The contention here, following our earlier discussion of objectives and priorities, is that this course should embrace the broader concept of the field, though, of course, including exposure of the student to the traditional personnel areas. The broad concept, it would seem, is particularly appropriate for the student whose primary interest lies in another area of business.

But of the many possible subjects that could be covered, which ones should receive emphasis in this course? Our earlier discussion of objectives and priorities should also help us answer this question. It suggests objectives such as these. First, the student should see how his earlier work in the social sciences may help him understand problems in this field. He should also be exposed to the historical development of these problems, particularly as portrayed by institutional, public policy, and labor force changes, and to the organizational adaptations of management to these changes. Finally, he should come to grips with the reality of this field by tackling a few sample problems, perhaps in the form of case material, and by exposure to the many sources of data that exist.

While there are many ways in which these objectives might be fulfilled, most of the variations may be included within this topical structure.

1. The evolving structure of the American labor force and of American

labor markets may be portrayed in relation to management's recruitment and compensation problems. Data about the labor force should be useful to men in any field of business.

2. Even brief study of the development and nature of trade unions is worth while because the institutions are important and because study of their formation should provide insight into employee response to management action.

3. Alternative management approaches to employee and union relations may be examined, with the role of the personnel specialist in the firm given special attention.

4. Study of a few problems, such as the installation of change, the maintenance of discipline, and the administration of wage structure and incentives in a changing environment, should help make the more general, earlier material concrete. Cases are plentiful on these subjects.

5. Finally, the student may examine some problems of public policy, so that he may see their relationship to the management task and think them through more intelligently as a citizen. This topical structure for the course required of all students should provide the instructor with ample opportunity to suggest strengths and limitations of social science as applied to this field, to discuss prominent developments, and to sample the reality of practical problems. If the course provides no practical answers, it can at least bring problems to the student's attention and suggest ways in which he may think them through.

A Program for Personnel Majors

We may turn now to the program for students concentrating in personnel management and industrial relations, having at our disposal three to four courses. The subject matter will, of course, include that presented in the terminal course described above, but presented in greater depth. It might be suggested, therefore, that those who intend to major in this field skip the terminal course, using the time saved for development of work in their major. This will not always be possible, since many students will elect this field for concentration only after taking the terminal course.

To what extent should this program of courses be oriented toward training for job skills? We have seen that this orientation is a strong one in many present programs, but we have argued that the orientation may more properly be toward a general understanding of the problems, institutions, ideas, and data in this field. In part, the argument rests on student objectives. Especially if they aspire to more than a technician's role in industry, those who seek careers in this field must build any specialized knowledge they acquire on a sound and broad base of understanding.

In addition, specific skills are often best acquired on the job in the context of each firm's somewhat unique requirements. Thus the firm may teach most specific skills more readily than the university.

The choice of an area for concentration in school, furthermore, is not necessarily a career choice. Many of those who specialize in personnel and industrial relations in school will, by accident or design, end up in jobs not directly related to this field. Finally, many students may be taking these courses as an adjunct to work in other fields, such as production management, or as a means to deepen their understanding of the problems of management more generally. As noted earlier, however, the reality of personnel and industrial relations may be woven into the curriculum throughout, as it will enhance the student's understanding of general principles. We may certainly hope that the study of general principles, supplemented by exposure to many types of concrete situations, will prove vocationally useful in the long run.

The basic materials for this area of concentration fall into four groups which may appropriately be handled in three to four courses. Material appropriate under each of these headings will be discussed briefly, and one proposed course will be discussed in detail, as a means of illustrating the recommendation.

1. An initial grouping of materials may be labeled "Data, Institutions, and Outstanding Issues." Included in this grouping would be the study of (a) the size and composition of and changes in the labor force, (b) the concept of the labor market and its limitations as a guide to management actions, (c) management organization for dealing with personnel and labor relations problems and the strategic policy alternatives open to management, (d) the nature and role of the trade union in a free economy, (e) the collective bargaining process and some of the outstanding issues dealt with in collective bargaining. Since various aspects of the wage issue are treated elsewhere in this recommended curriculum, wage problems may appropriately be omitted from this course. Ample data and case material exist to enrich study of these topics, and many opportunities are presented for the application of economic and behavioral science concepts.

2. A second grouping of material would place emphasis on the application of economic analysis to the problems and issues of personnel management and industrial relations. A central theme here would be study of wages and associated recruitment and motivation problems. Included would be extensive study of labor markets and economic determinants of the firm's demand for labor. Within the framework of such broad treatment of the firm's environment, problems of wage structure, incentive methods of wage payment, and various types of fringe benefits could be studied. Public policies related to the labor market,

such as minimum-wage legislation, provision for unemployment compensation, and national policies toward the level of employment, may also be examined.

3. A third set of topics would include much that is traditional in personnel management but would use the application of the behavioral sciences to the firm's personnel problems as an organizing concept. Appropriate subjects include methods of selection and appraisal and their limitations, employee and supervisory training, executive development and compensation, and studies of morale and its relation to productivity. The work and role of the personnel department in organizations of various sizes may appropriately be given special consideration here.

4. A final set of materials would be concerned with the government and its impact on the problems of personnel management and industrial relations. Included here would be the evolution of, and current national policy toward, the organization of unions and the conduct of labor management relations, as well as material dealing with problems of economic security. This course may emphasize historical developments, and it presents opportunities for pulling earlier material together, thus playing an integrating role in the curriculum. Useful case material of all kinds abounds and may form the basis for a variety of exciting term-paper assignments.

In addition to these four courses, some room should certainly be provided in the curriculum for student electives in the field of personnel management and industrial relations. Appropriate subject matter for these electives can hardly be specified in any generally applicable way. Ideally, they should reflect the special interests and talents of the particular school's faculty members. They would therefore vary between schools, and, in any given school, they would not necessarily be the same over any period of time. They might well represent current faculty research interests and therefore provide the student with methodological as well as substantive instruction.

A Course in Some Detail

Let us turn now to a more detailed examination of what might be done in a course applying economic analysis to the problems of personnel management and industrial relations. Such a course might take up five types of subjects: theoretical concepts, the relevance to wage determination of the structure of labor and product markets, institutional policy making on wage questions, typical wage issues within the firm, and governmental policy toward the labor market.

Economists have long been searching for a satisfactory wage theory. Though the state of wage theory is not satisfactory, it does offer a framework for thought about wage movements and differentials and an explanation for central tendencies. This course might well start with an exploration of various wage theories and of the empirical implications of applying the market concept to labor. This concept can then be used to organize information about labor markets, aided by reports on the labor-market research of economists over the past two decades. It may be noted that this research has provided a fruitful meeting ground for concepts drawn from the behavioral sciences as well as from economics. In recent years, economists have also produced a great many industry studies, which may be used to show the impact of industry demand conditions on wage levels and often on systems of wage payment as well.

These broad studies may be supplemented by discussion of company and union wage policies, again drawing on the extensive literature developed by labor economists over the past two decades. Here again, in analyzing institutions in action, we may draw on ideas from political science and sociology, as well as from economics. All of this material may be pulled together for students through discussion of three or four cases involving disputes over the wage level in a particular firm or industry. There are well-documented, published cases available for this purpose.

The course might then address itself to wage problems internal to the firm, such as those involved in establishing a wage structure, administering individual or group incentive plans, or determining appropriate fringe benefits. At this level, it may be useful to bring in some of the techniques of personnel management, such as job evaluation. The student may learn something about all such techniques by a detailed and sophisticated evaluation of the strengths and limitations of one of them.

Finally, attention may be turned to the broad policy level. Much material is available about the operation of minimum wage laws and the unemployment insurance system, and the wage-level problems that accompany a full-employment policy are almost constantly in the forefront of public debate. Perhaps one such area might be selected for intensive treatment, with the others covered by reading materials.

Throughout this course, use can be made of published research materials, and students could appropriately be required to do a small piece of research themselves. Field research, though quite time-consuming, is often most rewarding, though much also can be done with materials available in a good library.

The course outlined above is quite different from that often given in the business school under the title "Wage Administration." The student will not learn so well the various plans for administering the firm's wage structure, incentive program, or appraisal system. But he will have a broad background against which to evaluate these techniques and with which to acquire more detailed knowledge should that be needed in a subsequent job. If this course is more difficult for the student and the teacher, it should also be more challenging, more a part of the over-all business school curriculum, and more helpful to the student in the long run.

Summary

We may summarize these observations about the master's-level curriculum by pointing again to certain general ideas which underlie the more specific recommendations. The goal throughout has been to provide broad understanding of the problems encompassed by this field, though constant efforts have been made to make use of the knowledge developed through research and experience in personnel management and industrial relations. Emphasis has been placed on using concepts developed earlier in the general curriculum, in part to give real meaning to these concepts so that they may be applied elsewhere and in the future and in part to help shed light on the material encountered in this field. Students will have been exposed to the research process through study of the work of others and through independent work or group projects of their own. Finally, the student should emerge from the program with some grasp of the momentum of this field, so that he may better appreciate developments in future years.

RECOMMENDATIONS FOR THE UNDERGRADUATE CURRICULUM

The arguments for training oriented to general understanding rather than to job skills apply with even more force at the undergraduate than at the master's level. The student's career objectives are even more uncertain and the amount of time allotted for concentration in a particular field of business may often be smaller. If we may assume the undergraduate curriculum recommended elsewhere in this report, however, about the same program for the area of personnel management and industrial relations would seem to be appropriate for undergraduates as was suggested above for master's-level students. That program would call for a broad course required of all students and three to four additional courses in which those who concentrate on personnel management and industrial relations would work on the subjects described in connection with the M.B.A. program. One would expect, however, that with students who are somewhat less mature, the material would be covered less intensively.

Students in the M.B.A. program, we have suggested, may well be asked to do considerable independent work, with much of the reading material appropriate for the courses taken from original sources and from research monographs and journal articles. Under these circumstances, the student must bear much of the burden of integrating the material into coherent units. While undergraduates as well as M.B.A. candidates will derive significant educational benefits from thus grappling with material on their own, they are likely to need more help than graduate students in the organization of this material. Textbooks can perform this function and should probably be used more extensively in the undergraduate than in the M.B.A.-level courses.

It would probably not be possible, however, nor would it be desirable to rely completely on such secondary resources of information. Students should still be exposed to original research work, to original sources of data, and to the complexity and vitality of industrial relations problems. They will have had considerable background, given the program recommended here, in economics and behavioral science, and they should put these concepts to work as part of their undergraduate training.

STUDY FOR THE DOCTORATE

A program for the doctorate in business, with special emphasis on personnel management and industrial relations, should differ sharply from that recommended for students at the undergraduate and master's degree level. The objectives of the program and of the students in it are different from those prevailing at the less advanced levels. Career choice is more definite. Students are not as much oriented to work as an operating executive in business as they are to careers as teachers, research workers, or staff specialists in a business, with truly professional competence in the field of personnel management and industrial relations. The holder of a doctorate is more than a consumer of research results; he should be able to produce these results himself and be a sophisticated interpreter of research and other developments in his field.

Unfortunately, many current programs for the doctorate in business schools are basically extensions of the master's program, with broader exposure to various business fields and the addition of independent work in the form of a thesis. Thus the student's knowledge of business is broadened, but the conceptual depth in the disciplines underlying business study is not very different from that provided in a good master's program. A more appropriate distinction between these two programs might be just the reverse, with the research and professional orientation leading to increased emphasis on a basic intellectual discipline rather than to broader exposure to business fields.

The importance of thorough knowledge of a social science discipline for fruitful research in various aspects of personnel management and industrial relations is suggested by the fact that the best research available has been turned out by men with that kind of training. Since a continuing flow of students in these various disciplines may be expected, one may question whether study for the doctorate in business is preferable to study in a traditional social science department.

Three characteristics distinguish the discipline-oriented doctorate in a business school from one in a social science department. The student and faculty in a business school will tend to have more interest in problems of importance to business, to develop a special expertness in working with these problems and, as a general rule, to be somewhat more oriented toward empirical research. They will also bring to their research some understanding of broadly related business fields, such as accounting, production, marketing, and finance. Finally, since problems of personnel management and industrial relations provide a natural meeting ground for various social science disciplines, the doctoral program should include at least some work in more than one discipline. Thus, while students should surely emphasize some single discipline, most appropriately economics, social psychology, or sociology, they should also expose themselves to the basic ideas and research methods of the other disciplines.

Study for the doctorate in this field, then, should (1) emphasize a thorough working knowledge of the conceptual framework in one discipline, (2) require exposure to the ideas and research methods of at least one other discipline, (3) require basic knowledge of accounting concepts, a reasonable sophistication with statistics, and exposure to the ideas and problems in the various fields of business, (4) include a thorough familiarity with the area of personnel management and industrial relations, and (5) emphasize research and independent work, including, of course, a thesis.

Given the solid conceptual underpinning recommended here, the student should be able to dig deeply into the subject matter of this field. He should be able to comprehend more quickly and more fully the research and experience to which he is exposed, no doubt more intensively than is the M.B.A. candidate. The basic topics should be similar to those outlined earlier, since a broad and general understanding of this material is most important to the doctoral student. But he may also be expected to develop more specialized interests, particularly in conjunction with his thesis work.

Two aspects of the environment for fruitful specialized work in a doctoral program are worth mention. Strong courses in a variety of disciplines are obviously difficult to supply unless Ph.D.-level programs are offered in these disciplines at the university of which the business school is a part. Certainly the students working toward the doctorate in business should be encouraged to take some work in the relevant social science departments. At the faculty level, the existence of this tradition should help integrate the business school into the intellectual life of the university. Second, the thesis work is likely to be more fruitful if the student finds in the school an environment congenial to research. Faculty interest and participation in research are clearly essential. The establishment of a regular research seminar should also serve many useful functions. It can provide a forum for discussion of faculty and student research and of the work of visiting academic or business people. It can help the student in his transition from emphasis on courses to emphasis on research and expose him to a wide range of topics in his field, supplementing the coverage of his formal course work and adding depth to his understanding of the subjects involved. It may also give him some experience in presenting his work to an interested and critical group of people, thus helping him develop the skills of exposition necessary for the teacher.

This discussion of study for the doctorate in business, with emphasis on personnel management and industrial relations, has distinguished the doctoral from the master's program less in terms of material in the field of concentration and more in terms of conceptual underpinning and research effort. This kind of distinction is too often not the one made in business schools, but I believe it to be most important. It places emphasis on a solid foundation rather than an elaborate superstructure.

SOME SPECIAL PROBLEMS

There are a few special problems to which we may give brief consideration. To some extent they are general ones for the business school, but in each case they emerge as well from study of programs in personnel management and industrial relations.

Relationships among Different Levels in the Curriculum

We have already noted that programs at more than one level often exist side by side. No special problem is posed by a combination of undergraduate and doctoral work, since these two levels call obviously for separate treatment. But when an undergraduate and master's or master's and doctoral program are placed in a juxtaposition, there is danger that each one will be diluted. Since the more advanced program will usually have the smallest number of students, it is most likely to suffer. The problem is less acute at the lower levels, since undergraduate and master's programs are usually large enough to be self-supporting. In addition, the problem is solved by a number of business schools by simply not offering undergraduate work. But these schools must face the more difficult problem of articulating separately their doctoral program. To do so is very expensive, perhaps prohibitively so where the school cannot draw on the resources of other parts of the university for work on basic disciplines.

In the long run, however, good programs at the undergraduate and master's level depend heavily on demanding work at the doctoral level. In part, this is because the quality of tomorrow's teachers is at stake. Even in schools where the proportion of the faculty holding an advanced degree is small, those who have been thoroughly trained may have great influence on the sights set by their colleagues. In part, however, the quality of doctoral-level work is important because of its impact on the rate at which the field develops new and appropriate dimensions and reweights the relative importance of its various parts. Thus, the doctoral program, with its emphasis on research, operates on the frontiers of knowledge. These frontiers, in turn, are gradually explored, understood, and made part of the field's standard content.

This process of constant renewal and reappraisal is especially important for personnel management and industrial relations since, as we have already noted, this field has been and remains a changing one, deeply affected by the business and more general social environment. We remarked earlier, for example, on the changing industrial and occupational composition of the labor force. The magnitude of these changes is just now being appreciated, and their impact on the institutions of the labor market and on the tasks of personnel management is still primarily a matter for speculation. It is clear enough that the problems of white-collar workers must be given increased emphasis by those engaged in research and teaching, as well as by those charged with the duties of practical administration. But what are these problems? Are the old questions, let alone the old answers, appropriate? Should our public policies toward the labor market be changed? If so, what changes should be made?

If it is easy to show the importance of well-designed work at the doctoral level, it is more difficult to know how this work may be disentangled from the demands placed on faculty by large numbers of undergraduate and master's-level students. The path of least resistance seems to lead to making the doctorate a "master's with a thesis on top." The path suggested here is an expensive one, though, if its benefits are broadly conceived, the potential net gains may be great. At any rate, a clearly differentiated doctoral program with the content recommended earlier seems most likely to develop where there is (1) an atmosphere in the business school that gives more than lip service to the importance of scholarly work, (2) a teaching schedule that permits time for research and includes time to spend with small groups of advanced students, (3) a university environment on which the business school may draw for help in developing appropriate work in basic disciplines, and (4) enough administrative support so that the program itself and the students in it are clearly visible in the over-all activities of the school.

Development of Teaching Materials

We have noted earlier that the field of personnel management and industrial relations is blessed with voluminous material suitable or adaptable for use in the teaching program. Over twenty universities have formally established groups explicitly for work in this field, and many others have done so informally. While these groups vary widely in their purposes and activities, they have stimulated much research and been more or less responsible for organizing the voluminous raw material in many useful ways. Books, articles, special journals, the proceedings and special volumes of the Industrial Relations Research Association, and collections of cases and essays on various aspects of the field offer to the teacher rich and varied sources from which to select reading materials. As in most fields, there is also much trash to throw away, as well as a continuing need for new and fresh combinations of materials. Nevertheless, the teacher, with a little imagination should have no difficulty in finding adequate readings for his students.

But these readings may be supplemented to advantage with individual student assignments that bring them into direct contact with important raw material. Good students especially will find the experience of organizing this material for themselves to be a most educational one, even within the limited scope of a term paper. Sources of information that may be readily exploited are newspaper accounts of events important enough to be reported in some detail, the awards of arbitrators (often reproduced in full and classified by subject matter in the publications of several organizations), hearings and reports of congressional committees, the results of regular and special surveys conducted by various units of government, decisions of courts and of administrative agencies, such as the National Labor Relations Board, and, of course, direct contact with the organizations whose problems and operations are being studied. These direct contacts are sometimes expanded into limited spells of direct work experience and are conceived as a necessary part of the curriculum. Such work experience can be valuable, but its development as a regular part of any sizable program is a difficult and often frustrating undertaking.

The individual assignments suggested here are, in any case, likely to be time-consuming for student and teacher alike and therefore are most suitable where the size of classes is small. Nevertheless, the benefits derived from independent work on materials searched out by the student himself can be great enough to warrant the high costs in student and faculty time. Even where the number of students is large, then, it may be well to incorporate into the curriculum at least modest demands for independent work. The failure to do that much is a failure to take full advantage of the wealth of materials available to students of personnel management and industrial relations.

SUMMARY

These are the main points developed in this essay:

1. The scope of the field, personnel management and industrial relations, is a broad one, and the amount of material available in it is voluminous. The dimensions of the field and emphases within it have changed over time and may be expected to change in the future.

2. The field may be portrayed as applied social science and its evolution as an integral and important part of economic and social developments in the United States and in other areas of the world. Public policies have often played a strategic part in this evolution.

3. There are great variations in the personnel management and industrial relations programs offered in business schools. Many seem oriented toward training for job skills which may often become obsolete and, in any case, can usually be acquired more readily on the job. In a crowded curriculum, the time available may more profitably be oriented toward training for general understanding.

4. All the programs recommended seek to draw on economics and the behavioral sciences. Suggested components for undergraduate and master's-level programs are (a) understanding of the principal institutions and issues, (b) application of economic analysis to study of wages and related areas, (c) use of behavioral sciences to illuminate these and other problem areas, and (d) the development of public policies and the historical sweep of issues in this field. Experience and research have provided rich material for use throughout the curriculum.

5. Doctoral programs in business schools have a tendency to become simple extensions of master's programs, with more detailed and specialized courses and a thesis added. For study of personnel management and industrial relations at this level, it is more important to emphasize thorough work on basic disciplines and the development of capacity for research.

CHAPTER 18

PRODUCTION

Howard L. Timms

Production problems are generally confined to internal firm relationships having physical, economic, and human dimensions. Business schools should concentrate on the last two aspects of production, relying chiefly on microeconomic analysis and taking account of the human aspects through the exercise of judgment. The business curriculum in production should move in this direction just as rapidly as students can acquire the necessary background preparation in mathematics, statistics, and science.

INTRODUCTION

Production is a pervasive function in American business. On this account alone it ought to be a core course in the business school curriculum, if it can be offered at an intellectual level appropriate to the university course. This can be done, as will be shown, provided the student's mathematics-statistics skills are improved considerably over what they usually are now. For students with the appropriate level of talent in mathematics-statistics, and an interest in the production area of business, a concentration (major) can, and very probably should, be offered in production, so designed that it will promote maximum exploitation of their talents and interest. This can be done at both the undergraduate and graduate level in a 9- to 12-hour major.

The task undertaken here is to outline in general terms the direction which business schools should follow in the area of production. The ideas presented here are the outgrowth of a number of years of practice in production management, almost as many years of teaching in the area, followed by considerable discussion with many who are interested in improving the production curriculum. The recommendations for the future are in part an extrapolation of movements already under way in a number of schools of business and in part the outgrowth of faculty ideas which have been tested to some extent in teaching production at Indiana University and elsewhere.

FRAMEWORK FOR COMMUNICATION

It would hardly seem necessary to offer at the start a set of definitions and a framework for developing the curriculum ideas to be set forth here. However, in the course of discussions of this subject with a number of professors, students, and businessmen, I became acutely aware of the difficulty in achieving effective communication because of differences in the frameworks within which people think about the subject of production. Accordingly, I will develop at the outset a framework, including definitions, which is intended to preclude misunderstandings and, in the end I hope, contribute to general agreement with the ideas set forth here.

First is the matter of "production." What is or should be meant by this term in the business school? It has been said that production in the business firm is that activity not embraced by marketing and finance— which tells us little. Others have said production is concerned with the supply side of business, while marketing is concerned with the demand side. If supply is construed to include bringing the product to the ultimate buyer, the very important problems related to channels of distribution would be production rather than marketing problems. This would not conform to real world organization of business functions and is therefore inappropriate. It is certainly true that for purposes of developing theory we sometimes abstract from a total situation in a manner quite differently from that of the businessman in making his complex problems manageable. There would seem to be little reason, however, for doing this at the outset when not yet forced to it by theoretical considerations.

Accordingly, for purposes of this discussion, production is defined empirically in accordance with the schematic model of actual firms in Fig. 18-1. Being a generalized model of real world conditions, it represents a somewhat drastic abstraction for some firms, not very drastic for others. The three functions, marketing, production, and finance, are conceived as basic to business firms of all types, e.g., insurance companies as well as manufacturing firms, although the actual names and groupings of subfunctions within production are not always like those shown in the chart.

Study of the figure may raise the question of whether there is a production function in other than industrial-type businesses. In other words, do we produce only goods, or do we also produce services? Offering the above model as general for all types of business indicates that for purposes of this chapter, production will mean the creation of goods and services and thus is not confined to the industrial-type firm. Production in the nonindustrial firm, such as an automotive service station, a department store, or a bank, is frequently called "operations" in these businesses. Thus production is here defined functionally rather than institutionally.

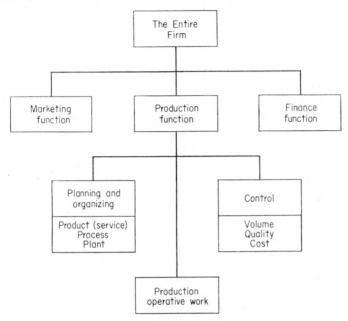

FIG. 18–1. Model of the firm.

Defining production in this manner raises the question of whether courses in the subject should be designed to show how the principles, practices, and problems of the function are typically handled (descriptive), and should be handled (prescriptive), in all types of firms. Put another way, should the course content be mixed, i.e., functional and institutional? To do a reasonably complete job on both poses two large problems. First is the problem of finding sufficient time in the curriculum, which is already stretched severely in most schools of business. Second is the great problem of finding instructors (and textbook writers) who are sufficiently acquainted with all types of business to do a respectable job of teaching both aspects. Typically, business schools have coped with this problem by taking a functional approach, using the manufacturing firm as a model, while using cases or problems to introduce the institutional aspect, e.g., cases and problems involving bakeries, restaurants, department stores, distribution warehouses. Professors usually make a point of acquainting students with the known adoption by

department stores and large banks of techniques used by the manufacturing firm for solving operating problems.

For various additional reasons, the curriculum should stress the functional approach, using the manufacturing firm as a model. First, the
manufacturing firm is a particularly useful model in that the production
function is most complex in such firms. Presumably, if the student can
cope successfully with the subject from that point of view, he can, with
very little academic institutional acquaintance, apply his knowledge in
later practice to other types of firms. Second, the typical student majoring
in production usually aspires to an executive position, staff or line, in a
manufacturing firm, not in a merchandising or a financial firm, although
a number of graduates have later changed to management positions in
"operations" in the latter-type firms. Their broad training in business,
together with their production know-how, is often demanded above the
more specialized training of others, e.g., the industrial engineer. Finally,
for reasons which are developed more fully in a later section, it would
seem that the functional approach should be stressed, since it lends itself
directly to a decision-making approach to a study of production.

Since this chapter is concerned with production management, there is
the question of what is meant by "management." Definitions of the term
frequently take the form of "getting things done through (other) people." From this, some conclude too hastily that the manager spends all his
time wheedling people into doing things, which raises the question,
"Who decides what should be done—the manager or the managed?"
Obviously, the manager must decide what it is he wants the managed to
do, and this is a very important part of the manager's task. It is fruitless
to argue that one, i.e., deciding what shall be done, is any more important
than the other, i.e., getting it done. They are equally important and
deserve attention accordingly.

Perhaps a more useful definition of "management" or, better, "managing" is one which describes rational management work in a more
specific but still generalized way. This is known in the literature as the
management, or administrative, process. One useful form is the following: (1) establishing the objective, (2) planning (work done by others)
to achieve the objective, (3) organizing (dividing up the work) to carry
out plans, (4) getting action (motivating the others to do the work),
and (5) controlling (the work of others to conform to the plan).[1] This
concept of management makes it abundantly clear that at the heart of
managing is a great deal of decision making. Rational planning, organ-

---

[1] See the description of "at least six fundamental concepts and steps in the process
of administration" on page 9 of the casebook by George Albert Smith and C. Roland
Christensen, *Policy Formulation and Administration,* Richard D. Irwin, Inc., Homewood, Ill., 1955.

izing, motivating, and controlling call for many managerial decisions on a continuing basis as the business situation and hence objectives (more decisions) change. It can be shown, quite logically I believe, that the rational management process is itself nothing more than the so-called "scientific method" of coping with the ever-changing business situation facing the firm. And, of course, the planning decisions, organizing decisions, etc. ought to be made as "scientifically" as possible if the practice of business administration is to warrant the status of a profession.

Next in the framework is the important concept of "levels of management." This conceives of there being only two types of work in the business firm, i.e., managerial and nonmanagerial (sometimes called "operative") work. It follows from this that there can be levels of management work. Some managers, both line and staff (which includes most specialized work, e.g., tax accounting, engineering), are themselves managed by a higher level of manager, the highest level being called "top management" or "administration" and the lowest level being often called "supervisory" or "operative management." The important point here is that the rational management process is equally applicable by and at all levels of management and, also, that there are interconnected levels of decision making in the firm.

From the above it seems clear that the business school should be concerned solely with business *management*. Certainly a professional school of business should not be concerned with the other type of work, i.e., the operative work of the firm which is essentially vocational, e.g., operating a machine tool in the manufacturing firm. Furthermore, it seems clear that there would be no logical reason for the business school to be concerned with only one level of management, e.g., top management. Presumably, top-management decisions are mostly of the "policy" type. The problems involved are typically broad in nature, cutting across all three of the basic functions of the firm, e.g., should the firm go through with a proposed merger? One can hardly classify the typical top-management problem (in the reasonably large firm) as a functional (production, marketing, or financial) problem. It is interesting to note that not many typical top-management problems have been researched to the point where formal decision processes, let alone decision rules, have been developed for their solution. On the other hand, many lower-level management problems, particularly in production, have advanced to this happy scientific state, e.g., balancing an assembly line, deciding economical production runs.

Perhaps the reason that business management is conceived and taught almost completely as top-management policy making by some schools lies in the background and training of the faculty. If, for instance, the faculty is not prepared to teach the rather involved formal (and frequently mathematical) decision processes which have been developed for coping with many lower-management (functional) problems, it is practically compelled to deal with little more than top-management policy making. As noted in Chap. 5, there is a strong argument for taking a top-management approach to the study of business, but, as also noted earlier, there is much in middle- and lower-management problems that is worth teaching or learning. For practice in rigorous analysis, a strong case can be made that the middle- and lower-level management problems are more useful.

On the other hand, one hears the complaint that students, excepting some scions of business families, will not graduate into top-management positions and, in fact, may never achieve this pinnacle of business success, by choice or otherwise. Therefore, why bother at all with top-management policy making (decision making)? One answer is that a knowledge of the nature of top-management problems and the difficulty of their solution is useful in the successful conduct of lower-level management work. The opposite is also true. A knowledge of lower-management problems and how good or poor their typical solutions are is useful in successful top-management decision making. Thus it would seem inappropriate to confine the study of business to any one level of management; all levels should be considered including, to some extent in production at least, the much-neglected foreman. In fact, one can hardly develop rational decision processes for many production problems without developing a sequence of interconnected decision processes down (or up) through all levels of management. One favorite graduate examination question of mine is to ask students to develop this set of interconnected decision processes for production volume, e.g., starting with the master schedule at the top (where they quickly point out the desirability of certain prior lower-level decisions) on down through shop-order scheduling to order dispatching (operation scheduling), showing where and why formal decision processes and rules have not yet been fully developed, e.g., dispatch decision rules for job-shop operations.

Summarizing to this point, a case has been made, albeit sketchy, that (1) the course in the production major should take a functional approach to the subject, using the manufacturing firm with its highly complex production function as a model but nevertheless showing clearly the generally universal nature of the production function through a secondary institutional approach; (2) the courses should be concerned with management and not with the operative (and thus vocational) work of the firm; (3) the courses should be oriented toward *application* of the rational management process to the work of production at all levels of management, not just top management; (4) that the professional core of applying the management process, e.g., planning, organizing, motivating, and controlling, is decision making and, therefore, the courses should be oriented toward problem solving in production management.

THE CASE FOR A PRODUCTION MAJOR

This discussion cannot include the whole range of issues facing higher education for business today. Therefore, a full case for or against the existence of an undergraduate production major in the business school curriculum cannot be made here. This question has been raised and treated earlier in this report. However, a few important points in favor of offering the production major are worth making here because they have a bearing on the design of the major curriculum if it is to be offered at all.

First and very probably foremost is the matter of student interest. Probably the most compelling problem facing higher education for business is that of making the four years a challenging and rewarding educational experience. The mere shuffling of various subjects into and out of the business school curriculum will not in itself solve this problem. The answer lies principally in the motivation of the student. If he is genuinely interested in the studies he undertakes, he will come closer to acquiring a sound education.

Rightly or wrongly, the highly motivated business student wants to learn a good deal about business during his four-year undergraduate program. If only to bolster his confidence in his ability to compete successfully for executive positions, he wants to be exposed to a number of business courses before graduation. And many students want exposure in some depth to a particular business function in which they at least believe they are highly interested, say marketing, accounting, or production. Accordingly, if high motivation on the part of the student is the key to achieving an education, perhaps educators would be better advised to turn their attention to upgrading the courses the student is interested in rather than dictating to the student that he ought to be interested in something else. It may be quite true that the best education for competence in professional business management would include none of the traditional business courses but rather a vigorous exposure to all the underlying disciplines. But it is probably a safe bet that in such a program the professor most successfully motivating his business-oriented students would be the one who draws most of his illustrative examples from the business world!

If the production major can be designed in such a way as to contribute heavily to the student's education, then, given a real or even fancied interest in production on the part of students, it would seem that a production major should be offered. Further, if the production courses can be made to contribute heavily to the student's education, little harm would befall the student if subsequent to graduation his interests changed.

The problem, then, is how to design the production major so that it contributes heavily to the student's education. This of course raises the question of what constitutes an education—a question which I am not prepared to explore fully here. However, if we narrow the problem to education for business, perhaps we can come up with a useful definition. It would seem that there are only two aspects of business with which we can deal in educating the student. The first is essentially descriptive information about business as opposed to theory and analysis of typical business problems. Presumably an educated graduate should be well informed in his subject. However, on the theory that within a year after graduation even the better students have forgotten most of the purely descriptive information to which they have been exposed, it would seem inappropriate to devote much of the production program to description on this account alone.

The second aspect of business with which we can deal in educating for business is training the student to deal effectively with the problems of business, a case for which was made in the preceding section. And of course "dealing with problems" should go beyond just recognizing them and beyond even a mere discussion of the pros and cons of taking various courses of action; such an approach often ends with the student's memorizing lists of advantages and disadvantages without, however, deciding on one course. Ideally, the student should go beyond this elementary level of analyzing problems and be exposed to making decisions, i.e., making judgments where formal quantification of factors and explicit decision processes cannot be developed and practicing the close-thinking analysis required where they can be developed. In short, in addition to the passing of information about business, we can train the student in analysis, or how to think.

In broaching these thoughts to educators, some have replied that a student cannot be taught to think—he either does or he doesn't! Then, if we cannot teach him to think and he cannot retain most of the descriptive information he is exposed to in college, it would appear that we cannot educate him at all—and we really have no problem!

Actually, the student of the requisite capacity can gain by exposure to rigorous analysis. If he can think to begin with, his ability to think rigorously can be improved considerably with practice. If he cannot think, and practice cannot teach him to do so, the issue becomes one of deciding whether he should be in college at all, not what major subject he should study. Production management peculiarly lends itself to practice in the type of analysis that should characterize a professional education. It should be remembered, however, that explicit decision processes, requiring close analysis for their understanding and implementation, are more highly developed for lower-level (internal-functional) management problems, and particularly production problems, than they are for top-management (external-interfunctional) problems.

DESIGN OF THE PRODUCTION MAJOR

A production major for students who are highly interested in production can be designed to contribute heavily to the student's education by taking a managerial decision-making approach to the subject. The courses can be designed as an extension of basic underlying disciplines by particularizing the application of these disciplines to production problems. Before getting into this, however, perhaps a quick discussion of the traditional production courses will be useful.

Traditional Production Courses

Schools of business offer variously in the undergraduate production major several or all of the following one-semester three-hour courses:

Industrial Management (a broadly descriptive basic course)
Materials and Processes (often including blueprint reading)
Tool Design
Motion and Time Study (including work simplification and job design)
Plant Layout
Materials Handling
Plant Maintenance
Production Control
Quality Control
Purchasing and Materials Control

Some schools include in the production area certain courses which in other schools are included in the personnel management area, such as Job Evaluation and Wage Administration, the latter conceived as a logical extension of the standards work taught in the Motion and Time Study course.

The metropolitan area business schools tend to offer more, and sometimes all, of these courses, particularly where two conditions exist: (1) the courses are also offered at night, and (2) the courses are offered in an affiliated engineering school (industrial engineering). In the nonmetropolitan school of business, particularly where the courses are not offered at night to working students and/or where there is no school of engineering in the university, only a selected few of these courses are customarily offered in the production major. Quite frequently the selection is: Industrial Management, the basic course often offered also as the core course in management per AACSB requirement, followed by Motion and Time Study, Production Control, and Quality Control. Purchasing is sometimes taught in marketing; if not, it is often taught in the production major either as a requirement or an elective.

In schools offering only a selected few of these courses, the usual justification for the choice comprising the production major involves personal conviction on the part of the professor that he can include in the courses chosen enough of what is worth while in the omitted courses. For instance, one professor feels that he can teach all that is worth while in materials handling and plant maintenance to the business student in his course in plant layout. Another feels that he can and should include work from materials and processes in his course in production control. Perhaps the real basis for selection lies in the background of the professor. At other schools a separate course in production control is considered unnecessary because a large portion of the basic course in industrial management is devoted to production control—following the content of several well-known basic texts in industrial management.

The course in motion and time study probably appears more frequently in the business school curriculum than any beyond the basic course. Perhaps the reason for this is that the skill acquired in this course can make the graduate almost immediately useful to his employer. The business graduate often starts his production career in staff work. Motion and Time Study represents such a start. Another course apparently chosen for job-getting reasons is Production Control, particularly where nearby industries look to the school for graduates to start in this staff work, often as expediters, as part of an in-service training program.

Relatively few schools of business offer in the production major a course in line management in production. However, in recent years the appearance of more employers' programs for training college graduates in line management has apparently induced a few schools to introduce a course in "supervision" as an elective. Most of these courses are designed as applied human relations courses, particularizing the substance of a general course in human relations to the work of the supervisor. Few business schools that are not part of a university which includes a school of engineering offer the tool-design course. Where it is offered, it is usually an elective in the production major.

In general, most of the list of production courses are taught on a functional-descriptive basis, not on a theoretical-analytical basis. The bulk of the content of the courses, and the texts used, is informational, intended to acquaint the student only generally with the nature of the work done in that functional area. Almost always, tedious communications systems called "procedures" are developed to show how information developed in one function is passed on at the right time and place for use by another function. While procedure design is an exercise in analysis and decision making, it would seem unnecessary to devote to it very much curriculum time. Relatively little attention is given to the decision making required to fill in the quantities, dates, and other information required on the forms involved. Where problem solving is introduced, it is often not developed as an exercise in analysis involving application of the scientific method but rather as an abbreviated sample calculation starting with a given formula. And since the scientific method is only mentioned, not implemented, there is little or no treatment of experimental design and data collection. Usually, only the course in motion and time study begins to approach the analytical level that characterizes professional work.

Only in laboratory exercises are the students exposed to analytical work of any depth, involving experimentation and data collection, but normally the laboratory problems are such that they do not require a high level of analysis, e.g., the typical plant layout problem. A recent study of the use of laboratory exercises in teaching production courses in both business and engineering schools[2] indicates that the laboratory is actually used in great part for demonstration purposes (description) rather than for exercises involving a high level of analysis.

As a side note, this study indicates that the use of the laboratory in teaching production management courses is apparently coming into greater use (from a low level of use) in business schools, and just the opposite holds for engineering schools. Still, however, they are used to a great extent for demonstration purposes in both types of school. Perhaps the excellent motion pictures now available in the production area would be a preferable alternative to the laboratory for demonstration purposes. Unfortunately the laboratory exercises are too frequently taught by graduate assistants who are too busy or insufficiently prepared to develop and exploit challenging exercises.

In any case, the typical production laboratory is ill-equipped to deal with problems involving much more than elementary analysis—unless the university electronic data-processing equipment is considered part of the production laboratory. The study mentioned earlier indicates that, for the most part, the equipment available in production laboratories is for use in motion and time study. Equipment for use in other production

[2] W. Nye Smith, "Production Management and the Laboratory Method," an unpublished doctoral dissertation, Indiana University School of Business, Bloomington, Ind., 1957.

courses, where any exists, is not usually measuring equipment but rather a collection of what amounts to physical models of various kinds for use in rather unsophisticated decision-making exercises.

While for the most part the list of production courses given earlier is taught on a descriptive basis, a number of schools have introduced the case method in conjunction with the text-lecture method in some or all of the courses comprising the major. This represents an improvement in that it gives the student practice in recognizing the existence of particular production problems in simulated real world settings—a necessary part of the student's training for professional practice. However, if the cases do little more than this, i.e., if they do not provide an exercise in analysis for the solution of the problems recognized, then it would seem that not many cases are needed in the production program.

Certainly there is more to education for professional production management than the recognition and discussion of problems. The production case can be designed to permit going beyond problem recognition through problem analysis and decision. Designed this way, the case takes on aspects of the old-fashioned problem. If it does not, i.e., if there are insufficient or incomplete data available in the case for developing an explicit and formal decision process, then the decision, if it is to be made at all, must be made by judgment. However, that form of decision making called judgment should not be the sole type of decision making treated in the business curriculum.

Individual professors in a few business schools are going beyond the relatively unsophisticated decision making required for the problems offered in the typical production course text by requiring supplementary readings in research literature, e.g., *Management Science* and *The Journal of Industrial Engineering*. However, the lack of training in mathematics and mathematical statistics typical of today's business student generally frustrates these attempts. The really conscientious professor is reduced to taking his students through relatively low-level decision processes, e.g., use of the Gantt chart in production scheduling, requiring his students to recognize the weaknesses and inadequacies of these processes for more complex problems, then lecturing them in lay terms on the nature of more sophisticated processes which he knows through his own study of research literature. Thus he brings his students only to the threshold of a rewarding educational experience.

The recommendations on mathematics made earlier in this report will redress this situation. For production majors, however, an additional semester beyond the recommended mathematics program would be, if not necessary, highly desirable. The undergraduate production course should include exposure to some of the current research literature in production as well as practice in analysis implementing the findings of research, if it is to attain the status of a professional course.

Another feature of production courses typically offered in today's school of business is their division along functional lines following actual industrial organization. To make this clear, another schematic model is necessary. Figure 18-2 shows the division of production managerial work

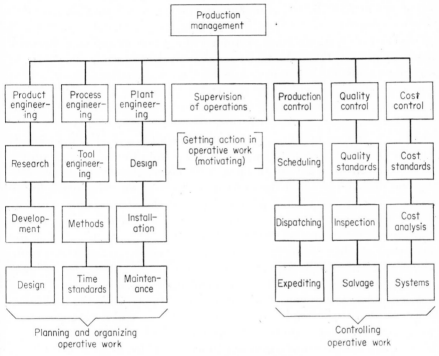

FIG. 18–2. Model of production managerial work.

in a generalized manufacturing firm. This does not mean that all, or even most, manufacturing firms are organized exactly this way in production, or even that the names are standard. For instance, in manufacturing firms with a highly complex product, product engineering may be a highly technical function reporting directly to top management, or parts of it, such as research and development, may report in this way. At the other extreme, the product may be so simple as to require no specialized staff product-engineering function, the work being done by line management. Again, process engineering and cost control may be organized as one staff activity called "industrial engineering." At the other extreme, the time standards function may be graced with the name "industrial engineering." Just what industrial engineering should comprise is not entirely clear even to many engineers, myself included.[3]

But this is a digression; the model is offered not as a typical organization chart in the individual firm or as the best practice in naming functions, but rather as a composite organization chart of the subfunctions of production as practiced in a number of reasonably complex manufacturing firms. Finally, the subfunctions shown are interpreted in terms of the management process, i.e., planning, organizing, motivating, and controlling the operative work of production. Thus the production manager uses specialized staff management personnel to aid him in applying the management process to production operative work. Generally, however, he will rely on his line supervisors to get action in operations.

Given the above model as a reasonably valid one, it appears that the production major has been divided into courses, according to the list given earlier, generally along the organizational lines shown in the model, except for the exclusion of product engineering and the inclusion of purchasing. Product engineering is excluded from the curriculum on the basis of a sensible division of labor with the engineering schools. Purchasing probably entered the curriculum back in the days when industrial purchasing was often a subfunction of production in many manufacturing firms. Recent industrial studies indicate that it is now more often considered a subfunction of finance, or a direct responsibility of top management; the reasons for this change are not fully clear, but it probably reflects the high percentage of product cost represented by purchased materials cost in many manufacturing companies.

Very probably the division of the production major into the traditional courses listed earlier came about through the adoption of texts which were written almost exclusively by men who had practiced one or more of the functions shown in the model either as employees or as consultants to manufacturing firms. Their texts reflected actual organization of production work and, therefore, the courses did the same. There would seem to be no good reason why this should be continued, particularly since it results in a flagrant waste of time.

Examination of the traditional texts on the subfunctions of production reveals that in general they overlap considerably in their content. For instance, texts for both tool engineering and motion and time study often start their substantive content (after the usual philosophical amenities) with process analysis, and it is one or several chapters later before they get into that which is different about their subject. Closing chapters are also inclined to be alike, usually dwelling on the need for working

---

[3] The name itself is confusing when set alongside other recognized engineering work, such as product engineering, plant engineering, or tool engineering. It is like saying there are Protestants, Catholics, and worshipers!

closely with other subfunctions without, for the most part, prescribing means of doing so. Finally, much of the same descriptive information about the over-all production function appears in each text in the chapters devoted to that which is peculiar to each subfunction. In short, much of each text is repetitious of what appears in at least several other texts. This tends to waste the time of students and faculty alike. Of course, professors could, and some do, redress the situation by omitting the repetitious materials, even going so far as reducing the course load, class meetings, and credit hours for the course. However, the tendency is to follow the text and to have a course per subfunctional text.

In defense of the repetitious materials, some claim that they show the interrelated nature of the work of the various subfunctions of production. It is claimed that the repetition enhances integration. Undoubtedly there is something to this argument, but the price paid in time is high. Actually, integration can be much more effectively achieved through the decision-making route. Students of mine, at least, almost unanimously assert that full realization and appreciation of the interrelated nature of business functions strike them only when they get into close analysis of business problems. In any case, since many business students wish to get their education for business in four years, the time available for all that should be done in this period puts a tremendous premium on curriculum time, and all reasonable steps should be taken to conserve it. One such step would be to reduce the repetition among courses. Ways of doing this in the production major are proposed in a later section.

Desirable Orientation of the Production Courses

A case was made earlier for orientation of the production courses toward decision making. The decision-making process is the subject of great study and debate among students of anthropology and others. For purposes of curriculum design, it seems to me that we can conceive of two types of decision making. First is that which involves an explicit, formal process usually developed by applying the scientific method, i.e., observation, building a hypothesis (usually a mathematical model in the more rigorous applications), testing the hypothesis, applying the decision rule developed from the hypothesis to prediction, and thus, eventually, controlling business operations. Decision making of this sort can involve analysis in all degrees of rigorousness.

The second type of decision making may be called "judgment," a process about which we know so little that I suspect it is this sort of decision making that is the subject of the inquiry and debate mentioned earlier. While formal decision making can be taught, it is my belief, and that of many businessmen, that we can teach very little judgment, at least at the level appropriate to a major concentration. Good judgment at this level comes with experience. It is difficult enough to school the student in formal, explicit decision making involving rigorous analysis, let alone in the informal, intuitive, and thus indescribable decision process we call judgment. The student can and probably should practice making judgments, however—and the case method is useful for this purpose. When the judgment of the professor and that of the student are in conflict in a particular case, the former is hard put to explain his position (if he could, it wouldn't really be judgment) and thus school the student in this elusive art. It is doubtful that the student's skill level in judgment, in the major concentration at least, can be very much improved in, say, a year of academic practice.

Accordingly, we should look to the case method in production, not to train the student in the close analysis that can characterize much functional problem solving, but principally to train the student in abstracting from the maze, which characterizes the usual business situation, the major production problems involved. If these problems lend themselves to solution by the rigorous analysis, usually quantitative, characterizing a formal and explicit application of the scientific method, then of course the case is useful for training of this type also. However, the typical case is often not so constructed, being lacking in data. For training the student in the problem analysis (decision making) appropriate to the production concentration, the old-fashioned "problem" is very likely the superior tool.

The rising interest on the part of forward-looking managers in so-called "operations research," which is essentially an application of the scientific method in problem solving, indicates that managers are not only discontented with their present practices but look to the scientist to help them develop better ones. One educator tells of an experience in an executive-development program where the businessmen in the class rebelled at being offered case practice. "We've been exposed to hundreds of such situations in business. What we want is ivory-tower thinking to help us develop better ways of handling them!" Apparently the businessman is beginning to look to the business school to show him the way. The business schools will do this best, not by confining the program to teaching present business practice either through the text-lecture method or the case method with its "realistic" practice in making judgments, but by stressing the development of better decision processes for more effective management. Better decision processes are almost always the result of close analysis implementing the scientific method of problem solving. Courses which stress this almost always offer a challenging educational experience to the better student.

Problem Solving in Production

Before getting into the structure of the production major, an analysis of the nature of production problems and what is involved in their solution may be appropriate. Also, this will serve as a basis for identification of the underlying disciplines for production management in later paragraphs.

Problems of the business firm can be classified as (1) external, i.e., the problems that arise from the reaction of society to the existence and operation of the firm, (2) internal, i.e., the problems arising in the operation of the firm, given the external environment. In the main, the external problems of business are dealt with principally through judgment, not through formal decision processes which produce explicit decision rules. Too many of the factors entering into complex external problems are outside the control of the manager, thus making it difficult if not impossible to implement formally the scientific method of problem solving.

Beyond those problems posed by labor laws, which normally would be covered in industrial relations courses, and a few relatively minor problems involving conformance to state industrial codes (typically handled by plant engineering) and to the standards of the American Standards Association and the Pure Food and Drug Act (typically handled by product engineering or its equivalent), production problems are confined to what might be called internal matters. For the most part, most of the factors involved in these problems are well within the control of management. The essence of their challenge is how best to control the factors involved. Another way of putting it is that production problems are essentially micro in nature.

For an understanding of the development of decision processes for the micro problems of production, the following abstraction is useful. The generalized production problem may be conceived as having three aspects or components, i.e., physical, economic, and human. The degree to which each aspect is involved in particular problems may vary from very little, if any, to very much. For instance, the physical aspect of a production problem in a highly complex and technical operation would be relatively high, but the physical aspect of many problems of internal operations in a commercial bank would be very low.

It would seem unnecessary to stress the fact that since the business firm is, or should be, first and foremost an economic institution, the economic aspect of production problems is central and universal. Finally, since the solution to most production problems involves people, there is the human aspect. From the standpoint of getting effective action in carrying out the solution of production problems, the human aspect is extremely important.

Putting the components together, we may generalize the complete decision process in production problems as follows: (1) the development of physically feasible alternatives, (2) identification of the more economical of these alternatives, (3) final choice of one alternative based upon the human aspects involved. The first step is essentially engineering (applied physical sciences);[4] the second step is essentially applied microeconomic theory; the third step is an application of the behavioral sciences, usually through judgment.

In the interests of a sensible division of labor with the engineering schools, the business school should teach only enough engineering (developing physically feasible alternatives) to acquaint the student generally with the nature of problem solving in the purely physical aspects of product, process, and plant planning; he should not attain depth in these aspects of the decision-making process. Accordingly, the student's exposure to engineering in the production major would, for the most part, be held to the descriptive level. This, on top of a heavy two-course sequence in the basic physical sciences (physics and chemistry), taken as part of his general education courses, should be sufficient for the business student. For the most part, in solving the micro problems of production, the business student will treat the physically feasible alternatives as given. The emphasis will be on microeconomic analysis followed by judgments in the human aspects.

Since the production function in business, particularly the industrial-type business, employs physical (material) factors to a much larger extent than do the marketing and finance functions, the temptation to call for some basic courses in engineering in the production concentration is great. However, very probably no more than a two-course sequence could be squeezed in. It is doubtful that such a sequence could be designed to lift the student's comprehension of decision processes in physical phenomena much beyond that acquired in a solid two-course se-

---

[4] In this chapter, "engineering" is defined more purely than its use today frequently implies, cf., *Webster's New International Dictionary, Unabridged,* 1953: "Originally, the art of managing engines; in its modern and extended sense, the art and science by which the properties of matter and the sources of power in nature are made useful to man in structures, machines, and manufactured products. . . ." This concern with "the properties of matter and the sources of power" implies that engineering is primarily concerned with physical phenomena and only secondarily with economic and human phenomena. This is the definition used in this chapter. Some modern definitions of engineering, particularly industrial engineering, given in terms of a "process" which may be applied to the solution of business problems in almost any basic function of the firm, sound suspiciously like "the scientific method" which, of course, is not a special province reserved solely for the engineer.

quence in physics and chemistry. Hence, at least until someone comes forward with such a sequence in engineering, the business student's exposure to engineering should be confined to its "mother sciences," i.e., physics and chemistry.

As a side note, it is interesting to observe the development of courses closely approximating business courses, i.e., industrial engineering, in the engineering schools. Perhaps the engineering schools responded to cries of the businessman that engineers did not know enough business (presumably to be effective administrators). One result was Grant's text, *Engineering Economy*, in 1930, incidentally a text which operations researchers respectfully acknowledge in their footnote references. Thus the engineer expanded his interests beyond developing physically feasible alternatives to include at least that part of the complete business decision process in which the more economical of these alternatives is identified, i.e., economic analysis. In fact, many engineers call this aspect of the complete decision process "the allocation problem," which brings to mind the economist Lionel Robbins' definition of economics.

It appears that in some of the latest industrial engineering curriculum changes the third aspect of the micro problems of production, i.e., the human, is given considerable attention. This, together with the increased stress on economic analysis, i.e., the allocation problem, has resulted in a reduction of the engineering emphasis (developing physically feasible alternatives) to the point where industrial engineering is increasingly losing its relevance to engineering. In short, the courses accept the physically feasible alternatives in production micro problems, much as was recommended earlier for the business school. This trend has apparently developed to such a point that some engineering schools have come right out and changed the name of the curriculum to Industrial Management or Industrial Administration.

One sensible division of labor, if indeed one exists, might be to roll back the industrial engineering program to provide a firm orientation in depth to the decision processes involved in developing physically feasible alternatives in product, process, and plant-planning problems and to require only enough of applied microeconomics and behavioral sciences to acquaint the engineer with the nature of the complete decision process in business problems. In other words, his exposure to the latter two aspects of the decision process would be mostly descriptive, not analytical. Just the opposite was recommended earlier for the business school, i.e., no depth in the physical aspects of business problems beyond that involved in physics and chemistry but considerable analytical depth in the economic and human aspects.

Such a rollback in the industrial engineering curriculum undoubtedly would be resisted vigorously, if only on proprietary grounds. In spite of the traditional orientation of most business schools to economics, they defaulted to the industrial engineers in developing decision processes in applied microeconomic theory, particularly in the production function. In fact, as noted in Chap. 9, about 60 per cent of the undergraduate schools of business have not yet developed a production major. Undoubtedly the persistent lack of emphasis on mathematics in the business curriculum, as compared with the engineering curriculum, contributed to this default. Lacking mathematics, the principal tool of rigorous analysis, the economist in the business school directed his interest in economics to building theoretical frameworks, not to applying the theory, i.e., economic *analysis*. These issues are discussed further in the next chapter.

The Basic Production Course

Enough building blocks have been fashioned up to this point to start assembling them into a structure of the desirable production major. The first course in the major ideally would be a general or basic course which cuts across the subfunctions shown in the generalized model of the production function presented earlier. It should treat in a one-semester 3-credit course these subfunctions: product engineering, process engineering, plant engineering, production control, quality control, cost control, and the line-supervision function. Purchasing can, and probably should, be included as a part of the treatment of production control, not because firms typically organize the function this way, but because purchasing can be taught as the beginning function in the flow of goods through the firm to the customer. It was suggested earlier that designing the curriculum with a course for each organizational unit of the firm is undesirable.

The orientation of the basic course will be analytical. Description will be necessary, of course, particularly in the engineering aspects of product, process, and plant planning, as indicated earlier. However, the necessary description will not be presented in the usual unorganized, almost eclectic, fashion. The description should be developed to achieve several desirable ends. First, it should explain production management work as an application of management principles of the Koontz and O'Donnell or the R.C. Davis variety, i.e., a system of thought about the management process involving a body of principles. Second, it should provide some depth in engineering (developing physically feasible alternatives) beyond the base provided by the prior physics and chemistry courses. The third purpose is to provide the description necessary for application of the scientific method in the development of decision processes in production control, quality control, and cost control problems. The analytical content of the course would be centered largely in the treatment of these three production subfunctions.

Purchasing would be treated mostly in a descriptive manner, with the description designed to show how the rational management process may be applied to the purchasing function. That portion of purchasing which lends itself best to the development of rational decision processes, i.e., raw material inventory control, can be covered along with the inventory decision making which is an essential part of production control. The decision processes are the same. To date, the central function of purchasing, i.e., buying, has not yet been researched to the point where formal decision processes have been developed. Hence, for practice in recognizing problems and exercising judgment in buying, as well as in all other sections of the basic course where treatment would otherwise be confined to description, cases should be used, the engineering sections excepted.

The level of the analytical content of the basic course in production would necessarily reflect the mathematical-statistical background of all business students, not just of production majors, as this basic course is intended to be a core course which should be required of all business students. With the higher level of mathematics-statistics indicated earlier in this report as background, the analytical content can be upgraded considerably over that offered in the typical general course in production in the business school today.

In the sections on production (volume), quality, and cost control the student can be exposed to simple model building and the application of statistical techniques to model testing. An elementary treatment of experimental design in production problems can be included at this point. In the scheduling part of production control and the indirect labor planning of cost control, he can be made aware of the need for applications of probability theory to the treatment of uncertainty and the treatment of waiting lines (queuing theory). However, awareness of this need is probably the limit in analytical level for this core course.

The great majority of business students would not be capable, mathematically, of going beyond this analytical level, despite the upgraded mathematics requirements recommended in Chaps. 8 and 9. An additional course beyond these requirements, probably in mathematical statistics, would be required of the production major prior to his taking his first senior-level course in this major. Obviously only those who have a relatively high aptitude for mathematical reasoning would care to take this advanced mathematics course which would be selected for the student's need in the light of his prior mathematical attainments.

In general, the core course in production management would be designed to accomplish the following: (1) provide the student with perspective in the production function, (2) acquaint him with the typical problems of production management and the situations in which they arise, (3) provide some practice in the analysis of these problems, (4) make clear to him the need for higher-level analysis in various production situations. The latter may be accomplished through a discussion treatment of a selected few research articles at appropriate points in the course. No appropriate text is available at present. However, several prospectuses of apparently suitable tests have appeared recently.

The Senior-level Professional Courses

A two-course sequence at the senior level should stress the rigorous analysis of problems in production management at all levels and in all subfunctions. An exception, for reasons given earlier, would be the purely engineering problems (developing physically feasible alternatives). In general, the two-course senior sequence will be an extension of the problem solving of the basic course but at a higher level, and for this the additional mathematics course mentioned earlier is a prerequisite.

Description will be introduced only to the extent necessary to implement the first step in the scientific method, i.e., observation, for each problem. Cases designed to include all the information of the traditional "problem," thus permitting the development and implementation of an explicit decision process as opposed to decision making strictly as an exercise in judgment, are an ideal method of combining the necessary description and the problem data in a manner which also gives practice in discerning the problem. Bowman and Fetter's *Analysis for Production Management* (Richard D. Irwin, Inc., Homewood, Ill., 1957) is a useful text for this purpose, but currently there is a shortage of suitable cases.

The senior courses should not be confined to problem solving at the intellectual level of Bowman and Fetter, however. Problems at both a lower and a higher level should be treated. In many problems, a kind of historical approach to the study of decision making is appropriate. This would take the student through the development of decision processes for a given type of problem, showing the inadequacies of earlier processes, e.g., use of the Gantt chart in production scheduling, through the development of more sophisticated processes, e.g., use of linear programming in production scheduling. Finally, in as many problems as possible, which will be few at the undergraduate level, the student should be taken to the frontier, i.e., to the research literature which leads business practice. I have in mind articles such as the following:

C. C. Holt, F. Modigliani, and H. A. Stone, "A Linear Decision Rule for Production and Employment Scheduling," *Management Science,* October, 1955.

A. C. Heyvaert and A. Hurt, "Inventory Management of Slow-moving Parts," *Operations Research,* October, 1956.

V. L. Smith, "Economic Equipment Policies: An Evaluation," *Management Science,* October, 1957.

The two senior problems courses should not be simply Selected Production Problems I and Selected Production Problems II. The production major should gain a comprehensive understanding of the flow of goods through the manufacturing firm from supplier to customer. This is undoubtedly the central functional aspect of production, i.e., the quantity-time aspect in the flow of goods through the firm. It embraces quantity-time (volume) planning and control from the sales forecast, back through master scheduling, finished goods inventory planning, work-in-process (shop-order scheduling), raw-materials inventory planning, and thence back to the supplier (buying).

One hesitates to call this course Production Control because of the relatively low analytical level (as well as procedural level) earlier texts bearing this name have achieved. However, John F. Magee's *Production Planning and Inventory Control* (McGraw-Hill Book Company, Inc., New York, 1958), is highly appropriate for this course. It provides the desired analytical approach in a functional setting. Also, the functional aspects are treated, not in relatively low-level procedural description, but in a systems-analysis approach. Hence, the first of the two senior-level courses for production majors would treat the complete class of problems associated with the flow of goods through the firm, including the associated systems (the system itself brings many of the problems into being). We can call it Production Volume Control.

The second senior production course in the major could appropriately be called Selected Problems in Production Management. In this course all the major problems encountered in the production subfunctions other than those directly associated with volume control can be treated. Selected problems in quality control, maintenance policy, equipment replacement, plant location and layout, scale of operations, make-or-buy decisions, etc. would comprise the course. For this, the Bowman and Fetter text noted earlier is appropriate. This could be supplemented with a few selected articles from the current research literature to bring the student to the frontier in at least a few of the problems treated.

At this point, three courses beyond the core course in production have been identified, i.e., (1) Advanced Mathematics-Statistics, (2) Production Volume Control, (3) Selected Problems in Production. One could have a highly rewarding program in production management with these three. However, the needs of some students would not be met, for example: (1) the student with definite career plans in production; (2) the student with plans for graduate work.

We would have to offer two electives to cover their needs: Selected Readings in Production and Motion and Time Study. For the student who plans a career in a given industry, say in a family business, the production function in that industry could be studied in depth and breadth through selected readings. The student with a functional career interest in, say, quality control or purchasing could pursue his interest through selected readings from among the many standard functional texts available in that subject. The student planning to go on to graduate study would pursue selected readings in the research literature.

For the student with a career interest in motion and time study, a reading course would not be appropriate. A laboratory course in which the student can set up experimental work situations, gather the appropriate data, treat it statistically, and make appropriate decisions will be required. Offered as an elective, this course would draw only those students who are clearly interested in it. Presumably this would be a relatively small number. This, together with the requirement that the course be taken only after completion of the required courses in the production major, would permit a high level of analytical work in the course, as well as coverage of more of the subject than is now undertaken in a single-semester course, e.g., Methods Time Measurement, Dimensional Motion Times, Universal Maintenance Standards, Ratio Delay Analysis, etc.

In summary, the undergraduate offering in the production major beyond the core course in production will be as follows, in the sequence shown:

Junior Year

Advanced Mathematics–Statistics.............. 3

Senior Year

Production Volume Control................... 3
Selected Problems in Production............... 3
Elective (not required)...................... 3
   1. Selected Readings
   2. Motion and Time Study

Total credits........................... 9–12

Underlying Disciplines for Production

The matter of appropriate basic disciplines for the business student has been thoroughly treated in earlier parts of this report. Special requirements for the production major would simply call for the choice of physics and chemistry in the laboratory science requirement. Available electives in advanced mathematics-science at the sophomore-junior level should not be preempted by the production major. They should be left open so that the student can gain more breadth. It is for this reason that an advanced mathematics-statistics course was included in the production major, rather than set up as a reduction of choice in an earlier elective area.

Inclusion of a sequence in the behavioral sciences along the lines recommended in Chaps. 8 and 9 will carry the treatment of production problems beyond microeconomic analysis to decisions for action. This feature of decision making, involving as it does the human factor in business problems, should be stressed throughout the production program, particularly through the use of cases in both the core course and the course in selected problems. Implementing specialized staff decisions is the essence of line-management production work, in the reasonably large and complex firm at least. Successful implementation is essentially an exercise in applied human relations which has its scientific base in the behavioral disciplines.

Obviously, the recommended stress on the economic aspects of production problems, which are essentially micro in nature, calls for an appropriate exposure to microeconomic theory as an underlying discipline. This also agrees with the curriculum proposals set forth in earlier chapters. Hopefully, this would include a treatment of pure production theory —that of the economist.

THE MASTER'S PROGRAM IN PRODUCTION

General Considerations

The production major in the master's program would be designed as an extension of the undergraduate major. It would merely be a notch higher in analytical stress. However, the conduct of the courses should stress self-development more than in undergraduate courses.

If the master's program is designed as a one-year program stressing breadth, it is very doubtful that a production major aimed at an analytical level one notch higher than the undergraduate level can be included. A two-year program would probably be necessary. In the one-year program, only a core course in production would be offered to all candidates. In the two-year program a major in production, involving three to four courses beyond the core course, would be highly rewarding to the interested student.

The Core Course

The basic production course, which presumably would be required of all master's candidates, should be designed to accomplish the same ends as the undergraduate core course in production discussed earlier, but at an analytical level one notch higher. The extent of this increase in analytical depth would depend for the most part on the depth of the accounting and mathematical-statistical tool courses required of all candidates, which should be taken prior to the core production course. If these are designed to lift all candidates significantly beyond that level of analytical skill acquired by the better graduates of the undergraduate business curriculum recommended in preceding parts of this report, the core course for master's candidates can be much more demanding than that of the undergraduate core course. If, however, the tool courses are designed merely to bring candidates with all sorts of differing backgrounds to the recommended level of the better business bachelor, then the core course in production cannot be lifted significantly above the analytical level of the undergraduate core course. If this were the case in a two-year master's program, admitted graduates of the undergraduate production major recommended earlier should not be required to take the core production course at the master's level. They would go directly into the next course in the master's sequence, Problems in Production Management.

Mathematical Prerequisites

In order to handle the analytical level of the master's problems course in production described later, the student would necessarily have to lift his quantitative analytical skill beyond that which I suspect will be reached in the accounting mathematical-statistical courses required of all candidates in the first year. For this purpose a course in mathematics-statistics beyond that of the general requirement for all candidates, appropriately chosen in the light of the student's background, will be the first offering in the production major.

The Key Course in the Major

The central course in the production major at the master's level will be a combination of the materials covered in the Production Volume Control and Selected Problems courses at the undergraduate level. The Magee text, supplemented by appropriately selected research articles, would carry the course to a higher level than the undergraduate course. In addition, problems would be selected from the new Bowman and Fetter text,

Analyses of Industrial Operations (Richard D. Irwin, Inc., Homewood, Ill., 1959). This text offers numerous applications of the latest analytical techniques drawn from various industries, thus giving the student some institutional breadth as well as analytical depth.

In short, the key production course in the major at the master's level would be designed to cover the essence, at a higher analytical level, of the two undergraduate courses, Production Volume Control and Selected Problems in Production, in one course. This could be done with the heavier mathematical background required of the major who has also generally higher abilities and greater motivation than the typical undergraduate. It is possible that the course so conceived may have to carry 4 hours credit, but this is doubtful.

Electives in the Production Major

The electives in the production major would be designed to meet the same ends as in the undergraduate program, i.e., career needs and preparation for the doctoral dissertation. The same approach could be taken to meet these needs, i.e., the course Selected Readings and the course Motion and Time Study could be offered. If the student had previously taken the motion and time study laboratory course at the level described earlier, he should not repeat it. His career interest in this subject could be better served by further readings in the area. Hence the mixing in the laboratory course of undergraduate production majors and graduate majors with no prior exposure would not be inappropriate. The graduate students would be expected to differentiate themselves from the undergraduates by pursuing additional readings beyond those required of undergraduates and, perhaps, reporting them to the class for the benefit of the undergraduates.

One graduate elective would be required and one left optional, whereas the undergraduate elective is optional. This reflects the desirability of having the master's candidate acquire depth in his specialty, since his undergraduate program would be quite broad, as recommended in earlier parts of this report.

The master's candidate who intends to do research in production for the doctoral dissertation will elect the selected-readings course in which he will pursue library research that will prepare him fully for his doctoral research, or alternatively, enable him to select a suitable research subject.

Perhaps a word is desirable on the conduct of the course in selected readings. Such a course can easily deteriorate. However, if the professor is as dedicated as he should be, he can conduct this course in a manner which would be gratifying to him as well as to the student. Written reports carefully studied by the professor, followed by an arranged discussion session open to all others taking the readings course that semester, regardless of subject, would put the student on his own and thus hasten his professional development as well as expose all the students to further breadth.

Concerning the reading load on the professor, there will probably be relatively few students in the production major designed as recommended here. Not many students, relatively speaking, are capable of going on to the advanced mathematics and statistics required of the production major at either the undergraduate or graduate level. But for those who can, the great university should provide an opportunity in the production area if they are so inclined. Otherwise, their talent may atrophy. Not all mathematically inclined people want to live their lives in the laboratory of the scientist!

On the other hand, there appears to be no good reason for offering in the university an undergraduate or a graduate major in production if the courses are not lifted well above the relatively low analytical level which currently characterizes most of them in the business school. A descriptive acquaintance with fork-lift trucks, roller conveyers, storage bins, and even production control systems can be obtained much more easily and effectively by going to work instead of to college!

Summarizing the recommended master's-level production major, it would be comprised of three to four courses beyond the core course as follows:

First Year

Advanced Mathematics–Statistics.   3

Second Year

Problems in Production Management.   3
Elective in Production (1 min., 2 max.).   3–6
  1. Selected Readings
  2. Motion and Time Study

                                            ———

Total credits.   9–12

THE DOCTOR'S PROGRAM IN PRODUCTION

The doctor's program in production would consist of research on a production problem of reasonable universality requiring a high level of analytical effort. The task should be such as to require the undivided attention of the candidate for at least twelve months, but not necessarily more.

Prior requirements for the doctoral dissertation should be satisfactory performance in a comprehensive as well as an analytical written examination designed to test the candidate's command of the content of the production field as indicated in the master's program recommended earlier.

An examination of the candidate's background, particularly at the master's level and in mathematics-statistics, would indicate the extent to which he would be required to take courses at the master's level, as described above, in order to prepare himself for the written field examination. Students showing up well in the recommended production major in the master's program would qualify for the doctoral program by passing the field examination and starting their dissertation research forthwith. A successful oral defense of the dissertation would be required for the doctor's degree.

PART FOUR

OTHER PROGRAMS
IN BUSINESS ADMINISTRATION

PREPARATION FOR BUSINESS
IN ENGINEERING SCHOOLS

W. Grant Ireson

A limited amount of business education is available in practically all engineering schools, but those schools having business administration departments and industrial engineering departments generally offer greater opportunities than the purely technical schools. Industrial engineering should concentrate its resources and professional development on the quantitative aspects of management. It should leave the typical business areas to the business administration schools. Where both industrial engineering and business administration are available in the same university there should be a general agreement on the division of courses to be taught by each, so as to take maximum advantage of the special qualifications of the staff of each division.

WHY BUSINESS EDUCATION AT ENGINEERING SCHOOLS?

The engineering school is usually devoted to the teaching of fundamentals of physical science and their application to engineering work, to research, and to the development of new and better aids to mankind. Few people think of engineering schools as places of business education, and, in fact, many such schools offer very little opportunity for the student to obtain basic education in business principles. The need, however, for such education has been shown in numerous surveys conducted by such organizations as the American Society for Engineering Education, American Society of Mechanical Engineers, and many other organizations.

The most important fact brought out by these surveys over a period of about thirty years is that more than 60 per cent of those persons who earned engineering degrees either became managers of some kind within ten to fifteen years or left the engineering profession entirely to enter various kinds of business ventures. This is adequate reason why engineering schools should provide opportunities for the student to obtain some basic knowledge of business principles, practices, restrictions, policies, and opportunities. Even those engineers who are very successful in research, design, construction, applications, or production eventually find themselves facing the prospect that the next promotion will take them into managerial positions where they will be making and carrying out administrative or managerial policies, with little background for the jobs. The best engineers frequently make the worst managers.

In recent years a small percentage of the engineering students have stated quite frankly that they have no intention of practicing engineering as a profession. They intend to use their engineering training as a background for graduate work in business administration and then to go directly into business as salesmen, personnel administrators, comptrollers, production supervisors, and the like. It is interesting to note that many industrial concerns have encouraged this educational plan by providing higher starting salaries for men with this background than for those who graduate from the same graduate schools of business but with a liberal arts undergraduate degree.

A third development, not quite so clearly defined, is that a great number of the graduates of engineering curricula never practice engineering professionally, even when employed by manufacturing, research, or construction industries. Many of these graduates are in fact well-educated technicians in these organizations, performing tasks that could be done by experienced high school graduates. Many of these people then progress into junior managerial positions without ever doing real engineering work. There seems to be no doubt that their engineering training helps them in those positions, because they understand the language of the technical people and can translate it into the language of management and make decisions for management.

BUSINESS EDUCATIONAL OPPORTUNITIES FOR ENGINEERS

The opportunities for engineering students to obtain some business education as undergraduates vary greatly with the type of college or university. Within most of the engineering colleges there are some limited opportunities. Where the engineering college or school happens to be part of a university, there are usually a greater number of opportunities. A side question, "How well do these engineering students avail themselves of these opportunities?" is discussed later.

The Engineers' Council for Professional Development, the accepted accrediting agency for engineering curricula, has exerted a powerful influence on the amount of general studies or humanities required in engineering colleges. While the intent of the ECPD was not to force these schools to require business training, some schools have used such courses as principles of economics, psychology, business law, sociology, industrial relations, report writing, and organization to satisfy their minimum requirements in the humanities. Most ECPD inspectors refuse to accept all of them as "humanities," but we would not argue the fact that all these courses contribute to the business education of the student. They certainly contribute to the student's understanding of the business world, personnel problems, and the social responsibilities of the businessman.

Most of the undergraduate engineering curricula accredited by ECPD will contain 15 or more semester units (or their equivalent number of quarter credits) of the 120 semester units required for graduation in some of these areas. The real value of these courses depends to a great extent upon the schools in which they are offered. Unfortunately, when these courses are offered within the engineering schools, there is a tendency to have the courses taught by teachers who would not be considered for appointment in top quality schools specializing in these areas. The courses are very likely to be taught "from the book" with little enthusiasm or imagination, and, consequently, without stimulating the students to do more than "pass the course." Those schools which are fortunate enough to have these courses available in liberal arts colleges or university colleges usually find a higher degree of enthusiasm on the part of the students for the courses and, as a result, greater benefit from the exposure.

The majority of the engineering schools in this country now require the engineering student to take at least one course in the principles of engineering economy. A recent survey[1] revealed that approximately 9,000 students enroll in this course each year in the nation's colleges. Its popularity has grown from recognition of its value as preparation for making sound business decisions. The subject matter of this course is applied economics with special emphasis on the formulation of the problem, the determination of the alternatives available, and the evaluation of the differences among the alternative solutions. For many engineering students this course is their first and only college exposure to the economic necessities of business, but it can become a powerful tool in the hands of the ambitious student.

Those schools that offer a curriculum in industrial engineering usually offer the largest number of opportunities for business education. The number of industrial engineering curricula has increased quite rapidly since 1943. In 1943, there were only 19 accredited industrial engineering

[1] A survey made by Dr. Gerald Matchett of the Illinois Institute of Technology for the Engineering Economy Division of the American Society for Engineering Education, to be published in *The Engineering Economist*, vol. 4, no. 2.

curricula or options in other curricula. In 1949 there were 23 accredited curricula or options and in 1957 there were 49.[2] Undergraduate enrollment in industrial engineering has grown from 2,303 in 1939 and 1,465 in 1946 to 5,991 in 1956–1957.[3] The growth has been the result of a number of important factors, but certainly one of the most important was the desire of engineering students to obtain the fundamentals of engineering (without any extensive specialization in one engineering field) together with a sound introduction to management and business practices.

There is no question but that part of the growth in the enrollment in industrial engineering was the result of the transfer of students from other engineering curricula to industrial engineering in the hope of finding an easier degree. Most departments of industrial engineering recognized this problem long ago and took steps to prevent a continuation of the practice. (Some few departments have not yet faced this problem.) The methods used by the departments have been varied, but one development has been the introduction of rigorous courses to replace descriptive, survey-type courses, and this has been especially true in the courses that tend to overlap or duplicate undergraduate business administration courses. Practically all industrial engineering departments offer and/or require courses in business or industrial organization, industrial management, production, inventory or materials control, industrial relations or personnel administration, accounting, and cost control or budgeting. Depending upon the availability of schools of business administration or economics, these courses may or may not be offered by the industrial engineering faculty. While these courses may be intended primarily for the industrial engineering major, they are usually available to the majors in other engineering branches as electives. The usual curriculum in the other branches seldom permits the students to elect more than one to three of such courses. The industrial engineering programs will be discussed more fully in a later section.

Within the last three or four years a new trend has been developing which promises to make more opportunities for business education available to engineering students. A number of engineering colleges have introduced "administration options" into the regular mechanical, civil, electrical, and chemical engineering curricula. Stanford University, Michigan State University, and the University of Illinois are a few of the colleges making this type of program available. These options usually permit the student to substitute ten to fifteen semester units of business

[2] Data extracted from annual reports of the Engineers' Council for Professional Development.

[3] Data extracted from annual issues of *Engineering Enrollments and Degrees*, U.S. Department of Health, Education, and Welfare, Office of Education.

or industrial engineering courses from an approved list for an equal number of units of the more advanced specialized courses within his major department. The objective of this program, as stated by a number of department heads, is to prepare the engineering student who has no interest in research or design for a career in the administration of engineering work. It must be recognized immediately that this program is similar in nature and intent to the established industrial curricula and, in a few cases, requires as much work in the managerial fields as the industrial engineering curriculum. These programs have a stronger appeal to some students than industrial engineering has, and a few companies have shown special interest in graduates of such programs. Probably more such plans will develop in the future. Joining a limited amount of management education to an established curriculum offers some definite advantages, but there is the hazard that this portion of the curriculum will be a superficial coverage and, consequently, mislead the student as to his qualifications for managerial positions.

OTHER PROGRAMS IN ENGINEERING SCHOOLS

A few engineering colleges provide opportunities for business education in programs that are slightly different from the usual industrial engineering programs. These curricula are given such names as Business and Engineering Administration, Administrative Engineering, Industrial Management, Industrial Administration, and Engineering Administration. Dartmouth College, Illinois Institute of Technology, Washington University, Rutgers University, University of Tennessee, Rensselaer Polytechnic Institute, and Yale University have used these or similar titles. Some of these programs are accredited by the ECPD as industrial engineering curricula, provided they meet all the requirements for the basic sciences, mathematics, engineering fundamentals, and humanities. An examination of the curricula that have been accredited in this way leads one to believe that the science and engineering content is on the lower side of the recommended ranges, but this is not always true.

The other types of programs (i.e., industrial management) usually require some basic work in engineering but not more than do the normal freshman and sophomore years. The other two years usually resemble the last two years of the usual undergraduate business administration curricula. These curricula are not accredited by the ECPD and are not presented as "engineering" curricula. They do, however, provide a specialized type of business education for the young man who has some tendency toward technical work but perhaps neither the capability nor interest in pursuing a regular engineering degree. The enrollment records of a few colleges where such programs are available show that a fairly large percentage of the graduates of these curricula started in engineering and transferred to these curricula. Interviews with faculty and administration officials of two such schools revealed that these students tended to be among the lower third or lower half of their class at the time of admission.

There is no definite pattern as to where the student obtains the business courses in these specialized curricula. In some cases such courses as accounting, marketing, personnel administration, and organization and management are provided by the business or commerce schools. In other cases, these are taught in the parent department or school, such as the School of Industrial Management. In still other cases, some of these courses are obtained from the industrial engineering department. It seems almost impossible to draw any valid conclusions regarding the benefit of having one source versus the others. The value of the courses seems to depend most heavily upon the teacher and not upon the department or school in which he is located. In some cases, the school or department policies regarding grading, tests and examinations, and outside work seem to influence the rigor of these courses.

An objective toward which effort should be exerted is a better basis for assigning areas of instruction to various schools within a university. Possibly one of the better bases would be to have courses that are based upon mathematics and science taught in the engineering schools with the traditional management functions taught in business administration. Again, the qualifications of the individual teachers should be considered heavily.

TRENDS IN THE UNDERGRADUATE INDUSTRIAL ENGINEERING CURRICULA

As previously indicated, the curricula in industrial engineering are strongly influenced by the recommendations of the ECPD and the desire on the part of most schools to obtain ECPD accreditation. Up until about five years ago, practically all industrial engineering curricula were inspected by nonindustrial engineers for the ECPD. The industrial engineering program inspectors were more likely to be civil engineers or business administration graduates (and faculty members) than they were to be industrial engineers. However, since the American Institute of Industrial Engineers became an associate member of the ECPD, the institute has been given the privilege of establishing the list of industrial engineering curriculum inspectors. As a result of this change, it seems apparent that there will be more consistency in the evaluation of the curricula in the several schools and colleges.

The accredited curricula will almost certainly consist of some combination of courses that approximates Table 19-1.

TABLE 19-1

	Semester hours
Physical sciences (physics, chemistry, etc.)	18–20
Mathematics (calculus, analytical geometry, differential equations)	18–20
Engineering mechanics (statics, dynamics, fluid mechanics, engineering materials, etc.)	15–20
Engineering fundamentals (electrical engineering circuits, electrical engineering machinery, thermodynamics, metallurgy, machine design, mechanical drawing, descriptive geometry)	24–36
Humanities (English, foreign languages, political science, social science, arts, psychology, economics)	18–20
Major field (motion and time study, organization and management, accounting, engineering economics, quality control, statistics, production planning and control, etc.)	25–40
Total	125–140

It is rare for the specialized courses in the major field to represent more than one-fourth of the four-year program. This statement depends to some extent upon what is considered as part of the major field. For example, some industrial engineering curricula show machine design in the major field and statistics as part of the mathematics program. However, it is believed that the stated generalities fairly represent the industrial engineering curricula.

Most colleges and universities impose certain restrictions on the curricula in the form of a minimum amount of general studies courses or languages, etc. The ECPD imposes certain restrictions, and the parent school or department may impose others. Consequently, the industrial engineering departments, just as all others, are trying to eliminate as much of the descriptive, survey-type courses as possible ("squeezing out the water") to make room for new courses or the expansion of other more demanding courses. In a number of instances, I found that the industrial engineering departments were establishing graduation requirements that were 5 to 10 per cent higher in units or credits than the university required. The purpose of this is to include some of the newer work. The nature of the courses being added and deleted depends again upon the personal interests and capabilities of the faculty members of the different colleges.

Some of the trends reflected in various courses are worth individual comment.

Organization and Management

A survey course in organization and management has for many years been the first course in the industrial engineering series of courses in many colleges. This course is usually descriptive in nature with some discussion case studies to add interest and bring the students into the classroom discussions. The industrial engineering majors are very critical of this course, and there is a trend toward eliminating it for them in favor of a later course in management science or operations research.

Another interesting development, however, is the increasing demand for this descriptive course by students enrolled in other engineering curricula. It appears that the course is serving an important need for the other engineers in that it introduces them to the complex organizational structure of a modern business and helps these students to visualize the relationships among such functions as personnel, purchasing, quality control, shipping and receiving, cost control, etc. in which they will be involved as engineers in the engineering, design, and production phases of the business. This is a healthy sign for it means that these engineers will understand the management's problems a little better, and the communication channels between management functions and engineering functions will be more effective.

Accounting

A trend has developed away from the usual general accounting and cost accounting sequence of the business administration school. Nine or more semester hours is normally required for the completion of the accounting and cost accounting sequence of courses in the business administration schools; the pressure of heavy curricula has caused most industrial engineering departments to either drop the accounting requirement or offer a specialized course within its own department. It should be noted that the educational objectives are quite different, and these differences seem to justify the changes.[4] The business administration courses provide the student with very thorough training in the mechanics of accounting, the various systems that may be encountered, principles of accounting and cost accounting, and a great deal of practice. On the other hand, the industrial engineer does not expect to engage in accounting practice but does expect to be engaged in cost control in the factory. He needs to understand the principles of accounting and cost accounting. He is more interested in interpretation of accounting statements than in

---

[4] Whether prevailing practices in the teaching of accounting at business schools need reexamination is considered at length in Chap. 14.

their preparation. The typical course given by the industrial engineering departments consists of about four semester hours and covers the basic principles of general accounting, cost accounting (job-lot, by-product, standard, process, and joint), and the interpretation of accounting statements. The course usually includes brief problems that illustrate each basic concept. Similar courses could just as well be taught in the business schools.

Statistics and Probability

The recent developments in management science have pointed up the necessity for the industrial engineer to have a good working knowledge of mathematical statistics and probability in order either to go ahead into other courses or to be able to read and understand the literature of the field. Practically all industrial engineering departments are now requiring three to four units of statistics and recommending three units of the theory of probability. The distinction should be clearly made between these courses in mathematical statistics and the typical business statistics courses. The mathematical courses treat the measures of dispersion and central tendency but go far beyond that in covering measures of significance, design of experiments, and specialized techniques, such as analysis of variance, Latin Squares, sampling, and statistical inference. This is one of the most important recent developments in the industrial engineering curricula; no doubt it will be developed extensively before the course content reaches a plateau. (This course is usually required in addition to a course in statistical quality control.)

Operations Research or Management Science

A number of departments of industrial engineering have added one or more courses at the undergraduate level in operations research (or some other title). This represents the most significant change in the philosophy of undergraduate industrial engineering education to date. The significance of this addition lies in the fact that it represents an elevation of the "management" courses from mere description and judgment to a scientific approach based upon factual analysis. It is evident that this is a move in the right direction, but it can have some adverse effects if it is allowed to overshadow all other industrial engineering techniques.

Numerous definitions of operations research have been used as the basis for establishing the content of these courses. Without trying to stimulate additional arguments, it can be said that the objective of the undergraduate courses is to present the student with a number of mathematical and statistical tools by which he can set up a decision rule for the guidance of management. The various techniques are just so many separate tools, and part of the courses must consist of learning the situations and conditions to which each is applicable. Part of the tools are used for analysis of data for use with other tools, so that guides to decisions or policies can be formulated. Very seldom are the techniques or the decision rules ends in themselves. Practically always, the decision rules must be applied with good management judgment. Here, it seems, is the real hazard, because so many of these courses are being taught by statisticians or mathematicians who do not appreciate the management aspects of the problems and in turn fail to transmit to the students a true appreciation of the contributions of the mathematical representation of the problems.

Data Processing

Electronic data processing, computer theory, and problem formulation have in the past been regarded as the exclusive preserves of the mathematicians, logicians, and electronic engineers. In recent years the industrial engineers have become more and more interested in these areas of learning. A few undergraduate courses in electronic data processing have been introduced into the industrial engineering curricula. These undergraduate courses are usually fairly elementary. They introduce the student to the computer language, basic programming, and the different types of computers (memory systems, coding systems, computer logic, etc.). They usually do not provide any extensive training in problem analysis, formulation, and solution.

The industrial engineer's need for extensive data for production control, cost control, personnel management, wage and salary management, work standards, etc., has never been satisfied under the manual data-handling systems. It quickly became evident that the large, high-speed computers for the first time allowed the industrial engineer to hope that he might be able to gather all the data and statistics necessary to accomplish the assigned tasks within the time and cost limits imposed by a rapidly changing industry. Furthermore, the use of computers to do repetitive computational tasks more economically and more rapidly than they can be done by humans fits right into the industrial engineer's purpose in life: to do things more efficiently and economically.

OBJECTIVES OF THE INDUSTRIAL ENGINEERING CURRICULUM

Interviews with a large number of industrial engineering department heads and practicing industrial engineers supported my initial hypothesis that the profession of industrial engineering has not been satisfactorily defined and that there are many different opinions about the objectives of industrial enginering education. Even the American Institute of Industrial Engineers has found it necessary to use a very general definition that is subject to a great deal of individual interpretation. Its definition is, *"Industrial Engineering is concerned with the design, improvement, and installation of integrated systems of men, materials and equipment, drawing upon specialized knowledge and skill in the mathematical, physical and social sciences together with the principles and methods of engineering analysis and design, to specify, predict, and evaluate the results to be obtained from such systems."*

There is general agreement that industrial engineers must be provided with a sound foundation in physical sciences, mathematics, and engineering fundamentals. It is recognized that industrial engineers may never be occupied in mechanical, structural, or electrical design or in engineering research in these fields. However, it is also recognized that most industrial engineers will be involved in coordinating the work of mechanical, civil, chemical, electrical, or other engineers and will have to understand, evaluate, justify, criticize, and perhaps authorize the work of these engineering specialists. Therefore, it is essential that industrial engineers have a basic knowledge of the special fields so that they can talk the same language.

Secondly, the industrial engineer will be involved with people. In the definition approved by the American Institute of Industrial Engineers, the one word that distinguishes that definition from one for mechanical or electrical engineers is "men." Man is the most unpredictable element of any system, and the industrial engineer's concern for man's part in the system distinguishes him from those in other fields of engineering. Consequently, the industrial engineering programs include such subject matter as work simplification, work measurement, industrial psychology, personnel administration, and so on.

A third element is the fact that the industrial engineer is concerned with economy. His job is to save or conserve the resources that go into the production of any goods or services. This can be interpreted in terms of saving money, if one likes, for practically everything in business can be reduced to monetary factors with some degree of accuracy. Top management must also be concerned with money, for it is only through the prospect of profit that men can be induced to invest their savings in businesses of any kind. The industrial engineer can be thought of as the right hand of management in cost control and cost reduction. He, therefore, must have an appreciation of the management aspects of the business and, again, speak the same language as management. Thus he must have a good working knowledge of accounting and cost accounting, salary and wage administration, sales, inventory control, materials control, finance, depreciation, taxes, and business law, to name just a few. In addition, he must know the "tools of his trade," those techniques of data collection, analysis and evaluation, problem formulation, and synthesis that will enable him to carry out his assigned tasks. These "tools" include motion and time study, statistics, statistical quality control, principles of engineering economy, and the other specialized engineering subject areas that deal with his particular business (machine design, electronics, chemistry, structures, production tooling, etc.).

Industrial engineers are being employed by industry in a wide variety of jobs after graduation. Literally hundreds of different types of jobs could be enumerated. These early jobs seldom represent more than in-plant or on-the-job training programs. Most of these graduates eventually find themselves in various managerial positions ranging from presidents of corporations downward. Just as mechanical engineers or electrical engineers are likely to find that they have reached the top positions in their chosen engineering functions and must accept managerial positions in order to advance further with the organization, the industrial engineer goes up the company ladder. The difference seems to be that the industrial engineer develops his managerial ability as he goes along. Part of his ability to develop thus stems from his undergraduate training. As the former head of one of the big industrial engineering departments expressed it, "It isn't so much what the student learns and remembers from his college courses as it is the recognition that there are many other activities other than his own job in any organization. The industrial engineering curriculum makes him keep his eyes open to the things that are going on around him, so that he will be growing with the whole organization while he is doing a small, specialized job."

The foregoing analysis of the objectives of an industrial engineering education is a composite of many individually expressed ideas. Some people do not agree with this broad statement. A few prefer to limit the objectives to "management of manufacturing activities"; others think the objective is "management of functions that require an engineering background in order to understand the technical problems." Most, however, believe that the scope of work for the industrial engineer is unlimited and is equally applicable wherever human beings are performing work.

GRADUATE PROGRAMS IN INDUSTRIAL ENGINEERING

Forty-six colleges and universities had students enrolled in graduate programs leading to the master's degree in industrial engineering in 1956–1957, and thirteen had students enrolled in programs leading to the doctorate. A total of 2,173 graduate students were enrolled. There were 4,138 graduate students in mechanical engineering and 7,959 in electrical engineering during the same year. In 1950–1951, only 1,128 graduate students were enrolled in industrial engineering. For the same year there were 3,046 enrolled in mechanical engineering and 5,147 in electrical engineering. This is indicative of the growth of interest in advanced degrees in industrial engineering.[5]

The last ten to twelve years have seen a radical change in the content of industrial engineering graduate programs. In the late forties most of the graduate programs emphasized motion and time study (and its various specialties) and the business type courses (such as principles of organization, personnel administration, labor economics, accounting, finance, and production control). A trend began to develop in the late forties with the introduction of statistical quality control and industrial statistics. As time has passed, the emphasis has gradually shifted more toward the quantitative aspects of industrial engineering and less emphasis has been placed on the business subjects.

As is to be expected, the graduate programs were influenced by the interests of the senior members of the various departments. Most of the departments tended to emphasize one or two special areas. As the number of associate and full professors grew and more diverse interests were brought into the departments, more specialties were developed into graduate courses. Within the industrial engineering departments one will find by examining the catalogs that the following special fields are relatively common now, most of them being major options under the degree of master of science in industrial engineering:

Engineering economy
Motion and time study (or work simplification)
Data processing
Industrial statistics
Operations research (or management science)
Personnel administration
Production (and tool engineering)
Statistical quality control

No one school, to my knowledge, offers all these specialties as options in the advanced degrees. In addition, the specialized course work and thesis requirements seldom make up more than two-thirds of the total requirements for the advanced degree. The student usually has the opportunity to elect about a third of his total requirements from the other areas of study.

The graduate programs in engineering are not subject to accreditation by ECPD. Therefore, there is considerably less conformity in course

[5] *Engineering Enrollments and Degrees,* circulars published annually by U.S. Department of Health, Education, and Welfare, Office of Education.

requirements among the several schools, or for that matter, between different options within the same school. It is impossible to give a meaningful summary of courses required for the advanced degrees. It is worth noting, however, that practically every department offering a graduate degree requires one or more courses in mathematical statistics beyond the undergraduate requirements. It seems evident, both from the academicians' and the practitioners' viewpoint, that statistics has become as important to the industrial engineer as differential equations is to the mechanical or electrical engineer.

It is interesting to note that a majority of the industrial engineering departments allow the graduate student to take several courses in the graduate school of business whenever they are available. The specific courses that are permitted cover a wide range, but most often they are the courses that are typically "business" courses, as opposed to those that may be available in both industrial engineering and business schools. In some universities there has been a formal or informal division of subject areas, so that duplication of offerings will not occur. For instance, a business school may offer both the undergraduate and graduate courses in accounting, finance, labor relations, personnel administration, organization and management, marketing, insurance, and banking. The industrial engineering school may offer all courses in industrial statistics, statistical quality control, work simplification, production planning, production engineering (as distinguished from production), operations research, engineering economy, and data processing. Students of both schools may then take a limited number of courses in the other school.

This arrangement can be both beneficial and detrimental. Normally it means that the teachers are specialists in the course areas and therefore should be able to stimulate the students to a higher level of understanding and accomplishment. If, however, there are no limitations on class sizes, they may become so large from both sources of students that a good part of the value of having a recognized authority as the teacher may be lost. If classes are limited, the parent department naturally gives preference to its own students, and students from the other department, even though they need the course to complete their educational plan, are excluded. Students with radically different backgrounds may tend to reduce the effectiveness of the teacher because too much time is taken in clarifying concepts and fundamentals. Thus one group may hold back the other group.

The graduate programs in industrial engineering are generally designed to give the student the opportunity to explore in depth one or two areas which he covered rather superficially as an undergraduate. The undergraduate industrial engineering curricula probably provide less opportunity for specialization than any of the other four major engineering curricula. The breadth of coverage, as explained earlier, simply does not leave enough time for such specialization. On the other hand, the graduate program permits the student to develop some skills in a particular area of work and to become thoroughly familiar with the subject matter and literature of his chosen field. In addition, the graduate programs place more emphasis on "why" than the undergraduate programs and attempt to place the student in situations where he will be forced to do creative thinking. In this respect, the industrial engineering programs are little different from all others.

At the present time only a few schools offer the Ph.D. degree in industrial engineering. The next decade should see a substantial increase in the number of such programs, because as the number of Ph.D.s on industrial engineering faculties increase, more schools will be capable of offering significant advanced work. Furthermore, as industrial engineering becomes more a science and less an art, more fundamental subject matter will be available for inclusion in the graduate programs.

A few current trends seem to indicate the direction in which the Ph.D. programs will develop. The strongest present trend is toward doctoral programs centering around statistics and mathematics as applied to industrial decision-making processes. This type of program is generally referred to as "operations research."

A strong interest in man-machine systems is developing, and some substantial work has been done by psychologists and others in this area. The engineering aspects of man-machine systems call for participation by engineers with strong interests in the human aspects of the problem. Industrial engineers are proving to be rather ideally suited to this new field. This area offers great possibilities for doctoral programs in the next ten years.

The availability of high-speed electronic computers is challenging the industrial engineers in two other fields. One is to simulate human actions and reactions to different stimuli. The other is to simulate economic problems. It appears that these fields may well develop into important areas of doctoral study.

RELATIONS BETWEEN BUSINESS ADMINISTRATION AND INDUSTRIAL ENGINEERING

A previous section pointed out that in some cases the business administration and industrial engineering departments have cooperated with each other to the extent of dividing subject areas between them. This cooperative attitude is not always present at either the undergraduate or graduate level.

Some faculty members of both industrial engineering and business administration feel that they are in competition for the same students. This seems to be most prevalent at the undergraduate level, perhaps more so between "industrial management" departments and industrial engineering than between regular business administration and industrial engineering. There is likely to be more competition where either department does not have enough students to operate efficiently than where both departments have all or more students than they can handle.

It is impossible to get a clear indication of how prevalent this competition is or to measure the importance of it. In discussions with representatives of both business administration and industrial engineering schools, I found that the department that seemed to be the aggressor refused to admit the existence of such competition and the aggrieved department either spoke of it freely or by sly innuendo. The competition took several forms. One method was to influence the college or university faculty body to write university or college requirements in such a way that a large number of students were forced to take certain courses that would, in effect, keep the less popular department alive. A second method was to prevent a department from offering a course on the grounds that this would tend to impinge upon the offerings of another department. An example of this occurred when an agricultural statistics department tried to prevent the industrial engineering department from giving a course in statistical quality control. Another was where a business and economics department of long standing refused to allow the new industrial engineering department to give the course in engineering economy which is normally taught in industrial engineering departments.

There is a tendency for each department to offer courses that duplicate the other's. This, however, is not necessarily bad. As was pointed out in the section on graduate programs, there are valid reasons why this duplication may be perfectly justified. The objectives of courses with similar titles may be different. The wage administration course of a business school will usually have an entirely different purpose and approach from one given by industrial engineering. Business administration students may need an introduction to quality control, but without a strong background in mathematics they should not be expected to take the same course in statistical quality control that would be required of industrial engineers. These are just examples of areas of apparent overlap between industrial engineering and business administration education that can become sources of friction.

One of the areas in which some overlap is taking place is discussed at length by Dr. Timms in Chap. 18, "Production." A number of business schools, both graduate and undergraduate, are offering work in production, and in some cases this tends to be direct duplication of industrial engineering courses. Even laboratory facilities are duplicated, and each in turn is used only a small portion of the time.

INDUSTRY'S USE OF INDUSTRIAL ENGINEERS

Information about industry's use of industrial engineering graduates was obtained from papers in the American Institute of Industrial Engineers' *Journal of Industrial Engineering*, papers given at ASEE conventions, local chapter meetings, surveys conducted by other individuals and institutions, and by talking with a large number of company interviewers who visited Stanford University in search of industrial engineers.

There are essentially three general plans for the utilization of recent graduates. A good many large industrial concerns have formal or informal training programs into which industrial graduates go. These training programs last from about six months to as long as three years. There may be only one training program for all types of engineering graduates, or there may be two or three different programs. Industrial engineering graduates usually find themselves in programs with graduates of other curricula in all the different types of training plans.

A second plan, common in both large and medium-sized companies, is to place the industrial engineers in operating departments or service departments and to rotate them every three or six months until they have learned a great deal about the company, its policies and practices, and its products and methods of manufacture. The objective is twofold: to let the young engineer learn as much as possible and "find" himself in the company and to permit the company to evaluate the man. After a period of time ranging from a year to two years, the young man is usually assigned to a specific department selected by mutual agreement.

The third plan is less formal than either of the first two. It usually is practiced by the small and medium-sized companies. In this plan the young engineer is normally hired for a specific department or task. After a very short time, he is expected to carry on the work with or without supervision and to "pay his own way" in the organization. In nearly all such cases observed, the young engineer was assured that the initial job was just a steppingstone to something higher and that the opportunities for advancement were unlimited.

There are many variations of these three employment plans, as Chap. 20 will show, and generalizations such as these are likely to be misleading unless the reader recognizes that the only purpose of such generalizations is to provide a basis for discussion of the adequacy of the engineer's education for his job and for the study of the company's reaction to the student's knowledge.

It should be immediately obvious that the young engineer's knowledge at the time of his employment is only one factor, frequently a minor one, in the determination of his success and satisfaction in his job. His performance and success (in the company's viewpoint) are influenced by his personality, personal desires, ambition, initiative, background, the other company personnel, his supervisor's ability and attitudes, and many other factors. Consequently, his success depends a great deal upon selecting a company whose policies, practices, etc., are compatible with his personal make-up. The student is not ordinarily in a very good position to make a wise choice in this matter. Such factors as location, salary, personality of the interviewer, and the "selling" job that the interviewer does are likely to be the real basis for his decision to accept a certain offer. The company usually has resources for evaluating a student's characteristics in reference to its objectives for him and should be responsible for assuring that it makes offers only to students who will be compatible with the whole company setting. This is seldom the case, however; the policies are more likely to be "hire two or three times as many young engineers as we need or expect to keep and be able to make the final selection after they have been with us some time." Few company representatives have admitted to this policy, but several have admitted that they prefer to hire young engineers for technicians' jobs (that could be filled by experienced high school graduates), because they obtain more responsible persons and the young engineers cost less than the experienced technicians.

During seventeen years of college teaching I have been asking company representatives questions about what kind of training they expect the young engineering graduate to have and what they would like them to have that they do not usually get in their college career. There is fairly general agreement that the young engineer lacks adequate ability to express himself clearly and concisely, either in written or oral form. Many representatives have stated that they did not care what special skills or knowledge the engineering graduate had attained, provided he had a strong foundation in mathematics and sciences and had learned to think. The other answers most frequently seemed to reflect specialized needs unique to the particular industry represented or personal gripes resulting from disappointment in a few engineering graduates.

The general philosophy of engineering education has been expressed on many occasions by prominent speakers in the American Society for Engineering Education. It has been more distinctly stated in the requirement for accreditation by the ECPD. Stated briefly, it is to turn out graduates with a thorough background in science, mathematics, and engineering fundamentals, with a basic appreciation of human values, and with as much skill and specialized knowledge in some broad area of specialization as time permits. Industry has accepted this concept, but the engineering faculties must be constantly on guard against complacency in designing courses and curricula.

The previous discussion has been in reference to engineering in general. The situation in industrial engineering is not very different. Recent trends in employment have indicated that industrial engineers are in demand in a wider spectrum of jobs and positions than any of the other engineering specialists. They are being employed for technical engineering work in competition with other types of engineers in addition to being employed for the classical industrial engineering positions in all kinds of companies. They are being employed by banks, merchandising establishments, hospitals, public utilities, common carriers, research laboratories, and many other nonmanufacturing industries. Certainly their introduction to business practices and problems through the business education courses available to them contributes to their widespread demand.

SOME INDICATIONS OF FUTURE DEVELOPMENTS IN INDUSTRIAL ENGINEERING CURRICULA

Several of the industrial engineering departments visited are currently reexamining their curricula, and the trends of the changes are worthy of note. The most pronounced change is toward the inclusion of more statistics and mathematics in the undergraduate curriculum. In a few cases the increase in statistics and mathematics is being accomplished by reducing the number of units devoted to the typical industrial engineering subjects, such as motion and time study, production control, economics, accounting, etc. The basis for these changes is the rapid development of operations research and management science. A representative of one business administration school said that the industrial engineering department's offerings had been so severely reduced that the business school would be forced to offer several courses that had previously been offered by the industrial engineering department.

As an inspector for the ECPD, I observed that one school was trying to retain the basic courses but also trying to add undergraduate work in data processing, operations research, modern algebra, and other new fields. The result seemed something less than desirable, because the students were receiving only the barest essentials in both the typical industrial engineering and business courses as well as in the new courses. It is my firm conclusion that a four-year curriculum does not provide enough time to encompass adequate educational opportunities in basic sciences, engineering fundamentals, and *all* these newer courses. It appears that these newer courses at the undergraduate level, if added at the expense of the more fundamental courses, tend to direct the student in a much narrower path than has been the case in the past. It will undoubtedly force some of the industrial engineering students to change curricula because they will not find the breadth of training they desire in the industrial engineering curriculum.

The foregoing criticism of the undergraduate curricula changes is not to be construed as a denial of the importance of the newer areas of activity. Instead, it should be recognized that these courses represent perfectly valid areas of specialization that are more appropriate for the graduate years than for the undergraduate. Both the ASEE and the ECPD have criticized the tendency of colleges to add engineering curricula and options for every possible field of specialization. These organizations have recommended that the undergraduate years be used to strengthen the foundations for engineering practice and that more of the specialization be left to the graduate years. A tremendous increase in knowledge has occurred in the last fifteen years. It has been reflected in science, mathematics, and engineering courses, and representatives of practically all engineering schools have expressed the feeling that it is becoming less and less feasible to include any large amount of specialization in the undergraduate curricula. At the very time when mechanical, electrical, and other engineering departments are reducing the number of options, some industrial engineering departments have been diluting their curricula by attempts to require more professional courses.

Curricula-planning Experiments

Some industrial engineering departments are doing some valuable experimentation in the matter of curriculum planning. New York University is providing the student the opportunity to elect several units of work in some other engineering field and, in turn, to relate his industrial engineering courses to the specific problems of the other field. For example, a student may take ten to twelve units in chemical engineering along with the usual number of industrial engineering and business courses; if he does, some of the usual courses in mechanics or mechanical engineering are eliminated from his program. The objective is quite obvious: to provide the student with the training that would enable him to be a better industrial engineer in the chemical industry.

This experiment has not been running long enough to obtain a fair evaluation of the results, but the faculty members feel that it is advantageous. Such specialization is not, however, in line with recommendations of the ASEE.

The Industrial Engineering Department of Northwestern University is following the basic philosophy of the Harvard Graduate School of Business in that it is not offering the industrial engineering courses under titles referring to the subject matter. The courses are listed as Industrial Engineering I, Industrial Engineering II, Industrial Engineering Problems I, and so on. The subject matter is organized according to relationships within the typical company rather than according to individual functions. The case method (which, for example, might require some accounting, cost control, quality control, and materials handling in one case) is used extensively.

In several schools, the industrial engineering program is a part of the mechanical engineering department, and the degree is granted in mechanical engineering with a subnotation of the option. A similar administration option is open to other students in electrical, civil, etc. Variations of this plan are being tried in a number of schools. In one school a bachelor of science degree in industrial engineering was once available but has been dropped in favor of optional programs in connection with other engineering curricula.

These rather new concepts in curricula planning are examples of the kind of thinking that is influencing industrial engineering education. The Engineers' Council for Professional Development encourages legitimate experimentation in engineering curricula planning in spite of the general standards that it uses for accreditation. Undoubtedly more experimentation of this sort will take place in a field of endeavor as new as industrial engineering. There are no strong precedents as in some other engineering fields; honest differences of opinion exist among the industrial engineering teachers as to what constitutes the ideal program. These differences of opinion account to a great extent for the rather wide variance among industrial engineering curricula.

As chairman of the Education Committee of the American Institute of Industrial Engineers from 1953 to 1956, I attempted to set up some broad guide lines for the formulation of accreditable industrial engineering curricula. The Committee consisted of eight prominent industrial engineering educators, each of whom presented preliminary, suggested criteria. It was impossible to obtain general agreement within the group on even a set of minimum courses and credits. The project was finally dropped. This incident is related only to show that any attempt to set up a model curriculum is certain to stimulate rather violent opposition from a large number of the affected teachers. On the other hand, some comments on general objectives, bases of evaluation, and the effects of the next ten to fifteen years of development on the curricula seem in order.

Planning the Future Curriculum

A look at modern business practices gives the best indication of the paths that will be followed in the development of curricula in the future. Modern business has become very complex as a result of growth in size, the accelerated pace of business activity, the fast reaction to market conditions, the increasing physical complexity of the products, and the expansion of governmental regulations and controls. The ratio of the number of people in administrative, clerical, coordinating, and control functions to the number in production has increased steadily for the last twenty years. Management must reduce its risk of making wrong decisions. The permissible margin of error in decision making is very small, and huge sums of money, perhaps even the future of the organization, may hang on the decisions. Thus we can see that the future will call for greater amounts of more exact information for use by management. The young industrial engineering and business administration graduates will be largely responsible for gathering, analyzing, and presenting these data in usable form to management.

Along with the need for great volumes of data there is a similar need for the development of techniques for analyzing the data so that the best possible predictions can be made about the future. The means and skills in communication must be improved so that less time will be involved in transmitting ideas, concepts, and recommendations. Communication difficulties are one of the most costly factors in business today. Also needed is a greater knowledge of man, his weaknesses and strengths, thought processes, motivating factors, and so on. Regardless of the technological advancements, men will still be the most important element in business management.

All this gives some indication of the way that our curricula should be planned for the future. The first necessity is to determine educational objectives of the various levels. Secondly, there must be a division of specialties so that the work can be accomplished in the most expeditious way with the minimum of confusion or "noise" in the process. Third, the educational program must be planned to give each person the maximum possible capacity in the area of work he has chosen within the time available.

Several years ago I presented a paper[6] in which I described three levels of accomplishment in industrial engineering. These levels were:

1. The technician level: that level of work accomplishment in which the person performs more or less routine operations, making minor decisions and perhaps supervising a small number of other technicians.

2. The level of professional practice: where the person is thoroughly familiar with all the techniques of the profession and is capable of analyzing and evaluating unusual situations and problems and of presenting a plan of action based on his findings. He keeps up with current develop-

---

[6] W. Grant Ireson, "Some Applications of General and Statistical Mathematics in Industrial Engineering," *Journal of Engineering Education*, vol. 43, no. 9, May, 1953, pp. 528–533.

ments and continues to improve his skills but does not contribute to the expansion of knowledge in his field.

3. The research and development level: where the person is perhaps more theoretical than on the second level and has the capacity to do fundamental research and to develop new techniques for use by the first- and second-level personnel. He contributes to the expansion of knowledge in his field.

These levels of accomplishment seem as applicable in business education as in industrial engineering. Obviously many of the bachelor graduates of both industrial engineering and business administration will serve out their lives in the first level of work, but most of the holders of a bachelor's degree will practice their professions at the second level. The third level will be filled primarily by the holders of advanced degrees. One of the objectives of the undergraduate programs should be to stimulate the undergraduate student so that he will develop those traits of character, professional knowledge, and ability that will prevent his being satisfied to spend his life in subprofessional activities. At the same time, students should be exposed to enough challenging ideas and concepts so that those with above-average capabilities will strive to earn advanced degrees and to spend their lives in exploratory work, creative activities, and the advancement of learning.

The rapid growth in the number of junior colleges, technical institutes, and vocational high schools will continue to provide the educational opportunities for those young people who will fill the technicians' positions in business and industry. Both business and industrial engineering schools should examine their curricula, course content, and faculties to assure that college and university education is not directed toward the training of technicians. There is pressure on colleges from all kinds of business concerns to tailor the curricula to the end that the graduates will be able to "earn their keep" immediately after joining the company.

The research minds of the future must be stimulated early in the graduate program, if not in the undergraduate years. Consequently, each graduate program should introduce the student to the scientific method of investigation and provide him with the basic tools for use in the conduct of research. If the student's graduate program consists only of learning what others have learned and if he does not realize the great challenge to do original work, we will find that few are inclined to go on to the doctorate level. Only through the training of a small percentage of the graduates for the third level of accomplishment will we assure the continuous expansion of knowledge in these fields.

In an earlier section of this chapter the discernible trends in curricula planning at the present time were described and a typical curriculum for industrial engineering was outlined. A careful analysis of those trends and the curriculum reveals a number of difficulties that will be encountered in not too many years. Recognition of these difficulties and corrective action as soon as possible will help to assure better curricula ten years hence. The following are some of the more pressing matters that need careful consideration.

Every field of learning has been expanding extremely rapidly, and more and more knowledge is considered to be fundamental. As early as 1945, serious consideration was given by engineering schools to a five-year program. A few schools, including The Ohio State University and Cornell University, adopted five-year engineering curricula. Most of the other schools either rejected the idea immediately or decided to wait and learn from the experience of those schools. After some ten years there is very little pressure for five-year bachelor programs. Over this period, the number of students enrolled in graduate programs has increased substantially. Many educators think that it is preferable to retain the four-year undergraduate program and to expand the graduate programs (and financial aid for graduate students), because this plan provides a terminal program for the students of average or below-average ability and permits the limited graduate educational resources to be made available to the more capable students.

In turn, there is considerable pressure to reduce the amount of specialization in the undergraduate programs in order to include the increasing amount of knowledge now considered fundamental. I believe that this is the direction that will be followed in the next two decades. Some movement in this direction was reported earlier in this chapter regarding mathematics and statistics. A high percentage of the industrial engineering curricula examined required more than the normal number of units for graduation. This is also true of other engineering curricula. This is, in effect, an increase in the requirements beyond a four-year program, but everyone recognizes that this slow, creeping increase cannot go on indefinitely. As a result, many departments have eliminated specialized courses, which were considered part of the professional training ten years ago, and have added *fundamental* courses or increased the coverage and units in mathematics, statistics, mechanics, electronics, psychology, etc. This is happening in most of the engineering curricula. This has the effect of bringing the four-year programs of the different fields of engineering closer and closer to a common curriculum. For example, at this time about 75 per cent of the requirements in mechanical, civil, and industrial engineering are common at Stanford University.

The future curricula probably will provide very limited specialization in the undergraduate programs; many of the courses now taught at the undergraduate level will become graduate courses. Along with this shift in the status of courses in any one department, there will be the necessity to change the required and elective courses outside the parent department. For example, the number of units now permitted for humanities and social science will not increase; yet the student will not be able to obtain an adequate foundation in those areas because they, too, are developing rapidly. More of the humanities and social sciences that contribute to business education will by necessity be carried over to the graduate programs.

There are many advantages to be gained from the changes just described. The undergraduate students will not be as channeled upon graduation and will be able to shift their fields of endeavor more easily. The graduate students will be more mature and capable of doing higher-level work in their professional courses. The teachers of graduate courses will be able to accomplish more in their courses than at present, because the students will have a better foundation in the sciences and mathematics. The graduate students will represent the upper one-third to one-half of the graduating classes and provide the teacher with a select group with which to work.

The changing pattern of curricula will force many departments of industrial engineering to re-evaluate their educational objectives. As mentioned earlier, a good many departments have added courses in such areas as data processing, operations research, statistics, probability, and human engineering by reducing the units for other courses or by deleting the second or third course of a series. These relatively new areas have received a lot of attention in the journals, professional societies, and educational organizations, and many departments have scurried to get on the "band wagon." It is perfectly obvious that the total number of subject areas in the undergraduate curriculum cannot be increased without diluting the original areas. The question becomes, "Will the variety of subject matter be continually increased at the cost of thorough coverage of fundamental work?"

Future curricula will probably develop along one or the other of two lines. One course of action will be to emphasize the quantitative aspects of industrial engineering and delete most of the psychology, industrial relations, and humanistic areas at the undergraduate level. This course will lead to the training of the type of industrial engineer represented by the operations analyst. In this case, the traditional business courses, like marketing and personnel administration, organization, management, and finance, will be left to the business administration schools.

The other course of action is to continue the traditional undergraduate industrial engineering curriculum with some readjustment to introduce quantitative techniques. Specialization in the several areas will be left for the graduate years. In this case, there probably will not be the clear demarcation between the industrial engineering and business school offerings that was mentioned in the previous paragraph; some duplication probably will continue.

The course of action that will be followed will probably depend more upon the special interests of the faculty members than on any recommendations of societies or research groups. Men who are presently teaching the traditional industrial engineering and management courses are not likely to agree to the discontinuation of these courses regardless of the introduction of newer concepts regarding quantitative aspects of the profession. Thus, for the existing departments, the future curricula are more likely to be the result of gradual evolution from the present subjective to the more quantitative type of curriculum. New departments yet to be formed and the presently young departments will have more opportunity to set up initially the more scientific curricula. These departments will be able to add new faculty members whose interests are in the quantitative area, thereby ensuring that the departmental program will follow that path. Furthermore, searches for faculty members by a number of different industrial engineering departments have shown that a larger number of the young Ph.D. candidates are interested in the operations research type of programs than are interested in the traditional industrial engineering programs. This tends to ensure that a supply of teachers for the quantitative type program will be more readily available than for the traditional programs.

FACULTY PREPARATION

The number of industrial engineering faculty members who hold doctorate degrees is low compared with the faculties of electrical and mechanical engineering departments. Part of this is due, according to department heads, to the fact that the supply of Ph.D.s in industrial engineering has been smaller than the number of new faculty positions. The best information available indicates that there are less than 100 men in the United States with Ph.D. degrees in industrial engineering. This is less than one year's output in electrical engineering. We cannot expect the number to increase rapidly until the financial incentive is greater.

The fact that few young men work for the doctorate in industrial engineering is due to some extent to the fact that business and industry have not expressed their desire for doctorate-level education by providing salaries as attractive as those for the research-minded electrical and mechanical engineer with the doctorate degree. It appears that most of the men working for the doctorate in industrial engineering are doing so as preparation for teaching careers.

The demand for industrial engineering teachers is increasing at a much faster rate than the supply of Ph.D.s. More financial support must be made available to outstanding students in order to entice them to work for their doctorate. One department head, when questioned as to how he expected to staff his department in the coming years, replied that he intended to "grow his own" teachers by hand-picking candidates and providing good salaries for part-time work while they worked for the Ph.D. Effort should also be devoted to securing research contracts in order to provide both financial assistance and challenging projects for dissertation research.

Industrial engineering faculties can also be improved by employing outstanding men from other disciplines. Several colleges have hired statisticians, economists, psychologists, and social scientists for their industrial engineering departments. In most cases, the successful integration of such men depends to some extent on their having some engineering background, whether it is actual engineering education or several years of work in close relationship with engineers. This means appears to offer the best possibilities for *immediate* upgrading of industrial engineering faculties, but the supply of such persons is still limited.

The need for both pure and applied research in areas of industrial engineering has not been recognized either by large industrial concerns or by government agencies. Very little research, in terms of money expended, has been conducted, and additional emphasis on this need must be made by department heads in order to make teaching jobs more attractive.

SUMMARY AND RECOMMENDATIONS

The opportunities for some amount of business education in the engineering colleges have been increasing quite rapidly in the last ten years. These opportunities are available primarily in the departments of industrial engineering or industrial management. However, some schools of business administration are making business courses available to engineering students.

A small percentage of the students in engineering curricula other than industrial engineering are taking advantage of the opportunities to take business courses over and above those required by their curricula. Most of those are doing so through the so-called "administration" options and fall into two main groups. The first group does not want to go into research and design jobs and prefers the operating or production phases of its chosen professions. The second group is made up of students who do not intend to practice engineering professionally but feel that it is the best preparation for graduate work in business administration or other nonengineering professions.

Potential areas of conflict between business administration schools and industrial engineering schools at the undergraduate level seem to be minor, and those that exist are apparently being solved without serious adverse effects on the students. The areas of conflict seem more important at the graduate level, and it behooves each university to identify these areas and take positive steps to overcome the conflict. Several suggestions were made in this chapter as to how to reach a basis of agreement.

It is recommended that the industrial engineering departments evaluate their curricula in light of the educational objectives of the American Society for Engineering Education and the Engineers' Council for Professional Development. The curricula should have as a first objective the training of competent engineers. Whatever time is available after that should be devoted to a balanced program of humanities and professional specialization. Flexibility should be provided to allow each student to plan his program to meet his personal objectives within the over-all objectives of the school. The industrial engineering curricula should concentrate on the quantitative aspects of business management where the engineering method is most applicable. The subjective and descriptive areas should be deemphasized, but the inclusion of great quantities of statistics and mathematics for the sake of these subjects should be avoided. Under no circumstances should the curriculum ignore, overlook, or deemphasize the industrial engineer's concern about the *man* in the system, because this is the principal factor that differentiates industrial engineering from all the other branches.

Industrial engineering should not attempt to provide teaching resources for all the areas of interest within its own department. The hazard is that the student will be exposed to extremely important subject matter being taught by nonexperts in those fields and consequently will receive a distorted picture of the principles involved in the subject matter. This comment applies particularly to such areas as marketing, personnel management, industrial psychology, sociology, sales management, and many others. This is not to say that all industrial engineering faculty members are incompetent in these areas but that only *thoroughly* competent teachers should be used in *each area*. The business administration and social science schools' courses should be used as much as possible for the engineering students' training in these traditional courses. Business and social science schools should recognize that different educational objectives motivate engineers and nonengineers to study these subjects and should plan their courses to accommodate the special needs of both groups.

The graduate programs in industrial engineering should provide truly graduate-level training. Many persons have questioned the graduate programs now in existence on the basis that they are merely additional courses of the same level of accomplishment as the undergraduate courses. The graduate programs should emphasize the quantitative aspects of all courses and should require a high level of competence in statistical methods, experimentation, and research. Originality and creativity should be primary objectives. In those universities in which there are graduate programs in both industrial engineering and business administration there should be a clear-cut division of areas of specialization and a clearly defined set of objectives for each school.

CHAPTER 20

COMPANY MANAGEMENT

DEVELOPMENT PROGRAMS

Donald S. Bridgman

One of the most important business phenomena of the years since World War II has been the increased attention devoted to development of a highly competent and forward-looking management team. Today a great majority of the country's large industrial organizations are carrying on formal programs with this objective. Programs such as these either increase the competence and breadth of all managers at specific organization levels in their present positions, prepare selected individuals of high potential for advancement, or cover particular topics of value to individuals or groups through increased knowledge or skill in a special field. Among the many unsettled questions in this area are those relating to the proper emphasis on individual methods of development as compared with training courses for groups, the appropriate roles of university as compared with internal-company courses, the development of suitable methods for appraising the contribution of such programs to improved management, and the influence these evolving programs should have on the content and methods of undergraduate and graduate curricula in business administration.

From a company's point of view, its management development program includes every activity designed to increase the effectiveness of its management forces in their present assignments and to ensure an adequate supply of qualified management personnel in the future. Since this volume deals primarily with courses of instruction in collegiate schools of business and other institutions offering business courses of college grade, this chapter will emphasize specific courses provided by companies themselves for such purposes. It will attempt, however, to place these courses in the perspective of such other activities for management development

536

as determination of requirements, recruiting and identification of persons with management potential, and individual development on the job through supervisory coaching and in university or other external courses. As indicated by the chapter's title, it will not cover training in such functions as accounting or sales, although such training contributes to individual development and, in some instances, may be designed in part to improve the management of the function.

While practice differs between industries and individual companies, it is now usual to regard as members of the management team all employees in supervisory positions at any level and in staff positions normally involving contacts outside the individual's own work group. In describing their management development programs, few companies would exclude foreman training, or even presupervisory training, where much of the content involves principles of supervision and human relations applicable at any management level. This broad definition of management will be used in this chapter and such programs, as well as those for executive levels, will be described. Adoption of such a definition does not disregard the fact that in industries where foremen's unions are recognized, foremen are not considered part of management, that many companies draw somewhat of a line within the management team between the foreman and higher levels, and that some consider only a few executives as truly management.

In securing material for this chapter, the author has been given access to publications and nonconfidential files of the American Management Association and the National Industrial Conference Board dealing with this topic. He has been privileged also to review records of interviews with executives of eighty-seven companies (and supplementary material) assembled by representatives of the Ford Foundation's current study of business education. These reports cover the companies' management development plans as well as other pertinent topics. In addition, he has obtained material directly from a number of companies and has interviewed representatives of a few others with programs of special interest for this discussion. Statements concerning companies named in the text have been reviewed by them, but undoubtedly changes have occurred in company programs since early 1959, when this material was reviewed. Grateful acknowledgment is given for the wholehearted cooperation received from all these organizations.

GROWTH AND PRESENT EXTENT OF PLANS

Management development programs, including the higher as well as the lower echelons of supervision, have had almost all their growth since the end of World War II. Although often not recognized, a real foundation had been laid for them over the previous quarter century through the growth and extension in scope of foreman training programs. While such training was confined to production departments and originally dealt mainly with the specifics of the foreman's day-to-day work, it came to include more and more material concerning the roles of interest and attitudes in the effective handling of men, broad principles of organizing work, and company policies, now primary elements in management training. The point of view gained by foremen through such training inevitably had its impact on their relations with their own supervisors and was one of the factors in breaking down the time-honored assumption that natural ability and ambition would provide competence needed by the higher supervisory levels and even more clearly by executives, currently and in the future.

Many other influences have brought about recognition of the necessity for direct attention to management development and the resulting rapid growth of active programs in the past ten years. During the war the value of formal training was demonstrated not only by the military services themselves but through activities stimulated by the War Production Board leading to the Engineering Science Management War Training, Training Within Industry, and other programs. Almost immediately after the war's close, business became aware of the serious gap which had developed in its flow of management material due to restricted opportunities for experience during the Depression and to limited new employment during that period and the war itself. Problems of management-employee relations became more critical with the growth of unionization and the danger of its extension to lower supervisory and professional levels, with governmental regulations affecting these relations, and with the changed attitudes of individual workers who had a better education and a broader outlook than formerly.

A more dynamic influence soon became apparent in the explosive growth of the country's population, national product, and technological knowledge. With this came a great increase in the scope and complexity of management problems, requiring particularly the ability to adjust quickly to the effects of technological change and to prepare for future change. Companies no longer could rely on established products and markets, and their ability to meet competition came to depend very largely on the caliber and flexibility of their management. One of the decisive elements in this whole pattern has been the recognition by many companies of their responsibility for the maintenance of a free society, for providing stable employment and opportunities for growth in their employees, and for playing a constructive role in the communities where they operate.

Finally, business has been able to draw upon an increasing body of organized knowledge concerning the science and art of management for use in its development programs. Contributions to this resource have come from collegiate schools of business, other branches of higher education, business consulting firms, management associations, and business organizations themselves. Wide acceptance was accorded the view stated by the General Electric Company that ". . . managing is a distinct and professional type of work which can be taught and can be learned."

As the result of these and many other factors, the growth in management development programs in recent years undoubtedly has been great, though measurement of this rate of growth or of the present scope of the programs would require a more precise definition of the field and more extensive surveys than have been made.

In 1935, some 3 per cent of about 2,500 companies and, in 1946, some 5 per cent of about 3,500 companies stated in response to general surveys of personnel practices conducted by the National Industrial Conference Board that they had "executive training programs." [1] In 1952 some 30 per cent of about 2,000 companies and two years later 54 per cent of some 500 companies reported "management development programs" (a broader designation than that of the N.I.C.B. surveys) in their answers to specific surveys of this field carried on by the American Management Association.[2] These respondents, however, included only 25 to 30 per cent of the companies addressed, a high proportion of them being AMA members. The first of the two mail surveys and a series of interviews supplementing it indicated a distinctly higher proportion of plans in the larger companies than in the smaller ones. In 1958, in a survey by H. F. Clark and H. S. Sloan that covered all types of large-company educational programs, 77 per cent of about 350 large companies stated that they were carrying on management development activities.[3]

Although other sources describe programs of individual companies, or particular features of them, apparently only the Ford Foundation study provides somewhat detailed up-to-date information concerning those of a number of companies in different businesses in the several areas of the country and, despite the high proportion of large firms, of varying size. That study includes forty industrial companies (manufacturing, construction, public utilities, and railroads) with 10,000 or more employees, twenty industrials with fewer than 10,000, twenty-one nonindustrials

[1] Stephen Habbe, *Company Programs of Executive Development*, National Industrial Conference Board, Studies in Personnel Policy 107, New York, 1950, p. 4.

[2] J. M. Trickett, *A Survey of Management Development*, sec. 2, American Management Association, New York, 1954. J. C. Sinnigen, *Current Practice in Management Development*, American Management Association, New York, 1954.

[3] H. F. Clark and H. S. Sloan, *Classrooms in Factories*, Institute of Research, Fairleigh Dickinson University, Rutherford, N.J., 1957, pp. 14–15.

(banks, insurance, distributing companies) among the largest in their fields, and six smaller nonindustrials. On the basis of purely subjective judgment by the author, the management development programs of these organizations may be classified as comprehensive, partial, distinctly limited, or negligible. Programs classified as comprehensive would be those including positive activities in cultivating sources of management material, in developing the individual on the job and through supervision, and internal management training courses above, as well as at, the foreman level, or the use of outside executive training courses for that purpose. Such a classification for the sixty-one companies, consisting of the industrials with over 10,000 employees and leading nonindustrials, would show, except for one company with a negligible program, about one-third of the group in each of the comprehensive, partial, and limited categories. Of the twenty-six smaller industrials and nonindustrials, one-half had negligible programs and about one-sixth each had comprehensive, partial, and limited ones. Relatively little significant difference was found between the larger industrial and nonindustrial companies; while the most highly developed programs seemed to be in the industrial companies, more of them also had very limited ones. There were necessarily only a few companies from each type of business, but among those covered, the textile companies and railroads had the most limited activities.

Undoubtedly a major factor in the need for a formal program is the size and complexity of the organization. Although up-to-date figures are not available, there appear to be only about 300 companies in the country with 10,000 or more employees. These companies have about 20 per cent of the nation's nonagricultural employees. Of all such employees, moreover, more than half are found in organizations with less than 500 employees.[4]

It is clear from this discussion that there are available only general indications of the actual extent of company management development activities. Although a review of the studies made over the past dozen years confirms the impression of substantially increased activity in the field, the limited rate of return to the AMA questionnaire for example, and the preponderance of member companies in that return, suggests that, four or five years ago at least, only a small proportion, even of the companies large enough to justify them, had formal programs. Today, it can be assumed that a majority of the leading organizations in their fields are giving major attention to this matter, but the programs of many are quite limited in scope. Although a number of relatively small companies have well-organized programs, most such organizations are likely to rely on day-to-day contacts with the boss and between associates and on

---

[4] *Survey of Current Business*, May, 1954, p. 18.

conferences dealing with the operations of the business for their indirect effects on management development. Given the right management climate, such methods may be the best ones for many organizations of moderate size. While, moreover, the word "program" has been used in designating these activities to indicate that those actually in existence usually are on an organized basis, even those companies with the most comprehensive plans regard them as experimental and, in some instances, prefer to call them only an approach to the problem. One large company has given up completely a formal course in management practices provided for several years and is now placing more emphasis on plans for individual development on the job and through supervision.

None of this discussion implies that top executives and boards of directors of progressive companies consider provision for high-caliber present and future management as anything but a serious challenge to American business. It merely recognizes that great gaps exist in this activity and that as yet there are no established patterns through which to achieve the results desired.

BASIC ELEMENTS IN MANAGEMENT DEVELOPMENT PROGRAMS

In spite of the great differences in the scope of these plans, there is general agreement that any effective program in this field must be based on a favorable management climate resulting from confidence in company objectives, belief in its integrity, and acceptance of high standards of performance. Factors in such a climate often mentioned as directly related to the management development program include its strong endorsement by top management, acceptance of responsibility by supervisors for their own development and that of their subordinates, widespread delegation of authority and willingness to live with its occasional costs, free two-way communications, and insight into the stimulating or inhibiting effects of interpersonal relations.

Elements usually regarded by company executives and other authorities as essential structural parts of a comprehensive management development program would include:

1. Organization planning
2. Sources and selection of management material
3. Appraisals
4. Management inventories
5. Development through both individual programs and training courses

The degree of emphasis placed on each of these steps and the extent to which the program is formally organized naturally vary greatly between companies. Some of the differences in approach will be touched upon in the following discussion.

In addition to its importance for the effective functioning of the business, organization planning provides the basis for determining the numbers and types of future management personnel needed. From the long-range point of view, this includes consideration of the probable growth of the business, changes in its characteristics likely to be reflected in management requirements, and the replacement rate of management personnel due to retirement, death, and other causes. On a more immediate basis, it involves periodic consideration and possible revision of the existing organization structure in the light of changing conditions. Some companies utilize detailed position descriptions and manpower specifications in this process, but evidence from a number of companies suggests that such procedures are found in only a minority of even the larger organizations.

In order to ensure that they have in their organizations an adequate supply of individuals with the intellectual and personal characteristics for development into management, companies are turning increasingly to the employment of recent college graduates, as is evident by the high level of recruiting at the colleges and the sharp competition for the abler men. Among the larger companies covered by the Ford Foundation study, about three-fourths were actively engaged in college recruiting, although this was true of only one-fourth of the smaller organizations. Of those seeking new graduates, the majority put emphasis on capacity for continued growth rather than on competence in an immediate job, but, in a number of cases, the high proportion of engineering and science graduates among those employed raises a question concerning the extent to which this purpose affected their employment program.

Among these companies, it is the general opinion that promotion of noncollege workers from the ranks in the future will provide few members of management beyond the foreman or comparable lower levels. Even at the foreman level a few of the industrial companies expect an increasing proportion of college graduates because of the technical character of their operations. A few others are making special efforts to identify employees with supervisory potential through appraisals of their working forces and testing programs which help to reveal those of high capacity. In general, however, the points of view expressed raise a serious question concerning the loss of potential talent and the blocking of opportunity for able persons without college degrees. Undoubtedly the scope of the problem has decreased in recent years with the higher proportion of able young persons completing college, and it is likely to decrease further. The question, however, involves many persons still young who began their careers before the recent rise in the graduation rate, and even today a large proportion of those with ability do not complete college.

Although few companies, especially smaller firms, rely wholly on promotion from within for management appointments, companies with organized development programs tend to follow this practice. The selection of individuals for promotion within management, therefore, is very largely from those originally employed as recent college graduates or promoted from the ranks. Examination of company practices on this point brings out clearly that executive judgment concerning the candidate's demonstrated ability in his work and his relations with associates and subordinates is by far the dominant factor in the final choice for a particular position. Only a few companies believe that experience and research have established as yet any particular pattern of abilities and personal traits for the successful executive, as men with various combinations of qualities appear to possess the essential ability to secure effective results through the work of other people. Even where formal position descriptions exist, except for positions of a technical or professional character, much adaptability to specific requirements in a position is expected from men with records of accomplishment. Development of such flexibility frequently has been the purpose of varied early assignments. Personnel records providing personal and work histories help to ensure that all appropriate qualified candidates are considered, and appraisal results and management inventories where available are useful aids to proper judgment. A substantial number of companies are convinced that psychological test scores, and in some cases clinical interview results by a psychologist, are of major importance in establishing an individual's executive potential. The National Industrial Conference Board's 1956 report *Selecting Company Executives* states that sixty-two company presidents reported that test scores were considered in 13 per cent of about 200 recent high-level appointments in their companies.[5] This report also describes extensive research projects now under way in this field.

Although appraisals of the performance and abilities of employees at all levels must be a part of the regular operations of the business, review of the limited evidence concerning the extent of formal periodic appraisals of management personnel indicates that their extent may be rather smaller than the emphasis placed on them in management literature would suggest. Such appraisals generally are considered to have two parts, the appraisal itself and its review by the superior with the subordinate. The first of these, in addition to providing information for the second, serves as a systematic basis for salary increases and promotions,

[5] Stephen Habbe, *Selecting Company Executives,* National Industrial Conference Board, Studies in Personnel Policy 161, New York, 1957.

transfers, or terminations. The second consists of a scheduled discussion with the individual of his performance, his strong and weak points, "how he stands" with his boss, and what plans should be made to overcome weaknesses, improve his work, and increase his opportunities in the future.

With regard to the appraisal process itself, there is a long history of experiment and difficulty in arriving at valid judgments. Today in many companies, forms listing personal characteristics for rating by numerical or graphic methods are being replaced by requests for statements concerning the individual's strong and weak points, specific incidents in which they were displayed, and performance on major elements of his particular job. In some companies, appraisals are based on discussions between individual supervisors and a personnel staff man or on group discussions of several coordinate supervisors who have some contact with the individuals to be appraised, frequently with a staff man present to stimulate emphasis on actual behavior and maintain balance within the group.

Recognition of the second major element in the total appraisal process as now generally conceived, the planned appraisal review with the subordinate, is a much more recent development and considerably less general than appraisals themselves. Many of the efforts to improve such reviews have grown out of the conviction that for the development of the individual, this step is an important one and that sound personnel policy should include advising the individual as to "how he stands" with his boss so that he himself may overcome his weaknesses. Both the need for and limitations in such plans are shown by results of surveys reported in the section "On the Job Coaching" in the AMA's volume *Developing Executive Skills*.[6] The surveys indicated that in companies with formal plans of this kind, 85 per cent of the respondents felt they understood what was required in their positions and about 60 per cent believed they had a good idea of their bosses' opinion of them and had received suggestions for improvement. In companies with only informal methods, the corresponding figures were about 60 and 30 per cent. Even in companies with formal plans, a considerable fraction of the respondents stated they had never had such an interview.

As the need for a high degree of skill in conducting such interviews has become better recognized, companies have developed materials and training programs for their managers which make clear the primary purpose of the review and stress the importance of planning, an appropriate atmosphere, emphasis on job performance rather than on personal characteristics, and listening rather than talking in order to stimulate the

[6] Myles L. Mace and Walter R. Mahler, "On the Job Coaching," in *Developing Executive Skills*, American Management Association, New York, 1958.

subordinate to reach his own conclusions and set his own goals. Some of these programs include case studies, practice reviews, and role playing.

In his article "An Uneasy Look at Performance Appraisals," Douglas McGregor ascribes the line manager's reluctance to carry through this process not only to dislike of having to criticize a subordinate and to recognition of his lack of skill in this role but to a deep, if unrecognized, conviction that the conventional approach which begins with the superior's judgment comes "dangerously close to a violation of the personality." [7] He proposes, referring to other writers on the subject and particularly to Peter Drucker's concept of management by objective, that the subordinate establish short-term goals for himself in his job, assess his own strength and weaknesses, and make specific plans to reach his goals prior to the interview with his superior. Agreement on such a program is then reached jointly by superior and subordinate, and accomplishment in carrying it out is reviewed after, for example, a six-month interval. McGregor cites two large companies which have undertaken work in this direction, and descriptions of somewhat similar approaches in other companies have appeared more recently. It is clear that such a plan would be time-consuming and expensive, but action by a number of companies indicates their faith in the worth-while results to be secured.

Individual appraisals provide the primary basis for management inventories, usually after review by higher management in connection with other data, such as experience and age and, in a few companies, psychological test results. The more formal type of such an inventory might provide for each unit of the organization and the key positions covered in it, lists of the present incumbents, and one or two designated replacements, showing their names, ages, company service, evaluations of performance in their present positions, and their potential ability. Another type of inventory provides a central file of management personnel whose appraisals and background indicate demonstrated potential for promotion to one or more levels. The first type of inventory provides a highly specific picture of the present and short-range future status of each unit's management structure; the second identifies, often early in their careers, men of special promise for development through experience or training and provides a pool from which openings may be filled without undue dependence on the unit in which they occur or on hasty selections.

Of the elements in a comprehensive management development program already discussed, organization planning, recruiting and selection of management material, appraisals of the competence and potential for promotion of management personnel—as distinguished from appraisal

---

[7] Douglas McGregor, "An Uneasy Look at Performance Appraisals," *Harvard Business Review*, vol. 35, no. 2, January-February, 1957, pp. 89–94.

reviews with individuals—and management inventories may be called "company-centered." They are essential for the building of a sound management team, and through their contribution to the company's success and the setting up of an effective framework in which the individual manager can function, they play a major part in his development. The most carefully designed framework, however, will have little value unless the individual is given the opportunity and stimulation to rely on his own abilities and devote them to the good of the company. The key element in the program then becomes development of the individual member of management and other employees with management potential. Obviously, as already stated, this may be accomplished by plans for individuals and by those for groups, primarily management training courses, participation in which becomes in turn a part of the individual's plan.

Even those companies, moreover, which have devoted the greatest effort to establishing management training courses agree that the development of individuals, primarily on the job, is by far the more important of these two channels. This stems from the conviction that all true development is self-development and that learning from experience is the most valuable. Such a concept leads directly to placing the heaviest emphasis on the day-to-day job and the decisive influence of the individual's supervisor upon him. In one company, the validity of such emphasis was indicated by a survey of several hundred managers, 90 per cent of whom said their greatest development occurred when working for a particular man. The efforts of many companies, therefore, have been directed toward heightening the effectiveness of the supervisor's part in this relationship through written materials, conferences, and training courses. Their content includes pertinent behavior principles, the different approaches to each individual person to build attitudes of mutual confidence, the great importance of genuine delegation of authority, techniques of observation, diagnosis, creating motivation, action and follow-up, and similar material. They point out the importance of clear understanding of job responsibilities, the need for high standards of performance, and a review of particular assignments under way and just completed. Although skillful conduct of the appraisal review is a key element in the desired goal, what is sought is a continual relationship of mutual planning and follow-up. Such a review generally provides the proper timing for the discussions of a program of self-development, often for the year ahead, which may include special job assignments, training courses (including out-of-hours study), planned reading, participation in professional, social, or community activities, and medical, psychological, or psychiatric counseling.

In addition to emphasizing the individual's development through his current job, companies are using a variety of other ways to broaden his background and better equip him for promotion. Among these are:

1. Job rotation, sometimes to an entirely different general function of the business. This might be as a training assignment, or as an understudy to an executive, but more generally through regular placement in a new position where he will remain long enough to demonstrate his capacity in the new field.

2. Assignment to a committee, with several departments represented in its membership, working on solutions to one or more special problems for recommendation to top management.

3. Election to a junior board of directors, in companies which have them, providing opportunity to participate in the consideration of a series of such problems.

4. Assignment to a management training course, either within the company or conducted by a university or other outside organization.

5. Assignment as a leader in a company training course or conference.

6. Assignment as the company's representative or speaker at a conference of a professional society or business association.

Company-conducted Management Training Courses

Although this discussion, in its attempt to place management training courses in the framework of the entire management development program, may appear up to this point to minimize their importance, the necessity for training in the supervisory skills required to stimulate and assist in the self-development of subordinates illustrates the integral place such courses have in a complete program. They include, of course, both those conducted by the companies themselves and those given by universities, colleges, and other agencies. This section will outline the general pattern of such company-conducted courses and give examples of their major types. Courses given by colleges and universities, either as extension courses which employees undertake on their own initiative and time or as special management courses for those selected by the companies and sent on company assignment, are described in other chapters of this volume. The following section, however, will touch on the place of such courses in the over-all company management development programs and describe briefly a few outstanding courses with similar or related objectives given by other agencies.

It is very difficult to classify the company-conducted courses in a way which takes into account their wide variety in purpose, content, and length. Their complete range includes both a thirteen-week full-time residential course on a number of topics considered of major importance for all top-level managers in one company and a free elective course of three sessions of 1½ hours each on personal efficiency. Some companies would include also regularly scheduled meetings which seek primarily solutions to current business problems or provide talks, mainly of an informative nature, by executives or outside speakers, but these are not included in this discussion. As already stated, courses dealing principally with a particular function, e.g., sales, are also excluded, as well as initial training courses for college graduates which are primarily for company orientation rather than for management development.

The principal evidence available concerning the extent of such courses of different general types seems to be contained in the material collected from the limited number of companies covered by the Ford Foundation study of business education.

With full recognition of its limitations, the following presentation classified these courses in accordance with their general objectives:

A. Courses for the primary purpose of increasing competence in the present job or level. They are generally regarded as essential for all management personnel at a particular level or at closely grouped levels. Their content in most cases has been selected to meet the special requirements of such a level and covers the various areas appropriate for that purpose.

B. Courses to assist in providing highly qualified management personnel for the future. These are primarily for selected personnel of high potential, designed to broaden their knowledge and perspective for expected promotion. As in Type A courses, their content covers a number of areas.

C. Unit courses covering specific topics provided for groups or individuals on either a company recommended or elective basis. Some such courses are designed for particular organizational levels; others are open to any member of management. Some may be primarily useful for the current job; more are mainly for the individual's development.

Courses designated as Type A or Type B are usually given on company time. Frequently they are full-time assignments for a week or several weeks away from the usual work location. Type C courses may be given on either company or the employee's time.

These objectives, of course, are closely related in that better performance today is of great importance for promotion tomorrow, and the breadth of understanding needed for a future higher position will make for greater competence in the present lower one. At present, there seems to be increasing emphasis on the first objective due to fuller recognition of the demands in all management positions today, of the constant changes in each job, and of the fact that, except in rapidly growing companies, less than half of those at one level today will move on to a higher one.

Of the larger companies covered by the Ford Foundation study, about three-quarters provided courses of one or more of these types. One-half their total number (or two-thirds of those with courses) carry on Type A courses for the first supervisory level, and about one-third apparently offer those of Type C. Only about one-eighth offer Type A courses for higher levels or courses of Type B. Of the smaller companies in that study, about one-quarter provide some management training course, including three or four with Type A courses for their first supervisory level. Among these companies, only single examples were found of a Type A course for a higher level or of the other types of courses.

Among the following examples of courses of these several types are some conducted by companies which were not included in the Ford study but which have outstanding courses of the type presented. The courses listed are, naturally, only one part of each company's total program in this field.

A1. General Programs for First-level Supervisors. Many courses for potential or new supervisors are given through weekly sessions varying in length and number up to a total of about 100 hours of presentation and discussion, with emphasis on company policy and organization, principles of supervision, and labor and human relations. A few courses given on a full-time basis are described below.

The Armstrong Cork Company's program for the training of new foremen is largely conducted on an individual basis and, except for the final group phase in some cases, is completed before actual appointment. Candidates are either nominated by plant management or apply for consideration and are selected by a comprehensive process which includes personal data, foreman's evaluation, testing, and interviewing.

The first phase of the training is designated as on-the-job and requires about three weeks, two of them with an experienced foreman, observing the entire range of his functions; the remaining time is devoted to discussion with appropriate plant officials of the foreman's responsibilities as related to plant objectives and product specifications and processes. The second phase, up to sixteen weeks in length, includes several days each with the plant industrial engineer, comptroller, production planning manager, inspection manager, and personnel manager on such matters as job evaluation and incentive rates, payroll and material reports, scheduling and inspection, and employment, inductions, and safety practices. It also includes several weeks on a staff assignment selected on the basis of individual needs. The final phase involves 94 hours of group instruction at company headquarters on such matters as company policies, history and financial reports, human relations and union relations, training methods, ways of tackling problems and improving methods, and basic economics.

Newly appointed first-level supervisors of salaried personnel—sales, accounting, engineering, etc.—in the *Westinghouse Electric Corporation* receive a one-week course in management techniques at company headquarters. This covers management functions and responsibilities broadly, presented through illustrations from Westinghouse by managers of headquarters staff departments. The opening sessions relate those functions to the supervisor's responsibilities for quality, quantity, cost, and employee relations and to the tools and philosophy of management. Later sessions deal with the principles of organization; planning; communicating; personnel selection; supervising, including understanding people, development of personnel, union contract administration, and human relations problems; controlling, including expense control, salary administration, and methods improvement. The topic of the final session is industrial leadership. Courses for first-level production supervisors are conducted at the company's individual plants.

In the financial and distributing organizations with a relatively high proportion of college graduates among first-level supervisors, training for this level is frequently part of an initial program, primarily for such graduates, in which some nongraduates from rank-and-file positions also may have been enrolled. In the *Mutual Life Insurance Company of New York*, experienced noncollege men are selected for one section of an extended program for college graduate home office management trainees. Topics covered in the four and a half months devoted to this section include reading improvement, effective speaking and writing, personnel and other administrative practices, conference leadership, and methods of instructing new employees. Principles found in standard management textbooks are emphasized with some use of the case method. There are, however, group projects for research and reports and an individual thesis usually on a company problem. Company officers present lectures on company objectives, management problems, and their own departmental operations, with emphasis on the methods used to reach over-all objectives. Such officers also hold discussions with each student.

A2. General Courses for Middle Management. Courses of this type, primarily for middle management, have been found in relatively few companies. Other large companies undoubtedly are providing training for their middle management with locally developed programs at their major locations.

One such course for all management levels is that of the *General Electric Company* entitled Professional Business Management I, given by its various components and requiring twenty 3-hour sessions. Several sessions each are devoted to General Electric's growth and future prospects, its philosophy of organization and management, the work of a professional manager, and planning for action. The theme of the course is "Managing My Job Professionally," and its stated objectives are to instill an understanding of the principles of management, to demonstrate how they can be applied in the work of particular groups and individuals, and to make clear company objectives and internal relations and the effect of business decisions and actions on the economic and social system. Although a common study guide is provided and the three-volume *Professional Management in General Electric* is used for basic information, it is expected that there will be substantial variation in the content for each group, with examples drawn from its own problems and experience to illustrate the principles presented. The method of training used is one of learning through discussion led by a specially selected trained manager, with participants providing the leader with "feed-back" comments concerning each session.

In the *Bell Telephone Companies,* third- and fourth-level managers participate in programs built around three- to five-day training units dealing with such various aspects of their jobs as: Handling Changes, Planning-Organizing-Controlling, Handling Barriers to Communication, and Line-and-Staff Relationships and Evaluating and Developing People. Where appropriate, these managers may take such a three-day unit as Talking with People, originally developed for the first level, which is primarily skill training in interviewing by the understanding-listening method. Material prepared by the American Telephone and Telegraph Company is arranged for the use of each company by its own personnel staff. There is much use of the case discussion method.

The Western Electric Company conducts two conference programs for middle-management levels at a rural location, one over a three-week period for superintendents, the other over a two-week period for assistant superintendents. Participants in the first of these consider the economic, political, and social environment in which the business operates; broad business policy and administrative problems; communications skills and the functions of planning, organizing, and controlling. The method used is primarily that of free discussion, sometimes with business cases as the basis. In addition to a number of university professors, outside speakers from government, the press, and other businesses discuss such topics as International Relations, Problems of Minority Groups in an Industrial Society, Major Forces in Our National Economy, and Ethical and Moral Responsibilities of Business Leadership. The other conference uses similar methods, but its orientation is largely toward personal development and the development of subordinates; the management skills of planning, organizing, and controlling; and the needs, objectives, and policies of the company as a business enterprise and corporate citizen. Most of the leadership is from universities.

A3. General Courses for Higher Management. It is probable that two of the courses at these levels have been the most widely discussed in the management development field, those of General Electric and the Bell System. These courses and similar ones more recently initiated by the Shell Oil Company and International Business Machines Corporation will be discussed later in this section.

Somewhat less comprehensive courses are found mainly in other industrial companies. Among these is the two-week course at company headquarters conducted by the *Aluminum Company of America* for its plant managers, their immediate staffs, and comparable men from sales and headquarters staff departments. It deals largely with company policies and functions, discussed by top executives of the company, but includes a few other topics with outside speakers. The *Johns Manville Corporation* gives a one-week course in administrative leadership for its key management men. Basic subject matter is presented by a staff specialist, and each group consists of only ten men, each from a different division or department in order to provide widely varied points of view in the discussions. In addition to certain management functions, content includes consideration of the bearing of outside forces on management decisions and the bringing of unity out of diversity through collaboration. For its top management, *Armour and Company* has conducted a series of conferences with nine weekly 4-hour sessions under the leadership of a business school dean; the emphasis is on human relations problems.

The only example found in a financial or distribution organization of a program at all comparable to these is the series of one-week conferences held by the *Wachovia Bank and Trust Company* in North Carolina for all its officers and their immediate staffs. Eight to ten men attend each conference, which is led by a staff specialist. There are no fixed agenda, but management practices and existing conditions are reviewed and ways to effect improvements are discussed. Careful reports of each conference are prepared and circulated to the participants of all of them. Other companies in these fields apparently feel that conferences dealing with the policies and specific problems of the business and day-to-day contacts with one another, added to long experience, provide the knowledge and skill needed by their higher executives.

Of the more comprehensive courses for higher management, the first was the *Bell System's* Executive Conference Program begun in November, 1953, and planned to cover all those executives of the Bell Telephone Companies who were at the level of functional department heads in those companies reporting directly to general managers, together with men at a comparable level in the other units of the System, the Western

Electric Company and Bell Telephone Laboratories. Men from this and other levels in these companies had been attending university management courses for some time, but those courses could accommodate only a fraction of the large number for whom a broader outlook seemed essential if they were to meet the problems raised by the expanding demand for telephone service and by a rapidly changing world. Originally planned by a committee of Bell Telephone Company vice-presidents and a staff from the American Telephone and Telegraph Company and other System companies with the assistance of outside consultants, the program has evolved through several stages as experience with it has accumulated. This has led to participation by the original registrants in a follow-up program, inclusion of general managers and vice-presidents, and increased application of the content and perspective provided by the original course to current and future general management problems of the business.

The program now includes a basic course three weeks in length for newly appointed department heads and also senior courses two weeks long for experienced department heads and one week long for general managers and vice-presidents, the great majority of whom had previously taken the original course. About forty participants make up the group attending each course. The purposes of the basic course are to increase the present effectiveness of the participants and to stimulate their interest in further self-development by broadening their outlook and helping them to evaluate social and economic trends and to consider their effects on the telephone business. Areas covered include economics, marketing and selling, finance, labor relations, earnings, administrative policy, foreign affairs, and political and social trends.

The emphasis in the senior courses is on the future of the business. Participants are requested to review in advance changes inside and outside the business during their own careers and to formulate their views about forthcoming changes. The course then aims to help them think more clearly about the future, anticipate changes in the economic and social environment and their effect on internal operations, recognize adaptation to change as management's greatest challenge and opportunity, and encourage establishment of realistic goals and specific plans to achieve them. The areas covered include most of those listed for the basic course, but the orientation is toward the future. A close look is taken at the years up to 1965 with a more general view taken beyond that in terms of specific management problems of another fictitious telephone company and projections of its operations.

This program has been conducted from the beginning at Asbury Park, New Jersey, away from company offices and a large city environment. The methods used include both lectures followed by discussion and case discussions in small groups. Speakers and moderators include business-men not associated with the Bell System, university professors, and the System's top executives. The director is an executive of extensive experience in several System companies. Other members of the small staff are loaned from line-and-staff telephone positions for a few months. There is a large amount of outside reading, and case material bearing on major company problems is sent out in advance.

The Advanced Management Course of the *General Electric Company* began its sessions in the fall of 1955 after about four years of research and planning concerned with the over-all problem of high-caliber management in a large and diversified company which had put into effect the basic policy of decentralized operation in 1951. In that year a research group was appointed, consisting of experienced General Electric men, consulting psychologists, business school professors, and management consultants, and was charged with study of the basic factors in the development of people. One of the major recommendations of its 1953 report was the establishment of the Advanced Management Course. Those eligible for and expected to participate in this course, now conducted at the company's Management Development and Research Institute in Crotonville, New York, include major executives, division managers, department managers of the operating components and their chief functional subordinates for manufacturing, sales, etc., and men of comparable levels in the service components, such as engineering or personnel and public relations. By the end of 1958, about half of these men had taken the course which is given over a period of thirteen weeks to groups of forty-eight "students."

The objectives of the course are to provide opportunity for participants to see the company as a whole in the total outside environment, to visualize future accelerating changes in that environment, and to explore improvements in managerial performance which will anticipate and help to shape the future. It aims also to increase participants' understanding of the managerial objectives and philosophy of the company and of the work of managing as a distinct kind of professional activity, to provide principles useful for better management performance, and to prepare the participants to be effective multipliers of their new knowledge.

About one-half of the course content covers the major elements of the planning, organizing, integrating, and measuring functions of professional managing work. The integrating function particularly is concerned with the application of human behavior principles to managerial climate, teamwork, communications, and the manager's role in self-development. Under the measurement function, there is discussion of the key result areas used in judging the performance of a company component which include personnel attitudes and development, discharge of public responsibility, and technical leadership as well as profitability and market position. Other subjects covered include the learning process, the national and international environment, the use in business management of data processing and operations research and synthesis, and the functions of the company's staff services as valuable resources to assist operating managers.

The permanent faculty responsible for the course includes men of long experience with General Electric, those with major experience in other companies, and former university faculty members. Outside speakers include executives of other companies, management consultants, and university professors. The work of each of the service components is presented by the major executive responsible for it. Resources of the management research group of social scientists, carrying on long-range research into future problems of business management and policy, are used constantly. The teaching methods emphasize principles rather than cases, with a major portion of the time devoted to discussion in both the entire group and smaller sections. There is a large amount of outside reading and assignment of individual and group projects for study and report.

As one of its activities to help managers accelerate self-development, the *Shell Oil Company* and its subsidiary companies established the Shell Management Course in 1956 and have conducted it twice each year using Columbia University's Arden House as its residential facility. Each group for the four-week program includes thirty key management members, such as plant superintendents, sales managers, research directors, pipe-line superintendents, and production managers.

Because of the varied activities of the Shell companies, about half the course is designed to increase the participant's knowledge of Shell as an integrated enterprise, its divisions, and their relationships to each other and to outside groups. About a quarter of the course is devoted to understanding the management function, with emphasis on the managing process, business organization, executive communication, and coaching and development of subordinate managers. Another quarter is concerned with economic, social, and political forces affecting American industry.

During each course the president and each vice-president of Shell Oil Company and its subsidiaries serve as instructors, discussing their respective organizations, objectives, policies, problems, and the application of management principles to them. Other instructors are professors, consultants, and leaders of other companies.

The basic instruction methods are study assignments and group sessions emphasizing informal presentations and free discussion with some cases. In addition, participants are given one group and one individual assignment. Individuals, small groups, and finally representatives of the groups draft a statement of their concept of Shell's objectives as a business enterprise, its corporate character, philosophy, and policies and give their suggestions for improvement. This statement is given to the president and serves as a basis for his discussion at the closing session.

Since the ultimate objective of the course is to help each participant develop himself, he is given a "Check List of the Managing Process" against which to review his managing ability in terms of what he would like to improve. After recording ideas he acquires in the course which are especially applicable to his needs, he prepares a summary plan for his use in his further self-development as a manager.

The Executive Development Program of the *International Business Machines Corporation* began operation in 1957 in realization of the company's management needs as a result of its extremely rapid growth in recent years and its anticipated future growth. It is designed for the functional executives reporting to its plant managers, sales managers responsible for large areas of the country, and others at a comparable level just below the company's senior executives. The program lasts four weeks, and only twelve men are enrolled in each session. Eight sessions are held during the year. Previously conducted at a country club in Westchester County, New York, it moved to permanent company-owned quarters on Long Island in 1959.

The major portion of the course period is spent in consideration of management problems with emphasis on finance, planning, organization, policy formulation, controls, and decision making. The remainder of the time is devoted about equally to economic, political, and social elements in the environment and to the organization of IBM and its financial and personnel functions.

The limited size of the group permits maximum participation by its members, and there is much discussion of case material, including role playing. A major activity is team competition in the Management Decision Making Laboratory, using an IBM computer for rapid policy decisions based on marketing, production, and financial data of a hypothetical company. Another project is the "In-basket Test," following methods developed by the executive study project of the Educational Testing Service and the National Training Laboratories. Lectures, however, are given on a number of topics, and there is a substantial amount of reading in management texts and other books. An experimental testing and appraisal program is being undertaken while the participants are in residence.

Leadership of the majority of the course meetings is provided by six permanent staff members, three of whom have had primarily IBM experience; one, other business experience; one, experience in college teaching; and one, experience in educational administration and adult education.

The remaining sessions are led by major IBM executives representing staff functions and by authorities from outside business and the universities.

B. *Courses for Selected Men of High Potential*. Individuals selected for these courses are generally, but not always, in middle-management positions since they have had the opportunity to demonstrate capacity for higher levels but are young enough to have many years of their careers ahead of them.

The present Management Training Program of the *Western Electric Company* has evolved from a Labor Relations Training Program, established in 1947 and subsequently broadened in 1949, 1954, and 1957 to provide an integrated course in management training. Participants, as in the past, are selected men from middle management. Two groups of approximately twelve men are trained each year for a full-time twenty-four-week period.

About one-quarter of the training time is devoted to administrative policies and practices, including in some detail those of the Western Electric Company and other Bell System companies, with roughly equal amounts of the remaining time given to labor relations, business in the American economy, managerial controls, public, community, and human relations, and personal development. Each of the fields listed is considered in terms of its broadest aspects, in the light of current conditions, and as applied to the company itself. This program is designed to develop in the trainees insight into the problems of managing, to provide stimulation and opportunity that will serve as a force for self-development, and to assist each man in gaining an understanding of economic, social, and political forces that affect operation of a business.

A variety of teaching techniques is employed. There is extensive use of the case method, with small group discussions to explore case material in depth and, in some instances, role playing by trainees. To stimulate the learning process and to sharpen communication skills, some written reports are required of the trainees and frequently oral presentations to the group. Leadership of a number of the sessions is provided by the course director or his assistant, but leaders and speakers also include all the principal Western Electric executives and men from other companies and universities.

The Special Management Trainee Course of the *International Harvester Company* was first established in its Manufacturing Department in 1953 and has since been extended to a number of other major departments. This is a three-year course which consists primarily of carefully planned individual development on the job but includes also completion of a special project and group training for two weeks each year at Harvester's Central School. The course is for men already holding significant positions in the company who are judged to have the potential for key management posts. Its objectives are to provide training that will develop leadership qualities and broaden experience in the general administration of a company operation and to identify those trainees who have the greatest potential for growth.

Topics covered in classroom training include company organization, policies, and function—presented by top executives; personal development methods, business management principles, economics, and organization relationships—presented by university professors. The principal theme the first year is "Problem Solving"; the second year, "Planning for Profit"; the final year, "Organizational Relationships."

During the first school period, each trainee selects an individual project concerned with a problem of current importance to his own function, which is submitted for approval to higher management. A substantial part of the ensuing year is devoted to investigation of this project, in some cases with the assistance of other men in his organization, and a report must be made on it during the second period at the Central School.

During the entire three years, the trainee carries out the individual development program agreed upon with the manager of his operation at the time of his admission to the course and later revised when desirable. This program may include special assignments to committees or to specific problems, job rotation, university courses, or other disciplines. Local management prepares a progress report every year, evaluating the training results of each man, and the course policy committee gives careful consideration to the further development of each trainee.

Other large industrial companies providing courses for selected management are the *Westinghouse Electric Corporation* and *United States Rubber Company*. There are two such courses in the Westinghouse Company, each given twice a year for a two-week period to groups of fifty men. The first of these is a course in basic business-management principles given by university faculty members to men at or near the middle-management level with potential for key positions. The second is the Westinghouse Policy Course, with presentation and discussion of company objectives and policies given by company staff officers to high-potential men already in or approaching upper-management positions. The U.S. Rubber course developed at its Mishawaka, Indiana, plant is given by that plant and others in its Footwear Division. Groups of about twenty-five relatively young management men spend two to three weeks full time away from the plant, mainly covering areas of the division's operations, such as production, industrial and product engineering, style and design, price setting, sales, industrial relations, etc. Each man prepares a report on the course and takes a final examination.

One of the electric utility companies of moderate size, the *Wisconsin Power and Light Company*, with 1,800 employees, conducts a Principles of Management course for fifteen selected employees, covering through case discussions fifteen topics, including management prerogatives, co-ordinating, decision making, personal efficiency, development of people, organization principles, and business ethics. A minimum of 4 hours is devoted to each topic, with meetings at two-week intervals. In addition, each participant undertakes a research project during the summer under the guidance of a top-management person.

Courses of this type seem distinctly rare in the financial and distributing fields. A different approach worth mentioning is that instituted by *McCormick and Company* over twenty years ago and often designated in management literature as "multiple management." Its essential feature is the setting up of a Junior Board of Directors which meets regularly, selects company problems for study, and, on unanimous agreement, recommends action to the Senior Board, composed of higher management. The Junior Board is now composed of administrative personnel and other office employees, and there are also factory, sales, and institutional sales boards. Each is composed of about fifteen members and is self-perpetuating. Members spend at least 5 hours a week attending meetings and in committee assignments. Membership on such a board is definitely considered executive training and an opportunity to demonstrate what one can do. Many other companies are now employing a somewhat similar approach.

C. Courses on Individual Topics. The principal characteristic of these courses is that they deal with single subjects in separate units, while in those already described a series of subjects provides a relatively broad background for management personnel, usually at a particular level. Some of these unit courses have also been designed for groups at particular levels, but many of them are for individual selection and, in this case, usually are taken out-of-hours. A few examples will illustrate the large number provided.

The Boeing Airplane Company offers courses of the latter type to all members of management, in subjects selected from analyses of individual development programs. These include effective reading, writing, and speaking, human factors in management, administration, conference leadership, and personnel management, economics, and applied imagination. Each of these courses meets for a 1½-hour period each week for about thirteen weeks. Boeing courses for the specific needs of groups of managers include, in addition to some of the broad types described earlier, short, one- or two-day seminars covering such topics as delegation of responsibility and authority and the administration of change for higher-level management men.

Management training programs carried on by *Johnson & Johnson* include a number of unit courses dealing with specific management functions, such as employment interviewing (for the supervisor rather than for the employment specialist), counseling, and conference leadership, or with general skills of management, such as communications, effective job organization, and cost improvement, or with fundamental skills, such as public speaking and reading improvement. The individual employee and his supervisor agree upon the trainee's participation in them to further his development program and to increase his competence in his job responsibilities. Each course usually involves five to ten 1½-hour weekly sessions and is always given on company time. For the higher levels of management, one course covers business economics for executives, with special application to Johnson & Johnson, and is usually given on a five-day full-time basis.

One of the major functions of the General Motors Institute is to provide management training material and instructors to the various divisions of *General Motors Corporation*. The courses offered, many of which can be tailored to local needs, include some of the types covered in earlier sections, such as the Basic Management Course for Foremen and many others on specific topics in both management skills and such general skills as effective reading. One of the more comprehensive management skill courses is called Working with Individuals and is given on company time for twenty-nine 1-hour sessions. Its aim is to help the supervisor improve his understanding of forces motivating individual employees and to use this understanding in supervision. In the more general area is a course in Creativity, which covers understanding the "laws of association" in mental processes, those processes used in creative thinking, and a problem-solving pattern organized to develop such thinking.

In general it appears that only the larger industrial companies have found it appropriate to offer elective courses for individuals on a variety of subjects. Elsewhere courses on specific topics are designed for particular groups, and many of them deal with the human relations aspects of management. For example, in the electric utility field, *Commonwealth Edison Company* of Chicago has offered at appropriate intervals since 1953 a course entitled Human Relations for Middle Management consisting of ten 2-hour sessions stressing bread-and-butter techniques of practical application. More recently it has introduced a Middle Management Coaching Program developed with the assistance of the industrial relations center of a nearby university and consisting of twelve 3-hour sessions for groups of not more than twenty men. The focus of this program, aimed to bring out desired changes in the knowledge, skill, and attitudes of subordinates, is a day-to-day coaching process involving observation, diagnosis, motivation, planning for improvement, action, and follow-up. Half the time is devoted to practice in such skills as questioning, active listening, and interviewing. Among the instruction methods used are role playing and assignments involving applications of suggested methods to actual situations with reports to the group.

Content, Leadership, and Methods of Management Training Courses

The material in this section has provided illustrations of a number of types of management training courses, classified primarily on the basis of their specific purpose. It may be worth while here to recapitulate very briefly their general content, leadership, and methods.

The extent of the concern about human relations problems in industry is especially well illustrated by the number of specific courses devoted to this area and the emphasis given to it in the comprehensive courses for lower-level management. In such courses for the middle and higher levels, there is less direct attention to it, but recognition of the importance of its principles underlies the approach to discussion of management skills generally, particularly those of supervision and communication. Those skills and such others as planning, organizing, and controlling are a major theme in most of the comprehensive courses for management above the first level but the dominant one in only a few of them. In the first-level courses, they receive less emphasis than human and labor relations and immediate elements of the job, such as getting out production, quality, and cost. Few unit courses deal with such skills broadly but are devoted to a single skill or function, such as conference leadership and personnel management.

Company organization, policy, and future development are major topics in practically all the comprehensive courses for middle and higher management and constitute the dominant theme in several of them. In the lower-level comprehensive courses, the discussion is more likely to be of company practices as related to the supervisor's job. Such practices are frequently the topic of management meetings of an informational nature.

Although on the basis of relative time, discussions of the economic, social, and political environment receive less emphasis in practically all the comprehensive courses than management skills or company policy and problems, this area is a significant one in most of those above the first level and receives greatest attention at the higher levels. It serves to provide perspective for discussion of the company's future under rapidly changing conditions and the public responsibilities of business. Specific courses in this area, except those dealing with the elements of the American enterprise system, are very rare.

Companies offering courses on an elective out-of-hour basis typically include some in the basic communication skills of reading, writing, and speaking. Some of the comprehensive courses for first-level management also give limited attention to these subjects, but they are seldom included in courses for other levels. Occasional examples of specific courses on problem solving or creative thinking were also found.

A number of the descriptions of individual courses also mention the type of instruction or discussion leadership used. For the comprehensive courses at the lower level and the courses on specific topics open to management employees generally, instruction is usually given by members of a special training staff, many of whom have had academic teaching experience and graduate training, or by a specialist in a particular subject who may come from within or outside the company. The courses in human relations given to middle-management men in companies of moderate size frequently are led by university teachers. In the comprehensive courses at the middle and upper levels, a reasonable generalization is that company executives, executives of other companies, and university professors all appear as speakers or discussion leaders. In some cases, members of the course staff are responsible only for its administration; in others, particularly where the content emphasizes management skills, they lead a substantial proportion of the sessions. Although the major experience of most of the men on such staffs has been in the company concerned, some of them include men whose background is largely in university teaching. Men selected from within the company are of high caliber, due both to recognition of the importance of the assignment and to the belief that the experience will be distinctly useful in their own careers. Top company executives, including presidents, are convinced of the need to give time to talks or to lead discussions in these courses and appreciate the values to themselves of such participation. Certainly the greatest care is used in securing speakers from universities and other companies, and it has proved possible to attract outstanding individuals. The research and other staff work as well as the executive attention which goes into management training courses, particularly those for the higher levels, is very great. In most cases, this involves extensive study of the needs of managers and exploration of educational approaches that might be applicable in academic institutions and other companies. The usefulness of special techniques, such as role playing, is examined. Wide differences have been developed in the extent to which the case method is used, based on strong differences of opinion concerning its value. A major purpose of the methods adopted, such as discussions in small groups and, in some courses, individual and group projects, is to stimulate active participation in the course program. Although no attempt has been made to estimate the cost of comprehensive courses, it is obviously substantial. The cost in salaries of participants, moreover, is so great that economy in other directions at the expense of even marginal effectiveness would be difficult to justify.

THE PLACE OF TRAINING COURSES GIVEN BY UNIVERSITIES AND OTHER AGENCIES IN MANAGEMENT DEVELOPMENT PROGRAMS

In view of the emphasis placed on self-development and the building of individual programs for that purpose, some reference should be made to training in knowledge and skills useful in management work and available generally on an out-of-hours basis and very occasionally on a full-time leave-of-absence basis. The exclusion of courses concerned with specific functions of business from discussion in this chapter would tend to exclude from consideration also most of the courses covered in Chap. 22. This in no way means that courses in such subjects may not play a significant part in an individual's development in or toward management. That chapter, moreover, indicates that management development is a recognized goal of some institutions' programs and gives one interesting example of what is essentially an out-of-hours program with this objective. At present, the evening and extension school offerings range from the most practical to the most general, and these schools are beginning to play an increasingly important role at all levels of management. The National Industrial Conference Board's *Tuition Aid Plans for Employees* states that some companies which have such plans give their contribution to management development as one of the reasons for carrying on the plan.[8] About one-fifth of the larger companies in the Ford study, moreover, mentioned their tuition aid plan as one of the methods used in their development programs.

A major extension of a tuition aid plan is that of the *Ford Motor Company's* Basic Management Training Program. Employees with at least a year of supervisory experience, or in certain staff positions, with above-average performance records and superior potential, are selected for this program by a plant manager or his equivalent. The program includes a minimum of 40 credit hours of prescribed and elective classroom work in nearby accredited institutions to be taken over a three- to four-year period and special development on the job through intensive coaching, job rotation, and the like. The prescribed courses are in the four general fields of people in industry, business organization and practice, control, and economic analysis; the electives may be in technical production courses, in writing and speech, or additional work in human relations

[8] Doris M. Thompson, *Tuition Aid Plans for Employees*, National Industrial Conference Board, Studies in Personnel Policy 151, New York, 1955.

or labor relations. This program is distinctly similar in purpose to the company-conducted courses for selected high-potential men described earlier in this chapter. Another program of this type is that conducted by the University of California for *United Air Lines* for which men are selected according to their need for broadening on their present assignment or for preparing themselves for greater responsibility. This is a three-year program consisting of four one-week summer seminars and three years of home study and reading in specific fields. Topics of the seminars are the psychology of human behavior, effective leadership, business fluctuations and forecasts, and advanced human relations and leadership, with the home study in the same general fields.

Before discussing the values which companies believe they gain from sending members of their management to the management training courses, or to other courses with related purposes conducted by universities and other outside agencies, and the extent of their participation in such courses, brief descriptions will be given of the principal courses, exclusive of those given by universities which are fully covered in Chap. 21.

Undoubtedly the organization with the most comprehensive and widely used program in this field is the *American Management Association,* which, in addition to its conferences, courses, and seminars in the major functions of business, offers several courses and seminars specifically in the management development field. The most comprehensive of the courses is the AMA Management Course, first offered six years ago, and given in four single-week units to permit flexibility in scheduling and designed to provide an integrated approach to management problems for men of substantial management experience. The four units deal with basic principles, including the aims, responsibilities, and scope of management and the skills and tools of management; planning and organizing; reviewing and improving performance; and management in action, applying management principles, skills, and tools to representative companies through simulation exercises. Presentations are made very largely by operating executives, with discussion sessions led by members of the course staff. For lower-level management, AMA has recently instituted a three-week presupervision series and clinic which provides a "take-home" program for in-company training for potential supervisors. Other management development courses deal with executive action and decision making and the use of "business games" and simulation techniques in in-company management training employing electronic computers. Among the shorter (three- to five-day) seminars AMA offers are a number in the general management field on such subjects as management in transition, organization planning, and management problems in small businesses, as well as more specific topics, and also several in the personnel field dealing directly with management development problems. AMA courses are given at its academy at Saranac Falls, New York, on the Colgate University campus during the summer, at its New York City headquarters, and, less frequently, in other cities.

A program in which increasing interest illustrates business' desire to learn of more effective approaches to problems of human relations is that of the *National Training Laboratories* sponsored by the National Education Association. Its staff is drawn as needed from leading social scientists, who are also experienced in training, from about twenty leading universities. It holds a number of two- to three-week sessions both in Bethel, Maine, and at Arden House for key executives in industry, middle-management personnel, and, in the case of one laboratory session, for individuals concerned with working with people in various capacities of government, education, social work, and similar fields, as well as business. These sessions include primarily nondirective group discussions designed to increase sensitivity to the significance of behavior in oneself and others and skill in group leadership through role playing, observation, and diagnosis. Other sessions are held at various locations throughout the year, including some for former participants in the basic program to prepare them for training activities or in staff or action leadership.

The psychiatric approach to human relations problems and its application to industry have been presented since 1956 by the *Menninger Foundation* in an annual six-day seminar. This seminar, held at Topeka, Kansas, for not more than twenty company presidents or vice-presidents has recently been supplemented by one- or two-day demonstration programs in some of the larger cities. The major topics discussed at the seminars are psychodynamics, or the basic theory of motivation from the psychoanalytic point of view, interpersonal communication, psychological factors in supervision, creative thinking about human relations, and emotional problems of executives.

Another program which has attracted marked attention is that conducted at Aspen, Colorado, by the *Aspen Institute for Humanistic Studies* during ten two-week periods each year. Designed primarily for the top-level executive, it seeks to develop his understanding of his role in society and his responsibilities in that role through readings in philosophy, history, and political science, emphasizing in part source materials from early American history; discussions at which outstanding leaders in the fields of labor, religion, government, and education are present; and evening lectures by authorities in international affairs.

The vigorous growth of the university management programs, noted in the following chapter and apparently paralleled by the growth of the other agencies just described, is obvious witness to their increased use by business, diminished in relatively small degree by the 1957–1958 decline in general business activity. Once again, except for AMA's statement that over 1,000 companies had been represented in its management course over the past six years, the principal evidence discovered concerning the proportion of large and small companies in the country using such programs is that based on the limited number of companies in the Ford Foundation study. Of the larger companies included there, about three-quarters indicated that they were participating in the university programs; of the smaller ones, about one-fifth were participating. In each group, such participation might be considered as substantial for about half the companies involved, relative to their size, and as limited for about half of them. Participation in the AMA management course was less common, but that in its seminars was equally frequent among the large companies and more frequent among the smaller ones. Seminars in functional fields, however, undoubtedly accounted for much of the representation in them. Companies represented in the AMA management course in almost all cases were participating in university courses also. These proportions may be understatements as this point may not have been covered with every company included in the study. At least one company had reduced its participation greatly, questioning the value of many of the courses tried, and several raised doubts concerning the longer university programs. Only one company made a point of its inability to secure a place over several years in the well-known university course it had selected.

Companies participating in the outside programs were, with only a few exceptions, those which also were conducting their own management training courses, at least at the lower-management levels or in specific subjects. Many of them, however, did not have comprehensive courses for middle- and higher-management levels and evidently had turned to university or AMA courses to fill such needs. Two or three large companies which had recently instituted or were planning courses for middle management or junior officers expected to continue reliance on selected university programs for their top levels.

In most of these companies where the point was covered, the men sent to such courses were representatives of middle management with high potential or, slightly less often, representatives of higher management, in some cases selected because of potential for top positions. Two companies indicated that they had sent all or a very high proportion of their top management to such a course. A few companies spoke of selections on the basis of special needs for individuals. A few were sending large enough numbers so that they were able to include men in many courses designed for different levels.

The Ford study inquiries ordinarily did not ask the executives interviewed to distinguish between the objectives of company-conducted programs and those sought by representation in outside programs. This may account, at least in part, for the fact that the only objective of the outside programs which was widely mentioned was the opportunity to exchange points of view with outstanding representatives of other businesses. One company emphasized this point by selecting for the outside programs men whose experience had been entirely or almost entirely in its own organization. In a few instances, such programs were credited with a heightened awareness of the range of management problems, a wider perspective, or the development of a specialist into a generalist. Usually, however, the purposes served by each type of program were essentially the same.

No information was secured in the Ford study concerning participation in the other programs mentioned earlier in this section. The Aspen Institute's announcement lists about 175 representative large companies and a substantial number of smaller organizations as past participants there. One company mentioned it as providing a complete change of pace for the men it had sent. The methods of the National Training Laboratory apparently have won the very great respect of a few well-known organizations, and their representatives have taken intensive training there and carried it back to significant groups in their own organizations, often including the highest executives. Attendance at the Menninger Foundation seminar has included representatives of a number of the country's major companies as well as of smaller organizations.

TYPICAL COMPANY PATTERNS IN MANAGEMENT DEVELOPMENT

The attempt in this chapter to present separately specific elements of management development programs and especially different types of training programs has obscured the way the programs of particular companies are constructed. This section will outline briefly those of five organizations with relatively highly developed programs in their specific fields.

In the great extension of its management development activities since the war, the *Bell Telephone System* has been able to draw upon long-range estimates of the growth of the business, the evolution of its management structure over many years, and information concerning the education and age of its present management personnel and of those currently reaching certain levels of management positions in order to estimate its current and future management needs. Such estimates are used in determining the size of the companies' college employment programs which have been conducted on an organized basis since World War I and have emphasized the importance of better identification of rank-and-file employees, many of whom have reached management positions at all levels. This has led to active search for better appraisal methods useful for that purpose and also applicable at higher management levels.

As has been true in that particular area, emphasis on research and experimentation is characteristic of all the System's management development effort. Since 1946, interview field studies have been made to determine what kinds of developmental experience would be most helpful to managers at various levels. The analysis of these interviews, together with estimates of needs, has been used as a basis for the design of development programs. As experience, further studies, and other knowledge indicate, changes are tried out and improvements made. As the studies have indicated different needs at the several levels of management, separate courses have been developed for them.

At the first and second levels, in addition to departmental training in the technical and basic knowledge of the business needed by the manager, courses covering three to five days are given in Personal Factors in Management, covering the human relations aspects of good management, Talking with People, and Leading Group Meetings. Third- and fourth-level managers with broader administrative duties participate in programs consisting of several three- to five-day units dealing with various aspects of their jobs, such as planning-organizing-controlling and evaluating and developing people. Higher-level managers, functional department heads, general managers, and vice-presidents attend the programs already described on pages 552 to 554.

While these courses are designed for and participated in by all management people in the several levels, selected third- and fourth-level managers attend special college programs in the humanities and social sciences, ranging from eight weeks at Dartmouth, Williams, and Northwestern to ten months at the University of Pennsylvania. Increased breadth of outlook and stimulation of interest in further self-development are the main purposes of these programs. Although their common base is study of the liberal arts, these programs differ in content and approach, and each one is arranged and staffed by the college responsible for it. Selected men from the third up to the sixth level of management also attend university and other outside programs in management development and related skills.

Individual coaching and extensive job rotation are also emphasized in the System companies. Special values for individual development are found in the conduct of the field studies in management training and related problems and in experience on the staffs of the training courses.

All programs are constantly studied to determine as far as possible the effects and benefits they provide and the criteria which should govern the selection of candidates. Research is in progress using interviews before and after attendance, questionnaires on knowledge, interests and attitudes, and direct observation of the program.

Among the forces which have shaped today's structure of management development in the *General Electric Company* have been its tremendous wartime and postwar growth, its confident expectation that such growth will continue, the diversification of its products, and recognition of the complex problems and obligations brought about by great size and rapid technological and social changes, all leading to adoption of a basic philosophy of decentralized operations carried into effect in 1951. At that time, a research group was established to examine intensively the basic factors involved in the development of people and their significance for management at all levels. Its report was made in 1953, but long-range research into future problems of management and business policy has been carried on since by a continuing group of social scientists as a regular part of the company's management consultation service. This major attack on management development was not a new enterprise in that the company had had long-established apprenticeship, foreman training programs, and other educational opportunities for employees enabling many of them to qualify for management positions. For over sixty years the company has employed and trained for its work selected graduates of the country's colleges and universities. Limited numbers of men with appropriate experience in other organizations have been employed to fill special needs, frequently in the newer areas of company operations. As a result, the company has had in the past, and continues to have, outstanding sources of management potential.

As the foundation for its operations under the decentralized form of organization and also for its management development activities, General Electric has formulated a set of principles and related methods covering the work of a professional manager, based on a conviction that it is a distinct kind of work which can be taught and learned. These principles emphasize the importance of leading by persuasion rather than command, of self-development, self-discipline, and competence by both managers and subordinates, and of seeing each individual job in its relation to the particular function of which it is a component, to the entire company, and to society as a whole.

As a result of findings of the research group, the heart of the company's manager development program has become the planned self-development of every individual willing to take the initiative and pay the price for it in time and effort, as distinguished from a policy of identifying and developing selected individuals of apparent high potential. This is achieved primarily through opportunities and challenges presented by the individual's immediate manager on his current job, with advancement as a secondary objective. The framework for it includes careful manager manpower planning, a managerial climate favorable for growth, and suitable educational opportunities. Comprehensive centrally developed material has been made available to each manager for his use in appraisals of subordinates and as assistance to them in self-development planning, but each manager is advised to feel free to modify the method suggested. Specific means for carrying out individual reading and study plans include a tuition refund plan for courses contributing to the employees' work, authorization for loans to employees undertaking a regular college course, and an extensive bibliography covering both business and other subjects.

Company courses of value to managers and available on a voluntary basis and on the individual's own time at many plant locations include, for example, effective presentation (both written and oral), economics, and labor law. Courses in the fundamentals of manufacturing and other foremen training courses are also given, at least in part on company time. At present, however, the major course provided for all employees responsible for the work of others and for those in comparable staff positions is Professional Business Management I, described on pages 550 to 551. It is expected that additional courses covering particular elements of professional management will be made available. In addition to the supervisory training and professional management courses given at its field locations, General Electric also conducts the Advanced Management Course described on pages 554 to 555.

General Electric also sends a substantial number of men, very largely from the upper levels of management, eligible for the Advanced Management Course, to appropriate management training courses conducted by universities and other outside agencies.

Consistent with its emphasis on measuring as one of the primary functions of professional managing, General Electric has devoted substantial attention to evaluating its management development program. Specific evaluation methods for the Advanced Management Course include a review of statements from each participant at the end of each major section, field interviews of graduates one year later concerning its usefulness to them, and a forced choice test before and after the course regarding attitudes toward different types of supervisors. Finally, questionnaires have been sent out to four graduating classes, covering observed changes in their behavior as managers after a one-year interval. Through such a range of evaluation instruments, together with others to be devised, a clear picture should be obtained of this course's value and the changes necessary for its further usefulness.

Despite its moderate size, the *Connecticut Light & Power Company*, with about 3,000 employees, is devoting major attention to a management development program. It carries on extensive training programs for the limited number of college graduates recruited each year to meet its requirements. A substantial number of its promotions to management, however, are of noncollege men from the ranks, and it is seeking definite means for improving the selection of such men. Appraisals of new lower-level supervisors are conducted at regular intervals by appropriate levels of higher management, and extension of the appraisal program is planned.

The training program for each new supervisor begins with one week of orientation by field management, followed by three days of group training at company headquarters to provide basic familiarization with the fundamentals of the supervisory-management job. This program includes discussions of such subjects as the union contract, safety, appraisal, and communications. The new supervisor returns to headquarters after a few months' interval for two more two-day sessions devoted to further instruction in the essentials of supervision.

More experienced lower-level and middle-management men now participate in a one-week course at company headquarters covering the economics of public utilities, the skills of management, and related topics. These sessions are conducted by company officers, consultants, and visiting faculty members. All of the company's higher executives and some of its middle management have attended the AMA management course, several of its middle management have attended the special university courses for public utility management, and staff men attend appropriate AMA seminars.

An active program of management development in the retail department store field is carried on by *Marshall Field and Company*. In addition to its long-established main Chicago store, this company, with over 10,000 employees, operates five branch stores in that area and a main store with one branch in the Seattle area.

It conducts an extensive college recruiting and initial training program for both men and women, as a major source of management personnel, and also promotes to management positions an approximately equal number of rank-and-file employees without college degrees. There is a comprehensive annual appraisal of each promotional employee and a review with the individual of his performance.

The individual approach to employee development through his job and supervision is supplemented by a series of training courses and conferences. Potential and new supervisors participate in the courses in principles of department store management, human relations, and principles of supervision given in a total of about forty weekly sessions of 1½ or 2 hours. For more experienced managers, one- and two-day seminars on various aspects of executive leadership have proved particularly effective.

Marshall Field supplements its own training staff and executives in the leadership of these programs with a number of university professors but has not participated regularly in university or other outside management training courses.

The Wachovia Bank and Trust Company is giving major attention to management development in part as the result of extremely rapid recent growth and problems incidental to the incorporation of six merged banks within the past three years. It now operates in twelve North Carolina cities and has about 1,600 employees.

Its principal source of management potential is now new college graduates, due to the recent upgrading of other competent men in the organization during its period of rapid growth, and the limited number of younger men in its rank-and-file positions. The number of graduates to be employed over the next five years has been estimated on the basis of expected requirements for replacement and growth. Included in this number will be a few carefully selected men with graduate training or valuable experience in banking or other business.

Individual development is emphasized through a plan requiring a progress report three months after employment or transfer, and an annual appraisal thereafter based on the individual's performance in relation to the requirements of his job and on a review of his job with his supervisor. Candidates for important promotions are given special assignments and committee posts as aids in their development.

The college graduate trainee program, about a year in length, includes more material concerning the broader aspects of the bank's work and its management problems than most courses for new graduates. Every fall and winter a series of monthly meetings is held for small groups of management employees under rotating leadership, each session being devoted to a specific topic. All officers and men at the next lower level attend a one-week, off-the-job conference in groups of eight to ten as outlined on page 552.

One or two high-level men each year attend the Executive Program of the University of North Carolina and twenty to thirty men a year attend the Rutgers Advanced School of Banking and other special banking courses, which include management material peculiar to the banking field.

COMPANY EVALUATIONS OF MANAGEMENT DEVELOPMENT PLANS

The report of the 1954 survey of the American Management Association, *Current Practice in Management Development,* includes the answers to a question concerning the value of their plans from 342 companies which then had some definite program.[9] One-third of these companies said they had made no appraisal of its value. Of the remainder, 20 per cent felt satisfied and gave specific reasons for it, 35 per cent felt general satisfaction, 23 per cent felt it too difficult or early to judge, and only 2 per cent expressed dissatisfaction. The AMA 1958 volume *Evaluation in Developing Executive Skills* contains a report of a University of Michigan survey on such programs which lists a number of advantages gained and, without specific figures, indicates general satisfaction.[10] Among such gains are improved supervision and leadership at each level, better interdepartmental cooperation, increased ability to promote from within, and knowledge of the qualifications of key men.

In the Ford study interviews, only the larger companies generally were asked for an evaluation of their internal programs or of their participation in outside ones. With almost no exceptions, they indicated satisfaction with the results, but about one-third stated they had made no attempt at evaluation. Those which had done so relied on general judgments concerning performance of individual participants, their expressed opinions concerning a course, and, in a limited number of cases, responses to questionnaires. The methods used by the Bell System and General Electric Company to evaluate parts of their programs are indicated in the statements concerning them. A few other companies with comprehensive courses are using detailed questionnaires to participants on completion of the courses and requests for further judgment a few months later. One company has found a conference discussion by participants in a particular course most informative.

By far the most comprehensive attempt so far to tackle this problem is that of Professor Kenneth R. Andrews of the Harvard Business School, who gives his opinions about evaluations of such programs in Chap. 21. His recent articles in the *Harvard Business Review*, "Is Management Training Effective?" [11] include discussion of internal company programs and document his findings to date but express the same concern regarding the validity of enthusiastic reaction from participants and the lack of clear evidence of changed behavior and greater efforts for self-development. It is apparent that more exact definition of the purposes of management development programs and better methods of measuring executive performance must precede valid judgments concerning the value of such programs.

---

[9] *Op. cit.*, p. 5.

[10] Walter R. Mahler, *Evaluation in Developing Executive Skills*, American Management Association, New York, 1958.

[11] Kenneth R. Andrews, "Is Management Training Effective?" *Harvard Business Review*, vol. 35, no. 1, January-February, 1957, pp. 85–94; *ibid.*, no. 2, March-April, 1957, pp. 63–72.

CONCLUSION

This rather detailed survey of company management development programs and particularly the management training courses included in them must leave the impression, perhaps fully expected, of an extremely uneven area, with quite limited activity in many of its important parts. This impression would apply not only to the training field but to other elements of these programs which authorities regard as fundamental, such as a clear picture of management needs, adequate sources of material, knowledge of the abilities and potential of present management, and supervisory interest and skill in assisting positively in the development of their subordinates. Even in the large companies, organized efforts for these purposes are far from universal. They are characteristic of only a modest minority of the smaller ones. It should be recognized that good results do not always depend on formal mechanisms, but such results are likely to be rare in large companies, at least, without them. If we accept the statements of Anshen[12] and Andrews[13] in their *Harvard Business Review* articles that a solid foundation in these respects is essential for the success of management training, early development by other companies, at least of the more comprehensive courses, would not seem sound.

With regard to the training courses themselves, the number of companies with substantial programs for the several levels of management or with comprehensive courses for management above the first or second level is distinctly small. The proportion of companies with general courses for the first level or unit courses on specific subjects, usually quite short, is much larger. It is the author's conviction that a well-developed presupervisory or first-level program is a major contribution to management development in directing attention to topics important at all levels and in helping to identify and give an early start to able individuals from a relatively large pool. The contribution of such courses, however, has received little attention in the literature. Similarly, a good bit of skepticism has been expressed about the effectiveness of short courses, often given once a week for an hour or two, but they would seem to have real value, if well-organized and conducted, when a group recognizes that they are helping to meet a specific need in its work, or when an individual sees them as filling a definite gap in his background. An example such as an effective course in appraisals and coaching, including adequate practice,

[12] Melvin Anshen, "Better Use of Executive Development Programs," *Harvard Business Review*, vol. 33, no. 6, November-December, 1955, pp. 67–74.
[13] *Op. cit.*, p. 57.

perhaps cannot be considered typical but serves to illustrate what may be invaluable.

With regard to the fundamental question of the appropriate role of company courses in this field, particularly those of a comprehensive nature, both company and university courses share the advantages of any program serving mature students actively engaged in the field they are studying. These include, in many cases, recognition of a definite need and of the opportunity to apply what is learned, the experience required to interpret its meaning, a homogeneous group of participants able to keep the pace and exchange points of view, and teaching material based on the contemporary scene and new knowledge not available when many of the participants completed their full-time education.

So long as the number of comprehensive company courses is relatively quite small, they are able to supplement the leadership of executives and professional staffs from within their own organizations with outstanding men from the universities, other businesses, and with management consultants. This opportunity is likely to diminish if the number of such courses increases substantially, particularly in view of the growing belief that all men in the levels involved should be covered rather than selected individuals only. This creates a dilemma, since there seem compelling reasons for company operation of courses for entire levels. With the tremendous demands on university teaching staffs that seem certain for the next decade at least, companies may have to draw more on their own and other nonacademic sources.

As already indicated, practically all companies conducting comprehensive courses also participate in those of the universities, recognizing the value of a varied group of participants to combat the inbreeding of ideas. Although the advantage of meeting a recognized, even an immediate, need was cited, companies appear to have avoided, through their own concepts of the management job, another danger of overspecialization and emphasis on narrow skills.

The possibility of dividing the field more effectively on the basis of the broad topics to be covered runs into the problem of dual programs, acceptable only on a limited scale. Universities and other outside agencies cannot provide the substantial segment of comprehensive programs devoted to company policies and problems, including an approach to them in the light of broad principles and the forces of the environment. Yet the university course appears most appropriate for presentation of those principles and, even more clearly, the economic and political scene generally. With regard to any program in the humanities for managers, there can be no question.

What, however, does this rise in courses for management both in companies and universities imply for business education of full-time undergraduate or graduate students? The advantages cited for the former clearly indicate the difficulties faced by the latter in the management area. The content of the courses for those already in management, however, does suggest points of emphasis in preparation for it. Certainly to the extent that college graduates find it necessary to seek company courses in basic communications skills, a grave question is raised concerning the adequacy of their education. The management functions of planning, organizing, supervising, and controlling may be illustrated by projects within the experience of most students. The stress put on human relations training in business leaves no doubt that the principles of human behavior are an indispensable part of the college man's training for business. History and political science, as well as economics, can lay the foundation for understanding the entire environment surrounding business. Even though courses in the humanities are not widespread, their steady growth in the Bell System bears witness to the need for broad interests and a reasoned philosophy of life in today's executive. Perhaps of greatest significance is the emphasis in management courses on principles, understanding, and perspective rather than on techniques.

In the wider area of all management development activities, three points stand out: the conviction that all development is self-development, the importance of continual growth, and the range and severity of the demands upon management generally and on key executives especially, demands which will hardly be met without a deep-seated sense of personal responsibility. These are points every college desires to make part of each graduate's equipment for life, recognizing the challenge they present to it.

The avowed aims and methods of management development programs present also a severe challenge to business policy as established by its top officers and boards of directors. There have been dramatic demonstrations of failure in the use of our deeper knowledge of human behavior for lower supervision with respect to the rank and file when its use stopped at the middle-management level. Only if company policy and practice through a long-range look even at the profit statement make a reality of its stated obligations to employees and the community, local or nationwide, will the plant manager be convinced that his contribution to these purposes and the prospect of promotion are worth the expenditure of himself which is expected.

CHAPTER 21

UNIVERSITY PROGRAMS
FOR PRACTICING EXECUTIVES

Kenneth R. Andrews

The recent development of university courses for business executives has led to expansion of internal training activities in business and to broader concepts of the tasks of management. For the schools, it has led to stronger relationships with business, increased revenues, and valuable experience for faculty. But the demands for special courses far exceed the capacity of schools to provide them. Devising and manning elementary courses in administration for special-interest groups distract faculty attention from research and innovation. Schools need criteria against which to accept or reject proposals from business. Rejection should occur often enough to permit attention to principal objectives and to permit development in the leading schools of new and more advanced courses at or beyond the present horizons of business practice.

A recent but very lively development in business education has been the multiplication of university-sponsored educational programs for practicing executives. These range in length from conferences of a few hours to degree programs of a full year. The purpose of this chapter is to examine the origin, growth, and variety of college and university business education for executives, the nature of the most influential of these programs, the quality problems which have arisen, the potential contributions of "continuing education" to business education generally, and ways by which the dangers in the rapid growth of this activity can be contained and the opportunities capitalized.

The information drawn upon in this chapter has been derived from three major sources. The writer surveyed 136 schools, including, besides the entire membership of the American Association of Collegiate Schools of Business, the nonmember schools which had indicated in their responses to this study's Survey Questionnaire sponsorship of some sort of educational program for men already occupying management positions. One hundred and twenty-four, or 91.2 per cent, of the schools queried responded to the inquiry. The writer has drawn also on information accumulated by interview during the three-year course of a research project designed to study the effectiveness of executive training programs.[1] Finally, publications of other students of this movement have been drawn upon.[2]

ORIGINS AND GROWTH OF SCHOOL-SPONSORED EXECUTIVE TRAINING

The Beginnings

The oldest continuing university program designed for men actually occupying management positions was begun in 1931 at the Massachusetts Institute of Technology. The present Executive Development Program (Sloan Fellowships) began in Professor Erwin H. Schell's successful attempt to secure the support of business leaders to make possible for a few young men a year's study away from their jobs. In the years between 1931 and 1942, seventy-eight men underwent this training. Since its suspension from 1942 to 1949, the program has gradually expanded in number until today thirty-four men are accepted each year.

In 1943, Harvard and Stanford Universities were requested by the U.S. Office of Education (Engineering, Science, Management War Training Effort) to offer a course known as the War Production Retraining Course to facilitate the transfer to war production of men displaced from their normal occupations. Originally fifteen weeks in length, this program was terminated after seven sessions in June of 1945. In response to requests from industry to continue the course, the Harvard Business School offered a thirteen-week program without government support and with substantial other changes in objective and course content.[3]

---

[1] For a description of this project, see Kenneth R. Andrews, "Is Management Training Effective? I. Evaluation by Managers and Instructors," *Harvard Business Review*, vol. 35, no. 1, January-February, 1957, pp. 85–94, and "II. Measurement, Objectives, and Policy," *ibid.*, no. 2, March-April, 1957, pp. 63–72.

[2] See, for example, George V. Moser, *Executive Development Courses in Universities*, revised, National Industrial Conference Board, New York, 1957; *1958 Guide to Intensive Courses and Seminars for Executives*, American Management Association, New York, 1958; and Jon R. Ivarson and Earl G. Planty, *An Analysis of Twelve University Executive Development Programs*, Management Publications, Champaign, Ill., n.d. In addition, all universities publish descriptive brochures.

[3] Stanford withdrew temporarily to conserve its resources for returning veterans.

From the beginning this program was designed for men older than the Sloan Fellows. It has been attended by approximately 4,000 men, averaging forty-four years of age and $20,000 in salary. Thus two main threads in the development of school-sponsored executive training—a relatively long course for junior executives and a shorter course for more senior executives—had their beginnings at institutions whose first efforts in business education for men of conventional student age dated back in the case of M.I.T. to 1914 and for the Harvard Business School to 1908. It is still possible to distinguish in the later programs offered in many schools two emphases, one close to the purpose of regular business schools to prepare promising young men for future positions of leadership and the other to attempt to broaden the perspective of men who have already proven themselves as executives in specialized functions.

The Varieties of Executive Programs

Since these beginnings in "middle management" and "advanced management" courses, a great many variations have appeared in many institutions. The current welter of college and university courses for managers can be ordered into six categories established after considering (1) whether the program is residential or nonresidential (which often means also whether the program is full- or part-time), (2) whether its subject matter is a broad approach to the administrative process and to "general management" offered to executives from a cross section of industry or is specialized in one way or another, (3) whether the course is primarily comprised of business or liberal arts subject matter, and (4) whether the course is relatively long or short. The importance of these characteristics, if not already self-evident, will become clear later.

1. The first and most important group of programs consists of forty-two *residential broad-coverage programs in general management or business administration* of two weeks or more in length. Examination of Table 21-1 reveals that twenty of these programs were established from 1953 to 1955, the peak years for the introduction of these courses. Four courses were initiated in 1957 and five in 1958, with several others deferred because of the recession. The longest programs (besides the twelve-month M.I.T. and the thirteen-week Harvard programs already referred to) are the new eight-month Stanford Program in Executive Management for twelve junior executives, the five-year-old Harvard Middle Management Program of eight months, and the ten-week M.I.T. Senior Executive Program begun in 1956. The other programs range in length from nine weeks for the Carnegie Institute of Technology's Program for Executives to five different two-week programs, one of which (North Carolina) begins with one week in residence, continues on for

TABLE 21-1

UNITED STATES RESIDENTIAL EXECUTIVE DEVELOPMENT PROGRAMS

Name of school	Title of program	Length, weeks	Year begun	Number of graduates 1949–1958
Massachusetts Institute of Technology	Executive Development Program	1 year	1931	218[a]
Harvard University	Advanced Management Program	13	1943	3,049[b]
University of Pittsburgh	Management Problems for Executives	8	1949	1,121
University of Pennsylvania	Executive Conference on Administrative Policies and Problems	2	1950	294
Northwestern University	Institute for Management	4	1951	661
Indiana University	Executive Development Program	6[c]	1951	268
Columbia University	Executive Program	6	1952	935
University of Southern California	Institute for Business Economics	6	1952	225
Stanford University	Executive Development Program	8	1952	332
Texas Agricultural & Mechanical College	Executive Development Course	3	1952	164
University of Washington	Advanced Management Seminar	6	1952	156
University of Buffalo	Executive Development Program	3	1953	107
Cornell University	Executive Development Program	6	1953	224
Cornell University	Executive Leadership	4	1953	300
University of Georgia	Executive Development Program	6	1953	137
Harvard University	Middle Management Program	8 months[d]	1953	311
University of Houston	Southwest Executive Development Program	6	1953	247
University of North Carolina	Executive Program	2[e]	1953	145
Carnegie Institute of Technology	Program for Executives	9	1954	140
University of Hawaii	Advanced Management Program	6	1954	300
University of Michigan	Executive Development Program	4	1954	223
Oklahoma State University	Executive Development Course	3	1954	68

Washington University	Management Development Conference	2	1954	115
University of Kansas	Executive Development Program	5	1955	71
Michigan State University	Executive Management Program	4c	1955	67
Ohio State University	Executive Development Program	4	1955	90
Ohio University	Executive Development Program	3	1955	103
University of Richmond	Program for Executive Development	5	1955	104
University of Texas	Executive Development Program	8f	1955	155
Case Institute of Technology	Management Development Program	10	1956	113
Massachusetts Institute of Technology	Senior Executive Program	4	1956	109
Pennsylvania State University	Executive Management Program	2	1956	166
University of Portland	Advanced Management Program	4	1956h	150
University of Illinois	Executive Development Program	5	1957	17
University of Oklahoma	Executive Development Program	2g	1957	49
University of Santa Clara	Management Development Program	2	1957	55
University of Utah	Executive Development Program	3	1957	56
University of California (Los Angeles)	Summer Executive Program	3g	1958	39
University of Chicago	Management Development Seminar	4c	1958	25
University of Colorado	Executive Development Program	6	1958	18
University of Georgia	Advanced Management Program	3	1958	25
University of Oregon	Executive Development Program		1958	18
Stanford University	Stanford Program in Executive Management	8 months	1958	12

a Number previous to 1949 = 78.
b Number previous to 1949 = 1,012.
c Divided equally over two years.
d Suspended 1958; to be replaced by a Program for Management Development of 14 to 20 weeks.
e One week each at beginning and end, 9 weeks in between.
f Spread over a 23-week period.
g Program also has a nonresidential part-time version.
h Discontinued in 1958.

nine alternate week ends, and closes with a second week in residence.

Nine of the programs listed are six weeks in length, nine are for four weeks, six last for three weeks, three last for eight weeks, and three for five weeks. More than 10,000 men, sponsored by their companies, have completed special on-campus courses designed to supplement their previous formal education and their considerable practical experience and to increase their ability to manage well.[4]

2. The survey revealed eight *nonresidential broad-coverage courses in business administration* designed for practicing managers which are *a year or longer in length*. The best-known of these is the Executive Program of the University of Chicago, which is for the college graduates who attend it a degree-granting program and for all an educational undertaking of considerable rigor, requiring two evenings a week in classes over a period of two years. Other evening and extension programs are considered in the next chapter, but such programs as the Executive Program in Business Administration at the University of California (Los Angeles) and the Executive Development Programs of the Universities of Missouri, Dayton, and Toledo seem to have been designed more to provide courses which companies would sponsor than opportunities for individuals seeking them at their own expense. Most of these nonresidential courses belong to the middle-management group.

3. A half-dozen *short, nonresidential, broad-coverage courses in business administration* designed primarily for working managers range in length from ten to twenty-four weeks. These are often courses meeting once a week as in the "Management Controls" and the "Techniques in Management" courses of the Advanced Management Program of Adelphi College, or somewhat more intensive courses like that of the University of Cincinnati, which has been offered to 200 men from fifty-five plants in the Cincinnati area from 2:00 to 4:30 P.M. on Tuesdays, Wednesdays, and Thursdays for each of twelve weeks. Other variants to meet the need of local industry and business appear in the twenty-four-week once-weekly course at Notre Dame, the Middle Management Program of the University of Oklahoma (one full day each week for twelve weeks), and San Diego State College, whose Middle Management Institute is comprised of five two-day sessions. Some of these programs will be referred to in the chapter on evening and extension work.

A subcategory of this group, though usually shorter than ten weeks in length, is the short course in administration supported by the Small Busi-

---

[4] Five programs belonging to this category are offered in Canada: the University of Western Ontario, the Atlantic Summer School (sponsored by the maritime universities and held at King's College), McGill University, and two programs at Banff sponsored by the four western universities. Thus forty-seven broad-coverage, full-time residential programs are readily available to American executives.

ness Administration. This is typically an eight-week program, meeting once weekly for 2½ hours to consider "planning, organizing, staffing, directing, controlling—rather than day-to-day operations of a business." [5] The Chief of the Management Services Division advises the writer that 12,350 executives of small businesses have attended 419 courses conducted by 156 educational institutions as of June 30, 1958.

4. At least ten *liberal arts courses* (two of which have been discontinued) have been devised for executives. Five of these have been full-time residential courses for executives of the American Telephone and Telegraph Company offered by Dartmouth and Williams for eight weeks each, by Swarthmore for fourteen weeks, and by the University of Pennsylvania for ten months. Wabash College, offering a three-week program in the first summer and a two-week program in each of the following four summers, has devised a combination residential and nonresidential liberal arts course. The University of Denver offers a nonresidential course in "Liberal Education for Business Leadership." The Aspen Executives' Program, although not university-sponsored, belongs in this category. Leadership in the liberal arts branch of executive training is firmly in the hands of the Bell System, which continues to experiment, currently at Northwestern in an eight-week combination of a liberal arts approach to materials relatively close to business.

5. There are at least twenty-four *special residential business courses, not broad-coverage but particularized either in subject matter or occupation of the participants.* These consist of a half-dozen consumer credit management, credit and financial management programs, and schools of banking at Columbia, Dartmouth, Stanford, Colorado, Louisiana State, Michigan, and Indiana; three four-week public utility executive courses at Georgia Institute of Technology, Idaho, and Michigan; transportation management programs at Columbia (one week) and at Stanford (four weeks); a six-week Hospital Administrators Development Program begun this year at Cornell; and a Blue Cross–Blue Shield National Executive Training Program at Michigan for three weeks in each of two successive summers. Syracuse has a four-week Executive Controls Program as well as a degree-granting course emphasizing financial management in the "Army Comptrollership School." Relatively technical courses in industrial engineering are offered by the University of California at Los Angeles (Engineering and Management Course—two weeks) and the University of Iowa (Management Course—two weeks). Courses like the Graduate School of Sales Management and Marketing at Rutgers University (five weeks), the short course in operations research at Case Institute (two weeks), a management development program for independent telephone executives at the University of Kansas (four weeks), and a two-week program for

[5] Small Business Administration, *Ninth Semiannual Report,* December, 1957, p. 88.

civilian employees of the Air Force Materiel Command at Western Reserve suggest the variety of residential programs which have arisen in the new cooperation between business and the business schools to fit special subject matter to special groups in response to specific needs.

6. In addition to the foregoing categories, there is an uncountable and lusty miscellaneous group consisting of *hundreds of institutes, seminars, workshops, conferences, and short courses* which would be impossible to detail in a short space. These range in magnitude of effort from the presentation of a single institute to the offering of 130 different programs put on by the Michigan State University through its Kellogg Center for Continuing Education. These institutes, ranging from a day to five days in length, may be tax clinics, C.P.A. review courses, transportation institutes, electronic data-processing conferences, special conferences—indeed, in all the functions of business—patents and patent law, office automation, personnel, retailing, procurement, etc. They may be courses in basic management designed for special groups, like the School of Management for Bedding Manufacturers or the Institute of Advanced Management for Appliance and TV Dealers, or seminars for news photographers and editors ("Be sure to bring your camera"), for roofing managers, and for cemetery superintendents. This list would include the second Southeastern School of Management for the Poultry Industry, the Pest-Control Clinic (with a curriculum about half entomology and half administration), the Business Management Institute for Florists, the Management Conference for Soft Water Service Operators, numerous management conferences for liquefied petroleum gas dealers, as well as one-day seminars entitled "Management Development Pays Dividends." Arising from the initiative of trade associations and the consent of colleges and universities, these are the miscellaneous progeny of the newfound need for some sort of postgraduate business training which in the last ten years has appeared everywhere. Many of these should not be considered management courses at all, for though the students are businessmen, the subject matter is often not administration.

Significance of the Rapid Growth

A definitive inquiry into the sociology of continuing business education has not been undertaken. It is immediately clear, however, that the great expansion in executive programs in the last ten years follows from the belief in companies that such programs are of sufficient value to justify the expense. It is clear also that the great majority of men attending have found such programs stimulating, enjoyable, and have at least supposed them instructive and applicable to executive tasks. Initial satisfaction by a few has led to the demand for similar training by many. Most schools report that their specific programs began in the request from business groups or individual companies who came to them with general or specific requests for programs. These requests arise from recognized needs.

The recognition by industry of need for school-sponsored formal training in management is part of the postwar interest in management development which has affected all but a handful of the country's largest corporations and many smaller companies as well. The basic assumption that it is possible to study management and then manage better dominates continuing education. The obvious growth in complexity of the present-day executive's responsibility supports the supposition that continuous study is appropriate. At any rate, a return to the classroom is not considered a degrading reflection upon an executive's present ability but an opportunity for improved performance and often a sign that his company has high hopes for his future.

This growth has been accelerated also by the willingness of most schools to accede to requests from business and even to proffer programs on their own initiative. The prospect of attracting students who for once would pay the full cost or more of their education has been tempting. The other advantages to the schools will be alluded to later. In the meantime, it is enough to say that many schools have more than met the business community halfway. Some have developed promotional programs to increase not only the number but the quality of applicants from business firms.

Durability of the Phenomenon

Despite the rampant enthusiasm apparent in the rapid growth of short courses for executives, it would be unwise to conclude that we are considering a temporary phenomenon like miniature golf or technocracy. Although it is quite possible that the movement will mature, that some schools will withdraw and some companies will be less in a hurry to educate their membership, it is probable that business education will one day be permanently altered by the concept that there is no natural end to learning and by the expansion of the business school's sphere of influence to the whole executive career. Companies are not merely standing by while the schools respond to their requests. Instead they have undertaken their own educational programs; the number of persons enrolled therein is said to be as great as the number of persons enrolled in all colleges and universities.[6] Their efforts open the way to a most promising partnership and new division of labor. That business enthusiasm is not

[6] See *Second Report to the President,* The President's Committee on Education Beyond the High School, 1957, p. 69. For the activities of business organizations in executive training, see Chap. 20.

wholly shallow may also be evident in the absence of collapse in the 1958 recession. Managerial activities have suffered, some new programs have small enrollments, and long middle-management programs are not oversubscribed, but a wholesale scrapping of training effort has not taken place. The extension into other countries of middle- and advanced- management courses (the Philippines, Chile, Venezuela, Turkey, Norway, France, Italy, Switzerland, and England) and the adoption even by the International Labor Office of the intention to educate management in underdeveloped countries indicate the viability of the concept.

This is not to say that all effort has been of high quality or that it has indeed contributed to better management. The proper conclusion is that despite naïveté and haste, support by business for the extension of business education to practicing managers has been seriously undertaken as a long-term investment. It is quite possible that the swift expansion of education for managers has a greater promise than most of the other changes which have taken place since business education began in 1881. Before inquiring into implications, however, we should look at what the most important and influential executive training programs are like and in what way they resemble and differ from ordinary business education in objectives, subject matter, and educational theory and practice.

PRINCIPAL CHARACTERISTICS OF THE ESTABLISHED RESIDENTIAL PROGRAMS

Objectives

Study of the announcements of the forty-two American full-time residential programs devoted to management broadly conceived reveals much similarity in stated purpose. Although some statements emphasize different elements, almost all say their programs are designed first to help executives function more effectively in their present positions and then to help them prepare for promotion to greater responsibility. All these programs provide, in the language of the Northwestern brochure, for making "generalists out of specialists" or, to quote Stanford, "to develop a top management perspective, an aptitude for considering problems from the viewpoint of the company as a whole." An increased tolerance and understanding of other departmental functions, recognition of the importance of human relationships in organization, an expanded awareness and broader understanding of the economic, political, and social environment of business are common purposes of all the major programs. Some universities make explicit the intention to stimulate self-development on the part of the executives attending, and others, influenced by the increased awareness of the relevance of a liberal education to the performance of top-management tasks, include (like Indiana and North Carolina) a small place for increased acquaintance with cultural traditions.

The extraordinary similarity in the objectives of these management programs can be attributed (1) to the influence of the schools upon each other, (2) to the conventional or stylized ritual of stating purposes, or (3) to a common perception of a clearly defined need felt in the top levels of company managements. Undoubtedly, all three are involved. But at least it has been clearly presumed with the assent of companies most interested in developing or perpetuating competent managements that the normal course of education and development of business executives in this country inevitably brings with it provincialism and narrowness as well as specialized competence and accomplishment. Intensive experience in research, engineering, manufacturing, and sales, for example, may not indoctrinate a man with attitudes, perspectives, and approaches to problems adequate for decisions affecting the company as a whole. It is this basic assumption, supposedly derived from common sense and observation, that is the principal guide to the formulation of objectives in the training of men for top-management responsibility. Consequently, all short programs for experienced executives aim to "broaden," to expose men to new horizons, and to change their outlook toward the things about them. This enlargement of vision of management responsibilities is a purpose akin to, but different in emphasis from, the usual goal of undergraduate or graduate business education.

Because the executive development programs presuppose experience, they emphasize change, increased awareness, re-examination of previous experience as ends rather than the acquisition for the first time of knowledge, analytical ability, techniques of management, or the orderly and systematic study of one or more business functions—the usual goals of undergraduate and graduate education. Programs that follow their stated objective do not emphasize vocational specialty, new developments as such, the history and description of business activity, or the development of explicit theory. This difference implies a difference in the curriculum and in the educational process through which learning, if any, is accomplished. Whether this approach, almost universal in executive education, is appropriate to undergraduate and graduate business education is a question better explored elsewhere in this book.

Subject Matter

The very great variety of course designations used in executive development programs does not obscure the possibility of categorizing the courses offered as falling into one of the following categories:

1. The human problems of administration and business organization
2. Labor relations
3. Policy formulation, general management, or the tasks of top manáge-
ment
4. The social, economic, and political environment of business
5. Marketing management
6. Financial management
7. Control, accounting, and other uses of quantitative data
8. Personal improvement courses such as public speaking, speed reading, conference leading, and executive health

Partly because of the shortage of time, not all curricula include all
these categories.

At least four basic approaches are made to the problem of com-
pressing a balanced course offering into a relatively short period of time.
The Harvard pattern, consisting of six related but separate courses (Administrative Practices, Business Policy, Business and the World Society,
Cost and Financial Administration, Labor Relations, and Marketing)
was derived originally from its postwar Elements of Administration
course for the first year of the M.B.A. program, with Business Policy
drawn from the second year to replace Production. It has been followed
and modified in various ways in other institutions. A second major approach has been to emphasize sharply the subject of human relations, as
in the Executive Leadership Course (formerly Human Relations in Administration) at Cornell, or the Management Development Seminar at
Chicago, with enough other general subjects included to keep the course
broad in appeal and scope.

A third major approach followed at Columbia, Northwestern, and
Cornell is to subordinate individual courses to such major subject headings as the determination of business policies, internal administration,
and the relation between business and its environment. Northwestern's
four-week course focuses upon the tasks of top management without
separate attention to traditional courses. The Executive Development
Program of the University of Illinois carries "the business environment"
and "the business organization" as two-thirds of the offering through all
four weeks, with financial control, labor relations, marketing, and "current developments" (that is, operations research, health and fitness,
executive compensation, etc.) for one week each.

At the University of Southern California, the intent is to stress a general point of view and the ability to think abstractly—to steer a course
between the sharpening of specific administrative tools and the unfocused
objectives of liberal arts programs.

A new, and still not fully explored, means for meaningfully integrating a wide-lens intensive study of management is visible in the efforts of the Case Institute of Technology and the University of Santa Clara to have their middle-management participants study a cross-functional problem in their own companies. This use of a laboratory, especially feasible in a part-time program like Santa Clara's nonsummer version and in Case's distribution of eight weeks over a twenty-three-week period, presumably serves as an urgent focus for the general studies and, in addition, brings them to potentially useful fruition in individual effort. The faculty members of executive programs who have wished to have senior managers apply themselves to specific individual projects to make concrete application of their new awareness may, if a greater zest for experiment ultimately invades these courses, make greater use of this approach.

At any rate, the nature of changes currently being considered in the leading schools suggests that some kind of integrated approach concentrating on subjects appropriate to top-management "decision making," for example, may displace the collection of courses in traditional subjects. In any manifestation, the proper subject matter of executive programs will differ from undergraduate and graduate curricula in its selectivity. If neither knowledge nor analytical ability as such is the aim so much as an enlargement in point of view, as an awakened sense of the scope of management competence and responsibility and the importance of approaching every problem from the point of view of the organization as a whole, then what is studied is less important than how it is studied. Although many courses, particularly those attended by junior executives very much bent on improving themselves and their position in life, contain courses of immediate and narrow utility, such as public speaking and speed reading, by and large the curricula of the executive training courses have been broadly conceived even if sometimes they are narrowly executed. These courses belong in theory to the tradition of liberal education, with its emphasis on what happens to the man rather than on what he finds out.

Educational Process

Differences between executive education and undergraduate or graduate education are especially clear in what actually goes on at an executive development program at a university. The formulation of objectives and the choice of subject matter are perhaps unfortunately less influential processes than the day-to-day interplay of the participants and faculty. The role of the faculty differs quite sharply from that usually assumed in a conventional academic program. The professor, likely to be the same age as the participants, appears as an equal rather than a superior and serves often, as the University of Southern California describes it, as a member of a committee of the whole. Except in the middle-management degree-granting programs and some certificate programs, grades are not assigned nor examinations given. Companies are ordinarily not furnished faculty estimates of executives' performance in the course, and as a result, the executive is not looking to the faculty for a grade. By and large, executive groups regard the faculty groups they meet with friendliness and respect. The stereotyped reaction of businessmen to professors —business school faculty are too theoretical, too far removed from real life, or radical in thought and action—does not often appear. Not all faculty members are highly regarded, of course, but disaffection, where it occurs, seems to arise as a result of personal idiosyncrasies, mannerisms, or attitudes, and lack of experience in the assignment rather than from prejudices of the practical against the academic. The true function of the faculty member in an executive training course is more catalytic than authoritative. His leadership appears to be based on the ability to provide a stimulating and useful experience for the participants rather than on his standing as a scholar or his rank in his profession. Lectures are used in many programs, but certainly much more discussion is planned for in executive training programs than in many undergraduate and graduate curricula. This circumstance is thoroughly consistent with the planned emphasis on a broadening exchange of experience rather than subject matter and on the attempt to draw from the total experience of the group rather than from the limited experience of the professor. The need to make so much discussion meaningful puts a heavy demand on faculty and means that those who are not able to teach via discussion are at a considerable disadvantage. Long years of teaching men of student age do not necessarily prepare a faculty to take over an executive program.

A further aspect of the educational process significantly different in executive programs is the place of association with other men in the program. Although it has been long recognized that students at any level learn much from each other, at no other level of business education is it possible for men to learn so *much* from each other. In informal associations outside class, at meals, at cocktail hours, at study sessions, and in conversation with roommates and neighbors, men whose previous associations have been primarily in the same specialized function and industry learn of other men's interest in other functions and industries and come to respect different experience. Even further, men from one business system learn of the executive's life in other countries, such as India, England, and the countries of Europe and Africa and South America. The well-established executive programs plan for such diversity to make this association rewarding and attempt to balance classes to achieve the widest possible interchange. Separation from family responsibilities as well as from the restrictions of job, company, and industry give an opportunity which can never be provided to younger men to profit from one another. This, incidentally, is the advantage which the full-time residential programs have over part-time programs which provide for interchange of experience almost exclusively in the classroom.

The social life important in all schools at all levels is once again sharply different in executive programs. The executive's standard of living and the present-day "executive way of life" carry over into the academic atmosphere, giving the effect usually that high thinking is never associated with plain living. Access to expense accounts makes more money available than students usually have. It is spent primarily on food and drink, sometimes in awe-inspiring amounts. The kind of social life varies, of course, with the location of the program. At Arden House (Columbia), in remote lodges and ranches, traffic with city amusements is impossible, except on week ends, which become more important than in city programs. At all programs, as would be expected, a considerable period is spent at cocktail hours at the program bar or elsewhere. Though certainly conducive to an exchange of experience, the amount of drinking which takes place when executives gather together has been of considerable concern to schools and companies. It is interesting to note that though it sometimes erupts in boisterous behavior which late at night sounds much like undergraduate activity in the spring, it does not often result in unpleasantness or even in complete lack of preparation for class. Attributed in part to the good fellowship which always prevails at programs of this sort and to the peculiar kind of tension and pressure which exists, this phenomenon has not been widely studied nor has it been a major deterrent in the progress of most courses.

The most striking difference between executive training courses and ordinary business education lies in the motivation of individuals. Despite the absence of examinations, grades, and other hurdles like reports to companies, it is the general belief that not more than 5 to 10 per cent of those attending most of the programs described here consistently avoid the work assigned or do other than attempt seriously to make the most of the opportunity. The level of preparation reported by faculty members teaching in both advanced management and other business programs is often higher in quality than in regular programs. Class discussions are usually rewarding. It is more difficult to interest executives in large amounts of individual or solitary work, and most programs have not successfully found ways to get men to do individual written work. Highly theoretical reading matter assigned in large amounts is often neglected, but prodigious research can be expected from a small group assigned to make a presentation to the total group.

Needless to say, what is possible is not always achieved. Some groups decide for reasons hard to evaluate that a given course or instructor is marginal. Barely polite attention to business is the outcome. Lapses in interest and attention are inevitable in the longer and more intensive programs, for concentrated study on a college campus has never been for anyone an unbroken joy. Confusion or frustration at the outset is sometimes followed first by euphoria and then by apathy near the end of a program. Men are usually glad, of course, to get back to their normal ways of life, no matter how rewarding they find their school experience. But a comparison of drive, interest, and attention to subject matter between executives attending management training programs and undergraduate or graduate students would lead most educators with experience in both kinds of programs to conclude that the harder problems of motivation lie with the inexperienced. Those teachers of undergraduates who had experience with returning veterans after World War II will remember how much difference one kind of motivation can make. Another, born of experience and first-hand exposure to management problems, has equally dramatic effect.

Part of the success of executive programs is the good feeling which seems to pervade groups chosen for diversity rather than for expected congeniality. Standards of conduct, mutual respect, and forbearance are very high. The norms quickly established make an ideal social climate for the encouragement of high motivation and the exchange of experience. Most men, including many who attend these programs against their will, feel that they are in the best company in which they have ever found themselves, and most succeed in relating themselves successfully to the formal and informal groups which become established. Experience becomes positive for many reasons. A noncollege man who has been obsessed by his lack of formal education finds himself not only on a campus but indistinguishable from his degree-holding associates. Others find how much pleasure experience and good company can lend to learning.

Evaluation

But though in faculty functions, classroom operations, social life, and warmth of relationships executive programs are significantly different from other levels of business education, it is just as difficult to measure the impact upon the men attending. It is possible at present to measure the effectiveness of a training program only when its objectives are very specific, ending in measurable skills, like the ability to read or to speak French or to program a computer. The best management development programs are ventures in general education. Multiple criteria are involved, cause and effect are impossible to trace, and the influence of a university program is hard to separate from other environmental and developmental factors. Some small progress is being made. So far the great growth of the executive education movement has proceeded not from proof of benefit but from the enthusiastic testimony of a majority of those undergoing the experience.[7] It is the belief of those attending most programs that only a small percentage of men return to their jobs without being affected at all. Men usually report a high degree of mental stimulation and significant changes in attitude toward executive responsibilities and other people. An awareness of many factors lost sight of in the press of business—the importance of other functions, the need to view functional problems in the perspective of the company as a whole, the responsibilities and dignities of management as a profession, the relation of the company to the economy and the American business system to the world society—is as undeniable as it is difficult to trace in terms of changed behavior. The areas in which it is far more difficult to prove the impact of the training program are in its direct contribution to executive behavior and to self-development. It is disappointing to researchers and to teachers to find so little scientific evidence of changed behavior and to find so little visible change in efforts toward "self-development." On the other hand, all education is subject to doubts about ultimate effectiveness.

To summarize the similarities and differences between training for practicing managers and education for men about to go into business, we should say chiefly that experience increases the voltage of the learning process. Properly led by adequate faculty, experienced executives can learn more in a shorter period of time, keenly interested as they are in their association with fully developed colleagues and in the problems put before them. With objectives adapted to the need for breadth after intensive and confining functional experience, with provocative subject matter leading to a breakout from previous narrowness, and with an educational process taking advantage of the experience, interest, and good will of the participants, there is possible an educational experience unique in the history of education which cannot be achieved with men of little experience. So dramatic is this possibility that many who have seen and felt the differences have concluded that the more education for management as such can be postponed until some experience with business has been accumulated, the better. The implications of this belief for the future of either undergraduate business education by itself or graduate business education following immediately upon undergraduate years are considerable. Needless to say, the possibility of postponing study of

---

[7] The writer, assisted by Professor Reed Powell, expects to query 10,000 alumni through a detailed questionnaire now being field-tested. The results from this questionnaire, available in 1960, supplemented by extensive interviewing, will make possible a fuller evaluation of executive programs.

business subjects does not make any less necessary the acquisition of a liberal education—one way or another—by the young.

PROBLEMS OF QUALITY IN EXECUTIVE EDUCATION

Criteria for Judgment

Before specifying the kinds of quality problems that exist, it is necessary to have some beginning presumption about the educational and administrative standards which a good management course should be expected to meet. We should presume first that a school is genuinely interested in providing an educational experience to the executives attending rather than, for example, a pleasant interlude in busy lives for public relations and financial reasons. It follows from this presumption that certain fundamental educational and administrative conditions must be met if a program is to merit a reputation for high quality.

To examine the educational requirements first, a diversified and able student body is the first necessity. Men between forty and fifty with a continuing interest in the professional aspects of management, drawn from the widest spectrum of functional, company, and industrial experience, constitute the ideal student body. Middle-management programs especially designed for men under forty apparently succeed best if drive and intelligence compensate for the reduced exposure to executive responsibility. Men over fifty in some instances suffer from the intensity of the program and the disruption it necessarily introduces into their normal lives.

Despite the importance of the exchange of experience and the obvious advantage that middle-aged executives have over young students in the attempt to educate themselves, a capable faculty is still a vital requirement. In addition to command of field, the professor must make the work he assigns appear relevant day by day to practical business decisions. This is an unfortunate limitation but one which is better accepted with resignation than fought against. The professor must be able to provoke successfully the recognition and dissipation of prejudices in the areas of labor relations, politics, human relations, and functional loyalty. He need not be himself a former executive, although firsthand experience helps if combined with required teaching skills. Most deans have found that not all their faculties are capable of successfully handling this responsibility. As a consequence, many schools bid for the summer services of a relatively small number of faculty people with proven experience.

In addition to providing the attractions of extracurricular association, a good program must command the intellectual interest of the group as a whole and of almost all the individuals in it. The artificiality of student life, separation from family, and relief from job preoccupations make it essential that the intensity of this interest be stimulated and restimulated. A good program will be an intensive program, then, with a substantial amount of meaningful work designed to occupy all but a few of each man's waking hours. The work will be study of a recognizably integrated pattern so that a host of separate courses are not being pursued simultaneously, and the study of business functions will be taken up explicitly in the context of the company as a whole. The distribution of time among courses is relatively unimportant so long as (1) the policy-making function, (2) the human aspects of organization, (3) the place of a business organization as a whole in its social and economic environment, and (4) the use of quantitative data are studied in some detail.

Of greater importance is the probable need for work that involves and requires hard thinking. So far the requisite quality of thought has been achieved in problem solving rather than in more abstract forms of mental activity. We know how to present problems posing the need to decide who could or should do what and why with what objectives in mind and with what values underlying their choice. It is more difficult to achieve as great an intensity in courses which, for example, present an abstract classification of management into such functions as organizing, staffing, directing, planning, and controlling, without concentrating upon the complex *how* questions which arise when these managerial functions are performed in actual situations. Current attempts, as at the University of Chicago and the Carnegie Institute of Technology, to approach subject matter more theoretically may enrich the intellectual content of theoretical courses. So far it is futile to charge executives with indifference to theory when the constructs available in the field of administration are too feeble or hackneyed to merit serious attention. What is crucial is not that executives should study problems rather than theory but that what they do study illuminates their lives and guides their performance.

To be educational, an experience should contain enough stimulation or confrontation with the unexpected to lead to some kind of personal readjustment. Courses which fit closely the expectations of those attending, confirming previously held positions or affirming popular platitudes never seen in conflict with each other, would under this approach be classifiable as possibly pleasant but not instructive. The participating executives and the faculty should be meeting with the objective of discovering things not apparent before. For the executive this will lie usually in himself and his past experience and will take form as a different attitude, a different picture of himself, or a different formulation of personal goals in the performance of professional responsibilities.

It is important also that our criteria for evaluating, however subjectively, a management training program or our approach to conceiving an ideal program should include the administrative requirements. Able administration of an executive program is required for two purposes—the internal conduct of affairs and long-range relationships with the companies who actually select nominees approved or rejected by the schools. The successful transplanting of an executive group from office to classroom and from home to dormitory requires expert scheduling and hotel-keeping skill. The very first impression of a registration procedure or of baggage handling can do much to color an executive's impression of the experience he is about to have and put him in a frame of mind which will influence what happens subsequently. Plain quarters are possible, but such items as the composition of study groups, the matching of roommates, and the handling of personal affairs must be of the quality to be expected of any first-rate organization, especially one which professes to know and teach administration.

But the administrative head of a high quality management course must also work continually with companies, not only to be able to turn down candidates he considers unsuitable for his group or those who cannot be admitted because of the press of numbers, but to work out with companies the most useful role his course can play in the company's total management development program. Establishing criteria for selection, persuading companies not to use programs for remedial transformations, helping companies deal with the meaning that selection for a given program has within the company as to status, imminence of promotion, and membership in a top group, providing some basis by which a company might decide which program is suitable for which men, all these matters affect the quality of a university program.[8]

These comments, which may provoke disagreement in detail, appear to represent in general the developing concept of what a good executive program should be. Incomplete examination of the full-time programs now being offered suggests two major dangers which imperil the quality of the courses being offered. In general, the criticisms of major import relate either to the strain on poorly equipped schools and distraction from the principal programs of all schools which the popular management movement makes possible or to the dangers of superficiality, a condition which may by its nature be especially virulent in highly esteemed places.

Distraction from Principal Mission

The presentation of executive courses of any sort, from the three-day institute which makes minor inroads into the time of its faculty to the

[8] See Melvin Anshen, "Better Use of Executive Development Programs," *Harvard Business Review*, vol. 33, November-December, 1955, pp. 67–74.

longer program which requires a full-time faculty for itself alone, is a demanding undertaking which may easily distract the administration and faculty of a business school from its primary mission—the presentation of its basic undergraduate or graduate program. It is not only the need to make a success of any program undertaken which gives power to this distraction. The occasion to offer a self-sustaining or a profit-making program while at the same time strengthening the relations of the school with the business community within its sphere of influence is a financial opportunity of unusual attractiveness. Although modest fees are charged by many institutions, substantial fees are charged by others. It would be too much to expect that any school would charge less than the program costs when the fees are paid as tax deductible expenses by business organizations. Some institutions deliberately charge more than the operating costs for a program as a means of supporting the acquisition of case material or some of the other activities of the institution. The discovery of a market which for the first time in educational history makes realistic pricing possible and opens up a new means of support is an understandable encouragement to a school to offer a substantial amount of its undermanned and overworked faculty effort to courses established for businessmen. Because these are received with considerable approbation and enthusiasm and appear as well to be addressed to a widely felt need, praise and recognition are added to financial return as inducements to extend further this new activity. It is small wonder if some schools have ventured prematurely into this new field and are competing under difficulties for company support.

But more than the financial, public relations, and competitive temptations, the sheer energy needed to meet the administrative and educational requirements of a good program constitutes an inevitable deflection from research and innovation. Although interesting new ideas have appeared in a few institutions, the basic pattern of objectives and course construction remains much the same within the executive courses. Further than this, the effort required for a program to hold its own and to keep operating discourages experiment. By and large, men attending the well-established programs expect to find what their colleagues in their companies found before; except where dissatisfaction exists, the pressure for change is negligible. It will be found in other segments of this survey (Chap. 11) and in the parallel study that is being made by the Ford Foundation that schools are already having problems finding the manpower and the financial resources to continue the study of the functions of business and to experiment with curricular innovation. If so, it is appropriate here to point out that establishing, operating, and recruiting executives for a successful management training program, while of unquestioned value to business, does not necessarily advance and may even hinder the efforts of a school to improve the quality of its basic programs. As an enlargement of current service, executive training has long-range costs not recovered in tuition fees.

As management development has become more popular, and as the concept of continuing education has been taking hold, an infinity of need has been stirred up. The notion that formal education should terminate at commencement was at least convenient. With a wide variety of executive courses, refreshers, and advanced seminars, the potential school population is countless, particularly if the idea of spending a couple of weeks every year or so in management training becomes more deeply rooted. In any case, individuals, companies, industry trade associations, and community organizations are conceiving of course opportunities with an energy which is not diminishing. The naïveté in this increased desire for further education is more than balanced by the good will and determination which accompany it. The need is real and worthy of respect. In the face of the large numbers of young people soon to appear, the business schools of the country are ill-equipped for filling the gaps in a complete program of continuing education. It is hard to say yes to one organization and no to another. It is apparently hard to follow a very simple rule—refuse all requests emanating from single companies or single-industry, special-interest groups. So far, therefore, the usual means of control has been to serve those who express their need first and deny the others when manpower is committed. It would be preferable, of course, to be able to do what most needs to be done.

The Dangers of Superficiality

Somewhat more ominous than the burden which educational programs for practicing executives place upon the business school is the resultant superficiality which must occur when tasks undertaken exceed resources. Optimistic views of the power of education have always characterized our society. Some sectors of the business community are at present more receptive to the role of education for management than may be justified by what business education has accomplished. Although this attitude provides a friendly climate for the improvement of education for the profession of management and is certainly preferable to skepticism or hostility, it means the school must be wary that its influence not be overrated. The expectation that a short course in anything, however it is taught, can have a pronounced effect may in part be the wishful thinking that arises from the difficulties of detaching executives from their jobs for a considerable period. It is easier for a school to be silent on the theme that education is a slow process and agree to give a little course than to challenge the premises of the interested and eager architects of such courses.

Superficiality thus manifests itself in the concept that a short course can do a big job. It can appear also in the way in which courses are conducted. The thinness of wide-survey lectures and the miscellaneous topicality of programs touching briefly on everything need not detain us, for these are perennial problems easily recognizable. More subtle is superficial teaching, as in the bull session about business. Out of the vivid experience of articulate businessmen can arise active conversation about management problems which is anecdotal, undisciplined, and entertaining without being instructive. Questions and answers after lectures do not necessarily constitute effective discussion. The pressures on an instructor may lead him to think more about preserving rapport than getting to a problem. It is easier to skim the surface of a subject than to risk diminishing enthusiasm by plunging into it.

Associated with the potential corruption of the educational process which the multiplication of executive courses can bring with it is the faddism which almost everyone acknowledges as an important ingredient in the development of management education in the last ten years. That schools, sensitive to pressure, anxious to serve, and needful of contact with practitioners might succumb to this is understandable. But even company presidents, meeting with their colleagues at industry meetings, are affected by each other's activities in executive development and are not necessarily critical or curious about objectives and results. When, as has happened, the president of one company in an industry well known for its participation in university programs finds himself embarrassed by reporting that he is not taking part by sending men, he is responding to a newly established expectation. When a dean reports that he is "sorry to say" that he has no executive programs, he acknowledges a norm. It is quite clear that at the present moment it is good to be giving and attending courses in management—whether discriminations between what constitutes useful and wasteful activity have been made or not. So long as participation in such programs continues to be the right thing to do and the propriety is supported by the pleasures and stimulus implicit in the associations made possible by executive courses, the voice of protest will doubtless be muffled by the announcements of new courses.

So far, the aspects of superficiality discussed here are mostly innocent in origin. But there may be in education, as in other human activity, an element of charlatanism and fakery less pleasant to contemplate. Although it is inappropriate to make specific charges here, it may be proper to say that there are said to be individuals, if not instituti whose principal intent is to earn fees and wide repute without providing the opportunity for learning and without running the risks which serious educational projects do run. Courses in the newest gimmicks and in popular developments sometimes seem to the bilious observer to be very nearly fraudulent in claims. Business has a reputation of being hard-headed in the face of spurious claims, but in the field of education it can be deceived.

The central problem which may give rise to such manifestations as superficiality, gullibility, and self-deception is the conflict between two contradictory needs—to be off the job long enough to learn what needs to be learned and to get back to the job fast. It is not impossible to balance these two needs successfully, but so far, in the early years of the movement for a continuous management education, inexperience and the desire to please have probably too much encouraged the idea that significant and permanent effects can be achieved in a matter of days. What can be done with seasoned executives is remarkable, but the true price in time has been unrealistically discounted.

Even further, trouble lies ahead if companies decide that they should specify the content and length of the courses they will support or if they expect schools to conduct courses especially designed to their specifications. Assent now to misconceptions about the educational process and willingness to conduct programs of a superficial sort may lead ultimately to either a loss of independence or the inability to get the kind of substantial support and sacrifice from participating industry which meaningful executive education may require.

POSITIVE CONTRIBUTIONS TO BUSINESS EDUCATION

The foregoing suggestions that the management education movement may have flourished so rapidly as to have suffered excesses should not obscure the genuine promise for the future in the association of practicing managers and institutions for formal education. Certainly in the eyes of management, ill-equipped though it is to measure definitively the contribution of the educational institutions, the movement has not been a failure. For the schools as well, the new opportunity, if properly managed, can be enrichment of resources and a contribution to professional practice.

Challenge to Faculty

Presiding over effective discussions of management problems with able ⸱⸱ ⁿn of proven experience is a highly educational task for faculty members ⸱⸱ have the opportunity to learn a great deal from such students.

The need for acceptance, the absence of the trappings of status, and the weapon of grades may lead an instructor to superficiality, but it may mean just as well that he increases his powers of leadership in ideas to command respect with skills that deserve it. The development of liberal arts courses for businessmen, exposing professors of art, music, literature, and history to businessmen for the first time is almost invariably reported as an illuminating experience for the faculty member who discovers between lectures how out of date his notions of business have become, derived as they are from effective but unverifiable novels of the 1920s and of the Depression. Discovery by faculty members in liberal arts colleges that men in responsible executive positions can be not only sensitive but intelligent has been met halfway by businessmen who are able to change their preconceptions about the inhabitants of the ivory tower. Because the hostility of teachers of the liberal arts has often been cited as one of the reasons why business is the residual profession, elected after the others have been discarded, the edification of liberal arts faculty members by their businessmen-students may be one of the most promising by-products of this development in management training. Other evaluation of liberal-arts executive courses must be left to a later occasion.

In courses devoted to business subject matter, the close and friendly contact of faculty member and business executive acquaints the faculty member with varieties of business practice, gives him access to confidential and unpublicized developments, and paves the way for future research and case-gathering opportunities. Consulting contacts, effective not only in alleviating professorial poverty but in advancing professional knowledge and providing some opportunity for responsible decision, also arise easily from acquaintances made in courses. Businessmen, learning the difference between the skills of practice and the skills of research and teaching, are not slow to see the opportunities for the latter in the conduct of business. The opportunity to participate in management training courses is, besides being a challenge, an important stimulus to faculty development in strengthening its sense of reality and in contributing to its search for openings to make possible the advancement of practice.

Further opportunity for college faculties exists in the problems posed by trying to plan proper objectives for short courses and to choose subject matter, issues, and problems appropriate to these objectives and to devise methods which make considerable progress possible within a relatively short period of time. Although it is clear that contemplation, reflection, and listening to lectures (all desirable activities) are not especially effective processes for an intensive course making the best use of very short time, much yet remains to be done in devising materials for discussion that effectively integrate the complex materials of management into an attainable whole and a perceptible pattern. In the leading schools the choice between specialized and general education has been made, but ways of conceptualizing an approach to general management which will stimulate subsequent self-development still have not been completed. The literature of business organization is not yet fully rewarding. The transition between the highly charged atmosphere of management training programs and the job in the company has not yet been adequately studied or successfully bridged. In addition to perfecting educational methods for a unique undertaking, there are many areas in which inquiry can be pushed and action taken when the time is right.

For an ideal opportunity—almost a faculty man's dream—exists here. Free from the drudgery of examinations, reading repetitive papers, and routine activities going again and again over the same ground, the professor is now dealing with experienced men highly motivated and interested in issues the importance of which they recognize. The teacher has for a brief period the opportunity to discover how far one can go with interested and knowledgeable associates. The tension, anxiety, and fatigue which accompany this kind of teaching may offset in part the potential advantages of this situation, but that the opportunity exists for testing, experimenting, and developing new teaching skills is undeniable.

So great, in fact, are the possibilities of professional association between business and the business schools arising from the successful execution of management training courses that it seems inconceivable a school would withdraw from such positive opportunities in the face of the problems that attend them. It is appropriate, therefore, to look now at how schools might contain the dangers and capitalize the opportunities which lie before them.

SETTING A COURSE IN CONTINUING EDUCATION FOR EXECUTIVES

The present range of business education, the variety in kind and quality of school, and the complexity of the needs of business make it very difficult to specify a plausible and desirable single future for university-sponsored executive programs. If maturity is to come, an orderly division of labor between companies and business associations on the one hand and college and university schools of business on the other should be developed. To company-managed programs would go specialization, vocational instruction, orientation in knowledge peculiar and essential to a given industry. To the schools would belong basic education in the principal functions of business, in business organization and the administrative process, and in the contextual subjects. A withdrawal by the schools from detailed specialized courses and from advanced functional instruction would clarify the mission of company training and free school resources for its basic mission—general education in management at three levels of experience—novice (undergraduate and graduate), middle management, and senior management.

If this should be the future course of the partnership, a further division of labor, for the purposes of conserving resources and concentrating effort, is desirable among the schools. It is not necessary that schools in private universities, in state universities, or in municipal institutions—with national, regional, or local spheres of influence—or church schools and departments in liberal arts colleges should all attempt the same range of activities. Since no master plan will be conceived and executed to assign specialized tasks to each type of institution, it will be necessary for academic leaders to make their own choice and chart their future accordingly.

Choice of Objectives

The dangers of overextension and the need to husband resources for maximum contribution make it especially desirable that a business school consciously formulate its objectives in the area of management education for practicing executives. These should have as much precision as the countervailing need for flexibility and freedom of initiative for individuals will permit. For a school to have as its purpose to "do all it can" in management development is as inadequate as for a company to state as its objective "to make as much of its product as it can." Neither general objective, obvious as it is, is precise enough to give guidance.

In attempting to formulate objectives, a school must resign itself to the likelihood that it cannot do all it would like to do. Assessment of its resources in physical facilities, in faculty, and in administrative personnel, analysis of present weaknesses and strengths, and study of the business community it wishes to serve will reduce the choices available. Such a study may result in a decision to offer *no* executive programs until adequate manpower and facilities are available beyond the minimum requirements of the degree-granting program. If the clamor for such service from surrounding business is difficult to stave off, a precise presentation of the kind of support necessary to increase the ability of the school to provide such programs may result in resources being increased.

A review of the strengths and weaknesses of an institution, besides leading to a definition of what is possible in the foreseeable future, may also help clarify answers to the basic question, "What kind of a school is this school to be?" The setting of objectives is in substantial measure a question of circumstance, charter, and desire, but enough freedom remains so that prior to decision all the practical alternatives should be reviewed.

Choice of what kind of executive program to offer follows in part from the kind of school an institution plans to be. It is not appropriate, for example, for a business department in a liberal arts college to offer a short human relations course for salesmen of prescription shoes any more than it is for the biology department to teach beekeeping. The character of an institution furnishes criteria adequate to deal with special interests and urgent proposals to study modish reincarnations of basic processes and subject matter. By defining the objectives of the school, by specifying, according to charter or voluntarily assumed responsibility, the degree of vocational or special interest a school is to serve, then the kind of program to be offered to what kind of executive can be clearly established.

The urgent need is for intelligent limitations that neither offend the business community nor blight the aspirations of faculties. Despite the variety of legitimate purpose, it seems clear that a basic, general part-time or full-time course in management deserves priority over individual institutes and three-day conferences. The latter, especially necessary in state and municipal institutions, should be grouped in a separate bureau of business services or extension division with at least administrative manpower of its own. Here, too, rather than proceed *ad hoc* from request to request, the possibilities of programming the variety of institutes to be offered, and the industries, associations, and other markets to whom they could be most profitably presented, can be planned in advance to avoid the helter-skelter profusion of meetings which, though they accumulate good will, add little else to the resources of the faculty or business community.

For the problem of the institutes, a specific recommendation, then, is to say no. As the condition for saying yes, certain minimum quality standards should be applied by the school to any program it sponsors. Scrutiny of the objectives, provision of adequate time to deal with any subject taken up, inquiry into what form of continuing study the institute is to contribute to or to awake interest in, all are questions which can be profitably raised with those making requests for programs. Conferences which seem worth while but which do not seem to merit official sponsorship can be turned over to another sponsoring organization with faculty help being furnished on an individual basis. Just as it is not usually considered appropriate for a school to sponsor officially an enterprise confined to a single company, so, too, special industry or trade groups should be encouraged to run their own programs with help from the schools. There are reasons for the properties in these relationships, and observance of them can improve the quality of the service to business of educational institutions.

A school, then, should ask itself these questions:

Where are we now able, or where will we be able in the foreseeable future, to make a contribution to management training *which will in turn make a contribution to the school?*

What kind of a school is this to be?

What are its relative responsibilities to liberal education in fundamentals as opposed to vocational specialization?

What is to be its relative emphasis on degree programs and other services?

What general purpose programs will we sponsor and hope to interest the business community in?

By what standards will we accept or reject proposals for special short courses made by companies and trade groups?

According to what criteria will we contribute help and encourage requesting groups to manage their own programs?

Relation with Associated Companies

The second major task for schools which would build on the strengths of recent developments in executive education requires faculty or administrative people to work with companies as, in a sense, coordinate educational institutions. The extraordinary growth of company-sponsored courses has exceeded in numbers even the remarkable expansion of executive courses in the colleges and universities. Because industry-employed educators are by and large less experienced and under great pressure for results, the first and continuing injunction is to keep companies constantly reminded of the difficulties in trying to teach knowledge, attitudes, skills, and behavior, of the impossibility of universal or predictable results. In particular, the representative of a school should never consent to the oversimplification common in industry training in nontechnical subjects. It should be wary of the inclination to attempt too much in too short a time and, in addition, of the inclination of some companies to turn their educational problem over to the schools for quick solution. Appreciation of the true costs of education, which schools have never charged and are only now beginning to make known, both in dollars and in effort, should be one objective of this association.

A closer partnership of school and company educators is necessary to make a living reality out of the division of labor recommended earlier. The developing pattern which suggests undergraduate education in liberal arts, science, or engineering, graduate business education, company training in relevant specializations, apprentice and actual experience in management, and finally a university executive program requires deliberate coordination between industry and academic educators. When the school can help educate the trainers, rather than do the training for the company, it will be multiplying its influence without dissipating its energy. Rather than raid faculties to get teachers, companies might seek, as many do, consulting help in becoming able to train their own people for internal training tasks.

What appears to be a significant example of conceiving a unique executive program with broad objectives but specific adaptation to local situations is the activity at the University of North Carolina. The combination of a full week's residence at the beginning and end of a six months' program, with nine week ends at Chapel Hill in between, makes possible a state-wide participation by managers from all sizes of companies comprising the state's industry. Attempt is made to combine the advantages of an on-campus program with the feasibility of a part-time course. The formation of a nonprofit corporation, "Management Development, Inc.," provides a mechanism for continued development of alumni of the programs and for providing institutes for managers of smaller firms who are unable to participate in the main program. The alumni of the main program instruct in these institutes and are given one share of stock for each hour of instruction.

The Executive Program is supported by apparently active cooperation between the School of Business Administration as a whole and the business community. A Business Executives Advisory Committee, comprised of state business leaders, in addition to assisting the School of Business Administration generally, recently appointed a research committee to make an outside study of business education. A painstaking inquiry was conducted in the business community to gather its ideas about the proper objectives of a business education, industry's expectations and criticism of business education, the responsibilities of industry, and its recommendations of what a business school should do.[9] From this kind of study, and from the discussions that followed it, can certainly come much of the information needed by a school in the crucial decisions involved in setting objectives and deciding what goals to pursue.

The Need for Creativeness

It is, of course, much easier to speak of the desirability of formulating objectives and of working out with business firms a division of labor and a common educational philosophy than it is to do either of these things.

---

[9] A report *Business Looks at Business Education* was published by the university in 1958.

The process of setting objectives involves more than choice of alternatives already recognized. It means frequently the achievement of a new combination of educational procedure and local circumstances. The short history of academic participation in the education of practicing executives has already led to a number of major adaptations of the basic innovations in middle management of the Sloan program and in advanced management of the Harvard AMP course, such as the part-time but rigorous executive program of the University of Chicago, the projected combination of work on a company research project started at Case Institute and appearing in different form at Santa Clara, and the devising of new ways of integrating a variety of subject matter as in the Executive Controls Course at Syracuse. There must be in every regional situation the basis for creating a unique approach to the task of acquainting working managers with the points of view, concepts, and means for self-development which our society is saying their position demands of them. The multiplication of management training courses should be paced to the painstaking development of such programs and carefully adapted to local needs and resources. The hasty reproduction of someone else's brochure, the borrowing of someone else's faculty, and the rounding up of some executives from somewhere have served their function in providing for the establishment and acceptance of the idea of university education for businessmen. Henceforth, the emphasis should be on what a particular institution can contribute in a particular area without apology for not being on a bandwagon.

Horizon Programs for the Leading Institutions

In essence, then, it is the conclusion of the writer that the effort by the universities to offer intensive courses in management for practicing executives has on balance been good for industry and good for the schools, but that the schools must exhibit firmness and discrimination in regulating and economizing their effort. To take the fullest advantage of opportunity, the next development in education for executives should probably be truly advanced courses offered to those who are already experts in the subject. Rather than merely risking exhaustion of its educational capital by presenting essentially the same course to class after class of managers drawn from a never-satisfied need, it has been proposed that a series of programs in new developments be presented to practitioners and scholars who would be invited to participate, not on the basis of how much they had to learn, but on what they might contribute to further progress in the field. Preceded by research, the program itself would be devoted to an attempt to chart the future of study in the field and to come to conclusions about problems in applying in actual management practice findings reached or caught sight of. The development of new concepts for business management or for business education to which both scholars and executives would contribute would carry with it the acquainting of leaders in scholarship and practice with what is going on in the field under discussion and with the opportunity to guide the future course of study and practice. The activity should bridge the gap between research and business in actual administration of business affairs by either exploring the implications of research findings or by making new and useful combinations of what has already been discovered. Each program, devoted to the farthest reaches of the basic curricular subdivisions of the business program, should help advance the teaching of even the traditional subjects.

Such a plan, now mostly in the discussion stage, is full of difficulties, not only because of the intellectual problem of making a genuine advance in a field, but because of the administrative problems of securing sufficient financial support and attracting to the program those persons essential to its success. Rather than to elaborate possible solutions to these problems or even to specify in detail examples of the subjects which might be taken up, it is appropriate here to point out only that some undertaking to add to the intellectual capital of business education is perhaps now more vital than establishing further programs to adapt present materials, ideas, and objectives to the education of new audiences. Schools which would preserve a capacity for innovation and maintain leadership in instruction must seek new knowledge in depth in the basic fields. The addition of such a program to the offerings now available would greatly enlarge the opportunity which the willingness of practitioners of management to undertake further formal education now makes for us.

CHAPTER 22

EVENING-EXTENSION PROGRAMS IN BUSINESS

John P. Dyer

Rapid growth in numbers and in programs within the past twenty years reveals the fact that the adult education divisions of major colleges and universities constitute an important phase of contemporary American higher education. In these programs business education is receiving heavy emphasis. These adult education institutions (evening colleges and/or extension divisions) are still in a formative stage, but are rapidly maturing. This chapter relates some of the progress and touches upon major problems with respect to the curricula, the faculties, the students, credit and noncredit programs, and graduate study.

INTRODUCTION

A number of liberal arts colleges and teachers colleges unaffiliated formally with national evening college and extension organizations offer a limited amount of business education in their evening or extension programs. The great bulk of work in adult education at the college level in the field of business, however, is offered by the 110 members of the Association of University Evening Colleges and by the 65 (after deducting memberships overlapping with AUEC) members of the National University Extension Association. For the year 1957, these institutions appear to have had a combined enrollment in credit courses of approximately 643,752 part-time students in all subjects. Of this number, some 35 per cent took credit courses related to business. This would mean, then, that approximately 225,000 adults took at least one credit course (including correspondence courses) in an evening college or university extension division in some phase of business education during 1957. Approximately half of these were enrolled in the evening colleges, another 35 per cent in land-grant and/or state university extension divisions, and the balance in assorted liberal arts and teachers colleges. These figures represent an increase of approximately 33 per cent over 1951 and about 110 per cent over the enrollment for the five years immediately preceding World War II.[1]

HISTORICAL BACKGROUND

In charting the development of the evening colleges and extension divisions, it is important to keep the similarities and differences between the two types of institutions in mind, for the relationship is often not well understood even by many educators. One may see in historical perspective, however, some of the points of convergence and divergence.[2] The half century between 1875 and 1925 witnessed the appearance in American higher education of new and powerful urges and influences. The sheer multiplication of institutions of higher learning was little short of astounding. In this period of time, some 604 full four-year colleges and institutions were founded. Older institutions found themselves developing programs which carried education off the campus to people not formerly considered the concern of the university. Throughout the land there appeared to be an educational and cultural renaissance. Chautauqua tents dotted the landscape, and almost every small town had its quota of lyceum concerts and lectures. Dr. Eliot's five-foot shelf of books became a national best seller. With the industrialization and urbanization of the country, commerce and industry began to make their wants and needs felt. They wanted trained accountants, sales managers, personnel managers, and a long list of other types of trained men. Thus it seems quite proper to describe this period as one of intellectual and educational ferment, and out of this ferment grew three types of institutions pertinent to this study: (1) the general extension divisions largely confined to the land-grant colleges and/or state universities; (2) the partially or wholly

---

[1] Exact figures on enrollment are impossible to obtain at the present time because of the irregular nature of statistical reporting by the institutions involved. These figures are based on statistics given in *School and Society*, Dec. 7, 1957, p. 372; on statistical reports in *Proceedings of the AUEC*, 1957; and on enrollment figures given in questionnaires submitted to the institutions. Figures released by the U.S. Office of Education quoted in the *New York Times*, June 1, 1958, give the day enrollment in undergraduate business administration as "about 300,000." See also *Statistics of Land-grant Colleges and Universities*, Bulletin 1958, no. 2, U.S. Department of Health, Education, and Welfare.

[2] There are only fragments of printed materials dealing with the recent history and practices of extension education. The evening college has been dealt with in John P. Dyer, *Ivory Towers in the Market Place*, The Bobbs-Merrill Company, Inc., Indianapolis, 1956. There is a brief historical sketch of the extension movement in John R. Morton, *University Extension in the United States*, University of Alabama Press, University, Ala., 1953, pp. 1–12. See also C. O. Thompson, *University Extension in Adult Education*, University of Chicago Press, Chicago, 1943.

tax-supported municipal universities; (3) new functions for the privately endowed colleges or universities in urban areas.

First to emerge, wilt, and then take on new growth was the university general extension plan which had its genesis in certain ideas being developed during the nineteenth century in England. First Cambridge, during the 1870s, and, somewhat later, Oxford put into practice an idea which had been germinating in many minds for how many years no one knew.[3] On its surface it was not a particularly recondite idea. It was simply: Why not take university education to people who cannot attend the university? But it was an idea likely to appeal to American universities fired with a zeal for more democracy and more utilitarianism in education. It was natural, therefore, that American educators should take steps to adapt the idea to American university education.

One after another, American universities—Johns Hopkins, Chicago, Wisconsin, Michigan, and many others—developed extension departments. Soon there was a veritable flood of extension classes all over the country, the contents of the courses being as multipatterned as a landscape seen from an airplane. Any group in any part of the country could get just about anything it wanted, either intellectual or practical. The state universities and land-grant colleges made entire states their campus. Thus, it can be seen that the extension movement was concerned with off-campus education and that the clientele was at first largely rural and small-town. The extension movement remained largely this type of operation until after World War II when certain changes, pointed out later, took place which somewhat altered its nature.

Meantime, the municipal university idea was spreading with the growth of the cities. Prior to 1875, only two municipal colleges or universities existed in the country—the College of Charleston and City College of New York. In the period roughly from 1875 to 1925, nine others were chartered—Louisville, Hunter, Brooklyn, Toledo, Akron, Cincinnati, Wayne in Detroit, Wichita, and Omaha.[4] These municipal universities were largely financed by local taxation; they operated both day and evening programs; and their curricula were geared to the needs of the immediate communities. Since these immediate communities were often heavily industrial and commercial, it is not surprising to find that these municipal colleges and universities early developed programs in business education.

The privately endowed institutions located in urban areas felt the rising pressure for adult educational opportunities and met it by estab-

---

[3] W. S. Bittner, *The University Extension Movement*, Bulletin 1919, no. 84, U.S. Office of Education, 1920, p. 14.

[4] R. H. Eckelberry, *The History of the Municipal University in the United States*, Bulletin 1932, no. 2, U.S. Office of Education, p. 7.

lishing residential evening divisions. The demand existed right at their own doors. They had but to open their facilities evenings and Saturdays to create on the campus a new adult education division serving the needs of the community. Soon buildings were ablaze with lights every night, and enrollment mounted. Seven of the fifty-five largest evening colleges were established before 1900; forty-one were established between 1900 and 1929. The balance came after 1929. Many are still in the process of formation.

It can thus be seen that the general extension divisions of the state universities and land-grant colleges originally had a rural and small-town orientation while the municipal universities and the privately endowed universities in urban areas were urban phenomena. To a limited extent this is still true. Few of the state universities and land-grant colleges have established evening colleges on their campuses, because most of them are located in small towns incapable of supporting an evening college. Only the administrative head is at the college or university. The body is scattered all over the state. Because of the facts outlined above, therefore, programs in business education developed more rapidly in the evening colleges than they did in the general extension divisions. It was not until after World War II that the extension divisions gave full and adequate attention to business education.

The evening college and the extension division also differ functionally. Approximately 25 per cent of the evening colleges have their own curricula, offer their own degrees, and are not necessarily compelled to follow the pattern of the day college. The general extension divisions, on the other hand, with one exception, are largely service divisions of the day colleges in credit programs. As such they administer the day college curricula, and all credits earned by the extension students are registered in the day college records. Naturally it follows that all degrees are awarded through the day college division. Thus the extension divisions by their very nature cannot be innovators with respect to credit courses.

It should be hastily added, however, that evening college and extension division programs in business education tend more and more to overlap and to resemble each other. Of primary importance is the fact that both have the same type of student, namely, the adult. There is also a strong trend among the extension institutions to develop residential centers in urban areas within the state.[5] These residential centers resemble very strongly the evening college. In fact many of them *are* evening colleges. Virtually every university extension division located in a state where there are extensive urban areas has set up such centers—Michigan, Michigan State, Wisconsin, Tennessee, Alabama, Georgia, Minne-

---

[5] In 1953, twenty-three institutions maintained ninety-four resident extension centers. Morton, *op. cit.*, p. 106.

sota, California, for example. These urban centers, of course, represent a rather sharp break with the past. In this chapter other differences and similarities between the two types of institutions will be brought out as the discussion proceeds. The discussion will include both a review and an appraisal of evening colleges and extension divisions.

In making the analysis, the author has depended largely upon the answers to a very comprehensive questionnaire submitted to the members of the Association of University Evening Colleges, the National University Extension Association, and scattered liberal arts colleges and teachers colleges. (From the members of AUEC, there was an 89 per cent response; from NUEA members, a 70 per cent response. From the fifty scattered institutions, the response was negligible.) After the results of the questionnaire were tabulated, the author held personal interviews with twenty leaders divided evenly between the two types of institutions. In order to avoid a space-consuming repetition of footnotes citing the questionnaire, the reader is advised that unless otherwise stated the facts are from the questionnaires. In addition to the above sources, bulletins and catalogs of the institutions were consulted. Secondary sources, of course, have been utilized.

The analysis is classified under five major headings: (1) the undergraduate curricula, (2) the faculty, (3) undergraduate students, (4) the noncredit programs, and (5) graduate programs.

UNDERGRADUATE BUSINESS CURRICULA

Two points about the business curricula of the evening colleges and extension divisions stand out. One is that their curricula are tied closely to those of the day colleges of business administration. The other is that, in theory at least, there is virtual unanimity of opinion as to what the curricula in the evening and extension divisions ought to be.

As stated previously, approximately 25 per cent of the evening colleges have the administrative autonomy customarily associated with any degree-granting college within a university. Despite this autonomy, however, their business curricula are virtually duplicates of the day college programs, although differing in their approach to subject matter and in teaching techniques. For the other 75 per cent of the evening colleges and for all the extension divisions reporting, the curricula in credit programs do not differ, at least formally, from those of the day college. Even course numbers and course titles are often the same. In short, they are satellites of the day colleges. Only nine institutions say their programs are designed especially for adults, without reference to the day college, but this may indicate the beginning of an important change of direction which could be contagious.

There is a high degree of theoretical agreement among the evening and extension divisions on what they hope to accomplish for the student. By and large, they agree that the general objective is the development of students oriented toward business but with a well-rounded general education. Sixteen institutions, however, admit that their purpose is to develop vocationally specialized students.

An examination of the bulletins and catalogs of the responding institutions reflects in general this trend toward an almost equal division between the so-called liberal arts and business subjects. Based on a 120-semester-hour degree program in business administration, the median minimum degree requirement in liberal arts is 54 hours. The median minimum degree requirement in business subjects is 51 hours. The range in liberal subjects, however, is from 21 to 73 hours minimum requirement.

When these figures are translated into nonstatistical language they assume added significance. The statement that the median minimum degree requirement in liberal arts is 54 hours can be misleading. One must be careful to observe that this means that there are as many institutions requiring less than 54 hours in liberal arts as there are institutions requiring more than 54 hours. The range, therefore, is perhaps more indicative than the median. Nine institutions require as little as 21 hours of liberal arts subjects in the business curriculum. Two require as many as 73 hours.

The fact is inescapable that the business curricula in at least half the institutions are from moderately to grossly inadequate in so-called liberal subjects.

Deans and directors were asked to list the most important subjects they would recommend to a business student if there were no specific degree requirements. These subjects are classified in two fields: (1) liberal arts subjects, (2) professional subjects. (For some unknown reason the replies of the evening college people were much fuller than those in extension.) The following listing of subjects, in order of their importance in the minds of administrative heads, seems significant.

For the evening college (relative importance):

Liberal Arts	Professional Subjects
English	Economics
Psychology	Finance and statistics
Philosophy	Accounting
History	Personnel and labor relations
Sociology	Business law
Mathematics	General management
Political science	Business communications
Science	Marketing
Speech	
Languages	

For the extension divisions (relative importance):

Liberal Arts	Professional Subjects
Social studies	Economics
English	Labor and human relations
Psychology	Accounting
Speech	Business law
Mathematics	
Philosophy	

It is obvious from these lists of subjects that there is a high degree of agreement between the evening colleges and the extension divisions on the most important subjects in both the liberal arts and professional fields. In the liberal arts field, English and social studies are ranked high. In the professional subjects, both groups rate economics, accounting, labor relations, and business law high. The surprising thing is that mathematics is given a relatively low position in the liberal arts field and is not listed at all among professional subjects. This may indicate a lack of understanding of the part mathematics is coming to play in the business field. It would be interesting to ask these same deans and directors ten years from now to make a similar list. The chances are that due to the new emphasis on statistical studies and the electronic computer, mathematics will rank close to the top.

It should be added that many of the deans and directors are concerned over sharp lines of demarcation between what is considered a liberal subject and what is considered a vocational or professional subject. They feel that this line is too arbitrarily defined and that labels are too readily accepted as designating liberal studies. They point out, for example, that although a course labeled "marketing" is ordinarily considered a professional course, it may give, if properly taught, as much of an insight into the way people live and think as a course in sociology. Similarly a course in labor relations may bring into sharp focus an important segment of American history. Other subjects, they point out, also have a great deal of liberal arts content.

This contention, of course, has considerable merit, assuming that the professional courses are taught with liberal values in mind. There is strong evidence, however, that both the liberal arts people and the business people operate in insulated compartments. A business professor who teaches a course in money and banking all too often teaches this as a technical course without regard for the significance of this business activity in the social and political history of this country, especially since the turn of the century. At the same time, the history professor in his course in recent American history will discuss such matters as free silver, the gold standard, and our national banking system with little regard for enough technical information to enable the student to grasp relationships between a banking and monetary system and the life of an individual. The two professors never seem able to work cooperatively. Undoubtedly a major reason is that the history professor as a student never saw the need for courses in money and banking and the business professor never saw the need for courses in history.

Although most deans and directors of both types of institutions say that their general objective is the development of students generally oriented toward business but with a well-rounded liberal education, a breakdown of course offerings with respect to major fields somewhat modifies this point of view. Approximately 80 per cent of the institutions reporting state that they have an undergraduate specialized major in a field of business. The median number of such undergraduate majors is five but the range is from one to thirteen majors. The most frequent undergraduate majors are as follows:

Accounting	Marketing
Advertising	Personnel management
Banking and finance	Real estate
Economics	Secretarial science
General business	Statistics
Industrial relations	Transportation
Insurance	

It does not require more than a modicum of profundity to see that if a student takes 60 hours in the liberal arts and is permitted an undergraduate area of specialization (the major) of some 30 to 36 hours, this leaves but 24 to 30 hours for courses designed to orient him to the whole field of business. The result seems to be that there is more vocational specialization in many of the curricula than the deans and directors are aware of or will readily confess.

The above, of course, raises the question of what the business curriculum ought to be in the evening colleges. (Extension divisions are excluded from discussion here because they strictly follow day college curricula.)

An intelligent answer to this question is hard to come by. Evening and day colleges ought to be making a continuing and comprehensive study of their curricula, but there is little consistent effort being made in this direction.

At the present time, thinking (or lack of it) on curricula may be divided into three segments: (1) The evening college curriculum is faulty if it imitates the day college curriculum; adult "needs," it is maintained, are different, and thus the curriculum must be different. (2) The evening college curriculum is bad unless it copies the day college's; this is based on the rather smug assumption that the day college curriculum is exactly what it ought to be. (3) In between these two conflicting points of view the rest drift to and fro on the misty flats, uncertain of what ought to be done.

A major portion of the problem lies in the fact that too many day and evening college faculties have no fundamental philosophical concept of what business education ought to be. This is perhaps more characteristic of evening college deans than of day deans. They have not intelligently faced up to the question of what the university's primary obligations are and what training can best be left to business itself. Nor have they developed a satisfactory rationale for what they are doing.

In the opinion of the author, there are at least three reasons why so little thinking and experimentation are going on regarding evening college business curricula: (1) Conformity to the day college pattern offers a more pleasant course for the evening college dean than significant departures from the norm. (2) The organizational patterns of evening colleges and the previous training of the deans inhibit unorthodoxy. (3) There is no leadership for the study of the problems of business education in the evening colleges.

The university evening college in its present form is a comparatively recent development in the field of higher education. As has been the case with every new form of higher educational activity, the evening college has had to struggle for recognition and status in the university complex. In the beginning (and in some cases even now) the evening college was viewed with distrust or animosity on the part of day college deans and faculties. In most of the better institutions, the evening colleges have won the battle for recognition, but in most cases it has been won on the principle that the evening college will do substantially the same work as the day college and will do it just as effectively. Having found some measure of peace, the evening college dean is reluctant to engage in experimental curricula which will bring down upon him the old charges of soft pedagogy and failure to comply with the requirements of academic traditions. Realizing that nothing is more likely to precipitate combat than curriculum changes, the evening college dean is loath to fight old battles again. It is much more comfortable just to follow the lead of the day college.

The evening college organizational pattern is one which brings into positions of leadership many deans who are unacquainted with the problems of business education. Evening colleges fall roughly into five types: (1) the strictly liberal arts evening college, (2) the strictly business administration evening college, (3) the noncredit evening college such as the University of Chicago's University College and the Division of General Education at New York University where courses for adults are offered almost entirely on a noncredit basis, (4) the strictly technical and engineering evening college, (5) the multidimensional evening college in which both liberal arts and commerce programs, among others, are offered.

The multidimensional type of organization is rapidly coming to be the prevailing one, and in the great majority of instances the deans of this type of evening college do not come from the field of business administration. More often than not (and the author is one of these) the background of the dean is in liberal arts. Thus he is at a disadvantage in dealing with curriculum revision in the business administration division of his college.

Perhaps most important of all, there is no leadership for the study of business education in the evening college comparable to that which exists for liberal education. The Fund for Adult Education supports an institution in Chicago known as the Center for the Study of Liberal Education for Adults. This organization, though small, has had a terrific impact upon the educational thinking of leaders in the field of evening college and extension *liberal* education. It has furnished the answers to a few questions, but its achievements have been more in the nature of putting the problems into sharper focus and then bringing to bear on them pertinent information which already exists or which may be discovered through research. Conferences and seminars supplement the written material. Resource people are made available for national and regional meetings of the Association of University Evening Colleges and the National University Extension Association. Proof of the influence which the center is exerting in the field of liberal education for adults can be obtained by walking into the office of any evening college or extension dean in the country and bringing up the matter of liberal education. The dean quite likely will be prepared to discuss knowingly the problems and possibilities of liberal education for adults. *But when the subject is switched to the matter of business education for adults, it is obvious that his grasp of it is much less adequate.* The day college dean, through the American Association of Collegiate Schools of Business, has access to pertinent materials and discussions. The evening college dean has little to guide his thinking on the philosophy and problems of business education. The establishment of a center for the study of business education for adults, or its equivalent, is the most important move which could be made to provide education for the evening college dean in the philosophy and rationale of what he is trying to do. Evening college and extension deans and faculties must have an understanding of their goals and objectives and clear concepts of what their problems are. They do not have these now.

The evening and day divisions of business education have many things in common, but differences are significant enough that specific questions must be raised and answered regarding evening college business education for adults. The problem is not neatly solved by an expression one often hears, "You have a good day college. Why don't you just follow it?" The injunction to the evening colleges that they follow the curriculum of the day colleges has its points. It has the virtues of simplicity and uniformity. It enables the day and evening college deans to say, "We have the same degree program for everyone. This ensures that degrees in business administration are on the same level and that uniform standards are upheld. The only difference in the day and evening program is one of techniques and teaching methods. These are adjusted so as to provide learning situations which take into account the differences in age levels. Otherwise the two curricula are exactly the same."

This is an attractive argument and has considerable validity, but at the same time it has in it some questionable assumptions. It assumes that the needs of the mature adult student and the immature day college student are the same, an assumption which will bear investigation. It also assumes there is no need to take into account discrete local needs which may not exist in the general region served by the university. There is the third assumption that "standards are best maintained if there is a complete duplication of curriculum." These assumptions ought to be studied very carefully, for the uncritical acceptance of them may lead to blind alleys.

Construction or revision of the evening college curriculum is more complicated and more difficult than the same sort of revision in the day college. This is due largely to the fact that the evening college must attempt to meet the needs of a heterogeneous group.

A typical evening college class of 25 members ordinarily will have a distribution somewhat as follows: 3 young and inexperienced people not long out of high school and looking for a place in the world of business; 7 people between the ages of 25 and 40 who are fully matriculated degree students; 10 people between the ages of 25 and 50 who are taking special courses to improve certain skills; and 5 junior executives about 35 years of age who already have degrees (usually a bachelor of arts or a bachelor of engineering) who are seeking to orient themselves more fully to the field of business.

Obviously it is difficult with this wide range of background and experience to devise any one curriculum which will satisfy the needs of all. In contrast to a single curriculum in the day college which serves a homogeneous group with similar objectives, the ideal evening college curriculum must be threefold: (1) There needs to be the degree curriculum, probably closely resembling the day college degree program. (2) In addition, there needs to be a series of package or certificate programs below the degree level for those who wish specialization at the undergraduate level or who wish only special courses. (3) Finally, there should be an assortment of noncredit courses for those seeking a wide orientation to the field of business but who have little concern with traditional college credit.

Even though the degree programs of the day and evening college probably should closely resemble each other, there are good reasons why they may need to differ in certain details. The evening college, by and large, serves a rather restricted local area, whereas the day college ordinarily serves a region. The evening college, therefore, must be more cognizant of the needs of business in its restricted area than the day college. In New Orleans, for example, Tulane's evening college serves the immediate community which is trade-oriented, especially toward Latin America. There is reason, therefore, why the evening college may require a foreign language and courses in the trade and transportation areas. The day college program can offer the student a choice between a foreign language and other subjects, and training in trade and transportation courses can be much more casual. Similar differences exist in institutions located in highly industrialized communities, or in others with special problems and needs which the day college is not in a position to meet.

The important thing, however, is not whether these suggestions are valid. The really vital consideration is that it is high time that the evening college curricula in business subjects receive searching study and analysis in the light of student and community needs. Regrettably this is not happening in most institutions.

THE FACULTY

In 1951–1952, evening colleges that reported showed a total of 3,789 faculty members, including nonbusiness as well as business instruction. In 1955–1956, the number was 4,945, an increase of approximately 31 per cent. During the same periods, extension divisions reported 1,669 and 2,369, an increase of approximately 42 per cent. Combining the two categories gives a total of 5,458 in 1951–1952 and 7,314 in 1955–1956, an over-all increase for both institutions of approximately 34 per cent.[6]

These faculty members were recruited from three sources:

1. Less than 10 per cent were full-time evening college or extension faculty.

2. Approximately 40 per cent (a few institutions went as high as 71 per cent) were part-time faculty recruited outside the university.

[6] Since all institutions did not report, it is obvious that this figure is too low. While the increase of 34 per cent is probably fairly accurate, the total number of faculty members in the combined institutions would be nearer 8,000.

3. Approximately 50 per cent were from the day college faculty, carrying these courses either as a part of their regular load or as an overtime load.

There is a pronounced trend toward using more day faculty members, making these courses part of their regular teaching load, and using more part-time teachers recruited outside the university. Extension institutions show a somewhat greater use of faculty members on an overload basis, but the difference is not significant. There is a trend away from the use of full-time evening college and extension teachers, despite the fact that most deans and directors are strongly of the opinion that they need more full-time people in their division. This apparent dichotomy is explainable in terms of what seems the most pragmatical of several choices.

While most of the deans feel that a better job could be done if the evening college had a permanent full-time faculty, at the same time they realize that the job of adult education is one in which the entire university ought to be concerned and in which it ought to participate. The evening college is by its very nature isolated chronologically in that it begins its work at a time when day college people are going home for the evening. If the evening college further isolates itself by having a separate faculty, the tendency is for the rest of the university to think of adult education as being the function of the evening college only. If the dean can secure on a regular and continuing basis the services of interested day college faculty members as a part of their regular load, he is more likely to find a greater understanding of the problems of adult education in the day divisions. What appears to be a gradually developing pattern is this: the evening college will come to have a relatively small core faculty augmented as much as possible by day college people teaching as a part of their regular load. Remaining vacancies will then be filled with part-time instructors from outside the university or by regular faculty members who teach as an overload.

It is the almost overwhelming opinion of the deans that under the circumstances faculty improvement should be in this order:

1. More and better day faculty teaching as a part of their regular load
2. More full-time evening college or extension teachers as a core faculty
3. More and better part-time faculty from outside the university
4. More and better day college people teaching as an overload

Almost all the deans and directors of both types of institutions, however, find considerable fault with both the part-time off-campus faculty member and, at times, with the full-time day college faculty member who teaches in the evening or in extension. The most frequent criticism of the off-campus teacher is that he often uses poor teaching methods and that he cannot or will not attend faculty and/or committee meetings. One out of three institutions report dissatisfaction with day college faculty members. The chief sources of difficulty in this category seem to be:

1. A tendency of the faculty members frequently to look upon evening or extension students as inferior

2. Their inability or refusal to adapt teaching methods to the interest level of the adult students

3. Their general lack of interest in evening college or extension work

Approximately 60 per cent of the evening college administrators feel that the salary scale for part-time faculty is satisfactory.[7] In extension divisions, however, there is more of an inclination on the part of the deans and directors to feel that the salary scale is unsatisfactory. This feeling may be due to the fact that travel of the extension faculty member to and from the extension center makes his work more difficult and fatiguing. In both types of institutions the pay scale for part-time overload and nonregular faculty is very low. This may be attributed to two factors: (1) With many of the off-campus teachers who have somewhat lucrative positions in the business world, the matter of income from teaching is unimportant. The fact that he is a member of a university faculty is his chief compensation. (2) In many universities the evening and extension divisions have been used as profit-making enterprises for the university. Unfortunately many deans have concurred in this in an attempt to secure status for their division of the university. If his division, he reasons, can turn over to the university an annual surplus of $300,000 to $500,000 he feels that this is an important factor in securing recognition from the university administration. Thus many of the deans themselves are responsible for the low salary schedule for part-time people.

Some 60 per cent of the institutions reporting say that the dean of the day business college is warmly cooperative; about 30 per cent say he is somewhat cooperative; and approximately 10 per cent say that he is cool and negative toward evening college or extension work. While this is encouraging, the attitude of day college faculties in many instances leaves much to be desired from the standpoint of the evening or extension dean or director. The difficulties may be grouped around what may be called "role conflicts."

[7] Figures are not available for extension divisions, but for the evening colleges the median salary for a 3-semester-hour course taught by an off-campus part-time instructor is $375. The median figure for the full-time faculty member teaching as an overload is exactly the same, although many institutions base their compensation on the rank of the faculty member, and thus the figure for them would be somewhat higher than $375 but ordinarily does not exceed $425. A sampling reveals that part-time teachers' salaries in extension divisions are somewhat higher. *Report of the Committee on Study and Research,* Association of University Evening Colleges, November, 1957.

The first of these is that of scholar versus popularizer. Many day college instructors feel that in the evening college they must lower their customary academic standards and merely popularize knowledge. In many instances they also feel that the time consumed in reorganizing course material and in devising new teaching techniques for evening college work takes time that they should be spending on their own research or on their graduate courses.

Secondly, the conflict over professional advancement is one of paramount importance. The requirement of a faculty member in the evening or extension division is good teaching and not research and scholarly production. Salary increases, tenure, and the like may depend primarily upon the faculty member's role as a scholar in the university, whereas success in the evening college may depend primarily upon the ability to "go over" with the adult students. The natural tendency of the faculty member is to devote himself largely to the phase of his work which brings the maximum tangible results in salary, tenure, and scholarly reputation.

Thirdly, the time when evening college classes meet and the fatigue factor set up certain conflicts. As one faculty member expressed it: "I like my evening class. It is stimulating. But the time it is offered almost destroys my pleasure in teaching it. There just isn't any good time to come back to the campus at night to teach a course."

Faculty attitudes toward evening college and extension work, on the whole, may be summarized under three headings: These attitude complexes are: (1) The evening college or extension work is the same as the day college. (2) Evening college and extension programs are different and better. (3) Evening college and extension work are different and worse. There appears to be at the present time no way of determining the prevalence of any of these categories.[8]

Both the evening and extension institutions show concern over the impending tide of increased enrollment in the day colleges, which situation they fear will result in the day colleges recalling many of their best teachers for work wholly in day classes. Three out of four answers reflect this fear. If their fears are realized, and they most probably will be, the deans have no alternative except to bring in part-time teachers from outside the university. This eventuality again raises the problem of the part-time teacher and the quality of his work.

Perhaps no problem strikes closer at the heart of good instruction in the evening and extension divisions than that of the widespread use of relatively untrained teachers who possess little or no academic orientation. A foundation-sponsored study of this problem was made by the

[8] See Dyer, *op. cit.*, chap. 5.

University of Bridgeport subsequent to the author's own research on this matter.[9] This study points up and amplifies several facets of the problem which were encountered by the author. Approximately 70 per cent of the large and 90 per cent of the small urban universities use part-time faculty members, it is pointed out. The chief advantages claimed most frequently are that these part-time people make for good public relations with business and industry and are less costly than full-time faculty members. The greatest disadvantages were listed as lack of institutional orientation, poor preparation for teaching assignments, poor teaching methods, unavailability for student conferences, and a high rate of absenteeism. The study clearly makes no good case for the part-time teacher. Unless this type of teacher has had previous teaching experience and has been put through a thorough program of training, "mediocrity is not only tolerated but positively encouraged under such conditions."

It is small wonder that many evening and extension deans are concerned, even alarmed, over the wide use they are forced to make of this type of teacher, but existing conditions and the fact that they are likely to become worse in the future put the institutions in the position of using these people or closing down many of their classes. Although the average evening college or extension dean shivers at the thought of turning away registrants, it actually seems desirable to restrict offerings to those which can be done well. This, of course, would be a move away from the colossus complex which is characteristic of so many institutions. With day, evening, and extension enrollments growing and the inadequate number of teachers being developed by graduate schools of business throughout the country, the deans feel trapped.

They recognize clearly that whatever difference, if any, there is in standards between day and evening colleges may be the result of the large number of part-time people they are forced to use. Probably none of these deans would deny that a faculty 50 to 60 per cent of which is composed of nonprofessional teachers is not likely to produce as high-type work as the professionally trained teacher whose entire career is devoted to teaching and research.

This is not meant to be a blanket indictment of part-time teachers, for many of them do good work and are anxious to learn more and more about the art of teaching. A particularly advantageous use can be made of these people in such courses as accounting, marketing research techniques, and other similar fields. Ordinarily these part-time instructors do not do well with courses involving theory and principles. There is also a severe limitation which ought to be placed on them as teachers of graduate courses.

[9] A condensed version of the study released in October, 1958, rather than the voluminous complete document has been used here.

The above comments on the part-time teacher also are not intended to indicate that the teaching of the full-time faculty member is always superior. Evidence collected for this study shows pretty clearly that there has been no substantial change or improvement in the teaching methods of the day and/or evening instructors during the past thirty-five years. The case method seems to be gaining an advantage over the lecture method of instruction, and more frequent use is made of visual materials, but, on the whole, the matter of effective teaching methods for adults or for the youth in the day colleges is receiving inadequate attention.

It is urgent that faculty development become a major area of joint action by the day and evening divisions. The problem is only complicated when the day division withdraws regular faculty members from their evening teaching. Such a procedure may solve the day dean's problem of teaching load, but the business community suffers. If American business is to continue to thrive, it needs two types of personnel in supervisory and management capacities. One of these is the young man or woman fresh out of a school of business administration, inexperienced but with many good ideas which he or she can bring to the employer. The other type of personnel is already on the job, already experienced in and oriented to many phases of the company's problems but lacking in college training. The day college can supply the first type of man or woman. The evening colleges and the extension divisions, *and they alone,* can supply the necessary training for the second type of man or woman. It is the unique role of evening colleges and extension divisions to give to the individual and to business an in-service type of training.

Day colleges must recognize the necessity for adopting policies which will help carry out both these types of functions. In too many instances that is not the case now. Information indicates that relationships between evening colleges and extension divisions and day colleges, on the whole, are pleasant and cooperative. But this attitude must not be too optimistically interpreted. This does not mean that the day colleges are willing, at the present time, to spend the time and effort necessary to assist in developing the evening colleges and extension divisions into a really strong segment of the university's services to the business community. In many cases the author has found the attitude of the day college dean to be this: "Yes, the evening college is coming along very well. Unfortunately, however, our best faculty people have such a heavy load in the daytime that we are not able to spare them for evening or extension work."

What he is really saying is that one half the program is to be strengthened at the expense of the other half.

UNDERGRADUATE STUDENTS

It would be very helpful if an accurate breakdown of figures on evening college and extension division enrollment in business education could be given, but this is not possible. The evening college and extension people, especially the evening college people, have developed no accurate and uniform method of reporting enrollment figures, and thus the Office of Education reports are inadequate. It is impossible to determine accurately even the total number of adult students in the two larger categories of credit and noncredit courses, to say nothing of a breakdown into smaller areas, such as liberal arts, engineering, business, etc. The questionnaires returned do not reflect accurate enrollment because 11 per cent of the evening colleges and 30 per cent of extension divisions did not reply. Table 22-1 gives a close approximation of enrollments.[10]

TABLE 22-1

Type of student	1951–1952	1955–1956	Per cent increase
Evening college (credit)............	100,230	128,500	28.2
Extension division (credit).........	78,763	88,150	12.0
Evening college (noncredit)........	10,500	15,000	42.9
Extension division (noncredit)......	14,800	38,500	160.1
Total........................	204,293	270,150	32.2
Other colleges (credit)............	12,000	16,000	
Other colleges (noncredit).........	?	18,000	
Grand total....................	216,293	304,150	

The period from 1951–1952 to 1955–1956 was not the time of greatest enrollment gains, however. Between 1945 and 1950, the immediate postwar years, enrollment in evening colleges and extension divisions slightly more than doubled. This was the time when the GI invaded the campus and sent administrators scurrying to provide classroom space and teachers. With the advent of the GI, adult education received the greatest stimulus in its history. Thousands of adults found they could learn and earn at the same time and do well in both fields. GI enrollment has dwindled almost to a trickle in 1958, but the impetus it generated still is felt.

[10] This table is a breakdown of the figures given in the introduction, adjusted to percentage figures for various enrollments given in answer to the questionnaire. The total figures given in questionnaire answers are inaccurately low, but the percentages of change appear fairly accurate.

The passing of the GI student did not, on the whole, mean a decrease in enrollment. Others took his place or, in many instances, he continued as a student after his benefits had expired. The sharp upward enrollment curve of the 1940s has leveled off into a plateau, but it is inclined upward. The heritage of this GI enrollment is reflected in the fact that in 1958, thirty-seven evening colleges have an enrollment in business education larger than the corresponding day college. Extension figures on this item are too sketchy to have relevance.

Describing adult students and their problems is more difficult than counting their noses. Ninety-one per cent of evening and extension students are part-time. Nine per cent of them are under twenty; 78 per cent are between the ages of twenty and forty; and 13 per cent are over forty. The median time required for a degree for adult students starting as freshmen is eight and a half years, with some students needing as many as twelve years to earn a degree. Approximately 10 per cent of those who enroll in a degree program complete it, but this is not surprising in view of the length of time required for a degree and because of the fact that many adults, who have no idea of completing the requirements, register in a degree program but merely take special courses or fall by the wayside. However, the number who do persist to the end is often a matter of considerable wonder to deans and directors.

It should be pointed out that a new type of student is making his presence felt in the evening college and extension division. Up until about 1950, almost all the students in these institutions were those who had missed an education in their youth. They, however, did not come within the classification of underprivileged, because most of them were holding down positions in business or industry which enabled them to maintain a fairly decent standard of living. Since 1950, the new type of student has become increasingly obvious. He already has a college degree, but he finds a need for more training in business education at the undergraduate level. The two most common degrees held by these, as has been pointed out, are in engineering and liberal arts. They received their degrees and went into business or industry only to find that they needed additional training. Many of them have reached the stage of middle management. They are, on the whole, junior executives who find that more training in business education is necessary if they are to progress.

This same type of student, as will be pointed out later, is also swelling the rising tide of demand for graduate work in the evening or through extension courses.

The adult student has certain characteristics which set him apart from the younger day student. He appears to be better motivated, more serious, and has more definite goals. He wants to apply immediately what he learns and thus is often critical of theoretical business courses or those in the liberal arts. His motivational patterns are not difficult to analyze. They are composed largely of urges toward success, toward improving himself in his present job, or toward securing a better job. Above all, he is much more sensitive to learning situations than the younger student; that is to say, he is more appreciative of good teaching and more intolerant of bad teaching. Many day college faculty members have found to their great amazement that the adult student will not tolerate the sloppy teaching sometimes foisted off on a hapless day student. He has paid his money for tuition and he wants everything he can get. He is also extremely sensitive to personal relations between himself and his instructors. Perhaps because he feels a bit insecure, he is likely to resent keenly any sarcastic or disparaging remarks which teachers sometimes resort to. The other side of the picture is that no one responds more readily to courtesy and good teaching than the adult student.

On the whole, he suffers from five major disadvantages. Deans and directors feel these are: (1) lack of time for study due to job pressures; (2) conflicting responsibilities between his course work and his home and social responsibilities; (3) fatigue; (4) difficulty in using the library or conferring with instructors due to the limited amount of time he spends on the campus or in the building where the extension center is housed; (5) courses too often not adapted to his mature levels of interest.

How effectively the adult student learns is a matter of some debate in certain quarters. There are those who accuse evening colleges and extension divisions of fostering "soft pedagogy." A number of deans and directors are in the midst of studies aimed at discovering the truth about the matter. One out of four institutions reporting say that they have objective evidence which sheds light on relative academic achievement. Those who report objective evidence uniformly indicate that the modal response shows a slightly higher median but a larger range for evening college students than for day students. There is a considerable body of evidence which indicates that the good evening or extension student is slightly superior (probably because of greater maturity) to the good day college student. It is also reported that the average student is slightly better, but that the poor student is much poorer. Undoubtedly this latter condition is due to the fact that the day colleges are often more selective in their admission policies.

A preliminary study completed recently by the Center for the Study of Liberal Education for Adults offers substantial evidence that adulthood is no deterrent to academic achievement.[11] "Evidence suggests that adult students both in evening colleges and in university extension have

---

[11] *Ability and Achievement of Evening College and Extension Students,* Center for the Study of Liberal Education for Adults, Chicago, 1958.

intellectual ability and achievement at least equal to that of their undergraduate counterparts," the report states. "Yet the assumption that adult students are less able stubbornly persists," it continues. "This misconception is itself an important cause of poor instruction since it misleads instructors into stretching out or watering down the subject matter of their courses in a kindly but condescending effort to ease up on the adult student. These procedures may produce mediocre accomplishment which is then interpreted as confirming the preconceived notion that adult students on the whole are not very capable."

In defending this thesis the study reports on research which has been done in a number of institutions in an attempt to discover the extent of differences between our adult evening college and extension students and regular day students.

At the University of Minnesota and at five other university extension divisions, the mental capacity of the extension students with that of the day students was measured by tests of high validity. The results are quoted as follows:

The evidence indicates that the measured abilities of extension and non-extension students are essentially equal. In some universities the extension students have higher abilities and in others the full-time students are slightly superior, but the differences are not very large at any university. They do indicate, however, that any existing superiority is found within the adult group. The scores of the poorest extension students are as low as, and sometimes lower than, those of the poorest residence students, but the best extension students are probably a little more capable than the best non-extension students.

Breaking this down further, the study shows:

No significant difference on the ACE Test, though the mean score of residence students was slightly higher

Extension students significantly higher (at the 1 per cent level of confidence) on vocabulary scores

No significant difference in speed-of-comprehension scores

Extension students higher (significant at the 5 per cent level of confidence) on the level-of-comprehension score

Studies of adult achievement made in both extension divisions and evening colleges reflect the same favorable comparisons between adult and day college students. It is reported that fifty pairs of comparable day and evening classes were studied to determine differences, if any, in achievement. In each pair the instructor, subject matter, and examinations were the same. Twenty-six extension or evening classes were superior, ten were equal, and fourteen inferior to the achievement of the day classes. In few classes were the differences very great, and the results were similar on either objective or subjective examinations.

At Roosevelt University twenty-four pairs of day and evening college students in the degree credit courses were selected from the registration records, matched on the basis of sex, number of credit hours completed, and the ACE Psychological Comprehensive Total Score Test. Each group was given the same battery of achievement examinations with the result that "the evening students demonstrated roughly the same achievement as the day students."

At De Paul University, thirty-seven pairs of male students in the College of Commerce were matched with an equal number from the evening division. Again differences were insignificant, with the evening college students scoring slightly higher in the Cultural Achievement Test.

At the University of Pittsburgh a slightly modified plan was developed with the result that "no statistically significant differences between the two groups emerged."

The study, of course, being a preliminary one does not claim to have settled the matter for all time. It does show, pretty clearly, however, that the notion of "soft pedagogy" in the extension and evening divisions is probably a myth. Nevertheless, evidence collected by the author suggests that the evening college and extension divisions would be better institutions if they could devise a method by which admission could be more selective. The rapid growth in enrollment has brought in a significant number of adult students who simply have no business being in college even on a part-time basis. It is estimated that approximately 25 per cent of the students in evening and extension classes should not be there, a percentage, one suspects, which would also apply to the comparable day divisions. A policy of greater selectivity is easier to adopt in the evening colleges which are largely parts of privately endowed universities than in extension divisions which are essentially limited to state colleges and universities.

Most deans agree that their divisions could do a better job if this lower group of poor students could be kept out. The absence of a selective process may be attributed to two sets of circumstances: (1) Evening college and extension divisions have been built on a volume basis, and some deans find it necessary to continue to boast of the fact that theirs is the largest college or division in the university. This volume enrollment, of course, greatly increases university income. In certain instances, higher administrative officials have encouraged the evening divisions in maintaining a large enrollment even though a significant percentage of enrollees were not capable of doing college work. (2) Administrative machinery which would make a more highly selective plan possible is extremely difficult, if not impossible. Most, if not all, of the most acceptable college entrance tests are not designed for students at the adult level, but even if they were, administering them to all adults seeking enrollment would be of the utmost difficulty. The enforcement of a regulation which would require all adults to take a preentrance test probably would deprive the evening or extension division of as many good students as it did of poor ones.

In the author's opinion, the present liberal enrollment policies of most of the institutions will have to continue for the foreseeable future. For practical reasons the weeding-out process will have to take place after the student has completed enough courses to demonstrate his inability to do college work. Even here, however, caution must be exercised, for in many instances the good adult student who has been out of touch with intellectual activity for a period of years does not hit his stride until he has completed several courses.

NONCREDIT PROGRAMS

The adult noncredit programs in business subjects are comparatively recent innovations for the evening colleges. This type of work has gone on for a somewhat longer period of time in extension divisions, but for both, the present major emphasis on this type of work is comparatively recent—that is, within the past ten years. At the present time, approximately half the evening colleges and 75 per cent of the extension divisions are offering noncredit courses in the field of business. The median number of courses being offered in the evening colleges is eight and for the extension divisions thirty-one. For noncredit courses for adults in the field of liberal education these figures are almost the reverse, with the evening divisions doing more in the field of liberal education for adults than the extension divisions and the extension divisions doing more work in noncredit courses in business education.

The noncredit course is exactly what the name implies. It is a course which ordinarily has no examinations and carries no course credit toward a degree. In form it may range from a one-day conference for electrical equipment distributors to a year's program for executive development. It may be held on the campus, at a local hotel, or at a residential center off the campus. It is a very flexible sort of program designed to meet the immediate needs of business groups for information, usually in a rather specialized field. The most frequent subjects for these courses are:

1. Executive training
2. Investments
3. Real estate
4. Insurance
5. Labor relations
6. Supervisory training

7. Accounting
8. Taxes
9. Transportation
10. Secretarial
11. Problems of special groups

There is nothing approaching unanimity of opinion among the deans and directors as to what the nature of these courses ought to be and of what their value is in the university offerings. The evening college people feel that the relatively short (six to eight weeks) course is the most effective. The longer course (eight to fifteen weeks) the extension people find preferable. Both agree that the short conference (one to five days) is the least effective. There is also a considerable difference of opinion between the evening college and extension people over the value of these courses. Approximately one-third of the evening college people feel the noncredit programs are of enormous value; another third feel that they are of value but that they should not be permitted to interfere with regular credit programs; another third feel that the programs are too experimental as yet to be evaluated. On the other hand, there seems to be little doubt in the minds of extension people about the value of noncredit courses. Half of them feel that they are of enormous value, and the balance feel that they are of considerable value. No extension people voiced any opposition to this type of course.

Four factors seem to limit the number of noncredit business courses offered by the evening college: (1) The evening college is probably more strongly attached to the academic tradition of credit courses. (2) Major emphasis in noncredit programs in the evening colleges is being placed on liberal education for adults. In this, one can see the influence of the Center for the Study of Liberal Education for Adults. (3) Faculty resources in business education are more limited. (4) The demand for credit courses far exceeds that for noncredit.

Noncredit courses are characterized, especially in the evening colleges, by a lack of planning. Probably because this type of work is still in an experimental stage, no pattern of planning has emerged. About half the evening colleges say they consult with business groups before planning a noncredit course. Those who do not consult with business groups beforehand determine the need for a course by guessing, faculty suggestions, or suggestions of prospective students. One dean perhaps expressed a common practice when he said: "We do it [plan noncredit courses] by trial and error but usually we check with someone." The extension people seem to have their ears more closely tuned to the needs of business and thus appear to work more closely with these groups in course planning. In neither type of institution is there any serious attempt made to evaluate, except possibly to find out whether the participants like the course or not. Virtually no one seems seriously to try to answer: "What did this course actually accomplish for the participants?"

From the standpoint of organization and administration, noncredit programs are classifiable in four categories:[12] (1) quasi-extension activities in business education for adults ordinarily carried out by day divisions which in most instances do not have a regularly organized extension division; (2) the residential type of courses carried on largely by land-grant and/or state universities; (3) courses offered by the extension departments off the campus; (4) courses offered by the evening colleges on the campus.

The quasi-extension type of activity is largely in the field of management and executive development. Since this phase of business education is discussed in Chap. 21, it will not be touched upon here except in very general terms.

Two illustrations will be sufficient at this point.

Perhaps the best-known of the executive development programs is the original Bell Telephone experiment under the auspices of Pennsylvania Bell and the University of Pennsylvania. Conceived as an experiment, it has been much studied and reported. The idea with modifications has spread to other institutions, such as Williams, Dartmouth, and Swarthmore. But this quasi-extension type of adult education activities is not confined to the larger institutions. An example of what may be done in the smaller colleges is the Institute for Executive Leadership at Southwestern in Memphis. Southwestern has no formally organized extension division, but it does have a community-wide leadership program for representatives of local business and industry.

The author thinks it is notable that so many of the smaller liberal arts colleges and other institutions which do not have extension or evening college divisions are developing adult programs for business executives. It is estimated that some 2,000 executives are attending fifty colleges and universities which have executive development programs.[13]

Residential centers are thus far confined largely to the extension divisions of land-grant and/or state universities. They are centers, usually on the campus, serving many different groups from the entire state. In a way, they represent a reversal of older ideas in extension education in that people are brought to the university for residence work instead of the university's being carried outward over the state.

It is impossible to give a complete coverage of the activities of all of

[12] Many of the various types of programs in this field are described in Peter E. Siegle and James B. Whipple, *New Directions in Programming for University Adult Education,* Center for the Study of Liberal Education for Adults, Chicago, 1957.

[13] *New York Times,* June 1, 1958.

these residential centers, but two institutions may be taken as examples: the Continuing Education Center at Michigan State University and the Continuing Education Center at the University of Georgia.

These two types of operations are similar. Both have been heavily supported financially by the Kellogg Foundation; both have similar basic arrangements and types of programs. In each case, the buildings are composed of a modern and comfortable hotel, administrative offices, and an educational wing containing conference rooms, auditorium, library, television facilities, etc.[14] Some idea of the services rendered to business education by these two centers may be gleaned from reports of their operations.

The Continuing Center at Michigan State held eighty-four conferences for 8,292 registrants during 1956–1957. Business conferences made up 23 per cent of the total number held and involved 16 per cent of the total number of registrants. The average business conference tended to be longer than the average nonbusiness conference and to involve smaller groups of people. In general, the people attending these conferences were not top executives taking liberally oriented courses, but they were from middle and lower management, taking courses actually involving techniques—courses such as real estate appraisal, insurance fundamentals, office management, advertising management, and small-business clinics and courses for ready-mix concrete dealers, traffic supervisors, savings and loan managers, electrical contractors, etc.[15]

During the first year of operation of the Georgia Center for Continuing Education (1956–1957), twenty-seven business groups with a total registration of better than 4,000 conferees were served. As in the case of Michigan State, a great variety of business groups was represented at the conferences, groups such as the lumber industry, the poultry industry, the railroads, Southern Bell Telephone Company employees, bankers, fertilizer dealers, accountants, women employed in business, tax appraisers, tire dealers, ice cream manufacturers, etc. Business groups at Georgia represented approximately 20 per cent of the total number of individual registrations.[16]

As mentioned previously, objective evaluations of the various types of

[14] Other universities, of course, have some type of residential centers—Minnesota, Louisiana State University, Oklahoma, Purdue, and Wisconsin, for example. One might also mention UCLA's Arrowhead Center, Columbia's Arden House, NYU's Gould House, Illinois' Allerton House, and the three Adirondack centers of Syracuse University.

[15] Annual Report of the Continuing Education Service, Michigan State University, 1956–1957, pp. 42–46. Also James Harrison, Assistant Director, Continuing Education Service, Michigan State University, to the author, May 27, 1958.

[16] Ernest A. Lowe, Associate Director, Georgia Center for Continuing Education, to the author, May 24, 1958.

conferences conducted at these residential centers have, in most instances, not been made. It appears, however, that this short course-conference type of education at the residential center possesses certain virtues that cannot be overlooked. The programs are usually well planned with university and business group leaders entering reciprocally into the planning. Most of the lectures and discussions are carried on by competent university faculty members with an occasional expert from the outside supplementing their work. This type of education also has the advantage of bringing groups together in a pleasant residential situation where they live and work together, even if for a brief period of time, free from business and other distractions. The question of whether the brevity (average length of conferences is 2.8 days) of the conferences is a serious defect or not cannot be answered at the present time. There is no question, however, but what this type of adult business education is gaining in favor with both the universities and business groups.

The most that can be said about informal, noncredit business education for adults, regardless of the techniques utilized, is that at the present they are in a formative and experimental period. With better planning, especially by the evening colleges, this type of education holds great promise for the future. The author feels that this type of assistance to business groups, even to the lower echelons of business, affords an excellent opportunity for the university and business to utilize the resources of each other. That this is good public relations for the university goes without saying.

GRADUATE PROGRAMS

Of all the topics covered in this study, the one involving graduate work is the most difficult because the whole field of graduate study in the evening colleges and extension divisions is less well organized and more amorphous than any of the other programs.

Only ten evening colleges report that they administer a graduate program in business. The term "administer" is used advisedly because the graduate work and the graduate degree in all instances is in the Graduate School of Business Administration. None of the evening colleges and, of course, none of the extension divisions offer the degree. A somewhat higher number of graduate programs are administered by the extension divisions, but accurate figures on this are not available.

The Master of Business Administration (M.B.A.) is the most common degree. It is the highest degree offered through extension divisions. Three evening colleges report that it is possible to earn the Ph.D. degree in the evening.

Other facts about graduate work are these:

1. The modal number of hours for the master's degree is thirty.

2. For the doctor's degree, the range is sixty to seventy-two hours above the bachelor's degree.

3. For the doctor's degree, all reporting state that a thesis is required. For the master's degree, however, only about half the institutions require a thesis.

4. None of the institutions reporting requires a foreign language for the master's degree, and only one requires it for the doctor's degree.

5. Approximately 22 per cent of the faculty in institutions offering graduate work were from outside the university; 78 per cent were from the day college faculty.

6. Although the figures are unreliable, they indicate that student enrollment in graduate programs has about doubled between 1951 and 1956.

Pressures for more graduate work in the evening and by extension are coming from all sides, but expediency seems to be the only guiding principle now being utilized. The result is that this important phase of business education can almost be characterized by aimless drifting. A need arises in a given area for graduate courses. The evening college or extension division hastily constructs a curriculum and employs whatever instructors are available and thereby inaugurates the graduate program.

There seem to be two cardinal principles which ought to be involved in the development of a graduate program: (1) Such a program must be carefully planned in terms of faculty and other instructional resources of the institution. (2) Graduate programs should function through the graduate division of business education and not through the evening colleges and extension divisions themselves. Otherwise the result may well be cheap graduate degrees.

In some institutions, strange things are happening to graduate programs outside the regular day college division. In one institution, for example, the evening graduate program has been abandoned entirely, because the graduate faculty in business administration found it had so many full-time graduate students that it could not properly administer an evening program.

Under such circumstances, what is the evening college dean to do? Pressures for graduate study in the evening continue to mount. He might devise some sort of nondegree certificate program which would satisfy some of the clientele, but the fact remains that most of the students want a graduate degree.

This and numerous, similar problems can only be approached within a frame of reference suggested in earlier portions of this chapter. Day college divisions must take a fresh look at the role of evening colleges and extension divisions in educating men and women for business.

OBSERVATIONS AND CONCLUSIONS

1. Evening colleges and extension divisions have shown an enormously rapid rate of growth since World War II. Enrollment estimates for undergraduate students show that the number enrolled in the evening and extension divisions in business programs is in excess of the number of students enrolled in day college business programs. The extension divisions and evening colleges, therefore, emerge as a new and potent factor in the training of people for business careers.

2. Rapid growth of numbers has prevented most of the extension divisions and evening colleges from taking stock of themselves and of determining directions in which they should go. This is particularly evident in curriculum revision or lack of it. Evening colleges and extension divisions serve a clientele quite different from that served by the day colleges, yet both types of clientele are necessary to the development of American business. What considerations should be taken into account in considering possible necessary differences in the curricula for the day and evening colleges? Not only has this question not been answered, but there is too little critical thinking about it. One of the major needs is for day and evening divisions to sit down together and think out their curriculum problems. On this matter both groups need guidance.

3. *The major and crucial problem of evening colleges and extension divisions in business education is faculty.* In most institutions a high percentage of the faculty is made up of relatively untrained faculty members from off the campus. This is a deplorable fact. If high standards are to be maintained in the evening and extension divisions, the great bulk of the teaching force must be composed of competent well-trained professional teachers. It is worth repetition to say that this is the most critical aspect of business education in the evening colleges and extension divisions. The evening colleges are particularly vulnerable on this point.

4. Noncredit programs in business education are growing in scope and usefulness. With better planning and more objective evaluation of results, this type of business education has enormous possibilities.

5. Business education at the graduate level in the evening colleges and extension divisions is in a state of uncertainty and flux. The great danger is that many institutions may yield to the increasing demand for graduate education when they do not have the faculty and facilities to do a first-rate job.

CHAPTER 23

PREPARATION FOR BUSINESS IN JUNIOR COLLEGES

Leland L. Medsker

The large number of students enrolled in transfer, terminal, and adult business programs in junior colleges, together with the successful record of former junior college business students, indicate that these institutions will play an increasingly important part in this field in the future. A greater amount of articulation than now exists is needed between two- and four-year colleges in identifying the requisites of business transfer and terminal programs. In both types of programs cognizance must be taken of the individual's role in society and of the growing complexities of business which place a greater premium on social understanding than on skills.

Any consideration of undergraduate business education programs—and, indirectly, of graduate programs—would be grossly incomplete without a review of these programs in the junior or community college. The person interested in business education programs generally is, therefore, inevitably concerned about what the junior college is doing in this field, how what it is doing fits in with the programs of other collegiate institutions, what the problems encountered are, and what the potential role of the junior college in business education appears to be in the immediate years ahead.

Two very discernible and significant characteristics of post-high school education in the United States are: (1) the increasing number of high school graduates who are enrolling in junior colleges either to complete the first two years of a baccalaureate degree or to complete a training program leading directly to employment and (2) the tendency for older youths and adults to enroll in junior colleges in extended day and adult education programs. These characteristics have far-reaching implications for business education at the collegiate level. The very fact that many students pursue a lower-division program in the junior college means that inevitably a certain percentage of them enroll as business administration majors. Many who do not intend to transfer to a senior college prepare for immediate employment in the business field. Of those who return to junior college on a part-time basis, the majority are high school graduates and many are either college graduates or have had one or more years of college work. A large percentage of this adult group enroll in business courses of all kinds. The junior college is, therefore, an important agency for preparing the vast number who are to engage in the managing and the doing of the operations in modern business. It is not an agency to be viewed in isolation, or as something "junior" or incidental, but rather as an important member of a team of institutions working toward common goals in the business enterprise.

The *1958 Junior College Directory* lists 652 institutions classified as junior colleges, though they did not all bear that name. Of this number, 377 or 58 per cent were public, and 275 or 42 per cent were private. Of the publicly controlled two-year colleges, the three principal types are: (1) junior colleges governed by local boards and usually financed by a combination of local taxes and state aid, (2) junior colleges supported and controlled by the state and usually serving as regional institutions, and (3) two-year extension centers of four-year institutions. Enrolled in these two-year institutions in 1957 were 428,511 freshman and sophomore students, 106,139 special students, and 335,070 adults. An analysis of data from the U.S. Office of Education shows that for 1956 the "Level I" institutions, which are essentially the two-year colleges, accounted for 12 per cent of *all* students enrolled in higher education and 18 per cent of all enrollments in public higher institutions. Even more significant is the fact that the Level I institutions enrolled 23 per cent of the students in college for the *first* time. In several states the proportion of students served by the junior colleges is considerably higher than the national average. For example, data from 53 of the 61 colleges in Michigan indicate that for the school year 1957–1958 the two-year colleges enrolled approximately 30 per cent of the students in college for the first time. In California in 1955, approximately 60 per cent of the freshman and sophomore students in all higher institutions, both public and private, were enrolled in the approximately 60 public junior colleges which blanket the state.

This background of the extent and purpose of the junior college makes its actual and potential contribution to the field of business reasonably apparent. The remainder of this chapter is devoted to the specifics of that contribution and is concerned with the nature and extent of business offerings in junior colleges, the general approach of these colleges to business programs, the types of students who enroll in such programs, the teachers of business subjects, and the major issues which demand attention. In the discussion the terms "two-year college," "junior college," and "community college" will be used interchangeably.

The principal source of the objective data to be reported is an over-all study made of the two-year college by the author during the 1956–1957 school year for the Center for the Study of Higher Education at the University of California in Berkeley.[1] This project, which was financed by the Carnegie Corporation of New York and which was limited to an intensive study of the two-year institution in fifteen representative states, not only utilized general questionnaire reports from the various two-year colleges in those states but also involved the specific cooperation of 76 two-year colleges and a number of four-year institutions. Each of the cooperating two-year colleges was visited by the director of the study, and each completed certain specific studies for the project. Other sources of information for the chapter include numerous publications dealing generally with the junior college and special reports from specific agencies and institutions. In addition, the author hopes that his earlier experience as a teacher of business subjects in junior and senior college and as an administrator in different types of two-year colleges will add some insight to the issues and problems at hand.

THE EXTENT OF BUSINESS ENROLLMENTS IN TWO-YEAR COLLEGES

While complete data on the number of students enrolled in any field in any type of institution are difficult to obtain, there is sufficient information to indicate a relatively high enrollment in business programs in junior colleges. Some approximation of the number of students in such programs is possible by the examination of data from several sources.

1. An analysis of the major curricula offered and enrollments in each curriculum for the majority of the public and private junior colleges in the country.[2] It was revealed that in the 342 junior colleges for which 1955 enrollments by curriculum were reported, more than 42,000 regular students (exclusive of students in classes for adults) were enrolled in business curricula. The percentage that business enrollments were of total enrollments varied greatly by institutions as well as by states. How-

[1] For further details and a report on this project, see Leland L. Medsker, *The Junior College: Progress and Prospect*, to be published by McGraw-Hill Book Company, Inc., in 1960.

[2] Data for this analysis were obtained from Jesse P. Bogue (ed.), *American Junior Colleges*, 4th ed., American Council on Education, Washington, 1956. This publication reports, among other items, the major curricula offered and enrollments in each curriculum in the majority of public and private junior colleges in the United States.

ever, the median percentage of students enrolled in business to total enrollments by states was 23.

In addition to the 342 colleges from which enrollment data were obtained, 111 colleges reported that they offered business curricula but gave no enrollment figures. Had such data been submitted, the number reported enrolled in business would have been considerably greater. In fact, there is little doubt that the number of students enrolled in business curricula in junior colleges is well in excess of 50,000.

A further analysis of the data submitted also revealed that, of all students enrolled in business curricula, 19,235 or 45 per cent were in transfer programs, whereas 22,764 or 54 per cent were in programs classified as terminal.

2. A report of enrollments in terminal business programs in a sampling of two-year colleges. From 163 two-year colleges in the fifteen states in which the Berkeley study was conducted, a total of 25,684 students were reported enrolled in business curricula which were designated as terminal in nature. This was the largest number reported in any subject field and even approximated the total of enrollments in *all* terminal curricula.

3. An idea of the extensiveness of enrollments in business education *subjects* (not curricula) in junior colleges in one state is obtainable from a report of the Bureau of Business Education of the California State Department of Education. Out of a total of 58 public junior colleges offering business subjects, 52 reported a total of 96,823 students enrolled in such subjects in 1956. The bureau reported that this represented an increase of 27 per cent over 1954.

Additional data could be cited on the extent of the program in the adult education phase of the junior college. For example, it was found that in the fall semester of 1956, enrollments in business courses accounted for 18 per cent of all adult enrollments in 37 of the cooperating junior colleges. After studying enrollment data and surveying the literature, Chomitz concluded:

It appears from the available studies of enrollments that business education is offered for adults in every classification of junior college surveyed, regardless of size, kind, or location of the institution. These studies show that of all the program areas offered for adults in the colleges surveyed, business education is the one offered by more colleges, covering more courses, and attended by more adults than any other single area. These studies indicated that although in 1936 there was found practically no business education offered for adults in the junior college, less than twenty years later, business was the most prominent area for adults in the junior college.[3]

[3] David L. Chomitz, *Business Education for Adults in the Junior College,* Monograph C-5, South-Western Publishing Company, Cincinnati, 1957, p. 22.

In every way, therefore, the two-year college must be considered an important contributor to the total effort of producing informed and capable workers in the business world.

CURRENT PRACTICES WITH RESPECT TO BUSINESS EDUCATION IN JUNIOR COLLEGES

In the interest of obtaining a complete overview of the nature of the junior college business curriculum, it is important to review each type of program, although special emphasis is placed on the transfer program.

The Lower-division Program

It is obvious that the principal manner in which a two-year college may organize its curriculum for the first two years of a four-year program is through a consideration of the general requirements of the four-year program. There are, however, some dangers in such a generalization. In the first place, a junior college that follows *in detail* the requirements of other institutions stands to lose its own individuality and perhaps to deviate from its own philosophy. In the second place, undergraduate programs in business tend to vary considerably among four-year institutions; thus, the junior college must make allowance for the different types of higher institutions to which its students will transfer. These limitations are discussed as problems in a later section of this chapter. They are merely posed here as partial exceptions to the general rule that the business transfer program in junior colleges must fit reasonably well into the usual undergraduate program.

From observation and investigation, it is apparent that certain evolving characteristics of business administration programs are being carried into the junior college. Since these characteristics are the subject of other chapters of this report, they are not enumerated here except by way of incidental referral to them. Certainly, one marked tendency is for junior college programs in business administration to reflect the trend toward postponement of specialization until upper-division or graduate years. This tendency was not only confirmed orally at the time of the visits made during 1956–1957 by the author to the 76 two-year colleges which cooperated in the Berkeley study but was reaffirmed by a study of the business administration program outlined in the catalogs of 55[4] of the same cooperating institutions. Fifty of these institutions were public (mostly junior or community colleges) and five were private junior colleges. They were distributed over the entire United States. The

---

[4] Included in the institutions studied were the extension centers of the University of Wisconsin and the Pennsylvania State University. The centers in each of these states were counted as one only in computing the total of 55.

majority of the institutions prefaced the catalog outline of required and elective subjects in the preparatory business curriculum by a statement to the effect that the basic lower-division program in the field is that of liberal arts or letters and science. A few of the colleges did not even outline a business administration curriculum but instead referred the reader to the section of the catalog in which the usual letters and science program was outlined and suggested that the student interested in business consult the catalog of the appropriate senior institution for the proper choice of electives while in junior college.

Most of the institutions which did outline the program followed the liberal arts curriculum, though there was some variation in the number and types of specialized or background courses required or recommended over and beyond the more academic courses. Accounting and economics were by far the most commonly recommended subjects, accounting being included in the outline of 40 of the colleges and economics in 38 of them. Business law was specifically mentioned in 14 colleges, introduction to business or business organization in 14, typewriting in 8, and other miscellaneous subjects in 7. Several of the institutions called attention to the variety of lower-division requirements among four-year colleges and in effect outlined separate sequences for the different colleges. There were expected variations in many of the outlines. For example, a number of colleges, though by no means the majority of them, included two years of accounting. Even the liberal arts pattern varied considerably. A few of the colleges required two years of English, others only one year.

An emphasis on mathematics was observed in many four-year colleges. Again the pattern varied. Thirteen of the colleges merely stated a general mathematics requirement—usually 6 semester hours or more. Seventeen specified a minimum of college algebra. A number included trigonometry and analytical geometry. Several in a state in which the state university requires calculus in its business school included it as a subject logically to be taken in the junior college. Nine institutions included statistics in the outline. Eleven included Mathematics of Finance. Two required Business Mathematics. In several catalogs were statements relative to the mathematics which a prebusiness student should have taken in high school. On the other hand, it was evident that most institutions were affording the entering student who was deficient in mathematics an opportunity to make up the deficiency in junior college.

Terminal Business Programs

As indicated earlier, terminal courses in business tend to outnumber those of any other field. It is, in fact, not at all uncommon for the smaller junior colleges to offer one or two organized terminal curricula in the business field and none in any other subject field. At the same time, the larger a junior college becomes, the larger and more diversified its business program for the terminal student tends to be. Some idea of the different organized curricula in this field was obtained through an analysis made from an inspection of the catalogs of the same 55 institutions for which the prebusiness program was reported. Categories of such curricula in a larger number of schools included the following: accounting, secretarial, general business, business management, merchandising and retailing, office practice, and medical secretarial work. More specialized curricula outlined in the catalogs of some of the larger colleges included: transportation, advertising, insurance, punch-card operation, and real estate. A program combining agriculture and business under the title of "agri-business" was listed by a number of California junior colleges. Of all the terminal business curricula, the one in the field of secretarial work was the most common, it being listed in the catalogs of 36 of the 55 colleges. A curriculum in the "general business" category was found to be second in frequency, although it was reported by different names and its objectives seemed to range from the training of general clerical workers to that of preparing students for general administrative and managerial positions on a semiprofessional basis. Twenty of the colleges outlined a two-year program in accounting. Only 17 reported programs in the field of retailing and/or merchandising.

While the sampling of the 55 institutions is small, the experience and observation of the author leads him to believe that the programs enumerated above are typical of the business curricula offered for terminal students in junior colleges throughout the United States. Somewhat the same picture is obtained from the study reported by Armsby, Eells, and Martorana in *Organized Occupational Curriculums,* which sought to determine the graduates and enrollments in organized occupational curricula of at least one but less than four years in junior colleges, technical institutes, and other institutions of higher education in the United States. In the 312 *two-year* institutions which submitted data on such curricula, the number of graduates and enrollment by different business curricula for 1956 were reported as in Table 23-1.

The mere listing of a structured curriculum does not necessarily mean that each student follows it to the last detail. As a matter of fact, the listing of a curriculum does not even guarantee that the demand for it is always sufficient to warrant its being offered in full or in part. But if it is offered, it should be, and usually is, sufficiently flexible for students to have some latitude in the selection of courses most appropriate to their individual needs and backgrounds.

The process of developing terminal business courses was observed

TABLE 23-1

INSTITUTIONS, GRADUATES, AND ENROLLMENT IN BUSINESS AND
COMMERCE CURRICULA, 1956

Curriculum	Number of institutions	Graduates July 1, 1955– June 30, 1956	Total enrollment on or near Oct. 1, 1956	
			Full-time	Part-time
Accounting..................	91	756	2,978	1,319
Business, general.............	135	1,560	5,470	2,465
Executive assistant...........	5	63	246	302
Hotel management............	3	92	293	—
Sales and distribution.........	42	413	1,164	325
Radio and TV production.......	12	56	111	13
Secretarial, general............	205	1,857	6,368	1,656
Secretarial, legal..............	9	57	114	49
Secretarial, medical and dental..	50	415	1,011	8
Secretarial, technical..........	9	67	151	9
Technical office assisting.......	8	77	138	17
Total.....................		5,413	18,044	6,163

SOURCE: Henry H. Armsby, Walter C. Eells, and S. V. Martorana, *Organized Occupational Curriculums, Enrollments and Graduates*, 1956, U.S. Office of Education Circular 512, 1958, p. 121.

to be quite in line with the procedure followed by most junior colleges in developing *all* terminal curricula. An attempt is generally made to work with community groups to determine the kinds of workers needed and the recommended preparation for them. This is especially true of more specialized programs, such as those involving medical secretaryship, real estate, transportation, and retailing. It seems, however, that many junior colleges *almost automatically* offer general business or secretarial work without any special effort to analyze community opinion with respect to the need for such training. Apparently it is presumed that students will migrate to other communities where they can make use of the training.

Business Education in Adult Programs

Since this subject is dealt with elsewhere in this volume, no attempt will be made to depict the scope and extent of business offerings in junior college adult education programs. They consist of both credit and noncredit courses. They may be organized into structured curricula or offered merely as individual classes. They may involve the teaching of skills or they may relate to the philosophical or managerial aspects of business. They may be in the nature of clinics, workshops, and seminars in such fields as sales promotion, personnel, industrial foremanship, real estate, insurance, and management. For the nation they tend to cover every conceivable facet of business (see Chap. 22).

WHAT TYPES OF STUDENTS ATTEND TWO-YEAR COLLEGES?

The nature and contribution of any program are naturally dependent in part upon the types of students the program serves. Some general understanding of the junior college student is, therefore, important. The very nature and purpose of the junior college results in its enrolling a somewhat different type of student body than may be found in many other institutions. In the first place, most junior college students live at home and commute. A large percentage of them hold part-time jobs while attending college. As a group, the socioeconomic status of their families is likely to be lower than that of students in residential colleges. Since the junior college generally admits all high school graduates and others eighteen years of age or over, regardless of academic status, many enter with subject or grade deficiencies which must be removed if they wish to pursue a baccalaureate program. Because of the unselective nature of the junior college, the students as a group are shown by normative data to be somewhat less able than four-year college students. However, great care must be taken in generalizing on any of the characteristics of junior college students due to the great range in the various items. Seashore has commented as follows on the overlap between two-year and four-year college students as found in his study data from the College Qualification Test:

The median score for junior college freshmen is near the 25th percentile for senior college freshmen.

About 24 per cent of junior college men and 20 per cent of junior college women are above the respective medians for freshmen in four-year colleges.

. . . There are many junior college students whose scores would be considered superior in senior colleges, and many low-scoring senior college freshmen would also rate low in junior colleges.[5]

An example of the range insofar as ability is concerned and the possible overlap with four-year institutions is illustrated by data presented in the *Restudy of the Needs of Higher Education in California* in 1955, which revealed that the median scores on the American Council on Education Psychological Examination of freshman entrants to a number of the California junior colleges were higher than in some of the state colleges despite the fact that there were selective admission require-

[5] Harold Seashore, "Academic Abilities of Junior College Students," *Junior College Journal,* vol. 29, October, 1958, pp. 74–80.

ments in the state colleges and none in the junior colleges. Such a situation can easily prevail when a substantial number of high-aptitude students, for a variety of reasons, go directly from high school to a junior college rather than to a four-year college.

Certain data collected in connection with the Berkeley study showed that junior college transfer students in business have about the same academic ability as transfer students in general but that they rank well below transfer students in some other fields. In one study, based on some 6,000 transfer students from 31 junior colleges, the mean score of the entire group on the American Council on Education Psychological Examination was 102. The mean score of the business transfers was 103. The business students, however, ranked in eighth place out of 11 transfer groups, with the highest mean score of 122 recorded for the transfer engineering students.

Another study was made of 6,000 students from 14 junior colleges which showed differences between students in transfer and terminal programs on the basis of ACE scores arranged according to class intervals. The median score of the terminal students was 91 compared with the transfer students' score of 100.3. More surprising is the fact that the terminal business students ranked lowest among the terminal groups. Their median ACE score was 84. The technical students attained the highest median score—95. No attempt was made to determine the level of ability of students in the various subdivisions of the business curriculum; but had this been done it is almost certain that basic differences would have appeared.

THE JUNIOR COLLEGE BUSINESS TEACHER

A more complete overview of business education in the junior college is possible by reviewing some information about the teacher of business subjects in this type of institution. Some interesting data on this matter were collected in connection with a study of the professional staff in 74 of the cooperating two-year colleges in the Berkeley project.[6] This phase of the project was designed for the primary purpose of discovering the basic attitudes held by staff members toward the two-year college and its purposes and problems, although certain objective information about the staff members was also obtained. Of the 3,282 individuals who returned a detailed questionnaire (which represented an 84 per cent response), more than 2,100 were devoting full time to classroom teaching, and of this number 211 or 10 per cent were full-time business teachers.

[6] Medsker, *op. cit.*, Chap. 7.

The background of the business staff indicates a combination of an M.A. degree, previous teaching experience at the secondary level, and some experiences in the field of business. Practically all (96 per cent) the business teachers held a baccalaureate degree, and 76 per cent held a master's degree. Only 1 per cent held a doctorate. Eleven per cent reported they were working toward an M.A., and 14 per cent that they were working toward a doctorate. The majority (69 per cent) reported previous teaching experience in a high school. A total of 87 per cent indicated they had experience in a "trade or profession," ostensibly meaning, in their case, that they had been employed in some kind of business activity.

Such a combination would suggest that, as a group, business teachers are oriented toward the "practical" aspects of teaching. The majority with high school teaching experience undoubtedly means that they take such experience as a reference point. This is not necessarily adverse to good junior college teaching, since the junior college must serve a student body with a wide range of abilities, aptitudes, interests, and motivations. The *good* high school teacher is almost always regarded as a potentially good junior college teacher. The small number of teachers with a doctorate obviously means that there is little emphasis on research, but this is not presumed to be the function of the junior college.

The attitudes expressed by business teachers concerning various phases of the junior college program were very similar to those expressed by other teachers of "applied subjects," which was a category that included all teachers in nonacademic fields. Moreover, the opinions expressed by the business teachers (and other teachers of applied subjects) were in many ways different from the attitudes expressed by teachers of academic subjects. In general, the business and related groups were inclined to put much greater stress on the terminal than on the transfer function of the college, yet they tended to agree with the academic staff that the principal emphasis of the junior college should *not* be on vocational education. It is significant that the business teachers were more liberal than their counterparts in other vocational fields with respect to the proportion of general education which should be included in a terminal program. In fact, almost 50 per cent of the business group said that half the terminal curriculum should be devoted to general education. The business teachers were also the most sure of all groups that "junior college instruction is usually as good or better than lower-division teaching in four-year colleges and universities."

These and other attitudes expressed by junior college business teachers indicate that as a group they are confident in their ability to carry on a business education program in a type of college that must serve students who will not transfer as well as those who will. It is also to their credit that so many of them place a high value on general education within the framework of a terminal program.

PROBLEMS AND ISSUES
IN JUNIOR COLLEGE BUSINESS EDUCATION

As in all segments and in all fields of education, certain questions and difficulties characterize the efforts of the junior college to conduct an effective program of business education. While many of the problems are of the expected normal nature and do not warrant special consideration in this chapter, others are sufficiently distinct and important to bear on the whole integrated process of business education and to justify some discussion of them. In general, these problems center around two categories: (1) determining the nature and content of the business education curriculum in the junior college and (2) matters pertaining to instruction.

Determining the Nature and Content of the Business Program

The junior college faces a general curriculum problem by reason of its being an autonomous unit with its own basic educational philosophy and objectives, yet necessarily occupying a middle position between high school on the one hand and either industry or the four-year college on the other hand. Ideally, it is committed to meeting the complex social needs of the larger society as well as of its own community. As an institution, it is entitled to its own ideas as to how best to meet these needs and to set its requirements and program accordingly. Yet, in its middle-ground position it must be cognizant of the demands made by higher institutions and by industry.

These circumstances make curriculum planning in the junior college a complex task. They generally require that attention be given to appropriate programs for those students who look to employment immediately after leaving the junior college. Also, in most cases they necessitate a curriculum which enables other students to transfer to four-year colleges to continue their work toward a baccalaureate degree in business administration.

But merely to say that a junior college must provide suitable programs for both terminal and transfer students is hardly sufficient, since there immediately arises a host of questions concerning the desirable nature of these programs. What should be the differences and the similarities in terminal and transfer curricula? Are they mutually exclusive? To what extent, if at all, can they overlap? What are the minimum essentials for each program?

Though there is by no means unanimity of opinion on such questions—and perhaps there should not be—it seems reasonable to propose some guidelines or principles which may be used in viewing present and future business education curriculum practices in junior colleges. These proposed principles, which emerge out of the increasingly complex social structure within which all business education must be expected to function, would logically include the following:

1. The terminal and transfer programs, though for different purposes, should have certain characteristics in common:

   a. They both should be planned in consideration of the student who must: (1) take his place in a business enterprise in which performance is dependent, not alone upon skills, but also upon understandings and attitudes which enable him to work cooperatively with others in synthesizing the complex elements of business with the equally complex elements of society, and (2) take his place as an effective person in the many phases of life outside his occupational sphere. This would indicate the necessity for including in both programs a substantial core of general education.

   b. They both should introduce the student to the more general aspects of business, so that his perspective of his chosen business specialty will have a relationship to the over-all business enterprise.

   c. They both must be concerned with giving the student whatever specific business knowledge and tools are necessary to enable him to continue beyond junior college in the business field—either as a worker or as a continuing student in business administration.

2. There are, however, some distinguishing features between the two programs:

   a. The transfer program by necessity must be broader in scope and contain fewer specialized courses in business than the terminal program. In fact, the nature of modern business is such that the baccalaureate program should aim at a wide perspective with the lower-division program particularly broad in nature. Depending on the requirements imposed by four-year colleges, it is possible that only a limited number of units in economics and accounting should be the extent of specialization at this level.

   It is increasingly true that the abilities required of students who become business administration graduates are primarily in the interpretative and social relationship fields. Even in the area of accounting, highly efficient and complicated machines are changing the process of record keeping so rapidly that less time is needed to teach the accounting process and more time is necessary to determine what it is the machines are to be called upon to do and to the interpretation of the data once they come from the machines. Furthermore, the determination of data to be compiled and the interpretation of such data are usually not judgments to be rendered in a vacuum or on some rule-of-thumb or expedient basis but rather in the context of many factors which require keen insight into the interaction of the business organism with the world about it.

b. The terminal program must, naturally, allow for some concentration on specific knowledge and tools. For example, where machines are involved in a particular curricular outlet, the student will be taught more about what the machines do, how they operate, and usually, to a somewhat limited extent, the factors involved in interpreting the data. The girl trained as a secretary must indeed be skillful in typewriting, shorthand, and related skills. But the principal difference in performance of a girl with an associate in arts degree plus secretarial training in a junior college and a girl direct from high school or from a concentrated business training course should *not* be her superior secretarial skills (though it is probable they will be superior). Instead, the difference should be the girl's skill in communication, her understanding of people, and her awareness of and interest in the outside influences which touch upon her employer's responsibility.

3. The two programs may usually, though not necessarily, overlap in varying degrees.

Since general education should constitute a considerable share of the background for both programs, it is logical that many students should follow the same program for this phase of their education. This is also quite essential in the small junior college where there is not the possibility of duplicate class sections that exist in larger colleges. There are, however, limitations to this plan, such as those that arise when certain students enter the junior college unqualified to pursue courses which regular transfer students take. Another factor which often reduces the feasibility of having both groups follow the same general education program grows out of the requirements imposed by the four-year colleges on the business transfer students. For example, the junior college may offer certain general interdisciplinary courses for meeting the objectives of general education, and the terminal students may be encouraged to take them. On the other hand, the transfer students may not find it possible to gain credit for such courses in certain universities; thus they must pursue the conventional departmental courses in liberal arts.

What specific courses in business can double for both terminal and transfer courses is a moot question. It appears that the possibility is becoming restricted due to the tendency for most of the work of the transfer student to be in liberal arts. Thus the terminal student who follows this program is in reality not following a business education program. And since the transfer student has no alternative if he meets requirements in the next institution, the "specialized" phases of the programs are different by their very nature.

Stated briefly, the process of planning the different business terminal programs is not necessarily easy. The programs must be sufficiently flexible to meet individual student needs. They must be intensive enough to develop the competencies needed, yet they should be designed with recognition of the fact that elements of general education are also important to the development of the individual both as a worker and as a person. In this connection it is fairly apparent that there is room for improvement in most junior colleges. This contention is based upon information drawn from an examination of all the terminal curricula outlined in more than seventy-five junior college catalogs. This examination made it clear that general education for terminal business students, as well as for all other terminal students, is confined largely to some two or three courses in communicative arts and in the social sciences. The students generally may elect two or three courses which may or may not pertain to general education. Any other course work allowed or recommended in a general area is sparse. Little or no general education is provided for students in one- and two-year certificate programs, which are distinct from programs leading to an associate in arts degree.

Yet the junior college that tries to increase the amount of general education in its terminal program immediately encounters numerous difficulties. The time required to teach the various skills considered necessary for employment constitutes a heavy demand on the total time the student has available within a two-year period. A question soon arises as to the relative importance of (1) subjects which concentrate either on business skills or concepts and (2) greater academic content in the curriculum. Teachers of business subjects are wont to emphasize the business subjects. Students are also prone to consider the business subjects of prime importance. As noted in Chap. 5, employer opinion is divided and may vary among industries or even among individuals in the same industry or in the same company. The high-level executive of the company may make statements on the importance of workers with broad understanding, capable of assuming leadership positions. The employment officer and the office manager, on the other hand, may be concerned with more specific vocational training. Such differences of opinion on the part of employers with respect to the types of programs and training needed make it difficult for the junior college either to interest students in pursuing a terminal business program or to broaden the scope of the program to include more general education.

If industry sincerely believes that structured business programs at the junior college level can produce workers who are more valuable and whose opportunity to assume satisfying and rewarding positions is greater by reason of their having completed such programs, the fact should be made known. Since World War II, employers have often hired beginning workers without differentiation from those with training. Too seldom is there any specified place for the two-year business student. A reclassification of the positions in industry which would identify positions for which junior college training is a necessity would be of tremendous help. Also, if there is a fundamental interest in including more general education in business programs, it would be well if business would be more articulate in indicating such interest. It may be necessary for the junior college to help business interpret and express its needs and ideas concerning the most valued kind of training.

But even if industry should attempt to go "all out" to specify its needs, there is still the problem of what can be accomplished in two years. It is a well-known fact that every phase of business is becoming more complex with each passing year. If junior colleges are to produce workers who are skillful and knowledgeable about business, both skills and theory are involved. Even the junior college administration devoutly dedicated to the idea of including in the business curriculum a considerable amount of liberal education has to deal with the serious question of what *can* be included. In discussing the same problem having to do with the training of engineering technicians, a representative of the National Association of Manufacturers recently said: "We may, in developing these technician programs, have to eliminate about all of the so-called liberal arts courses except English, economics and political science. We may have to devote much of the two years to actual basic courses in science and engineering." It would seem lamentable if the same philosophy were to be considered applicable to the preparation of workers for a social institution as complex as modern business.

Problems in Organizing a Transfer Program

Planning the program for the first two years of a four-year business administration curriculum involves numerous problems. Mention has been made of the difficulty arising from the variation in patterns among four-year colleges and of the attendant difficulty on the part of junior colleges in following the different programs of the institutions to which its business students transfer. Some of this difficulty arises from the grade placement of certain key subjects, such as economics, law, accounting, etc. In some four-year colleges these subjects are a part of the lower-division program, and in others they are not. Students enrolling for business law in junior college, for example, may be required to enroll for another law course in the senior college. Advanced accounting and cost accounting are considered upper-division courses in many institutions, and students taking such subjects in junior college are required to make adjustments when they transfer. In other four-year colleges such subjects are considered lower-division. Even for the business subjects taught in junior college, there are various opinions concerning the year in which they should be taught. For example, some senior institutions prefer that the subject of accounting not be introduced until the sophomore year.

These variations all have far-reaching implications for the junior college and obviously support the need for close articulation with senior colleges. In some states there is formal institutional machinery which seeks to coordinate the efforts of both types of institutions in the region. In other states or regions much of the articulation is dependent upon some type of informal liaison machinery. In California, for example, there is an over-all conference committee to consider relationships among the junior colleges, the state colleges, and the university. In addition, there is in several subject fields a special liaison committee to consider the problems of curriculum and teaching in those fields. Included among such committees is one on business administration which meets periodically to exchange points of view, discuss contemplated curricular changes, results of research studies on performance of students, and other considerations concerning the undergraduate business program in all three types of institutions.

The variations in requirements also indicate the need for adequate counseling programs in the junior college. The very fact that the four-year colleges vary in their requirements means that individual programs must be tailored accordingly. A number of the junior college catalogs examined called attention to the difference in requirements in the state university and in other state institutions. Making sure that each student takes what he needs in order to fulfill the requirements of the next institution would be easier if students were always sure of the four-year college to which they will transfer. Unfortunately, this is frequently not the situation. The result is that some flexibility must be maintained and changes effected as the student progresses through the first two years. The varying backgrounds of students also make for counseling problems. Since most junior colleges do not have selective admission practices, some entering students may not satisfy admission requirements of four-year institutions. Their academic record may be less good and their pattern of high school subjects not the same as that required by some higher institutions. The responsibility of the junior college in these cases is to advise students concerning the realism of their entering certain programs, to set up criteria for admitting students to individual courses where background and skill are needed to succeed in the course, and to arrange a program by which subject prerequisites can be made up. Even though guidance programs in junior colleges have certain weaknesses, there is probably no type of institution that takes its counseling obligation more seriously and attempts to serve its students in an advisory capacity more completely.

Problems Related to Instruction

A number of problems perplex those who are responsible for the content and teaching of individual business education courses in the junior college. An examination of the minutes of several meetings of the liaison committee on business administration in California revealed that two of the topics most frequently discussed in the committee related to the content of individual courses and to points of emphasis in certain business courses. Concern about the same problem was expressed by a number of junior college people interviewed in connection with the Berkeley study. Determining the content of a course so basic as economics with its many possible approaches and theories should require a high degree of articulation with the senior colleges to which students will likely transfer. Placing the most appropriate emphases in an introductory accounting course is highly important. There is always the danger of stressing the mechanics of record keeping to the exclusion of giving the student a knowledge of accounting as an orderly means of sifting, classifying, presenting, and interpreting data and of acquainting him with the basic language of business. The types of examinations used by junior colleges in the basic business courses were found to be a subject of discussion, with a consensus that objective-type means of evaluation should not be overstressed at the expense of requiring the student to show interrelationships of data and to demonstrate proficiency in problem solving.

The entire problem of content and emphases is complicated by the diversity of students in the junior college courses. The basic subjects—such as economics, law, and accounting—are often recommended for terminal students as well as for transfer students. Thus in most junior colleges both types of students are enrolled in the same classes. To complicate matters, many students who plan to transfer will not do so. In fact, it was discovered that although at least two-thirds of the entering students in the junior colleges which cooperated in the Berkeley study declared themselves to be transfer students at the point of entering junior college and enrolled for programs accordingly, only one-third of the class entering in 1952 subsequently transferred. Thus, in each course normally considered as meeting transfer requirements, there are those students who by design as well as by chance are not enrolled as transfer students. The knowledge of this fact places a special responsibility on those who plan and teach the courses to meet the needs of the terminal student as well as the needs of the student who is to transfer.

Such a responsibility raises the question of how best, if at all, to adjust content, emphasis, and methodology to the terminal student and yet to prepare the transfer student to fit into the long-range program of business administration. It also raises such questions as to whether or not students in a prebusiness curriculum should be screened by a selection process and segregated in special classes. Even if special classes for transfer students were considered desirable, this would be difficult to implement in many junior colleges that are too small to afford multiple sections of the same or similar courses.

Still another aspect of the teaching problem has to do with the factor of producing quality of performance on the part of the students. While this problem is equally acute in the case of terminal and transfer students, it looms large in the consideration of the role of the junior college in the baccalaureate business administration program. Certainly, the transfer business student must have the ability, motivation, work habits, and background which enable him to take his place alongside others in the business program after he transfers. Instruction in the junior college must, therefore, be geared to this end. Students who are presumed to be transfer students must be expected to perform at a level commensurate with their later plans. Instruction for them cannot be geared to lesser standards.

In connection with the Berkeley study, some data on the relative success of junior colleges in preparing business students to transfer were obtained from four universities. The retention and academic performance of students who transferred to these universities as juniors in 1955 were compared with that of the group of juniors in the same class who had entered the university as freshmen and who were thus classified as "native students." It was possible to compare the business students with both native students and transfer students in other subject fields. The four universities submitting data specifically on business students were the University of California at Berkeley and at Los Angeles, the University of Illinois, and the University of Mississippi.

As may be observed from Table 23-2, in most categories a slightly higher percentage of the business students obtained a baccalaureate degree "on time," i.e., within the normal two-year period following junior classification, than did the *total* students in the corresponding categories. However, except in one university, the percentage of the transfer business students who received degrees within the normal period was considerably smaller than for the native business students. In terms of academic performance, as measured by median grade point averages,

Table 23-2

COMPARISONS BETWEEN JUNIOR COLLEGE TRANSFERS AND NATIVE STUDENTS
IN BUSINESS ADMINISTRATION IN FOUR UNIVERSITIES

Institution	Students receiving degrees within two years following junior classification in 1953				Median grade point averages (based on a 3-point scale)	
	Business students		All students		Business students	All students
	Number	%	Number	%		
University of California—Berkeley:						
Native students*	98	61	864	57	1.59	1.78
Transfer students (eligible)†	17	60	184	57	1.71	1.84
Transfer students (ineligible)‡	25	32	213	35	1.60	1.60
University of California— Los Angeles:						
Native students*	76	47	587	49	1.73	1.88
Transfer students (eligible)†	13	31	141	28	1.49	1.75
Transfer students (ineligible)‡	42	31	288	26	1.51	1.57
University of Illinois:§						
Native students*	186	57	1040	61	1.68	1.83
Transfer students	38	47	168	40	1.56	1.68
University of Mississippi:						
Native students*	69	78	200	75	1.63	1.76
Transfer students	38	84	88	60	1.63	1.65

* Students who entered the university as freshmen.
† Eligible for entrance to the university upon graduation from high school.
‡ Ineligible for entrance to the university upon graduation from high school.
§ Data for students classified as juniors in 1952.

the total group of business students made only a slightly lower average than the students as a whole. Further, except in one instance, the record made by *business* transfers was slightly less than that made by *business* native students. In both instances, however, the differences were so slight that it could be said that the transfer students performed *almost* as well as the native students and that business students generally did work of *about* the same quality as other university students.

On the basis of the evidence from this somewhat limited sample, it would be concluded that business students who transfer tend to achieve grades about as good as do those who begin their business program in the university but that it is less likely that the transfer students will complete the requirements for their degree within the normal two-year period after transfer.

IN RETROSPECT AND PROSPECT

The junior college is now an important unit in American higher educa-tion, both with respect to the number of institutions and the number of students it serves. In view of the fact that business is among the subjects receiving the greatest emphasis, the junior college must be viewed as an important member of a team of institutions charged with the responsi-bility of upgrading the business process in a complex society.

So far this discussion has dealt primarily with the present status of business programs in junior colleges and with the attendant problems and issues in connection with these programs. It has been observed that the transfer program conforms quite generally to the lower-division requirements of the business administration program in senior colleges and universities. Furthermore, it was observed that the tendency is for the freshman and sophomore years of this program to consist largely of a prescribed liberal arts program with only a few fundamental courses, such as economics and accounting, included by way of introduction to the business specialty. In a sense, this tendency simplifies the task of the junior college, although, as was mentioned, there are numerous prob-lems of articulation. It could be argued that the situation leaves the junior college little opportunity to be original or to develop its institu-tional personality. Though this is true to a certain extent, the basic fact remains that students who transfer must be prepared to fit into the required program in the next institution. A peculiar difficulty does arise when the senior institutions are inflexible with respect to the exact nature of the junior college courses in a given field which are permitted to satisfy specific requirements. Greater latitude on the part of the senior colleges would be of assistance to the junior colleges.

In the preparation of workers for immediate employment, the junior college has a wide-open field and is bound neither to tradition nor to the influence of other institutions. Here it can, and to some extent does, play its own unique role. The problems it encounters in this function are, as previously discussed, those which grow out of the relatively undefined concept of middle-level occupations and of the cultural bias in favor of baccalaureate-type programs.

The prevalence of business education programs in junior colleges would seem to bespeak the appropriateness of this type of institution as a business training agency. Furthermore, as was indicated earlier, there is evidence that the junior college has been reasonably successful in its efforts to conduct the lower-division business administration program as well as to produce workers who can perform the skills and semiman-agerial functions which do not demand a four-year program. This is not to assume that all has been well as far as business education in the junior college is concerned. The record made by transfer students indicates that for some reason many students who begin their business administration program in junior college and transfer to a four-year college do not attain their degree, or, if they do, it takes them longer to acquire it than it does the native students. The relatively small emphasis on general education in the terminal program can also be regarded as a shortcoming. The tendency for some of the subjects to be taught in the same way as they are taught in high school, with no attempt to make the business education program in the junior college really distinctive, may be regarded as an additional criticism. Also, the tendency for many junior colleges to "follow the leader" in planning business programs— imitating those commonly given in other institutions without making an all-out effort to determine what is best for the particular college at hand —is a weakness. While the point was made that junior colleges have little alternative but to follow the prescriptions of the four-year colleges in determining the program for the transfer student, it may be that they have succumbed too much to the prescription and have not been sufficiently active in injecting their own ideas relative to what constitutes a desirable lower-division program.

Future Probabilities

While predicting the future role of an institution is always hazardous, there seems little doubt that some type of two-year college will serve an increasing number of freshman and sophomore students in the immediate years ahead. In practically every state there has recently been completed a study of the future needs in higher education. In most states a plan has been proposed to establish a new system or to expand an existing system of two-year colleges for the purpose of meeting future enrollment demands. The proposed systems vary among the states. In some states the new units will be extension centers of four-year colleges, in a few states they will be state or regional institutions, and in a number of states there are proposals to give the local community college considerable financial assistance from the state. Regardless of design, it all adds up to an increasing recognition of and reliance on two-year colleges.

Such a situation inevitably means that more students will attend these institutions and that an increasing percentage of the future business administration majors will complete their first two years of work in a two-year college. Also, it is possible that increasing numbers of junior college graduates prepared for some type of immediate employment in the business world may be available. In any event, the total role of the two-year college looms even larger in the future than it has in the past.

Implications

The necessity for very close cooperation and articulation between two- and four-year colleges is apparent. The divided plan inherent in a system which utilizes two types of colleges cannot work to the advantage of the student unless there is a high degree of joint planning and of communication between and among the institutions involved. Furthermore, such a relationship is a two-way street. It is not enough for the senior institutions merely to inform the two-year colleges of new requisites and plans; rather, it is of prime importance that both institutions jointly make the plans and design the program. Of all implications, this is of the highest order. The four-year colleges from now on must take the junior college planners into partnership, with both parties responsible for the planning of the best possible baccalaureate program.

A second implication is that greater consideration must be given to the matter of one- and two-year terminal programs in business. It may well be that industry's needs cannot and should not be met by four-year business programs. For one thing, there may not be sufficient facilities to afford baccalaureate programs for everyone. Further, it is probably true that just as in other phases of industry, there are many supporting positions at the technician's level which can be well filled by the person with two years of training. Many youths who can profit from that amount of training may not be able to profit materially from four years of more rigorous training. Yet as a nation it is extremely important that talent of all kinds and at all levels be salvaged if adequate manpower is to be made available to the economy in the next decade.

If the status of the two-year college training program is to be strengthened, several things will have to happen. The jobs at that level will have to be identified and dignified. Business itself will have to play a leading role in this. But educational institutions must also look at the problem realistically. The two-year colleges must assume that there is dignity and purpose in planning and expanding terminal programs. They will need to help the public overcome some of the natural prejudices against a program that does not lead to a four-year degree. The four-year colleges not only must lend support to the less-than-four-year programs, but they must generally refrain from offering such programs. If the two-year college is to have this special mission, it would seem better for the higher institutions to concentrate on the sufficiently large task of providing the baccalaureate program, particularly for upper-division students.

Other implications of the total situation to business education include the prime importance of adequate counseling and guidance programs in high schools and junior colleges, the necessity of emphasizing a high degree of quality in business education, and the desirability of developing adequate means of evaluating the business program at the junior college level. Students need and desire assistance in formulating their educational and vocational plans. They need help in becoming realistic about their goals. Often they are not cognizant of opportunities in the various levels of business. Though highly important in the junior college, the same services are needed in high school in order that students may look toward educational programs and to the training institution in a logical context.

The stress on quality should become a matter of great concern. Present emphases on the so-called "softness" in American education, together with the extent to which facilities are taxed in meeting enrollment demands, would suggest that academic standards must be emphasized and that students must in the future, more than in the past, earn their right to remain in any type of collegiate situation.

Finally, it is reasonable to look to better evaluation of what junior colleges are doing in business education. It will be important for them to know how their graduates perform both on jobs and in the next institutions. It will be even more important to know *why* they perform as they do. Most of all, it will be important to know the contribution which the junior college makes in producing workers with broad social understanding and with appreciation of the place of the business enterprise in the greater society.

It can be assumed that the better job the junior college does in producing personally effective individuals, the better able those individuals are to contribute to the welfare of business and to their own development.

CHAPTER 24

PREPARATION FOR BUSINESS IN
LIBERAL ARTS COLLEGES

Joseph D. Coppock[1]

> The liberal arts colleges cannot compete effectively with the
> university schools of business in offering business administration
> courses. They can, however, provide their students with excel-
> lent preparation for actual business administration or later spe-
> cialized study by providing suitable liberal arts subjects, espe-
> cially economics, English, mathematics, history, government,
> philosophy, psychology and sociology. Some colleges may find
> it feasible to institute "prebusiness" programs consisting of
> selected courses from these subject-matter fields.

For about forty years small colleges in the United States have struggled
with the question of special education for students who want to be business administrators or enterprisers. The question has been particularly
trying for colleges devoted to the liberal arts tradition. No clear-cut
answers have emerged from their experience during those forty years.

PROBLEMS

As colleges look ahead to the 1960s and 1970s some of the questions
they must answer concerning the pattern of undergraduate education for
students preparing for business careers are:

1. In view of the rising demand for college education, should the
liberal arts colleges decrease or increase their emphasis on subjects which
are expected to provide "practical" preparation for business administration?

2. Should the liberal arts colleges support the concept of business ad-

[1] With the assistance of Margaret Parsons Apgar.

662

ministration as a profession—like medicine, law, or college teaching—by expecting students who want business careers to take specialized graduate training after college? If so, what should be the characteristics of the prebusiness undergraduate program of study?

3. Will the alternative ways that are developing for obtaining specialized education for business—in graduate schools, community colleges, colleges of commerce in universities, in-service training programs, executive development programs, etc.—affect the demand for business administration courses in liberal arts colleges?

4. Will the demand from business firms for liberal arts graduates be strong enough to induce relatively more students interested in business careers to study liberal arts rather than business administration in colleges? In other words, are increasing numbers of students, parents, and employers convinced that liberal arts education is of practical value in opening up jobs leading toward management opportunities?

5. To provide adequate, practical preparation for business administration, what conditions must a college meet? What courses should it offer? How many teachers of business administration and economics does it need? How can it recruit and retain them? How many students does it need to justify the necessary number of teachers?

6. If, on the other hand, a college plans to emphasize economics and other liberal arts subjects as preparation for business, what courses are essential? How many teachers does it require? How can it obtain and retain good teachers?

This chapter should throw some light on these and related questions. The first part is a survey of what various types of liberal arts colleges—each with an enrollment of less than 2,000—are now doing in the field of education for future business administrators. The second part sets forth the author's conclusions as to the most promising lines of action with respect to educating students for business careers.

"LIBERAL ARTS" AND "EDUCATION FOR BUSINESS ADMINISTRATION"

"Liberal arts" means the fields of study which enable a person to understand something of the fundamental nature of the physical and biological world, the main characteristics and problems of the social world, and the spiritual, artistic, cultural, and intellectual achievement of mankind.[2] *Understanding* is the basic purpose in th-

[2] According to contemporary categories, the liberal arts comp
matics, astronomy, physics, chemistry, geology, biology, psyc
sociology, geography, economics, political science, history, phil
guage and literature (English and foreign), music and the other

ception, and it involves not only knowledge but also the development of an inquisitive mind, good judgment, and the ability to think logically. The liberal arts conception does not imply primary devotion to the scholarly pursuit of new knowledge, to pushing back the frontiers of knowledge. It does not intentionally develop vocational skills and detailed knowledge of production. Nor does it properly include the essentially precollege subjects of English composition, elementary foreign language study, elementary mathematics, and rudimentary knowledge of the natural and human worlds, although it builds on these subjects. The liberal arts provide "higher education" in the general areas listed. The essence of liberal arts education lies (1) in its purpose—understanding— and (2) in the selection of "important" subjects for the "whole" person.[3]

In contrast, education for business administration is, by intention at least, education for a career or profession. Hence, like other vocational or professional education, it differs in *purpose* from liberal arts education. As generally understood, it differs also with respect to *content*, although some people take the extreme position that the liberal arts, especially the more rigorous traditional fields, provide the best preparation for business administration. We shall take the generally accepted position, however, that there is a body of knowledge which can be denoted as education for business administration without implying that such education is the only, or even the principal, route to a business career.

Education for business administration obviously relates to the numerous and varied tasks the business administrator has to perform.[4] He directs the activities of other persons in his organization, hires and fires personnel, arranges financing, selects his firm's sales commodities, purchases the means of production, arranges for marketing, etc. The larger the firm, the more he is concerned with directing and coordinating the efforts of others in the various departments of the enterprise. In practically every line of business there are specific technological processes involved in turning out the sales product or service which frequently require the services of specialists inside or outside the firm. Also, business firms of any size have on their staffs, or have access to, specialists in such fields as accounting, law, finance, personnel, production, and

---

[3] This statement does not pretend to compete with eloquent and inspiring essays on this subject. A notable, recent contribution is by Robert D. Calkins, "Professional and Graduate Education and the Liberal Arts," *Georgia Review*, Summer, 1952.

[4] Economics, as a field of study, is often confused with business administration. Economics is the study of the use of scarce resources, whether by individuals, small groups such as business enterprises, or whole nations or societies. Business administration, as a field study, is concerned with the profitable conduct of a business firm within a given type of economic system. It draws on parts of economics, but it properly draws also on subject-matter fields other than economics.

marketing. The business administrator, however, in coordinating the work of these specialists, must keep a perspective on the operations of the company as a whole and take ultimate responsibility for their proper conduct. He must pursue the goals of the firm, the first of which is to make adequate profits, mostly through the cooperative efforts of his employees or coworkers. He is not, except incidentally, a technician who knows how to operate an office machine, balance a set of books, or run a lathe. The kind of business education that will best equip a person to meet such varied demands is our concern here.

The liberal arts college, in trying to decide what it should do to prepare students for future careers as businessmen, faces a basic difficulty: there is no well-defined body of knowledge or set of principles which students must learn in order to become successful business administrators. Business executives and enterprisers have had diverse educational backgrounds. It is impossible, on the basis of studies made thus far, to determine with any precision the desirable elements of education for future businessmen.[5] Educational prescriptions of practicing businessmen are equally diverse, tending to be autobiographically oriented and to drift off into maxims like "Work hard," "Keep your eye on the ball," "Don't watch the clock," "Take responsibility willingly," "Think." Business contrasts sharply with law and medicine, for example, with respect to educational prerequisites. If a person can get through medical school or law school, he is well on his way to being a doctor or lawyer, but nobody would dream of considering a person a business administrator because he had completed a graduate program in business administration, to say nothing of an undergraduate program. There is no professional licensing of business administrators; with minor exceptions all persons are legally free to engage in business. And the ways of entry are diverse. Furthermore, there is no generally accepted code of conduct for businessmen—beyond the legal and moral minima of society generally.[6]

The function of the businessman in the economic system of private enterprise is primarily to conduct a profitable business enterprise according to prevailing law and custom. Generally he has to see that his firm produces some salable goods or services in order to make profits. But the aim of the business firm as just stated—the standard formulation—is not universally accepted, even by businessmen. Some people contend that business firms, especially large corporations, which administer most of the productive resources of the country, are "social trustees" of the resources, particularly the funds and physical assets subject to their direction, and that profit considerations are secondary, even incidental,

---

[5] Mabel Newcomer, *The Big Business Executive,* Columbia University Press, New York, 1955. Other studies are cited there.

[6] These issues are discussed at greater length in Chaps. 5 and 6.

to the drive for power, prestige, fulfillment of a deep desire to render social, national, or similar service. Without attempting to analyze or rationalize these various objectives and their relation to profits, it should be evident that the lack of agreement, at least in some quarters, as to objectives of business firms and administrators complicates the problem of education for future businessmen.[7]

REASONS FOR AND AGAINST BUSINESS ADMINISTRATION IN THE COLLEGE CURRICULUM

The expansion, since World War I, of public universities and colleges, with their vocational and professional curricula and low tuitions, made them formidable competitors with private schools for students and funds. College education was increasingly viewed not as cultural and preprofessional education but as job training that would accelerate a student's climb up the economic and social pyramid. Already plagued by dwindling financial support from individuals and religious organizations—especially after 1929—private colleges were pressured by boards of trustees, financially minded administrators, college departments ambitious to expand, and business-minded alumni, parents, and friends to initiate programs in business administration that would attract students who otherwise would attend public institutions. College public relations officers gave further impetus to the idea in the hope that provision of courses which even mediocre students could pass would gain broader and more lucrative support for the private-college cause. Another, less materialistic reason for urging the addition of business courses to the private college's curriculum was voiced in the statement that "business has become so important that an understanding of it is essential for the truly educated person."

All these forces were felt in varying degrees in various colleges between the early 1920s and the early 1950s. Three general patterns of response to the demand for business education emerged. The first was set by colleges that made a fairly rapid and rather large-scale shift into the field of business administration (Group A colleges below), generally following the patterns of the schools of business created in the large universities after World War I. The second was defined by colleges that adapted only slightly to the increased demand for business administration (Group B colleges below). And the third was comprised of colleges that made practically no changes to attract students interested in studying business administration (Group C colleges below). The problem was

---

[7] See A. G. Papandreou, in B. F. Haley (ed.), *A Survey of Contemporary Economics,* vol. II, Richard D. Irwin, Inc., Homewood, Ill., 1952, for an excellent discussion and numerous references.

not so trying for colleges in the first and third categories as for those in the middle position that wished to offer only "some" business training—and those were the majority.

In many cases, adaptation has consisted only of including the name "business administration," or something similar, along with "economics" in the title of a department. In other cases, it has consisted of permitting a student to have a business administration "major" within the department of economics, which has usually meant that he would have to take a year of accounting but would not have to take economic theory and that his diploma would show his bachelor's degree in business administration. Another form of adaptation has been to grant a B.S. degree in business administration, enabling the student to graduate without meeting any foreign language requirement. These adaptations, and variations of them, have served to ease the pressure by students and others for business studies in many institutions.

Not all colleges were able to deal with the problem in such superficial ways. Many changed their subject offerings. The most common addition was accounting. Business law was usually second.[8] Other adaptations were offered by the economists, for example, corporation finance as a supplement to money and banking, personnel relations as a supplement to, or substitute for, labor problems, and marketing as a supplement to, or possibly a substitute for, economic theory. Mathematics departments frequently added mathematics of finance and statistical methods; English departments, "practical business English" and "business speaking"; and psychology departments, courses in selling, human relations, etc.

A closely related aspect of such adaptations was the relaxing of academic standards. Much of economics, the subject generally considered, rightly or not, to be most closely related to business administration, has long struck the typical business-minded undergraduate as abstract, difficult, and largely irrelevant to his purposes. Many practicing businessmen have shared this view. So the changes in the name, content, or array of courses, in response to the pressure for education for business, generally involved a reduction in the theoretical, an increase in the descriptive

---

[8] Many coeducational and women's colleges introduced secretarial studies, either alone or in conjunction with a teacher-training program in high school commercial subjects. Of the 95 coeducational colleges among the 119 colleges selected for intensive investigation, 48 offered secretarial programs in 1955–1956. None of the 24 men's colleges in the 119 offered secretarial programs. The larger the coeducational college, the more frequently secretarial work was offered; and the greater the emphasis on business administration generally, the higher the incidence of secretarial studies. Someone asserted that secretarial courses had no more to do with business administration than the washing of test tubes had to do with chemistry, but the fact is that colleges responded to the demand to prepare women for business careers mainly by expanding their secretarial offerings.

and mechanical, and a relaxation of grading standards to accommodate the relatively weak students. The traditional course in principles of economics was retained, although it was occasionally moved up to the junior year because of its difficulty for freshman or sophomore business students. Money and banking was also retained. The number and types of business courses offered, beyond accounting, corporation finance, business law, marketing, personnel relations, and business organization and management, varied widely according to the training and interests of teachers, the number of teachers available, the number of students, and special outside pressures. Most liberal arts colleges offered no more than a semester in any one business subject, except in accounting, which was often considered the primary business subject. In some colleges, there was a tendency toward proliferation in the marketing area which probably launched the reputation for "snap" courses in business, although more recent courses in management have apparently become rivals for this distinction.

There are very few instances of colleges reversing the movement toward business administration, but the movement was retarded over three or so decades by various barriers. We have discussed the barrier represented by the nonvocational liberal arts tradition that was breached in nearly all institutions in the 1920s. Financial necessity widened this breach in the 1930s. One barrier to the introduction of more business courses was the shortage of trained teachers in this field. Persons qualified in some measure as economists generally taught business administration subjects. The great majority of teachers and administrators believed that business students should have some economics before, or along with, their business courses, but enrollments and the financial situation in many colleges did not warrant hiring business teachers in addition to the necessary number of economists, even if such business teachers were available. As a result, there was a tendency for economists to teach business subjects closely related to economics and for the college to enlist part-time people, especially for accounting and business law, and to have faculty members from other departments teach such courses as statistics, mathematics of finance, geography, economic history, business English, public speaking, and psychology (of salesmanship, advertising, personnel relations, etc.). Thus the response of some colleges to the pressures for business courses tended to be unenthusiastic because of the professional background of many of the teachers. Uncertainty regarding the subject matter of a business curriculum and shortage of good teaching materials also retarded adaptation.

Such barriers have not been great enough, however, to resist the general movement, except in some of the financially strongest liberal arts colleges. After World War II only a few institutions made any pretense of confining their offerings to the liberal arts and sciences, even generously construed.[9]

EXTENT OF BUSINESS ADMINISTRATION IN COLLEGES

Of the 493 accredited liberal arts colleges with less than 2,000 students in the United States in the mid-1950s, 199 offered "many" courses in business administration (Group A), 158 offered "some" (Group B), and 136 offered "few" or none (Group C). (See Table 24-1 for details on the selection of the 493 colleges and for basic classification according to Groups A, B, and C.) The colleges in Group A tended to be publicly rather than privately controlled, large rather than small, and coeducational rather than for men only or women only. Group C colleges tended to be small, privately controlled, and not coeducational. The pattern for Group B colleges was mixed. Fairly full secretarial programs were offered in 32.4 per cent of the 108 women's colleges and in 32.7 per cent of the 327 coeducational colleges. Men's colleges did not offer them (Tables 24-1 and 24-2). Of the 108 women's colleges, 11 were in Group A, 32 in Group B, and the rest in Group C. The median number of teachers of business administration and economics in the 43 women's colleges in Groups A and B was 3.

Although women make up about 37 per cent of the United States labor force and comprise 15 to 20 per cent of the business administrators, enterprisers, etc., it became clear from this survey that women's colleges generally do not place much emphasis on business administration as a field of study. Even economics is given only scant attention in half or more of the women's colleges. Questionnaire comments indicated in various ways that women interested in business administration could be educated for it more satisfactorily in graduate schools or in other types of undergraduate institutions than in women's colleges. In view of these facts, it does not seem necessary to give further attention to women's colleges in this chapter.

Other characteristics of the Group A, B, and C colleges were derived from a study of an *un*representative sample of 119 of the 493 liberal arts colleges. The 119 colleges consists of 95 coeducational and 24 men's colleges which are probably the top one-third, academically, of the nation's 385 coeducational and men's liberal arts colleges.[10] The other 266 colleges presumably have similar problems in providing satisfactory education for business administration. Of the 119 colleges, only two are

[9] E. J. McGrath, "Are Liberal Arts Colleges Becoming Professional Schools?" Institute of Higher Education, Teachers College, Columbia University, New York, September, 1958.

[10] See Table 24-2 for the list and how it was compiled.

TABLE 24-1

DISTRIBUTION OF 493 LIBERAL ARTS COLLEGES BY (1) EXTENT OF OFFERINGS IN BUSINESS ADMINISTRATION, (2) SIZE, (3) CONTROL, AND (4) SEX OF STUDENTS*

Sex of students and extent of business administration	Size and control											
	300–699 students			700–1,199 students			1,200–2,000 students			Total		
	Priv.	Pub.	Both	Priv.	Pub.	Both	Priv.	Pub.	Both	Priv.	Pub.	Both
Coed	129	13	142	90	26	116	42	27	69	261	66	327
A	38	4	42	47	17	64	28	21	49	113	42	155
B	63	6	69	31	3	34	11	1	12	105	10	115
C	28	3	31	12	6	18	3	5	8	43	14	57
Secretarial	39	4	43	33	5	38	22	4	26	94	13	107
Women	82	3	85	13	2	15	7	1	8	102	6	108
A	4	2	6	1	1	2	2	1	3	7	4	11
B	25	1	26	6	0	6	0	0	0	31	1	32
C	53	0	53	6	1	7	5	0	5	64	1	65
Secretarial	24	1	25	7	1	8	2	0	2	33	2	35
Men	23	0	23	19	1	20	14	1	15	56	2	58
A	9	0	9	12	0	12	11	1	12	32	1	33
B	7	0	7	2	0	2	3	0	3	12	0	12
C	7	0	7	5	1	6	0	0	0	12	1	13
Secretarial	0	0	0	0	0	0	0	0	0	0	0	0
Total	234	16	250	122	29	151	63	29	92	419	74	493
A	51	6	57	60	18	78	41	23	64	152	47	199
B	95	7	102	39	3	42	13	1	14	147	11	158
C	88	3	91	23	8	31	9	5	14	120	16	136
Secretarial	63	5	68	40	6	46	24	4	28	127	15	142

* A college was put in Group A if it had three or more (full-time equivalent) teachers of business administration (excluding economics) and/or offered 40 or more semester hours of business administration; in Group B if it had one or two (full-time equivalent) teachers in business administration and/or offered 10–39 semester hours in business administration; and in Group C if it had less than one (full-time equivalent) teacher in business administration and/or offered less than 10 semester hours in business administration. All accounting courses were counted as business administration courses.

For the purposes of this investigation liberal arts colleges were defined as those accredited institutions of higher education which consider themselves liberal arts colleges, have no more than two professional or graduate schools, with a few exceptions, and have total enrollments of 300 to 2,000 (in the mid-1950s). Ten colleges of slightly less than 300 and two of slightly more than 2,000 are included. Colleges of arts and sciences (or with similar names) in large universities are excluded, mainly on the ground that they are faced with different problems in connection with education for business administration, because their universities, almost without exception, have set up separate schools of business—undergraduate, graduate, or both. Teachers' colleges are included only if they offer some liberal arts and have a four-year program. Junior colleges are excluded.

The colleges which qualify according to these standards number 493. They were selected by means of the *Education Directory*, 1955–1956, Part 3, "Higher Education," published by the Office of Education, U.S. Department of Health, Education, and Welfare. Specifically, 472 were selected from columns II and III, rows b, c, e, f, and j; and 21 were selected from II-k, III-k, IV-k, IV-j, and II-h, page 8, because basically they met our qualifications. The use of the term "college," "university," "institute," or such in the name was not a criterion; all are referred to as colleges here.

TABLE 24-2

LIST OF 119 COEDUCATIONAL AND MEN'S COLLEGES SELECTED FOR INTENSIVE STUDY*

Group A	Group B	Group C
Albion, Mich.	Alfred, N.Y.	Amherst, Mass.
Antioch, Ohio	Allegheny, Pa.	Bates, Maine
Baker, Kans.	Beloit, Wis.	Bowdoin, Maine
Baldwin-Wallace, Ohio	Bethany, W. Va.	Carleton, Minn.
Berea, Ky.	Capital, Ohio	Charleston, College of, S.C.
Birmingham-Southern, Ala.	Colgate, N.Y.	Dickinson, Pa.
Bucknell, Pa.	Cornell, Iowa	Drury, Mo.
Carroll, Wis.	Davidson, N.C.	Earlham, Ind.
Central, Mo.	Denison, Ohio	Hamilton, N.Y.
Centre, Ky.	DePauw, Ind.	Hampden-Sydney, Va.
Clark, Mass.	Doane, Neb.	Haverford, Pa.
Claremont, Calif.	Franklin, Ind.	Hiram, Ohio
Coe, Iowa	Grinnell, Iowa	Kenyon, Ohio
Colby, Maine	Hamline, Minn.	Lawrence, Wis.
Colorado College	Heidelberg, Ohio	Middlebury, Vt.
Elon, N.C.	Hendrix, Ark.	Pomona, Calif.
Fisk, Tenn.	Hobart, N.Y.	Reed, Ore.
Franklin and Marshall, Pa.	Hope, Mich.	Ripon, Wis.
Furman, S.C.	Illinois College	Swarthmore, Pa.
Geneva, Pa.	Juniata, Pa.	Talladega, Ala.
Gettysburg, Pa.	Kalamazoo, Mich.	Wabash, Ind.
Grove City, Pa.	Knox, Ill.	Wesleyan, Conn.
Howard, Ala.	Maryville, Tenn.	Williams, Mass.
Illinois Wesleyan	Monmouth, Ill.	Wooster, College of, Ohio
Jamestown, N. Dak.	Mount Union, Ohio	
Lafayette, Pa.	Muskingum, Ohio	
Lake Forest, Ill.	Oberlin, Ohio	
Linfield, Ore.	Occidental, Calif.	
Loras, Iowa	Ohio Wesleyan	
Macalester, Minn.	Park, Mo.	
MacMurray, Ill.	Randolph-Macon, Va.	
Marietta, Ohio	Rice Institute, Tex.	
Millikan, Ill.	Rockford, Ill.	
Millsaps, Miss.	St. Olaf, Minn.	
Mississippi College	Sewanee (Univ. of the	
Muhlenberg, Pa.	South), Tenn.	
N.C. College at Durham	Southwestern at Memphis,	
North Central, Ill.	Tenn.	
Otterbein, Ohio	Trinity, Conn.	
Pacific, College of the, Calif.	Ursinus, Pa.	
Puget Sound, College of,	Washington and Jefferson,	
Wash.	Pa.	
Redlands, University of,	Wheaton, Ill.	
Calif.	Whitman, Wash.	

LIST OF 119 COEDUCATIONAL AND MEN'S COLLEGES SELECTED FOR INTENSIVE STUDY*

TABLE 24-2 (*Continued*)

Group A	Group B	Group C
St. Lawrence, N.Y.	William Jewell, Mo.	
Simpson, Iowa	Wofford, S.C.	
Wake Forest, N.C.	Yankton, S. Dak.	
Washington and Lee, Va.		
Westminster, Mo.		
Westminster, Pa.		
Whittier, Calif.		
Willamette, Ore.		
Wittenberg, Ohio		

* From "List of Approved Colleges, Universities and Technological Institutions Whose Qualified Graduates Are Admitted to Graduate Schools of the Association of American Universities," in A. J. Brumbaugh (ed.) and Mary Irwin (asst. ed.), *American Universities and Colleges*, 1948, American Council on Education, Washington, 1949. The list also includes about fifty women's colleges. The list was discontinued in 1949.

publicly controlled, and only 26 had over 1,200 students in 1955–1956.

Of the 119 colleges, 51 are in Group A, 44 in Group B, and 24 in Group C (Table 24-3). Only one-fifth of the top 119 coeducational and men's colleges in the country make no serious attempt to offer business administration courses. Examination of the list of Group C colleges (Table 24-2) shows that some of the outstanding colleges are included. The men's colleges are divided almost equally among Groups A, B, and C, but their emphasis on business administration varies directly with their size. Of the 95 coeducational colleges, nearly half are in Group A and over four-fifths in Groups A and B. The percentage of coeducational colleges in Group A increases with size—from 18 per cent of the small colleges to 61 per cent of the large colleges. Coeducational colleges tend to emphasize business administration more than men's colleges; the explanation lies in the tradition, clientele, and financial strength of the men's colleges, not in the absence of women.

There is some regional variation in the emphasis on business administration, although it is not great. The ranking of regions from high to low, according to the percentage of colleges in Groups A and B, is: West, South, Middle West, and East. Group A colleges are relatively more numerous when the percentage of day students, as distinguished from resident students, is high. Group A colleges are also relatively more common when the percentage of students from out of state and from foreign countries is small. Group C colleges are at the other end of the scale

TABLE 24-3

DISTRIBUTION OF 119 SELECTED COEDUCATIONAL AND MEN'S COLLEGES BY (1) EXTENT OF OFFERINGS IN BUSINESS ADMINISTRATION, (2) SIZE, AND (3) CONTROL

Extent of business administration	Size and control														
	300–699 students			700–1,199 students			1,200–2,000 students			Total		
	Priv.	Pub.	Both	Priv.	Pub.	Both	Priv.	Pub.	Both	Priv.	Pub.	Both
Coed.	33	1	34	38	0	38	22	1	23	93	2	95
A.	11	0	11	19	0	19	13	1	14	43	1	44
B.	17	0	17	11	0	11	8	0	8	36	0	36
C.	5	1	6	8	0	8	1	0	1	14	1	15
Secretarial.	14	0	14	20	0	20	14	1	15	48	1	49
Men.	11	0	11	10	0	10	3	0	3	24	0	24
A.	2	0	2	4	0	4	1	0	1	7	0	7
B.	4	0	4	2	0	2	2	0	2	8	0	8
C.	5	0	5	4	0	4	0	0	0	9	0	9
Secretarial.	0	0	0	0	0	0	0	0	0	0	0	0
Total.	44	1	45	48	0	48	25	1	26	117	2	119
A.	13	0	13	23	0	23	14	1	15	50	1	51
B.	21	0	21	13	0	13	10	0	10	44	0	44
C.	10	1	11	12	0	12	1	0	1	23	1	24
Secretarial.	14	0	14	20	0	20	14	1	15	48	1	49

with respect to these characteristics. If endowment is small, colleges tend to fall into Group A, and if large into Group C. The same pattern prevails with respect to educational expenditures per student and tuition: low for Group A colleges and high for Group C colleges. The Group C colleges tend to attract students from families which can afford the higher charges; these families tend to have a greater interest in liberal arts education. Classification of the 119 colleges by religious connection shows a relatively high percentage of Group A and B colleges among Methodist, Presbyterian, Baptist, and Lutheran institutions, and a relatively high percentage of Group C colleges among those which are non-sectarian (except public), Congregational, Episcopal, and Quaker. Group C colleges among the 119 have faculties (in all subjects) with a higher educational level than the Group A and B colleges. The faculty of the median Group C college has 50 per cent doctors of philosophy; of Group B colleges, 41 per cent; and of Group A colleges, 44 per cent. These figures are much higher than those for the typical college (among the 493 in the country) in which Ph.D.s comprise approximately 20 per cent of the faculty. Group C colleges tend to have larger library collections than do colleges in Groups B and A, even though they are typically smaller. Group A colleges have the highest rate of attrition, Group B the next highest, and Group C the lowest.[11] Phi Beta Kappa chapters are more common in Group C colleges (83 per cent) than in Group B colleges (50 per cent) and in Group A colleges (24 per cent).[12]

Course Offering in Business Administration

In the 119 colleges 35 different business administration courses were offered in 1956–1957, even with some combining. The following courses were offered in 50 or more colleges: principles of accounting (113); marketing (86); business law (84); business finance (81); cost accounting (70); intermediate accounting (62); tax accounting (56); investments (56); personnel management (54); advanced accounting (53); business organization and management (51); economic geography (51); mathematics of finance (50).

The emphasis on accounting is very clear: 5 of these 13 most common courses are in accounting. The pattern is different, however, when the colleges are classified into Groups A, B, and C. The most common courses for the separate groups are as follows:

Group A: principles of accounting (51); business law (51); marketing

---

[11] "Attrition" refers to students' dropping out of college before graduation.

[12] Statistical tables supporting the statements in this paragraph are available but proved too bulky to be included in this volume.

(48); cost accounting (47); business finance (42); tax accounting (42); intermediate accounting (41); auditing (41)

Group B: principles of accounting (44); marketing (36); business law (33); business finance (31); intermediate accounting (21); cost accounting (21); investments (21); business organization and management (17)

Group C: principles of accounting (18); business finance (8); mathematics of finance (8); business organization and management (6); economic geography (4)

There is clearly consensus among the colleges in the offering of business courses. Additional evidence of agreement was provided by the replies of college departments of business administration and economics when the author asked them which four business administration courses they considered most valuable for business administration students. The six most frequently mentioned courses were: accounting principles (98 per cent), business law (70 per cent), management (54 per cent), marketing (53 per cent), business finance (43 per cent), and business organization (34 per cent). This evaluation coincides almost perfectly with those courses which occur most frequently in the catalogs of the 119 colleges. This high correlation may reflect the fact that those who answered the questionnaires were largely the same people who chose the courses. Four of the first five courses in both lists are the same: principles of accounting, business law, marketing, and business finance. It is evident that principles of accounting is the most esteemed single course. The low position of personnel management in both lists is perhaps surprising. In the survey conducted under the auspices of the American Economic Association in the late 1940s, accounting, corporation finance, and management ("industrial") held the top places.[13] The substantial agreement among teachers as to the most important half dozen business courses should not be construed to mean that these teachers believe the study of these and other business courses constitutes the best college preparation for business careers; in fact, they ranked economics, English, and mathematics ahead of business administration (Table 24-6).

Course Offerings in Economics

Economics courses are discussed here because they are frequently grouped with business courses under college administrative arrange-

---

[13] "Undergraduate Economics and Careers in Business," *American Economic Review,* Supplement, December, 1950, pp. 128–134. The questionnaire in that survey tried in vain to obtain information on the relative value of certain economics courses and roughly corresponding business administration courses, so detailed comparisons with the present survey are not possible.

ments. Sharp differences of opinion prevail, however, as to the relative value of economics, business administration, and other subjects as preparation for business careers.

The 119 selected colleges offered 29 different courses in economics in 1956–1957, according to their catalogs. The following courses were offered by 50 or more of the 119 colleges: principles of economics (116), money and banking (110), public finance (105), international economics (98), statistics (88), history of economic thought (80), individual studies, etc. (69), government and business (66), comparative economic systems (63), business cycles and fluctuations (60), labor problems (55), and labor economics (53). When the colleges are grouped according to the extent of business administration (in Groups A, B, and C), the ranking of economics courses does not vary significantly.[14]

The relative valuation placed on various economics courses as preparation for business administration showed that principles of economics (98 per cent), money and banking (73 per cent), and statistics (58 per cent) were clearly favorites. Labor scored 44 per cent, fluctuations, etc. 18 per cent, managerial economics 15 per cent, and the rest of the subjects smaller percentages. Each respondent was asked to choose four subjects. Since economics courses serve other purposes than as preparation for business administration, the ratings obtained from the catalogs could hardly be expected to hold from the point of view of business administration. Of the six most common courses in economics—principles, money and banking, public finance, international economics, statistics, and history of economic thought—only principles, money and banking, and statistics were among the top six considered most valuable for business administration students.

The respondents' rather low ranking of managerial economics (economics of enterprise, economics of the business firm, business economics) in sixth place and of price and distribution theory (intermediate economic theory, price theory, etc.) in seventh place is worth noting, since these subjects are in the branch of economic analysis which bears most directly on the operations of the business firm. It is well known, despite lack of statistical evidence, that students majoring in business administration tend to avoid theoretical courses of this type, but it is surprising to find their teacher-advisers apparently supporting this attitude. In departments combining business administration and economics, students taking

---

[14] The American Economic Association survey, *ibid.*, p. 99, found money and banking second and public finance third, after the principles course. Then followed labor, economic history, statistics, international economics, corporations (roughly approximating our government and business), theory. The 71 respondents to the American Economic Association questionnaire were from a wide variety of types of institutions.

the business option are frequently excused from economic theory, and those taking the economics option are often excused from accounting.[15]

TEACHERS OF BUSINESS ADMINISTRATION AND ECONOMICS IN THE LIBERAL ARTS COLLEGES

The average number of full-time (or full-time equivalent) teachers of business administration and economics in 385 coeducational and men's liberal arts colleges was 4.5 in 1955–1956 (Table 24-4). The median was

TABLE 24-4

DISTRIBUTION OF 385 COLLEGES BY (1) NUMBER OF TEACHERS OF BUSINESS ADMINISTRATION AND ECONOMICS, (2) EXTENT OF BUSINESS ADMINISTRATION, AND (3) SIZE OF COLLEGE

Extent of business administration and size	Number of teachers					
	1–2	3–4	5–6	7–8	Over 8	Total
Group A................	6	45	51	37	49	188
Small................	5	24	15	4	3	51
Medium..............	1	16	24	21	14	76
Large................	0	5	12	12	32	61
Group B................	38	67	17	2	3	127
Small................	29	43	4	0	0	76
Medium..............	9	19	7	1	0	36
Large................	0	5	6	1	3	15
Group C................	37	21	7	2	3	70
Small................	28	9	1	0	0	38
Medium..............	7	7	5	2	3	24
Large................	2	5	1	0	0	8
Total..................	81	133	75	41	55	385
Small................	62	76	20	4	3	165
Medium..............	17	42	36	24	17	136
Large................	2	15	19	13	35	84

SOURCE: *American Universities and Colleges*, 1956.

3.8; 50 per cent had fewer, 50 per cent had more. The median number of business and economics teachers (combined) for Group A colleges

[15] In a sampling of 20 colleges offering a major in business administration, 95 per cent required principles of accounting of business majors, well over half required money and banking, less than half required statistics, and only two required economic theory. One correspondent wrote that "the business administration major without the theory of the firm resembles the engineer without physics," but his is a minority view.

was 5.8, for Group B colleges 3.4, and for Group C colleges 1.9. Small colleges had a median of 2.6, medium-size colleges 5.3, and large colleges 7.5. Only 55 (14 per cent) of the 385 colleges had over 8 teachers of business administration and economics; 32 of these were large Group A colleges. For the 195 colleges showing business administration as a separate department, the median number of teachers of business administration was 4.0—4.8 for the Group A colleges and 2.2 for the Group B colleges (Table 24-5).

TABLE 24-5

DISTRIBUTION OF 195 COLLEGES HAVING SEPARATE DEPARTMENTS OF BUSINESS ADMINISTRATION IN 1955 BY (1) NUMBER OF TEACHERS OF BUSINESS ADMINISTRATION, (2) EXTENT OF BUSINESS ADMINISTRATION, AND (3) SIZE OF COLLEGE

Extent of business administration and size	Number of teachers of business administration					
	1–2.9	3–4.9	5–6.9	7–8.9	9 and over	Total
Group A..................	25	56	31	25	7	144
Small..................	9	20	10	0	1	40
Medium...............	6	24	14	10	4	58
Large.................	10	12	7	15	2	46
Group B..................	42	8	1	0	0	51
Small..................	31	4	0	0	0	35
Medium...............	9	1	1	0	0	11
Large.................	2	3	0	0	0	5
Total*..................	67	64	32	25	7	195
Small..................	40	24	10	0	1	75
Medium...............	15	25	15	10	4	69
Large.................	12	15	7	15	2	51

* No Group C colleges, since they offer little or no business administration.

These figures on the number of teachers become significant when they are set against the large variety of courses the teachers conduct. Even the Group A colleges have less than 6 teachers, on the average, to cover all of economics and all of business administration. The plight of the Group B colleges—with an average of 3.4 teachers in both areas—is much worse. The Group C colleges, though having an average of 1.9 teachers in economics, at least have the advantage of offering only economics. The extent to which the teachers, especially in the Group B colleges, are spread out can be fully appreciated only by examination of the catalogs of the individual colleges and by conversations with the teachers.

The average course load of teachers in the colleges is about four per semester, or three per quarter (in colleges on the quarter system). A few colleges—the wealthier, usually—require teaching loads of only three courses per semester, or four courses with only three, or possibly two, preparations. In such colleges the teachers tend to take on additional responsibilities for supervision of individual studies, special outside extracurricular activities, special examination programs, etc. In the great majority of colleges the teachers teach different subjects the first and second semesters (or the first, second, and third quarters). Frequently, courses are given only in alternate years. Teachers often teach both business administration and economics. There is little opportunity, under these conditions, for the teachers to develop more than the barest acquaintance with the subjects they teach beyond the textbooks they use.

Are departments of business administration and economics adequately staffed? Replies to the questionnaire show that the respondents consider the *minimum adequate number* of teachers of business administration to be 2.8 and of economics to be 2.8, regardless of the size of the college. Yet only one-third (130) of the 385 colleges actually have more than 5.6 teachers in both subjects (Table 24-4). The teachers think that 6 teachers would be the *optimum* number. The optimum number rises from 4.6 in the small schools to 7.0 in the large schools. The Group A colleges actually have the largest number (6.4) in business and economics combined; they also set their optimum at the highest (8.2), which is not surprising in view of the number of specialties in business administration. The respondents from Group B colleges think 5.6 an appropriate number of business and economics teachers. The Group C respondents would like to have 4.8 teachers in economics alone.

Indications are that the number of students handled by the teachers is not excessive, judged by the usual standard of four classes with 20 to 30 students in each. Very frequently introductory classes are larger, but upper-class courses often have fewer than 10 students. The smaller number of students is largely a result of a proliferation of courses, which results from a variety of pressures: from the administration for the teacher to teach four, or sometimes more, courses each semester, from the students for various specific courses, from the teacher (or department) bidding for more students, and from the admissions office hoping to show that the array of courses offered in business administration compares favorably with the array offered by nearby universities. Courses listed in the catalog are sometimes given irregularly or not given at all, or are offered by teachers who have not had graduate work, research, or other experience in those subjects. Since the quality of teaching of business and economics in college depends above all else on the teacher's knowledge of his subject, the typical situation foredooms the students to mediocre teaching or worse. (It is not intended here to praise under-graduate teaching in universities by implication.) Teachers in the colleges do not, with few exceptions, have assistants to do clerical and routine grading tasks, secretarial help to handle paper work, associates with whom they can discuss their subjects, or good library facilities. Moreover, they find themselves almost inevitably involved in administrative work, faculty committees, and student extracurricular activities, little of which contributes to the intellectual quality of their teaching. This situation, almost universal in the small colleges, means that most faculty members are not intellectually active in their chosen fields.[16]

It should be self-evident that business and economics teachers in lib-

[16] A statistical study of appearances on the programs of the annual meetings of the American Economic Association (the principal professional association for the college teacher of business and economics) shows that participants from small colleges are extremely rare. "There was an almost complete absence of papers from the nation's liberal arts colleges. . . . Only six colleges were represented, accounting for eight papers (less than four per cent)." Daniel R. Fusfeld in *American Economic Review*, September, 1956, p. 643. These eight papers were all that were presented in five years (1950–1954)! At the 1958 meetings of the association (and allied associations), only three persons from colleges presented papers.

The president of the Midwest Economics Association in 1957–1958, Leland J. Gordon of Denison University, fully aware of the lack of participation by small college members, was able, even through personal solicitation, to obtain only four faculty members from smaller institutions to present papers.

In recent years the Ford Foundation, directly and through the Brookings Institution, has designed study and research programs especially to attract teachers of economics (including economists teaching business administration). The applications have not been numerous and have tended to come mainly from a few prominent colleges; there are some indications that the situation is improving. Even a casual perusal of the professional journals and of the announcements of new books shows that very few articles or books are written by teachers in the colleges. Part of the explanation is provided by the statistics on the degrees held by teachers of business administration and economics in the small colleges. Even in the 119 selected colleges, only 44.8 per cent have completed their Ph.D.s. In the 51 Group A colleges among the 119, 38.0 per cent of the teachers of business administration and economics have the doctorate, in Group B colleges 44.0 per cent, and in Group C colleges 66.4 per cent. Colleges emphasizing business administration thus have a smaller percentage of teachers of economics and business with the Ph.D.

Mention should be made of external barriers to publication. Professional journals are edited from the large universities and there is an understandable—though hardly commendable—tendency for articles to be chosen and reviews to be assigned on the basis of acquaintance and professional prominence. The organizers of programs for professional meetings have a strong tendency to put on the programs "names," persons who press hard for places (important for their advancement in universities, not in colleges), and acquaintances or former graduate students. Heavy teaching and administrative duties, poor library facilities, and lack of research assistance combine to discourage scholarship in the liberal arts colleges. Various professors in these colleges who have done reputable writing told the author that they did it in spite of the circumstances at their colleges.

eral arts colleges cannot maintain the intellectual vitality required to be good teachers if they do not engage in scholarly activity. Writing is a severe discipline in its own right. Research involving the use of documents, books, and periodicals is the surest way to keep sharp one of the principal tools the teacher can train his students to use: the judicious use of written materials. Quantitative research, especially with original data, is one of the basic disciplines involved in business and economics. The formulation of theoretical or policy questions in systematic form and the search for their answers are right at the heart of teaching these subjects. The passive teacher—who reads rather than writes and reads less and less as time goes on—is or becomes the poor teacher. The alleged dichotomy between scholars and teachers is false for college teachers of business and economics; some scholars may not be teachers, but teachers of any competence must be scholars to some degree.

There is a fairly strong belief among administrators, students, parents, prospective employers, and some faculty members that the teachers of business administration must have had some practical experience in the subjects they are teaching. The promotion, by colleges, of business administration as a practical subject warrants the expectation that the teachers of it be familiar with the actual practice of business. We do not know how many teachers of business administration have had practical experience with the main problems of business. Some teachers of accounting have worked as accountants or carry practice along with their teaching. Many teachers of business law do practice or have practiced law. Most other teachers of business subjects have also had part-time or summer experience doing manual labor, factory work, sales or office work, but it is the author's impression that very few have actually run a business—even a small one—or have occupied an important executive position in a business of some size. Even the experiences they have had—all to the good, of course—could touch only a small part of the major problems of administering a business. This situation is widely recognized, and various large firms have made arrangements for college teachers of business and economics to work close to top executives during summers. The Economics-in-Action program, sponsored by the Foundation for Economic Education, is consciously designed to acquaint teachers with business practice.

It is simply impossible, however, for the college teacher to acquire and maintain a body of knowledge from direct experience which will enable him to teach his various courses on the basis of personal experience. Inevitably the teacher must rely upon other means of learning about business practice if he is to avoid a painfully anecdotal, limited, and out-of-date approach to his subject. He can maintain contacts with businesses, he can draw on businessmen for some classes, and he can try to broaden his own work experience, but these efforts can only supplement the basic method of using written materials. The world of business, not the academic world, is the place for students to learn the immediately practical.

The task of the teacher of business subjects is to study business behavior and the environment within which business operates in the hope of understanding business behavior and of conveying this understanding, together with the ways of developing it, to his students. This is the genuine task. The best schools of business have learned, after much experimentation, that their faculties should be composed mainly of teacher-scholars, not exbusinessmen. Exact statistics are not available, but most teachers of business administration subjects other than accounting and business law view themselves as economists, rather than as members of some other professional group. Even those teachers holding advanced degrees in business administration tend to view themselves as economists. If the field of business administration as an academic subject develops a more distinctive—not necessarily more specialized—body of subject matter for pursuit at the graduate level, teachers of business administration will become available who are not limited to this academic background. (See Chaps. 11 and 12 on faculty and doctoral programs.)

Not more than one-fourth of the full professors of business administration and economics in colleges had salaries of more than $6,000 for the academic year during the mid-1950s, according to estimates. Instructors tended to receive salaries corresponding to the earnings of factory operatives, around $4,000 per year. Assistant and associate professors typically received between $4,000 and $6,000.[17] It is probably correct to say that college professors had supplementary income from summer earnings or other sources of not more than one-fifth of the above amounts. The students of these teachers typically received nearly as high pay on their first jobs as their teachers, and many received more. Also, the students' prospects were for considerably higher incomes than their teachers' if they stayed out of academic work. Much has been written in recent years about salaries in college teaching as compared with other lines of work calling for similar qualities. The present study has made only too evident the shortage of competent personnel in business and economics departments of colleges, a shortage which would undoubtedly not have existed if the academic salaries of the 1940s and early 1950s had been, say, double their actual levels, or had maintained even the same relative position, compared with other occupations, that they had before World War II.

[17] Survey of Business Education Questionnaire.

Income prospects for the liberal arts college teacher of business and economics are not very good, despite increased demand for college teachers and sluggish increase in supply. The main reason, quite aside from the tendency toward inflation, is that the shortage is not expected to be as acute in other subjects, except for some sciences, and that administrators find it difficult, from the point of view of faculty morale, to pay members of some departments distinctly higher salaries than members of others. Since college administrators have rarely tried to bid for top-level teachers in business or economics, it seems unlikely that they will run the risk of upsetting faculty morale and unbalancing always precarious budgets by putting the salaries of the teachers of business and economics well above the general average. The individual teacher of business or economics who has competence and initiative can find attractive work elsewhere at higher pay, so the tendency will increase for colleges to keep only the academic dregs. There are not enough qualified teachers with inheritances, rich wives, or monkish tastes to fill the positions.

One cannot avoid the judgment that many college teachers of business and economics are poorly trained, badly overworked, and sadly underpaid. It is an illusion to think that such persons can, by and large, be great teachers or great inspirations to their students. Their training, their jobs, their accomplishments, and their pay should be such that they can be persons of pride and dignity.

REQUIREMENTS OF BUSINESS ADMINISTRATION MAJORS AND METHODS OF TEACHING BUSINESS ADMINISTRATION

General graduation requirements for majors in business administration tend to differ from those for other students only with respect to foreign language requirements. In a sample examination of catalogs of the 119 colleges, one-fourth had no foreign language requirement for business administration students but did have it for most other students.

An almost universal requirement of business administration students is an elementary course in accounting. This requirement is not a psychological burden to most students concentrating in business administration, although many of these students find it exacting. The standard course is in the principles and practice of double-entry bookkeeping for the proprietorship, the partnership, and the corporation.

Business administration majors are usually relieved of a requirement customarily made of economics majors in the better colleges—a course in economic theory beyond the principles course. The public explanation of this difference is that the theory course is not relevant for business administration majors; the private explanation is that the business administration majors find it too difficult. This situation is likely to exist where business administration is used as a dumping ground for weak students (see Chap. 4). Economic theory is a moderately difficult subject, as compared with many college subjects; for most students, it is probably on a level with calculus, physics, or philosophy, for example. The comparison for the business students, however, is not with these subjects but with the relatively easy subjects of management, marketing, personnel relations, or business finance.

Several of the colleges within the purview of this chapter allow majors in one or more of the specialties of business administration, but the cases are too few and varied to warrant statistical statement. Specifically, some of the majors are in insurance, banking, finance, accounting, marketing, personnel administration, and production management.

A sample survey of catalogs of Group A and B colleges in the list of 119 colleges showed the minimum number of semester hours for a major in business administration runs from a low of 24 to a high of 49. The typical figure is 30 to 36 hours. This is often exclusive of economics courses in Group A colleges. Some colleges place no upper limit on the number of hours in the major field. Specified limits ran from 39 to 58.[18] Colleges show great variation in the courses in business administration they require or strongly recommend for majors, but these courses are not numerous in any one institution.

Teaching methods in business administration courses resemble those in economics courses very closely. The all but universal system in the colleges is the lecture-discussion class of twenty to thirty students, more or less, that meets three times per week, for 50 minutes per meeting, for a 15 to 17 week semester. The textbook is the backbone of the course, so far as reading is concerned. Examinations are given two to four times per semester and are both essay and objective, although the objective type is increasingly common.

Variations occur around this basic pattern. Accounting and statistics differ from other subjects in the business and economics curriculum in that problems are assigned and answered regularly in most colleges. Office machines are generally available. In other subjects, the basic class-text-examination process may be supplemented by required reading from books (usually on reserve) in the library, reading certain newspapers or magazines, writing a book report on the basis of a book read, writing a term paper, visits to a business establishment, class visitors from businesses, "solution" of business case problems, small research assign-

[18] A few colleges, in order to save their students from themselves in their passion for the supposedly practical, have called a certain program of studies "business administration" or a similar name and have included in it several subjects generally considered to be of a liberal and rigorous character. Query: Is it appropriate for administrators to become such "hidden persuaders"?

ments involving the use of the library or direct interviews. Variations on academic methods used in other subjects in colleges are generally applicable to business administration subjects, for example, seminars, tutorials, independent study, senior theses, audio-visual aids, extracollege experiences, comprehensive examinations, graduate record examinations, outside examiners. These variations on the basic pattern differ from college to college, from teacher to teacher, and from year to year. Widespread opinion exists that methods can and should be improved, but the extent of departure from the basic pattern could easily be exaggerated. The teachers are spread too thinly over the subjects to be able to give very much attention to experimental methods. Teachers of business administration, except as they are also teachers of economics, are, however, spared the burden of developing "integrated" or survey courses in the social sciences, since business administration is considered to be beyond the pale of "general education."

Another facet of this problem of teaching methods and requirements in the field of business administration is the character of the teaching materials. There is no lack of materials, as such, but some teachers think the materials lack form and system. One explanation is that the authors of the materials rarely give evidence of a coherent conception of the nature of the business enterprise and its place in the economy. Some critics contend that there are no ascertainable principles of business administration, so that writings on various aspects of the firm's operations are necessarily only collections of facts, or of problems for which there are no principles or theories to serve as firm guides in their solution. A less critical way of stating the same idea is to say that business decisions involve so many variables, few of which can be known with much certainty, that it is hopeless to expect principles or theories to be of much help. Recognition of this point leads the colleges toward the simulation of real situations or efforts to reconstruct them: the case method. This method undoubtedly works better with people who have had some business experience, who are saturated with the facts of particular cases, and who have acquired some acquaintance, or even mastery, of the disciplines which can throw light on business problems: economics, statistical methods, accounting theory, psychology, government. For undergraduates the case method is of questionable value.

The respondents to the author's questionnaire think that some academic subjects are better than others as preparation for business administration. It is interesting that the field of business administration ranks fourth on the list (Table 24-6). Economics, English composition, and mathematics are ahead of it. Other highly valued subjects for this purpose are history, psychology, political science, and speech (including drama). One should not leap to curricular conclusions from this ranking.

TABLE 24-6

RANKING OF ACADEMIC SUBJECTS AS PREPARATION FOR BUSINESS CAREERS

(Replies to questionnaire from 39 teachers of business administration and economics)

Subject	Number of replies	
	"Very valuable"	"Of some value"
Economics....................	39	0
English composition...........	34	3
Mathematics.................	27	11
Business administration........	27	6
History......................	22	11
Psychology..................	22	11
Political science..............	21	11
Speech, drama...............	20	12
Sociology....................	12	17
Philosophy..................	11	17
English literature.............	10	20
Geography...................	9	18
Foreign languages.............	8	13
Religion.....................	5	10
Physics.....................	4	11
Chemistry...................	3	13
Geology.....................	1	13
Anthropology................	1	11
Home economics..............	1	4
Fine arts....................	0	13
Music.......................	0	8
Astronomy...................	0	5
Zoology.....................	0	5
Botany......................	0	4
Education...................	0	3

The top ranking for economics, for example, may merely reflect the fact that most of the respondents were economists!

With business administration, as a subject or collection of subjects, in such a formative and fluid state, it is no wonder that college teachers, almost inevitably not deeply saturated with business facts and problems because of their background and current duties, find it difficult to give high-quality courses in this field.

THE STUDENTS WHO TAKE
BUSINESS ADMINISTRATION COURSES

A good many observations have been made earlier in this chapter about the students who take business administration courses, but a few additional comments are offered. They are based on statements of teachers rather than on statistical analysis and for the most part coinicide with the findings reached in Chap. 4. As a group, business administration majors tend to be below the college average with respect to scholastic aptitude, rank in high school class, college grades, and graduate record examination scores. According to many teachers, they tend to come from families of only moderate incomes, without college backgrounds, and with only casual interest in intellectual, cultural, or public affairs. College is often viewed by them as a means of financial and social advancement, and the students, with parental blessing, tend to gravitate toward the supposedly most practical program of study—business administration. For students of such social-economic origins and with a flair for mathematics and the natural sciences, especially the applied physical sciences, other ways up the income-prestige ladder are available. Few young men of this background have the family encouragement or the financial backing needed to pursue programs pointing toward graduate school in law, medicine, pure science, the fine arts, humanities, social sciences, or even in business administration. They and their parents fear—rightly, no doubt, in many cases—that concentration on some nonvocational subject, without the prospect of graduate school and without family or social connections in business, is likely to find them graduating from college unable to get a job at other than common labor or routine sales work. With such an outlook, one wonders why such students go to small colleges, nearly all of which are poorly equipped to provide specific skills. Part of the explanation lies in religious affiliations of families, part in apprehension or dislike of large universities, part in ignorance of college offerings, part in the proximity of the colleges to the homes of the students, and part in the belief, often correct, that student competition and academic standards are lower at small colleges. Opportunities to earn part of one's way probably do not differ much between universities and colleges.

The children of parents who have been to college, who have executive or professional positions, who have relatively high incomes, or who have interests in various subjects in the liberal arts curriculum, tend to take more liberal and fewer vocational subjects. Their high school or preparatory school courses have also generally been in standard academic subjects. The economic position of such families reduces the pressure for the immediately practical and enables the students to look forward to graduate school for specific vocational training if they show the interest and aptitude. A home atmosphere congenial to the liberal arts makes the study of those subjects much easier for the student who is at all disposed to study. Such families may also doubt the proposition that specific vocational studies in college are the most profitable, even in money terms, in the long run, and they are more likely to believe that liberal education is a good thing regardless of its financial consequences.

These contrasting attitudes, perhaps overdrawn here, seem to explain in considerable measure why some students study business administration (or other subjects intended to be practical), and some do not. They also help explain why some colleges make no pretense of offering business administration while others strive to offer many courses in it. As a dean of a heavily endowed men's college told the author, "Our graduates have done very well in business without having had any undergraduate courses in business, so they see no need for them. We are under no pressure at all." In contrast, the head of a business administration department in a relatively poor college, with half or more of its students commuters, said: "Liberal arts are fine for students from families of some means or with the right connections, but they do nothing to put a poor boy on a payroll when he graduates from college." Then he told of the ease with which his best majors in business administration could outdo the liberal arts graduates of nearby "name" colleges in getting hired by business corporations, even while the heads of these corporations were making commencement speeches on the value of liberal arts. As he put it, "The recruiters didn't read the speeches." Similar comments were made by many persons interviewed. On the other hand, there were few reports that students majoring in economics or other arts subjects had unusual difficulty in obtaining jobs. A period of general prosperity, such as has prevailed since 1942, tends to minimize the competition for jobs among students with different major fields.

There are, and no doubt will continue to be, many thousands of students who seek in small colleges courses which they think will be of cash value in the short run. They do not think in terms of the subjects which will best enable them to learn on the job or will provide them the essential background for special training, evening school work, or their own individual study. They do not think of learning as a continuing process which college simply helps along. Even less do they think of the more philosophical, social, and cultural subjects which can help them become well-rounded persons and, eventually, wise business administrators. Perhaps even sadder is the fact that a great many students who pursue some so-called practical program of study do not obtain jobs in this particular field; many that do at the outset often change soon to other lines. Thus their college studies have been substantially devoted to specialties which they do not even use in the short run, while they have missed the best chance in their lives to broaden themselves.

OPINIONS OF TEACHERS OF BUSINESS ADMINISTRATION
AND ECONOMICS REGARDING COLLEGE PREPARATION
FOR BUSINESS ADMINISTRATION

This section summarizes the views of several hundred persons engaged in teaching college-level business administration and economics. Questionnaires and interviews were employed.[19]

The first of four questions on the questionnaire was:

1. Should a liberal arts college attempt to shape its curriculum to meet the needs or wishes of students who look forward to careers as business administrators or enterprisers?

Of the responses, 58.1 per cent said yes and 22.3 per cent said no. The remaining 20 per cent included those qualifying their answers to such an extent that it was apparent they did not wish to make the sharp choice, even in principle, and cases in which respondents from the same institutions disagreed. It is not surprising that 70 per cent of the replies from Group A colleges said that liberal arts colleges should shape their curricula toward this end. The interesting thing is that 30 per cent of these respondents did not think so, or had doubts. It is also interesting that nearly 30 per cent of the Group C respondents thought the colleges should so shape their curricula. Obviously, there are dissidents in both camps. Group B colleges are understandably on the fence, 60 to 40 in favor.

Surprisingly, opinions do not vary significantly according to size of college: between 55 and 60 per cent of all three groups answered yes to the question. The breakdown according to the sex of students shows only 38 per cent of the respondents from women's colleges answering yes as compared with 48 per cent from the men's and 64 per cent from the coeducational colleges. The reason for the relatively low percentage from the men's colleges, despite the predominance of men students in business administration, would seem to be that many of the men's colleges which have remained relatively small liberal arts colleges are well established and are rather firmly devoted to the liberal arts curriculum. The control breakdown shows the expected preference of public institutions for voca-

[19] Questionnaires were sent to the 493 accredited liberal arts colleges. Three copies were sent to each college in order to facilitate expression of a diversity of views. There were 326 replies from 215 different colleges. Extensive comments were made by many respondents. The author interviewed scores of college presidents, deans, department heads, and teachers of business administration and economics from all parts of the country. He also had reports from other persons working on other chapters in this volume. This summary of the various points of view cannot possibly do justice to the thoughtful contributions of hundreds of informed and experienced persons, but an attempt is made to show the main patterns of thought.

tion-oriented curricula. The replies to Question 1 are summarized in Table 24-7.

TABLE 24-7

REPLIES TO QUESTION 1 OF QUESTIONNAIRE BY (1) EXTENT OF BUSINESS ADMINISTRATION, (2) SIZE OF COLLEGE, (3) SEX OF STUDENTS, AND (4) CONTROL*

	Yes		No		Qualified answer†		Total	
	No.	%	No.	%	No.	%	No.	%
1. By extent of business administration:								
A...............	62	70.4	8	9.1	18	20.5	88	100.0
B...............	50	61.0	16	19.5	16	19.5	82	100.0
C...............	13	28.9	24	53.4	8	17.7	45	100.0
2. By size of college:								
Small..........	59	58.4	27	26.7	15	14.9	101	100.0
Medium........	40	59.7	11	16.4	16	23.9	67	100.0
Large..........	26	55.4	10	21.2	11	23.4	47	100.0
3. By sex of students:								
Coed..........	100	64.2	28	17.9	28	17.9	156	100.0
Women........	12	37.5	14	43.8	6	18.7	32	100.0
Men..........	13	48.2	2	22.2	8	29.6	27	100.0
4. By control:								
Private........	106	55.8	45	23.7	39	20.5	190	100.0
Public.........	19	76.0	3	12.0	3	12.0	25	100.0
Total...........	125	58.2	48	22.3	42	19.5	215	100.0

* "1. Should a liberal arts college attempt to shape its curriculum to meet the needs and wishes of students who look forward to careers as business enterprisers or executives?"

† Different views from same college and qualified views by respondents.

Question 2 sought to discover the preferred approach of the respondents to education for business administration by posing three alternatives. These alternatives had emerged from interviews.

2. There are sharply differing views regarding desirable programs of study for college students who look forward to business careers. Please check the statement which is *closest* to your view.

__ a. The college student looking forward to a career in business administration should take a liberal arts program. The exact field of concentration does not matter very much, although the more rigorous arts and sciences are to be preferred. The important thing is that the student learn how to think, that he be able to express himself well, and that he acquire some degree of mastery of his chosen field. Excellence in a subject shows intelligence and determination. A student does not know what kinds of jobs he will have later, but if he has done well in solid subjects in college he will have developed the intellectual discipline which will enable him to learn on the job, in special training programs, or in graduate school. His broad education will become increasingly useful to him as his executive opportunities and responsibilities increase.

___ b. The future business executive or enterpriser needs many talents, but above all he needs good judgment. He must have the capacity to choose people, to choose wisely among alternative courses of action, and to elicit the cooperation of other people in pursuing chosen courses of action. Although many college subjects can contribute something to the background of the future businessman, some subjects are more likely to help the student develop the essential executive talents than others. (If you prefer this view, which of the subjects below—typically offered by liberal arts colleges—do you think would be (1) very valuable, (2) of some value, or (3) of nominal value for students looking forward to business careers?) Anthropology, Astronomy, Botany, Business Administration, Chemistry, Economics, Education, English Composition, English Literature, Fine Arts, Foreign Languages, Geography, Geology, History, Home Economics, Mathematics, Music, Philosophy, Physics, Political Science, Psychology, Religion, Sociology, Speech-Drama, Zoology, Other.

___ c. A student hoping to become a business executive or enterpriser should devote about one-third of his time in college to business subjects. In addition to or as a part of the usual distribution requirements in liberal arts and sciences, he should take some courses in subjects closely related to business, such as economics, psychology, English composition and public speaking. Additional liberal arts subjects are fine for students who have jobs waiting for them, regardless of their training, and for those going on to graduate school, but for students who plan to start their business careers upon leaving college, concentration in business administration is best. (If you select this view, will you please rank or check the four business subjects and the four economics subjects you consider most important for students planning business careers?)

Business: Accounting (Principles), Accounting (Advanced), Business Finance, Business Law, Business Organization, Economic Geography, Insurance, Investments, Management (General), Management (Personnel), Management (Production), Marketing, Mathematics of Finance, Other.

Economics: Principles (or other name), Comparative Economic Systems, Consumer Economics, Economic Development, Economic History, Fluctuations, National Income, Government Control of Business, History of Economic Thought, Industrial Organization, International Economics, Labor Economics and Problems, Managerial Economics, Money and Banking, Price and Distribution Theory, Public Finance, Statistics, Other.

Comment: (If neither a, nor b, nor c reflects your viewpoint, please indicate changes you would make, or sketch out your own approach.)

The 305 individual respondents divided up as follows among the three alternatives: 33.1 per cent (101) favored the most general (a); 36.4 per cent (111), some degree of concentration but not necessarily in business administration (b); and 30.5 per cent (93), concentration on business administration (c). Some respondents wanted all three alternatives! College is too short to permit such luxury. The approximately equal division among the three alternatives brings out with painful clarity the divergent views of people actively engaged in college education.

Question 2 also invited respondents to indicate the academic subjects (following departmental lines, generally) which they thought would be "(1) very valuable, (2) of some value, or (3) of nominal value for students looking forward to business careers." The ranking, noted earlier, was as follows: economics, English composition, mathematics, business administration, history, psychology, political science, speech, and then a scattering (Table 24-6). The omission of philosophy among the top subjects was the only surprise to the author.

Option c of Question 2 provided the opportunity for respondents to check the four business subjects and the four economics subjects they considered most valuable for students concentrating in business administration. The results, discussed above, showed a striking consensus among college teachers of business administration and economics as to the most important courses.

The respondents who prefer alternatives a and b in Question 2 of the questionnaire *ipso facto* conceive of preparation for business as permitting a much wider range in choice of subjects. Of course the selection of a major field, such as economics, mathematics, English, psychology, history, or political science, entails the meeting of certain general or distribution requirements and certain requirements in the major field. Teachers who select the a option in Question 2 would, by this choice, recommend to students the presumably traditional liberal arts subjects, without any deliberate reference to the problems of business. Any of many programs of study available in colleges with high academic standards would do. Teachers who select the b option presumably think they can recommend courses to students which will help the students develop "good judgment" and the other qualities listed under this option. The comments on the questionnaires indicate that these teachers do not, in general, think in terms of set patterns of courses. They just think some college subjects are better than others as education for business leadership.

The results of the tabulation of Question 3—the actual, minimum satisfactory, and optimum number of teachers of business administration and of economics—were discussed previously. In general, the respondents thought that they had the "minimum adequate" number of teachers at the present time, but that they were understaffed with reference to the optimum by 25 to 35 per cent. The question of appropriate size of staff is considered further in the concluding section.

Question 4 was as follows:

4. If you think that the liberal arts colleges are not doing as good a job as they might reasonably be expected to do in preparing students for business careers, could you indicate some of the reasons?

Over half the respondents accepted the invitation to comment. Opinions regarding preparation for business administration clearly reveal a genuine diversity of views, although they seem to fall quite easily into the three categories represented by options *a*, *b*, and *c* of Question 2 of the questionnaire. Evidently, the different viewpoints will continue to be represented in the liberal arts colleges of the country, despite the trend over the past four decades for colleges to shift from Group C (no explicit preparation for business) through Group B (some) to Group A (several or many specific courses in business administration). Many teachers of business administration and economics in the colleges covered in this survey are convinced that the movement toward and into Group A has gone too far. This view derives in part from the recognized inability of the colleges to compete with the schools of business in the universities in the various specialties of business administration and in part from convictions regarding undergraduate preparation for business. Whatever its merits, educationally speaking, once the road toward intensive specialization has been selected, the large institutions, with enough finances and students to support at least a dozen teachers of business administration, can easily outshine the college that can support, all things considered, only a few. The author always asked the teachers, in the interviews, whether they thought their colleges could do as good a job of teaching business administration as the large universities. The answer was invariably no. The answer to another question— "If your departmental teaching resources were devoted to the teaching of economics, could you do as good a job as the universities?"—was different. Many replied that they could do just as good a job; several replied that they could do much better, because teaching undergraduates is their main duty. Others said they would have to have more and better colleagues and easier teaching loads. The basic reason for greater optimism with respect to economics seems to be that economics is a fairly coherent, systematic discipline— a method of dealing with scarcity problems as well as a collection of information and generalizations from this information—whereas business administration is not such a subject. While eventually it might become such a discipline, at least at present it is not.

According to this investigation, the overwhelming majority of teachers of business administration and economics in the colleges believe that they could, even with as few as three economists, provide good offerings in economics but that they cannot do so in business administration and economics even with twice that number of teachers. All liberal arts colleges recognize the need for economics, whether or not they offer much in the way of business administration. When asked why they did not simply concentrate on economics and leave business administration to the schools of business in the universities, the teachers and administrators advanced the usual reasons for the existence of business administration recited earlier in this chapter. It was generally recognized that the decision lay with the college administrators rather than with the teachers, but that the college administrators were hamstrung by fancied or real pressures by boards, students, alumni, and parents—and by derivative financial considerations.

In a word, most teachers in the small colleges know they are offering poor or mediocre courses in the field of business administration, but they do not know how to extricate themselves or their colleges from the situation.

ALTERNATIVE COURSES OF ACTION

The preceding sections of this chapter should have made it clear that very few of the approximately 500 accredited liberal arts colleges with less than 2,000 students have satisfactorily solved the problem of college education for students looking forward to careers as business administrators or enterprisers. Moreover, the answers to the problem are not readily apparent from a survey of the facts.

In this concluding section the author sets forth (1) his opinions on the questions raised at the beginning of the chapter and (2) four alternative approaches to the basic problem. There is no intention of implying that all colleges should follow the same pattern. College administrators, trustees, and teachers will recognize the ideas applicable to their own situations. First the author's opinions on the questions:

1. It seems likely that many colleges will be able, if they wish, to increase the relative emphasis on liberal arts subjects as preparation for students looking forward to business careers.

2. Colleges should support the concept of business administration as a profession which can best be pursued academically on the graduate level or in conjunction with actual work experience. The characteristics of undergraduate "prebusiness" programs are discussed below, but there is obviously room for variation and experimentation.

3. The numerous and developing alternative ways of obtaining specialized education for business—outside the undergraduate framework—may be expected to relieve the colleges of many pressures for immediately practical business courses to which they have been subject for the past three or four decades.

4. There is much evidence that business firms increasingly seek college graduates who have excelled in any of several liberal arts programs. There is little evidence that liberal arts graduates have unusual difficulty in finding and retaining positions of responsibility.

5. If a college wishes to offer a fairly adequate program of studies in

business administration, it should be certain that it is able to support a fairly large staff of teachers (10 to 12) in economics and business administration. See Alternative 2 below for details.

6. If a college wishes to offer few or no courses in business administration, there seem to be three main curricular patterns from which it can sensibly choose. These are discussed below under Alternatives 1, 3, and 4.

The four alternative approaches are as follows:

1. Omit business administration but offer good courses in economics as well as other liberal arts subjects.

2. Develop a strong business administration program along with good courses in economics.

3. Offer a few key courses in business administration that are closely related to economics along with good offerings in economics.

4. Offer a "prebusiness" program, or set of programs, which would consist of liberal arts subjects which are especially good as background for business, but omit courses in business administration.

Alternative 1. Some colleges may wish to omit business administration as a subject of study but want to have adequate offerings in economics. A very acceptable rationale can be provided for this course of action,[20] and a number of well-known colleges follow this course.[21] Every liberal arts college with a total undergraduate student body of less than 1,000 to 1,200 should seriously consider this alternative.[22] A principal reason is that a smaller college, all things considered, cannot afford adequate teaching staffs in both economics and business administration, but it can afford the minimum adequate staff of three in economics. Even in a coeducational college of 1,200, which would mean 100 teachers under a 12 to 1 student-teacher ratio, probably not more than five teachers would be allotted to economics and business administration. Five teachers can do a very reputable job in economics in a college of this size; they can only do poorly if they are spread over both economics and business administration. The basic reason is that business administration, if not

[20] See, for example, "A Businessman Looks at the Liberal Arts," by Clarence B. Randall, published as *The Randall Lectures*, by the Fund for Adult Education, New York, January, 1957.

[21] Of the 119 coeducational and men's colleges included in our smaller list, the following approximate this pattern: Amherst, Bowdoin, Carleton, Dickinson, Earlham, Hamilton, Haverford, Kenyon, Lawrence, Middlebury, Pomona, Swarthmore, Wabash, Wesleyan (Conn.), Williams, and Wooster. Women's colleges which approximate it are: Bryn Mawr, Connecticut College, Mount Holyoke, Smith, Vassar, Wellesley, Wells, and Wheaton (Mass.). All these colleges have three or more full-time teachers of economics.

[22] Small size is by no means the only reason for following this pattern. Several larger institutions, not included in this study, omit undergraduate business administration, e.g., Chicago, Harvard, Princeton, and Yale. Columbia and Cornell have dropped their undergraduate business programs.

superficial in the extreme, is a collection of quite specialized subjects which require specialists as teachers.

Some colleges may *want* to choose the liberal arts path but feel that they have to use the term "business administration" in the catalog, as a department name, as the name of a program of study, on diplomas, and for other publicity. It should not be beyond their ingenuity to explain and to eulogize the liberal arts as preparation for business careers for public relations purposes without misrepresenting it. Many prominent businessmen, as brought out in Chap. 5, will support them.

The positive point about the straight economics approach, in the liberal arts context, is that it is within the capacity of a great many colleges. There are few colleges, regardless of size, which cannot afford three economists, the minimum satisfactory number for an economics department under contemporary conditions. With as many as five economists, a college can obtain all the specialization needed for undergraduate work in economics; additional manpower should be used to improve teaching effectiveness. With three or more, there can be flexibility in teaching assignments, mutual intellectual stimulation, opportunity for worth-while outside experiences for the teachers, and regular yearly offerings of the courses.

This course of action is increasingly open to colleges that wish to provide primarily a liberal arts, cultural, or preprofessional type of education. True, it is *not* a practicable alternative for community colleges and others that are convinced they must offer various forms of vocational education. Nonetheless, the straight liberal arts course of action will be increasingly open to many colleges because of certain external factors: (a) the mounting number of students eligible for college, (b) the expanding economic capacity of families and the country generally to support college education in the liberal arts and sciences, (c) the growing interest in liberal arts which derives from higher standards of living, and (d) the increasing availability of good graduate schools of business, evening schools, and specialized training programs provided by businesses themselves. Colleges wishing to prosper as purveyors of liberal arts education in the coming decades will move promptly to reshape their curricula and their teaching staffs to provide more and better solid liberal arts subjects and fewer vocational subjects. There can be no serious question about the expanding market for liberal arts education.

Mention should be made of the variant of this first alternative which gives no precedence to economics among the liberal arts subjects as preparation for business administration. Ninety-nine questionnaire respondents (30 per cent) approved this approach. This variant is undoubtedly satisfactory for students going on to a graduate school of business, although these students should have enough undergraduate economics to gain some idea of the nature of the economic system within which the business firm operates, or they should prolong their graduate studies sufficiently to learn this much economics.

Alternative 2. A second major alternative is for a college to expand in size sufficiently to be able to afford, all things considered, an economics staff of at least the minimum acceptable size, taking into account the size of the college, *plus* a business administration staff of sufficient size to warrant having on it specialists in at least some of the key branches of the subject.[23] A plausible *minimum*-size college for this approach would have 1,000 to 1,200 *men* students. A minimum of five teachers of economics and five in business administration would be feasible. The business administration offerings could then approximate those recommended in Chaps. 8 and 9 for undergraduate schools of business. In business administration this minimum acceptable arrangement would permit, say, two specialists in accounting and in other quantitative methods related to business, one in finance, one in marketing, and one in either general management or personnel management. Even a staff of this size would not permit (perhaps fortunately) specialists in various industries or in various functional fields other than those listed and it would leave to economics the teaching of business or managerial economics, statistics, business fluctuations, governmental control of business, international trade, public finance, and other subjects which relate closely to business management.

If a college selects this second course, it should recognize that it will have a very hard time attracting good teachers of business subjects, since such teachers, really scarce, tend to go to the large universities where they can pursue their specialties intensively, teach at least some graduate students, publish, obtain special grants for research more readily, and engage in remunerative consulting work.

Another result which will almost certainly be encountered by a college selecting this second course is the placing of the economics department— or the regular economist members of a combined business and economics department—in a secondary or "service" capacity. Economics then tends to be viewed by administrators, faculty, and students more and more as background or supplementation for business administration and less and less as a liberal arts subject designed to provide an understanding of the economy. This has happened long since at many large universities. In due time the economists will tend to convert themselves into business administration specialists of some sort or seek jobs elsewhere; the best ones are most mobile. A college should be alert to this probable development.

It should be apparent that Alternative 2—the offering of a minimum

[23] Davidson College is moving in this direction.

satisfactory program of business administration—is beyond the competence of practically all liberal arts colleges of less than 2,000 students. To try to pursue this course of action means, on the one hand, waging a losing competition with the university schools of business and, on the other, using scarce resources that could be used advantageously for other college needs.

Alternative 3. A third alternative is to try to work out a combination of economics and business administration that will be acceptable but less ambitious than that just described. *This third position consists of selecting a few key courses in business administration to supplement adequate offerings in economics.* It is obviously a compromise between straight economics, in the liberal arts context, of Alternative 1 and the substantial business administration program of Alternative 2. All but a handful of the 385 coeducational and men's liberal arts colleges have been pursuing this intermediate course of action for many years. This course is full of pitfalls, as the first part of this chapter should have made clear.

If a college must, for whatever reasons, attempt this alternative, it can at least avoid some major mistakes. The first injunction is not to try to offer any business administration subjects unless more than three teachers are available to teach economics. Nobody seriously questions the need for economics as one base for the study of business administration at the collegiate level, and nobody seriously questions the essentiality of a good department of economics in a liberal arts college. Second, the limited teaching resources available for business administration, probably one or two teachers in addition to the three in economics, should be concentrated in only two or three areas, at most, of the broad field of business, not spread over the whole field. It must constantly be borne in mind that the business offerings, under this alternative, are only tokens or gestures.

The exact subject-matter areas in business might well vary from college to college, but those selected, unless there are very special reasons, should be from the list of generally accepted key business subjects: accounting, business law, management, personnel, marketing, and finance. Selection must be based primarily on the availability of teachers. Consider accounting first. Not many economists want to teach accounting, although some will teach one course for a limited time. Practicing accountants can rarely give enough time to their courses or their students to be good teachers. Should the college hire a full-time accounting teacher? If so, should it expect him to concentrate entirely on accounting or to teach also, for example, business finance or business law? It would seem better to have him concentrate on accounting. How competent an accounting teacher can the college hire, all things considered? The chances of obtaining an excellent one are not good. If the college decides to offer business law, it usually has the choice of using a practicing lawyer as a part-time teacher or of having an amateur in legal matters (an accountant, economist, or political scientist) teach the subject. Neither alternative is very satisfactory.

In the field of management the chances of the college's being able to hire a competent specialist are slim, so it would have to rely on a nonspecialist, presumably an economist, or possibly a psychologist or political scientist. In some situations a business executive might be available on a part-time basis. This is a good field to omit unless unusually favorable conditions exist.

Personnel relations, labor-management relations, etc. can be developed by an economist specializing in labor economics, if he has the inclination, or by a psychologist interested in "industrial relations." Part-time teachers might be available in this field in some communities. Production management is likely to be beyond the competence of colleges.

In the field of marketing, the choice will tend to be between hiring a marketing specialist and having an economist teach the subject as a side line. Marketing can be taught in many different ways. It can be linked with consumer economics, industrial organization, economic theory, statistics, psychology, or sociology, according to the ability and inclination of the teacher.

With respect to business finance, the answer is fairly easy. The subject can be competently taught by a well-trained economist. The broad field —including investments, financial institutions, and security markets as well as business or corporation finance in the narrower sense—is closely related to money and banking, public finance, economic theory, mathematics of finance, and government control of business. A college could add to its staff an economist who would specialize in this area.

Is there any priority among these fields for a college seeking to provide a few courses? Probably. Any attempt to offer business courses should include enough accounting to enable students to read financial statements critically and to understand the accounting references in finance and other subjects. One year, or even a semester, of "managerial accounting" or "basic accounting concepts" can serve the purpose; of course, adequate economics offerings should include a course in basic accounting concepts applicable to various economic units, including the business firm. If a college undertakes the larger task of providing detailed training in advanced accounting, auditing, cost accounting, tax accounting, etc., it should expect to have two full-time accounting teachers or the equivalent manpower with more teachers. If the college is not going to have this minimum number, it might well confine its accounting to a single basic course, taught by a practicing accountant, an academic accountant from a nearby university, or an economist.

Business law, taught by a practicing lawyer, might well take the second place, although the discussion in Chap. 9 raises serious doubt about the way this subject is usually approached. Business finance seems to be the next most important field. It should be taught by an economist who would devote his major energies to it. This economist should be in addition to the minimum three economists needed for the standard economics offerings.

More or less on a par, after accounting, finance, and business law, would be business organization and management, marketing, and personnel management. With three regular economists, an accountant, and a financial economist, the addition of any of these subjects would imply having more than five teachers of economics and business administration. Many colleges found and will find it hard to resist the temptation to offer courses in these three fields, along with the other three principal business fields, without increasing staff, even though the inevitable result is dissipation of teaching resources and mediocre offerings. If a college feels that it must offer something in business organization and management, marketing, or personnel management, the choice should probably be made on the basis of the interest and capacity of available teachers. Business organization and management is probably the best single catchall; it might be taught by the economist who teaches industrial organization and public policy.

No matter how carefully a college pursues this intermediate course of action—Alternative 3—it is doomed inevitably to mediocrity in the business field, and it may easily impair its economics offerings. It should thus devote to business courses only the minimum resources necessary to meet the public relations or other pressures to which it is subject.[24]

Alternative 4. The fourth and final alternative leans toward the liberal arts just as the third alternative leans toward business administration. *It is a "prebusiness" program, parallel in conception to the prelaw and premedical programs in liberal arts colleges.* Since it represents something of a departure from contemporary practice, it is described in some detail. It is a logical counterpart of the recommendations developed in Chaps. 8 to 10 for undergraduate and graduate business programs. It consists of selections of courses from the standard liberal arts departments which seem most likely to be of long-run value to the future business administrators and, at least experimentally, some new courses. There would be no attempt to teach business administration as such. This program is an adaptation of the approach suggested in option *b* in Question 2 of the

[24] Some of the few colleges with enough teachers and an adequate sense of restraint to pursue this course of action are Beloit, Denison, Grinnell, Kalamazoo, and Oberlin.

questionnaire.[25] It differs from Alternative 1 mainly in its conscious focus on the ultimate vocational or professional objectives of students.

It is true, as many advocates of pure liberal arts would critically contend, that this approach treats the liberal arts subjects as vocational instruments rather than as broadly cultural subjects. It is true also that this approach would not satisfy people who wish, for themselves and others, courses of study which relate directly to actual business operations. Thus it would require careful explanation by college administrators to the clienteles of many colleges. College catalogs and brochures would have to explain such a prebusiness program fully, especially for the benefit of students and parents who view college education as primarily and directly vocational. Numerous prominent business executives support this approach strongly, and deans of graduate schools of business would tend to endorse it enthusiastically.

Explaining the philosophy of this approach is one thing; carrying out such a program is quite another. Here are some ideas on its execution: First, the interested college should examine its offerings in economics, English, mathematics, history, government, and the other key prebusiness subjects among the liberal arts to see whether they are reasonably adequate from the point of view of liberal education. Second, it should rearrange the offerings or expand them—almost certainly with some new, and probably additional, personnel, in accordance with the results of the examination, in order to provide the prebusiness students with better course opportunities. Third, the college should designate a faculty member (not a committee) as coordinator or adviser on prebusiness programs who would, among other things, formulate some model prebusiness student programs of study, advise prebusiness students on their programs, and review periodically for the benefit of all concerned the operation of the program. Prebusiness students would major in some standard field, or possibly in some acceptable combination of fields. There would be no prebusiness major, just as there is no prelaw or premedicine major. Fourth, the college should establish a full-fledged student placement service covering both postcollege jobs and graduate study.

These suggestions require some elaboration. It is not intended that the courses in the various departments be revised to fit into a hard mold,

[25] See above, pp. 690–692. This alternative bears a family resemblance to the line of thought advanced by Howard R. Bowen in his pamphlet, *The Business Enterprise as a Subject for Research*, published by the Social Science Research Council, New York, 1955. The only experimental program in education for business within the liberal arts framework that the author knows of is being conducted under Bowen's general guidance at Grinnell College, where he is president. Several of the ideas advanced in this conclusion derive from a discussion with the members of the Grinnell economics department.

as premedical education has tended to do at times; it is intended only that the main subjects in the various fields be offered regularly and be taught competently, so that the prebusiness students may be able to select from a good array of courses. Every college department serves a variety of purposes, and its offerings have to take these purposes into account, but the prebusiness purpose, according to the approach being described here, would involve very few courses that good liberal arts departments should not have anyway.

Examples of courses which might be added, however, if they are not taught already, are: economic history, including some biographies of businessmen and histories of businesses; the systematic, objective study of the business enterprise in modern society (in economics or possibly in sociology); consumer and social economics; a mathematics course, such as finite mathematics, with a selection of topics and problems oriented toward the social studies instead of toward physics and other natural sciences; a second course in statistical methods, with laboratory work; a philosophy course which would include business ethics and the social responsibilities of businessmen; a course in the theory of administration and organization (probably in political science). These or similar modifications should not pervert or distort offerings in these departments. They should bring the light of each discipline to bear on economic behavior generally and on business behavior in particular. Understanding, not near-term cash value, should be the objective in each case. The objective study of business activities—along with love, politics, war, and religion—is clearly within the framework of liberal education.

It is not entirely satisfactory to be specific about courses without referring to an actual college situation, but the following courses, in various departmental fields, seem especially desirable for prebusiness students.

In *economics:*[26] principles (introduction), accounting fundamentals, business enterprise in modern society,[27] comparative economic systems, consumer and social economics, economic development (of less developed areas), economic history (with some geography), economic stability and growth (fluctuations, national income), capital markets, gov-

---

[26] Principles two semesters, others generally one. This is a list of *all* courses (alphabetically arranged after principles) which an economics department of four to six members might well offer. This list is also valid under Alternative 1. With fewer teachers some hard choices would have to be made or some courses would have to be alternated.

[27] "Business enterprise in modern society" is a proposal for a conscious attempt to examine the business enterprise, particularly in the corporate form, in its historical and contemporary setting, to examine it objectively in the best scientific spirit of the social sciences. The author has experimented with such a course since 1953. Some of the materials used are contained in his *Economics of the Business Firm*, McGraw-Hill Book Company Inc., New York, 1959.

ernment control of business (including some actual market structures and problems of particular industries), history of economic thought, international economics, labor, money and banking, price and distribution theory, public finance, and statistical methods.

In *political science*:[28] introduction, American government, comparative political systems, international politics, law or organization, public administration, political parties and public opinion, constitutional law, American foreign relations.

In *history:* recent world history, modern European history, American history, British, Russian, other areas.

In *psychology and sociology:* introductory courses, social organization, social psychology, learning.

In *philosophy:* introduction, ethics, logic and scientific method, aesthetics, comparative religions.

In *English:* composition, speaking, modern literature (especially writings dealing with complex human situations).

In *mathematics:* introductory college mathematics, analytic geometry, introductory calculus, statistical methods (mathematical version), mathematics for economists (or social scientists).

No one student could, in four years, take all these subjects, or similar ones, and meet his other college requirements. A student would do best to major in one field and to supplement the courses in his major field with several in one or two related fields. Prebusiness students should be steered away from excessive concentration in their major field, for college is by far the best time in their careers to obtain some disciplined breadth. The contemporary emphasis on senior comprehensive examinations in the major field and the increasing use of the graduate record examinations are powerful forces causing students, usually with teacher encouragement, to increase the number of courses they take in the major field. This tendency is counter to the conception advanced here. Faculty advisers for prebusiness students should seriously try to hold semester hours in the major field to a maximum of 36, preferably less. Breadth means more for the student's education than additional courses in the major field. Comprehensives and graduate record examinations could be altered—not made easier—to take this breadth into account, so that prebusiness students would not be at a disadvantage in trying for college honors.

A careful selection of these subjects—with the advice of the prebusiness adviser—can provide the student with the intellectual equipment to master, with relative ease, any of the subjects covered under business administration, whether in formal study, on his own, or in connection

---

[28] The courses listed under other departments than economics do not presume to constitute complete offerings.

with jobs, so far as these subjects can be mastered by study as distinguished from practical experience. Moreover, the subjects listed above are of sufficient breadth to enable students to shift vocational directions later. Numerous experienced deans and teachers have commented on the fact that few students, especially business students, actually pursue the specific vocations for which they have prepared themselves in college. It is a commonplace for businessmen in the intermediate levels who have had a highly specialized education to feel the lack of more general education and to find themselves unable, all things considered, to overcome the lack. Executive development programs are the latest response to this lack. The same point is made frequently by senior business executives in praising the liberal arts as background for their work.

An effective placement system, primarily for graduating seniors, can go far in overcoming the hesitancy of students, parents, and others to accept this type of prebusiness program. The director of the placement office must show initiative in discovering the businesses which are looking for future executives and managerial personnel rather than for office boys, technicians, or specialists. The placement director can also handle the arrangements for admission, fellowships, etc. to graduate schools.[29]

This discussion of Alternative 4—the prebusiness approach—will close with some illustrative four-year programs for a prebusiness student in a liberal arts college which wishes to provide valuable basic education for future businessmen without attempting to offer courses in business administration. Obviously, actual programs have to be constructed from the courses available, which depend mainly on teacher capacities. Student aptitudes and interests are obviously important too. In the first illustrative program in Table 24-8 it is supposed that the student is majoring in economics, that he has learned enough of a foreign language in high school to be able to enter the second-year course in college (assuming a foreign language is required or desired), and that he can write the English language well enough to be able to take a literature course in English rather than the most elementary freshman composition course. It is supposed in this case that the student has only moderate mathematical aptitude or interest. The familiar distribution requirements—in the natural sciences, social sciences, and humanities (frequently specified within these groupings)—are included in the program.

What economics courses are best for the prebusiness student and when should they be taken? It is very desirable, motivationally, for the prebusiness student who thinks he knows his general vocational plans to be able to take a prebusiness subject in his freshman year. The introductory

---

[29] Carleton College has a fully functioning placement system of this type. It is the author's impression that most of the more strictly liberal arts colleges have tended to be less efficient than their competitors in this respect.

(principles) course in economics is obviously the appropriate course for the student to take first, though experience over the country indicates that many freshmen find it quite difficult. In view of the importance of the principles course as background for other courses, including accounting, statistics, and economic history, it is recommended that the principles course be opened to freshmen generally. The course might then be more descriptive than analytical. The principles course should be insisted upon as a prerequisite for other courses in economics; it is also by far the best survey of the subject for nonspecializers regardless of their college class. The prebusiness student majoring in economics should probably have, in addition to the principles of economics: accounting fundamentals, statistical methods, money and banking, capital markets and/or public finance, business enterprise in modern society and/or government control of business, labor, price and distribution theory, economic stability and growth (fluctuations, national income), and one or more other courses (comparative economic systems, history of economic thought, economic history, economic development, or international economics). The order, after the principles course, does not matter very much, although money and banking and other rather institutional subjects might well precede the upper-college theory courses for most students.

The methods used in teaching economics courses are very important in this context. Small empirical research projects can be of immense value, especially in the upper-class courses. Students can actually study wage rates, commodity prices, geographic differentials, interest rates, stock prices and yields, foreign trade, unemployment rates, national income projections, etc. within the customary theoretical frameworks. The small colleges are at no disadvantage in this respect if teaching loads are reasonable—in general, not more than three courses per semester or two per quarter, with upper-college classes small enough to function as seminars, at least part of the time.[30]

In Program 2 (Table 24-8) the economics and mathematics courses take up just about all the available time, outside the distribution requirements. This program would be especially suited for students expecting to do graduate work. Program 3 allows for minimal mathematical interest or aptitude and assumes that the student will need the fundamentals of speech, composition, and foreign language. Many college students now enrolled in business administration programs would gravitate toward Program 3. Programs 4 and 5 illustrate prebusiness schedules with concentration in fields other than economics or mathematics. History, because of its breadth, is a particularly good field from the point of view

[30] One highly qualified commentator, not connected with a liberal arts college, stated: "Approached in this way it seems to me that the curriculum in economics is a highly desirable curriculum for a man anticipating a career in business."

TABLE 24-8

ILLUSTRATIVE PREBUSINESS PROGRAMS IN A LIBERAL ARTS COLLEGE*

Program 1: Economics major
Political science or history minor
Good college preparation

Year 1	Year 2	Year 3	Year 4
Economics	Economics	Economics	Economics
Foreign language	Philosophy/religion	Economics/elective	Economics
English	Humanities	Psychology/	Humanities
		sociology	
Science/	Mathematics/	History	History
mathematics	science		
History	Political science	Political science	Political science

Program 2: Economics or mathematics major
Mathematics or economics minor
Mathematical aptitude

Year 1	Year 2	Year 3	Year 4
Economics	Economics	Economics	Economics
Foreign language	Foreign language	Economics/elective	Economics/
			mathematics
Mathematics	Mathematics	Mathematics	Mathematics
Science	Psychology	Philosophy/religion	Political science/
			history
English	Political science	History	Humanities

Program 3: Economics concentration
No minor subject
Only fair college preparation

Year 1	Year 2	Year 3	Year 4
Economics	Economics	Economics	Economics
Foreign language	Foreign language	Economics	Economics
English	English	Speech	Humanities
Science	Science/	Philosophy/religion	Political science/
	mathematics		history
History/political	Political science/	Psychology/	Sociology/
science	history	sociology	psychology

* The slant bar (/) means "and/or."

TABLE 24-8 (*Continued*)

ILLUSTRATIVE PREBUSINESS PROGRAMS IN A LIBERAL ARTS COLLEGE

Program 4: History major
Economics minor

Year 1	Year 2	Year 3	Year 4
History	History	History	History
Foreign language	Foreign language/	History	History
	humanities		
Economics	Economics	Economics	Economics
Science	Science	Philosophy/religion	Humanities
English	Political science	Political science	Political science

Program 5: "Behavioral sciences" major†
Economics minor

Year 1	Year 2	Year 3	Year 4
Psychology/	Psychology/	Psychology/	Psychology/
sociology	sociology	sociology	sociology
Foreign language	Foreign language/	Psychology/	Psychology/
	humanities	sociology	sociology
Economics	Economics	Economics	Economics
Science/	Science/	Philosophy/religion	Philosophy/religion
mathematics	mathematics		
English	English	Speech	History/political
			science

† These subjects are mainly in psychology and sociology; either of these fields could serve as a major subject. Similar programs could plausibly be devised with other fields of concentration, e.g., political science, philosophy, or English.

of a prebusiness student. Economics and government are treated essentially as minors in this example and thus use up nearly all the available time above the history and distribution requirements. The "behavioral sciences" (mainly psychology and sociology) represent another sound focus. Satisfactory student programs could also be developed for prebusiness students who wish to major in government, English, philosophy, and perhaps other subjects.

SUMMARY

A college that is concerned with the problem of what to do about education for business administration can rationally select one of four courses of action. One course is to omit business administration and to strengthen economics and other liberal arts departments. A second course—sensible only for colleges which can afford, actually hire, and effectively use ten or so competent faculty members in economics and business administration—is to offer a minimum acceptable program in business administration along with the indispensable offerings in economics. A third line of action is to offer a few key courses in business administration along with adequate offerings in economics. The fourth course of action is to provide prebusiness programs of study composed of various combinations of subjects in economics, mathematics, English, history, government, and other liberal arts disciplines which are considered especially good background for business.

It is the opinion of the author that many of the 500 or so liberal arts colleges are able to choose the first alternative. Some undoubtedly consider it "too pure" in the face of strong vocational pressures. The second alternative is far too expensive for all but a handful. The third acceptable pattern, involving a few key business courses in addition to good economics offerings, is already in operation in a few colleges. It is the minimal direct response to pressures for vocational offerings in business administration. If a college must relieve these pressures to some extent, it is well advised to concentrate its efforts on only one or two of the fields of business administration, but it should first have a minimum of three teachers of economics. Far too many colleges are trying to offer some business training without having the minimum adequate offerings in economics and other essential liberal arts subjects. Dissipation of resources and mediocre teaching are the constant hazards in pursuing this third alternative.

The writer thinks that the fourth course—the prebusiness concept—is a feasible one and a desirable one for many colleges. It is in line with the liberal arts tradition; it is preprofessional; like premedical and prelaw programs, it can be explained readily to constituencies; and it relieves the colleges of the impossible task of competing directly in the field of business administration with the schools of business in large universities or with the in-service training programs of businesses themselves. The colleges can, if they will, organize to provide adequate or even excellent undergraduate offerings in economics and the other liberal arts subjects which are valuable preparation for business. And their graduates will be well prepared to learn the art of business administration on the job and in graduate or other special schools.

APPENDIX 1

First Degrees Conferred by Universities, Colleges, and Technological Schools
in the United States, 1918–1958*

Year	First degrees in arts and sciences	First professional degrees
1917–1918	20,587	16,566
1919–1920	27,671	19,518
1921–1922	31,269	28,704
1923–1924	39,713	40,188
1925–1926	47,691	44,447
1927–1928	55,208	48,266
1929–1930	59,821	51,540
1931–1932	59,036	79,910
1933–1934	54,007	81,754
1935–1936	56,920	84,882
1937–1938	63,345	101,663
1939–1940	66,280	120,387
1941–1942	66,348	119,017
. . . .	. . . . .	. . . . . .
1947–1948	108,406	156,843
1949–1950	163,963	265,329
1951–1952	120,978	208,956
1953–1954	106,000	186,036
1955–1956	115,919	194,547
1957–1958	135,778	229,292

* For the academic years 1917–1918 through 1929–1930, earned degrees in the "arts and sciences" include earned degrees listed in the *Biennial Survey of Education* under the headings "Arts and Sciences," "Fine Arts and Music"; for the academic years 1931–1932 through 1941–1942, earned degrees in the arts and sciences include earned degrees listed in the *Biennial Survey of Education* under the heading "Total Arts and Sciences" *less* degrees in arts and sciences with specialization in Agriculture, Commerce and Business, Education, Engineering, Home Economics, Industrial Arts, Journalism, Library Science, Nursing, Predentistry, Prelaw, and Premedicine, *plus* degrees given by professional schools in Fine Arts and Music; for the academic years 1947–1948 through 1954–1955, earned degrees in the arts and sciences include earned degrees listed in *Earned Degrees Conferred by Higher Educational Institutions* under the following headings: Anatomy, Anthropology, Astronomy, Bacteriology, Biochemistry, Biology, Botany, Chemistry,

709

Economics, English, Entomology, Fine Arts, Geography, Geology, History, International Relations, Languages, Mathematics, Metallurgy, Meteorology, Music, Natural Sciences (n.e.c.), Philosophy, Physical Sciences (n.e.c.), Physics, Physiology, Political Science, Psychology, Religious Education and Bible, Social Sciences (n.e.c.), Sociology, Zoology, and Arts and Sciences (n.e.c.). Data for 1955–1956 and 1957–1958 were grouped so as to conform as closely as possible with the classifications used for the earlier data in the series.

Earned degrees in professional fields include all earned degrees listed by field in the *Biennial Survey of Education*, 1917–1918 through 1941–1942, and in *Earned Degrees Conferred by Higher Educational Institutions*, 1947–1948 through 1957–1958, except degrees in the arts and sciences as defined above and degrees listed in the latter source under the heading "Other."

SOURCES: U.S. Bureau of Education, later U.S. Office of Education, *Biennial Survey of Education*, 1917–1918 to 1941–1942. U.S. Office of Education, *Earned Degrees Conferred by Higher Educational Institutions*, 1947–1948 to 1957–1958.

APPENDIX 2

FIRST DEGREES CONFERRED BY UNIVERSITIES, COLLEGES, AND TECHNOLOGICAL SCHOOLS
IN THE UNITED STATES, 1918–1958*

Year	Business and commerce	Education	Engineering	Law†	Medicine†
1917–1918	640	1,169	3,079	2,369	2,423
1919–1920	1,559	797	4,400	3,273	2,806
1921–1922	3,562	1,662	6,431	5,068	2,598
1923–1924	4,948	3,721	7,476	6,842	3,642
1925–1926	5,435	5,318	7,376	7,938	4,122
1927–1928	6,621	7,109	7,607	8,652	4,342
1929–1930	6,213	9,054	7,371	8,874	4,769
1931–1932	10,177	25,824‡	10,374	8,906	5,274
1933–1934	9,591	29,788	11,409	7,882	5,311
1935–1936	9,869	32,359	10,629	7,423	5,571
1937–1938	14,652	37,173	11,039	7,969	5,444
1939–1940	19,036	44,905	14,348	7,168	5,490
1941–1942	18,117	43,132	15,519	5,733	5,601
....	.....	.....	.....	.....	.....
1947–1948	38,371	29,694	31,096	10,990	6,867
1949–1950	72,137	46,635	52,246	14,312	8,836
1951–1952	46,683	52,060	30,549	12,558	9,159
1953–1954	40,944	47,383	22,329	9,298	8,954
1955–1956	47,203	45,355	26,312	8,285	8,557
1957–1958	57,669	50,292	35,332	9,433	8,833

* For the period 1931–1932 through 1941–1942, earned degrees in commerce and business administration include degrees in arts and sciences with specialization in commerce and degrees given by professional schools in commerce and business. Earned degrees in engineering, education, and other professional fields were computed in the same manner.

Before 1955–1956, degrees listed under "Education" by the Office of Education include the subclassifications: Education, Industrial Arts, and Physical Education. The figures for the years before 1955–1956, given in Appendix 2, are for the subclassification Education which does not include industrial arts and physical education. It is stated in a footnote in *Earned Degrees Conferred by Higher Educational Institutions*, 1954–1955, that degrees in secondary education for students majoring in particular subjects such as English, music, and commerce were distributed in that year and in previous years according to the major field of specialization and were not counted as degrees in education.

711

In 1955–1956, the system of classification was changed, and "Education" included degrees in specialized teaching fields. In order to make the data conform as closely as possible with the classifications used for the earlier data in the series, 25,261 degrees in specialized teaching fields had to be subtracted from the total degrees in education in 1955–1956 and added to the appropriate major fields. For example, 4,148 degrees in business education were subtracted from "Education" and added to "Business and Commerce." The same procedure was used in dealing with the data reported for 1956–1957 and 1957–1958.

† The law degrees and medicine degrees are considered first degrees in the Office of Education classification, because they are the first degrees in these fields. They are actually post-bachelor degrees, whereas the degrees in business, education, and engineering are chiefly bachelor's degrees.

‡ The sudden increase in 1931–1932 in first degrees granted in education is accounted for in part by a change of the Office of Education method of reporting these degrees. This is about the time when a great many normal schools became degree-granting institutions.

SOURCES: U.S. Bureau of Education, later U.S. Office of Education, *Biennial Survey of Education*, 1917–1918 to 1941–1942. U.S. Office of Education, *Earned Degrees Conferred by Higher Educational Institutional*, 1947–1948 to 1957–1958.

APPENDIX 3

Questionnaires were sent in March, 1957, to all accredited four-year undergraduate and all accredited graduate institutions of higher education offering programs in business administration. The original list was made up of 621 institutions. This list consisted of all schools conferring degrees in business and commerce as reported in U.S. Office of Education, *Earned Degrees Conferred by Higher Educational Institutions,* 1954–55, Circular 461. Excluded from this list were all institutions not fully accredited, junior colleges, institutions which were exclusively teacher-preparatory or offered only secretarial and closely related courses. Sources consulted were the U.S. Office of Education, *Education Directory,* 1955–56, *part 3;* American Council on Education, *American Universities and Colleges, 1956;* and the catalogs of the institutions. Of the 621 institutions, 34 were later dropped from the study because 23 of them were found not to be accredited, and 11 of them were engineering schools with no general program in business administration.

There were two forms of the questionnaire: a long form sent to 187 larger institutions most of which have separate schools or colleges of business administration and a short form sent to 400 institutions with departments or divisions of business administration. The longer form of the questionnaire consisted of 16 pages and followed the outline shown below; the shorter form covered the same general areas, but less comprehensively.

Outline of Survey Questionnaire

General information:
 Name and administrative unit
 Date program was organized
 Budget of business program
 Types of business programs offered: undergraduate, graduate, summer school, etc.
Faculty data:
 Number and rank of faculty, with salary for each rank, 1951 and 1956
 Number of part-time faculty
 Highest degree held by members of regular full-time business faculty
 Comparison of salaries of business faculty with other divisions of the university
Curricula data, 1955–1956:
 Undergraduate curriculum
  Nonbusiness subjects required
  Business and economics courses required
  Major fields of concentration

713

Graduate curricula
  M.B.A. or other master's programs
  Requirements for the doctoral degree
Most popular fields of concentration: undergraduate and graduate
Student data:
  Number of admissions, 1951 and 1956
  Extent of scholarship aid
  Home residence of business students
  Prior education of graduate students in the business program
  Student-faculty ratio
  Number of earned degrees, 1951–1952 and 1955–1956
  Enrollment data for business program, 1951 and 1956
  Estimates of growth in enrollment to 1970
  Distribution of earned degrees in business program and other divisions of the
    entire institution

In January, 1958, a "Summary of Preliminary Findings" based on the questionnaire returns was prepared and distributed to all cooperating schools. At the time
this summary was prepared, questionnaires had been returned by 159 (or 85 per
cent) of the 187 schools and divisions receiving the long forms and by 240 (or 60 per
cent) of the 400 institutions receiving the short forms. These responses represent
more coverage in terms of degrees granted than in terms of numbers of institutions,
the 399 schools responding accounting for 86 per cent of first-level business degrees,
95 per cent of second-level business degrees, and 99 per cent of third-level business
degrees. (These figures on degree coverage were calculated from data given in the
U.S. Office of Education Circular 461 mentioned above.)

After the preliminary findings had been summarized, questionnaires were returned
by twenty-five more institutions. These were received in time to be incorporated in
tables prepared for this report.

Data derived from the Survey Questionnaire have been used at many points in the
study. The tables given below deal only with business schools and cover data which
are not discussed extensively in the main body of the report; data on departments
and divisions of business are summarized in Chap. 24. The 138 questionnaires
summarized in these tables came from 98 schools of business with 4-year undergraduate programs, 34 schools of business with 2-2- or 1-3-year undergraduate programs,
and the 6 exclusively graduate schools of business. When a table refers specifically to
undergraduate programs, the total number of schools is 132. Of these 132 schools,
90 had some graduate work in 1955–1956, so the total for tables referring to graduate
programs is 90 plus the exclusively graduate schools, or 96.

TABLE 1

DATE BUSINESS SCHOOL STARTED*

Date	Number of institutions
Before 1900	3
1900–1909	10
1910–1919	33
1920–1924	20
1925–1929	22
1930–1934	6
1935–1939	9
1940–1944	5
1945–1949	17
1950–	13
Total	138

* Of the 138 institutions answering this question, 30, or 22 per cent of the total, were business schools established after 1944, and 75, or 54 per cent of the total, were established between 1910 and 1929.

TABLE 2

BUDGET OF BUSINESS SCHOOL, 1956–1957*

Amount	Number of institutions
Over $500,000	15
400,000–499,999	15
300,000–399,999	15
200,000–299,999	27
100,000–199,999	30
50,000–99,999	18
Under $50,000	4
Total	124
Not given	14
Total	138

* Of the 124 institutions answering this question, the highest number (30, or 24 per cent of the total) reported annual academic business program budgets in the interval $100,000–$199,999; 75 institutions, or 61 per cent of the total, reported business budgets between $50,000 and $299,999 per annum.

TABLE 3

HIGHEST DEGREE HELD BY REGULAR FULL-TIME BUSINESS FACULTY, FALL 1956

(Includes both undergraduate and graduate)*

Number on faculty (regular full-time)	Number of institutions	Total number of faculty members	Number with doctor's degrees	Per cent with doctor's degrees
60 or more	13	1,364	701	51.4
50–59	11	596	288	48.3
40–49	8	353	152	43.1
30–39	28	952	437	45.9
20–29	35	874	354	40.5
10–19	34	487	166	34.1
5–9	11	84	36	42.9
Total.............	140	4,710	2,134	45.3 (avg.)
No data	1			
Total.............	141†			

* Of the 140 institutions answering this question, the proportion of the business faculty with a doctoral degree varied from 34 per cent among schools with 10 to 19 business faculty members to 51 per cent among schools with 60 or more business faculty members; the average for all faculty members in this group of business schools was 45 per cent.

† Three of the 138 institutions sent in data for graduate and undergraduate faculties separately. Both were included in this table.

TABLE 4

MEDIAN SALARY OF FULL PROFESSORS, 1956–1957

(Includes both undergraduate and graduate)*

Salary for 9–10 months	Number of public institutions	Number of private institutions	Total institutions
$12,000 or more	2	4	6
11,500–11,999	1		1
11,000–11,499		1	1
10,500–10,999	3		3
10,000–10,499	3	2	5
9,500– 9,999	3	3	6
9,000– 9,499	2	1	3
8,500– 8,999	5	2	7
8,000– 8,499	9	4	13
7,500– 7,999	11	12	23
7,000– 7,499	15	11	26
6,500– 6,999	10	5	15
6,000– 6,499	5	14	19
Under 6,000	5	2	7
Total.................	74	61	135
Not given	1	5	6
Total.................	75	66	141†

* Of the 135 institutions answering this question, 22, or about 16 per cent of the total, paid full professors in the business school a median salary of $9,500 per annum or more, and 83 or 61 per cent of the total paid a median salary between $6,000 and $7,999.

† Three of the 138 institutions sent in data for graduate and undergraduate faculties separately. Both were included in this table.

TABLE 5

PERCENTAGE OF INCREASE IN MEDIAN SALARY OF FULL PROFESSORS
FROM 1951–1952 TO 1956–1957

(Includes both undergraduate and graduate)*

1956 *as per cent of* 1951	*Number of institutions*
160 or more	3
155–159	1
150–154	1
145–149	1
140–144	6
135–139	10
130–134	18
125–129	16
120–124	20
115–119	19
110–114	14
105–109	9
100–104	3
Total	121
No data	20
Total	141†

* Of the 121 institutions answering this question, 97, or 80 per cent of the total, increased the salary of full professors between 10 and 39 per cent over the period 1951–1952 to 1956–1957; the median increase was 24 per cent during this period.

† Three of the 138 institutions sent in data for graduate and undergraduate faculties separately. Both were included in this table.

TABLE 6

ESTIMATED GROWTH IN BUSINESS ENROLLMENT TO 1970*

1970 as per cent of 1956	Number of institutions	
	Undergraduate students	Graduate students
300 or more	2	31
200–299	30	22
180–199	14	4
160–179	19	4
140–159	17	6
120–139	12	3
100–119	10	5
Less than 100	3	1
Total...............	107	76
Not given	25	20
Total...............	132	96

* Of the 107 institutions answering this question for undergraduate students, 32, or 30 per cent, expected their enrollment will more than double by 1970. Of the 76 institutions giving estimates for graduate students, 53, or 70 per cent, expected the enrollment to double by 1970.

TABLE 7A

MOST FREQUENTLY CHOSEN MAJORS IN UNDERGRADUATE PROGRAM, 1956–1957*

Majors	Number of institutions indicating each major by rank of student choices				Total institutions
	1st	2d	3d	4th	
Accounting............	52	46	13	3	114
Marketing.............	18	23	38	19	98
Management..........	12	20	31	12	75
General business.....	31	12	10	6	59
Finance..............	0	1	7	23	31
Secretarial...........	0	5	1	13	19
Labor relations, etc.....	0	1	6	15	22
Economics............	4	4	2	4	14
Production...........	0	1	1	3	5
Miscellaneous.........					30
Not given............					15

* Among the 123 undergraduate institutions answering this question, the most frequently chosen majors (first four highest choices combined) were accounting, marketing, management, and general business in that order. On the basis of first choices only, accounting and general business were the most frequently chosen.

TABLE 7B

MOST FREQUENTLY CHOSEN MAJORS IN GRADUATE PROGRAM, 1956–1957*

Majors	Number of institutions indicating each major by rank of student choices				Total institutions
	1st	2d	3d	4th	
Accounting............	18	18	9	5	50
Management..........	28	10	4	0	42
General business.....	1	2	5	1	9
Marketing.............	6	11	16	9	42
Finance..............	3	5	6	6	20
Taxation............	0	4	3	5	12
Labor relations, etc.....	3	3	4	5	15
Economics............	3	7	4	4	18
Production...........	1	0	3	3	7
Miscellaneous.........					16
No major fields........					14
Not given............					18

* Among the 64 institutions with graduate programs answering this question, the most frequently chosen majors (first four highest choices combined) were accounting, management, marketing, and finance in that order; on the basis of first choices only, management and accounting were most frequently chosen by a wide margin.

TABLE 8

PRIOR EDUCATION OF GRADUATE STUDENTS IN BUSINESS, FALL 1956*

% of students with prior business degrees	Number of institutions	% of students with prior liberal arts degrees	Number of institutions
0–9	5	0–9	15
10–24	8	10–24	25
25–49	18	25–49	23
50–74	21	50–74	9
75 or over	22	75 or over	2
Total.................	74	Total................	74
No data	22	No data	22
Total.................	96	Total................	96

* Of the 74 institutions answering this question, 43, or 58 per cent of the total, drew 50 per cent or more of entering graduate students in 1956 from undergraduate business programs; there were also 48 institutions which drew between 10 per cent and 49 per cent of their graduate students from liberal arts programs.

TABLE 9

LOCATION OF ECONOMICS DEPARTMENT, 1956–1957*

Undergraduate Programs

	Number of institutions
In business school...	65 (52%)
In liberal arts college..	42 (34%)
In both business school and liberal arts college......................	17
Total...	124
Other or not given..	8
Total...	132

Graduate Programs

	Number of institutions
In business school...	44 (50%)
In graduate school of arts and sciences.............................	33 (38%)
In business school and graduate school of arts and sciences...........	11
Total...	88
Other or not given..	8
Total...	96

* In 52 per cent of the undergraduate institutions and in 50 per cent of the institutions with graduate programs, the department of economics was located in the business school.

TABLE 10

RELATION OF NUMBER OF FULL-TIME FACULTY MEMBERS
TO PART-TIME FACULTY MEMBERS, 1956–1957

(Includes both undergraduate and graduate)*

Size of faculty	Number of institutions	Total number full time	Part-time		Evening or extension	
			Number	% of full time	Number	% of full time
5–9	8	62	24	39	148	239†
10–19	37	526	156	30	278	53
20–29	34	857	237	28	484	57
30–39	28	947	390	41	231	24
40–49	8	353	116	33	175	50
50 or more	23	2,054	527	26	1,213	59
Total.........	138	4,799	1,450	30	2,529	53

* In the 138 institutions answering this question, the average ratio of part-time to full-time business faculty was about 30 per cent; the average ratio of evening and extension business faculty to the full-time business faculty was about 53 per cent.

† One of the eight institutions in this group reported eighty-eight evening or extension faculty, which raised the percentage for the group markedly.

APPENDIX 4

INSTITUTIONS OF HIGHER EDUCATION WITH BUSINESS PROGRAMS, 1955–1956

Exclusively undergraduate business schools........................... 46
Undergraduate business schools, also offering graduate work........... 105
Exclusively graduate business schools.............................. 6
Engineering schools with general programs in industrial management..... 6
                                                                    ———
Total business schools... 163
Divisions and departments of business in colleges and universities........ 424
                                                                    ———
Grand total of all institutions with business programs................ 587

APPENDIX 5

Baylor University (Texas)
Bowling Green State University (Ohio)
Bridgeport, University of (Connecticut)
Cincinnati, University of (Ohio)
Creighton University (Nebraska)
Drake University (Iowa)
Eastern New Mexico University
East Tennessee State College
Fenn College (Ohio)
Fordham University (New York)
Georgetown University (D.C.)
Georgia State College of Business Administration
John Carroll University (Ohio)
Kansas City, University of (Missouri)
Lamar State College of Technology (Texas)
LaSalle College (Pennsylvania)
Louisiana Polytechnic Institute
Loyola University (Illinois)
Loyola University (Louisiana)
Loyola University (California)
Manhattan College (New York)
Memphis State University (Tennessee)
Millikin University (Illinois)
Nevada, University of
Niagara University (New York)
Notre Dame, University of (Indiana)
Oklahoma City University (Oklahoma)
Omaha, University of (Nebraska)
Portland, University of (Oregon)
Rider College (New Jersey)
St. John's University (New York)
St. Mary's College (California)
St. Peter's College (New Jersey)
San Francisco, University of (California)
Santa Clara, University of (California)
Seattle University (Washington)

724

South Dakota, University of
Southwestern Louisiana Institute
Stetson University (Florida)
Tennessee Polytechnic Institute
Utah State University
Villanova University (Pennsylvania)
Virginia State College
Wake Forest College (North Carolina)
Washington and Lee University (Virginia)
Youngstown University (Ohio)

105 Schools or Colleges of Business with Both Undergraduate and Graduate Programs, 1955–1956

Akron, University of (Ohio)
Alabama, University of
American International College (Massachusetts)
American University (D.C.)
Arizona State College
Arizona, University of
Arkansas, University of
Atlanta University (Georgia)
Boston College (Massachusetts)
Boston University (Massachusetts)
Bradley University (Illinois)
Brigham Young University (Utah)
Buffalo, University of (New York)
Butler University (Indiana)
California, University of (Berkeley)
California, University of (Los Angeles)
City College of New York (New York)
Colorado, University of
Connecticut, University of
Denver, University of (Colorado)
DePaul University (Illinois)
Detroit, University of (Michigan)
Drexel Institute of Technology (Pennsylvania)
Duquesne University (Pennsylvania)
Emory University (Georgia)
Fairleigh Dickinson University (New Jersey)
Florida State University
Florida, University of
Georgia, University of
Golden Gate College (California)
Hawaii, University of
Houston, University of (Texas)
Idaho, University of
Illinois, University of
Indiana University
Iowa, State University of
Kansas, University of
Kent State University (Ohio)

Kentucky, University of
Lehigh University (Pennsylvania)
Long Island University (New York)
Louisiana State University
Louisville, University of (Kentucky)
Marquette University (Wisconsin)
Maryland, University of
Massachusetts, University of
Miami University (Ohio)
Miami, University of (Florida)
Michigan State University
Michigan, University of
Minnesota, University of
Mississippi State College
Mississippi, University of
Missouri, University of
Montana State University
Nebraska, University of
New Mexico, University of
New York University (New York)
North Carolina, University of
North Dakota, University of
North Texas State College
Northeastern University (Massachusetts)
Northwestern University (Illinois)
Ohio State University
Ohio University
Oklahoma State University
Oklahoma University
Oregon State College
Oregon, University of
Pennsylvania State University
Pennsylvania, University of
Pittsburgh, University of (Pennsylvania)
Rhode Island, University of
Richmond, University of (Virginia)
Roosevelt University (Illinois)
Rutgers University (New Jersey)
St. Bernadine of Siena College (New York)
St. Louis University (Missouri)
Seton Hall University (New Jersey)
Simmons College (Massachusetts)
South Carolina, University of
Southern California, University of
Southern Illinois University
Southern Methodist University (Texas)
Suffolk University (Massachusetts)
Syracuse University (New York)
Temple University (Pennsylvania)
Tennessee, University of
Texas Christian University

Texas Technological College
Texas, University of
Toledo, University of (Ohio)
Tulane University (Louisiana)
Tulsa, University of (Oklahoma)
Utah, University of
Virginia, University of
Washington University (Missouri)
Washington, State College of
Washington, University of
Wayne State University (Michigan)
Western Reserve University (Ohio)
West Virginia University
Wichita, Municipal University of (Kansas)
Wisconsin, University of
Wyoming, University of

6 Schools or Colleges of Business—Exclusively Graduate, 1955–1956

Chicago, University of (Illinois)
Columbia University (New York)
Cornell University (New York)
Dartmouth College (New Hampshire)
Harvard University (Massachusetts)
Stanford University (California)

6 Schools or Colleges of Business—Engineering Schools or Other Institutes, 1955–1956

Babson Institute of Business Administration (Massachusetts)
Carnegie Institute of Technology (Pennsylvania)
Georgia Institute of Technology
Massachusetts Institute of Technology
Purdue University (Indiana)
Virginia Polytechnic Institute

APPENDIX 6

This group of 75 institutions was selected so as to be representative of the major institutions with business programs; most had separate business schools, but a few had departments or divisions of business. In choosing the group, the following factors were considered:

1. Date of founding of business program
2. Size of the program in terms of number of degrees granted
3. Type of undergraduate program
4. Type of graduate program
5. Type of control of the institution
6. AACSB membership
7. Ratio of business degrees to total degrees granted
8. Geography, including rural versus metropolitan as well as regional considerations

The director of the survey and his staff of twelve interviewers visited most of the following institutions during 1957 and 1958; however in several instances the information was limited to a few topics and was secured without personal interviews. The personal interviews covered from one to three days per school and, in a number of cases, return visits were arranged. Discussions were held first with the deans and then with as many members of the business and liberal arts faculties and general administration spokesmen as time permitted. The major questions followed a uniform outline prepared in advance, but latitude was left to follow up particular topics raised in the course of the discussion. The questions pertained to the following general issues: history of school, objectives, curriculum plan and content, faculty, teaching methods and conditions, research, students, management development programs, and relations with other branches of the university. Each interviewer then prepared a detailed report ranging from twenty to fifty pages in length, and all the reports were later summarized for purposes of the general survey.

New England states:
  Bridgeport, University of (Connecticut)
  Connecticut, University of
  Dartmouth College (New Hampshire)
  Harvard University (Massachusetts)
  Massachusetts Institute of Technology
  Massachusetts, University of
  Northeastern University (Massachusetts)
  Norwich University (Vermont)

Rhode Island, University of
Yale University (Connecticut)

Middle Atlantic states:
Buffalo, University of (New York)
Carnegie Institute of Technology (Pennsylvania)
City College of New York
Columbia University (New York)
Cornell University (New York)
Fairleigh Dickinson College (New Jersey)
Fordham University (New York)
George Washington University (D.C.)
Johns Hopkins University (Maryland)
Lafayette College (Pennsylvania)
La Salle College (Pennsylvania)
Lehigh University (Pennsylvania)
Maryland, University of
New York University
Pennsylvania State University
Pennsylvania, University of
Rutgers University (New Jersey)
Temple University (Pennsylvania)

Midwestern states:
Akron, University of (Ohio)
Antioch College (Ohio)
Bowling Green State University (Ohio)
Bradley University (Illinois)
Chicago, University of (Illinois)
Cincinnati, University of (Ohio)
Illinois, University of
Indiana University
Marquette University (Wisconsin)
Michigan State University
Michigan, University of
Minnesota, University of
Northwestern University (Illinois)
Notre Dame University (Indiana)
Ohio University
St. Louis University (Missouri)
Washington University (Missouri)

Southern states:
Alabama, University of
Chattanooga, University of (Tennessee)
Davidson College (North Carolina)
Emory University (Georgia)
Florida, University of
Louisiana State University
Miami, University of (Florida)
Mississippi, University of
North Carolina, University of

Tennessee, University of
Tulane University (Louisiana)
Vanderbilt University (Tennessee)
Virginia, University of
West Virginia, University of

Western states:
Baylor University (Texas)
California, University of (Berkeley)
California, University of (Los Angeles)
Denver, University of (Colorado)
Hardin-Simmons University (Texas)
Houston, University of (Texas)
Oklahoma State University
Oklahoma, University of
Oregon State College
Santa Clara, University of (California)
Stanford University (California)
Texas Agricultural and Mechanical College
Utah, University of
Washington, State College of
Washington, University of
Wyoming, University of

APPENDIX 7

MANAGERS, OFFICIALS, AND PROPRIETORS IN THE LABOR FORCE (EXCEPT NEW WORKERS) IN 1940 AND AS GAINFUL WORKERS IN 1930, 1920, AND 1910; ADJUSTED FIGURES FOR MANAGERS, OFFICIALS, AND PROPRIETORS IN THE LABOR FORCE IN 1950

	1910	1920	1930	1940	1950*
Labor force or gainful workers......	37,271,360	41,236,185	48,594,592	52,020,023	58,998,943
Managers, officials, and proprietors, except farm......	2,447,090	2,793,125	3,653,477	3,958,937	5,092,615
Latter as per cent of labor force or gainful workers......	6.5	6.8	7.5	7.6	8.6
Wholesale and retail dealers.........	1,245,801	1,401,751	1,786,996	2,037,900	2,274,055
Other managers, officials, and proprietors, except farm..	1,201,289	1,391,374	1,866,481	1,921,037	2,818,560
Latter as per cent of labor force or gainful workers......	3.2	3.4	3.8	3.7	4.8

* Data for 1950 were derived by applying the complete count for appropriate employments given in the 1950 Census reports to the employments listed under the headings "Wholesale and retail dealers" and "Other proprietors, managers, and officials" on p. 178.

SOURCE: A. Edwards, *Comparative Occupation Statistics for the United States, 1870 to 1940*, U.S. Government Printing Office, Washington, 1943, p. 187.

INDEX

Abegglen, James C., 99, 100–102, 104, 108, 130
Accounting, 77, 80, 81, 141–142
  degrees, 357–358
  history of development, 8, 40, 42, 51, 52, 358–366
  programs, evaluation of, 366–378
    graduate, 381–389
    doctoral, 389
    undergraduate, 208–211, 223–224
  recommendations, graduate, 383–389
    undergraduate, 373–381
  (*See also* Curriculum)
Adams, John F., 72
Adelphi College, 582
Admissions policies, 59–65
Adult education, 13, 108
  (*See also* Evening-extension programs; Management development programs)
Alderson, Wroe, 450
Aldrich, Morton, 36
American Association of Collegiate Schools of Business, 45, 53, 59, 173, 174, 202, 272, 273, 289, 366, 392, 577, 618
  history, 51–52
  requirements, 47, 165, 174, 199, 277, 285, 299
American Council on Education, 74, 298, 672
American Institute of Certified Public Accountants, 360
American Management Association, 537, 564
American University, 230
Amherst College, 69, 695
Andrews, Kenneth R., 288, 573, 574, 578

Anshen, Melvin, 574, 596
Anthropology, 38

Babson Institute of Business Administration, 61
Baker, George P., 299
Bartels, Robert, 426
Behaviorial sciences, 192–195, 213–214, 250–251, 267, 326–328
Bittner, W. S., 611
Blauch, Lloyd E., 26
Bogue, Jesse P., 640
Bokelman, W. Robert, 4
Bossard, James H. S., 40, 44, 45, 47, 52
Boston College, 61
Boston University, 61
Bowen, Howard R., 252, 701
Bowman, E. H., 496, 500
Brooklyn College, 611
Brown, Lyndon O., 425
Brown University, 69, 107
Brubacher, John S., 19, 273
Brumbaugh, A. J., 672
Business education, branches of, 10–12
  goals and purpose, 149–159, 232–233, 237, 295, 323–324
  graduate versus undergraduate programs, 134, 147, 150–152, 186, 232, 241
  major issues, 13–15, 52–58, 78–86
  prospects, 9–10
Business environment, 49, 89–93
Business law, 51, 52, 213, 251–252, 267
Business policy courses, 245, 257, 290
Business schools, administration, 196–197
  and employers, 84–123
  enrollments, 7, 50, 170–171

Business schools, four-year, 59, 62–64,
169–176, 187, 192, 200–202,
218–219, 225–226
graduate, 12, 66, 229–267
history, 14, 34–54, 297–299
three-two programs, 263–265
two-year and one-three programs, 64,
169–176, 187, 193, 200–202,
218–219, 225–226
types of, 238–248, 268
undergraduate, 12, 163–228

Calkins, Robert D., 19, 664
Cambridge University, 71, 611
Canadian universities, 582
Carnegie Corporation of New York, vii,
xvii, 24, 640
Carnegie Foundation for the Advance-
ment of Teaching, vii
Carnegie Institute of Technology, 12, 53,
61, 64, 189, 230, 231, 243, 244,
256, 274, 313, 315, 325, 334,
348–351, 396, 431, 579, 595
Case Institute of Technology, 583, 589,
607
Case method, 38–39, 48–50, 153, 216,
245–248, 287–290
Chomitz, David L., 641
Christensen, C. Roland, 478
City College of New York, 60, 291,
611
Clague, Ewan, 94
Clark, Charles E., 28
Clark, H. F., 539
Clark, J. M., 46
Coffman, Lotus D., 19
Colgate University, 565
College of Charleston, 611
Columbia University, 5, 12, 28, 30, 34,
43, 47, 64, 107, 230, 231, 242,
290, 297, 354, 442, 583, 588
Communication skills, 157, 167, 179–181
English courses, 142, 175–182
Community colleges (see Junior col-
leges)
Company training programs (see Man-
agement development pro-
grams)
Conant, James B., 440
Converse, P. D., 424
Copeland, Melvin L., 39, 48, 49, 180

Cornell University, 12, 64, 231, 354, 530,
583, 588
Curriculum, 21, 22, 26, 81
core, graduate, 237, 240–241, 249–
254, 256–260
undergraduate, 164, 198–216, 227
graduate, 50, 52
doctoral, 296–310, 346–351
master's, 229–267, 324–336
recommendations, 266–267
nonbusiness subjects, 45, 157, 163–195,
227
requirements, 43, 47, 163–166, 198–
201, 306
for majors, 198, 201–202, 218–225,
258–260, 335–336
undergraduate, 163–228
lower division, 165–195
recommendations, 226–228
upper division, 196–228
(See also Admissions policies; Liberal
arts; specific courses, subjects,
fields)
Currie, Brainerd, 29
Cutler, Howard, 254

Dartmouth College, 12, 34, 38, 40–42,
45, 47, 48, 107, 230, 231, 242,
263–264, 325, 396, 410–411,
431, 511, 568, 583, 633
David, Donald K., 287
Davis, Ralph C., 96, 494
Decision making, 48–50, 153, 211, 216–
218, 242
as organizing concept, 319–354
Degrees, 7, 11, 13, 40, 50, 108
bachelor's, 24, 104
doctor's, 276, 297, 307
master's, 13, 116, 117, 229–230, 241,
245, 258–267
De Paul University, 630
Dewey, John, 22
Dewhurst, J. Frederic, 40, 44, 45, 47,
52
Dixon, Frank H., 38
Doctoral programs (see Curriculum,
graduate)
Donham, Wallace B., 48–49
Douglas, Paul H., 46
Drake University, 61
Drexel Institute, 291

Drucker, Peter F., 96, 545
Dyer, John P., 36, 610, 623

Eckelberry, R. H., 611
Economics, 41, 42, 51, 80, 104, 142, 252–
    256
  courses, graduate, 252–256, 267, 304–
    305, 328–329
    specific, 38, 42, 212
    undergraduate, 211–214
  departments of, 46
  location of, 254–256
  relation to business, 35–37
  (*See also* Curriculum)
Electives, 77, 80, 226–228, 249, 267
Eliot, Charles W., 21, 24, 38
Emory University, 64, 168–169
Employers (*see* Management)
Employment (*see* Hiring policies)
Engineering, 7, 11, 70, 104, 105, 109,
    114, 116, 122
  curriculum, 28, 96
  degrees, 107
  undergraduate programs, 25
  (*See also* Industrial engineering; Pro-
    fessional education)
Engineers Council for Professional De-
    velopment, 508–513
English courses, 142, 175–182
Enrollments, 7–8, 10–13, 229–230
Evening-extension programs, 146
  faculty, 620–626
  graduate, 635–637
  history of development, 610–612
  noncredit, 631–635
  students, 626–631
  types of, 612–613
  undergraduate, curriculum, 613–614
    evaluation and recommendations,
    614–620
Executive development (*see* Manage-
    ment development programs)

Faculty, 41, 268–286, 339–341
  attitudes, 25, 279–282
  characteristics, 268–279
  graduate, 233–234
  recruitment, 38, 273–277
  teaching conditions, faculty-student
    ratio, 284–285

Faculty, teaching conditions, load, 277–
    278, 282–286
  outside work, 277–279
  salary, 4, 50, 282, 283
  (*See also* Business education; Business
    schools)
Fetter, R. B., 496, 500
Finance, history of development, 393–
    397
  programs, evaluation of, 402–408
    graduate, 400–402
    doctoral, 417–418
    undergraduate, 397–400
  recommendations, graduate, 413–417
    undergraduate, 408–413
  teaching materials and methods, 419–
    422
  (*See also* Curriculum)
Fine arts, 185
Flexner, Abraham, vii, 21
Florida State University, 37
Ford Foundation Study of Business Edu-
    cation, xvi, 103, 105, 113, 115,
    117–119, 121, 164, 537, 539,
    542, 548, 549, 563, 566, 567,
    573, 597
Fordham, Jefferson B., 29
Fordham University, 61
Foreign language, 167, 183–186, 306
Fortune, 104, 106
Foster, Louis O., 411
Fredericksen, N. F., 75
Functional fields, 47–48, 121, 157, 214–
    216, 227, 256–257, 267, 269–
    270, 331–333
  (*See also* specific subjects)
Fusfeld, Daniel R., 680

Gay, Edwin F., 38
General business or management, 216–
    218
General studies (*see* Liberal arts)
George, Claude S., 97
Georgetown University, 61
Georgia Institute of Technology, 583
Gilman, Daniel C., 24
Goetsch, Helen B., 74
Goldstein, Harold, 3
Gordon, Leland J., 680
Gordon, Robert A., xvi, 103, 164
  (*See also* Ford Foundation Study of
    Business Education)

Government and business, 92, 212
Graduate programs, 8, 53, 229–267, 296–310
  curriculum, 38, 234–236, 324–336
  dissertation or thesis, 260–261, 307–308
  evaluation, 231–234, 299–302, 309–310
  examinations, 64, 260–262, 302–306
  preparation for, 262–263
  requirements, 297–298, 306
  types, 237–244, 265–266
  (See also Curriculum; Enrollments; Faculty; Students; specific subjects)
Grant Study, 73
Greenewalt, Crawford H., 88
Grether, Ewald T., xvii
Grinnell College, 700

Habbe, Stephen, 539, 543
Hansen, Alvin H., 208
Hardy, C. DeWitt, 21
Harno, Albert J., 23
Harrington, Fred H., 294
Harris, Seymour E., 5
Harrison, James, 634
Harvard University, 12, 21, 24, 30, 34, 38, 40–42, 45, 47–49, 64, 69, 72, 86, 94, 107, 129, 137, 147, 153, 180, 211, 214, 230, 231, 242, 244–248, 257, 261, 262, 276, 290, 297, 298, 303, 310, 319, 325, 396, 439, 449, 526, 573, 578, 579, 588, 607
Haskins, Charles W., 37
Havemann, Ernest, 110, 111
Havighurst, Robert J., 76
Hazard, Leland, 213, 252
Heath, Clark W., 73
Heilbroner, Robert L., 208
Hemphill, John K., 95
High schools, 60
Higher education, 134
  enrollments, 3–9
  goals and purpose, 5, 10, 16–23, 149, 151, 157
  professional versus liberal arts, 6–7, 16, 23, 155–156
Hill, Karl A., 264

Hiring policies, 53, 78, 112–115, 120–122, 137, 221, 291
History, 38, 42, 77, 80, 192–194
Hofstadter, Richard, 21
Hollis, E. V., 298
Howell, James E., xvi
  (See also Ford Foundation Study of Business Education)
Humanities, 106, 175–186, 207–208, 227
Hunt, Pearson, 288
Hunter College, 611
Hutchins, Robert M., 17, 46

Illinois Institute of Technology, 509, 511
Indiana University, 34, 43, 230, 262, 265, 276, 297, 304, 396, 432, 583, 587
Industrial engineering, 507–535
  curriculum, 512–516, 518–521
  evaluation and recommendations, 516–518, 525–535
  faculty, 532–533
  relation to business schools, 521–523
  types, 508–512
Industrial relations (see Personnel management)
Insurance, 51, 111
Ireson, W. Grant, 528
Ivarson, Jon R., 578

Jacoby, Neil H., 419
James, Edmund J., 37
James, Henry, 21
Johns Hopkins University, 21, 24, 611
Johnson, Emory R., 37, 39
Joslyn, C. S., 100
Junior colleges, business enrollment, 638–642
  evaluation and recommendations, 649–661
  faculty, 647–649
  students, 646–647
  terminal programs, 643–645
  transfer programs, 642–643

Keller, S. I., 99
Kent State University, 64
Knight, Frank H., 46
Kozelka, Richard L., 52

LaSalle College, 61
Laughlin, J. Lawrence, 36, 37
Law (*see* Professional education)
Lehigh University, 61
Lewis, John P., 273
Liberal arts, 163–195
  prebusiness programs, 262–263
  relation to business, 37–38, 45–46, 96–98
Liberal arts colleges, business courses in, 669–677, 683–686
  as business preparation, 663–669
  evaluation and recommendations, 689–708
  faculty, 677–683
  students, 687–688
Literature, 181–182
Littleton, A. C., 361
Livingston, Sir Richard, 17
Loeb, Martin B., 76
Long Island University, 61
Louisiana State University, 34, 583, 634
Lowe, Ernest A., 634
Lowell, A. Lawrence, 38
Lyon, Hastings, 404

Mace, Myles L., 544
McGrath, Earl J., 7, 24, 669
McGregor, Douglas, 545
McNair, Malcolm P., 287
Magee, John F., 497, 500
Mahler, Walter R., 544, 573
Majors, 50, 218–225, 258–260
Management, 91, 94, 242–244
  advanced or top, 9, 49, 85
  attitudes, 96–98, 109–115, 120–122, 138–145
  careers in, 86–88, 135–142
  educational backgrounds, 99–109, 114, 126, 128–142
  functions of, 94, 95, 98
  implications, 84–89, 109–112, 122, 145–148
  lower or middle, 94, 98, 118
  requirements for, 92–96, 98–99, 115–120, 124–148
  three-company study, 125–148
  trends in, 89–93, 320–323
  (*See also* Decision making; Hiring policies; Management development programs)

Management development programs, 13, 51, 52
  company, 11, 54
  elements in, 541–563
  history of development, 537–541
  implications of, 572–576
  place of university programs in, 563–567
  types of, 567–572
  university evaluation and recommendations, 592–608
  history of development, 578–579
  types of, 579–592
Manhattan College, 61
Marketing, history of development, 423–427
  majors, 166
  programs, graduate, 430–432
    doctoral, 432–433
    undergraduate, 223, 427–430
  recommendations, graduate programs, 433–447
    undergraduate programs, 447–449
  research, 450–451
  teaching methods, 449
  (*See also* Curriculum)
Marshall, Leon C., 44–47
Massachusetts Institute of Technology, 12, 17, 29, 30, 54, 64, 189, 230, 231, 257, 274, 325, 354, 396, 578, 579
Master's programs (*see* Curriculum; Graduate programs)
Matchett, Gerald J., 509
Mathematics, 49, 90, 186–191, 227
Mead, Edward S., 404
Medicine (*see* Professional education)
Medsker, Leland L., 640, 647
Metropolitan schools, 6, 41, 43, 62, 238–239
Michigan State University, 325, 510, 584, 612, 634
Million Dollar Round Table, 72, 102, 103, 105, 108, 111, 112
Mills, C. Wright, 99
Morton, John R., 610, 612
Moser, George V., 578
Municipal University of Wichita, 611

National Analysts, Inc., 127
National Industrial Conference Board, 537, 539, 563

New York University, 12, 20, 36, 39, 53, 61, 181, 230, 231, 297, 526, 617
Newcomer, Mabel, 99–101, 665
Newman, William H., 96
Nickerson, Albert L., 96
Northeastern University, 61, 291
Northwestern University, 37, 49, 61, 64, 207, 230, 449, 526, 568, 583, 586, 588
Norton, Thomas L., 53

Oberlin College, 69, 700
Ohio State University, 43, 230, 297, 432, 530
Ohio University, 37
Olsen, Marjorie, 64
Ortega y Gasset, José, 21
Oxford University, 611

Pace, C. Robert, 79, 178
Papandreou, A. G., 666
Parkinson, Northcote, 208
Paton, W. A., 361
Patten, Simon N., 42
Pattillo, Manning M., 273, 283
Pennsylvania State University, 292–293
Person, Harlow S., 42
Personnel management, curriculum, 460–462
    history of development, 456–457
    programs, doctoral, 469–471
        evaluation of, 457–460
    recommendations, graduate, 462–468
        undergraduate, 468–469
    teaching materials and methods, 473–474
    (See also Curriculum)
Pfnister, Allan O., 273, 283
Philosophy courses, 17, 185
Placement programs, 117–119, 121–122
Planty, Earl G., 578
Political science, 192–194, 212–213
Powell, Reed, 593
Princeton University, 107
Private schools, 12, 172
Production, 215
    curriculum, 476–488
    doctoral programs, 502
    recommendations, graduate, 499–502
        undergraduate, 488–499
    (See also Curriculum)

Professional education, 23–33, 149–152, 154
    advanced professions, 27–32
    growth of, 6–8
    implications, 32–33
    specialization, 24, 79, 80
    types of, 23–27
Psychology, 192–194, 213–214, 250–251
Public schools, 12, 172
Purdue University, 12, 64, 231, 634

Quantitative subjects, 208–211, 249–250, 267, 329–331
    mathematics, 49, 90, 186–191, 227
    statistics, 90
    (See also Accounting)

Randall, Clarence B., 97, 695
Rensselaer Polytechnic Institute, 511
Research, 235–236, 310–316, 351–354
Richardson, Bellows, and Henry, 102, 106, 107
Rockefeller report, 10
Roosevelt University, 630
Roper, Elmo B., 74
Rudy, Willis, 19, 273
Russell, Charles H., 7
Rutgers University, 61, 64, 230, 511, 572, 583

San Diego State College, 582
Schmidt, George P., 18
Schrader, W. B., 75
Science, 186–191, 227
Scott, Walter Dill, 425
Scovill, H. T., 40
Seashore, Harold, 646
Seminars, 241, 293–294
Seton Hall University, 64
Seybold, John W., 101
Shartle, Carroll L., 95, 98
Sibley, Elbridge, 69
Siegle, Peter E., 633
Sloan, H. S., 539
Sloan program, 578, 579
Smith, George Albert, 478
Smith, W. Nye, 485
Social sciences, 192–194, 211–214, 227
Sociology, 192–194, 213–214, 250–251

Specialization, 21–25, 39–45, 96–98, 117–120, 222–225, 232, 234
Stanford University, 12, 43, 45, 49, 64, 72, 94, 230, 231, 263, 304, 396, 510, 523, 530, 578, 579, 583, 586
Starch, Daniel, 102
State College of Washington, 36
State universities, 20, 43
State University of Iowa, 230, 297, 583
Statistics, 90
Students, aptitudes, 62, 65–72, 153
  characteristics, 55–83, 129–135
  goals, 5, 70, 76–83, 132, 178
  motivation, 14, 57, 70, 72–83, 131–133, 137
  needs, 31, 57
  performance, 136, 137
  ranking, 65–72
  superior, 14, 53, 69, 79, 291–294
  testing, 61, 62, 66–68, 70, 71, 82, 136
Summer, Charles E., Jr., 217
Swarthmore College, xvii, 583, 633, 695
Symes, James M., 97
Syracuse University, 64, 79, 178, 583, 607

Taussig, F. W., 100
Teaching methods, 286–295, 336–339
Teele, Stanley F., 248
Temple University, 34, 81
Thesis, 260–261, 307–308
Thompson, C. O., 610
Thompson, Doris M., 563
Trickett, Joseph M., 98, 539
Tuck School (see Dartmouth College)
Tucker, William J., 38
Tulane University, 34, 36, 37, 41, 61, 189, 325, 620
Turner, R. H., 36
Tyack, David B., 299

Ulich, Robert, 18
Undergraduate programs, curriculum, 163–228, 341–343
  types, 163–169, 197–199
U.S. Office of Education, 3, 11, 52, 80–82, 229, 578, 610, 626, 645
University, of Akron, 611
  of Alabama, 43, 612

University, of Bridgeport, 624
  of California, Berkeley, 12, 34, 40, 42, 64, 80, 180, 189, 231, 325, 396, 564, 613, 640, 656
    Los Angeles, 12, 64, 189, 231, 261, 263, 315, 325, 396, 419, 582, 583, 656
  of Chicago, 12, 34, 39, 41, 42, 44–48, 53, 64, 69, 153, 230, 231, 242, 244–248, 256, 262, 274, 276, 297, 298, 306, 315, 325, 396, 431, 442, 444, 582, 588, 595, 607, 611, 617, 618, 628, 632
  of Cincinnati, 291, 396, 582, 611
  of Colorado, 199, 583
  of Dayton, 582
  of Denver, 583
  of Georgia, 612, 634
  of Idaho, 583
  of Illinois, 34, 40, 43, 361, 510, 588, 656
  of Kansas, 43, 325, 583
  of Louisville, 611
  of Michigan, 43, 45, 47, 64, 72, 230, 297, 354, 361, 396, 442, 573, 583, 611, 612
  of Minnesota, 19, 34, 43, 230, 297, 396, 431, 612, 629, 634
  of Mississippi, 656
  of Missouri, 582
  of North Carolina, 43, 64, 304, 325, 396, 572, 579, 587, 606
  of Notre Dame, 396, 582
  of Oklahoma, 582, 634
  of Omaha, 611
  of Pennsylvania, 29, 34, 35, 37–40, 42, 44, 47, 61, 64, 107, 230, 265, 355, 568, 583, 633
  of Pittsburgh, 630
  of Rhode Island, 61
  of San Francisco, 396
  of Santa Clara, 589, 607
  of Southern California, 588, 589
  of Tennessee, 511, 612
  of Texas, 230, 297
  of Toledo, 582, 611
  of Virginia, 12, 37, 43, 64, 231, 396
  of Washington, 64, 294
  of Wisconsin, 64, 230, 304, 611, 612, 634
Urban schools, 6, 41, 43, 62, 238–239
Urwick, Lyndall F., 87

Villanova College, 61
Viner, Jacob, 46
Vocationalism, 17, 23, 83

Wabash College, 583, 695
Wallis, W. Allen, 246
Ward, Lewis B., 86
Warner, W. Lloyd, 76, 99–102, 104, 108, 130
Washington University, 12, 64, 231, 265, 511
Wayne University, 611
Weissman, Jacob, 213

West, Patricia S., 110, 111
Western Reserve University, 61
Wharton, Joseph, 37, 355
Wharton School (see University of Pennsylvania)
Whipple, James B., 633
Williams College, 568, 583, 633, 695
Wolfle, Dael, 4, 65, 66, 68, 74, 136
Women's colleges, 667, 695

Yale University, 28, 107, 511
Young Presidents' Organization, 105, 108